CW01183462

**Jesko Perrey, Tjark Freundt, and Dennis Spillecke**
**Power Brands**

Jesko Perrey, Tjark Freundt, and Dennis Spillecke

# Power Brands

### Measuring, Making, and Managing Brand Success

Third edition

**WILEY**

**WILEY-VCH Verlag GmbH & Co. KGaA**

Third edition

All books published by **Wiley-VCH** are carefully produced. Nevertheless, authors, editors, and publisher do not warrant the information contained in these books, including this book, to be free of errors. Readers are advised to keep in mind that statements, data, illustrations, procedural details, or other items may inadvertently be inaccurate.

**Library of Congress Card No.:**
Applied for

**British Library Cataloguing-in-Publication Data**
A catalogue record for this book is available from the British Library.

**Bibliographic information published by the Deutsche Nationalbibliothek**
The Deutsche Nationalbibliothek lists this publication in the Deutsche Nationalbibliografie; detailed bibliographic data is available on the Internet at http://dnb.d-nb.de.

© 2015 Wiley-VCH Verlag & Co. KGaA, Boschstr. 12, 69469 Weinheim, Germany

All rights reserved (including those of translation into other languages). No part of this book may be reproduced in any form – by photoprinting, microfilm, or any other means – nor transmitted or translated into a machine language without written permission from the publishers. Registered names, trademarks, etc. used in this book – even when not specifically marked as such – are not to be considered unprotected by law.

**Design:** pp030 – Produktionsbüro Heike Praetor, Berlin
**Cover design:** init GmbH, Bielefeld
**Typesetting:** Inmedialo, Plankstadt
**Printing and binding:** CPI, Ebner & Spiegel, Ulm

**ISBN:** 978-3-527-50781-8

Printed in the Federal Republic of Germany on acid-free paper

# Why you should read this book

Brands. Is there any other topic in modern management about which so much has been published in recent years? The authors range from university professors to practitioners, advertising »gurus,« and consultants. On paper, their collected works would weigh many tons, leaving the impression that all aspects of branding have been covered in rich detail. Why then a book from McKinsey on brands?

The initial idea emerged in response to the concerns of many managers about the shortcomings of existing concepts and tools. At the one extreme, many texts are so theoretical that companies can't use them without major adaptations. At the other extreme, you find easy-to-read popular points of view on the world of branding that everyone can agree with, but which fail to offer practical tools or guidance. But the middle ground of a substantial yet pragmatic branding toolkit was nowhere in sight. In dealing with this concern over the course of many branding projects we have conducted, we became increasingly confident that we would be able to fill this »white space« by covering the topic in a practical, realistic, and analytically robust way. Many McKinsey teams have developed effective instruments in their marketing projects, which we know help our clients to improve their understanding of the complex issues of branding, and to manage their brands more effectively. Some concepts and tools evolved through intense cooperation with leading academics and practitioners over a number of years – in particular, the concept of brand relevance, developed in cooperation with Professors Meffert and Backhaus of the University of Münster, and with our McKinsey alumnus Professor Marc Fischer of the University of Cologne (formerly of the University of Kiel).

These concepts and tools have proven successful in many projects in completely different industries. The results motivated us to pull together McKinsey's diverse know-how on individual aspects of successful brand management into a holistic approach that top management could quickly grasp and apply. We also knew from discussions with our own McKinsey Editorial Review Board and external parties that brand management was a hot topic on the top management agenda. The total amount of money potentially spent ineffectively and inefficiently is just too large to leave decisions on branding to lower-level specialists or third parties.

Brands are an increasingly important issue not only for top management, but also in top management's discussions with analysts. For many acquisitions, for example, the questions often revolve around how to handle the acquired brands. Which ones have high value? Which ones can be abandoned? And what potential for value creation can be extracted from the acquired brands? Some companies excel at exploiting the potential of the brands they acquire – as BMW has shown with the Mini brand, or Marriott with Ritz Carlton. Others simply kill acquired brands or let them fade away over time. We believe that these decisions should not be based on gut feeling or left to luck. Instead, top management should have a fact-based, quantitative approach to making brand decisions and to explain them to their stakeholders.

We saw this as a challenge, an ideal one for McKinsey. Our traditional strengths could be exploited: careful attention to detail, fact-based approach, analysis-driven recommendations, and systematic follow-up and impact tracking. The challenge of applying this approach to brand management – where a belief in gut feeling and luck still largely prevails – beckoned irresistibly and drew us into what proved to be a highly motivating and satisfying journey.

When you take a closer look, you realize that marketing – unlike other management functions – really lacks great unifying breakthroughs. Marketing science has developed more and more into a niche field, where scholars talk to one another in their journals, while marketing practitioners have trouble understanding their theories or have simply stopped listening. Brand managers, on the other hand, along with advertising agencies and the media, have followed their own course. The media have all developed their own specific quantitative metrics. Brand managers can define their own market research so that the results will prove their hypotheses. Under these circumstances, it is no surprise that senior management's trust in branding decisions has declined, reducing any willingness to spend increasing amounts of money. Faced with growing pressure for business performance and transparency, boards and investors expect clear plans and quantified results.

To meet these expectations and regain credibility, marketing and brand management need to demonstrate much greater professionalism: they need to take a more systematic and a more quantitative approach to brand management. Power brands are just pure luck? That won't fly today. Brand success can be managed. This book will show you how. Our holistic approach – McKinsey BrandMatics® – provides senior executives with a complete framework for evaluating brand performance better, and gives marketing and brand managers a rich toolkit, illustrated with many examples, to manage brands more effectively. McKinsey BrandMatics® will help you make better brand decisions on the basis of data and facts, and thus equip you to manage your company's brand success systematically.

When we published the first edition of this book for the German market in February 2004, our ambition was to get the ball rolling on systematic brand management in German-speaking countries. The examples and illustrations we chose were therefore very well known in those markets. We were thrilled by the book's success and many positive reactions from readers. After adding to and improving our concepts, we published the second German edition in August 2005. By then, many global clients were asking us for an English version. Thus, we proceeded to adapt our book to global markets. In doing so, we have tried to choose brand examples known or readily understood around the world. *Power Brands* has German roots, but we are convinced that it will be useful in your home market as well. We know from many international projects that – as different as individual country markets may be – a unified global approach to the science, art, and craft of branding is the only way to manage the complexities of global brands successfully in a rapidly changing world.

## Why even readers of prior editions should read the new edition

Now is the best of times for brand managers. Consumers have never been hungrier for a unique experience, a golden promise, a good story. Rich rewards will fall to those who provide the thrills, keep the promises, and tell the stories that resonate with their target audience. What's more, people will readily collaborate with their favorite brands as co-creators and recommend them to their peers, both online and offline.

Now is the worst of times for brand managers. Consumers have never been as demanding, as fickle, and as well-informed as they are today. Technology gives them near-total transparency – and it lets their voices travel faster and farther than ever before. If a beloved brand lets them down, chances are they will not only walk away, but also share their disappointment with the entire world.

How rapidly things are changing becomes apparent when we take a look at some of the things that have happened since the last English edition of this book was published in 2009. That was only five years ago, and already the world of brand management is a different place:

**Brands in motion.** Five years ago, there were some 16 million internationally registered trademarks. In 2013, that number had climbed to 24 million, a 50 percent increase over the course of just five years. The World Intellectual Property Organization (WIPO) alone has received more than three million new applications for brand registration since 2009. At the same time, long-established brands, such as Nokia, have changed hands, and major brands, such as Pontiac, have vanished. Google, on the other hand, became the world's second most valuable brand in 2013, now valued at USD 93 billion by Interbrand, up from USD 32 billion in 2009. At the same time, Apple took the top spot from Coca-Cola as the world's most valuable brand in 2013 according to Interbrand. In 2014, Millward Brown ranked Google as the world's most valuable brand, valued at USD 159 billion.

**Advertising is back.** After the slump that started a decade ago, advertising has come back with a vengeance. Global advertising spending is estimated to have totaled some USD 500 billion in 2013, a sum that exceeds the GDP of medium-sized national economies like Austria, Thailand, or Denmark. The way this money is spent and allocated is also changing. Google, for example, has not only pushed the limits of contextual online advertising, but also pioneered auction sales of classic above-the-line media space. Since 2009, online advertising spending has doubled globally, and mobile advertising revenues have increased tenfold, reaching USD 17 billion in 2013. Print, on the other hand, has seen the dramatic rise of free papers. In five European countries, more free than paid papers are distributed, and in a dozen countries, the paper with the largest circulation is a free newspaper.

**Digital marketing.** Second Life may have come and gone, but the Web remains a major marketing opportunity for the foreseeable future. Active users of Facebook, for example, have increased more than fivefold, from some 250 million in 2009 to more than 1.3 billion in 2014. Smartphone penetration has more than doubled between

2009 and 2013 in the US. In China, an estimated 800 million smartphones are now in circulation. The online world has become a multiple-platform network of content generated by marketers, third parties, and consumers themselves. Much of this content is brand-related, be it branded entertainment (promotional mini movies), price comparisons (check24 or verivox), or consumer blogs (Yelp or epinions). As a consequence, digital marketing holds opportunities for a wide range of branding applications, such as insights gathering, outbound communication, viral marketing, or a combination of all three.

**Branded life.** Brands increasingly evolve from sheer labels to clusters of experience, often spilling over into entertainment and art. Above the line, brands such as Louis Vuitton are hiring feature directors, A-list actors, and mainstream musicians for their commercials – and award-winning architects for their flagship stores. Below the line, brands are trying hard to create tangible and lasting impressions; examples include Volkswagen's, Mercedes', BMW's destination outlets that are half museum, half amusement park, as well as Audi's new-generation showrooms that feature large-scale interactive displays and lounge areas. Luxury brands – such as Armani, Givenchy, and Cavalli – have successfully entered the hospitality sector with cafes, restaurants, and hotels, while Ikea is hosting sleepover events at its stores to create a unique experience for the brand's followers.

To stay relevant and attractive, brands must keep up with the pace of change without severing their roots. To help our readers come out on top, we have treated *Power Brands* to a thorough makeover. Highlights of this edition include:

- New research on the evolution of brand relevance, both in B2C and B2B
- Two modular additions to the proven brand purchase funnel framework
- All-new chapters on brand delivery, marketing return on investment (MROI), and digital brand management
- Dozens of new case studies from insights generation to brand promise definition
- Five new in-depth interviews with distinguished international brand managers.

We trust that even diligent readers of prior editions will find something new and helpful to guide and inspire them in coping with the increasing complexity and accelerating change in the world of brand management. They not only shape millions of purchase decisions and countless company decisions, but entire markets and the people who live in them; they also influence our perception and behavior, our self-esteem, our impression of others, and our value judgments. Put simply: brands shape people and markets alike.

# Third edition acknowledgements

Successful brand management is all about storytelling. To get our own story straight, we have called on the finest in their fields. We gratefully acknowledge the contribution of our interviewees: Kasper Rorsted of Henkel, Erwin van Laethem and Dorkas Koenen of Essent, Jean-Christophe Babin of Bulgari, Matt Jauchius of Nationwide, and Oliver Bierhoff of the German national soccer team. Professor Marc Fischer of the University of Cologne and Professor Christoph Burmann of the University of Bremen have helped us advance our thinking on brand relevance and brand image. Numerous experts among our colleagues were kind enough to infuse this book with their knowledge. In alphabetical order, they are: Reinhold Barchet, Thomas Bauer, Klaus Behrenbeck, Jochen Böringer, Peter Breuer, Benjamin Brudler, David Court, Linda Dauriz, Sandra Durth, Oliver Ehrlich, Dave Elzinga, Harald Fanderl, Thomas French, Jonathan Gordon, Omar El Hamamsy, Carina Kauter, Mathias Kullmann, Sascha Lehmann, Thomas Meyer, Yvonne Staack, Andris Umblijs, Kai Vollhardt, and Lorenz Zimmermann.

Thank you to our dedicated editorial team for putting together a great book: Birgit Ansorge, Kasia Bednarz, Lena Bolanz, Adriana Clemens, Heike Ditzhaus, Carmen Horn, Tobias Karmann, Sabrina Peltner, Scott Reznik, Sanya van Schalkwyk, Stephanie Schröder, Caroline von Schwerin, Ewa Sikora, Ola Swierzynska, and Alexandra Tuttas.

Finally, a special thank you to Cornelius Grupen, our executive editor. He has been with *Power Brands* from day one, and has kept it sounding fresh ever since.

December 2014

*Jesko Perrey*
*Tjark Freundt*
*Dennis Spillecke*

# Second edition acknowledgements

The first English edition of this book, originally published in early 2007, was well received by marketing practitioners, academics, and colleagues alike. Their positive reactions encouraged us to publish an updated and extended second edition. It incorporates a wide range of new tools, refined approaches, and recent insights rooted in the daily work of leading international companies, researchers, and consulting teams.

We are also grateful to the companies that have granted us permission to reproduce their proprietary graphics and texts, among them Apple, Audi, BMW, Coca-Cola, IBM, Ikea, Nestlé, Procter & Gamble, Sixt, Sony, Starbucks, Unilever, Virgin, and Volkswagen, and also for their cooperation regarding case examples and other contributions. We also thank Jens Lorenzen for renewing his permission to reproduce his full-page illustrations that have been inserted between chapters.

Again, many colleagues at McKinsey helped make the second edition of *Power Brands* possible. The evolving BrandMatics® toolkit in general is built on the support and expertise of McKinsey's global branding leadership group: David Court, Mary Ellen Coe, Dave Elzinga, Jonathan Gordon, Jean-Baptiste Coumau, Claudia Meffert, and Thomas Meyer. Specifically, Hemant Ahlawat, Christoph Erbenich, Harald Fanderl, John Forsyth, Maarten Schellekens, Vicky Smith, and Ansgar Hölscher all contributed to the development of new contents and updates in some way or another. The support of Nils Liedtke and Michael Egli was instrumental in bringing facts and figures up to date. We are also grateful to Ruth Balcombe, Terry Gilman, and Ivan Hutnik for their editorial supervision, as well as to Frank Breuer and Luisa Kaumanns for handling exhibits and illustrations. Publishing coordination and process management were in the capable hands of Marie Luise Cöln, Michaela Dülks, and Pia Verbocket at McKinsey and Jutta Hörnlein at Wiley-VCH.

Last, but not least, very special thanks to Thomas Meyer, our Senior Knowledge Expert for Branding and Marketing ROI, and to Cornelius Grupen, our Expert for Marketing Knowledge Development, for coordinating this project, as well as for updating and expanding large parts of the book.

Over the course of two German and two English editions, *Power Brands* and its German equivalent, *Mega-Macht Marke*, have, to some extent, become brands in themselves. We hope this new edition will inspire previous and new readers alike, help them to stay at the cutting edge of fact-based brand management, and act as a stepping stone for the creation of the power brands of the future.

Düsseldorf  
November 2008

*Hajo Riesenbeck*  
*Jesko Perrey*

# First edition acknowledgements

The many positive reactions to the first two editions of *Power Brands* in German (entitled *Mega-Macht Marke*) encouraged us to publish a version more accessible to an international readership. For the English edition, we have updated and internationalized many examples, added new steps, and described advances in our thinking and further ranges of application.

Many people participated in the writing of this book. We would like to thank our advisors outside of McKinsey, Professors Klaus Backhaus and Heribert Meffert of the University of Münster, who not only contributed to the rich exchange of ideas between scholarship and practice, but also participated actively in the development of some individual concepts and instruments. We also thank our alumnus Dr. Marc Fischer of the Department of Innovation, New Media, and Marketing at the University of Kiel for his research and analysis and for his suggestions on the chapters about brand relevance. Furthermore, a special thank you to Professor Henrik Sattler of the University of Hamburg for his support in advising and coordinating the international market research on brand relevance.

Many people at McKinsey helped make *Power Brands* possible: Jürgen Schröder, our partner colleague in Düsseldorf, contributed materially to the development of many of the tools we discuss, very often in collaboration with the University of Münster. Thomas Barta, Nicole Baumüller, Jens Echterling, Christoph Erbenich, Harald Fanderl, Tjark Freundt, Fabian Hieronimus, Ansgar Hölscher, and Patrick Metzler supplied valuable insights and examples from their consulting practice. Our expert researchers, Saule Serikova and Geoffrey Sherburn, devoted countless hours to researching and verifying individual brands and brand stories, with support from their colleagues in McKinsey Research & Information Services.

We also owe a special debt of gratitude to our colleagues Thomas Meyer, our European Branding Practice Manager, and Mathias Kullmann for their great support in coordinating this project and in updating, internationalizing, and expanding the book. A very special thank you also to Ivan Hutnik, our editor, for his incisive questions, practical suggestions, and expert editing of our drafts. As for the first two editions, publishing coordination was again in the capable hands of Hella Reese, Rainer Mörike, and Daniel Münch. With their unstinting dedication and expert support, our assistants, Michaela Dülks and Denise Kranepoth, also once again helped us to advance steadily towards completion of the manuscript.

This book would never have come to be without the thoughtful and detailed comments we received on our very first drafts. We sincerely thank Winfried Wilhelm and Dr. Axel Born, both members of our Editorial Review Board, as well as Professor Heribert Meffert for their valuable critical examination and suggestions regarding the original manuscript of the first German edition. Very warm thanks for their support of this first international edition go to our partner colleagues in McKinsey's European

Marketing Practice, Johanna Waterous and Yoram Gutgeld, and especially to Trond Riiber Knudsen, who has been advocating an international edition of *Power Brands* for a long time.

Finally, we want to thank Jens Kreibaum and his colleagues at our publishers, Wiley-VCH, for their enthusiastic and experienced support.

We wish our readers interesting discoveries, rewarding insights, and every possible success in implementing BrandMatics® and hope that sharing our experience will contribute to the creation and development of new power brands.

Düsseldorf *Hajo Riesenbeck*
November 2006 *Jesko Perrey*

# LUCKY STRIKE

IT'S TOASTED

CIGARETTES

# 1. What Brands Can Do

What has led companies to commit USD 1.6 billion in sponsorship fees alone to the 2014 FIFA Soccer World Cup in Brazil, or USD 2.2 billion to the 2016 Summer Olympics?[1] Why does Procter & Gamble buy over EUR 10 billion worth of media each year?[2] What is it that made companies spend more than USD 500 billion on advertising during 2012?[3] Why are some people willing to pay enormous sums for a Rolex watch or a Louis Vuitton bag? Why do consumers »google« information on the Internet, instead of searching for it? And how did matte-white in-ear headphones – the Apple iPod's trademark accessory – become the hallmark of urban trendiness all over the world?

The answer is simple: brands. Brands, as the examples in this chapter show, are the true giants of the modern world of consumption, dominating the household budgets of consumers and the investment calculations of companies. They not only shape millions of purchase decisions and countless company decisions, setting prices and determining profits; they also influence our perception and behavior, our self-esteem, our estimation of others, and our value judgments.[4] Put simply: brands shape people and markets alike.

## 1.1 What Brands Mean for Consumers and Companies

Brands are omnipresent. They address us directly in public, and subtly in the most intimate spheres of our lives. They stimulate our desires and form the hubs in the network of goods that typifies advanced consumer societies. No one can escape their influence. They are the emblems of a global economy, reaching new markets well ahead of the rest of the economy and visible from much farther away than the turrets of any company's headquarters.

The message is clear: there is hardly a bank or an insurance company, a company in the automotive or telecommunications sector, a machine tools manufacturer, or a chemicals, electricity, or gas supplier that now ignores the growing importance of brands. Even public institutions such as regions, cities, the armed forces of several countries, state pension providers, and the EU have sat up and taken notice.

### Brands shape our perception and our behavior

Perception is reality. It can also determine success or failure. Largely subconsciously, we pigeonhole people according to the car they drive, the clothes they wear, and the accessories with which they surround themselves. We use brands as beacons in the flood of signals and information we are subject to. And the imagery strong brands create to articulate the lifestyle they stand for extends well beyond the product. Their campaigns feature visuals of cityscapes, leisure activities, or other slices of the luxurious life in which the brand's products may feature as precious props, but not necessarily as the centers of attention.

Take the example of Louis Vuitton. The brand has gone to great lengths to create an entire world that consumers want to be part of. Founded in 1854, Louis Vuitton first ran its »Spirit of Travel« campaign in the late 1970s, emphasizing the adventure and the allure of traveling in style[5] (Figure 1.1). In the new millennium, the spirit of travel was rekindled by a series of star-studded ads shot by the likes of Annie Leibovitz and Peter Lindbergh: Keith Richards lounging in his hotel room with a branded custom guitar case by his side; Mikhail Gorbachev with his trusted monogram canvas travel bag riding in a taxi against the backdrop of the Berlin wall; Zinedine Zidane engaged in a game of table soccer, with his Vuitton trolley barely visible on the fringe of the frame; Sean Connery lounging on a tropical beach, traveling light with nothing but his Vuitton weekender for luggage. Other celebrities featured in the campaign include Francis Ford Coppola, Angelina Jolie, Catherine Deneuve, and Bono.

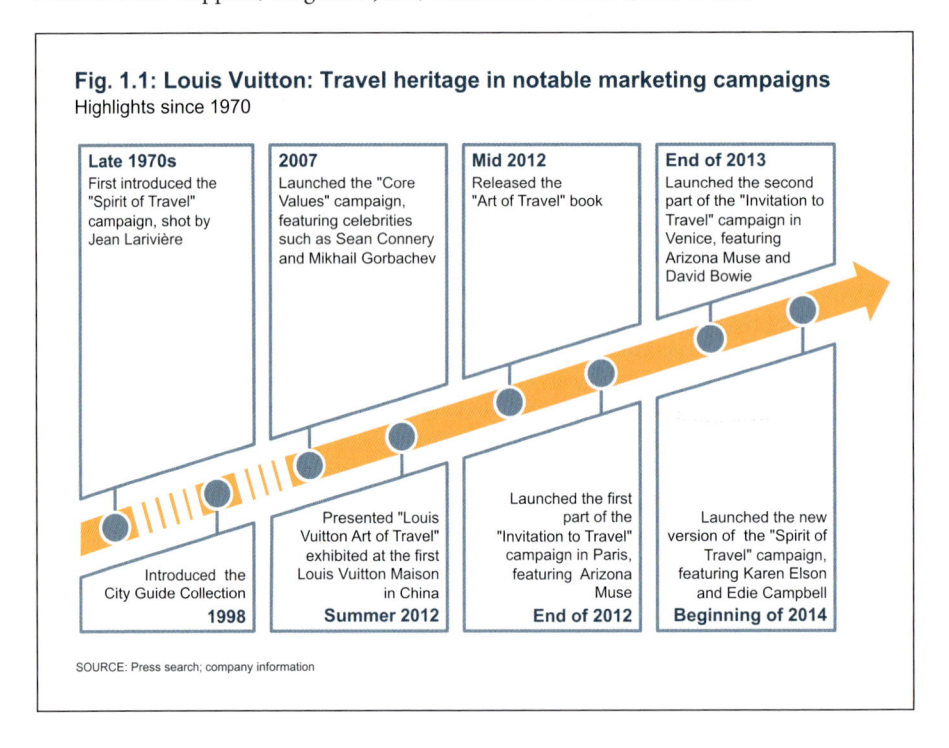

**Fig. 1.1: Louis Vuitton: Travel heritage in notable marketing campaigns**
Highlights since 1970

| Late 1970s | 2007 | Mid 2012 | End of 2013 |
|---|---|---|---|
| First introduced the "Spirit of Travel" campaign, shot by Jean Larivière | Launched the "Core Values" campaign, featuring celebrities such as Sean Connery and Mikhail Gorbachev | Released the "Art of Travel" book | Launched the second part of the "Invitation to Travel" campaign in Venice, featuring Arizona Muse and David Bowie |

| Introduced the City Guide Collection **1998** | Presented "Louis Vuitton Art of Travel" exhibited at the first Louis Vuitton Maison in China **Summer 2012** | Launched the first part of the "Invitation to Travel" campaign in Paris, featuring Arizona Muse **End of 2012** | Launched the new version of the "Spirit of Travel" campaign, featuring Karen Elson and Edie Campbell **Beginning of 2014** |

SOURCE: Press search; company information

More recently, Louis Vuitton extended its »Invitation to Travel« to consumers worldwide. Featuring Arizona Muse, the first part of the campaign was shot at the Louvre museum in Paris in 2012. In the brand's first ever TV commercial, a girl discovers a mysterious envelope at the museum and departs in quest of unknown adventures aboard a giant hot air balloon. Reminiscent of Jules Verne's *Around the World in 80 Days*, the balloon also featured prominently in full-page print ads. Additionally, the company published a travel guide book directing readers to the world's most inspiring destinations. In 2013, David Bowie joined Arizona Muse for the second part of the campaign: a romantic encounter set in Venice.[6] Touching down on the Piazza San Marco, Muse arrives at a lavish masked ball. Carrying the brand's Vivienne bag, she is duly serenaded by Bowie playing the harpsichord. In mid-2012, Louis Vuitton staged a similarly extravagant real-life event to celebrate the opening of its first Louis Vuitton Maison in China, at Shanghai's prestigious Plaza 66 mall. Arriving from Paris by way of Eastern Europe and Mongolia, the iconic Paris/Shanghai Express train was the centerpiece of the event. All this shows that strong brands go well beyond advertising in their efforts to engage consumers. They aspire to create a world you would want to live in.

How can you resist such corporate seduction? Brands save us time in that we do not have to check, challenge, classify, or critically weigh up everything before we make a decision to act. They are »an established, unmistakable mental representation of a product or service in the mind of the potential consumer.«[7] This representation is formed at all the points where we come into contact with the brand, including the product itself, advertising, customer service, and word of mouth.

Brands can mark class boundaries – or blur them. For some, owning a Rolex, a BMW, or a Louis Vuitton bag helps demonstrate – to themselves and to others – their membership in a particular social stratum. For others, brands can be used as a way of breaking free from their class shackles. Maybe they starved themselves to be able to afford that BMW – but once in the driver's seat, they moved into a different milieu.

Branding reaches ever more traditionally unbranded areas. Many formerly anonymous (i.e., no name) products or private labels (also referred to as »own brands,« »store brands,« or »house brands«) are giving themselves distinctive profiles by differentiating their value proposition and investing large amounts in publicity and uptrading. The previously clear-cut differences between branded, no name, and house brand products are blurring in the face of increasing competition for the consumer's affection and loyalty.

Over the past few years, some retailers have even started to promote their private labels with mass media advertising. In a series of TV commercials, discount retailer Aldi compared branded products with their private label equivalents. The main message was: »You can get the quality of a branded product at a fraction of the cost when you buy our private label equivalent,« implying that the only discernible difference was price: »Aldi. Like brands, only cheaper« (Figure 1.2). Featured products included champagne, gin, frozen fish, candy, and tea. The campaign won a gold trophy for creativity at the 2011 Epica Awards.[8] Ten years ago, the French grocery chain E. Leclerc ran a similar print advertising campaign, promoting private labels as affordable equivalents to branded products (»The same quality, 30 percent cheaper.«).[9] German coffee chain and general retailer Tchibo has teamed up with fashion designer Michael Michalsky to establish their range of sports apparel as a kind of budget designer label in its own right, »Mitch & Co.«

As a result, consumer spending on private label packaged goods is rising quickly, having increased from USD 172 billion in 2000 to USD 307 billion in 2012 to account for about a quarter of total consumer goods consumption in most countries.[10]

**Fig. 1.2: Private label advertising at Aldi**

Visual from "Like brands. Only cheaper" campaign
UK example, aired in 2013

SOURCE: YouTube, press search

Producers of branded products are taking this private label threat very seriously. When the German retailer Rewe launched a mass-media campaign for private label products, the German Brands Association was not very happy. In the past, the Association saw Rewe as an ally of manufacturers of branded products in their struggle against discount retailers and their store brands. Other brands associations even go one step further and are no longer mincing their words. For example, the 2005 campaign run by the Austrian Branded Goods Association treats the competition with private labels as »a battle between good and evil.«[11]

No product group is invulnerable to private label encroachment. Even the »safest,« most established areas, where the newcomers were long powerless, are now reporting a dent in sales due to competition from private labels. In some categories, private labels account for a third of the entire market in terms of value. Examples include frozen foods, tissues, dried foods, and even snacks (Figure 1.3). In the past, private labels were often perceived as the affordable alternative to manufacturer brands. But, as branding evolves into a source of differentiation for retailers, private labels start playing a more strategic role – and some of them are evolving into brands in their own right.[12]

The success of private labels should, however, not be interpreted as a sign that brands have lost their former power. On the contrary, it shows that brands have become increasingly important, even in areas previously thought immune to the lure of branding. Some retailers, in fact, are taking brand management so seriously that they have established entire portfolios of their own brands.

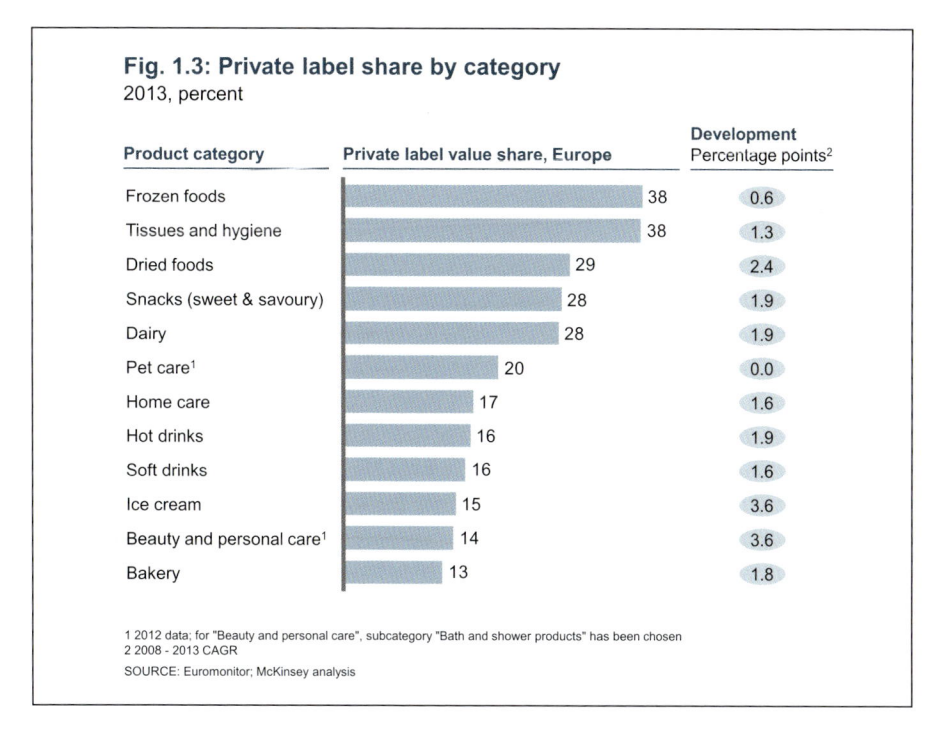

**Fig. 1.3: Private label share by category**
2013, percent

| Product category | Private label value share, Europe | Development Percentage points[2] |
|---|---|---|
| Frozen foods | 38 | 0.6 |
| Tissues and hygiene | 38 | 1.3 |
| Dried foods | 29 | 2.4 |
| Snacks (sweet & savoury) | 28 | 1.9 |
| Dairy | 28 | 1.9 |
| Pet care[1] | 20 | 0.0 |
| Home care | 17 | 1.6 |
| Hot drinks | 16 | 1.9 |
| Soft drinks | 16 | 1.6 |
| Ice cream | 15 | 3.6 |
| Beauty and personal care[1] | 14 | 3.6 |
| Bakery | 13 | 1.8 |

1 2012 data; for "Beauty and personal care", subcategory "Bath and shower products" has been chosen
2 2008 - 2013 CAGR
SOURCE: Euromonitor; McKinsey analysis

Examples include:

- Edeka's »Edeka Bio,« »Edeka Selection,« and »Elkos,« as well as Rewe's »Erlenhof« and »Today« in German grocery and personal care.[13]
- Dixons' »Essentials,« »Logik,« and »Sandstrom,« as well as Tesco's »Technika« in the UK's consumer electronics retailing.[14]
- MediaMarkt's »OK,« »Koenic,« »Peaq,« and »Isy« in European consumer electronics and household appliances.[15]

In 2010, German retailer Rewe went even further when it introduced Pro Planet, a proprietary sustainability label that indicates high ecological and social standards. It is awarded based on a standardized five-stage process that has been developed in cooperation with external experts specializing in sustainable consumption, climate change, and innovation. Pro Planet was first used in the produce department and has since been expanded to other categories, such as processed food, clothing, and paper goods. At the time of writing, there were more than 500 products carrying the Pro Planet label. Launched in Germany, it was rolled out to 13 other European markets. In 2012, the Rewe Group received the German Corporate Social Responsibility award recognizing its commitment to sustainability along the entire supply chain, and specifically, Pro Planet's contribution to sustainable consumption.[16]

In effect, the old battle between manufacturer brands on the one hand and private labels on the other is obsolete. These days, brands are simply fighting other brands.

*Brands both need and fear publicity.* In today's information society, our beliefs, thoughts, and behavior are increasingly subject to external stimuli. Companies that do not communicate well across all channels or ones that fail to publicize their company and brand profile soon stop being noticed by consumers and ultimately vanish from the market. What is more, public opinion acts as an independent force and can praise a company or brand to the skies one day and write it off the next. Such word of mouth – powerful as it may be – cannot always be steered by the companies themselves.

FedEx, the international logistics company, recently came under pressure when someone shot a video of a courier throwing a parcel marked »fragile« over a gate, never stopping to even ring the doorbell. The video was posted on YouTube and got five million hits in five days.[17] Realizing that the company's reputation was on the line, FedEx took the incident seriously and moved swiftly, shooting their own video and posting it on YouTube only two days later. In the video, a senior FedEx executive apologizes for the incident on behalf of the company and describes the actions they were taking to remedy the mishap, saying they would even use the original video as a negative example for internal training purposes. More than 80 percent of the subsequent social media buzz was neutral or positive, with many users applauding the company's responsiveness.

In contrast, Adidas Originals took control of multiple channels to generate beneficial viral effects for its brand and a series of new products inspired by cult figures. As part of an effort to launch a limited edition collection, Adidas partnered with the Star Wars franchise and the 2010 FIFA soccer World Cup. The theme of the campaign was »a neighborhood of originality.« One of the videos made for the campaign recreates a legendary scene from the 1977 Star Wars movie. The new version combines original footage of characters such as Obi-Wan Kenobi with appearances by celebrities like David Beckham. Uploaded to YouTube prior to its official TV launch during England's opening group match against the US in the World Cup, the clip got 2.5 million views within one week. It was the tenth most watched commercial on YouTube that year, generating a total of 4.7 million views. Other campaign touch points included a series of local launch parties, an app that lets users control a Death Star to vaporize their friends via Google Maps, product features on Facebook, and iconic product badges tied in with the campaign theme.[18]

It turns out that in the peer-to-peer world of opinionated, user-generated content, brands may benefit, but can also easily suffer from publicity. According to Keith Pardy, Nokia's former Senior Vice President of Strategic Marketing, now CMO for cx.com, a cloud computing company: »Brands are going to be made and destroyed on the Internet, and there's a whole set of new marketing rules for it. If you start playing games with people, they'll find out and eat you alive.«[19] For more examples, see the section on digital brand management (4.4) in Chapter 4.

As the YouTube videos show, brand communication doesn't necessarily equate to advertising spend. The Spanish fashion chain Zara operates in a world where marketing spend generally amounts to 3 to 4 percent of sales revenues,[20] but it manages to do without any advertising at all. Zara's sole means of advertising is its network of highly styled stores, always located on the best city streets and designed by a sizable team of top window dressers. Potential customers see the merchandise in the store windows as they walk through the city and hear the store recommended by satisfied customers – no more is needed to sell fashionable items of clothing by the millions. It works beautifully: Zara's sales revenues have seen double-digit annual growth rates over the past decade. Between 2008 and 2012, revenues have grown at an average rate of 14 percent each year. At the beginning of 2013, Zara had 2,280 stores around the world including the Zara Home stores, up from 531 in 2003.[21]

Jägermeister is another example of successful brand management without expensive mass media advertising. In the 1990s, after decades of being imported to the United States as a dark horse of sorts, the German brand's managers decided to change Jägermeister's communication strategy completely. The brand started to target younger drinkers, particularly college students, and focused its communication on inexpensive but targeted activities like the sponsorship of student parties and promotions in student bars. The result speaks for itself. Between 2001 and 2006 sales grew at over 30 percent per year, making Jägermeister the fastest-growing imported liqueur in the United States at the time.[22] At more than two million cases sold annually, Jägermeister is now one of the country's top 15 spirit brands (2013).[23]

More recently, Nestlé was facing severe budget constraints when the company launched its Kit Kat Chunky Cookies and Cream candy bar in Australia. The company had allocated only USD 500,000 to the launch, a sum that would not normally get a traditional advertising campaign noticed in a highly competitive and cluttered market. Nestlé opted for an all-digital campaign to target male adolescents, a premiere in the Australian fast-moving consumer goods (FMCG) market. Half the budget was spent to create the »Chunga« campaign featuring insatiable Hans Fagerlund as its hilarious role model, and half to buy rich banner advertising that would attract initial attention. The »Chunga Championship« – including Web episodes and an online game – went viral and generated a total reach of 46 percent in the target group. Consideration, purchase intent, and recent consumption went up. The campaign exceeded its sales target by 150 percent, generated an ROI of more than 6 percent, and received an Effie award.[24]

### Companies and their brands: A special relationship

*Brands can immunize.* While a media push is often very helpful for a company, negative publicity can be very dangerous. Nevertheless, companies that have continually built and promoted their brands in a well-founded and fully rounded way can survive media attacks relatively intact. Leading toy producer Mattel, for example, had to recall over 20 million toys between the summer and autumn of 2007 due to toxic lead-based paint and magnets that could be swallowed by children. Nevertheless Mattel still managed to exceed analyst expectations in the fourth quarter of 2007, and increased both sales (by 4 percent) and net profit (by 15 percent) compared with the fourth quarter of 2006.[25]

Apple launched Apple Maps in 2012 to replace Google Maps on the company's iPhones. Apple Maps quickly became notorious for its numerous glitches. According to Associated Press, the app directed users onto an airport runway in Fairbanks, Alaska. Forbes reported a similar issue with Washington's Dulles airport. The Huffington Post found that the Statue of Liberty was missing from the app's 3-D view, and that the software was giving incorrect coordinates for major cities such as Hong Kong and Kiev. Eventually, Apple's CEO Tim Cook issued a public apology, conceding that the application »fell short,« and suggesting users download competitors' products to replace Apple Maps. Yet iPhone sales didn't suffer. Apple sold 125 million iPhones, 35 million iPads, and 18 million computers in 2012.[26]

*Brands live and survive.* The best product names can even survive attacks of quite a different kind. Entire companies can go under, yet their brands are not sucked into the depths after them. Rover, a mainstay of the British automotive industry, ran aground in the 1990s and was acquired by BMW in 1994. The deal included the rights to the Mini brand. Originally launched in 1959, the Mini had brought mobility to the masses in post-war Britain and sold four million units in total. The car appealed to all levels of society and had long gained cult status when it went out of production in 2000. That same year, BMW sold Rover to the Phoenix consortium, but retained the Mini brand. Mini was relaunched in 2001 by BMW and has since sold almost three million cars – perhaps the biggest comeback in automotive history. Between 2001 and 2012, sales grew at a compound annual growth rate of 25 percent.[27]

Even without advertising, brands do not simply disappear. They can survive the drought like plants in a desert, waiting for the warm rain of fresh investments, to flower once again in abundance.

Strong brands are like living organisms. Their potential for adaptation and renewal seems almost unlimited. Strong brands such as Patek Philip (1839), Nestlé (1867), Heinz (1869), Coca-Cola (1886), Johnson & Johnson (1887), General Electric (1892), Maggi (1897), Mercedes (1902), Osram (1906), and Nivea (1911) have reached a legendary age and yet remain forever young. Classic brands such as Harley Davidson and Mini or Sinalco can be revived and even attain new heights.

It is the brands that truly claim this longevity, not the companies themselves. After 50 or a 100 years, who can remember a company's founders, its managing directors, its first board, or its core production plants or headquarters? But everyone still knows the brands.

*Brands generate strong impressions and powerful feelings.* When consumers hear the name Marlboro or just see the red Marlboro box, they immediately associate it with freedom and adventure, the cowboy riding across the plains. Nike evokes similarly strong, if quite different, associations with its images of athletics, performance, and lifestyle. The Lacoste crocodile immediately triggers thoughts of sporty luxury, or even the tennis court at Wimbledon, while the McDonald's logo makes many people's mouths water.[28]

Apart from creating strong impressions, brands also generate tangible value. They create price premiums, help to recruit the best talent, and save sales cost due to their inherent appeal to customers. Perhaps most important of all, companies with strong brands frequently outperform the stock market. A McKinsey analysis shows that a portfolio of 40 stocks, with their brands (or parent companies) being top ranked in Interbrand's annual »Best Global Brands« report, has outperformed traditional benchmarks like the MSCI World or the S&P 500 index in 9 of the last 13 annual periods. From a total return to shareholders perspective, the MSCI World was outperformed by a more than respectable 62 percent since the ranking was first published in 2000. Based on stock price alone – that is, when disregarding dividends – the gap would be even more dramatic. Top brands have beaten the stock market both in its bear and bull phases. Brand strength, it turns out, is a reliable indicator of economic performance (Figure 1.4). This analysis is one of the first to avoid the self-fulfilling prophecy of assessing the *past* economic performance of strong brands. Since brand strength, to some extent, reflects past economic performance, top brands will come out as strong stock market performers almost by necessity. This effect is eliminated in the analysis by assessing stock market performance *after* – rather than *before* – the publication of the annual brand strength ranking.

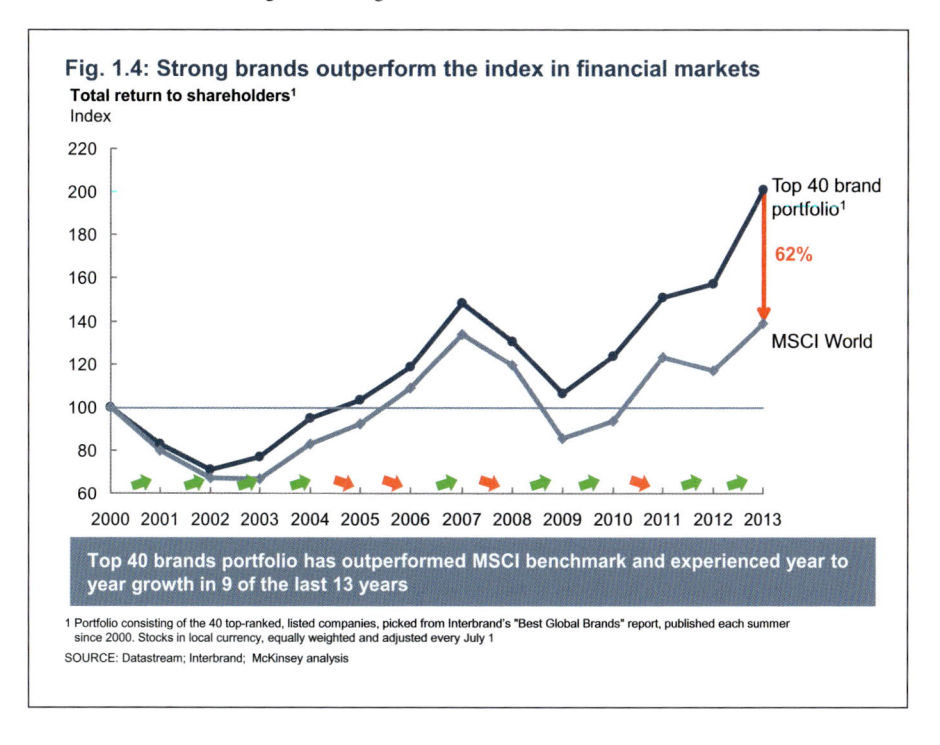

**Fig. 1.4: Strong brands outperform the index in financial markets**
Total return to shareholders[1]
Index

Top 40 brands portfolio has outperformed MSCI benchmark and experienced year to year growth in 9 of the last 13 years

[1] Portfolio consisting of the 40 top-ranked, listed companies, picked from Interbrand's "Best Global Brands" report, published each summer since 2000. Stocks in local currency, equally weighted and adjusted every July 1
SOURCE: Datastream; Interbrand; McKinsey analysis

Three factors determine the brand's added value as perceived by the consumer – and thus its value for a company (Figure 1.5).

1. **Information efficiency (the »time« factor)**. Brands are information carriers. They say something about the provenance of the item, help with recognition, and provide

### Fig. 1.5: Brands fulfill three basic functions

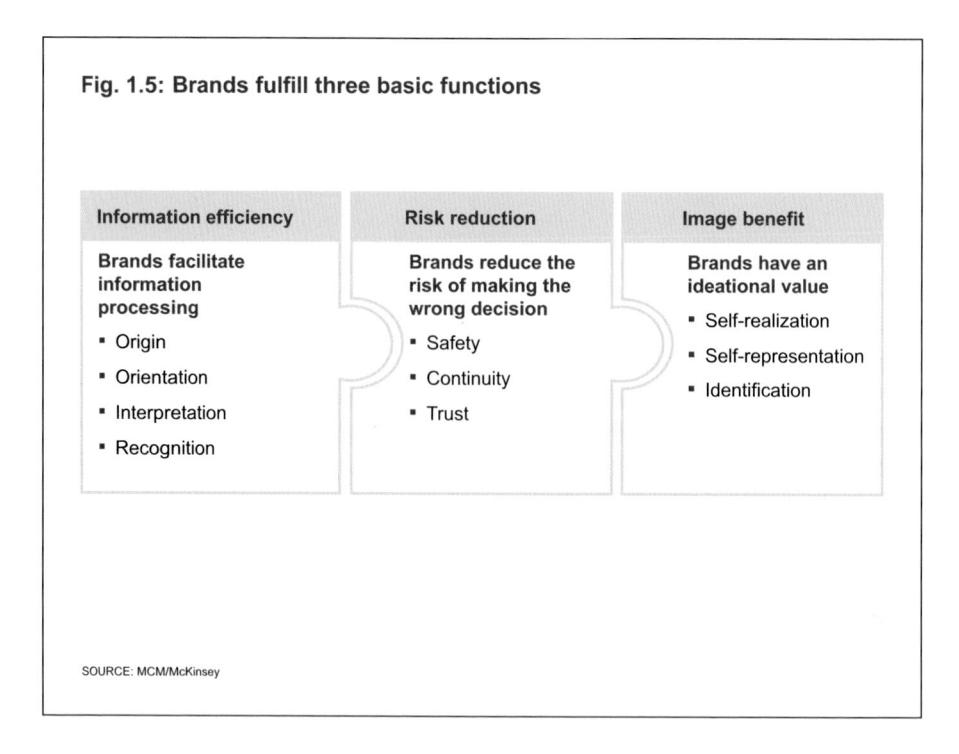

| Information efficiency | Risk reduction | Image benefit |
|---|---|---|
| Brands facilitate information processing | Brands reduce the risk of making the wrong decision | Brands have an ideational value |
| • Origin | • Safety | • Self-realization |
| • Orientation | • Continuity | • Self-representation |
| • Interpretation | • Trust | • Identification |
| • Recognition | | |

SOURCE: MCM/McKinsey

orientation. They act as consumer beacons in the flood of signals and information, making it easier to gather and process information about a purchase option. Brands as carriers of information help save time.

2. **Risk reduction (the »trust« factor).** Brands reduce the consumer's (subjective) risk of making a purchase mistake. Branded products promise consistent quality and a lower level of depreciation. Brands offer a safe choice, creating a basis of trust between the manufacturer and the consumer and then providing continuity in this relationship, for example, continued predictability of the product benefit.

3. **Image benefit (the »identity« factor).** Brands help consumers express who they are, contribute to self-esteem, communicate this to others, and enable them to claim allegiance to particular ideas or social groups.

The Volkswagen Golf brand provides a good example of these three components of added value. For decades, the Golf brand has been a constant, almost universal presence on European roads. The Golf brand bundles together everything that the consumer needs to know about the vehicle. Reliable quality and solid construction combined with decent prices in the used car market limit the risk in buying a Golf. Combining a well-balanced drive with time-tested reliability and resale value, the Golf is a widely accepted safe choice for all but the most expressive drivers.

Today, however, even the strongest brands must make headway in turbulent waters. The number of registered brands is increasing dramatically. Five years ago, there were some 16 million internationally registered trademarks. In 2013, that number had climbed to 24 million, a 50 percent increase over the course of just five years.[29]

The dramatic increase in the number of brands has inevitably given the consumer almost too much choice. Two decades ago, a typical supermarket carried some 7,000 different products (stock keeping units, or SKUs for short). Today's hypermarkets often carry more than 40,000 SKUs. The number of products advertised on television has seen a similar increase. At the same time, the consumer goods sector has also seen some concentration, with fewer manufacturers and a greater focus on core brands.

To complicate the situation even further, proliferation is by no means limited to brands proper. The number of distribution channels, consumer touch points, and marketing messages is constantly increasing. At the same time, complexity is also increasing on the demand side. Partly driven by the wide variety of options available, consumer choice is harder to predict than ever. For many consumers, it's coffee-to-go in the morning, fast food at lunch, and a three-course dinner at a fancy restaurant in the evening. But on the weekend, the same person may go for a healthy breakfast with whole grain cereal and fresh fruit from an organic food store, no lunch at all, and a late-night microwave TV dinner after a long day on the road, driving back from the in-laws. Old patterns no longer apply in the world of proliferation. While a business traveler will often fly with major airlines arranged through a trusted travel agent, the same person will book cheap tickets online from no-frills carriers for private travel. As a result, companies that find themselves stuck in the middle are facing increasing challenges and are showing much lower growth rates than both premium and no-frills providers. Alex Myers, formerly the Senior Vice President for Western Europe at Carlsberg, summarizes the dilemma as follows: »Historically, brewers have been big in the middle of the market. Now there is a polarization between the top and the bottom, and the risk is getting stuck in the middle.«[30] (Mr. Myers was appointed CEO and President at the Hilding Anders Group in 2013.)

**Tougher times require more effective brand management tools**

In this environment, efficiency is more important than ever. The good news: proven tools and approaches are available to fine tune branding investments for the highest possible impact. »Scattering losses« of 50 percent or more are by no means a law of nature. They are the result of insufficient analysis, shaky methodology, and dubious strategies.

It's no longer just the advertising gurus who dominate the branding scene with their creativity. Admittedly, creativity helps to increase advertising effectiveness; compare the findings from an analysis by McKinsey and the Art Directors Club on the success of creative campaigns in the next section. But brand managers cannot do without deep customer insights and thorough market analysis to complement creativity. After all, investing in brands is in many ways similar to other investments. Who would invest in a production facility, a research and development center, or a new head office without first examining the necessary commercial and financial groundwork to make a clear assessment of the probable payoff?

A shift toward a more professional approach to marketing and more efficient processes has been gaining pace recently. In the past ten years, almost 80,000 articles on branding have been published in leading international journals and news media.[31] Despite this flood of academic and practice-oriented publications, the right tools for effective and efficient brand management are still under debate. Experts are currently analyzing the basic factors underlying brand power, how best to describe them, and what their precise functions are for consumers. They are also looking into what makes brands strong, and what makes them weak.

While this debate continues, McKinsey has developed and continuously refined its own approach called BrandMatics®. This book uses this approach to reveal how companies can measure, make, and manage brands effectively without throwing creativity overboard. In the next section, we will discuss some recent additions to BrandMatics® that help companies capture the changes in how consumers interact with brands, arrive at their purchase decisions, and form lasting bonds of loyalty.

## 1.2 The Secret of Strong Brands

What makes a brand strong? What distinguishes Marlboro from Camel, Samsung from Nokia, and Giorgio Armani from Pierre Cardin? One answer that is commonly given to this question is that a brand becomes dominant and full of life when everyone in its target group has internalized it as »well known.« Though this might be a very common assumption about what makes a brand successful, it fails to distinguish the great brands from the also-rans.

Brand awareness – and the often corresponding high scores for brand recognition in market research evaluations – is not enough in itself to secure a place among the front-runners. Such indicators, however popular they are, actually say very little about consumer buying preferences. Nokia, for example, was probably never more widely known than at the time when it stopped making mobile devices and sold its core business to Microsoft in 2013, following five years of dwindling sales and two years of record losses.[32] Market share and profit margins are far more revealing when it comes to describing a brand's position. Companies that achieve a bond with buyers and generate customer loyalty that cannot be matched by the competition are the brand winners. The right strategy for brand management can be summed up in a single, simple sentence: strong brands need buyers – and repeat buyers.

Coca-Cola is a good example. Coca-Cola drinkers are particularly attached to their brand. In BrandKey's Customer Loyalty Index, Coca-Cola is ahead of Pepsi.[33] And according to Interbrand, the value of Coca-Cola as a brand is more than four times that of Pepsi.[34] These facts are enough to indicate the relative strength of those two major cola brands in that market. Pepsi's numerous celebrity endorsements – including Britney Spears, Michael Jackson, David Beckham, and Beyoncé Knowles (to name but the most prominent) – may have increased the public's general awareness, but they have failed to turn around cola drinkers' choices in many markets. Specifically, Coca-Cola is far ahead of Pepsi in much of Europe and South America.[35] From a total company perspective, the trade volume share of Coke (20.9 percent) is more than twice that of Pepsi (9.6 percent).[36] Compare the discussion of brand consistency below to find out how Coke does it.

## Three elements of success: The trinity of *science, art,* and *craft*

For management, the strongest indicators of brand success are market presence, profitability, and customer loyalty. Companies that want to ensure this sort of brand strength for the long-term need to achieve a harmonious blend of three elements underlying good brand management: *science, art,* and *craft*.

The *science* is measuring and understanding the brand's performance to create a fact base for strategy development and positioning. The *art* is in endowing the brand with a superior brand proposition, keeping it consistent yet up-to-date and executing it as creatively as possible. The *craft* is managing the brand rigorously in all its individual aspects throughout the organization.

Naturally, brands do not have to attain perfection in all three areas in order to be strong. Great brands have found different ways of mixing and balancing these elements to create unique propositions and differentiate themselves from competitors. Nonetheless, however well a company masters an individual element, this will be of little use to them unless they achieve a minimum standard in the other two elements as well (Figure 1.6).

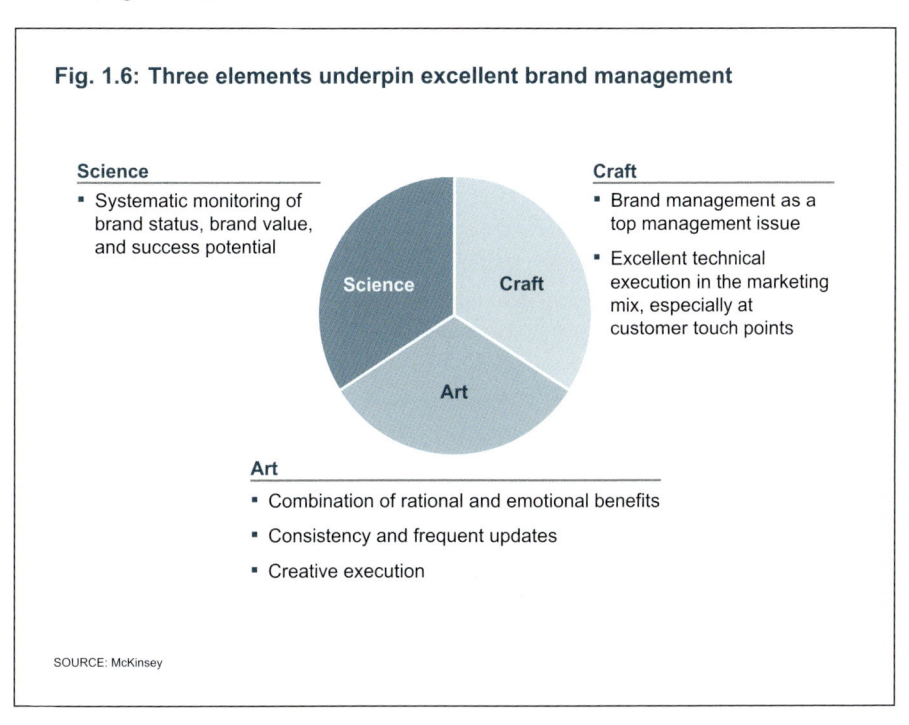

**Fig. 1.6: Three elements underpin excellent brand management**

**Science**
- Systematic monitoring of brand status, brand value, and success potential

**Craft**
- Brand management as a top management issue
- Excellent technical execution in the marketing mix, especially at customer touch points

**Art**
- Combination of rational and emotional benefits
- Consistency and frequent updates
- Creative execution

SOURCE: McKinsey

In general, the authors of this book consider *science* to be the first among equals. Many marketing departments will readily develop, and even shoot, TV commercials before spelling out what the brand is supposed to stand for, or who its products target. But frankly speaking, we believe it is foolish to create – let alone produce or activate – advertising or other brand communication without some sense of direction, and science is the key to its development. Branding without a fact-based strategy is nothing but a blind flight.

### *Science:* The challenge of accurate measurement

Science is the hallmark of good brand management. Only comprehensive and accurate measurement can provide and sustain the fact base that is essential for lasting success. Many marketing managers and agencies use primarily – some, even exclusively – brand awareness and advertising recall to measure the success of their brand management. But experience shows that this is an insufficient basis to assess the specific strengths and weaknesses of a brand. In some cases, such limited measurement can even create the illusion of a healthy brand, when in fact the brand is in trouble. The way out is to expand the toolbox of brand metrics, and to leverage it more comprehensively in brand management.

Despite recent innovations in brand measurement, advertising tracking instruments used to confirm the value of advertising investments still tend to focus on the level of awareness and recall. Determining that the brand enjoys a high level of awareness and recall can all too easily lead to the conclusion that the investment is well spent and the brand is strong. But often this is a false inference. This problem can be seen in teaser campaigns, for instance. Companies have wasted millions on advertising aimed at attracting attention to a brand before it actually appeared on the market or in situations where general brand awareness was of little relevance to a company's success.

Take Evonik Industries, for example. Evonik is the current name for the German RAG (»Ruhrkohle«), which was renamed after spinning off its former mainstay, coal mining. The company worked on the new name and the launch campaign for almost two years, but never disclosed anything. Halfway into the relaunch, Evonik found they had struck an overly early sponsorship deal with Borussia Dortmund's soccer team worth EUR 12 million in licensing fees. Since they were not ready to launch the brand, they put a simple exclamation mark on the players' jerseys for two seasons. A few weeks before actually introducing their new name, Evonik started a mass media teaser campaign that showed creative images (such as an elephant stuck to the side of a building) and the question »Who is doing this?« In September 2007, the company gave the answer: »We are doing this. Evonik Industries.« Evonik spent over EUR 20 million on advertising within one month to make the brand known and establish innovation as its core promise. It is questionable whether this level of mass media investment is justified for a business-to-business (B2B)-focused company that generates two-thirds of its revenues from its chemicals business unit. The objective of the mass media campaign was therefore not to sell, but to generate attention for the company's upcoming initial public offering. A few months later, however, Evonik announced it would postpone the initial public offering until at least 2009. It remains unclear whether Evonik will ever achieve its branding objectives. Suffice it to say that simple brand awareness is obviously an inadequate metric in a complex, multistakeholder situation such as this.[37]

The experience of E.ON was similar. Arising out of the merger between Veba and Viag in June 2000, E.ON needed to establish itself both as a corporate brand and as a product brand for electricity. When the campaign started, it only showed a red screen accompanied by dramatic music. After two weeks, the brand name E.ON and the nametag »new energy« appeared. Another three weeks later, E.ON started to position itself as an innovative brand by showing new energy initiatives like the possibility to switch off your light from a distance via a hotline. Finally, E.ON launched its »Mix it, baby« spots with Arnold Schwarzenegger, introducing a product that allowed the consumers to create a personal energy mix by choosing from several energy sources like wind or water. From a corporate branding point of view, the E.ON campaign was successful. E.ON certainly was able to strengthen awareness of its corporate brand among corporate stakeholders, for example, the capital markets.

Just four months after its launch, market research showed aided brand awareness of 93 percent and unaided advertising recall of 66 percent. Fifty percent of Germans knew the »On« slogan, and 85 percent knew it came from E.ON.[38] The challenge wasn't recall, the challenge was revenues. From a product marketing perspective, the impact was limited. Customers were simply not used to switching providers.

The German power sector appears to have learned from these early days. In 2004, the sector invested just over a fourth of the level spent five years earlier. But the fight for precious market share in an increasingly dynamic environment was quickly resumed. Says Matthias Kurth, formerly of the Federal Network Agency, Germany's energy and telecommunications regulatory body, »It took some getting used to for consumers, but these days they are well aware of the possibility to switch providers.«[39] (Mr. Kurth was appointed to a supervisory board position at Cable Europe in 2012.) In reaction to this growing opportunity, media spending by energy companies soared again, growing at ten times the market average between 2005 and 2008 according to Nielsen Media Research. Many players launched no-frills second brands, competing primarily on price. But after a series of failed attempts to build working business models for their widely publicized low-cost offerings, almost all energy providers are moving towards more differentiated brand positions. They now aspire to generate serious consideration among likely switchers, brought about by clearly communicated brand benefits, rather than sheer notoriety in the general population. Examples of recent repositioning efforts in the German energy market include:

- Yello Strom, established in 1999 as EnBW's second brand, has been repositioned as a service-focused provider.
- E-wie-einfach, launched in 2007 by E.ON as the prospective price leader, now emphasizes simplicity (»only pay what you use,« no monthly fee).

- eprimo, launched in 2005 and owned by RWE since 2007, is evolving towards a soft-discount player focusing on care-free supply and service.

See our discussion of brand relevance in the next section for an update on the evolving role of branding in the energy sector, as well as in a range of B2B industries from banking and chemicals to IT and logistics. Also compare our interview with Erwin van Laethem and Dorkas Koenen of Essent, the Dutch energy provider.

Strong brands generate strong sales and profits. They need buyers, repeat buyers, and a price that ensures they will continue developing and bringing in revenues and reasonable profits. Accordingly, the tool used for measuring the brand needs to be one that is able to dissect brand performance in terms of its bottom-line impact and not just its effect on consumer consciousness.

Even the notoriously advertising-savvy automotive industry sometimes misses the mark. Assuming attention was what would help them conquer the compact car category in Germany, Toyota focused on generating the maximum amount of advertising noise prior to the introduction of the Auris. In March 2007, Toyota launched its new model with the largest outdoor advertising campaign in German history. Toyota spent over EUR 30 million in March alone (EUR 43 million in 2007) to present the Auris on over 200,000 billboards in 82 major cities, more than 60 percent of all available billboards in Germany. Although Toyota achieved an impressive 300 million advertising impressions in one month, it turned out that 85 percent of all viewers were not even interested in buying a new car. With 18,561 cars sold in 2007, the Auris fell far short of Toyota's expectations. The company ended up spending EUR 2,334 per Auris on advertising. This amounts to 15 percent of the car's starting price (EUR 15,500).[40]

When Toyota launched the third-generation Prius in the United States and Canada in 2010, the company took a very different approach. Focusing almost exclusively on interactive content in online social networks and out-of-home advertising, Toyota reportedly spent less than USD 2 million on bought media and generated more than USD 20 million in free PR coverage, according to some estimates.[41] This equals about USD 185 per car sold in 2010. The Prius has since sold more than 800,000 units in the US and Canada, including the Prius Alpha body type.[42]

The main lesson from these examples is that any measurement focused on awareness does not provide sufficient insight into whether the advertising investment will translate into a tangible payoff for the company. If you look only at brand awareness, you remain in the dark as to whether the consumer is clear about the product benefits and – if they are clear – whether these benefits are relevant to consumer purchasing behavior. To get closer to measuring advertising impact on actual purchase decisions, what brand managers need is a measurement approach that helps them understand how advertising can promote the emotional and rational benefits of the brand itself.

Naturally enough, measuring brand strength will always take brand awareness as its starting point. But high awareness is only the start for a strong brand. Though a prerequisite for success, high brand awareness is not enough in itself to make a brand truly strong. For this to happen, consumers must also be familiar with the contents of the brand in terms of the product or service offer, and the target group must be willing to give greater consideration to the brand than to its competitors when making purchase decisions. In other words, the brand must perform well along the entire purchase funnel (see the next chapter for details on the purchase funnel).

This is not to say that a strong brand performs equally well at each stage of the purchase funnel. It is rare that a brand outperforms the competition at every stage from initial awareness right up to brand loyalty. Most brands reveal slight weaknesses at one stage or another. Nevertheless, for strong brands these weaknesses are rarely severe.

Accurately measuring a brand's relative strengths and weaknesses in the brand purchase funnel is the starting point for making further improvements to the brand. Nivea is an example of a brand that has strengths throughout the funnel. Nivea is currently one of the leading cosmetics brands in Europe and a world leader in skin care and in many other personal hygiene segments such as baby care, sun care, and deodorants. Brand awareness for Nivea Creme is very high; in Germany, 85 percent of the population are aware of the brand, 48 percent say they like it, and – most importantly – 39 percent use it regularly.[43] This funnel performance has been richly rewarded with revenues. Between 1990 and 2006, Nivea's global sales have increased five times over, reaching EUR 3.1 billion in 2006.[44] In 2013, NIVEA generated EUR 3.7 billion in global sales.[45] In early 2014, Nivea's parent company, Beiersdorf, reported its highest sales growth in five years.[46] At each stage, Nivea's brand managers measure the brand's success in the funnel, dissecting every aspect of the indicators, reinforcing positive trends, and taking immediate action to target even the slightest negative change.

Another emerging leader of scientific brand and marketing management is Amazon. Specifically, the company has perfected data-driven customer value management through its recommendation engine. Amazon applies advanced algorithms to a given users' browsing behavior, purchase history, and product ratings to derive new products for consideration. The engine also factors in what other customers have viewed and bought – a system Amazon calls »item-to-item collaborative filtering.«[47]

Good brand managers look below the surface at their brand's strengths and weaknesses. They make detailed measurements using objective standards and constantly hone their measurement techniques. Companies such as Procter & Gamble, Henkel, and Unilever spend millions of euros each year on market research, and the heads of their market research departments are some of the best-known experts in the field. Top management listens to them before making decisions.

### *Art:* Superior content generates emotions

For many of us, creativity is the first thing that comes to mind when we think of strong brands and the secrets they hold. And in fact, experts agree that brands must have the right content in order to appeal to customers and to generate demand. According to a recent survey among the judges for the North American Effie Awards, marketers are »officially hooked on content.« In fact, they consider it one of the most important drivers of MROI.[48] The challenge is to tell the story that is true to a brand's roots and will resonate with its target group. In other words, creative content is not enough. It also needs to be the right kind of content.

Brands need to move us emotionally so that we find them appealing. They need to appear trustworthy in their claims. Faced with the challenge of choosing the right attribute from among a mass of similar-looking technical and non-technical features, companies hardly know where to start. Should they focus on rational elements or on the more emotional elements that they think will speak to customers' feelings?[49]

Strong brands, in fact, always do both, although the balance between the two varies. There are hardly any strong products or services that are not at least as good as the competition in their rational elements, and they are usually better in one or two attributes. At the same time, real brand champions – Marlboro, Nike, or Porsche, for example – show champion-like qualities in their emotional elements as well.

Apple, now the world's most valuable brand according to Interbrand,[50] has created one of the most iconic communication efforts that combines rational benefits with emotional appeal. Working with ad agency TBWA's Media Arts Lab, the company launched its »Get a Mac« campaign in 2006. The minimalist TV commercials and print ads feature actors John Hodgman as the boring PC and Justin Long as the hip Mac. In a series comprising more than 60 episodes, the campaign uses personalization and metaphor to illustrate that Apple's hardware and software are more intuitive, more flexible, and more inspiring than PCs and Microsoft products. While the PC character, usually wearing a suit and tie, comes across as polite, yet formal and work-minded, the Apple persona, in T-Shirt and jeans, is portrayed as modern, casual, and fun-loving. In one of the most celebrated episodes, the PC has caught a virus. He warns Mac to stay away from him, citing 114,000 known viruses that infect PCs. But Mac isn't worried, as viruses don't affect him. PC then announces that he's going to crash and falls backward onto the floor. The campaign ran for more than three years and received a Grand Effie award in 2007. *AdWeek* declared it the »best advertising campaign of the decade« in 2010.[51]

Nivea is another good example. Every Nivea product features a rational product benefit and backs this claim up with research and information. This approach goes back to its introduction in 1911, when Nivea produced the first long-lasting oil-in-water emulsifier that was not based on animal and vegetable fats and so would not go rancid. This scientific approach continues. The company's research center employs over 150 dermatological and cosmetics researchers, pharmacists, and chemists. Today, according to the company, Nivea's latest skin care innovation, the Cellular Anti-Age care series »brings together the virtues of effective anti-ageing ingredients. Short chain hyaluronic acid improves the skin's own ability to bind water, magnolia extract increases cells' resilience to oxidative stress and creatine improves the energy system of cells.« In order to prevent premature skin ageing as a result of sun exposure, the day cream in the series also contains SPF 15 and a UVA filter system.[52] Most recently, Nivea received a brand award for its »In-Shower« range, an innovative kind of body lotion that can be applied while showering.[53]

The rational product benefits are not just displayed on the packaging, they are also backed up by numerous product tests and – even more importantly – by the trust placed in them by large numbers of customers. Since 2005, Nivea has won the award as the most trusted skin care brand by *Reader's Digest* every single year in every one of the 16 participating countries. At the same time, the brand is positioned in a clearly emotional way as a »gentle care« brand, supported by soft-focus photos and carefully chosen images that build a consistent identity, closely tied to central values of the blue »aura,« true values, and a code for genuine »close to touch« human togetherness. This softer side of Nivea became even more apparent when the logo was changed from a rectangle to a circle in 2013. The product's appeal is thus aimed equally at customers' emotional and rational sides; this is what gives the brand its competitive advantage.

This combination of emotional and rational elements is also part of the brand appeal for luxury goods, even though these are commonly perceived to be purely emotional. For Louis Vuitton products, for example, the customer's self-profiling plays a major role in the purchase and justifies the price difference compared with competitor products. At the same time, however, the materials used in the products are of very high quality: the finest leather, tanned by hand (using plant extracts), is water- and scratch-resistant. It is this combination of quality (rational) and prestige (emotional) that is fundamental to the brand's strength.

Audi is another example of a brand that successfully blends rational and emotional elements. The brand stands for technological leadership as well as emotional appeal. Audi's technological assets are condensed into the claim »Vorsprung durch Technik« (»advanced engineering«). They include the »Quattro« permanent all-wheel drive technology (a major factor in Audi's longstanding success in the World Rally Championship), the TDI diesel engine concept pioneered by Audi engineers to wide acclaim in the late 1980s, and the FSI injection technology derived from successful trials in motor sports. On the emotional side, recent milestones along Audi's development towards more progressive design include the introduction of »halo« cars such as the company's first modern convertible in 1991, the immensely successful TT model in 1999, and the launch of the R8 mid-engine sports car in 2006. In 2014, the company announced that the all-electric version of the R8 – originally conceived as an experimental project only – would enter limited production.[54] As a consequence, the Audi brand radiates both technological excellence and technological sex appeal. In a recent brand image survey examining attributes such as appeal and innovation, Audi took the number two position, trumped only by BMW and well ahead of Mercedes and even Porsche.[55]

At the same time, emotional positioning alone will not make a brand strong if rational benefits are missing. Apparel manufacturer and retailer C&A faced this problem in the early 1990s with its television and cinema commercials, including its Daydream campaign. The commercials appealed greatly to the young target groups and even won industry awards, but the reality in the stores was different. The no-frills ambience conflicted with the emotional world depicted in the commercials in terms of store design and product presentation. Potential customers were so disappointed that they seem to have avoided the shops for a long time afterwards. C&A managed to resolve this problem at the end of the 1990s. It did so by refocusing on the brand's traditional core positioning and values, such as honesty and trustworthiness. This change in focus in its campaigns has seen C&A become increasingly successful in attracting its target group of families with below-average to average incomes back into its stores. As a result, the company is managing to hold its ground.[56] According to Benedikt Spangenberg, C&A's Director of Country for Germany, the company weathered the first half of 2013 relatively well, and increased its market share slightly. He describes the privately held company as »profitable and very healthy.«[57]

For consumers, emotional advertising without a rational basis is like a vacation brochure's misleadingly attractive pictures. This is ultimately a form of advertising that can have a negative impact.

### *Art:* Modern creativity and consistency are no contradiction

Strong brands are consistent, preserving and maintaining their brand names. They do not make constant changes to their positioning, their target group, or their image. At the same time, strong brands innovate constantly, building on the brand promise.

At first sight, being both consistent and innovative might appear something of a contradiction. Nivea provides a good example of how a brand can be both highly innovative while always remaining consistent with its brand values. Nivea Creme's distinctive packaging – a blue tin with the Nivea name spelled out in prominent white script – is a vital part of this. Today's packaging has a long pedigree and can be traced back to 1924, when the distinctive blue tin was first introduced. In an effort to refocus on its origins and core strengths, Nivea took inspiration from this trusted tin when the formerly rectangular brand logo was relaunched as a circle in 2013. Just as important is that Nivea's brand promise from its introduction has been that of providing high quality and gentle skin care at a reasonable price, using a straightforward approach. It is this reputation for dependability and trustworthiness that has stood the company in good stead throughout the decades.[58] At the same time, Nivea has innovated constantly. As far back as the 1930s, Nivea introduced sun screen into its product range. Regular product innovations have followed since then, with a large expansion in products from the 1980s onwards. Today Nivea's products include specific care products for different skin types, shampoos designed for various hair types, and products for men as well as women. All these innovative products are distinguished not only by their packaging, but also by Nivea's brand values of gentle care. Nivea's consistent innovation and brand promise are well recognized in the industry, and Nivea has won many international prizes for its products, including the 2006 Beauty Glammies Award in Greece for Nivea Visage DNAge and the 2007 New Best Product Award in Canada for Nivea Lip Care Effect Q10 Plus. In 2013, Nivea's parent company Beiersdorf decided to refresh the brand by introducing »a new global design language based on the iconic blue tin. The new design consistently translates the successful Nivea brand values into a product that consumers can see and feel. Beiersdorf has consistently developed the Nivea brand with a focus on its global core values.«[59] Developed with the help of industrial designer Yves Béhar and San-Francisco-based fuseproject studio, the new design language received the Red Dot Design Award in 2013: »Using characteristics of the Nivea tin, this new packaging design makes products in all categories immediately recognizable.«[60]

Let's look at an industry many would say is dominated by engineering and rational buying factors: cars. BMW's well-known and successful brand promise of »The ultimate driving machine« has been at the heart of the brand since the 1960s and has made a large contribution to BMW's global success. »Our brand delivers performance and sportiness. That's our brand promise,« as the company board was quoted in early 2008.[61] In 1962, BMW launched the 1500, a dynamic compact sedan with front disc brakes and independent suspension. This innovative specification cemented BMW's reputation for fast sports cars, especially when the car won races in motorsports. Since the 1970s, BMW has been building its M models as especially powerful cars. After the launch of the M1 in 1978, BMW started to create extra sporty versions of the (already sporty) regular BMW vehicles. Not surprisingly, the 3-Series M model is the most successful motorsports car in the world, having won more than 1,500 races since its racing debut in 1987. More important, BMW has pledged never to introduce a car that does not fulfill the brand's promise of performance and sportiness. Even BMW's way of communicating the improvement of the carbon footprint of its fleet still incorporates the promise of sportiness (»Efficient Dynamics«). Commercials highlighting the fuel efficiency of the latest BMW models make sure to point out that a BMW is sportier than most. This combination of a consistent message and constant innovation has led to worldwide success for the company. Global sales have increased at a compound annual growth rate of 8 percent since 1991.[62] And even as BMW enters the electric age under its »i« sub-brand, the company sticks to performance and sportiness as its core values. One of the first »i« models to hit the trade fairs was the i8, a plug-in hybrid sports car with an electric motor in the front and a three-cylinder gas engine in the rear, achieving a combined performance of 300 HP. The i8 was shown at the IAA as a concept car in 2009 and as a production model in 2013. The car went on sale in 2014.[63]

An all-electric mid-range car that seats five, the i3 can reach a range of up to 190 km (120 miles). A prototype was showcased at the 2012 Summer Olympics in London. Commercial production of the i3 began in September 2013. In a nod to the car's unique combination of sportiness and range, the first vehicle off the production line went to Jan Fitschen, a long-distance runner and sometime European champion. The i3 was also the lead vehicle at the 2013 Berlin Marathon. According to company information, BMW had received 11,000 global orders as of January 2014. The i3 has received awards both for sustainability and design, including the World Green Car of the Year award and a Gold iF Product Design Award.[64]

Compare this with the example of Skoda's decision not to introduce a convertible for consistency's sake. Despite the considerable revenue potential, management decided against it because a convertible would inevitably be more expensive and more extravagant than a sedan, hence contradicting the Skoda brand's no-nonsense promise of solid quality at attractive prices.

The contrasting example of Pontiac shows what can happen to a brand that is not consistent. In the 1950s, Pontiac started to focus on young and performance-oriented drivers and managed to climb to third place in car sales in the United States. Over the next 20 years, Pontiac continued along this path with the launch of sporty models like the Firebird and the GTO, which became an icon for power and performance and was instrumental in starting the »muscle car« era in the US. But when insurance and fuel costs increased at the beginning of the 1970s, Pontiac shifted towards a positioning that included safety and economy by decreasing the power of its engines and by launching models like the Astre, the brand's first venture into the fuel-economy category. Pontiac tried to be all things to all people. As a result, the brand image became fuzzy and satisfied fewer and fewer customers. In the 1980s, Pontiac refocused its positioning with performance as the core attribute, supported by the redesign of the Firebird in 1982 and the launch of the Fiero in 1984. This »back to the roots« approach was rewarded by car buyers almost instantly. For the first time in more than a decade, Pontiac was the number three brand in the United States. The median age of its buyers dropped from 46 in 1981 to 38 in 1988. More recently, Pontiac went off track again by launching a range of cars out of line with the brand's performance promise, including minivans and family SUVs. But what was even worse, the brand continued to claim it was first choice for performance-oriented customers, when in fact its products could not fulfill this promise. Models offered aggressive styling, but lacked actual performance. This was partly due to the fact that Pontiac's models often used the same engines as other, less performance-focused General Motors brands. Between 2000 and 2009, Pontiac's sales plummeted by 68 percent. Despite numerous restructuring efforts and government-assisted bankruptcy proceedings, the Pontiac brand was discontinued by General Motors in 2010.[65]

Of course, there are always multiple factors at work when it comes to sales development. Products, prices, dealers, competitor moves, portfolio considerations, and external factors such as the 1973 Arab oil embargo may well have been at least as influential as Pontiac's brand identity in the case in question. General Motors is now focusing on its remaining four major brands: Chevrolet, Cadillac, Buick, and GMC.

Coca-Cola provides another example of the advantages afforded by consistency. While Coca-Cola has always stuck to its classic curly logo and the color red, Pepsi has changed its logo many times since the brand was created. Perhaps the most radical change was made in 1998. With a budget of USD 500 million, Pepsi changed its colors from red, white, and blue to just blue. The reason given by the company for the redesign was that the old logo was not distinctive enough and that it was imperative for Pepsi to distinguish itself from Coca-Cola.[66] In 2003, the next update occurred, aimed at stressing the brand's youthful image.

The Pepsi logo and its appearance on the company's products have seen another three revisions since – in 2004/05, 2007/08, and 2009/10. In 2004, the typeface and the Pepsi »globe« visual were updated. In 2007, Pepsi introduced different backgrounds for different types of beverages. In 2008, the biggest redesign since 1991 was unveiled.[67] As the much more consistent player, Coke leads the market globally today. The jury is still out on how Pepsi's strategy of relatively frequent updates will affect its brand and its business in the long term.

Marlboro has shown nearly the same persistence as Coca-Cola. Since Marlboro's makeover by Leo Burnett in the 1950s, it has never questioned its positioning as a cigarette brand associated with freedom and adventure. The image of the cowboy (since 1963) and the Marlboro red (since the 1950s) have remained constant over a very long period, while the contents of the advertising campaigns have been adjusted many times in line with current fashions, and new innovations in cigarettes have been used to refresh the brand. The umbrella brand name Marlboro was only extended with the launch of Marlboro Lights in 1986. In 1994, Marlboro Medium was introduced, and there have since been more product extensions such as Marlboro Menthol, Marlboro 100, and Marlboro Blend 29 (Figure 1.7).[68] In recent years, Marlboro made some changes on the product brand level in response to legal requirements, for example, from Lights to Gold, from Medium to Flavor Mix, and from Menthol to Blue Fresh.

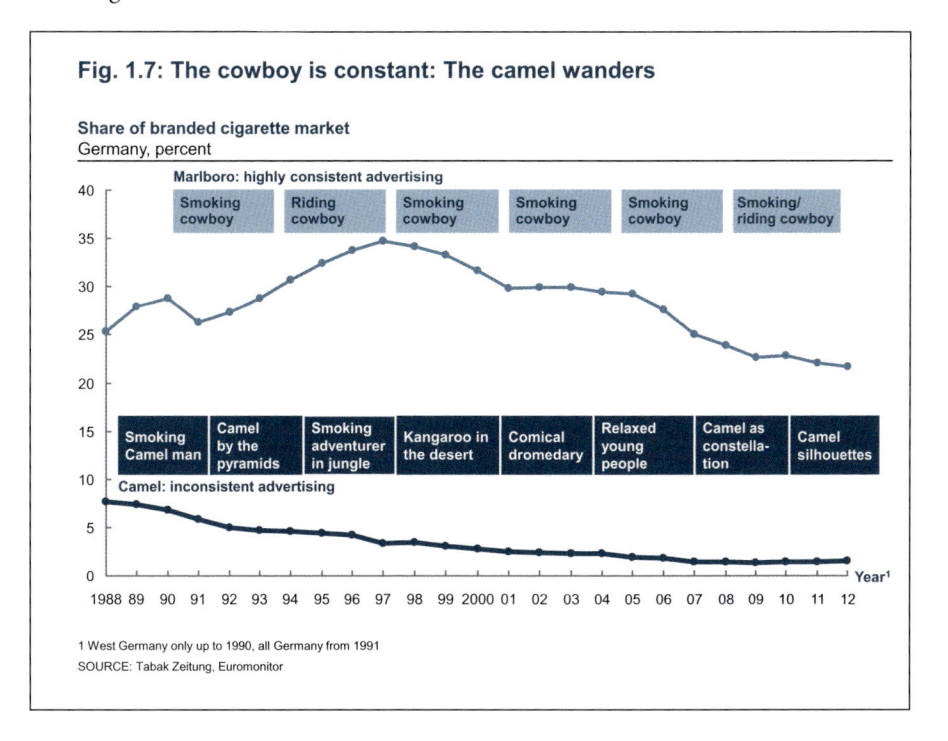

**Fig. 1.7: The cowboy is constant: The camel wanders**

Share of branded cigarette market
Germany, percent

Marlboro: highly consistent advertising — Smoking cowboy, Riding cowboy, Smoking cowboy, Smoking cowboy, Smoking cowboy, Smoking/riding cowboy

Camel: inconsistent advertising — Smoking Camel man, Camel by the pyramids, Smoking adventurer in jungle, Kangaroo in the desert, Comical dromedary, Relaxed young people, Camel as constellation, Camel silhouettes

Year¹: 1988 89 90 91 92 93 94 95 96 97 98 99 2000 01 02 03 04 05 06 07 08 09 10 11 12

1 West Germany only up to 1990, all Germany from 1991
SOURCE: Tabak Zeitung, Euromonitor

Recently, Marlboro changed both the packaging of its signature Marlboro Red product and its brand communication.[69] Launched in 2011, the campaign »Be Marlboro« features young people partying, falling in love, and playing music. The campaign explicitly advocates risk-taking; claims include »Maybe never fell in love« and »Maybe never reached the top.« The long-term impact of these changes on the Marlboro brand and its market success remains to be seen.[70]

Outside the United States, where there has been somewhat greater consistency, Camel, the number two brand, has changed its positioning constantly over the same period. In Germany, for example, it has moved from the Camel man as an adventurer with a hole in his shoe in the 1970s and 1980s to the leather-clad toy camel in the 1990s, to the image of the relaxed young professional between 2001 and 2004, and finally back to the camel. The image of the brand has been altered so many times that it has become almost devoid of meaning. Today, while Marlboro controls almost 18 percent of the Western European market, Camel has a share of just over 4 percent.[71] It remains to be seen to what extent Philip Morris, the owner of the Marlboro brand, will use this brand to market e-cigarettes or other substitutes, such as heated tobacco sticks.[72]

The results of a survey conducted in late 2006 among 300 marketing experts also shows the importance of consistency. When asked about the aspects of successful branding in an open-ended question, consistency was regarded the most critical aspect by far with 38 percent of all responses.[73]

However, consistency is not to be confused with stagnation. Without the courage to change, brands that were once weak or undifferentiated – like Puma, Audi, and Burberry – would never have managed to become the premium brands they are today. Samsung Electronics is another good example of a brand making the journey from a mass-market image to a quality brand, a transition that requires careful management of brand positioning – and a great deal of patience.

Until well into the 1990s, the Korean electronics manufacturer Samsung earned its way by producing cheap Samsung-branded products, and by acting as a third-party manufacturer of components for premium brands such as Sony.[74] The transformation began at the end of the 1990s. This was prompted by the Asian financial crisis, which led to staff reductions of around a third and the realization that – as an increasingly high-wage country – Korea would soon no longer be able to compete with China in the mass-market segment. As a first step, management established a global marketing function, thus underlining the importance of marketing for a company that had previously been dominated by an engineering mentality. Next, Samsung supported the development of the brand by bundling marketing activities across the company, stopping the production of cheap products in many countries, and concentrating instead on innovative digital products with exclusive design. While many competitors were still clinging on to cathode ray tube technology for television sets, for instance, Samsung made the strategic move into new digital technologies such as liquid crystal displays and plasma screens. This helped it overcome its image as a budget manufacturer and move into the category of premium manufacturer. At the same time, the company tried to strengthen the emotional promise of the products and raise the brand's profile. As part of this strategy, Samsung became a leading sponsor of major sporting events, such as the soccer World Cup and the Olympic Games, and paid EUR 73 million to have its name displayed prominently on the chests of the London soccer club Chelsea.[75] Between 1999 and 2007, Samsung spent an average of 3 percent of its net sales on marketing and advertising to position itself globally as a provider of appropriately priced leading-edge technology.[76]

Today, the results of this transformation are evident. The company's claim to be »leading the digital convergence revolution« is reflected at the product level (Figure 1.8). Samsung developed the first-ever speech recognition phone in 2005, launched the world's first Blu-ray Disc player in 2006, and released the world's thinnest liquid crystal display (a mere 0.82 mm) in 2007.[77] At the same time, Samsung has increased its brand value continuously. In 2000, the company had not even been listed in Interbrand's top 100 »Best Global Brands.« Five years later, Samsung had outgrown Sony, a 1990s icon, in terms of brand value and was ranked twentieth. By 2013, the Samsung brand was ranked number eight and valued at almost USD 40 billion – four times its value ten years prior. More recently, Samsung has also been trying to strengthen the emotional elements of the brand in order to develop it further. In an interview with *Business Week*, Gregory Lee of Samsung Electronics stated: »In the past, our communication was all about the product. There wasn't a real story to it. We are really trying to tell a story about how it fits into consumer lives in our newer communications.«[78]

**Fig. 1.8: How Samsung uses customer insights to drive product innovation**

**Need**

| An affordable device for mobile Internet access with a touch screen, set up for instant updates on Facebook | A device for handwriting and drawing. Asian users, in particular, find writing with a pen easier than typing | A light-weight, wrist-worn device that synchronizes with smartphones and offers basic phone and PDA functionality |
|---|---|---|

**Product**

| Corby entry-level smartphone | Galaxy Note smartphone | Galaxy Gear smartwatch |
|---|---|---|

**Impact**

| - Launched in 2009<br>- 1.6 million units sold in the first year<br>- Accounted for almost 10% of Samsung's smartphone sales at the time | - Launched in 2011 (tbc)<br>- 1 million units sold in the first two months<br>- A total of 10 million units sold in less than a year | - Launched in 2013<br>- 800,000 units sold in the first two months<br>- To be supplemented by Galaxy Gear Fit, a wrist-worn fitness device |
|---|---|---|

SOURCE: Samsung, press clippings; interviews

(When the interview was conducted, Mr. Lee was Samsung's Global Chief Marketing Officer. He is now President and CEO for Samsung Electronics in North America.) To accelerate Samsung's transformation into a true premium brand, the company launched its »Imagine« advertising campaign in 2005. In 2012, the group marketing budget reached a historic high of USD 12 billion, about ten times what Apple was spending that year.[79] Between 2007 and 2013, Samsung has achieved an average profit growth of 22 percent (CAGR).[80] But more important, there was a shift from the company's traditional semiconductor component B2B business towards consumer sales of devices, such as mobile phones, liquid crystal displays, and television sets.[81] Most recently, the company's popular Android-based range of Galaxy smartphones was the chief growth driver. In 2009, Samsung Electronics sold 6 million units, compared with the 25 million iPhones Apple sold. By 2012, the tables had turned. Samsung led the market with 215 million units sold, almost twice Apple's 135 million.[82]

This shift lends further momentum to Samsung's aspiration to break free from its past as an original equipment manufacturer to offer upscale products that are bought not only for their functionality, but also for their appeal as branded items. Today, Samsung is widely regarded as a strong brand: »Samsung has created a strong brand around innovation, cutting edge technology, and world-class design.«[83] In early 2014, Samsung reached a new level of marketing savvy as a sponsor of the 2014 Academy Awards: »It did not go unnoticed that Ms. DeGeneres used for her selfie a smartphone made by Samsung, a major sponsor of the Academy Awards. The company also bought more than five minutes of commercial time during the broadcast, promoting products like TV sets and tablets in addition to smartphones. The integration of the Samsung Galaxy Note 3 into the show itself offered another example of why marketers have become so fond of programming like the Oscars and the Super Bowl. They are live shows that tens of millions of viewers deem each year as must-watch television, and they provide numerous alternative ways to engage with consumers beyond traditional commercials.«[84]

### *Art:* Creativity doesn't necessarily mean winning prizes

In addition to ensuring that the brand has superior content and stays up-to-date (while consistent), a very important aspect of the art of brand management is the creativity of its communication. As a source of creative ideas, the advertising industry has always been an important partner to brand management. Today, however, in a society flooded by multimedia, many believe that advertising is no longer as effective as it once was. As a result, many companies are questioning the service provided by advertisers, and greater financial discipline is being brought into marketing, moving it into line with other functions in terms of measuring profits and losses. The demand is that advertising must deliver measurable results.

Plainly, some brands do manage to achieve consistent competitive advantage by means of superior creativity in their communication; they know exactly where to place the bait so that the fish will bite. Strong brands are highly effective in how they use creative campaigns to distinguish themselves from the competition, to strengthen their brand image, and thus ultimately to also generate correspondingly high sales. Examining the advertising used by brands over many years reveals a number of particularly successful long-lasting examples: Lucky Strike's minimalist approach limited to the packaging and a witty headline, Red Bull's unique scribbles, and Sixt's smart and often provocative advertising tag lines.

Creativity can take different forms, as the results of the »creativity in advertising« study show (compare the insert on creative advertising on page 46). Often, really successful creative advertising contains something that might be irritating, provocative, or funny, whether in pictures or in words – as the aforementioned illustrate. Many other major brands take a less radical approach, however, and are no less successful for it. For brands such as Nivea, Beck's, and Marlboro, creativity is primarily about constantly renewing a consistent brand in as simple and catchy a way as possible, occasionally introducing new elements to revitalize the message. This ensures that the brand remains up-to-date over the years and, although it may appear less original to the judges of creativity contests, it often delivers higher dividends.

Even if the advertising industry has stopped focusing exclusively on creativity, prizes remain as important as ever. One of the most respected advertising awards worldwide is the Effie, which recognizes ideas that work commercially. Mary Lee Keane, executive director of the Effie Awards, says, »Effie winners share the honor of finding the perfect combination of strategy, creativity, and media to resonate with consumers«.[85]

Bartle Bogle Hegarty's campaign for Unilever's Vaseline brand »Keeping Skin Amazing« won the global top prize in 2008. The campaign repositioned Vaseline as the skin authority in 15 countries and led to double-digit growth for the brand.

The Global Golden Effie in 2007 was awarded to Cayenne Communication for their campaign »It's Playtime« for Canon's EUR 1,000 single-lens-reflex camera EOS 350D. The big idea was to position the product not as a professional tool, but as license to play, a toy for adults to explore the world. As a result, Canon's sales in the segment grew by 135 percent and its market share increased by nine percentage points while its main competitor, Nikon, lost 12 percentage points.[86]

The 2013 Global Silver Effie was awarded to Grey for their Febreze campaign. In 2010, Procter & Gamble announced its global Olympic partnership lasting from 2012 through 2020. Febreze, a household odor eliminator brand that was first established in the United States in the 1990s, took this opportunity to make its debut on the global stage. To create a campaign that would stand out among all the other advertising for the Olympic games, Febreze decided to sponsor the Azerbaijani Wrestling Team, demonstrating to shoppers that Febreze will remove even the toughest sports odors (Figure 1.9).[87] Eleven different documentary short films were created and shared with more than a million Febreze followers on Facebook to activate the sponsorship.[88]

Fig. 1.9: Febreze 2012 Olympics campaign visuals

SOURCE: Febreze Facebook profile

Recently, several high-ranking executives have explicitly declared their ambition to win more advertising awards, suggesting that they believe in awards as indicators of brand performance. Mark S. Pritchard, Global Brand Building Officer for Procter & Gamble, pointed out the motivational aspect of awards in an interview with *AdWeek*: »Creative awards are really important to me and P&G in general. And the reason why is that we have a fairly clear philosophy on awards. Recognition is something that people really get energized by. Because you get energized when you get to see your great program is reviewed by others as being the best. It's also inspiring – it inspires people to try new things and look at other ways in which they can innovate. It also unites people – because it unites the team. And it shows what you think is important. And so our view is that winning the award in Cannes, especially for the integrated type of activity – that's important.«[89]

While the authors of this book agree that creativity matters, we are also convinced that it is just part of the puzzle. The challenge is to make sure creative content is relevant to a given company, its industry, and its target group. See the insert below for details.

**Art meets science: Creative advertising examined**

Who doesn't like creative advertising? It surprises, amuses, and inspires. We all love it, remember it, and tell our friends about it. But does creative advertising work? Everybody knows recall isn't everything. Some go as far as claiming creativity doesn't matter at all. The head of marketing at a major fast-moving consumer goods company says, »Creativity is irrelevant at best. Often, it is downright harmful to advertising success.« Traditionalists focus on making sure advertising content and messages are tailored to the brand, the product, and the target group in question. For them, »content fit« is much more important than creativity. Campaigns based on this belief may sometimes come across as conventional, but often have credibility on their side.

But can there even be a winning strategy irrespective of the industry? McKinsey, the Art Directors Club of Germany (ADC), and the Berlin School of Creative Leadership have teamed up to quantify the success of German marketing campaigns. Some 100 television commercials submitted for the Effie award have been examined; advertising recall and changes in market share were used to measure their respective psychological and business impact. The findings are likely to surprise the »purists.« Both types of advertising – creative and conventional, content-fit-focused – in fact work. But not for just any product, and not always in the same way. The more creative a campaign, the higher the likelihood that the featured product will sell. At the same time, however, not all successful campaigns are particularly creative.

### Advertising success can be measured

Despite the best intentions, most past attempts to measure advertising success have been controversial, simply because there are no widely accepted, objective indicators. This is especially true for the creative quality of campaigns. Creativity is typically assessed by jury votes that many would say are mostly subjective. The ADC/McKinsey study has chosen a different course. To determine the relative importance of creativity and content fit, a set of five criteria each was used, as shown in the checklist (Figure 1.10).

**Fig. 1.10: Criteria for advertising assessment: Creativity and content fit**

| Creativity | | Content fit | |
|---|---|---|---|
| Originality | New? Surprising? Innovative? | Relevance | Reflects target group needs? Fits strategy? |
| Clarity | Content easily and quickly understood? | Differentiation | Stands out from the clutter? |
| Conviction | Arguments persuasive and coherent? | Consistency | In line with former executions/general brand communication? |
| Execution | Execution consistent and professional? | Credibility | Value proposition believable? |
| "Want-to-see-again" factor | Enjoyable? Entertaining? Likable? | Activation | Moves consumers to buy? |

SOURCE: ADC of Germany, McKinsey

Using these criteria, all advertisements submitted as Effie contenders were assessed on a scale from 1 (poor) to 5 (excellent). A panel of art directors – including the author of this insert – assessed the creativity criteria, while a group of McKinsey marketing experts analyzed each advertisement's content fit. This assessment was then tested for correlation with advertising recall and post-campaign changes in market share.

Although both highly creative and – in terms of content fit – highly relevant campaigns can be economically successful, there are some notable differences. While successful creative campaigns come mostly from the automotive industry, the campaigns that succeed thanks to their content fit were typically created for FMCG companies. A similar category bias can be observed among the low performers. Many of the advertisements that the jury's verdict dubbed as »boring losers« came from financial institutions. Their messages are often abstract and hard to bring to life, which frequently leads to less exciting and less appealing spots. As a consequence, these campaigns also have lower sales impact. As a general rule, one could say that the more emotionally charged the product, the more creative the campaign should be. This is especially true for high-involvement products characterized by long life cycles and high purchase prices: cars, watches, jewelry, or high-end consumer electronics. By contrast, fast-moving everyday products and items with low ticket prices typically derive high sales benefit from campaigns with a good content fit (Figure 1.11).

**Industry in focus: Automotive advertising**

The German car industry thrives on emotional benefits, and creativity is the instrument of choice to make them come to life. The price of a new car is so high

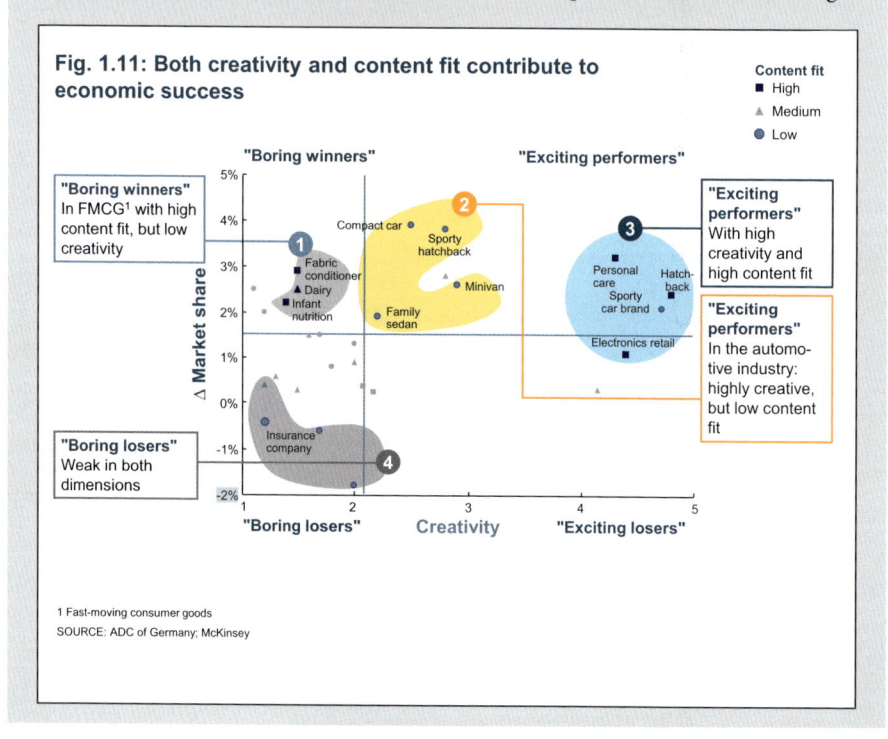

**Fig. 1.11: Both creativity and content fit contribute to economic success**

Content fit
- High
- Medium
- Low

"Boring winners"
In FMCG[1] with high content fit, but low creativity

"Exciting performers"
With high creativity and high content fit

"Exciting performers"
In the automotive industry: highly creative, but low content fit

"Boring losers"
Weak in both dimensions

[1] Fast-moving consumer goods
SOURCE: ADC of Germany; McKinsey

that buyers will have the basics covered anyway. Most of them are sure to research features, fuel economy, resale value, and the like by studying catalogs, checking test results, and visiting the dealer lot. This makes it imperative for automotive advertising to appeal to the heart and soul rather than reason. It must strive to generate desire by conveying emotional benefits: freedom, power, luxury, or simply »fun to drive.« This makes the creation of successful automotive advertising a real and present challenge for advertising executives. Compared with other industries, an above-average creative effort is required to make a given brand or model stand out among its competitors. Unsurprisingly, automotive advertising is considered the hallmark of creativity. Car campaigns have long dominated the advertising award scene. The Cannes Golden Lion – seen by many as the equivalent of the Oscar for creative advertising – has been awarded to car manufacturers such as Volkswagen, Honda, Mercedes, and Mini in recognition of their leading positions among the most creative advertisers in the world. According to the Gunn Report, an independent publication listing award winners from multiple competitions of this type, Volkswagen has consistently emerged as one of the most creative global advertisers in past years.[90] This study underpins the economic payoff of creative excellence in the automotive industry.

Creativity, however, is not the only success factor, not even in automotive advertising. Especially in the market's budget segment, most buyers make their decisions largely based on rational benefits. They want to see their buying factors reflected in advertising campaigns: small on the outside, yet roomy on the inside, and high mileage per gallon. In other words, low- to mid-range cars call for advertising with high content fit, ideally combined with creative delivery, of course, since nowadays even an affordable compact car needs to be more than just a vehicle. It remains to be seen whether the current trend of eco-advertising focusing on rational benefits like fuel efficiency and low carbon emissions will change the way automotive advertising works.

What are the practical implications of these findings for day-to-day brand communication planning and campaign management? The analysis conducted by McKinsey and the ADC yields three guiding principles:

- Content fit and creativity both have a substantial impact on advertising success. Even the biggest budget can't make up for a weak campaign that misses out on both dimensions.
- The appropriate mix depends on the category. Emotional products call for highly creative advertising; while for fast-moving goods, a high content fit is a necessary condition for success. Having said that, higher creativity almost always translates into higher impact regardless of the category.
- The biggest hits among advertising campaigns tend to combine creativity and content fit.

Once and for all, this study refutes the trusted prejudice that advertising can only be either of two things: innovative or informative, noticeably different or optimally adjusted. It's the appropriate mix that makes advertising successful. The criteria identified in the analysis will help to find the right proportion of creativity and content fit in a given situation, and they will help to make advertising success more predictable. If they get it right, advertisers will walk away with real returns – and real beauty.[91]

Creative content is a key success factor for strong brands. In some cases, however, creativity is called for in other respects as well. Consider the case of fluege.de, a German online flight booking portal operated by Unister Holding GmbH. When fluege.de was looking for suitable sponsorship engagements to promote its brand, the company came upon ski jumping because of its intuitive and strategic fit. The international skiing federation (Fédération Internationale de Ski, FIS), however, prohibits third-party branding to be displayed on athletic equipment. Only manufacturers' brands are permitted. In an act of creative compliance with regulation, fluege.de actually became a ski manufacturer. Unister Holding acquired Germina, a maker of jumping skis rooted in preunification East Germany, and relaunched the company as fluege.de Sprungskiproduktions GmbH, a company that employs no more than six people (jumping skis are hand-made for professional athletes only; they are not commercially available).[92]

Now officially recognized by the FIS as a ski manufacturer, fluege.de was able to display its brand on skis, creating about 15 seconds of exposure during TV broadcasts, and on slope-side banners.[93] Despite its affiliation with prominent athletes, such as former world champion and Olympic gold medalist Martin Schmitt, the fluege.de branding was banned from the 2014 Winter Olympics in Russia after four successful years on the world cup circuit. The company was required to conceal its brand and supply athletes with plain blue skis instead. The stunt seems to have served its purpose though. As early as 2011, Unister reported a brand awareness of 69 percent among Germans aged 14 to 60 for fluege.de, according to a survey conducted by TNS Emnid.[94] Later that year, fluege.de was ranked 8 out of 12 flight portals by mafo.de, chiefly because of its high brand awareness.[95] Other brands, have attempted to replicate Unister's strategy. Sporting goods retailer Sport 2000 attempted to cooperate with the leading maker of jumping skis, Fischer, but failed to be recognized as manufacturers by the FIS.

*Craft:* **Brand management is CEO business**

Ultimately, brands can only survive if their management is top notch. Such excellence requires continuity and a steady hand. This usually means the leadership of one person who has the depth of experience to ensure that the brand core remains unchanged over years (better yet, decades), while being kept up-to-date based on innovation and advertising. The more senior the manager, the more likely that brand management will be successful. At Amazon, for example, founder and CEO Jeff Bezos makes brand management his personal priority: »A brand for a company is like a reputation for a person. You earn reputation by trying to do hard things well.«[96] Amazon has been rewarded with record growth, reaching USD 1 billion in sales within just five years. More recently, the company has successfully leveraged its brand to spin-off a range of services surrounding and expanding its core retail businesses – both for consumers and business partners. The most prominent offering to end users is Amazon Prime, a subscription-based service model. Introduced in the US in 2005, it includes free express shipping, video streaming (Amazon Instant Video), and access to the company's e-book library (Kindle books). By 2013, Amazon Prime had enlisted about ten million subscribers. The company says it is targeting 25 million by 2017. Services for business partners include Amazon Marketplace, where 2 million vendors offer some 30 million items for sale at any given time. Other B2B services include cloud computing, content delivery, and supply chain management.[97] Collectively, these new ventures contribute 80 percent to the company's total operating margin. See Chapter 4, Section 4.4 on digital brand management for details.

Too much tinkering is more likely to damage the brand than enhance it. Deciding what will add to the brand's strength and what will not is a top management decision. The Smart car did not fit the Mercedes-Benz image, so it was better to choose a new brand name. Nivea can offer deodorant and shampoo alongside its creams and care products, but it should probably not offer a household detergent. The core of the Porsche brand will always be in its sports cars, even if certain models, such as the Cayenne, the Panamera, and the Macan may succeed in breaking down category barriers to transfer the brand's sporty core to new body styles.

The CEO or other chief caretaker of a brand must have internalized the brand core in order to be able to manage the trade-off between generating additional revenue potential and weakening the brand. Brand management is a top management issue. It should not be delegated to product managers, external agencies, or any other third party.

**Craft: Using the brand's strength to its greatest extent**

Beyond requiring an experienced guiding hand, craft also means translating the power of the brand concept into a reality on the street. In a word: execution. Companies with strong brands ensure attention to detail.

Apple is an example of a company that shows excellence in executing its brand strategy. Focusing on features that really matter to ordinary people, Apple has created a legacy of consumer-centric innovation. In the 1970s, Steve Wozniak and Steve Jobs set out to make computers easy to use for everybody. At the time, most computers were geared toward scientists and other specialists. Typically, they were delivered without keyboards, monitors, or software. In contrast, the Apple II featured an all-in-one design, including all the necessary components. It sold well and enabled Apple to go public in 1980. In 1984, Apple introduced the Macintosh. While other computers still required users to memorize DOS commands, the Macintosh was controlled by pointing and clicking with a mouse, a revolutionary device at the time. In 2001, Apple launched the iMac, a desktop computer fit for easy Internet access. During the first five months alone, Apple sold 800,000 units. Subsequent innovations included the iPod (2004), the iPhone (2007), and the iPad (2010). Today, the company's branded stores in the United States generate average revenues exceeding USD 3,000 per square foot, making Apple the most productive US retailer, well ahead of second-ranking Tiffany & Co. As of 2013, Apple is regarded as the world's most valuable brand.[98]

But it took much more than superior products to make Apple the strong brand it is today. In fact, it was on the brink of extinction in the late 1990s. Apple's moment of truth arrived when Steve Jobs, the company's cofounder, rejoined its ranks in 1997. Apple's share of the computer market had plummeted from a peak of 14 percent in 1993 to below 3 percent four years later. Jobs cut the product portfolio radically and put an end to more than two dozen different advertising campaigns. In September 1997, Apple launched its USD 90 million »Think Different« campaign, featuring stark black-and-white photographs of maverick thinkers, creative minds, and real-life adventurers such as Bob Dylan, Thomas Edison, Pablo Picasso, Nelson Mandela, Charlie Chaplin, Buzz Aldrin, Miles Davis, Jane Goodall, Francis Ford Coppola, and Albert Einstein.[99] The campaign »celebrates the soul of the Apple brand – that creative people with passion can change the world for the better,« Steve Jobs told the Wall Street Journal in 1998. Subsequent to »Think Different,« Apple reported two straight profitable quarters after nearly two years and USD 2 billion in losses, and the company has been growing ever since. The brand alone is now valued at almost 100 billion dollars.[100]

Porsche's 911 is one of the world's most successful models. Porsche has shown outstanding execution in branding, positioning the product for that small segment of the market that values well-above-average acceleration, a sporty chassis, and unmistakable design. Porsche has implemented this positioning in the 911's development from the design phase right up to vehicle testing. The concern for detail is particularly noticeable in the design itself. The typical Porsche boxster engine (featuring horizontally opposed cylinders) should sound »powerful, somewhat metallic in places, unmistakable, but always pleasantly sonorous and restrained.« This sound is monitored by no less than 50 engineers in Porsche's acoustics and vibration technology section. They listen not only to the six-cylinder engine but to wipers, blinkers, door locks, and light switches as well. The sound technicians check every moving part and correct even the slightest dud note. Every 911 has the distinct 911 sound.[101] In a proud display of its commitment to consistency, Porsche launched the 50-year anniversary edition of the 911 in 2013. The company says it puts special emphasis on balancing tradition with innovation. Like the original 911, the anniversary edition is a coupé with a flat-six rear engine and rear wheel drive. The special edition was limited to 1,963 cars, a number that reflects the year of the 911 world premiere.[102]

Excellent execution is not necessarily limited to the product. Price, sales channel management, and details of communication can form key characteristics in strong brands. For the discount retailer Aldi, for example, price is the key. This is the competitive advantage that has made the brand strong. Right from the outset, Aldi stressed that every article they sold was cheaper than the equivalent elsewhere.

Aldi has turned simplicity of execution into a guiding principle, from its spartan stores to its narrow assortment of around 750 products. Logistics costs play a role in the renting of space for new stores: it must be accessible for articulated trucks and the aisles wide enough for maneuvering pallets. Aldi's stores are usually located either on side streets near high-traffic areas, or on the edge of town where ample parking is available and rental costs are low. The comparatively narrow assortment of goods ensures simplicity in purchasing and handling, and the scale advantages lend bargaining power in negotiations with suppliers. Aldi also keeps labor costs down by reducing management to an absolute minimum and having notoriously low headcount in central functions.[103]

The rapid rise of Lidl – Germany's second largest discount retailer – is challenging Aldi in its market leadership. Lidl has copied many basic business processes from Aldi, but offers a wider assortment of products. While Aldi now has approximately 1,000 stock-keeping units (SKUs), Lidl has about twice as many, including substantially more branded items than its competitor. At the end of 2007, Lidl surpassed Aldi for the first time in terms of the number of outlets in Europe. In response to this, Aldi has also started stocking branded articles such as Ferrero's Kinder Country, Mars, or Bounty.[104] Yet, in mid-2014, Lidl was still growing faster than Aldi in terms of number of stores.[105]

One brand that has always been excellent in every aspect of execution is Coca-Cola. As early as 1923, the then-CEO Robert Woodruff made execution a key part of the brand by announcing that Coca-Cola should always be »within an arm's reach of desire.«[106] Coca-Cola has stuck to this motto, implementing it around the globe with great attention to detail.

To realize this objective, Coca-Cola has systematically developed new sales channels: beyond traditional food retailers, gasoline stations, and kiosks, it targets major sporting events and the like. Any remaining gaps in distribution are closed using vending machines. Some one million of these can be found in Japan alone.[107] Coca-Cola continues to develop and perfect these machines, some of which feature the very latest technology, such as in allowing customers to pay using their mobile phones.

Similarly, Coca-Cola's supply chain management is excellent: the product is always available at every sales channel. This is a critical competitive advantage for an impulse drink such as Coca-Cola, which needs to be available whenever and wherever the customer wants it. The product quality is reliable, the packaging is constantly being improved, and the brand has an enormous emotional appeal.[108]

It is top management's job to ensure that day in, day out, the core elements of the brand retain their quality in every aspect. This is no easy task, of course, and things can go seriously wrong, as was demonstrated by the Howard Schultz Starbucks memo, leaked to the public in 2007. Schultz bought the Starbucks chain in 1987 – then only a medium-sized enterprise – and transformed the company into a global coffee shop chain with more than 23,000 stores today.[109] In 2000, he stepped down as CEO and became Chairman. In 2007, Schultz had seen enough of what he called »the commoditization of the Starbucks experience.« In a memo to the top leadership group of the company he criticized a series of decisions that had seemed right on their own merit, but in sum, diluted the Starbucks brand. For example, the introduction of automatic coffee machines increased the speed of service and efficiency, but destroyed much of the romance and theater that was in play with the old machines. Moreover, the height of the new machines blocked the line of sight the customer previously had to watch the drink being prepared, and they made eye contact with the barista nearly impossible. The introduction of flavor-locked packaging clearly improved the quality of the fresh-roasted bagged coffee, but the aroma filling the premises was lost – the perhaps most powerful non-verbal signal Starbucks had in its stores, a signal which stood for tradition and heritage. Streamlining the store design enhanced economies of scale and satisfied the financial side of the business. But the shops lost their former soul, the warm feeling of a neighborhood store. Instead they seemed increasingly like just a random chain. Finally, the increasing number of merchandising articles, such as music CDs, took Starbucks even further away from its heritage as a coffee shop. »In fact, I am not sure people today even know we are roasting coffee. You certainly can't get the message from being in our stores,« Schultz wrote. Less than 12 months later, Schultz returned as CEO to help the company to refocus on the original Starbucks experience. More recently, Starbucks ordered all-new espresso machines from Thermoplan, a relative newcomer in a category long dominated by traditional Italian manufacturers. Thermoplan's USP: Coffee is ground individually for each cup of espresso. What is more, the machines are much lower than the current models, making customer-to-staff eye contact once again possible. Schultz says the new machines are meant to bring back some of the old charm: »Once again, it will be all about the coffee.«

Thermoplan has since been delivering automated espresso makers to all Starbucks coffee shops globally. In 2008, the company introduced a brand new machine, the Mastrena, designed specifically for Starbucks over the course of more than five years of joint development. For Howard Schultz, focusing on the best brew is all about consistency: »Coffee will always be the core of what we do. So many companies have made mistakes by not sticking to their knitting and they start believing their own press. That's not going to be us.«[110]

Google – now the world's second most valuable brand according to Interbrand[111] – is going to great lengths to make sure the strength and the reach of its brand is used to the company's full advantage in all walks of consumers' lives. Google is notorious for dedicating substantial resources to new products and services, testing these new ventures thoroughly, and phasing out those that fail to meet the company's rigorous standards for excellence and mass appeal. Prominent recent examples of such forays include self-driving cars – now licensed to operate on public roads in Nevada, Florida, California, and Michigan[112] – and Google Glass. The first batch of the futuristic device sold out within hours when it was first made available for one day only in April 2014 at a unit price of USD 1,500.[113] In effect, the company has grown from its search engine core to a technology leader across many platforms and touch points, including advertising, operating systems, and enterprise solutions (Figure 1.12).

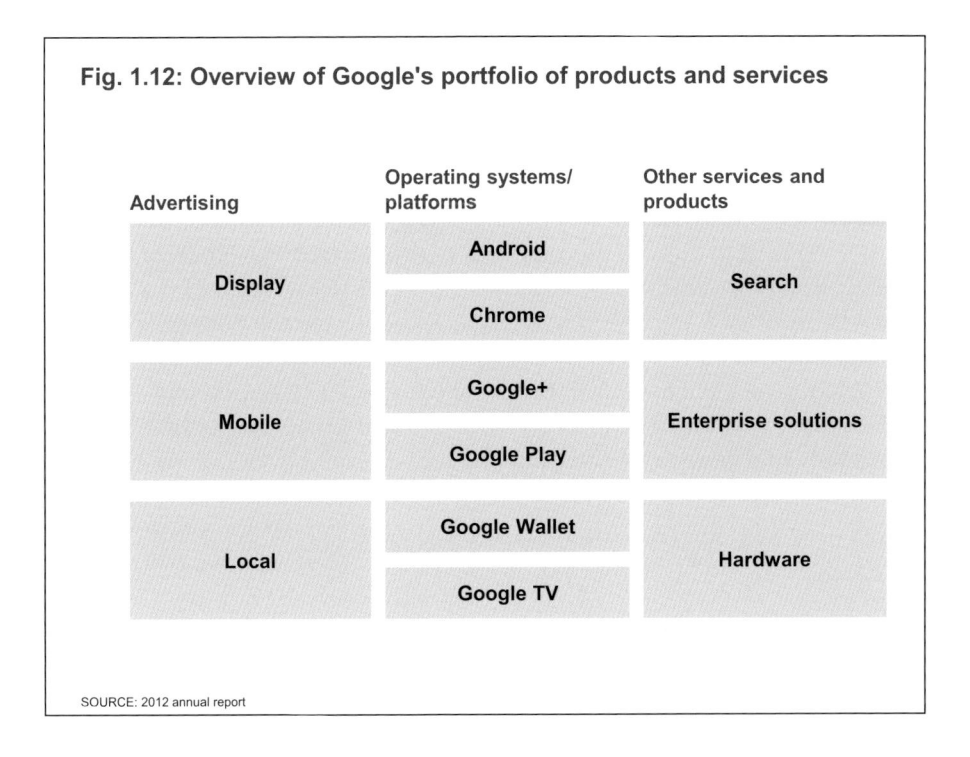

### Fig. 1.12: Overview of Google's portfolio of products and services

| Advertising | Operating systems/ platforms | Other services and products |
|---|---|---|
| Display | Android | Search |
|  | Chrome |  |
| Mobile | Google+ | Enterprise solutions |
|  | Google Play |  |
| Local | Google Wallet | Hardware |
|  | Google TV |  |

SOURCE: 2012 annual report

## The secret of brand success: The brand trinity

Strong brands develop and prosper by achieving a harmonious trinity of *science, art,* and *craft,* whatever their particular focus. High-powered brands need powerful content – in both emotional and rational terms – and an image that remains consistent over many years without ever becoming outdated. Top brands maintain and develop their strength by tracking their status continuously according to qualitative criteria – such as their image – and quantitative indicators – such as market share and customer loyalty. Strong brands are also executed in a consistent and effective manner, as reflected in the marketing and through the actions of the entire organization, from CEO to the front line.

Only a few brands have been able to achieve this balance and maintain it over the longer term. Top brands do not usually excel in all three disciplines, as already mentioned. Instead, they tend to have one or two areas where they really shine, and they keep plowing away at the others.

## Ikea: Brand trinity, Ingvar's way

Ikea, the largest furniture retailing chain in the world, provides another good example of how it is possible to produce harmony in the trinity of *science, art,* and *craft*. As of 2013, the Swedish furniture empire operated some 300 home furnishings stores in 28 different countries (345 stores if one includes franchised stores), drawing more than 770 million visitors and generating revenues of EUR 29.2 billion in 2013, up from

EUR 19.8 billion in 2007.[114] Around the globe, Ikea still stands for the concept launched by founder and owner Ingvar Kamprad in the 1940s: furniture and home accessories that combine function and design at affordable prices (Figure 1.13). What is it that makes Ikea so successful? It is a unique combination of the three pillars of successful brand management: *science, art,* and *craft*. Ikea excels in all three areas, with particular spikes in *art* and *science*. The combination leads to a just as unique, almost cult-like relationship between the brand and its customers, a deep attachment rivaled by only a handful of other brands. Ikea reports its stores were visited 775 million times during the year 2013. This is a magnitude achieved by very few companies and certainly by no other furniture retailer. In a report published by Millward Brown in mid-2014, Ikea was named the world's fiftieth most valuable brand, and one of the five fastest risers in terms of brand value. Let's look at the three components of the brand trinity in some more detail to find out how Ikea does it.

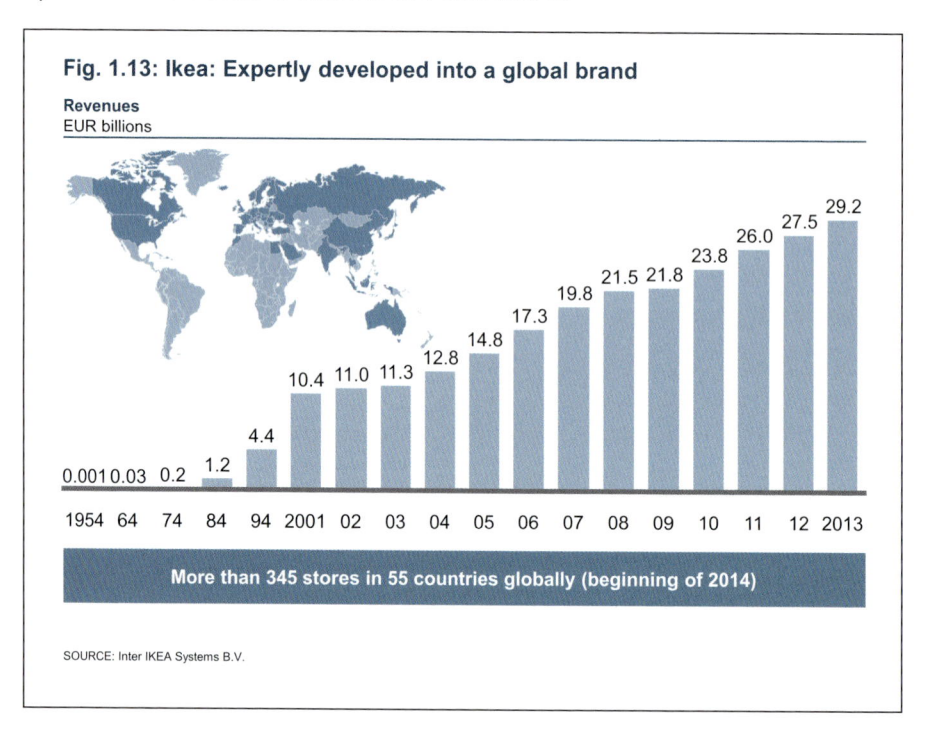

**Fig. 1.13: Ikea: Expertly developed into a global brand**

Revenues
EUR billions

| Year | 1954 | 64 | 74 | 84 | 94 | 2001 | 02 | 03 | 04 | 05 | 06 | 07 | 08 | 09 | 10 | 11 | 12 | 2013 |
|---|---|---|---|---|---|---|---|---|---|---|---|---|---|---|---|---|---|---|
| Revenue | 0.001 | 0.03 | 0.2 | 1.2 | 4.4 | 10.4 | 11.0 | 11.3 | 12.8 | 14.8 | 17.3 | 19.8 | 21.5 | 21.8 | 23.8 | 26.0 | 27.5 | 29.2 |

More than 345 stores in 55 countries globally (beginning of 2014)

SOURCE: Inter IKEA Systems B.V.

*Science: Systematic consumer research ensures fact-based brand management.* Ikea engages in extensive market research to ensure the brand meets consumer needs at key touch points, such as the product and store experiences. Partnering with AC Nielsen, Ikea explores what it calls the »three moments of truth« in its research: the shopping planning in the consumer's home, the core brand experience at one of the Ikea stores, and the product experience back at home. Using a wide range of observational techniques, Ikea aspires to generate the type of insights that enables the company to develop inventive interior decoration solutions that actually solve consumer problems rather than (just) pieces of furniture.

The opportunity to experience the entirety of Ikea's assortment during a store visit is a core element of the company's value proposition. Ikea conducts extensive store design tests to ensure customers are guided so that they get to see the entire assortment. Wim Neitzert, former Head of Ikea Southern Germany, explains: »We tested what happens when we let customers roam freely in the store. They made straight for the exit, missing the bulk of our floor space. Also, 40 percent of the shoppers never get to the second level in a traditional store. That's why we make them start on the second level.« Products are also thoroughly tested to ensure their quality and generate improvement ideas. For example, children's furniture is deliberately pressure-tested in the rough environment of child-care facilities.

Consumer feedback management is another area in which Ikea adheres to strict and systematic standards to ensure continuous input on the quality of its products, stores, and services. To get consumers' help in the area of product innovation (and foster loyalty at the same time), Ikea runs design contests (»fiffiga folket«). The winning designs are made into prototypes. As far as the store experience is concerned, consumers are rewarded with food vouchers for their improvement ideas, the best of which are presented directly to the store manager.

*Art: Creative communication leads to emotional appeal.* Since 1985, the company's campaigns have spotlighted ingenious solutions using Ikea products. When launching new stores in Tokyo, Ikea ran a major outdoor campaign in the city center and near the stores. Among other things, Ikea built 14 small »Ikea 4.5 museums.« In an area measuring just four and a half tatami mats (around 7.5 square meters) – slightly smaller than the standard room size in Tokyo – Ikea showcased how to make the most of small rooms by using Ikea furniture. The campaign led to a new record in store visitors and was awarded a Cannes Golden Lion.

In Russia, Ikea has created a new way for users to experience the company's kitchen range in the virtual realm. Working with Instinct/BBDO Russia, Ikea created an interactive film combining various slices of domestic life, from family breakfasts to spontaneous parties. As users navigate the story in real time, they can switch from one viewpoint to another. Seeing through the eyes of different characters, including those of the family dog, they can explore a nearly limitless number of kitchen solutions. As the footage plays, information snippets providing product details and practical hints pop up. In the first five months after the interactive film premiered, consumers experienced more than 850,000 kitchen features through the characters' eyes.[115]

In the UK, Ikea combined virtual and real-life touch points to bolster its emotional appeal. In 2011, the company's social media listening team discovered a Facebook page entitled »I Wanna Have A Sleepover In Ikea.« In 2012, Ikea decided to grant the wish and invited 100 of the page's 100,000 followers to spend a night at the Ikea store in Lakeside, Essex. Perks included snacks, massages, sleep advice from an expert, bedtime stories, and goodie bags. A strict pajamas-only dress code was enforced. Thanks to countless postings by enthusiastic winners, the search phrase »Ikea Essex sleepover« now gets close to half a million hits on Google (as of May 2014), including pages and pages of free favorable media coverage.[116]

Ikea's catalog is its most important tool for building relationships with its customers – apart from the stores themselves. With a wealth of ideas, inspiration, solutions, and products, the catalog shows how the company's product range contributes to a better everyday life. The catalog was first distributed to consumers in 1951. Today, more than 200 million copies are printed worldwide in more than two dozen different languages. In most countries, the catalog's circulation is rivaled only by Harry Potter books or the Holy Bible.[117] Today's catalog is complemented by online and mobile versions, along with interactive digital content that gives users a richer experience of the solutions and provides more in-depth home furnishing knowledge. Examples include online planning tools for kitchens, bathrooms, storage, and offices.[118] The catalog app was downloaded close to 10 million times in 2013, up from 3.5 million times in 2011, the year it was first introduced. The company's Web site drew more than 1.2 billion visits in 2013.[119]

*Craft: Consistent global brand promise, carefully adapted to local needs.* At Ikea, brand management is all about consistency. The store experience (size, number of stockkeeping units, corporate identity, and color scheme) is largely standardized globally. The same is true for the product lineup. Former product development manager Tomas Lundin says: »A product must do well in all countries to be successful.«[120] (Mr. Lundin was appointed Sustainability Manager for Ikea Trading in 2012.) The catalog, however, can be more easily and cost-efficiently adapted to make Ikea come across as a company that thinks globally, but acts locally. Although produced in Sweden for all countries, the props reflect local peculiarities. Television sets in the American edition are bigger than anywhere else, while the Chinese edition features kitchen supplies with Chinese *kaishu* characters.

To ensure a stream of consistently well-designed and innovative products, Ikea shares the common language and standards of its »design culture« even outside the organization, especially with its supplier community. Innovative designs and materials are consistently requested and rewarded to ensure a steady influx of simple, reliable, and profitable products. Ikea summarizes its brand promise as follows: »To offer a wide range of well designed, functional home furnishing products at prices so low that as many people as possible will be able to afford them.«[121]

To make sure all frontline personnel are up to date about the company's solutions, Ikea operates a retailer training center in Delft in the Netherlands. Retailers go there to experience the latest innovations in the hands-on environment of a mock-up store. Specialists are at the ready to provide additional information and advice. The center is also used to test new ideas and get feedback from retailers prior to the rollout of new products and store design features. At the same time, the center also deepens retailers' bonds with the brand as its foremost ambassadors.[122]

So successful is Ikea's version of the brand trinity of *science*, *art*, and *craft* that it is even spinning off its unique approach to a new category. In 1996, Ikea set up a joint venture with the building company Skanska with the aim of building apartments and houses. For decades, Ikea had been providing furnishings for homes, so it seemed logical to start building the homes as well. BoKlok (Swedish for »smart living«), as the joint venture was called, set itself the task of developing living spaces that were of high quality, yet affordable. Priced competitively at around EUR 150,000 per unit, more than 1,000 houses are built every year in Scandinavia. To date, the company has completed some 250 projects and built over 5,500 units in Sweden, Norway, Denmark, Finland, Germany, and the UK.[123] Who knows what's next?[124]

**Strong brands can survive occasional mistakes**

Trying to maintain the consistency of a brand at the same time as keeping it up-to-date is a tall order, and managers sometimes make mistakes. But consumers forgive strong brands for such mistakes. If they are corrected quickly and in full, brands can, in fact, become immune at least to minor or medium hiccups in corporate conduct. A classic example is that of New Coke in the 1980s. In the attempt to counter falling market shares and consumers' preference for Pepsi-Cola in taste tests, Coca-Cola's management decided to change the recipe of Coca-Cola, a closely guarded secret that had remained unaltered for 99 years.[125] After extensive testing, the company believed it had come up with a mixture that people would prefer to both Pepsi-Cola and traditional Coca-Cola. The results of consumer acceptance tests looking into the psychological aspects of a new Coke were also positive. Thus in April 1985, the company decided to break all taboos and launch New Coke, spending a substantial amount on advertising.

New Coke was something of a disappointment.[126] The introduction was accompanied by a storm of protests from customers. »It's as if God had dyed the grass pink,« complained a Coca-Cola fan. The company had to deal with up to 8,000 calls of complaint each day and was bombarded with tens of thousands of letters of protest. Coca-Cola was taken by surprise by this massive rejection of its product but soon took appropriate remedial steps: it admitted to making a mistake and asked its customers for forgiveness. Within three months, in July 1985, the old Coca-Cola was reintroduced under the name Coca-Cola Classic and enjoyed a massive comeback. New Coke was still supplied to retailers, but its market share plummeted until it was finally dropped by the company. The big surprise for many was that the New Coke affair did not inflict any serious damage to the company's sales: between 1984 and 1985 sales rose by 7 percent. Coca-Cola had inadvertently proved that no brand is stronger.

It is not only Coca-Cola that can survive shooting itself in the foot. Mercedes-Benz shows how a strong brand can overcome even serious issues. In November 1997, the company had assembled journalists from the Swedish automobile journal *Teknikens Varld* to watch its brand new A-class compact perform the 50-m slalom-shaped »Avoidance Maneuver Test,« commonly known as the »elk test.« At 60 km an hour, tracked by television cameras and with journalists aboard, the A-class teetered on two wheels and then turned over. One of the journalists was injured. Soon the television footage was being broadcast around the world, and the A-class had been labeled unstable and unsafe. New deliveries of the A-class were suspended until February 1998 while engineers considered the situation. In just 19 days, Mercedes had announced a plan and a timetable by which to rectify the problem. The introduction of an »electronic stability program« (ESP) cost Mercedes a little more than EUR 80 million. Within two months, the number of positive articles about the A-class's stability had overtaken the negative. Brand perception for attributes like high safety standards or high reliability did not even suffer from October to December 1997. Up to 95 percent of sales targets for the first year were achieved even though delivery was stopped for a few weeks.[127] During the whole product life cycle of seven years, Mercedes sold 1.1 million A-class cars. For any lesser brand, failing the elk test so spectacularly would have inflicted severe, long-term damage. For Mercedes, there was no lasting damage to its reputation for producing well-engineered cars.

Companies also make mistakes with B2B brands, but even here the strong brands survive. In 1994, a calculation flaw came to light in the Intel Pentium chip, which according to Intel advertising was the best on the market. Thomas Nicely, a professor of mathematics at Lynchburg College, Virginia, had noticed that his new PC, fitted with an Intel Pentium processor, made rounding errors from the fifth digit onwards, even when making simple divisions. He complained to Intel straight away, but the company's reaction was dismissive. It said that it saw no grounds to take action, since the rounding error would be a problem for only a few specialists and thus not significant for the average user.

That this position wasn't sustainable should have been immediately evident to Intel. Intel's response provoked Professor Nicely to vent his anger publicly on the Internet at the end of October 1994. This led to over 10,000 further responses, all of which expressed outrage at the calculation flaw on Intel Pentium processors. The problem was discussed in more than 20 chat rooms, and soon a parody of Intel's co-branding slogan was making the rounds: »Intel inside. Can't divide.« The stakes rose and soon news media from around the world were reporting on the plight of the dumb chip.

Somewhat surprisingly, Intel was still unwilling to listen. Andy Grove, CEO of the computer chip giant, even went so far as to demand that customers prove they were carrying out such advanced mathematical calculations before he would replace the faulty chips. This led to practically full scale mutiny against Intel.

The problem escalated still further in early December 1994. Computer giant IBM – then one of Intel's major clients – announced that it would replace all personal computers fitted with Intel Pentium processors and that from now on no computer would leave IBM's production sites with the faulty chip fitted. The stock markets were not slow to react; within minutes Intel's stock fell dramatically, reaching the point where trading was temporarily suspended. To top it all off, *The New York Times* awarded Intel a Consumer Deception Award. After having made a mountain out of a molehill, Intel finally reacted a few days before Christmas 1994. Three board members publicly apologized to customers and offered to replace all processors free of charge, no questions asked.[128]

The most surprising thing was that following these events, Intel's sales did not ultimately suffer: between 1993 and 1995, sales revenues almost doubled from USD 8.8 billion to USD 16.2 billion.[129] The lesson is clear: strong brands like Intel can even compensate for temporary lapses.

Strong brands that get the trinity of *science, art,* and *craft* right have such power over customers that – in extreme cases – they can even function successfully without any research and development, production, logistics, or sales of their own. Branded companies such as Red Bull and Adidas can ignore certain parts of the value chain altogether, outsourcing specific steps to third parties without damaging brand perception.

Red Bull, for example, has concentrated from the very beginning on the concept of the drink and its communication. The company does not own a single bottling plant, warehouse, or delivery truck. The fruit juice company Rauch, based in Rankweil in western Austria, takes care of worldwide production, and forwarding agents transport the product to the various national distribution companies.[130]

Similarly, the Adidas brand is so strong that consumers aren't worried about how the shoes are produced. This enabled Adidas to switch its production strategy in order to copy that of its major competitor Nike, which has never had its own production facilities since its creation in 1962. It has had all its goods produced in Asia. »We don't need production expertise,« said CEO Herbert Hainer.[131] To minimize production cost, Adidas outsourced all production to independent third-party manufacturers, primarily located in Asia. As a consequence, only 6 percent of all employees worked in production in 2007, compared with 27 percent in 2001 when Hainer took over.[132]

It is undoubtedly the case that brands such as these are highly valuable assets, but for those struggling on the periphery, the question remains: How does one develop a strong brand? The remaining chapters set out the right approach to brand management, analyze what makes a strong brand strong, lay out the tools that managers will require for a full understanding, and look into the ingredients for success when developing a strong brand.

## 1.3 McKinsey BrandMatics® – Mastering Brand Management

More myths surround the process of creating and developing a brand than any other area of business management. This is because the art of a brand flatters the consumer, appeals to the emotions, and develops a resonance that is hard to quantify. Indeed, the wit, originality, and imaginativeness of successful brands such as Red Bull and Apple show the importance of the intuitive and the creative. Strong brands are able to create their own myths. Iconic brands such as Chanel have even been immortalized in the works of artists like Andy Warhol (Figure 1.14).

Despite the undoubted importance of art, strong brands are seldom developed by art alone, but by a careful mix of *science, art,* and *craft*; the role of science and craft in this

**Fig. 1.14: Samples of "branded" artworks: Chanel by Andy Warhol**

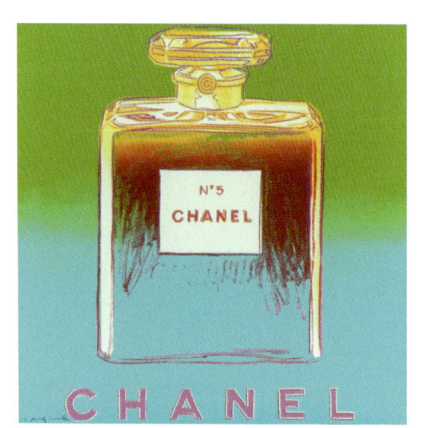

Andy Warhol, *Chanel*, 1985
From the *Ads* portfolio, Screenprint
38 x 38 inches, Trial proof 7/30
Courtesy of Ronald Feldman Fine Arts, New York

Andy Warhol, *Chanel*, 1985
From the Ads portfolio, Screenprint
38 x 38 inches, Trial proof 1/30
Courtesy of Ronald Feldman Fine Arts, New York

SOURCE: The Andy Warhol Foundation, Inc; Art Resource, NY

mix often being underestimated. Take Red Bull, for example, a brand with strong appeal to the younger generation. Science played a vital role in developing a detailed understanding of the brand's market appeal to target groups. Craft was also central in ensuring outstanding execution and consistency in the management of the brand.

The story of Red Bull is illustrative of how *science*, *art*, and *craft* intermesh. Dietrich Mateschitz, the founder of Red Bull and former marketing manager of Blendax (later acquired by Procter & Gamble), spent five years developing his idea for launching a sweet, caffeinated beverage. His idea was to introduce a pick-me-up of the type he had come to know and appreciate during his travels in Asia. The brand concept was carefully planned. He developed every process in detail, from packaging to communication. Mateschitz then ensured the precise coordination of all the processes before launching and distributing the beverage in its first market, Austria, in 1987.

He was equally meticulous in introducing the drink into each subsequent market. For example, the US market was divided into »cells,« in which the objective was to make consumers aware of the new product within three to six months.[133] The initial customer base was sought out and developed by specially trained teams that focused on locations where the young congregate, such as universities or clubs and bars. Once a loyal customer base had been developed in this manner, wide-scale distribution followed, typically two to three months later, using all the normal distribution channels with a slight preference for restaurants over food retail. Only then did classic advertising begin, focusing primarily on cinema, television, and radio. The focal point of the Red Bull communication was and remains the product itself, with its clear positioning: stimulation of mind and body. The design and color scheme of the drink cans reflect the product's positioning and demonstrate the meticulousness of the brand's planning. Some 100 different draft designs were commissioned before the final ones were chosen. The intention of the final design is carefully thought out. The bull embodies strength, courage, and stamina. Cold colors – blue and silver – represent the intellect; hot ones – red and gold – symbolize emotion. On the Red Bull Energy Drink, the logo is rounded out by the claim, »vitalizes body and mind.« This claim was reinforced with the slogan »Red Bull gives you wiiings!« This catchy motto is designed to convey individuality, innovation, fun, and agility, thus promoting the emotional values of the brand.

Red Bull's advertising creativity is kept direct, simple, and fun, using cartoon sketches that – through their humorous depiction of a bull – have achieved a high degree of consumer recognition. New motifs and ideas for advertisements follow the same design principles, ensuring that the product remains unmistakable for its market.

Red Bull has gone well beyond traditional media in many aspects of its campaigns. Nowhere is this better exemplified than in its sports event Red Bull Flugtag (or »Flight Day«). These events are an innovative and creative form of marketing that supports the claim »Red Bull gives you wiiings!« Teams have to build and fly their own aircraft. What constitutes an aircraft is left to the imagination of the teams participating in the event. The teams are judged on three criteria: distance, creativity, and showmanship. The first Red Bull Flugtag took place in Vienna, Austria, in 1992. To date, almost 500 events have been held around the world – from Wellington, New Zealand to San Francisco, US – attracting huge publicity and up to 300,000 spectators each time with dozens more scheduled for 2014 and 2015.[134] The brand's most spectacular achievement to date was perhaps the sponsorship of Felix Baumgartner's space jump in 2012. According to the *Financial Times*, eight million people watched the event on YouTube alone. The jump, referred to as »Red Bull Stratos« by the company, is both impressively original and fully consistent with Red Bull's brand image. The event received worldwide media coverage; estimates of the advertising value equivalent range from USD 300 million to several billions.[135] In light of this impact, the total cost of the event – estimated at EUR 50 million[136] – seems like a real bargain. By 2013, Red Bull achieved sales of more than 5 billion cans, the equivalent of EUR 4.9 billion in revenues (Figure 1.15).[137] Red Bull succeeded in achieving high brand recognition and market success through a well-measured combination of *science*, *art*, and *craft*.

There is no question that the creativity of advertising agencies and the craft of brand activation specialists are crucial in brand management – and will remain so for the foreseeable future. But their skills need to be applied in the systematic context of the science and of brand management, rather than at random. For many companies, accepting this simple fact requires stepping back from their current way of doing things. It involves a complete readjustment of their brand management approach. Senior management must set this course.

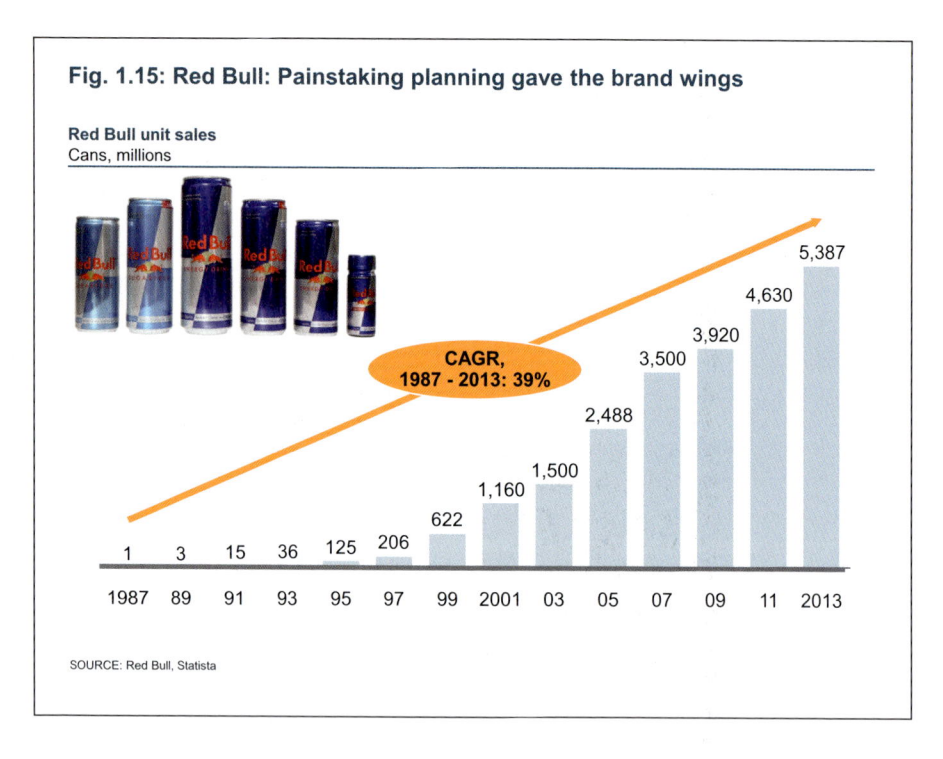

### Fig. 1.15: Red Bull: Painstaking planning gave the brand wings

**Red Bull unit sales**
Cans, millions

CAGR, 1987 - 2013: 39%

| Year | 1987 | 89 | 91 | 93 | 95 | 97 | 99 | 2001 | 03 | 05 | 07 | 09 | 11 | 2013 |
|---|---|---|---|---|---|---|---|---|---|---|---|---|---|---|
| Units | 1 | 3 | 15 | 36 | 125 | 206 | 622 | 1,160 | 1,500 | 2,488 | 3,500 | 3,920 | 4,630 | 5,387 |

SOURCE: Red Bull, Statista

It is clear that management, in its desire to integrate the creative aspect of brand management with its other management processes, is looking beyond market research institutes, turning increasingly to academia and strategic management consultants. Until now, there has been little light shed even here. Instead, management is presented with a nearly incomprehensible jungle of concepts that all make the claim that they lay bare the economic value of the brand without producing the necessary transparency. That this situation should prevail today is somewhat surprising. Whereas top management is used to receiving concrete business figures in terms of revenues, returns, capital ratios, costs, volumes, and productivity every Monday from virtually all areas of its business, branding has so far been the exception to the rule. This handicaps sound decision making and alienates top management from the management of one of the most vital components of success – the control of the brand. This is something we seek to redress here.

We believe that top management requires the integration of *science*, *art*, and *craft* for systematic, fact-based brand management. This means creating a degree of transparency that has so far been lacking in the branding world. Transparency is essential if executives are to base their brand management decisions on sound foundations. The following chapters present a holistic approach to brand management. This includes systematic, qualitative indicators (e.g., brand image) and quantitative ones (e.g., observed behavior at different stages of the purchase funnel). We refer to this approach as BrandMatics®, since it provides a systematic framework for brand management. On the following pages, the individual tools and detailed concepts are organized into three topic areas: measuring, making, and managing power brands.

## Measuring brands

When setting out to measure the brand, the starting point should always be a thorough survey of the current perception of the brand, from the perspectives of both established customers and potential new customers, a distinction that we have strengthened as part of an addition to the proven BrandMatics® approach; see Chapter 2 for details.

The brand purchase funnel gauges the strength of the brand in comparison with competing brands – from the point of initial consumer awareness to that of repeat product purchases by loyal customers. This analysis provides information to refine the brand. It also helps to identify which brands in a brand portfolio will be the most effective in reaching a target group of customers. In its most recent version, the brand purchase funnel reflects and captures new patterns in consumer behavior, especially as far as purchase decision making and observed loyalty are concerned.

## Making brands

Building on the results of the brand diagnosis, the next step is to identify what actions need to be taken to build the brand (Chapter 3).

First, *brand driver analysis* helps identify those factors and customer needs that distinguish strong brands from weak ones in the purchase funnel. This defines the strategic direction and the initiatives that need to be taken to grow the brand. In most cases, the fundamental *brand promise* will need to be adjusted (or even completely reformulated) to take the brand's current weaknesses into account. Of course, for this process to be effective in growing the brand, the brand promise needs to be anchored in the actual capabilities of the company's operating units (rather than those that the company might wish for).

While the professional management of a single brand requires the right mix of *science, art,* and *craft,* the task of managing an entire portfolio of brands is substantially more complex. With the support of some selected portfolio instruments, however, the BrandMatics® approach can also be used for systematic and successful brand portfolio management.

## Managing brands

Even a brand with a well-defined brand promise can fail, if it is not established consistently across all the relevant stakeholders within and beyond the organization. A positive brand image is created through the individual's experiences of the brand on a daily basis. This image will only become anchored in the customers' minds if it is consistent over a long period and at all customer touch points, not just in advertising. The internal brand activation approach provides a systematic way to create a brand mindset in the organization, to translate the brand promise into concrete actions along all customer touch points, and to ensure its longer-term institutionalization.

BrandMatics® is a holistic and consistent approach to brand management. Having said that, successful brand management is nearly always the result of strong partnerships. Frequently, one key factor for success is the involvement of external service providers, that is, hiring a market research agency to conduct surveys or commissioning a creative agency to design ways to communicate the brand proposition. The following chapters cover all these topics. They reflect the experience of McKinsey's Marketing and Sales Practice regarding how senior management teams have used the BrandMatics® tools and concepts to put brand decisions on a more objective footing, combining qualitative brand features with precise and reliable economic data – thereby maximizing brand value.

# Interview with Matt Jauchius of Nationwide: »The journey from art to science«

Based in Columbus, Ohio, Nationwide Mutual is a group of companies focusing on insurance and other financial services, such as strategic investment and asset management. The company was established in 1926 and started out in automobile insurance. Today, Nationwide generates more than USD 30 billion in annual sales and employs some 36,000 people.

Matt Jauchius is an Executive Vice President with Nationwide and the company's Chief Marketing Officer. He is responsible for marketing, brand management, digital marketing, advertising, social media, multicultural marketing, sponsorships, research and analytics, customer advocacy, public relations, and communications for all Nationwide companies. We spoke to him in 2013 about marketing analytics. The text is adapted from the transcript of a video interview.

**McKinsey:** What marketing decisions have advanced marketing analytics helped you make?

**Matthew Jauchius:** Marketing analytics have allowed us to improve the fact base for all our decisions. Before we invested in marketing analytics, we were already spending hundreds of millions of dollars on promotional activities. And of course we had to make allocation decisions: How much goes to television? How much goes to digital? How much goes to sports marketing or sponsorships? We had to decide how many commercials to run per year, and whether to have a spokesperson or not. These decisions were often more art than science. They were gut. They were instinct. And they were experience. Marketing analytics allows us to expand the fact base for all these decisions. Marketing is definitely on a journey. I don't know if it has hit the tipping point from art to science yet. But there is no question in our mind at Nationwide that it is on that journey from art to science. And marketing analytics is the science of marketing.

Let me give you an example of how we use marketing analytics. It is a tactical one, but quite important nevertheless. Should we spend money in regions, or metropolitan areas, in which we already have a high concentration of agents? Or should we spend our money across the entire country? You can do media buying either way, and there are differences in efficiency. And depending on whether you are doing television or digital, there are all kinds of additional considerations. We engaged in detailed analysis across all of those fronts. This enabled us to make the right decision, which, for us, was to take more of a national approach and put less money in local activities. This gave us a double-digit increase in marketing efficiency – as measured by quality demand generated per dollar.

**McKinsey:** How important is big data and advanced analytics to Nationwide?

**Matthew Jauchius:** The way we think about it is this. If we have sufficiently large data sets, we can apply statistical techniques to that data to distinguish the essential from the irrelevant. What is more, we can apply predictive modeling to hundreds of millions of dollars in marketing spend to drive better responses: more requests for quotes, an improvement in unaided brand awareness, and so forth.

The property and casualty insurance industry in the United States is characterized, first and foremost, by an arms race of promotional spend. From 2009 to 2012, promotional spend in this category went up 62 percent. In contrast, our own investment went up 0 percent. Now you may ask, what about demand generation? We increased demand generation across all channels – clicks on the Internet, calls to our call center, and quotes requested through our exclusive agents – by 15 percent. Ever since we started investing in marketing analytics in 2009, we have increased marketing productivity by almost 20 percent annually. By the way, we even saved almost USD 5 million in market research and data cost.

**McKinsey:** What are the three most important lessons you've learned in setting up your advanced analytics program?

**Matthew Jauchius:** The first one might come as a surprise. In my experience, you need to invest in organizational support outside of marketing. This includes your board of directors. This includes senior management, the chief executive officer, the chief financial officer, the chief information officer, and the other C-suite executives, as well as your colleagues at the business unit level. This is because marketing analytics will ultimately affect the way that hundreds of millions of dollars are spent. For example, when things get a little tough, the first thing my board of directors will want to cut is promotional activities, which we are spending hundreds of millions on: »Hey, call the marketing guy. Cut his ad budget.« What we were able to do is show the board that competitive spend has increased by 60 percent over the last four years. And while we didn't get any more marketing dollars, we've actually increased demand generation. And we've increased the quality of the generation. All of what I just said was backed up and proven by marketing analytics. Without those tools, I'm not sure I would've prevailed.

The next thing you need to do is build support inside of marketing. You invest in people. You invest in technology. And you invest in data. Make no mistake, I use the word invest deliberately. Because it will cost money. And you have to believe it's going to pay off in the decision making later on.

Speaking of decision making, that's the third point. As a marketer, you have to think about your own marketing organization. Because the goal of marketing analytics is to change the way decisions get made, to make them better. But what this means is that you will need to change the way creative people do their job. They have been brought up thinking of this as an art. Then you are coming in with a bunch of folks with spreadsheets. And you will change the way they do things. This is what CMOs need to be the most aware of with respect to their own organization.

**McKinsey:** What are the big challenges in using big data and advanced analytics?

**Matthew Jauchius:** Big data and marketing analytics drive the journey from art to science in marketing. But the concept I would urge marketers to think about is the notion of what you're really doing with that big data. You are trying to change the way decisions get made in marketing. And academically, we can say, »Well, of course I do it. I apply big data. I have statistically more valid techniques. And, therefore, I have better decisions.«

But ultimately, every organization is about people. Marketing is no exception. And in marketing, creative people have had the control and the power for generations. And when it comes to art and science, these people are often the most artistic. And they have a point. The creative process may start with data. But at some point, you need inspiration. You need creativity. And it's the CMO's job to think about this: »How do I meld analytics and statistically driven techniques with creativity to provide better decision making and better results?« If you forget the people part, the journey from art to science could end in a disaster.

**McKinsey:** How do you transform your marketing organization to get better at advanced analytics?

**Matthew Jauchius:** We often form what I call marketing councils to connect with folks outside of marketing – in product management, pricing, distribution, finance, and so on. These councils help us leverage data for better decisions. And what I'm suggesting is that you use the same concept inside marketing. Typically, most marketing departments are broken down into various shops: a creative shop, an analytics shop, and a research shop. All of these groups hold critical pieces of the puzzle. But they may not work together in the way you need to get the right decisions. What you need to think about is, how do I get a group of people coming from different subdisciplines within marketing to work together and think in a common way? The notion of a council united by a common set of goals is a form of collaboration I've found to be effective.

**McKinsey:** How is the CMO role evolving?

**Matthew Jauchius:** The CMO needs to be both more strategic and more analytical than in the past. Think about business unit strategy. The foundation of any business unit strategy is the value proposition. What am I going to sell? To whom will I sell it? And why should they buy my product or service instead of those of my competitors? You also get into the trade-off between value and price. Well, that's business unit strategy. And increasingly, in any customer-centric strategy, marketing is at the heart of it. If the CMO cannot speak with a strategic voice and cannot articulate these concepts in a way that the business can rally around it, marketing isn't doing its job. Marketing analytics helps CMOs engage with finance folks and IT folks and business unit presidents on their own terms. For a marketer to talk about value propositions and data-driven segmentation is extremely powerful.

**McKinsey:** How have you been able to make Nationwide more agile?

**Matthew Jauchius:** Digital technology is forcing organizations to become more agile. But the question is, do you try to change the entire organization? Or do you put in place coordinating mechanisms that allow parts of your organization to move at a digital speed? I succeeded by doing the latter. I invested in talent. I made modifications around digital decision making. What I mean by that is how much money do I devote to digital, and what decisions get made? In many companies, online and mobile expertise is rooted in large business units. But the decision making has to be fast as lightning. This is why we concentrated a core set of digital capabilities in the corporate center, which I control in my capacity as chief marketing officer: advertising, mobile marketing, social media management, and digital infrastructure. And I also control the promotional budget, so I control how many dollars go towards digital channels.

You have to put the decisions and dollars under one senior executive, such as myself. That's the only way I know how to do it. If you don't, you have committees. And committees do not move at the speed of digital. You have to avoid them.

**McKinsey:** How has the marketing organization built bridges to other departments in Nationwide?

**Matthew Jauchius:** Reflecting on it, one of the most important lessons we've learned is that marketing is not an island. It may sound kind of funny to say that. But in many companies – and Nationwide is no exception – marketing is thought of as slightly separate. »Well, we're going to give a certain amount of dollars to those guys. They're going to make ads and do whatever it is they do. And let's hope it generates demand.« Some companies are far more integrated than that. It depends on the company.

To change this, I have built bridges to three main partner groups within my organization. The first is with my chief information officer. He's my best friend now. Big data and analytics are impossible without having the technology and the data storage and the interfaces to pull it off. Fortunately, the technology folks, they get it. They understand that the application of technology to data for decision making is the way of the future. So that, quite frankly, was natural. But you have to do it.

In addition to the IT folks, you need to do this with the finance folks. They are charged with the efficient and effective use of dollars across the company. And they measure everything. Well, you know what? When you have marketing analytics to enable better decision making, they can be your best friend. Because they can help you tell the story of the value marketing has. We have regular meetings with our finance partners. And we think it adds a lot of value to the process.

The final piece is connecting marketing to the business unit presidents and the CEO. They will always ask the question: »What do I get from all those dollars?« And the CMO has to have an answer that is worded in a way that a general business person relates to – in terms of »I spend this, and I get this.« The only way I know how to do that is with marketing analytics. And we've built the answers to those questions into the management forums and the regular management meetings, so that marketing is not a separate thing anymore. It's integrated into what we do.

# Notes

1 http://www.sponsorship.com/About-IEG/IEG-In-The-News/Marketers-Brace-For-Big-Shows-In-Crisis-Torn-Brazi.aspx.
2 Zenith.
3 McKinsey Global Media Report 2013.
4 Kenning, Peter et al, »Die Entdeckung der kortikalen Entlastung,« Neuroökonomische Forschungsberichte, No. 1, 2002. University of Münster, Institute for Trade Management and Network Marketing, Prof. Dieter Ahlert. See also »Monetäre Markenbewertung: Die Marke als Kapitalanlage, «Absatzwirtschaft 2, 2004, pp. 26–41.
5 http://hautetoday.wordpress.com/2011/06/23/louis-vuitton-core-values-campaigns/.
6 http://en.vogue.fr/fashion-videos/fashion-story/videos/louis-vuitton-s-invitation-to-travel/4855.
7 Meffert, Heribert, and Christoph Burmann, »Markenbildung und Markenstrategien,« Handbuch Produktmanagement, ed. Sönke Albers and Andreas Herrmann, Wiesbaden: Gabler, 2000, pp. 167–187.
8 http://de.adforum.com/award/showcase/6650180/2011/ad/34470341.
9 E. Leclerc, press release, Aug 2004.
10 »How to Resist the Private Label Threat in 2006,« Datamonitor, 26 Dec 2005; McKinsey analysis.
11 »Auftritt der Woche,« Horizont, 10 Feb 2005.
12 Bavagnoli, Giuseppe and Lars Köster, »Private Label Branding«, in Jesko Perrey and Dennis Spillecke, Retail Marketing And Branding, Second Edition, Wiley, 2013.
13 Lattmann, Christian, »Handelsmarken zahlen auf die Händlermarke ein,« Lebensmittelzeitung, 30 May 2008.
14 Bavagnoli, Giuseppe and Lars Köster, »Private Label Branding,« in Jesko Perrey and Dennis Spillecke, Retail Marketing And Branding, Second Edition, Wiley, 2013.
15 Giuseppe Bavagnoli and Lars Köster, »Private Label Branding,«, in Jesko Perrey and Dennis Spillecke, »Retail Marketing and Branding,« Second Edition, Wiley, 2013.
16 http://www.storebrandsdecisions.com/news/2010/04/20/rewe-launches-new-eco-friendly-pro-planetlabel; http://www.rewe-group.com/en/sustainability/pillars/green-products/more-sustainableproducts/pro-planet/; http://www.rewe-group.com/en/sustainability/awards/germancsrprizeforproplanetlabel/; retrieved in May 2014.
17 http://newsfeed.time.com/2011/12/23/fedex-apologizes-after-video-of-driver-throwing-fragile-package-goes-viral/.
18 http://www.utalkmarketing.com/pages/article.aspx?articleid=16575&title=beckham-takeson-%E2%80%98star-wars%E2%80%99-in-newadidas-advert; http://www.chrisrawlinson.com/2010/01/adidas-originals-star-wars-collection/;http://www.viralblog.com/viral-social-videos/star-wars-used-in-ad-from-adidas-originals/#sthash.tkjMAgIf.dpuf; http://theinspirationroom.com/daily/2010/adidasoriginals-star-wars%E2%84%A2-cantina-2010/; retrieved in May 2014.
19 Knudsen, Trond, »Confronting Proliferation in Mobile Communications,« The McKinsey Quarterly Web exclusive, May 2007, www.mckinseyquarterly.com.
20 Based on H&M (4 percent of sales volume), GAP (3 percent), C&A (4 percent). See also »Mode zum Anfassen,« manager magazin 1, 2004, p. 74; »Gestreifte Schals wärmen die GAP-Aktie,« 28 Feb 2003, www.faz.net; »Zu modisch: C&A verlieren Kunden,« Stuttgarter Nachrichten, 7 Jun 2005, p. 10.
21 Annual reports, Inditex Group, various years; http://www.uniquebusinessstrategies.co.uk/pdfs/case%20studies/zarathespeedingbullet.pdf.
22 The US distilled spirits market, Impact Databank, 2007.
23 http://www.marketwatch.com/story/another-shotfor-jagermeister-2013-10-04.
24 Effie award winners showcase.
25 Capital IQ database.
26 http://www.dailymail.co.uk/news/article-2432906/Dangerous-Apple-Maps-glitch-directs-driversairport-runway.html; http://www.huffingtonpost.com/2012/09/20/applemap-fails-ios-6-maps_n_1901599.html; http://www.forbes.com/sites/petercohan/2012/09/27/apple-maps-six-most-epic-fails/; company information.
27 IHS Inc. database.
28 Fischer, Marc, Fabian Hieronimus, and Marcel Kreuz, »Markenrelevanz in der Unternehmensführung: Messung, Erklärung und empirische Befunde für B2C-Märkte,« Arbeitspapier Nr. 1, ed. Klaus Backhaus, Heribert Meffert, Jürgen Meffert, Jesko Perrey, Jürgen Schröder (McKinsey), Düsseldorf: 2002.
29 »World Intellectual Property Indicators – 2013 Edition«; IP Finance insights & Institute profile 2009.
30 Knudsen, Trond, »Confronting proliferation in beer: An interview with Carlsberg's Alex Myers,« The McKinsey Quarterly, Web exclusive, May 2007, www.mckinseyquarterly.com. 18 Results from a search performed by ABI/Inform of international academic publications.
31 GENIOS search 2003-2013 (as of March 2014).
32 27 http://www.faz.net/frankfurter-allgemeine-zeitung/verkauf-der-handysparte-das-ende-von-nokia-wiewir-es-kennen-12670155.html; Bloomberg.

33 http://brandkeys.com/wp-content/uploads/2014/02/2014-CLEI-PRESS-RELEASE-FINALFeb1-public.pdf.
34 http://www.interbrand.com/en/best-global-brands/2013/Best-Global-Brands-2013-Brand-View.aspx.
35 Martin, Andrew, »I'd Like to Sell the World a Coke,« New York Times, 27 May 2007; Euromonitor; http://www.statista.com/statistics/225388/us-market-share-of-the-coca-cola-company-since-2004/5.
36 Passport Global Company Shares by global brand owner, 2013.
37 »Kullmanns Moment,« Brand Eins, Feb 2008; »Weg mit der Kohle,« Werben & Verkaufen,« 20 Sep 2007.
38 Michael, Bernd M., »Wenn die Wertschöpfung weiter sinkt, stirbt die Marke,« Zeitschrift für Betriebswirtschaftslehre 1, suppl. vol., 2002, pp. 35–56.
39 »Klimaschutz-Tarif vom Billiganbieter,« Energie & Management, 15 Jan 2008; and Flauger, Jürgen, »Billigstrom – der zweite Anlauf,« Handelsblatt, 17 Apr 2008, www.handelsblatt.com; »Strompreise beflügeln E.ON-Geschäfte – E wie Einfach gut gestartet, « dpa/verivox, 15 Aug 2007, www.verivox.de; Bernotat, Wulf H., »Ausführungen zur Ordentlichen Hauptversammlung der E.ON AG,« 30 Apr 2008, www.eon.com; »FTD: Jeder vierte Stromwechsler bei ›E wie einfach‹,« 20 May 2008, www.clever-stromvergleich.de.
40 Ad spend per car according to »Wir wollen wieder auf Platz eins,« Werben & Verkaufen, 6 Mar 2008; and »VW ist Werbekönig,« Telebörse, 28 Jan 2008, www.teleboerse.de.
41 Toyota: Prius Launch – Harmony Installations, Effie Worldwide Bronze, North America Effies, 2011.
42 IHS Inc., 2014.
43 Stern MarkenProfile, No. 10, Nov 2004. 37 Stern MarkenProfile, No. 10, Nov 2004.
44 Annual reports, Beiersdorf AG, various years; company Web site.
45 Company Web site.
46 http://uk.reuters.com/article/2014/03/04/ukbeiersdorf-results-idUKBREA230D120140304.
47 JP Mangalindan, »Amazon's recommendation secret«, Fortune, July 30, 2012.
48 http://www.forbes.com/sites/jenniferrooney/2014/04/16/annual-effies-survey-content-is-king/.
49 Recent scientific research shows that the influence of rational vs. emotional rand aspects on the purchase decision varies across different industries, and that it can be measured analytically. See, for example: Freundt, Tjark: »Emotionalisierung von Marken,« Wiesbaden: DuV 2005.
50 http://interbrand.com/de/best-global-brands/2013/top-100-list-view.aspx.
51 http://www.adweek.com/adfreak/apples-get-maccomplete-campaign-130552.

52 http://www.beiersdorf.com/newsroom/press-news/all-news/2013/07/2013-07-29-news-a-masterpiecefor-cell-rejuvenation.
53 http://www.absatzwirtschaft.de/content/marketingstrategie/news/marken-award-2014-fuer-alproebike-und-nivea-in-dusch;81837.
54 http://www.auto-motor-und-sport.de/news/audi-r8-e-tron-comeback-kleinserie-fuer-denelektrosportwagen-7983373.htmlhttp://www.automotor-und-sport.de/news/audi-r8-e-troncomeback-kleinserie-fuer-den-elektrosportwagen-7983373.html.
55 http://www.auto-motor-und-sport.de/news/marken-image-umfrage-bmw-liegt-im-trend-8032921.html.
56 »Bekleidungskette C&A zeigt Expansionsgelüste,«Frankfurter Allgemeine Zeitung, 7 June 2005, p. 20; Weber, Stefan, »C&A trotzt der Krise im Textilhandel,« Süddeutsche Zeitung, 3 June 2003, p. 22; Werner, Markus, »Werbung und Wirkung,« Textilwirtschaft, 20 Feb 2003, p. 54.
57 http://www.finanzen.net/nachricht/rohstoffe/ROUNDUP-C-A-Weltweit-der-groesste-Abnehmer-von-Bio-Baumwolle-2677115.
58 http://www.beiersdorf.com/brands/brand-history/nivea.
59 »Nivea gets a new global design«, Beiersdorf AG press release, January 15, 2013.
60 http://red-dot.de/cd/online-exhibition/work/?code=05-2031&y=2013.
61 http://www.germancarforum.com/community/threads/why-bmw-deep-sixed-its-people-mover-plan.22011/.
62 Annual reports, BMW Group, various years; Ward's Automotive Yearbook; »BMW: We may need a green brand,« Automotive News, 21 Jan 2008; »Why BMW deep-sixed its people mover plan,« Detroit News, 22 Jan 2008.
63 http://live.wsj.com/video/bmw-launches-i8-hybridall-wheel-drive-supercar/89A7C998-6E40-4C00-880C-CC2ABEB9D489.html#!89A7C998-6E40-4C00-880C-CC2ABEB9D489.
64 http://en.wikipedia.org/wiki/BMW_i3#Design_and_technology; http://www.bmw.com/com/en/newvehicles/i/i3/2013/showroom/technical_data.html#m=i3_range_extender; retrieved in May 2014.
65 http://www.bizjournals.com/austin/stories/2009/04/27/daily3.html; http://media.gm.com/media/us/en/gm/news.detail.html/content/Pages/news/us/en/2009/Apr/0427_AcceleratesReinvention.html
66 Roosdorp, Alexander, »Coca-Cola: Leistungspflege durch agile Marktkommunikation,« Best Practice in Marketing, ed. Torsten Tomczak and Sven Reinecke, Vienna: Wirtschaftsverlag Carl Ueberreuter, 1998, pp. 241–251.

67 »Corporate Identity – nur anders,« Wirtschaftswoche, 25 Apr 1996, p. 134.
68 Dingler, Rolf, »Der Prototyp für erfolgreiches Markenmanagement,« FVW International, No. 22, 14 Oct 1997, p. 112.
69 http://www.talkingretail.com/products-news/tobacco/marlboro-red-gets-a-new-look/.
70 The Guardian; Huffington Post; Campaign for Tobacco-Free Kids Report.
71 Die Tabak Zeitung, various years.
72 http://online.wsj.com/news/articles/SB10001424052702304626804579360552508696542.
73 Brand Marketers Report, 2007.
74 »Das Comeback der Wow-Wows,« Brand Eins, Mar 2005, pp. 44–50.
75 »Hippe Handys, träges Marketing,« Werben & Verkaufen, 13 Jan 2005, pp. 22–24.
76 Roman Maurer and Volrad Wollny, »The Rise of Samsung Electronics,« Mainz University of Applied Sciences 2013.
77 www.samsung.com.
78 »Samsung's Goal: Be Like BMW,« BusinessWeek, 1 Aug 2005, www.businessweek.com.
79 Roman Maurer and Volrad Wollny, »The Rise of Samsung Electronics,« Mainz University of Applied Sciences 2013.
80 Capital IQ; annual reports.
81 Frankfurter Allgemeine Zeitung, 26 Apr 2008.
82 Strategy Analytics; annual reports.
83 http://www.venturerepublic.com/resources/Samsung_Building_brand_equity_through_brand_community.asp.
84 Stuart Elliot, »Selfies, Pizza, and Promoting Brands at the Oscars,« New York Times, March 3, 2014 (http://www.nytimes.com/2014/03/04/business/media/selfies-pizza-and-promotingbrands-at-the-oscars.html).
85 http://www.businesswire.com/news/home/20060608005264/en/Doves-Campaign-Real-Beauty-Created-Ogilvy-Mather.
86 http://current.effie.org/winners/showcase/2007/2029.
87 http://effie.org/case_studies/case/2235.
88 https://www.facebook.com/febreze/photos/a.10151434141960368.827954.260464885367/10151679423255368/.
89 http://www.adweek.com/news/cannes-2009-videos/qa-pgs-marc-pritchard-94334.
90 www.canneslionslive.com and www.gunnreport.com. For details on the ADC/McKinsey study, »Der Code erfolgreicher Werbung,« Werben & Verkaufen, 4 Oct 2007; Perrey, Jesko, Nicola Wagener, and Carsten Wallmann, »Kreativität + Content Fit = Werbeerfolg,« 2007.
91 This insert is based on a more comprehensive description of the ADC study by Sebastian Turner. Please see earlier editions of this book and its German version, Mega-Macht Marke, for details and case studies.

92 Fluge.de's ownership of Germina is contested by competitors. See »Springt Simi bald mit Quattro?«, Blick, 27 Nov 2010; retrieved 19 May 2014.
93 »Ski der deutschen Springer verboten,« Handelsblatt online, 26 Nov 2010; retrieved 19 May 2014; »Fischer gehört die Lufthoheit in Sotschi,« WirtschaftsBlatt, 14 Feb 2014; retrieved May 19, 2014; Georg Mannsperger, »fluege.de – ein neuer Player in der Skiindustrie debütiert auf der Vierschanzentournee«, 31 Dec 2011, http://wissensserver.info/2011/12/.
94 http://www.presseportal.de/pm/63094/2034059/tns-emnid-77-der-deutschen-kennen-ab-in-denurlaub-de-69-fluege-de-und-57-unistergrosse; retrieved 19 May 2014.
95 Allgayer, Florian »Mafo.de-Markenranking: Wie stark sind Flugportale?«, 8 Sep 2011; http://www.wuv.de/medien/mafo_de_markenranking_wie_stark_sind_flugportale; retrieved 19 May 2014.
96 Bloomberg Businessweek Magazine, August 1, 2004 http://www.businessweek.com/stories/2004-08-01/online-extra-jeff-bezos-onword-of-mouth-power.
97 McKinsey research; https://aws.amazon.com/releasenotes/; http://en.wikipedia.org/wiki/Amazon_Web_Services; retrieved in May 2014.
98 http://www.interbrand.com/de/best-globalbrands/2013/top-100-list-view.aspx.
99 Tim Nudd, The Greatest Marketer of the Age, AdWeek, October 2011; INSEAD.
100 http://www.interbrand.com/de/best-globalbrands/2013/Apple.
101 Rücker, Martin, »Der gute Ton macht die Musik,« Süddeutsche Zeitung, 19 Nov 2003, p. 36; »Vivaldi unter der Motorhaube,« Bonner Generalanzeiger, 1 Mar 2003, p. 72.
102 http://press.porsche.com/news/release.php?id=789.
103 Brandes, Dieter, »Die 11 Geheimnisse des ALDI-Erfolgs«, Frankfurt: Campus Verlag, 2003.
104 »Discounter Lidl wächst abermals schneller als Aldi,« Die Welt, 31 May 2005, p. 11; Schlitt, Petra, and Steffen Klusmann, »Angriff des Super-Krämers,« manager magazin, Sep 2003, p. 38; »Lidl bleibt dem Rivalen Aldi dicht auf den Fersen,« Financial Times Deutschland, 21 Oct 2003, p. 7.
105 Euromonitor; expert estimates.
106 http://www.coca-colacompany.com/history/the-chronicle-of-coca-cola-a-global-business.
107 »Japan's Vending Machines Want to Talk to You,« The Industry Standard, 2 April 2001, www.thestandard.com.
108 »Das Ende der Leidenschaft,« Werben & Verkaufen, 13 Jan 2005, p. 17.
109 http://www.statisticbrain.com/starbucks-company-statistics/.

110 Geoff Kirbyson, »Howard Schultz – uncommon grounds«, August 2004, http://www.brandchannel.com/careers_profile.asp?cr_id=47.
111 http://www.interbrand.com/de/best-global-brands/2013/Best-Global-Brands-2013-Brand-View.aspx.
112 Muller, Joann »With Driverless Cars, Once Again It Is California Leading The Way«, Forbes.com, September 26, 2012.
113 http://edition.cnn.com/2014/04/15/tech/mobile/google-glass-public-sale/.
114 Company information.
115 http://www.digitalbuzzblog.com/ikea-multi-viewinteractive-kitchen-stories/; http://adsoftheworld.com/media/online/ikea_change_your_view_in_the_kitchen; retrieved in May 2014.
116 http://www.mackcollier.com/ikea-fans-ask-for-asleepover-so-the-company-gives-them-one/; retrieved in May 2014.
117 Stevenson, Suzanne, »Ikea catalogue beats the Bible,«, Evening Standard, 27 Aug 2002, www.thisislondon.co.uk. For further details on Ikea, »Innovaro Innovation Briefing,« Nov 2005, www.innovaro.com; Furniture report on »fiffiga folket,« Mar 2008; Klingner, Susanne, »Der Spion, der aus der Kälte kam,« Süddeutsche Zeitung Magazin, No. 3, 2007; Meuli, Kaspar, »Blonde Möbel: Ikea ist überall gleich, einzig in Amerika macht man Konzessionen,« NZZ Folio, Oct 2001, www.nzzfolio.ch.
118 http://franchisor.ikea.com/Theikeaconcept/Pages/Ikea-stores-and-more.aspx; retrieved in May 2014.
119 Company information.
120 Meuli, Kaspar, »Blonde Möbel: Ikea ist überall gleich, einzig in Amerika macht man Konzessionen,« NZZ Folio, Oct 2001, www.nzzfolio.ch.
121 »IKEA Facts & Figures 2007,« www.ikeagroup.ikea.com.
122 http://franchisor.ikea.com/Theikeaconcept/Pages/Ikea-concept-center.aspx; retrieved in May 2014.
123 http://www.boklok.com/upload/Documents/Downloads/Downloads_EN/ The%20BoKlok%20story,%20fact%20sheet.pdf.

124 For further details on Ikea, »Innovaro Innovation Briefing,« Nov 2005, www.innovaro.com; Furtuniture report on »fiffiga folket,« Mar 2008; Klingner, Susanne, »Der Spion, der aus der Kälte kam,« Süddeutsche Zeitung Magazin, No. 3, 2007; Meuli, Kaspar, »Blonde Möbel: Ikea ist überall gleich, einzig in Amerika macht man Konzessionen,«NZZ Folio, Oct 2001, www.nzzfolio.ch. »EXTRA: Ikea ist Kult – Ein Mann vermöbelt die Welt,« 23 May 2003,www.stern.de. »IkeaIkea Facts & Figures 2007,« www.ikeagroup.ikea.com.
125 http://content.time.com/time/specials/packages/article/0,28804,1913612_1913610.1913608,00.html.
126 Schmeh, Klaus, »Die 55 größten Flops der Wirtschaftsgeschichte: Krimis, Krisen, Kuriositäten,« Frankfurt: Redline Wirtschaft, 2002, p. 33.
127 http://www.autokiste.de/psg/archiv/a.htm?id=5877.
128 Case study by Töpfer, Armin, »Rechenfehler im Pentium-Prozessor von Intel im Sommer 1994,« www.krisennavigator.de.
129 Annual report, Intel Corporation, 1998.
130 Clef, Ulrich, »Die Ausgezeichneten: Unternehmenskarrieren der 30 deutschen Marketing-Preisträger,« Munich: Clef Creative Communications, 2003.
131 Hirn, Wolfgang and Heide Neukirchen, »Fabrik-Verkauf,« manager magazin, Nov 2001, pp. 294–302.
132 Annual reports, Adidas, various years.
133 Keller, K.L (2003), »Red Bull: Building Brand Equity in New Ways,« in *Best Practice Cases in Branding: Lessons from the World's Strongest Brands*, pp. 69-92, Prentice Hall, Upper Saddle River: NJ.
134 Company Web site.
135 http://www.jeffreyvocell.com/post/33824436646/red-bull-stratos-was-an-astronomical-success-for.
136 http://www.nachrichten.at/sport/mehr_sport/Red-Bull-Stratos-Milliardenhoher-Werbewert;art109,984382.
137 Company information.

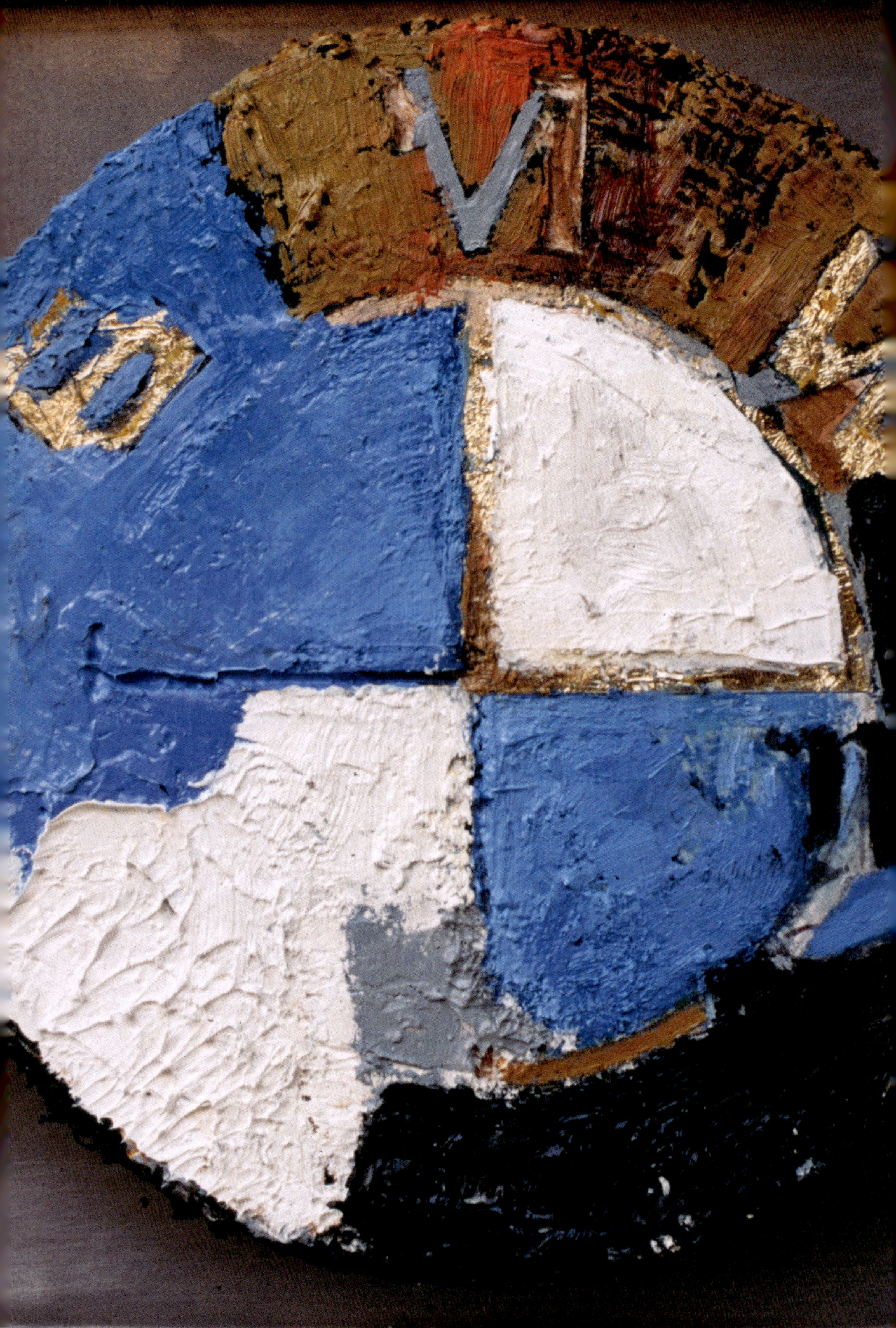

## 2. Measuring Brands

### 2.1 Brand Relevance: Assessing the Relative Importance of Brands

From financial services to telecommunications or electricity supply, there is hardly an industry today that does not hope to profit from the growing value of brands. And it is not just in established areas, such as consumer goods, where brands are important. Take retail banking, for instance. In a survey of 6,000 banking customers from ten different European countries, respondents rated the brand as the second most important decision-making criterion (following their proximity to a branch) when choosing a bank. Furthermore, customers are willing to pay higher prices and fees for branded banking services. For a standard commodity, such as a current account, for example, some strong branded banks are able to charge more than twice as much as their lesser competitors. In 2013, six banks were ranked among Interbrand's best global brands, collectively valued at more than EUR 50 billion: HSBC, J. P. Morgan, Goldman Sachs, Citi, Morgan Stanley, and Santander.[1] Apparently, banks are on the rebound from the 2008 financial crisis. In Germany, consumer banking was one of the biggest winners in terms of brand relevance in 2013. For the first time since 2002, private bank accounts made the top ten as a category.

Though brands are increasingly important, they are not a panacea. A closer examination of the business-to-business (B2B) sector makes this point well. A study by Sattler and PricewaterhouseCoopers reveals that the B2B picture is much more complex than it appears at first sight. Whereas brands overall represented only 18 percent of company value in B2B markets in 2005, in the consumer goods segment, this figure came to an average of 53 percent for durable goods and 62 percent for non-durables at the time.[2] In other words, brands are much more relevant to certain businesses than they are to others. A recent update of the survey revealed that the overall importance of brands continues to increase in many industries; see the B2C insert on page 88 for details. While brand value accounted for 56 percent of company value in 1999, this rose to 67 percent in 2005.

Although the power of brands is certainly increasing, one shouldn't jump blindly onto the brand wagon. Fact-based brand management requires a good understanding of the role the brand plays in consumer decision making in a given industry. The mere assumption that »brands are always important« is misleading and can result in poor investment decisions. Like all marketing tools, brand investment must be assessed in terms of its potential economic impact and, specifically, in terms of its influence on consumer purchasing behavior. If a brand is unlikely to have a significant impact on consumer behavior, there is little point in making considerable investment in it. Nonetheless, this is a mistake that has been made time and again.

The German electricity sector shows that brand recognition does not automatically generate sustained bottom line impact. Mirroring the consumer goods industry, German electricity suppliers attempted to introduce a number of brands to the market –

for example, PreussenElektra's ElektraDirekt and EnBW's Yello, both launched in 1998. These brands were all relatively successful in securing name recognition at a level similar to that of leading consumer goods companies. However, only Yello was still around ten years later. Following its large initial investments in brand building, it has achieved almost 100 percent aided brand awareness. The fact that other first-generation energy brands didn't survive shows that brand recognition is only one building block of commercial success. High brand relevance, a robust business model, and compelling propositions are equally important. Perhaps these pioneers also suffered from what might be called a first mover disadvantage. In 1998, German consumers may simply not have been ready for energy brands. Right after deregulation, many energy users were barely aware they now actually had a choice of providers, and were free to switch. Even in 2006, when German authorities first started tracking provider changes in a standardized way, the switch rate only came to 1.3 percent.[3] In contrast, many experts consider the UK energy market a somewhat more favorable environment for brands as sources of differentiation and value creation. Since British authorities regulate products and control prices,[4] brands are more relevant to consumer decision making than in other, less severely regulated markets with greater product variety.

At the time, private electricity consumers in Germany considered other criteria more important than the brand in determining their choice of electricity provider. If brands have had any role in shaping the German electricity market over the course of the decade after its deregulation in 1998, it is only at the local level. Surveys conducted in 2008 indicated that some 80 percent of consumers preferred their electricity to be supplied by their local public utilities company.[5] While this factor may not take priority for consumers anymore, it is still relevant today. According to our analysis of brand drivers in the energy market, »strong presence in the region« is the second most important purchase driver for potential new energy customers. Compare Chapter 3 for details. This clearly shows that, prior to any brand investment, it is crucial to have a sound knowledge of the relevance of branding in shaping consumer purchase behavior in the specific sector in which the company operates. Making generalizations or abstractions derived from other sectors that might well have little relevance to the sector concerned is likely to lead to poor investment decisions.

### Determining brand relevance

The starting point of BrandMatics® is thus to create transparency regarding the extent to which the brand shapes purchase behavior in a given industry and market. The brand is only relevant and worthy of increased management attention if it can influence the behavior of consumers or intermediate companies, or a company's position in the war for talent.

In order to establish the relative importance of brands in various product segments, McKinsey conducted research into the German B2B and business-to-consumer (B2C) markets in collaboration with a group of researchers from three well-respected German research institutions: the Marketing Centrum Münster at the University of Münster, the Institute for Innovation Research at the University of Kiel, and the Institute for Retail and Marketing at the University of Hamburg.[6] To measure brand relevance, a comprehensive scale was developed and validated according to scientific standards. The brand relevance measurement scale not only captures the overall relevance of brands as perceived by customers, but also breaks it down into the three functional components touched on in Chapter 1:

- **Information efficiency as the time factor:** Brands make it easier for the consumer to gather and process information about a product.
- **Risk reduction as the trust factor:** Selecting a brand-name product reduces the consumer's (subjective) risk of making a purchase mistake. Brands create trust in the expected performance of the product and provide continuity in the predictability of the product benefit.
- **Image benefit as the expressive or »identity« factor:** Brands may offer the additional benefit of helping the customer foster a desired image. This benefit can be directed either outward or inward. It is directed outward when the customer uses the brand to cultivate a certain public image. The benefit is directed inward for purposes of self-expression or in identification with certain values and ideals.

The three brand functions cover the entire purchasing and consumption process. Information efficiency assists customers prior to the purchase decision, risk reduction influences the actual decision making, and the image benefit emerges in the subsequent consumption phase.

The measurement instrument was applied in two large-scale national and international studies to a broad selection of B2B and B2C markets. The results provide interesting insights that are of high managerial relevance. For Germany, we have also conducted a longitudinal study of brand relevance in 30 B2C industries, comprising four waves from 2002 to 2013. See the insert below for details on variation over time, long-term trends, and the impact of factors such as macroeconomic development, consumer confidence, and regulation on brand relevance.

**The importance of brands in B2C markets across the world**

More than 12,000 consumers across the world took part in a representative online survey during the summer of 2006.[7] The original survey covered nine countries and 18 product categories. The countries covered were France, Germany, Japan, Poland, Russia, Spain, Sweden, the United Kingdom, and the United States. The product categories included fast-moving consumer goods, consumer durables, services, and retailers. In 2013, the survey was updated for Germany. See the insert below for details on this latest wave.

Across all countries and the 18 selected product categories, the 3 with the highest brand relevance in 2006 were cars, beer, and mobile phones (Figure 2.1). This trend continued in 2013 in Germany. Cars, beer, and mobile phones consistently made the

German top ten from 2002 to 2013, although beer lost the number one position in 2013. In the mid-field rankings, the survey consistently identified mail order, express delivery services, and scheduled flights. Finally, and unsurprisingly, the product categories in which brands were least relevant across all countries in 2006 were drugstores and paper tissues.

### Which brand functions are important for which products?

The survey made it possible to determine the strengths of the selected brand functions in the individual product markets. The combination of these values with the relative importance of the individual brand functions produced the overall brand relevance shown in Figure 2.1. The analysis of consumer evaluations across the nine countries indicates that risk reduction was the most important brand function, followed by the image benefit and the information efficiency function. Analysis of the specific brand functions provides a number of further insights (Figure 2.2).

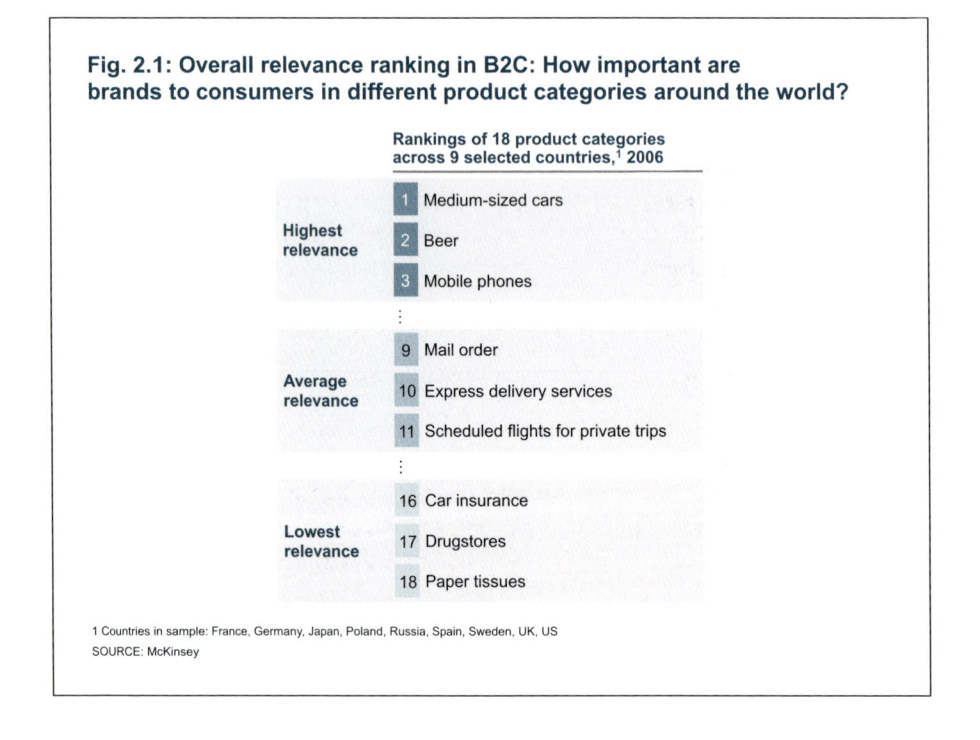

**Fig. 2.1: Overall relevance ranking in B2C: How important are brands to consumers in different product categories around the world?**

Rankings of 18 product categories across 9 selected countries,[1] 2006

Highest relevance
1. Medium-sized cars
2. Beer
3. Mobile phones

⋮

Average relevance
9. Mail order
10. Express delivery services
11. Scheduled flights for private trips

⋮

Lowest relevance
16. Car insurance
17. Drugstores
18. Paper tissues

[1] Countries in sample: France, Germany, Japan, Poland, Russia, Spain, Sweden, UK, US
SOURCE: McKinsey

### Information efficiency for recurring purchase decisions

Information efficiency was the dominant brand function in the case of fast-moving consumer goods in 2006. The common factors in these markets are that the consumer can select from many brands, that the consumer must make a decision relatively quickly, and – of particular relevance – that the consumer makes decisions on a regular basis. It should come as little surprise that information efficiency is particularly important in the case of beer and cigarettes: the packaging of these products is largely standardized, that is, there is little variation in the shape and size of beer bottles and cigarette packs. What little space isn't taken up by health warnings consists almost entirely of brand-defining elements that reveal little else about the product. Since in-store trial is not an option, consumers are entirely dependent on the brand to remind them of past associations or their previous experience with the product (if any) to guide them in their purchase.

Information efficiency loses importance when the consumer takes more time to make purchase decisions in order to collect information about various offers. This is the case, for instance, with durable consumer goods such as television sets and computers, but also in service sectors, such as car insurance.

### Risk reduction for high-end consumer goods

The higher the purchase price and the lower the purchase frequency, the more important the brand becomes as an instrument of risk reduction. If a given purchase accounts for a large share of the consumer's budget and this item will not be replaced for a long period of time, the consequences of a poor decision are much greater than is the case, for example, in fast-moving consumer goods with a low purchase price. Unsurprisingly, medium-sized cars topped the ranking for the role of brands in risk reduction in 2006,[8] followed by mobile phones and television sets. For drugstores or paper tissues, risk reduction played only a secondary role. Even high-profile services such as banking were only located in the middle of the list.

**Fig. 2.2: Ranking of selected B2C product markets by brand function**

Rankings of 18 product categories across 9 selected countries,[1] 2006

| | Information efficiency | Risk reduction | Image benefit |
|---|---|---|---|
| **Highest relevance** | 1 Beer | 1 Medium-sized cars | 1 Medium-sized cars |
| | 2 Cigarettes | 2 Mobile phones | 2 Designer sun glasses |
| | 3 Medium-sized cars | 3 TV sets | 3 Mobile network operators |
| | ⋮ | ⋮ | ⋮ |
| **Average relevance** | 9 TV sets | 9 Scheduled flights for private trips | 9 Express delivery services |
| | 10 Express delivery services | 10 Designer sun glasses | 10 Scheduled flights for private trips |
| | 11 Mail order | 11 Banking accounts | 11 TV sets |
| | ⋮ | ⋮ | ⋮ |
| **Lowest relevance** | 16 Drugstores | 16 Car insurance | 16 Detergents |
| | 17 Car insurance | 17 Drugstores | 17 Drugstores |
| | 18 Paper tissues | 18 Paper tissues | 18 Paper tissues |

1 Countries in sample: France, Germany, Japan, Poland, Russia, Spain, Sweden, UK, US
SOURCE: McKinsey

### Image benefit for publicly displayed products

Not only were cars at the top of the 2006 ranking for risk reduction, but they were also at the top of the global list for image benefit. They were followed by designer sunglasses and, more surprisingly, mobile network operators. Image benefit was also an important brand function across all countries with respect to mobile phones, beer, and cigarettes in 2006. By contrast, image benefit is of limited relevance in retail categories like drugstores and product types like paper tissues.

Image benefit is derived from influencing the perception of others as well as from one's own identification with the brand. The results of the study make sense intuitively. Sunglasses, for instance, are a prestige object visible to all. The same is true for cars and mobile phones. Even beer and cigarettes, although fast-moving consumer goods, are on display when consumed and possess very specific attributes, about which consumers care a great deal. Beer drinkers send very different messages about themselves by being seen with a pint of Guinness or a glass of Heineken, a half-liter bottle of Newcastle Brown Ale or a can of Bud Light. The same goes for cigarettes.

The results clearly demonstrate that the relevance of brands and the importance of brand functions vary considerably across product markets. Although brands play an important role in consumer decision making in all countries covered in the survey, the question arises whether brands are equally important in every country. The answer to this is important in shaping a company's global marketing strategy.

### Brand relevance across countries

Figure 2.3 provides a ranking of the overall brand relevance across the nine selected countries.[9] Russia, the United States, and Poland headed the list in 2006. Brands possessed the lowest overall relevance in Japan, Sweden, and Germany. Is this ranking useful? We believe it is. It is not surprising that brands have such a high importance in a country such as the United States where the ideas of economic freedom and individual choice have been paramount for a long time. After all, it was in the United States that the principles of modern marketing were born. In the highly competitive American market, brands play an important role in guiding consumer decisions and providing means of self-expression. By contrast, consumers in Poland and Russia were confronted with a high level of uncertainty subsequent to the rapid transition of their economies from a fully regulated system to one of liberal markets. Individual accountability for the choices one makes as a consumer is a very recent development. The former communist markets have gone from hardly any choice at all to an almost infinite number of alternatives. This can lead to information overload for consumers. In this context, brands are an important instrument for reducing uncertainty and risk. Thus, brands serve as a compass to guide consumers through the jungle of products and services.

This helps explain why respondents in Poland and Russia considered information efficiency and risk reduction as highly important brand functions in 2006, ranking these

**Fig. 2.3: Brand relevance ranking across countries: In which countries do consumers focus most on brands?**

| Deviation from average[1] | Brand relevance by country, 2006 |
|---|---|
| Deviation > +10% | 1 Russia |
| | 2 US |
| | 3 Poland |
| Deviation +/- 10% | 4 France |
| | 5 Spain |
| | 6 UK |
| | 7 Japan |
| Deviation < -10% | 8 Sweden |
| | 9 Germany |

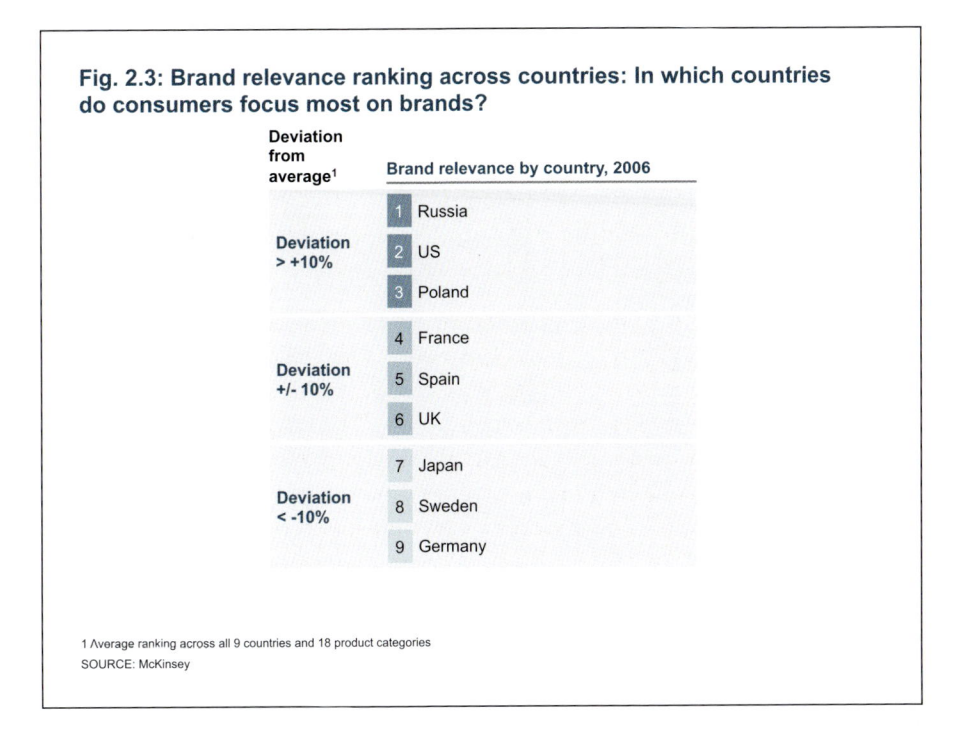

1 Average ranking across all 9 countries and 18 product categories
SOURCE: McKinsey

higher than respondents in any other country (Figure 2.4). The United States headed the list as far as the image benefit of brands is concerned, followed by Russia and the United Kingdom. It makes perfect sense for the United States and the United Kingdom to score high on this dimension. The Hofstede system, which differentiates countries along several cultural dimensions, such as power distance, individualism, and uncertainty avoidance, assigns the highest degrees of individualism to the United States and the United Kingdom.[10] Brands are a perfect means of self-expression in today's individualistic societies, a trend certain Eastern European countries seem to be adopting very quickly.

One may be surprised to find Japan, Sweden, and Germany at the bottom of the 2006 ranking lists in Figures 2.3 and 2.4. First of all, it should be noted that although these lists rank countries relative to each other, they do not tell us anything about the absolute level of brand relevance. The analysis of individual product markets shows that brands were highly relevant to consumer decision making in all three of these countries in 2006, even though this relevance was higher in others. In Japan, Sweden, and Germany, collective values – such as common welfare and a sense of duty – play an important role. In addition, Germans and Japanese are said to be very rational and to strive for perfection. It is probable that these values influence the decision making of consumers in these countries; this might explain why brands displayed a somewhat lesser importance compared with countries such as the United States or Russia in 2006.

**Fig. 2.4: Ranking of brand relevance by function across countries: Which brand function is most important?**

Brand relevance by country and brand function, 2006

| Deviation from average[1] | Information efficiency | Risk reduction | Image benefit |
|---|---|---|---|
| Deviation > +10% | 1 Russia<br>2 Poland<br>3 US | 1 Russia<br>2 Poland<br>3 US | 1 US<br>2 Russia |
| Deviation +/- 10% | 4 Spain<br>5 France | 4 France<br>5 Spain<br>6 UK | 3 UK<br>4 Poland<br>5 France<br>6 Japan<br>7 Spain |
| Deviation < -10% | 6 Japan<br>7 UK<br>8 Germany<br>9 Sweden | 7 Sweden<br>8 Germany<br>9 Japan | 8 Sweden<br>9 Germany |

1 Average ranking across all 9 countries and 18 product categories
SOURCE: McKinsey

## Brand relevance of product categories within countries

We saw that the product categories beer and medium-sized cars headed the list of brand relevance in 2006 worldwide. However, this ranking was not uniform across all countries in every product market. For example, the importance of airline brands for private trips varied substantially across countries (Figure 2.5). In France and Japan, airline travel belonged to the group of categories with the highest brand relevance, whereas it was in the group with the lowest brand relevance in the United Kingdom and Sweden. Again, a look at the Hofstede system of cultural characteristics might provide an explanation for this outcome. The French and Japanese both score high in terms of the »uncertainty avoidance« scale developed by Hofstede, while the United States and Sweden score lowest on this scale. Airline travel is perceived as risky by many people, and this can be a source of serious stress for some travelers. Brands are an important signal of quality and risk reduction, increasing the relative importance of brands in societies that are more focused on uncertainty avoidance. These intercultural differences regarding brand relevance are also reflected in the success of discount airlines with consumers in different countries. In the United Kingdom and Sweden – where the relevance of airline brands for private trips was relatively low – the market share of discount airlines was, not surprisingly, relatively high with around 34 percent in the United Kingdom and some 31 percent in Sweden when the research was conducted.[11] In Japan, only 1 percent of international flights were made with low-cost airlines at the time. This low market share reflects the relatively high importance of brands and perceived quality in this product category.

### Fig. 2.5: Variance of brand relevance across countries in selected product categories

Rank in overall brand relevance among 18 selected product categories

| | Scheduled flights for private trips | Medium-sized cars |
|---|---|---|
| France | 1 | 2 |
| Germany | 9[1] | 2 |
| Japan | 4 | 1 |
| Poland | 9[1] | 2 |
| Russia | 14 | 3 |
| Spain | 15 | 3 |
| Sweden | 17 | 1 |
| UK | 14 | 1 |
| US | 10 | 1 |

[1] Shared rank
SOURCE: McKinsey

Although brands are equally important across all countries, their relative importance in specific categories varies significantly by country. It is therefore necessary to look at product markets country by country in order to identify any differences that might exist in brand relevance.

**Brand relevance in Western European countries**

The ranking of product categories within the three largest economies of the European Union reveals some significant differences. While cars belonged to the highest brand relevance group in all three countries in 2006, scheduled flights for private trips and fast-food restaurants were part of this group in France, but not in Germany or the United Kingdom (Figure 2.6). We have already provided an explanation for the high rank of scheduled flights. The importance of brands in the fast-food business in France – the home of fine cooking – is somewhat unexpected. However, it mirrors the market situation fairly well. One would expect that in markets with high brand relevance for fast food there would be more room for the development of multiple brands, and this is indeed the case in France. Strong national chains, such as Quick Burger, have been established alongside the dominant American players such as McDonald's and Burger King.

At the same time, it comes as no surprise to see that brands were highly relevant to beer consumers in Germany and the United Kingdom, both home to notoriously passionate drinkers of barley-based beverages. In Germany, beer held the number one position for overall brand relevance from 2002 through 2010. At the bottom of the list, car insurance belonged to the group of categories with the lowest relevance. This was

### Fig. 2.6: Brand relevance by country: How important are brands to consumers across product categories in Western European countries?

Selected rankings of 18 product categories in 3 Western European countries, 2006

|  | France | Germany | UK |
|---|---|---|---|
| **Highest relevance** | 1 Scheduled flights for private trips | 1 Beer | 1 Medium-sized cars |
|  | 2 Medium-sized cars | 2 Medium-sized cars | 2 Cigarettes |
|  | 3 Fast-food restaurants | 3 Mobile phones | 3 Beer |
| **Average relevance** | 9 Cigarettes | 9 Scheduled flights for private trips | 9 Department stores |
|  | 10 Mobile phones | 10 Mail order | 10 Fast-food restaurants |
|  | 11 Banking accounts | 11 Banking accounts | 11 Designer sun glasses |
| **Lowest relevance** | 16 Detergents | 16 Car insurance | 16 Drugstores |
|  | 17 Car insurance | 17 Express delivery services | 17 Car insurance |
|  | 18 Paper tissues | 18 Paper tissues | 18 Paper tissues |

SOURCE: McKinsey

also true for paper tissues in all three countries. The low relevance of brands in car insurance accords with the fact that – at least in the German market – car insurance is a low-involvement category for most consumers and, as a consequence, was driven almost purely by price competition when the survey was conducted.

### Brand relevance in the United States and Japan

Different categories headed the list of brand relevance in the United States and Japan in 2006 (Figure 2.7; note that the lists have been shortened; they do not include all industries mentioned in the text below). In the United States, the importance of brands was especially pronounced in service markets. Express delivery services was ranked number three and categories such as mobile network operators and fast-food restaurants were among the top ten categories. As in the United States, brands were perceived as highly relevant in Japanese service markets (in categories such as mobile network operators and scheduled flights for private trips), but we also find consumer durables – such as television sets and designer sunglasses – among the categories that had the highest relevance. Japan has strong brands in consumer electronics, and this might have contributed to the higher importance of these brands compared with other categories. Japanese customers are among the most valuable customers for luxury goods.

### Brand relevance in Eastern European countries

Although the Cold War ended a quarter of a century ago, Eastern Europe still felt the long-term effects from decades of centrally planned production well beyond the year 2000. A closer look at Poland and Russia provides a number of interesting insights into

**Fig. 2.7: Brand relevance by country: How important are brands to consumers across product categories in the world's largest economies?**

Selected rankings of 18 product categories in the US and in Japan, 2006

| | US | | Japan |
|---|---|---|---|
| Highest relevance | 1 Medium-sized cars | | 1 Medium-sized cars |
| | 2 Beer | | 2 TV sets |
| | 3 Express delivery services | | 3 Mobile network operators |
| | ⋮ | | ⋮ |
| Average relevance | 9 Mobile phones | | 9 Banking accounts |
| | 10 Scheduled flights for private trips | | 10 Beer |
| | 11 Designer sun glasses | | 11 Cigarettes |
| | ⋮ | | ⋮ |
| Lowest relevance | 16 Department stores | | 16 Detergents |
| | 17 Banking accounts | | 17 Drugstores |
| | 18 Drugstores | | 18 Paper tissues |

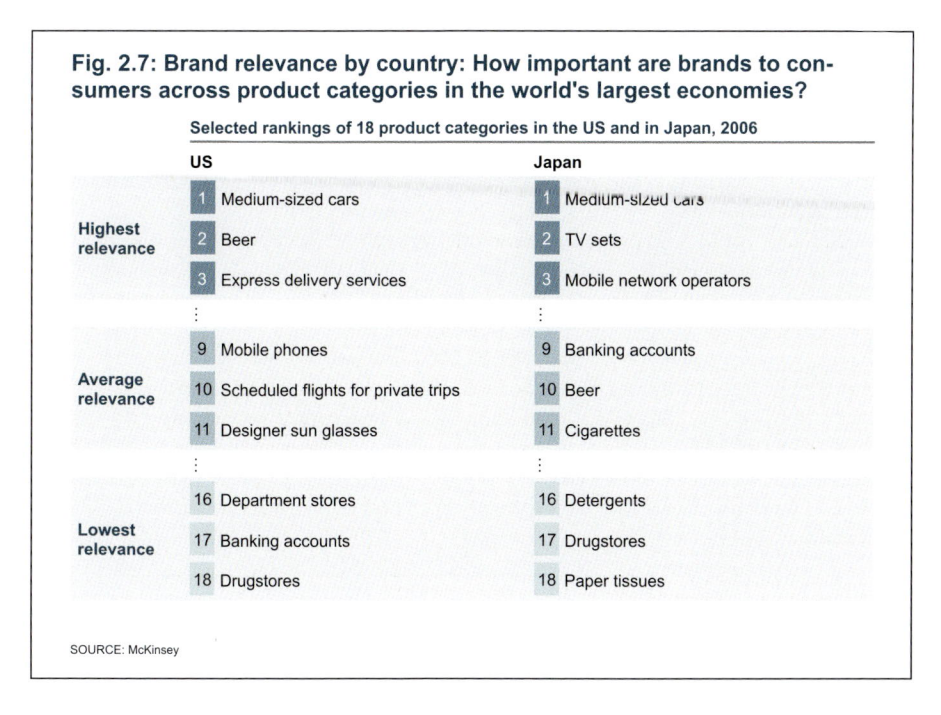

SOURCE: McKinsey

this area. While cars and mobile phones lead in both countries in 2006, mail order was a category with high brand relevance in Poland but with significantly lower relevance in Russia (Figure 2.8). Although there are many parallels in the economic and political histories of these two countries, it is not correct to assume that there will be complete consistency in the consumption behavior of the two groups of consumers.

**Fig. 2.8: Brand relevance by country: How important are brands to consumers across product categories in Eastern European countries?**

Selected rankings of 18 product categories in 2 Eastern European countries, 2006

| | Poland | | Russia |
|---|---|---|---|
| Highest relevance | 1 Medium-sized cars | | 1 Mobile phones |
| | 2 Mail order | | 2 Cigarettes |
| | 3 Mobile phones | | 3 Medium-sized cars |
| | ⋮ | | ⋮ |
| Average relevance | 9 Scheduled flights for private trips | | 9 PCs/computers |
| | 10 Detergents | | 10 Express delivery services |
| | 11 Cigarettes | | 11 Fast-food restaurants |
| | ⋮ | | ⋮ |
| Lowest relevance | 16 Fast food restaurants | | 16 Department stores |
| | 17 Car insurance | | 17 Mail order |
| | 18 Paper tissues | | 18 Paper tissues |

SOURCE: McKinsey

## The Development of Brand Relevance in Germany

To capture the development of brand relevance over time, we have been measuring brand relevance across 30 categories in Germany since 2002.[12] The online survey covers general brand relevance as well as the three principal brand functions as introduced above – risk reduction, information efficiency, and image benefit. The sample consists of at least 1,000 consumers who have been selected to be representative of the German population. Categories include fast-moving consumer goods, durable goods, services, and retail. The most recent wave is from 2013. We also conducted the survey in 2002, 2006, and 2010. Because of a change in panel composition, the original 2002 data set is not fully comparable with the subsequent waves. When we look at the ranking of categories across all waves, however, we find that the fundamental architecture is robust, especially as far as long-term developments and general trends are concerned (Figure 2.9).[13] In general, the spread of brand relevance scores is relatively low; most scores are in the 3 to 4 range. This is why we focus on ranks and tendencies, rather than absolute values in the following.

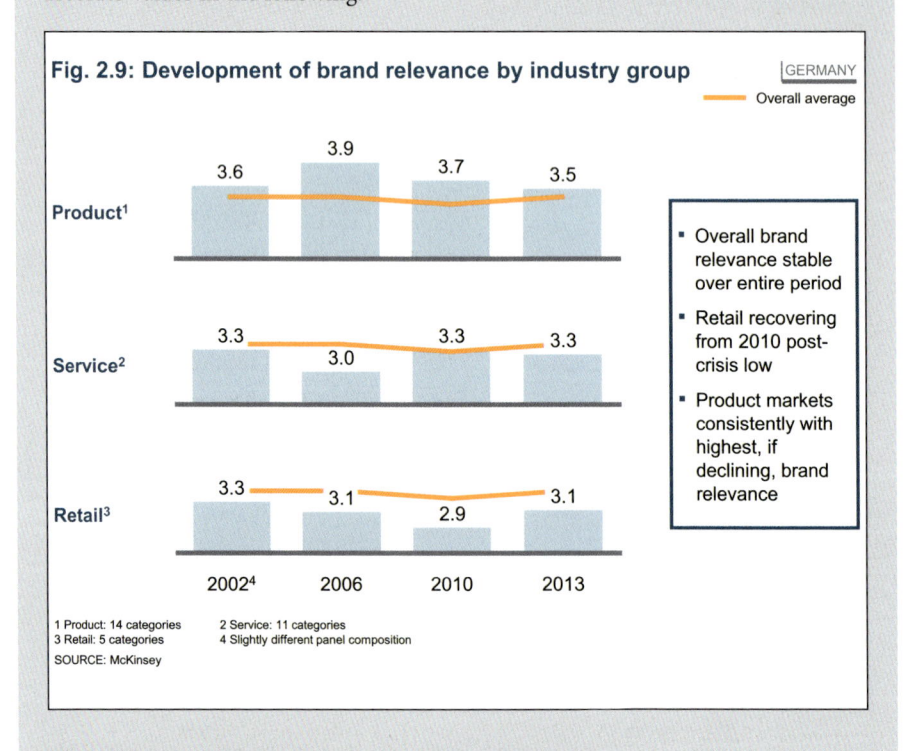

**Fig. 2.9: Development of brand relevance by industry group** | GERMANY
— Overall average

Product[1]
- 2002[4]: 3.6
- 2006: 3.9
- 2010: 3.7
- 2013: 3.5

Service[2]
- 2002[4]: 3.3
- 2006: 3.0
- 2010: 3.3
- 2013: 3.3

Retail[3]
- 2002[4]: 3.3
- 2006: 3.1
- 2010: 2.9
- 2013: 3.1

- Overall brand relevance stable over entire period
- Retail recovering from 2010 post-crisis low
- Product markets consistently with highest, if declining, brand relevance

1 Product: 14 categories  2 Service: 11 categories
3 Retail: 5 categories  4 Slightly different panel composition
SOURCE: McKinsey

### The 2008 economic crisis led to a dip in brand relevance

Overall brand relevance in B2C industries in Germany is high and stable since 2002 with little change over the course of the entire 11-year period. However, there was a slight, but statistically significant, dip in brand relevance in 2010 that is widely attributed to the economic crisis that started in 2008 and the subsequent recession. In times of economic duress, consumers tend to look for bargains as buying factors, at the expense of brands that carry a higher price ticket. While this is true across categories, the decrease in brand relevance was most obvious in retail, especially department stores. The effects of the crisis were further aggravated by the growing stronghold of private labels in Germany, discount stores, and other no-frills business models. At the time, department stores had come under pressure from two fronts: increasing differentiation and widespread digitalization. As a result, even former champions, such as the Karstadt chain of department stores, found themselves fighting for survival.[14] Traditional players – such as Hertie or Horten – had all but disappeared at the time of the 2010 survey. With fewer players around, brands had become less important as differentiating factors.

**In 2013, brands rebound across categories**

In 2013, brand relevance regained precrisis levels across most categories, up three percent from 2010 on average. The change from 2010 to 2013 is positive for almost all categories we examined; we will discuss one notable exception in more detail below. Consumers' appetite for strong brands has obviously been rekindled. This general trend is consistent with recent increases in both consumers' willingness to spend as reported by GfK, and actual consumer spending as tracked by the Federal Statistical Office. By the end of 2013, GfK reported the highest consumer sentiment score since the beginning of the economic crisis in 2007. Economists predict an overall acceleration of growth, with estimates for 2014 in the magnitude of 1.6 to 1.9 percent.[15] Beyond this, unemployment is now down to 6.8 percent, compared with more than 8 percent in 2009.[16] Despite the enduring depression in Southern Europe, the grip of the crisis is apparently loosening in Germany. The importance of all brand functions is generally stable compared to 2010, with a minuscule decrease in the importance of risk reduction – possibly another sign of a somewhat more optimistic outlook of German consumers. Increasingly, they use brands to express themselves and enrich their lives, rather than just to minimize the risk involved in a given purchase (although risk reduction remains the most important brand function in absolute terms).

Again, the effect of the general economic outlook is particularly apparent in retail. Compared with 2010, DIY stores and department stores have seen increases in brand relevance by 27 percent and 18 percent, respectively – some of the most dramatic among such changes in the survey's 11-year history. This effect may be partly due to an evolution of late-generation private labels. Private labels now account for 44 percent of retail sales in Germany according to PLMA.[17] Because a substantial share of a retailer's assortment now carries the retailer's own brand, these banners become more prominent in turn. Another factor might be the substantial investments by German DIY chains in brand building in recent years, Hornbach perhaps being the most prominent example. Its 2013 »The Hornbach Hammer« campaign (by creative agency Heimat) won multiple awards, including New Media Awards for »Integrated Campaigns« and »Efficient Communication.«[18] In 2013, both Hornbach and its competitor Obi made the top ten for advertising awareness in Germany, alongside heavyweights such as Volkswagen and Samsung.[19] In general, however, we see this sharp increase in brand relevance as evidence of Germany's all-around economic recovery and the optimistic outlook that prevails among consumers.

In the DIY category, Germany saw the bankruptcy of Praktiker – one of the country's largest home improvement chains – in July 2013, just three months before our survey was conducted.[20] This widely publicized event was unsettling for many consumers and may well have contributed to the increase in brand relevance in the category, especially since Praktiker had been focusing on aggressive discounting in the years leading up to its demise. Press reports said that »everybody felt cheated, even though there was no cheat.«[21] Praktiker suffered Germany's biggest insolvency in 2013, and experts believe that it left both consumers and investors looking for reliable brands they can trust.

As a group of categories, consumer goods still show the highest average value for brand relevance. Beyond this, all four categories that have consistently made the top ten across all waves are product categories: beer, mobile phones, painkillers, and cars (Figure 2.11). These observations are in line with the high share of voice consumer goods achieve through high advertising spending. Manufacturers of food, beverages, and personal care products alone spent a staggering EUR 17 billion on advertising in Germany in 2012, the equivalent of about two-thirds of total gross spending in Germany. There is, however, an exception to the prevalence of consumer goods: ever since the first wave of the survey, paper tissues were consistently ranked near the bottom of the table. It seems that some categories are immune to brand relevance, probably because of low consumer involvement. Then again, many insiders would have said the same thing about the energy industry ten years ago. It seems that once the dynamic of competitive differentiation through branding is set in motion, even the most mundane categories can be transformed.

While retail is regaining brand relevance quickly, services come in second to consumer goods. Some of the biggest winners of brand relevance are, in fact, service industries. Examples include consumer banking and energy, at compound annual growth rates of 4 and 6 percent respectively since 2010. This rise of service categories was already apparent in 2010, when express delivery was among the fastest climbers. In general, we observe a growing contribution of service categories to value creation in saturated economies such as Germany. This leads to an increase in competition and differentiation. Consumers, however, have little indication of the quality of a given service provider. For want of first-hand experience, they use brands as proxies of quality to aid in their decision making and reduce uncertainty. German consumers rely on brands as beacons as they navigate an ever more differentiated service landscape.

### Electricity is no longer a commodity

The most striking change compared with 2010 is a continued increase in brand relevance in the energy category. Although still low in absolute terms, energy has seen a steep increase in brand relevance by 18 percent since 2010, the biggest such change among all service categories (year-on-year growth: 6 percent). Over the seven-year period starting in 2006, brand relevance has increased by almost two thirds in the energy market. Fifteen years after deregulation in 1998, more and more consumers are getting wise to the fact that they actually have a choice.[22] However, the differences between providers and products are often minor and frequently intricate. This makes it hard for consumers to make an informed decision. In this situation, brands are welcome signposts for the growing share of households ready to switch providers. In Germany, the willingness to switch almost doubled from 2006 to 2008 alone. Reliability is top of mind for

2.1 Brand Relevance: Assessing the Relative Importance of Brands

**Fig. 2.10: Development of brand relevance in retail over time**  GERMANY

CAGR[1]

- Overall average: 0
- DIY stores: +2
- Department stores: +1
- Mail order: -1
- Retail average: 0
- Discount: +1
- Drugstores: -1

X-axis: 2002[2], 2006, 2010, 2013
Y-axis: 2.5 to 3.5

1 2006 - 2013, percent
2 Slightly different panel composition
SOURCE: McKinsey

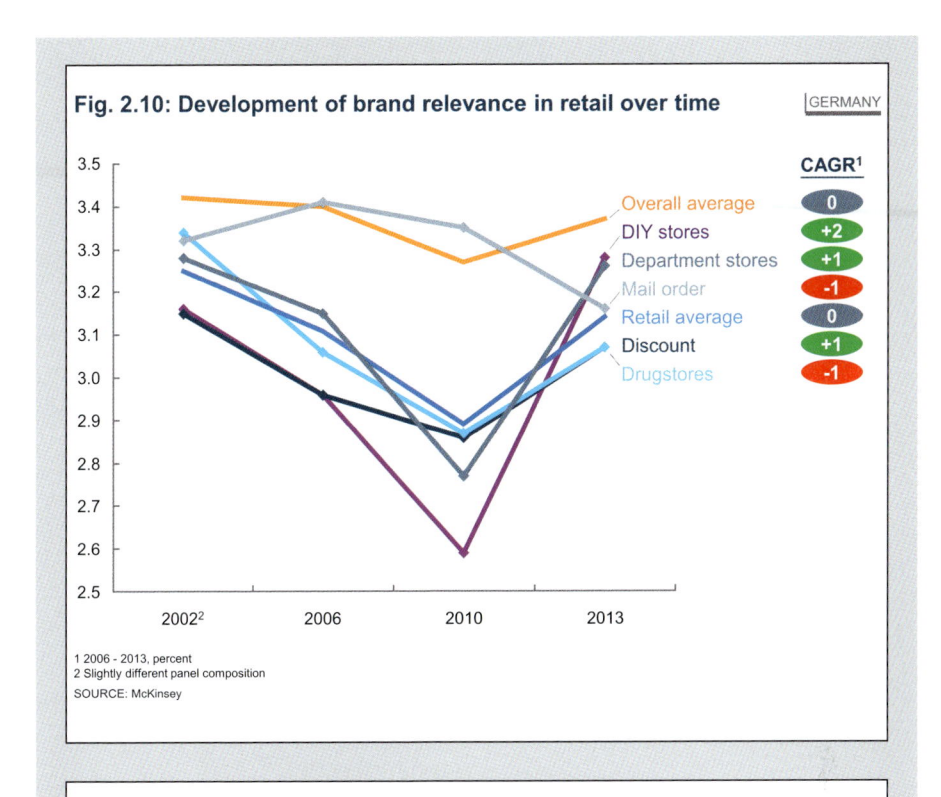

**Fig. 2.11: Four categories[1] made the top 10 in all waves**  GERMANY

Rank (overall brand relevance score)

| Category | 2002[2] | 2006 | 2010 | 2013 |
|---|---|---|---|---|
| Beer | 1 | 1 | 1 | 7 |
| Painkillers | 4 | 7 | 10 | 6 |
| Medium-sized cars | 5 | 9 | 8 | 4 |
| Mobile phones | 10 | 3 | 4 | 9 |

1 Out of 30
2 Slightly different sample composition
SOURCE: McKinsey

these switchers, making risk reduction the most important brand function. Systematic research conducted by McKinsey's Energy Practice since 2010 reveals that a large proportion of energy customers will gladly pay extra for reliable service from a known brand (»creatures of habit«), while others consider convenience and flexibility to be more important than the best deal (»comfort seekers,« Figure 2.12). Another important trend is the »green« consumer. Environmentalists account for up to 10 percent of clientele. They value low emissions and renewable energy sources, along with the social prestige that comes with their environmentally conscious choice. Increasingly, providers are using environmental concerns among consumers to refine their product propositions. Only a minority of consumers, however, is willing to pay a substantial premium for energy from sustainable sources so far. What little commercial success is seen in the UK, for example, is largely driven by the fact that British regulation favors small providers, a description that currently applies to all dedicated »green« players in that market.

To take advantage of these trends and attract a fair share of switchers, German electricity providers are spending heaps of money. Overall advertising spending in the category has tripled since 2005; it now reaches a total of EUR 78 million annually (Figure 2.13).

This development puts an end to the price war that ensued after the liberalization of the German energy market in 1998. Since energy is an elusive product, many providers initially assumed that price would be the most important decision factor. This resulted in a widespread launch of low-price energy brands. But this aggressive strategy proved hard to sustain. It brought about low margins, it was easy to copy, and it ended up destroying value for all players. It seems that – 15 years after deregulation – the category has finally overcome the commodity challenge.[23] Also see our interview with Erwin van Laethem and Dorkas Koenen of Essent.

**Brands matter as banks recover from the crisis**

The year 2008 was one of the worst in recorded history for the banking industry. Lehman Brothers filed for bankruptcy protection, countless other banks around the world had to be bailed out with government money, and investors lost assets in the magnitude of USD 4 trillion according to estimates by the International Monetary Fund. In leading German news media, the term »banking crisis« was mentioned almost 16,000 times in 2008, up from 2,000 the previous year. This development triggered a dramatic loss in consumer confidence. Subsequent to the crisis, many consumer banks also suffered drastic decreases in brand equity. In 2009, the half dozen banks included in Interbrand's top 100 ranking all lost brand value compared with 2008, with losses ranging from 10 to 50 percent.[24]

In 2013, only one of these brands had reclaimed its absolute precrisis value. At the same time, the number of leading news stories mentioning the »banking crisis« was still at more than four times the precrisis level.

In reaction to this enduring loss of confidence, brand relevance in consumer banking has been increasing ever since the crisis hit – by 12 percent since 2010 and by 22 percent over the seven-year period starting in 2006 (year-on-year growth: 4 percent and 3 percent respectively). When trust is scarce, consumers flock to providers that they believe will manage their assets reliably and responsi-

## Fig. 2.12: Needs-based customer segmentation reveals key buying factors beyond price

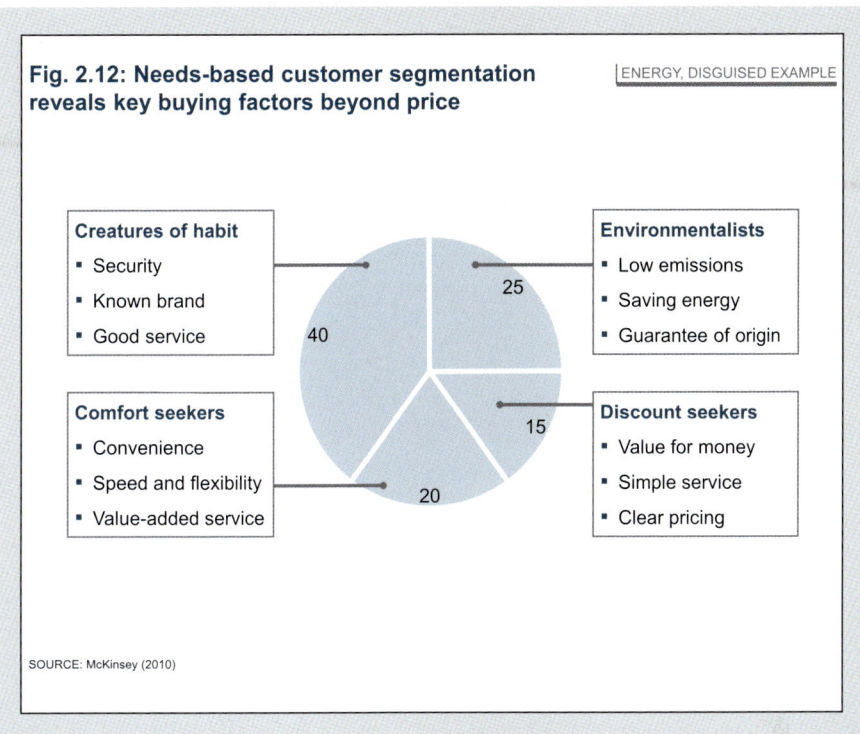

ENERGY, DISGUISED EXAMPLE

**Creatures of habit**
- Security
- Known brand
- Good service

**Environmentalists**
- Low emissions
- Saving energy
- Guarantee of origin

**Comfort seekers**
- Convenience
- Speed and flexibility
- Value-added service

**Discount seekers**
- Value for money
- Simple service
- Clear pricing

Pie chart values: 40, 25, 15, 20

SOURCE: McKinsey (2010)

## Fig. 2.13: Advertising spending by providers of electrical energy

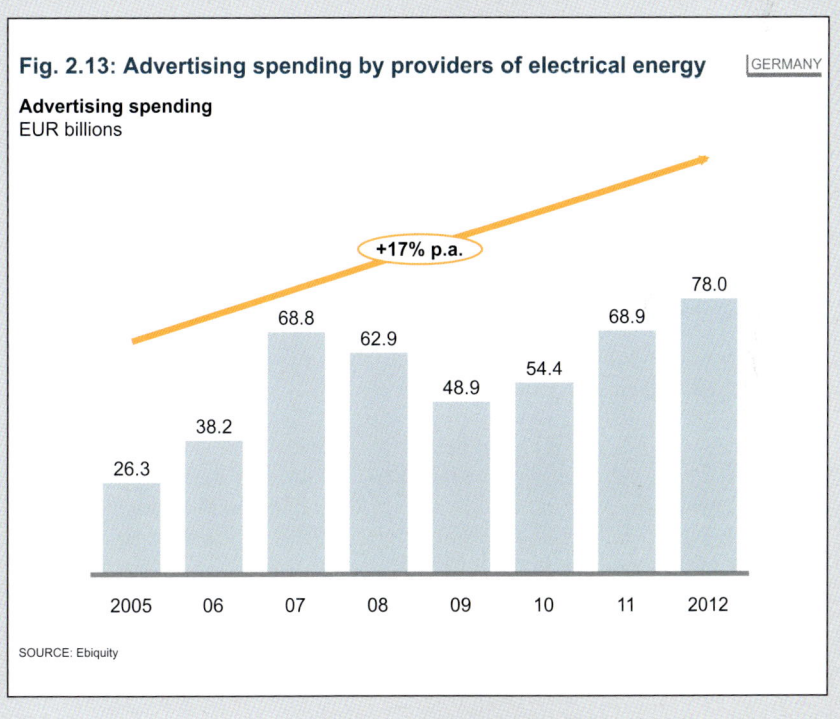

GERMANY

Advertising spending
EUR billions

+17% p.a.

| 2005 | 06 | 07 | 08 | 09 | 10 | 11 | 2012 |
|---|---|---|---|---|---|---|---|
| 26.3 | 38.2 | 68.8 | 62.9 | 48.9 | 54.4 | 68.9 | 78.0 |

SOURCE: Ebiquity

bly. This makes risk reduction the most important brand function in the consumer banking industry.

In our sample, consumer banking is also the service industry with the highest absolute value for risk reduction, ahead of categories such as telecommunications and hospitality. Remarkably, consumer banking also tops the list for image benefit as a brand function, well ahead of categories such as cars or sneakers. This may be due to the fact that few people want to be caught with an account at a bank of ill repute, especially since the industry has been shattered by so many scandals ranging from embezzlement to fraudulent insolvency at the taxpayer's expense. And given the increasing use of bank-issued debit and credit cards for everyday purchases in Germany, a consumer's bank of choice is now perhaps more visible than ever before.

**Advertising restrictions curb brand relevance for stimulants**

Ever since the first wave of our survey, cigarettes were ranked as number two in terms of overall brand relevance through 2010, despite a slow erosion of absolute values. In 2013, cigarettes have dropped to rank 14, below supposedly inconspicuous categories such as fast-food restaurants or detergents. At a loss of 21 percent, cigarettes have seen the biggest decrease in brand relevance of all product categories since 2010 (year-on-year growth: -8 percent). This is an acceleration of a development that was already apparent between 2006 and 2010, with a loss of 7 percent (year-on-year growth: -2 percent).

This decline is an effect of increasingly restrictive European regulation that makes it ever more difficult to activate tobacco brands. Many advertising vehicles and sales channels are already banned or severely restricted. TV sponsoring and daytime cinema advertising have already been prohibited for more than a decade. Manufacturers are also required to dedicate large areas of their cigarette packs to warnings. In 2007, the European Union also banned tobacco advertising from online media.[25] Sponsoring international events is now also prohibited. Most recently, Australia introduced legislation that requires all cigarette makers to use plain packaging for their products. Instead of branding, the olive green packets carry large, graphic health warnings.[26] Switzerland is also contemplating new legislation to impose more severe restrictions on tobacco advertising, sponsoring, and sales.[27]

In effect, cigarette makers have very little leeway to differentiate their brands. In reaction to advertising restrictions, tobacco companies have made dramatic changes to their marketing mix, effectively slashing their classical advertising budgets. In 2005, the industry spent about 23 percent of total marketing spending on classical advertising in Germany – chiefly on print and cinema (Figure 2.14). In 2010, classical ad spending was down to EUR 2 million or 1 percent of the total. During the same period, the share of promotional expenditure increased from EUR 86 million to EUR 127 million or from 47 percent to 64 percent. This split has since remained stable. In 2012, a meager 2 percent of total spending was allocated to classical advertising – almost exclusively in the form of late-night cinema spots, the only form of classical advertising still permitted by law.

A similar, although slightly less dramatic development is riddling the market for beer, with a loss of 19 percent in brand relevance since 2010 (year-on-year

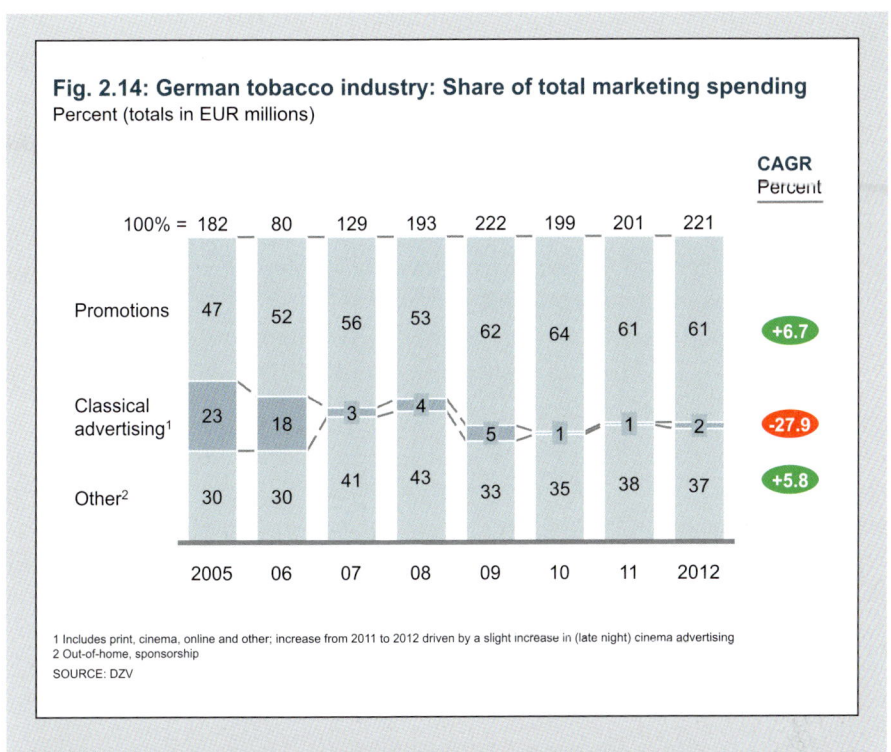

**Fig. 2.14: German tobacco industry: Share of total marketing spending**
Percent (totals in EUR millions)

| | 2005 | 06 | 07 | 08 | 09 | 10 | 11 | 2012 | CAGR Percent |
|---|---|---|---|---|---|---|---|---|---|
| 100% = | 182 | 80 | 129 | 193 | 222 | 199 | 201 | 221 | |
| Promotions | 47 | 52 | 56 | 53 | 62 | 64 | 61 | 61 | +6.7 |
| Classical advertising[1] | 23 | 18 | 3 | 4 | 5 | 1 | 1 | 2 | -27.9 |
| Other[2] | 30 | 30 | 41 | 43 | 33 | 35 | 38 | 37 | +5.8 |

1 Includes print, cinema, online and other; increase from 2011 to 2012 driven by a slight increase in (late night) cinema advertising
2 Out-of-home, sponsorship
SOURCE: DZV

growth: -7 percent), pushing the category from number one to rank seven. In this category, the effects of advertising restrictions may have been reinforced by market consolidation. Global players are scooping up ever more regional breweries. Currently, there are still about 1,350 beer brands in Germany,[28] but experts believe only about one in three will survive. At the same time, per capita consumption is decreasing. Over the course of the past two decades, consumption per capita has gone from some 120 liters to about 100 liters per annum. In 2014, Germany's Federal Statistical Office reported a record low of 95 million hectoliters in total annual sales, the lowest value since 1989. In the UK, an analogous development is in progress: some 12,000 pubs have closed over the course of the past ten years, bringing the total down by 20 percent.[29] It seems beer is going out of style, perhaps because it does not conform to the ascetic ideals of an increasingly popular lifestyle of health and sustainability. Breweries are fighting back with ever new varieties, mixed drinks, and nonalcoholic brewed beverages. However, experts are skeptical whether such product innovations will help stem – let alone reverse – the negative trend.[30] Even the 2014 soccer World Cup will probably only have afforded a few major breweries temporary reprieve.

## Implications for brand managers

The survey provides a number of important insights into the functioning of consumer markets across the world. First, it should be noted that brands play an important role in many categories irrespective of the country. We identify a remarkable consistency in the high ratings for cars and mobile phones. Second, brands apparently fulfill important functions in consumer decision making in emerging economies such as Russia and Poland. This observation suggests that despite the lower buying power of their populations, focusing on a low-price strategy might provide short-term success but is unlikely to be sustainable. Building the brand might well be equally successful in the short term and is likely to establish the roots for future growth. This is especially true given the dramatic rise of Eastern Europe as a market for luxury goods. The Polish luxury goods market, for example, had been growing at a compound annual growth rate of 27 percent for several years when our original research was conducted in 2006. Although this pace had slowed somewhat at the time of writing in mid-2014, Euromonitor reports that the luxury category »still presents a strong long-term development tendency [in Poland], as potential demand is still much above current sales.«[31]

Consumers in Eastern Europe appear to be skipping the value-for-money economy that focuses on brands as efficient carriers of information. After a short period in which brands are used to reduce risk, the most sophisticated brand function – image benefit – quickly becomes the most important one in these markets. As a result, sales of luxury goods are booming. Other examples of this boom include Dom Perignon fine champagne (Czech sales grew by two thirds from 2004 to 2005, for example) and Daimler's prestigious Maybach luxury sedan. Although now discontinued, Maybach is said to have sold more cars in Moscow than in any other city in the world, totaling some 130 vehicles by mid-2007.[32] In mid-2014, Rolls Royce Motor Cars named Russia as its third-largest export market.[33]

Finally, the results reveal considerable differences in brand relevance for categories across countries. Marketing managers can use these insights to identify the countries where brand relevance is highest in order to allocate scarce resources effectively. This will also help managers identify and evaluate the strategy options for the international market entry of new products.

**Brand relevance in German B2B markets**

A 2006 analysis showed that the corporate brand can account for up to 20 percent of B2B companies' stock performance – especially in trust-based industries, such as medical supplies or mail services.[34] The significance of brands in the B2B sector has also been investigated comprehensively in market research in cooperation with Professor Backhaus from the Marketing Centrum Münster (MCM). A total of 769 businesses were surveyed in 2002 in an analysis of 18 German product markets. The study yielded results similar to those for the B2C sector, showing that the relevance of brands varies significantly between product markets.[35] Brand relevance was very strong in switchgear equipment, machine tools, and company cars (Figure 2.15). Brands have the lowest relevance for industrial chemicals; apparently they play a secondary role in such largely commoditized areas. One surprising result of this analysis is that brand relevance for some product markets in the B2B sector was rated as high as in B2C markets. This observation points to much untapped potential for B2B branding. In a separate analysis of the industrial vehicles sector, for example,

**Fig. 2.15: Relevance ranking in B2B: How important are brands to business people?**

Selected from 18 product category rankings Germany, 2002

Highest relevance
1 Switchgear equipment
2 Machine tools
3 Company cars

⋮

Average relevance
7 Freight forwarding services
8 Commercial kitchen services
9 Automation equipment

⋮

Lowest relevance
17 Call center services
18 Industrial chemicals

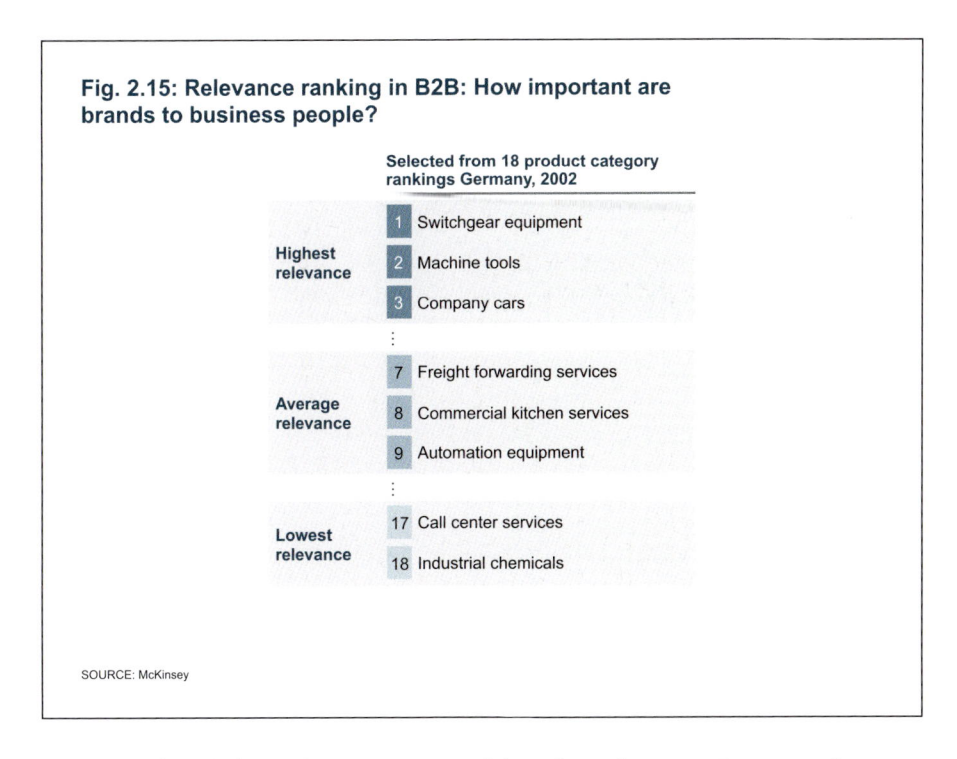

SOURCE: McKinsey

McKinsey found that soft, even emotional brand attributes, such as »good name,« »good design,« and »long tradition,« can be of the utmost importance – at least to certain groups of purchasing officers. In one case, »brand followers« turned out to be the second-largest segment of buyers at 28 percent of the total market, exceeded only by »value seekers« at 35 percent, but easily outnumbering the »hard bargainers« you might think would dominate this type of category.

These observations should not create the impression, however, that it is sufficient for a business to determine brand relevance merely at the industry-specific level. It is much more important to understand the nature of the functions from which this brand relevance derives on a case-by-case basis. In order to make wise investment decisions, it is necessary to first understand the relative influence of each function and how it applies to certain brands. Not surprisingly, the three brand functions are also highly relevant to the B2B sector because they reveal interesting aspects of sector-specific brand relevance. In B2B, brands carry information about a wide range of attributes of the respective product or service. Brands reduce the degree of complexity and facilitate communication between those involved in the purchase process: buyers, users, and managers.

**High importance of information efficiency for machinery**

The information efficiency function of the brand was at its most important for machines and equipment in 2002. Such purchases involve complex goods for which brands offer the customer an important orientation aid. For example, Siemens makes orientation easier for its customers by using the »Sie-« prefix for numerous product names (e.g., SieMatic); the origin and thus the quality of the product are quickly recognizable. The situation is quite different for industrial chemicals or alarm systems, where information efficiency plays only a secondary role.

**Risk reduction matters most for major investments**

»Nobody ever got fired for buying IBM,« or so they say.[36] Opinions differ about this oft-cited statement, but it does serve to highlight the fact that even in the B2B sector, brands can minimize the risk of making wrong investment decisions. Brands often represent a guarantee of consistent quality, and – especially in the area of complex systems – one of compatibility. This is a strong selling point for Microsoft programs or Apple hardware, sometimes dubbed the »network effect.« In the B2B sector, brands thus appear on occasion to act as a type of insurance – at least against senior management reproach.

**High importance of image benefit for publicly visible goods**

In the B2C sector, the image benefit of a product assists in cultivating the individual consumer's image or in fostering self-expression, as illustrated by the high relevance of brands in the designer sunglasses category. Somewhat less obvious is that image benefits are also an important function of brands in the B2B sector, especially in terms of the reputation of the company and its employees. This effect is strongest for publicly visible products and services, such as company cars, shipping, or accounting services. B2B brands are often used as a way of adopting a partner's reputation as part of one's own. This phenomenon is often referred to as »component branding« or »ingredient branding« and can be observed among computer manufacturers who advertise with the »Intel inside« logo as well as among makers of textiles who highlight the use of GoreTex fabric or Scotch 3M functional elements. The value of a company's own products is enhanced by association with the image of the worldwide market leaders in these categories. There is also an upside for the component brand in this relationship. Following the introduction of Intel's co-branding campaign »Intel inside,« the joint market share of its competitors (AMD, Cyrix, Motorola, etc.) shrank from 44 percent in 1989 to 17 percent in 1998.

In contrast, the public takes little notice of products such as chemicals or alarm systems, so the image function is not important in these sectors. Such goods are found near the end of the 2002 image benefit ranking (Figure 2.16).

As one might expect, the average general brand relevance in the B2B domain was somewhat lower than in the B2C sector in 2002. What might be more surprising is that the gap between the two is not overly large and that brands remain highly significant even for the B2B sector.

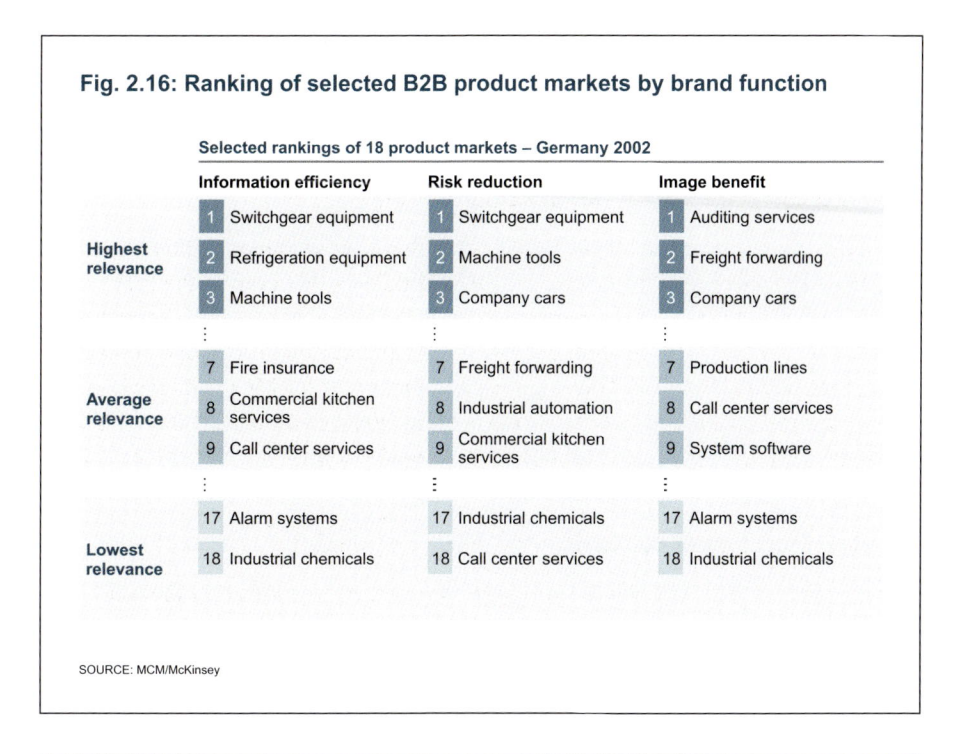

**Fig. 2.16: Ranking of selected B2B product markets by brand function**

Selected rankings of 18 product markets – Germany 2002

| | Information efficiency | Risk reduction | Image benefit |
|---|---|---|---|
| Highest relevance | 1 Switchgear equipment<br>2 Refrigeration equipment<br>3 Machine tools | 1 Switchgear equipment<br>2 Machine tools<br>3 Company cars | 1 Auditing services<br>2 Freight forwarding<br>3 Company cars |
| Average relevance | 7 Fire insurance<br>8 Commercial kitchen services<br>9 Call center services | 7 Freight forwarding<br>8 Industrial automation<br>9 Commercial kitchen services | 7 Production lines<br>8 Call center services<br>9 System software |
| Lowest relevance | 17 Alarm systems<br>18 Industrial chemicals | 17 Industrial chemicals<br>18 Call center services | 17 Alarm systems<br>18 Industrial chemicals |

SOURCE: MCM/McKinsey

**Brand Relevance in Global B2B Markets (2012)**

To complement and update the B2B branding research conducted in Germany in 2002, we conducted an online survey among some 700 respondents in three countries (Germany, India, and the US) in mid-2012. All respondents were decision makers with substantial influence on supplier selection at companies with more than 100 employees. The survey revolves around the relevance of branding in purchasing and aims to identify the drivers of successful business branding in seven different sectors. Topics of the survey included:

- The influence of the brand relative to other factors
- The dimensions, or brand functions, that make brands relevant
- The drivers of brand strength at various touch points.

Relative to other purchasing factors, the brand emerges as an important element in their decision making (Figure 2.17). While the research confirms the general importance of products, prices, and distribution, we have also found that branding matters. In fact, decision makers consider the brand a central rather than a marginal element of a supplier's proposition. The survey indicates that a company's brand is on par with sales as an influencing factor. In India, brand-related factors are perceived as especially important. In Germany, the brand is perceived as less important, consistent with other observations of this market as a more value-driven environment.

From the perspective of corporate decision makers globally, brands are particularly relevant for the selection of suppliers of machines and components. The market for chemicals, commodities, and basic materials is characterized by medium brand relevance. Brands are generally perceived as somewhat less important in categories such as financial services and utilities. In the United States, however, the brand is a bigger factor in the selection of providers of financial services than in India or Germany. This may be due to the fact that the enduring effects of the banking crisis are particularly severe in the US, where prominent merchant banks have foundered or required government aid to survive.

Across countries and industries, decision makers are willing to pay a premium for strong brands because they make their lives easier, particularly by aggregating information and reducing risk (Figure 2.18). Information efficiency emerges as the most important brand function in all three countries, on par with risk reduction in India. In general, information efficiency is particularly important for purchases that involve complex goods, such as machines and components or IT-related products and services. This result is consistent with the B2B brand relevance survey conducted in Germany a decade ago. Strong supplier brands may even aid companies in building their own reputation by association. For example, working with a prestigious logistics provider can help companies project a more upscale image to their customers.

B2B brands do not only help purchasing officers make informed decisions, they also provide ample opportunity for differentiation on a supplier's part. Already, providers of products and services to other businesses are sending plenty of brand-related messages, emphasizing topics such as corporate social responsibility, sustainability, or global reach. But these are not necessarily the issues decision makers in companies are most concerned about. Our research shows that they often pick suppliers based on perceived honesty and specialized expertise. Fact-based business branding provides a unique opportunity to close this gap between a supplier's message and the needs of decision makers. Early movers can expect to reap disproportionate rewards by differentiating their propositions accordingly. Examples of good practices include:[37]

- IBM. Ever since its incorporation more than a century ago, IBM has had to contend with rapidly evolving customer needs. The company's continued success rests on its ability to adapt its value proposition without putting its brand on the line. At the heart of the brand today is Smarter Planet, a positioning that reflects IBM's stance in the post-PC era. Originally conceived as the working title for the company's emerging public sector business, Smarter Planet now epitomizes the way IBM operates in a data-driven world. Smarter Planet guides product development, employee engagement, and all forms of external communication – from specific stakeholder engagement programs to global marketing campaigns. Under this roof, IBM has developed dozens of platforms, including Smarter Education, Smarter Energy, and Smarter Cities. Touch points range from a series of short films on the future of the city – showcased at the British Film Institute – to an interactive exhibit at Disney's Epcot Center. In a nutshell, Smarter Planet demonstrates the company's unique ability to balance innovation with sustainability. Today, IBM is widely regarded as one of the world's most valuable brands, on par with the likes of Coca-Cola and Apple.
- Established in 1850, American Express has been the most valuable credit card brand for a number of years now. In an effort to grow its business with small and medium enterprises (SMEs), the company recently set out to create a win-win partnership with these customers. By helping independent retailers attract

## Fig. 2.17: Brands drive decisions in B2B

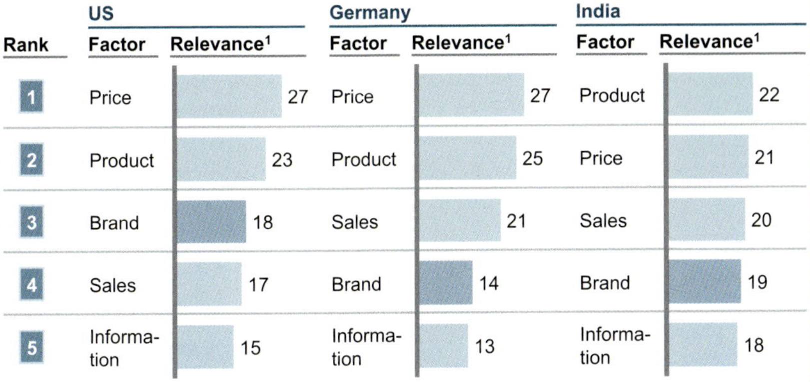

| Rank | US Factor | Relevance[1] | Germany Factor | Relevance[1] | India Factor | Relevance[1] |
|---|---|---|---|---|---|---|
| 1 | Price | 27 | Price | 27 | Product | 22 |
| 2 | Product | 23 | Product | 25 | Price | 21 |
| 3 | Brand | 18 | Sales | 21 | Sales | 20 |
| 4 | Sales | 17 | Brand | 14 | Brand | 19 |
| 5 | Information | 15 | Information | 13 | Information | 18 |

[1] Percentage of influence on purchase decision
SOURCE: B2B Branding survey

## Fig. 2.18: Brands help companies reduce risk in B2B

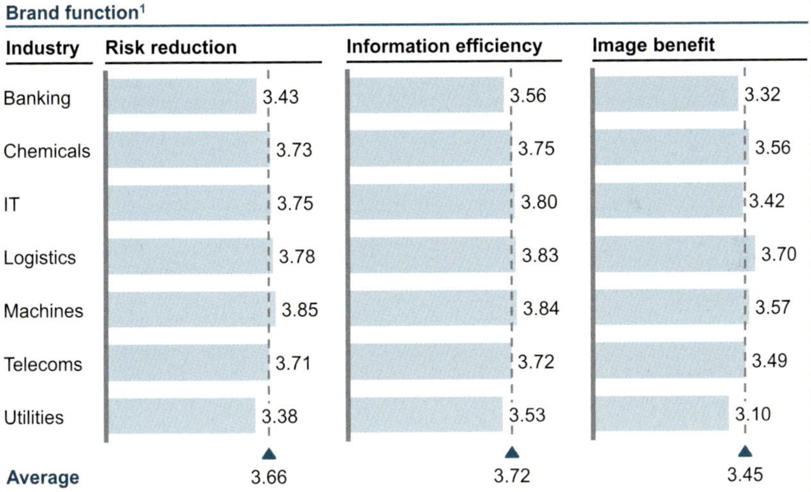

Brand function[1]

| Industry | Risk reduction | Information efficiency | Image benefit |
|---|---|---|---|
| Banking | 3.43 | 3.56 | 3.32 |
| Chemicals | 3.73 | 3.75 | 3.56 |
| IT | 3.75 | 3.80 | 3.42 |
| Logistics | 3.78 | 3.83 | 3.70 |
| Machines | 3.85 | 3.84 | 3.57 |
| Telecoms | 3.71 | 3.72 | 3.49 |
| Utilities | 3.38 | 3.53 | 3.10 |
| Average | 3.66 | 3.72 | 3.45 |

[1] Scale: From 1 (lowest) to 5 (highest)
SOURCE: B2B Branding survey

> more shoppers, Amex would benefit from the increase in transaction volume. To make it happen, the company initiated the Open Forum, a virtual platform for small business owners to connect with Amex and one another. Open Forum works as a catalyst that helps small businesses become more successful. The platform features various educational resources and tools. As a result, a growing community of SMEs has come to appreciate Amex not just as a credit card company, but as an advisor. The culmination of this effort is Small Business Saturday, an annual event held the weekend after Thanksgiving to help small businesses claim their share of the US holiday rush. The Small Business Saturday Facebook page attracted more than one million followers in less than three weeks, now totaling almost five million. Even President Obama tweeted about the event repeatedly, encouraging fellow Americans to »shop small.«[38]

**Implications for management**

What lessons can be learned from these findings? The significance of brands for corporate success is indisputable, but this study on brand relevance shows that – because the leverage effect of brands varies from market to market – brand building is not likely to have the same impact in all cases. Companies first need to analyze what relevance brands possess in specific markets as well as the reasons for this pertinence. It is important to note that brands target several markets simultaneously (e.g., B2B, B2C, capital market, recruiting). It is thus important to analyze the brand relevance in each individual segment, then prioritize target audiences and branding decisions accordingly.

Where there is market saturation in the end-consumer market, an analysis of brand relevance can help to avoid serious investment mistakes. In the B2B sector in particular, brand relevance analysis reveals that there are a number of significant market opportunities that companies have yet to capture. Examples include the high relevance of image benefit for B2B brands in India, the apparent trust gap left by the financial crisis in the US, and the role of component brands as sources of differentiation. Logistics providers in particular can count on their customers to care a great deal about brands, and to be willing to pay a price premium for a strong and reputable brand.

## 2.2 From Insight to Impact: Customer Insights and Segmentation for Better Brand Management

As we have seen, any meaningful examination of brand relevance has to be differentiated by country and product category. But it doesn't stop there. Even within a single national product market, you have to go a lot deeper to capture the diversity of perceptions and desires. Successful brand managers go beyond the concept of »the consumer« and embrace the fact that several consumer profiles and segments coexist in the same market. Their value will increasingly be captured by companies that excel at understanding and serving their respective needs. There is no such thing as »the perfect product« or »superior service.« These days, it's almost always a question of »perfect for whom?« and »superior in which respect?« Take car insurance. While one policyholder favors a no-worries deal with extended personal advice and doesn't care too much about the rates, the next person may simply be looking for the best bargain – be it from his next-door agent or from an anonymous Web site. Needs, attitudes, values, consumption or usage patterns along with brand perception depend almost entirely on who you are dealing with (Figure 2.19). The trend described in this clipping from 2008 persists today. In the US, for example, the same person will shop at Aldi or Walmart for low-priced basics and at Whole Foods or a local farmers' market for organic produce.[39] Hanna Ehrnrooth of the Hanken School of Economics sums up a recent study of this phenomenon as follows: »Hybrid consumers opt for both premium and budget alternatives but ignore midrange alternatives. [...] As hybrid consumers do not fall into distinct and stable categories, traditional marketing and segmentation strategies may need to be rethought. Consumers cannot be categorized in such a straightforward manner as conventional segmentation practices suggest.«[40]

**Fig. 2.19: Press report about hybrid consumption**

**Patchwork consumers: They want it all**

Consumers are erratic creatures. Their behavior is only partially rational. Take environmental friendliness. People will drive their Volkswagen Touareg or Mercedes M-Class SUV to an organic food store. They will buy a crate of "Bionade" [herbal lemonade], a pack of organic water buffalo mozzarella cheese and a pound of pesticide-free tomatoes. Then they store the whole stuff in a power-guzzling monster fridge equipped with "Bioshield" antibacterial coating. If they feel like it, they will watch a documentary on endangered backstroking catfish from the Kongo, on their 150 inch plasma screen once their done with the shopping. But the opposite is no less common: The consumer rides his bicycle to a discount supermarket and "ends up frying rotten meat on a designer stove," as Rainer Grießhammer of the Freiburg-based Öko-Institut puts it. He says we are dealing with "patchwork consumers" pursuing several lifestyles at the same time."

*Sascha Lehnhartz, "Bionade im Monsterkühlschrank," Frankfurter Allgemeine Sonntagszeitung, March 9 2008, No. 10, P. 59*

As consumer needs, shopper behavior, and competitors' moves become more complex and changeable, the importance of market intelligence for brand management grows. An increasing number of touch points, brands, channels, and messages – as well as increasingly erratic consumer behavior – make it all the more critical to anticipate what customers want. The challenge is to develop ever-more refined propositions without damaging profits through excessive customization. The value pool is deepest where marketing management and customer insights generation intersect, that is, at the so-called »insight cells.« Increased proliferation leads to a higher number of cells, resulting in more opportunities to innovate in areas such as products, varieties, packaging, and channels. Pioneers in targeted marketing succeed by understanding and leveraging what happens at these cells. In short, brand managers need to ramp up their game in customer insight management to stay competitive. It's a simple insight, but like all insights of consequence, it isn't easy to generate and it's even harder to implement. This chapter outlines critical steps along the way towards insights-driven brand management, highlighting the most comprehensive customer insights application of all: segmentation.

**Infusing your brand with the consumer's perspective**

Customer-insights-driven brand development can take many shapes. It doesn't always have to take the form of a revolutionary product like Apple's iPad that quickly achieved market dominance in the computer tablet category, Toyota's Prius, the prototypical hybrid car, or Procter & Gamble's category-defining WhiteStrip teeth whitening product that generated more than USD 500 million in new sales annually. Understanding what consumers value can also lead to innovations in the areas of individual product features or even packaging. After all, packaging is one of a brand's most important consumer-facing touch points, especially in the fast-moving consumer goods arena. Henkel's insights-driven product development helped it discover the need for well-designed air fresheners. A lot of potential customers simply considered existing products too ugly for their high-end bathrooms. In 2006, Henkel introduced the FreshSurfer – an attractively packaged air freshener designed by Alessi – and managed to increase market share by 5 percentage points, as well as to capture a considerable price premium over its competitors.[41] Similarly, Henkel pioneered the Theramed toothpaste dispenser and the two-in-one combination of toothpaste and mouthwash. Both innovations – eventually combined in a Theramed two-in-one product – have contributed significantly to the sales of Henkel's oral care division and been copied by many competitors in the same and in neighboring categories. Theramed is Henkel's best-selling oral care brand to this day and generated EUR 117 million in revenues in 2012 according to Euromonitor estimates (toothpaste and mouthwash). In 2012, Henkel extended the Theramed brand when it launched Theramed X-ite, a range of oral care gels geared to young people in search of unique flavors. In a 2013 social media campaign, Henkel took the legend of the tooth fairy to social networks and mobile applications.[42]

So is it all about thinking out of the box? When we take a closer look at how highly innovative companies differ from their competitors, we find that combining creativity with a systematic approach is the key to success. Highly original and very successful brand communication as presented in Chapter 1, Section 1.2 doesn't happen by chance or coincidence. It is the result of careful planning that reflects deep consumer understanding.

Successful innovations are often the result of active, open-minded, and diligent research well beyond the established frame of reference, combined with the will and skill to act swiftly and decisively on the insights generated. Says former L'Oréal chairman Lindsay Owen-Jones: »If you wait until the consumer has told you everything, it's too late. The battle has already happened, somebody has taken the prize, and it's gone.«

So what does it take to stay ahead of the pack? Successful marketers generate customer insights that go well beyond the concept of the customer-centric company. They define consumer touch points much more comprehensively to include trial use, after-sales experience, and word of mouth. They also dedicate a surprising amount of time and effort to generating and analyzing details that often seem irrelevant at first. Many observations unfold their power only when seen from a bird's-eye perspective that combines the experience and expertise of multiple departments. By combining shopper data with sales feedback and branding information, cutting-edge marketers move from a wealth of information to actionable insights. In many cases, these insights can overturn long-established beliefs and necessitate leaving the trodden path. Let's take a quick look at some compelling cases of brand management informed by market research – and specifically, at insights-driven innovations that have led to substantial changes in the way companies do business and manage their brands.

**Product feature innovation at Alcoa.** Alcoa makes aluminum beverage cans for Coke. Traditionally, as the »owner« of the consumer relationship, Coke would dictate the product specifications. Alcoa took a chance and looked at consumers' refrigerators. They found that the usual outer packaging of bundled cans didn't fit most fridges. Consumers had to take apart the bundle and refrigerate the cans individually. By developing a crate that fits the standard fridge and can be easily replaced as soon as it is empty, Alcoa boosted Coke's repurchase levels. This led to a 10 percent increase in US can sales within three months and helped strengthen Alcoa's reputation as a brand that listens not only to its customers, but to their customers' customers as well.[43]

**Product brand innovation at Pepsi.** Pepsi's company Stokely-Van Camp produces Gatorade. They understood there was significant demand for a low-calorie fitness drink in the US market, but assumed their product Gatorade Light was sufficient to meet this need. When they researched their target audience in more detail, however, they found it primarily consisted of health-conscious women who prefer water to soft drinks when they work out. But Gatorade Light was considered a soft drink by this audience. So Stokely developed Propel, a flavored water brand, and discontinued Gatorade Light. Today, Propel contributes EUR 138 million in annual sales (2013) according to Euromonitor, making it the number three functional bottled water globally in terms of volume. Effectively, this helped Pepsi to expand its brand portfolio from sweet fizzy drinks to lifestyle beverages.[44]

**Brand positioning at Yellow Tail.** Originally an export cooperative of minor Australian winemakers started by the Casella family, Yellow Tail was established as a brand in 2001. The brand management team behind Yellow Tail, at W.J. Deutsch & Sons, understood that many American wine drinkers were confused or put off by complicated, old-school wine labels spelling out provenance and quality in a mix of jargon and foreign languages. They went for a clean-cut label featuring clean lettering and the prominent trademark image of a leaping yellow-tailed rock wallaby. According to Libby Nutt, a marketing manager for Casella Wines, Yellow Tail aspires to reduce complexity – both in terms of terminology and range – and to create an easy drinking experience. Supported by a USD 24 million advertising campaign – one of the most aggressive ever for a wine brand – Yellow Tail leapt from zero to 112,000 cases in its first year as a branded product. By 2003, the brand had overtaken Concho y Toro and became the number one imported wine in the United States. In 2006, Yellow Tail surpassed Sutter Home and became the number one US supermarket brand. In 2013, it sold 9.2 million cases. Yellow Tail enjoys similar success in other countries. In 2007, the brand entered the British market. In 2008, three million bottles were sold in the UK within three months according to trade reports. In March 2014, *Drinks International* named Yellow Tail one of the world's 50 most admired wine brands, as well as »the most successful wine brand launch in history.«[45]

**Packaging innovation at General Mills.** In 1998, the market for yogurt was stagnating despite ever-increasing product quality and taste. General Mills, the US food manufacturer, launched an ethnographic study to explore yogurt consumption by young people. Researchers observed the eating patterns of children, both in their homes and at school. They found that many parents had trouble getting their sleepy kids to eat before rushing to school. At school, children who had not eaten breakfast often started eating their packed lunches as early as one hour after arriving. From these observations, General Mills derived a need for an on-the-go breakfast option that could be consumed in the car or during a mid-morning break at school. To address this need, the company created Go-Gurt, a specially treated yogurt variety delivered in a tube (sold as Yoplait Tubes in Canada and Frubes in the UK). Jeanine Bassett, the VP of Global Consumer Insights at General Mills, says: »We launched […] a campaign to assure moms that tossing a frozen Go-Gurt into the lunch bag in the morning would deliver a healthy, tasty treat a few hours later. That was a real winner for both moms and kids.« The product achieved first-year sales of USD 37 million and helped General Mills capture market share from Danone.[46]

None of these innovations would have happened without the generation and application of true customer insights across the entire value chain, from product development and channel management to brand communication. Taking insights seriously, generating them systematically, and applying them comprehensively are sure signs of a truly customer-centric, brand-driven company; these building blocks are described in Figure 2.20. Pioneers in this area move from insight to impact by infusing their brands with the consumer's perspective on an ongoing basis. Most of all, successful customer insights management is about the will to do things differently. Most successful cases of customer-insights driven growth include the following key success factors:

Successful brand managers combine internal strengths and continuous innovation with **systematic gathering and processing of customer data**. Ensuring data quality and depth is the necessary first step. Leading companies collect data at all important touch points, ranging from checkouts and call centers to online chat rooms and pro-

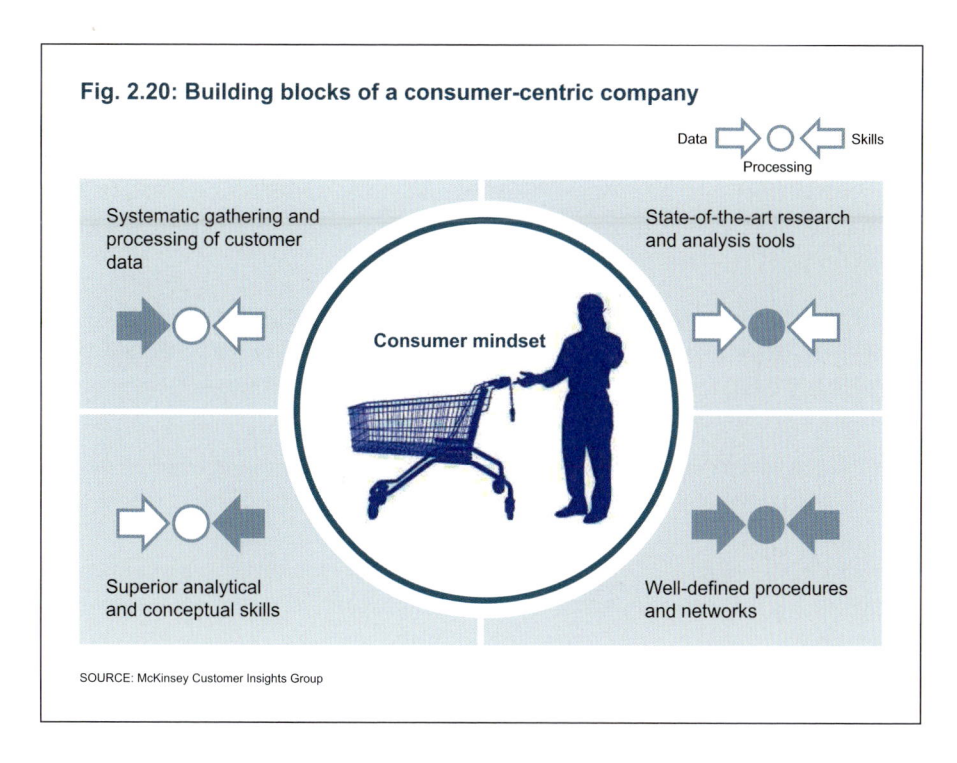

**Fig. 2.20: Building blocks of a consumer-centric company**

- Systematic gathering and processing of customer data
- State-of-the-art research and analysis tools
- Superior analytical and conceptual skills
- Well-defined procedures and networks

Consumer mindset

SOURCE: McKinsey Customer Insights Group

---

prietary research or observation. Leading retailers, for example, combine customer data derived from loyalty programs with market research to achieve new levels of store optimization and customized customer relationship management. Capital One, the credit card company, stores several megabytes of information per cardholder and uses it to tailor their terms and conditions, as well as for cross-selling purposes.[47] Establishing exclusive access to third-party data is another powerful component of integrated customer insights management. Some fast-moving consumer goods companies buy scanner data from gas stations and other such outlets to monitor their front-line performance. Best-in-class players include Procter & Gamble, Henkel, and Beiersdorf in fast-moving consumer goods, and Philips in consumer durables.

**State-of-the-art research and analysis tools** should be a matter of course, but many companies underestimate the effort required to ensure their research captures actual customer behavior, rather than stated preferences. It is a proven fact that customers are often wrong when asked to describe how they make their choices. Car buyers, for example, will say that safety or fuel economy matter most to them, when in fact design, performance, and value for money drive their choices (compare Figure 3.7). But even observational techniques don't get you to the holy grail of latent needs – dormant or inexplicit needs – that consumers themselves are unaware of or unable to realize because there are no products to match these needs. Because it is the very nature of these needs that consumers are not aware of them, they will not articulate them even in focus groups. The insert on ethnography/netnography provides examples of the latest explorative techniques to help customer insights departments go beyond the obvious. Bear in mind, however, that while successful players keep innovating on the tool front, the true power of customer insights comes from continuity. If you change your approach too often, you are likely to miss important trends. A McKinsey survey of 20 leading North American consumer goods companies revealed that high performers in the areas of insights management tend to have three things in common: standardized data collection processes and formats, frequent updates, and continuous trend observation. So executives at the intersection of insights and branding are well advised to think »motion picture, not snapshot.«

Since the finest tools are useless unless willingly applied, a **consumer mindset** is critical, but having insights is not enough. Their power comes from being applied effectively all across the value chain. As a consequence, well-defined **procedures and networks** are a prerequisite of real insights-driven impact.

Leading companies make sure insights are reflected throughout their business system from product development to distribution and aftersales management. Customer insights experts act as information brokers and are involved in all consumer-related strategic decision making. Consumer-centric companies move from a »make and sell« to a »sense and response« approach, as Hans-Willi Schroiff of Henkel's business intelligence unit is quoted in a 2005 press release by the company. Building networks includes being open to outside input from the best experts in their fields. At Procter & Gamble these days, up to 50 percent of all innovations are triggered by specialists outside the company.[48] At the other end of the value chain, Coca-Cola goes to great lengths to integrate the data gathered at various touch points to support superior execution at the store level. In the UK, the company employs a database of outlets that either currently sell or have the potential to sell soft drinks. Referred to as the »total retail opportunity« by specialists, the database covers more than half a million stores clustered into 16 distinct shopper environments and includes sales, volume, competitor information, shopper demographics, and behavioral data. The database is used to provide retailers with the right tools and incentives to lure consumers into stores – and ultimately to maximize the return on POS marketing investment.[49]

It takes superior analytical and conceptual skills to process and understand the data. Leading companies invest heavily in this area, either by training in-house specialists or hiring external experts on an as-needed basis. Because of the many trade-off decisions involved in insights management (tool innovation versus research continuity, depth of insight versus applicability of findings), customer insights excellence is ultimately about finding and developing the right kind of people. You'll be looking for candidates who combine the mindset of a manager with the skill set of an egghead. They're hard to find, so you'd better start looking today.

A word of caution: just as airlines don't trust autopilots to fly their planes without the supervision of human professionals, even the most sophisticated research cannot and should not dictate your brand management actions. It is a combination of deep insights that go beyond the obvious and the kind of business judgment only entrepreneurial experience can bring that will separate the leaders from the followers in insights-driven brand management.

## Qualitative Research Helps Identify Hidden Needs

Quantitative research and measurement are essential to fact-based brand management. But how do you know what exactly you should measure? Quantifying brand driver performance is all well and good, but which attributes should you even be looking at? One of the key challenges in brand related insight generation is to go beyond the obvious, to move from diagnosis to prognosis. To stay competitive, understanding today's consumers is not enough. Your brand's future performance will depend on preempting, even shaping, tomorrow's trends and fashions. This is particularly important when it comes to determining the appropriate needs dimensions for a strategic segmentation. But how do you find out what even consumers themselves are not (yet) aware of? This is where qualitative research techniques come in.

While proven tools such as focus groups and in-store shopper observation are still widely used, new ways of generating insights outside the status quo are emerging. One of the most promising techniques is ethnographic research, including its online version known as »netnography.« To identify unfulfilled or hidden needs, you have to develop a deep understanding of consumers in broadly defined purchasing and consumption situations that reflect consumers' general living conditions. There are two advantages to this approach: it allows you to explore new ideas (rather than just test existing concepts), and it centers on the actual brand-consumer interaction experience. It's not meant to off-load the creative achievement to the consumer, but it gives brand managers and product developers much richer input than previously thought possible.

Perhaps the most prominent examples of ethnographic research are street sports events used by companies like Nike and Adidas to investigate brand image and product usage first hand. Procter & Gamble famously took market research from the studio to the bathroom, visiting consumers wherever and whenever shampoo or toothpaste is actually used.

Heinz, the Pittsburgh-based maker of condiments and other processed foods, invested in ethnographic research to improve its ketchup packets.[50] Consumers complained that the company's single-serve packets were messy, hard to open, and that they did not provide enough ketchup. To get to the bottom of the issue, Heinz researchers constructed a fake minivan interior and sat behind one-way mirrors to observe consumers putting ketchup on fries, burgers, and chicken nuggets. The VP of global packaging innovation even personally bought a used minivan and took it to various local drive-through restaurants to order fries and apply ketchup in the confined space of the car. Based on these observational and experiential efforts, Heinz redesigned the packets. The new design, »Dip & Squeeze,« is bright red, bottle-shaped, and holds three times as much ketchup as the traditional packet. Additionally, it gives consumers a choice: they can either peel back the cover for dipping, or tear off the tip for squeezing. Tests at restaurants indicated that customers prefer the new packages. It also won the National Restaurant Association Innovations Award in 2011.[51]

Ethnographic research is by no means limited to the B2C arena. Hilti, a maker and brand of premium power drills and other hand-held tools, uses its own sales force to act as ethnographic researchers. By interviewing and observing construction workers on site, Hilti discovered that construction teams often include workers and engineers from multiple countries and backgrounds. As a result, there are often difficulties with written instructions, no matter what the language. To ensure that tools can be safely and easily operated nevertheless, Hilti introduced a color-coded tool design system: the company's trademark red for working parts, solid black for switches, and black trimming for handles and grips. The resulting color scheme doubles as a signature look reinforcing the brand identity. Hilti also developed a revolutionary self-sharpening power chisel when sales agents reported there is often no time for sharpening on construction sites, and that workers end up using dull chisels most of the time. Hilti CEO Marco Meyrat admits that direct sales is the most expensive distribution channel, but would not want to miss out on the instant, actionable feedback provided by his sales agents. Hilti has been rewarded with a 30 to 50 percent price premium over its competition.[52]

John Deere, the well-known manufacturer of agricultural equipment and other heavy machinery, has been exploring multichannel insights generation. On the occasion of CONEXPO-CON/AGG in 2011 – North America's largest construction trade show – the company launched the Chatterbox. The Chatterbox is both a Web site and a portable recording studio. Its main objective is to generate customer suggestions that will help improve the company's equipment and services. Ideas were peer-rated by the company's growing online community, and John Deere provided feedback on a regular basis. Accompanied by an advertising campaign revolving around a »designed by users« theme, the Chatterbox debuted to more than 5,000 attendees at the live unveiling. The related microsite attracted 150,000 hits. At the time of writing, John Deere had more than two million followers on Facebook. As a traveling exhibit, over the course of the subsequent three years, the physical Chatterbox was taken to construction sites, trade shows, and dealer locations across the US and Canada to get the perspective of hundreds of construction industry professionals. *B2B Marketing* short-listed the campaign as one of the best in 2011. At a press conference in early 2013, John Deere showcased its 644K hybrid wheel loader. It uses two energy sources: diesel and electric (Figure 2.21). The new loader is an example of the company leveraging customer input, including in-the-field feedback, in the design of innovative products. John Deere generated net sales of USD 36 billion in 2012, up 39 percent from USD 26 billion in 2010.[53]

Online insights generation is often collectively referred to as Netnography, for example, in the form of topical blogs, Web-based communities, and discussion groups that allow researchers to observe as well as to interact with current and future customers directly through text discourse. Platforms for consumer reviews such as Yelp – a company that acquired its European competitor in 2012 – have effectively turned netnography into a mass phenomenon, and companies are trying to capitalize on this source of customer insights. Manufacturers of hiking shoes and other sports gear, for example, have been known to refine and modify their products based on feedback from online outdoor communities. Electronic Arts (EA), the maker of entertainment software, uses consumer input from its moderated chat rooms to refine its products. Games that are released periodically incorporate feedback from consumers who have played earlier versions – for example, the football video game Madden NFL, a new version of which EA Sports releases every summer. In 2011, EA established »Origin,« a platform for software downloads that doubles as an online player community. EA's net revenues increased from USD 3.7 billion in 2010 to USD 4.1 billion in 2012.[54]

**Fig. 2.21: Example of insights-based product innovation at John Deere**

Ethnography: The Chatterbox space

Netnography: The Chatterbox microsite

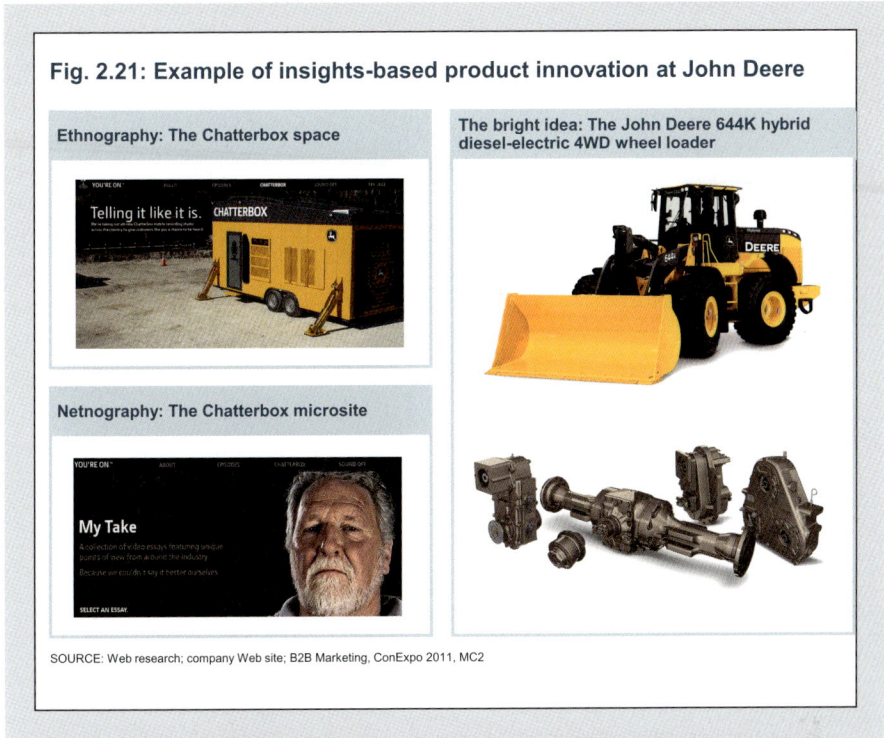

The bright idea: The John Deere 644K hybrid diesel-electric 4WD wheel loader

SOURCE: Web research; company Web site; B2B Marketing, ConExpo 2011, MC2

An even more refined example of netnography is the kind of online store that allows consumers to create their own products, for example, Puma's successful Mongolian Shoe BBQ. By analyzing the kinds of shoes created, the company learns what trendsetting consumers want and applies these insights to future product development. Increasingly, companies also use social networks to reach out to loyal brand followers and generate insights on a continuous basis. One example is Mountain Dew, the soft drink brand produced and owned by PepsiCo. Mountain Dew engages in an open dialog with consumers on Twitter, Facebook, and YouTube. The brand's most prominent program is called DEWmocracy. More than 4,000 of the brand's most loyal fans participated in consumer cocreation. The grass-roots effort has resulted in the introduction of three new flavors. Some 36 million cases of the new products were sold, 85 percent of which were considered incremental by the company. PepsiCo's Frank Cooper explains: »By maintaining an open dialog with our consumers [...] we've offered them an opportunity to leave their imprint on a brand they truly love and have solidified an even stronger relationship with fans who matter most.«[55]

Important and insightful as qualitative research techniques may be (Figure 2.22), their main function is to help enrich and complement the quantitative research approaches that are the backbone of brand measurement, such as the brand purchase funnel (discussed in more detail in Chapter 1, Sections 1.2 and 1.3; see Section 2.3 in this chapter for details on this core brand measurement framework). Ideally, qualitative and quantitative research should work hand in hand. Typically, qualitative methods as described above would help identify relevant attributes that might be potential brand drivers. Subsequently, the actual relevance of these attributes will be tested in quantitative funnel research (Section 2.3), refined

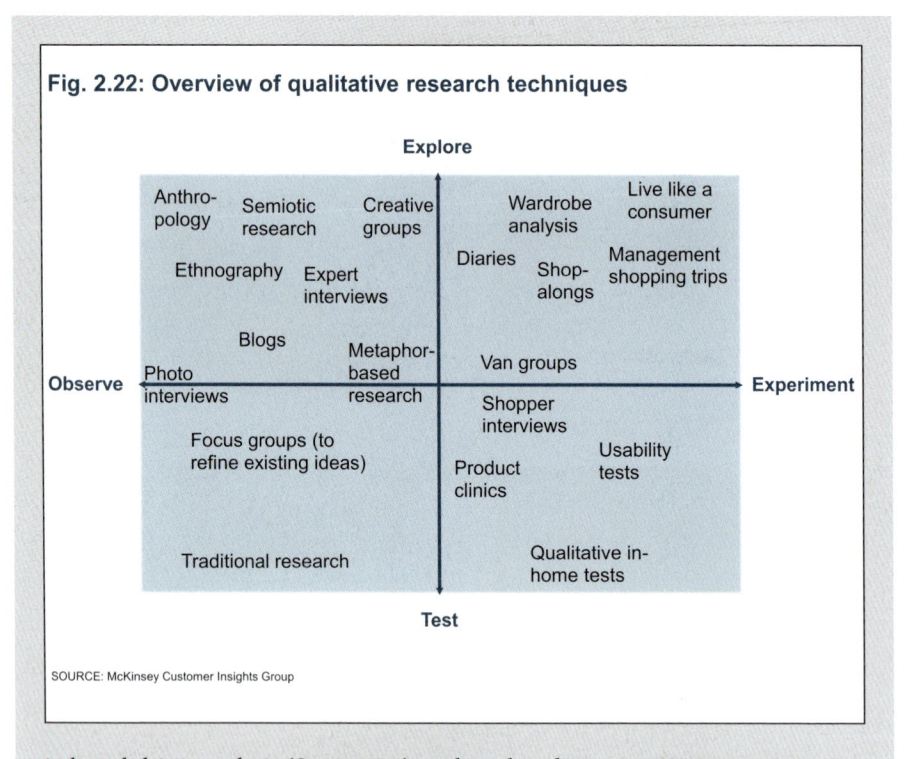

**Fig. 2.22: Overview of qualitative research techniques**

```
                         Explore
                            ↑
   Anthro-   Semiotic   Creative      Wardrobe    Live like a
   pology    research   groups        analysis    consumer
                                 Diaries          Management
        Ethnography  Expert            Shop-      shopping trips
                     interviews        alongs
              Blogs
                     Metaphor-
   Photo             based         Van groups
Observe ← interviews research                              → Experiment
                                   Shopper
          Focus groups (to         interviews
          refine existing ideas)              Usability
                                   Product    tests
                                   clinics

          Traditional research     Qualitative in-
                                   home tests
                            ↓
                          Test
```

SOURCE: McKinsey Customer Insights Group

in brand driver analysis (Section 3.2), and used to derive positioning options (Section 3.3). Research is yet another area in which you need art (open-ended qualitative research) as well as science (dependable quantitative research), held together by craft (good judgment based on marketing and business expertise) to succeed.

### Segmentation is the centerpiece of insights-driven brand management

In the age of IT-enabled one-to-one marketing, what would you need segmentation for? »As a map,« the former CEO of Esomar, Mario van Hamersfeld, said in an interview with McKinsey. The world of branding has become a jungle, and segmentation imposes order and provides orientation. Both are vital given the increasing pressure on the marketing function from ever-increasing numbers of brands, products, and channels along with the increasingly fierce fight over each and every customer. One indicator of the growing pressure is that, today, two out of every three customers are »brand switchers.« Take the example of fragrances in the German market. Back in the early 1990s, of every 100 new fragrances, 33 were still on the market two years later. Today that figure has shrunk to just three.[56] Decreasing loyalty and shortening life cycles make marketing more expensive than ever. Despite all the progress in information processing and logistics, one-to-one direct marketing is not the answer, particularly in the consumer goods industry, which depends on economies of scale to cover the fixed cost of product development and product launches. Even pioneers in »individualization,« such as Dell Computers, have recognized the limits of customization and tailoring and are now selling through traditional retail formats such as supermarkets or hypermarkets. In B2B sales, Dell has started segmenting its small and medium business customers to help them develop the most popular preconfigurations and limit the number of product models. But how do you decide which horse to bet on? When marketing resources are scarce, which products and customer groups should you concentrate on?[57]

Segmentation may seem old-fashioned, but as products, brands, and channels proliferate, segmentation is precisely the antidote a company needs to ensure that marketing is profitable. Twenty years ago, the challenge was to promote customer-centric marketing and help it prevail over the notion that »Good products sell themselves.« In the future, however, customer segmentation will become crucial in the search for the most profitable position between customization and mass marketing. Most corporations can be expected to serve five segments in a tailored manner without going to rack and ruin, but fifty thousand or five million customers? Not likely. This is also why nine out of ten executives say their companies have a segmentation (B2C), used for both daily operations and long-term strategy development. In a recent survey, »segmentation« was one of the top three marketing concepts named by US executives.[58] Companies that know how to use market segmentation achieve growth rates far higher than the market average. Done well, segmentation can unlock significant growth opportunities. For example, a needs-based segmentation helped PepsiCo discover a previously unserved segment in the 1990s: health-conscious young men who were reluctant to drink a »girl's drink,« such as Diet Pepsi. Specifically developed for this segment and introduced in 1993, Pepsi Max quickly became the fastest-growing sugar-free soft drink in the UK and prompted the introduction of Coke Zero by Pepsi's long-standing rival.[59] Launched in 2006, Coke Zero's signature black cans and bottles have fared well in many other markets. According to *Beverage Digest*, it was among the top ten carbonated soft drinks in the US in 2013. Pepsi Max wasn't introduced to the US market until 2007 (originally as Diet Pepsi Max, renamed Pepsi Max in 2009).

In short, proliferation in the market calls for granularity in brand management. But which cells, or segments, hold the biggest potential given the position of your brand and the benefits of your current product range? What should the value proposition for a promising, but currently unserved segment look like? The importance of this type of question for the profitability of targeted marketing makes segmentation the most comprehensive and perhaps the most important customer insights application of all.

**Unlocking the power of segmentation with explicit objective setting**

If segmentation is more important than ever, then why do so many marketing managers complain about expensive segmentation projects that just wind up gathering dust on the shelf? The complaints are well-known: the segmentations are hard to understand, difficult to communicate, and insufficiently actionable. Many segmentations are not total failures, but they fall short of executive expectations. It can't be lack of data. Never before has so much data been available. Thanks to turnkey solutions such as the New Car Buyer Survey (NCBS) in the automotive industry, market researchers can get thousands of data sets in just a few clicks. Analytical weaknesses can be excluded, too. Few other types of data analysis have received so much attention in the past 20 years. Leading experts agree that the possibilities for further statistical refinement have been exhausted. In fact, the biggest issue is much closer to home. According to a McKinsey survey of marketing executives, the success of a segmentation depends primarily on the objectives set for it and on its implementation, and much less on market research and modeling.

The way forward is to treat segmentation as a structured process to create a foundation for strategic brand management, not as a piece of research or a tool. The process comprises (1) objective setting, perhaps the most important step in light of the issues described above; (2) the actual segmentation research and analysis; and (3) implementation of findings (Figure 2.23). This process is more than worthy of a senior management decision, especially in its critical early stages. In the past, the emphasis was on refining the second step, while the first step was often underestimated and, hence, neglected.

**Fig. 2.23: Three-step segmentation process**

| Set objectives | Derive segmentation | Implement findings |
|---|---|---|
| • Specify clear objectives<br>  – Prioritize sources of future growth<br>  – Determine appropriate frame of reference for the business<br>• Ensure buy-in among all stakeholders<br>  – Involve segmentation "owners" and future users<br>  – Resolve conflicts of interest among stakeholders<br>• Identify key issues and decisions the segmentation must inform<br>  – Actions to take<br>  – Decisions to be made | • Ensure top quality research design and methodology<br>• Conduct qualitative research that informs development of quantitative survey<br>• Conduct quantitative research executed by trusted vendor partner and carefully monitored by market research<br>• Generate segmentation solution via iterative process that combines best-in-class analytics with solid business judgment | • Clearly communicate segmentation throughout organization, tailored to the needs of each audience<br>• Incorporate segmentation findings in planning process<br>  – Reprioritize all current activities by each functional group<br>  – Revise planning processes as necessary to ensure use of segment-specific insights<br>• Regularly monitor key metrics at segment level<br>• Implement organizational changes necessary |

SOURCE: McKinsey

## Phase I: Clarify segmentation objectives and frame of reference

Only a solution created with clear objectives in mind can serve as an effective guide to action. The wide variety of applications becomes tangible as soon as you think about the different stakeholders and what they are looking for:

- The division heads want to know which product categories have the highest growth potential. From their perspective, »type of product« should be the primary segmentation dimension.
- The CMO is struggling to position the brand globally and is looking for values and attitudes common to all markets in which the company operates.
- The product developer has to decide what ingredients to use for a new product and suggests consumers' specific product needs as segment-building variables.
- The media planner at the agency needs to pick vehicles for the latest advertisements and wants segments profiled by media usage.
- The sales department is looking for an approach to help them prioritize existing customers according to their potential value.

Even at first sight, it's clear that a single segmentation solution cannot possibly satisfy all of these demands at the same time – let alone with equal depth and precision. So why have a single solution at all? Why not have as many as it takes to keep everybody happy? The reason is simple. If you want one brand with one position, speaking to the customer with one voice and offering a consistent value proposition, you need a common basis. Without a unified understanding of who customers are and what they want, different departments will wander off in different directions, creating conflicting messages and inefficient investment decisions. Given the wide variety of questions, any unified segmentation approach will always involve compromise. To make sure the interests of all relevant stakeholders are sufficiently balanced, the responsibility for setting segmentation parameters should reside as high up in the organization as practically possible. However, a unified segmentation approach does not rule out the use of additional, more granular segmentations for operational purposes – such as loyalty management or media planning – as long as these secondary segmentations are compatible with the strategic segmentation that is used for brand positioning and proposition development.

To achieve an ideal balance of unity and granularity, Phase I is all about setting clear objectives, defining the frame of reference, and managing stakeholder expectations. It may sound absurd at first, but if you ask two different executives in your company to describe the relevant market, you are likely to get three different answers (Figure 2.24). But in fact, this is a critical factor in pretty much every segmentation. For if you don't know who your (potential) customers are, you don't know whom you should segment, profile, and target. If you think growth is most likely to come from new markets, you will want to ensure a broad market definition that includes neighboring categories. Is a brand like Nivea, for example, necessarily limited to beauty products, or might it be extended to include day spas or even wellness resorts? Do coffee shops really deal in coffee, or should they aspire to become the much-touted »third place« beyond home and work? Howard Schultz of Starbucks is famously quoted as follows: »We're not in the coffee business, serving people. We're in the people business, serving coffee.«[60]

If you don't think fundamentally about your frame of reference, you're likely to miss out on major growth opportunities. Gatorade would never have attained its unique market position had its managers not expanded their frame of reference from »isotonic beverages« (US market volume of USD 18.7 billion) to »sports beverages« (US market volume of USD 85.8 billion) (Figure 2.25).[61] The relevant market should, of course, also reflect brand heritage and in-house capabilities: Lamborghini is as unlikely to become a mass manufacturer as Kia is to go premium. In short, defining the frame of reference is a case-by-case decision that deserves senior management attention.

Any segmentation should have clear objectives, and its frame of reference should reflect your growth aspirations as well as your company's strengths and weaknesses. If the solution is intended to help design (rather than deliver) your value proposition, there should be only one of its kind. Additional, more tactical segmentations may be admissible to the extent they help you deliver your value proposition in distinctive ways. Holding-type companies operating in multiple industries will want to think about a segmentation architecture driven by the dynamics of their businesses and the portfolio of their brands as discussed at the end of this section.

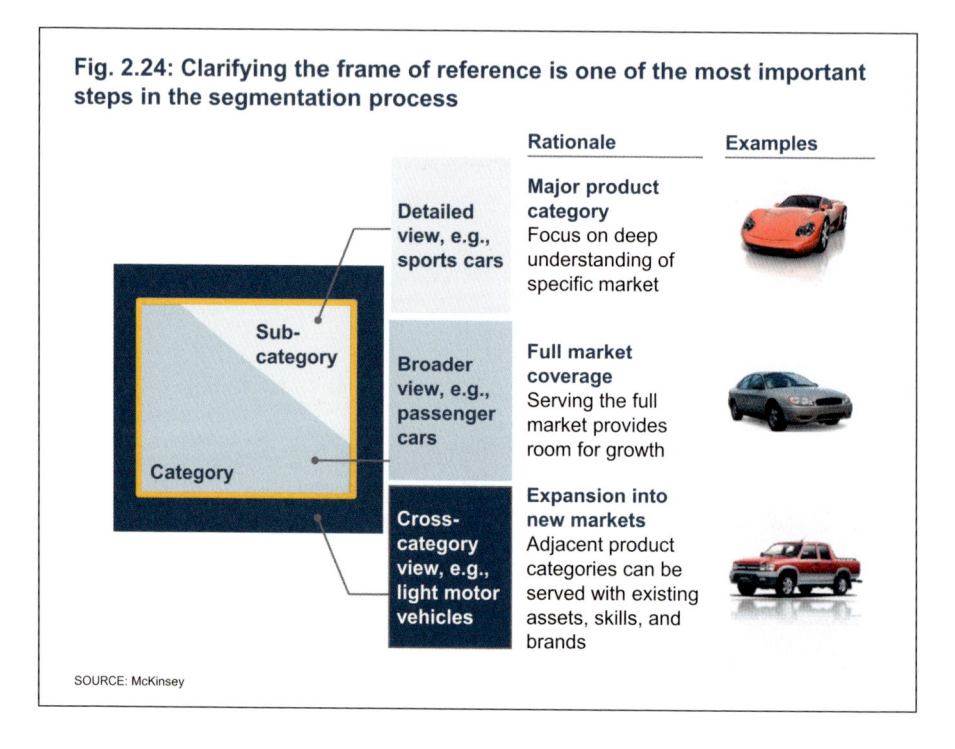

**Fig. 2.24: Clarifying the frame of reference is one of the most important steps in the segmentation process**

| View | Rationale | Examples |
|---|---|---|
| Detailed view, e.g., sports cars | Major product category — Focus on deep understanding of specific market | |
| Broader view, e.g., passenger cars | Full market coverage — Serving the full market provides room for growth | |
| Cross-category view, e.g., light motor vehicles | Expansion into new markets — Adjacent product categories can be served with existing assets, skills, and brands | |

SOURCE: McKinsey

### Fig. 2.25: Relevant market definition determines revenue potential

| Brand | Frame of reference | Competitive set | Innovation options | Market size USD billions[1] |
|---|---|---|---|---|
| Gatorade | Narrow: sports drinks | Powerade, other sports drinks | Flavor extensions, package sizes | 18.7 |
| Gatorade | Broad: functional beverages | Bottled water, sports drinks | Fitness water, performance bars | 85.8 |
| Uncle Ben's | Narrow: rice | Goya, Minute Rice | Flavor extensions | 68.9 |
| Uncle Ben's | Broad: ready meals | Hamburger Helper, Lipton, frozen meals, Progresso | One-bowl meals, multiple times of day (e.g., breakfast) | 90.8 |
| Nivea | Narrow: skin care | Oil of Olay, Lubriderm | Fragrances, skin type formulations | 107.2 |
| Nivea | Broad: personal care | Gillette, P&G, L'Oréal | Deodorant, sun protection, shampoo | 454.1 |
| Listerine | Narrow: mouthwash | Scope | Flavor extensions, efficacy improvements | 4.8 |
| Listerine | Broad: oral care | Wrigley's, Altoids, Crest, Palmolive | Tooth paste, gum, electric toothbrushes | 43.1 |

1 2013 data, at retail selling price
SOURCE: Euromonitor

## Phase II: Conducting research and deriving segmentation

Even once the relevant market (or frame of reference) has been defined as part of objective setting in Phase I, it is not necessarily self-evident whom to segment. Should you be looking at consumers, shoppers, or intermediaries? To find out, it is essential to analyze the decision-making process in the relevant market you have defined, using qualitative market research if needed. Take the example of a US processed meat manufacturer. The company knew that roughly 80 percent of the products (by volume) were consumed by men, yet 80 percent of the purchases were made by women. The company felt that a segmentation of purchasers would be missing a key part of the equation, especially the needs of consumers. But a quick survey revealed that purchasers did in fact make the bulk of brand decisions. The company came within an inch of a misleading segmentation. Had it segmented consumers rather than purchasers (who also tend to be preparers), they would have looked at the needs of a group of people that has little say in the actual decision. Similarly, pharmaceuticals companies typically look at prescribing physicians rather than patients, at least for prescription medication. But things are changing. For some types of drugs, such as sleeping pills or painkillers, physicians may continue to select the active agent, but consumers pick the actual brand they want.

In the market for shampoo, Procter & Gamble literally turned heads when it invested in an international need state segmentation to help tailor its formulations to local consumer requirements. One of the objectives was to grow the Head & Shoulders brand in Asia. The segmentation revealed that the hair of Chinese women differs from that of Caucasian women in its reaction to care products. Additionally, the research showed that many Chinese women wash their hair in cold water. Based on these insights, Head & Shoulders developed a special formula to meet the needs of Chinese consumers, and the company continues to invest in market research to deepen its understanding of local consumer needs. According to press reports, Head & Shoulders is the best-selling shampoo in China, despite fierce competition from lower-end local brands.[62]

Obviously, the cost of a short questionnaire or a few focus groups to determine the de facto decision maker in a given category is very easily justified considering the after-effects of a misguided segmentation – especially if it's meant for strategic applications such as brand positioning and future product development. Other than the segmentation sample, the fundamental parameter driving any segmentation solution is the variable or set of variables used to build the segments. Forty years after Russell Haley's groundbreaking 1968 article on »Benefit Segmentation,« benefits (or needs) are well established as the preferred segmentation dimension. At least that's true from the point of view of deep insight creation, simply because needs are the roots of consumer behavior: needs drive decision making, and understanding needs helps to develop relevant propositions. In this respect, needs are superior both to demographics and behavior (Figure 2.26).[63]

Having said that, it is important to acknowledge that there is almost always a conflict of interest when it comes to selecting the segmentation lens. Many users of segmentation solutions equate a good solution with a solution that enables them to identify segment members in the marketplace and to reach them easily through media or direct marketing. This is especially important for industries driven by personal relationships or direct interactions with their customers. An insurance company's sales agent may be able to grasp the key demographics and life stage of a potential policyholder quickly and adapt his pitch accordingly. But within the short time frame of a typical consultation, it is nearly impossible to assess the needs segment that same customer is in. The same goes for pharmaceutical sales agents trying to guess what type of physician they are dealing with. To select the right kind of sales pitch, the detailer would ideally want to know whether the physician is an experimental, a conventional, or a flexible prescriber of drugs, since such attitudinal factors largely determine their choice of drug. But it is next to impossible to glean such information from how a physician looks, dresses, and responds to a few simple questions. Using demographics as a proxy of needs can be the more pragmatic choice in such situations; for example, physicians who are in their late 50s now will typically have received their education and training around 1980 and hence will often be averse to treatments devised later – or at least depend on the sales representative to bridge the gap to drugs and treatments with which they are familiar.

Useful as they may be in time-constrained situations, the downside of demographics and other such descriptors is that they rarely correlate with needs. Consider this ex-

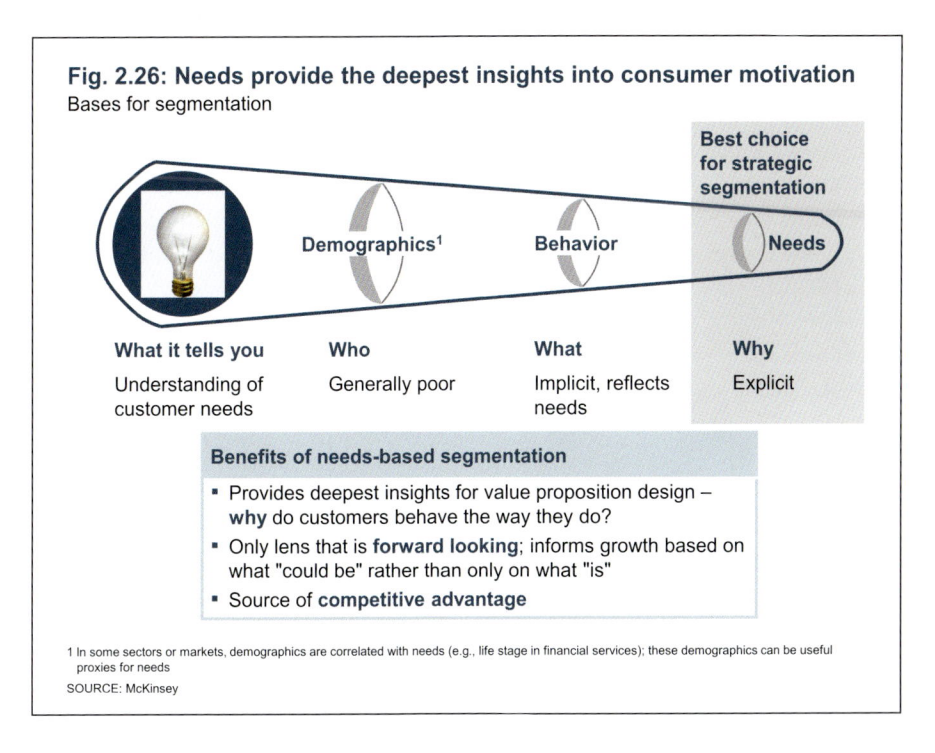

**Fig. 2.26: Needs provide the deepest insights into consumer motivation**
Bases for segmentation

|  | Demographics[1] | Behavior | Needs |
|---|---|---|---|
| **What it tells you** | **Who** | **What** | **Why** |
| Understanding of customer needs | Generally poor | Implicit, reflects needs | Explicit |

Best choice for strategic segmentation

**Benefits of needs-based segmentation**
- Provides deepest insights for value proposition design – **why** do customers behave the way they do?
- Only lens that is **forward looking**; informs growth based on what "could be" rather than only on what "is"
- Source of **competitive advantage**

[1] In some sectors or markets, demographics are correlated with needs (e.g., life stage in financial services); these demographics can be useful proxies for needs

SOURCE: McKinsey

ample: think of two British subjects, both male, both born in 1948, both in their second marriage, both affluent and from well-known families. The first is Charles, Prince of Wales, and the other is Ozzy Osbourne, Prince of Darkness. You can tell by their outfits and hairstyles alone that their purchasing behavior is probably pretty different despite the demographic similarities. So while demographics can be a helpful needs proxy in one situation (compare the example of the physician), they may be misleading in another.

Ultimately, the choice of segmentation lens in a given situation should be driven by the primary purpose of the segmentation: the more it is about developing the value proposition, the more the success of the solution depends on a deep understanding of the needs. Only insights at the needs level – the »Why?« of consumer decision making – will enable marketers to develop a superior value proposition, set the right price, make their products available in the right channels and create meaningful messages. If, however, the focus of the segmentation is to optimize the delivery of your value proposition – be it because of the nature of the industry or for other reasons – demographics, life stage, or, in B2B contexts, firmographics (such as number of employees or revenues) should feature prominently in your segmentation solution. At the very least, such external, easily observable factors should be used as profiling parameters to enable the sales team to derive insights into the needs of the person they are dealing with.[64]

To combine the advantages of insightful needs segmentation and more pragmatic demographic or behavioral approaches, there have been many attempts to create »dual objective« or »multi-lever« solutions. In some cases, this works surprisingly well, particularly when demographic or behavioral attributes themselves reflect latent needs. Take the example of a leading global manufacturer of consumer electronics. This company took its needs-based segmentation and added channel preference, primarily because that makes segment targeting much easier. Managers were astonished when they found that this step not only left the needs segments undamaged, but even improved their distinctiveness. It turned out that shoppers' choice of store actually reflected their latent needs: while bargain hunters would prefer Wal-Mart or Target, the more technically savvy buyers typically ended up at Best Buy or Circuit City. Despite such promising approaches, selecting the appropriate segmentation lens will have to remain a case-by-case decision reflecting the specific circumstances of the industry and market environment in which a given brand is operating.

### Segmentation should reflect that needs can vary with occasion

In many cases, ethnographic research and other deep-immersion techniques help researchers discover that needs can be highly dependent on the situation in which a product is purchased or used.[65] This is often the case in categories like food or apparel, since such products are used in a variety of different situations. For example, food can be consumed as a snack on the go, as a sit-down meal at home, or to cater to friends and family on special occasions. It goes without saying that one and the same person will have different food-related needs in these situations. Similarly, most people will have different demands on clothes worn to work, during a night out with friends, or on a quiet evening at home. In categories such as jewelry and fragrance, the principal question is whether someone is buying a treat for themselves or a gift for someone else. In such industries, state-of-the-art segmentation solutions should differentiate needs by occasions/situations, or »states« for short. This is especially true as the proliferation of brands, products, and channels, and the fragmentation of demand continues. Needs do not only differ from country to country, category to category, and customer to customer. Until recently, conservative buyers may have bought conservative brands through a conservative channel. But today, even the same person will have different needs in different purchasing or consumption situations. The same traveler will buy discounted flight tickets from a no-frills carrier for most short-haul travel, but will buy fully priced, fully flexible tickets from leading airlines for intercontinental or business flights. Buyers of apparel or furniture gladly mix budget with luxury. Compare the discussion of hybrid consumption above. Leading retailers such as H&M, Zara, or Ikea have recognized this development by complementing their portfolios with upmarket brands like Cos, Massimo Dutti, and Habitat respectively. To pick up on this kind of trend, state-of-the-art segmentations use states as a second dimension. Let's look at three cases in which differentiating needs by states led to far more practical insights:

**Fig. 2.27: Need states combine attitudes and needs in occasions worn**

RETAIL APPAREL EXAMPLE

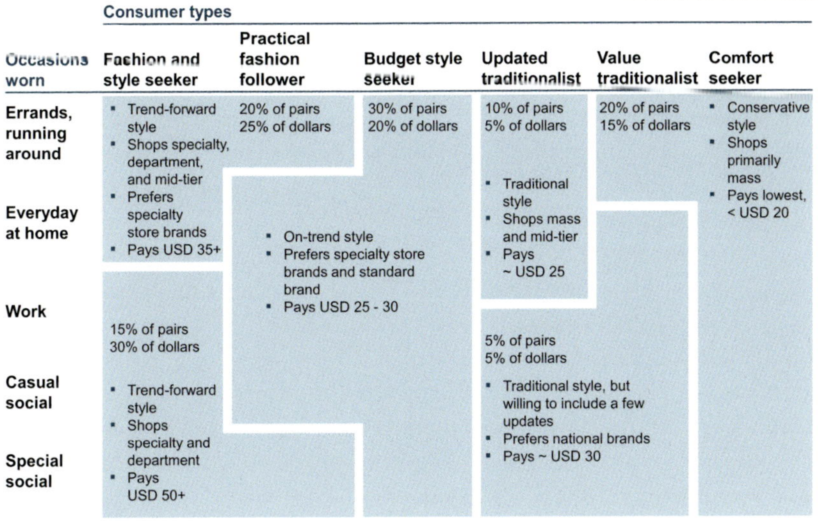

| Occasions worn | Consumer types |  |  |  |  |  |
|---|---|---|---|---|---|---|
|  | Fashion and style seeker | Practical fashion follower | Budget style seeker | Updated traditionalist | Value traditionalist | Comfort seeker |
| Errands, running around | • Trend-forward style<br>• Shops specialty, department, and mid-tier<br>• Prefers specialty store brands<br>• Pays USD 35+ | 20% of pairs<br>25% of dollars | 30% of pairs<br>20% of dollars<br><br>• On-trend style<br>• Prefers specialty store brands and standard brand<br>• Pays USD 25 - 30 | 10% of pairs<br>5% of dollars<br><br>• Traditional style<br>• Shops mass and mid-tier<br>• Pays ~ USD 25 | 20% of pairs<br>15% of dollars | • Conservative style<br>• Shops primarily mass<br>• Pays lowest, < USD 20 |
| Everyday at home |  |  |  |  |  |  |
| Work |  | 15% of pairs<br>30% of dollars |  | 5% of pairs<br>5% of dollars |  |  |
| Casual social |  | • Trend-forward style<br>• Shops specialty and department<br>• Pays USD 50+ |  | • Traditional style, but willing to include a few updates<br>• Prefers national brands<br>• Pays ~ USD 30 |  |  |
| Special social |  |  |  |  |  |  |

SOURCE: McKinsey

**Apparel.** A US-based manufacturer of jeans found that needs in its category are predominantly driven by whether a pair of jeans is worn at work, after work, or to go out at night (Figure 2.27). The company conducted a survey that included statements such as »When buying fashion for a special occasion, I am willing to spend more for a certain designer brand.« It turned out that the intended usage situation determines what people are looking for in terms of style, cut, material, and price point. They found the situation to be so important that there are hardly any overarching needs other than »good value for money.« Based on this insight, the company developed a segmentation that combines needs, or consumer types, with occasions worn. For example, while a dressy pair of jeans to wear for a »special social« occasion should be fashionable, form-fitting, and lightweight (and can be more expensive than others), a pair of jeans worn for gardening or running errands should be comfortably cut, durable, and comparatively low-price. That said, »fashionable« or »low-price« can, of course, still mean different things to different segments. In fact, the company used the segmentation to differentiate its multibrand portfolio in close cooperation with selected retail partners and to develop new products.

**Bakery.** An Italian manufacturer of wheat-based snacks found that consumer needs are primarily driven by consumers' eating habits: Are they looking for a balanced diet, for quick calorie intake, or for lots of tasty treats? But even within these needs segments, preferences vary so widely that the company found it needed an additional dimension to inform its brand portfolio management and product development (dependent factors range from salt, fat, and sugar content to package size and design). The relevant second dimension turned out to be purchasing occasion: Are consumers buying something to eat at work or on the go? Are they buying a snack or a main meal? Are they eating alone or with others?

**Beer.** An Eastern European brewery segmented beer drinkers by needs and attitudes and, predictably, came out with a range of segments based on varying mixtures of taste orientation, image benefit, and average beer intake. Unfortunately, the segments, such as the »taste enthusiasts,« the »beer patriots,« or the »brand loyalists« were blurry at best. Based on previous qualitative research, the brewery then added contextual factors as a second dimension: Are consumers drinking at home or in the pub? Alone or with others? If with others, with their spouse or their friends? If with others, on a regular basis or to celebrate a special occasion? This second dimension made the solution much more informative, especially to derive concrete actions for the marketing mix, such as in-store promotions versus tastings and brand advertising in pubs. While the use of drinking occasions as a second dimension is common practice, other companies in this industry work with even more general types as the primary dimension, such as value-based archetypes (traditionalists, social climbers, adventurers, etc.) instead of beer-related needs and attitudes.

### Phase III: Defining actions and implementing findings

The implementation challenge is threefold. First, you have to select the most promising target groups for your brand or brands. Second, you have to derive and monitor action plans to serve these segments; actions may range from brand (re)positioning to proposition development and channel mix optimization. Third, you have to make sure segmentation findings are communicated broadly and absorbed by the organization.

Roughly speaking, target segment selection should recognize two types of criteria: segment attractiveness, comprising factors such as size or volume and (potential) value, on the one hand, and segment accessibility – recognizing elements such as brand image fit, need fit, or switching probability – on the other. While attractiveness should be the same for all players in a given category, accessibility is determined by the specific positioning of your brand (or brands), including its current position as well as any potential to stretch or reposition the brand.

Once the target segments have been selected and profiled, it is time for action. Successful action planning is all about using insights generated by the segmentation to do things differently. Because the range of actions taken based on a strategic segmentation is so wide, let's look at two companies that have started doing things differently after major segmentation efforts.

**Convenience food.** A maker of precooked meals and other convenience foods selected »time-pressed cooks« as its new key target segment based on a needs-driven segmentation. These people enjoy cooking as a creative activity, wish they had more time to cook, and want products that reduce preparation time without limiting their creativity. To cater to these needs, the company stopped producing ready-to-eat precooked meals, prepared salads, and savory snacks. Instead, it started offering a wide range of semi-prepared ingredients to speed up the cooking process, like the prepared components many professional chefs use: sliced deli meats, washed and chopped vegetables, and ready-to-use marinades.

**Mobile telecommunications.** A mobile operator created a strategic segmentation of current and potential customers based on their needs (ranging from affordability focus to convenience focus) and their commitment level (prepaid versus flexible versus long-term contract). Having selected convenience-focused, heavy off-peak users as one of its key target groups, the company revamped its entire marketing mix based on the insights generated. Actions ranged from a tailor-made value proposition (e. g., attractive off-peak rates, 24/7 service promise, basic handset) to segment-based market share goal setting and monitoring to make sure the action plan was adhered to (Figure 2.28).

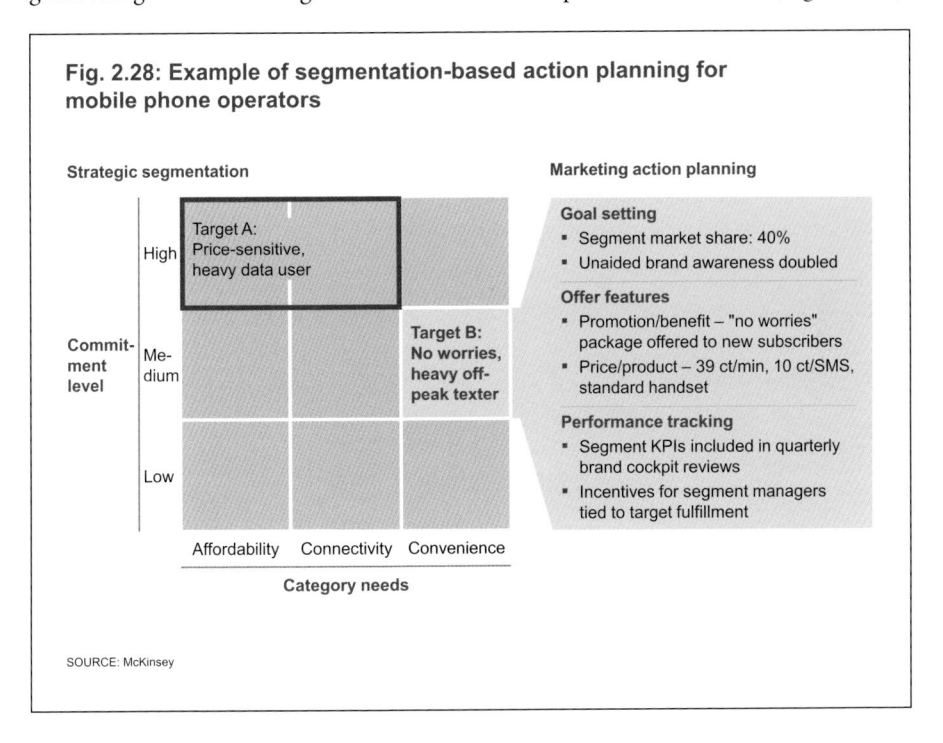

**Fig. 2.28: Example of segmentation-based action planning for mobile phone operators**

Strategic segmentation

Commitment level: High / Medium / Low
Category needs: Affordability, Connectivity, Convenience

Target A: Price-sensitive, heavy data user
Target B: No worries, heavy off-peak texter

Marketing action planning

Goal setting
- Segment market share: 40%
- Unaided brand awareness doubled

Offer features
- Promotion/benefit – "no worries" package offered to new subscribers
- Price/product – 39 ct/min, 10 ct/SMS, standard handset

Performance tracking
- Segment KPIs included in quarterly brand cockpit reviews
- Incentives for segment managers tied to target fulfillment

SOURCE: McKinsey

Using segmentation not only as a way of synthesizing insights and planning actions, but also as a tracking and controlling tool makes it even more powerful as a strategic platform. Having a strategic objective – be it brand image, market share, revenue growth, or subscriber adds – set and monitored for individual segments makes it much easier to derive targeted actions and track their effectiveness.

The third and final step to making sure segmentation insight leads to tangible business impact is to make target segments come to life for an audience beyond the actual segmentation team. To unleash the full power of a segmentation and transform the way your organization thinks about its customers, all marketing and sales staff and part of the product development staff need to be aware of what the target segments are, what they are like, and what they are looking for.

There is a wide range of creative approaches to bring segments to life. Examples include segment handbooks, »quick identifier« segment typing tools (tools that allow employees to determine a customer's segment membership from a narrow set of questions), and true-to-life segment experiences conveyed in movies, rooms, and role plays (Figure 2.29). A leading consumer goods company has created an »exploration and training ground« for marketing employees by renting a warehouse, setting up fake living areas, and training actors to stand in as segment representatives. Marketing staff circle through the various rooms and interview the actors to investigate their needs, determine their segment membership, and understand their brand preferences. In similar spirit, the customer insights team at General Mills has established what they refer to as Consumer Treks: »A key element in solving a pain point for consumers is in experiencing them yourselves. In an effort to supplement our quantitative approaches with increased consumer intimacy, we launched a new program last year called Consumer Treks. […] We announce a new Trek each month, tying an immersion experience to a specific consumer pain point or target. […] For example, we have asked our employees to live on a consumer's budget for a week, or shop at a bodega to experience shopping in an unfamiliar retail channel.«[66]

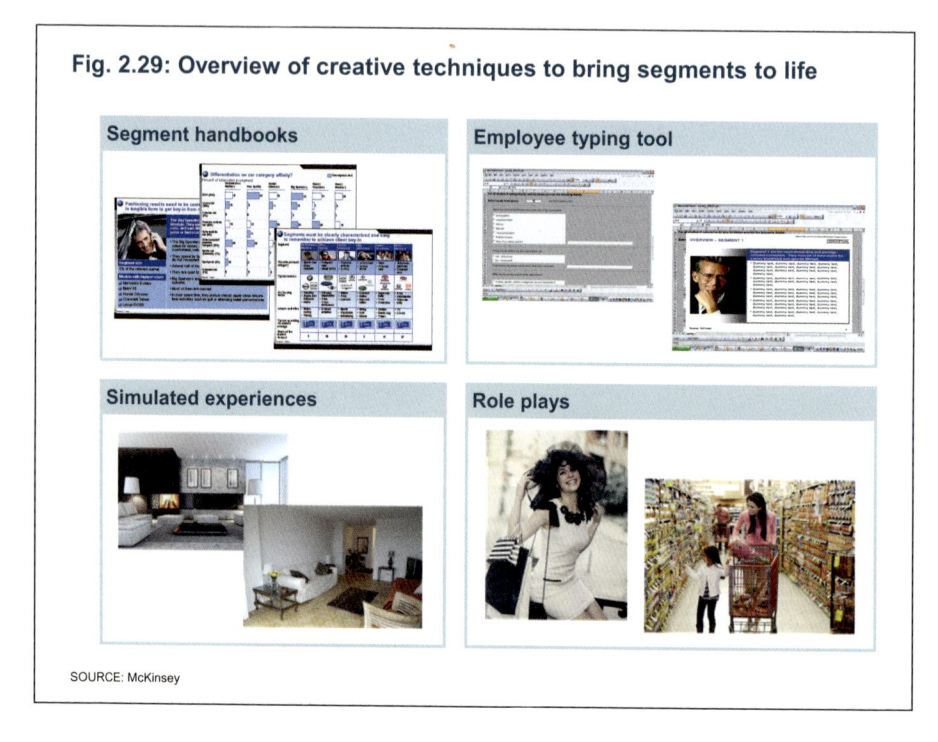

**Fig. 2.29: Overview of creative techniques to bring segments to life**

Segment handbooks

Employee typing tool

Simulated experiences

Role plays

SOURCE: McKinsey

## Characteristics of good segmentation

Segmentation is not an end in itself. It is a superior way to generate and integrate insights, and it provides a strategic platform for brand positioning and marketing action planning. Its ultimate purpose is to provide your brand with a more solid footing in the battle for customers. For segmentation to be successful in its execution, it needs to be both robust and practical. Even the most sophisticated segmentation is of little use if the resulting target groups are not embedded in the company's structures and processes. A robust and practical segmentation has the following characteristics:

- The segments are distinct from one another in terms of brand and product preferences.
- Segmentation provides evidence of untapped customer needs.
- The segments are reachable through the channels or media that matter in your business.
- The segment names relate clearly to the market, are easy to comprehend, and are limited in number to remain manageable.

So, what changes after you complete a strategic segmentation project in line with these criteria? Most people notice three things. First, the target segments are no longer only profiled by income, gender, and level of education. Instead they are defined based on customer needs in various situations and selected based on customer value. Second, the brand management and product marketing are already working on attractive propositions for the growth segments of the future. Third, everyone in the company – from the department manager to the front line – and at the lead agency can name the current target segments in their sleep. The result: from insight to impact.

## McKinsey's core beliefs about segmentation

A one-size-fits-all segmentation solution is impossible given the differences between industries, markets, and company structures. Jointly working out the objectives and general conditions lies at the heart of every segmentation project. Still, in our experience – since 2005, McKinsey has supported clients in all industries on more than 1,100 segmentation engagements worldwide – there is clearly a handful of »golden rules« that executives can apply to get better results. They have proved their merit in many different situations and serve as guidelines for developing tailored segmentation.

**Establish a clear hierarchy.** Use as few segmentations as possible. Build only one strategic segmentation in each major product category to drive value proposition development. The essential objectives of a strategic segmentation are the ability to manage the brand, product, and channel strategy. Additional, more granular segmentations for specific purposes – such as loyalty management or media planning – are admissible. Make sure that these additional segmentations are compatible with the strategic segmentation.

**Link choice of lens to segment objective.** Wherever possible, focus on customer needs to understand why they make the choices they do. The more segmentation is meant to inform value proposition development, the more it should use needs to build segments. The more it is about delivering the value proposition, the more important observable factors such as demographics and behavior will be, at least as profiling parameters. Although lens selection is a case-by-case decision, using needs and demographics as the two dimensions of a segmentation matrix is often the best solution.

**Embed results in the planning process.** Translate segmentation findings into action plans for each functional group, simplifying the communication as needed. It is vital to anchor the results of the segmentation in the marketing planning and controlling processes. This is especially true for the prioritized target segments and for the activities and campaigns developed. Segment targets such as market share objectives should be monitored and incorporated into the performance target agreements of the responsible employees. Try to simplify the solution as much as possible for communication purposes and make sure segments come to life in profiles and handbooks.

---

**Fact-based customer targeting in telecommunications**

Let's look at an example to illustrate how insights-driven market segmentation can shape the marketing mix, enable competitive differentiation, and create value for companies. A telecom operator, formerly the state-owned monopolist, faced increasing competition in a deregulated market that was forecast to grow very slowly if at all over the course of the next five years. Most recently, the government had authorized the establishment of mobile virtual network operators (MVNOs), which were expected to increase competition for mobile users dramatically. To make things worse, the company's standing was already weak among part of the population. While the company was the first choice for the majority of the adult population, only about one in three younger users had committed to the brand as their main provider. The marketing department, however, was unclear about the root causes of this relative weakness among younger users.

To get to the bottom of this issue and prepare the company for the imminent increase in competition, the company decided to conduct segmentation based on user attitudes in areas including communications, entertainment, and lifestyle, rather than just based on demographics. Using statements such as »I am willing to pay more for a well-established brand,« »I need to get access to the Internet everywhere,« or »I prefer a brand that is for young, modern, fashionable people,« three main target groups were identified (Figure 2.30):

- *Pragmatic professionals.* Most of these customers travel frequently, but they only use basic telephony. They are extremely price sensitive, especially regarding roaming fees.
- *Smart onliners.* These young locals are constantly looking for the best deal to accommodate their heavy data traffic at reasonable prices.
- *Affluent locals.* These users have an above-average income, low price sensitivity, and care a lot about the latest handset as a lifestyle accessory.

While the company's existing positioning and product portfolio was closest to the needs of pragmatic professionals, their value propositions to the other two target segments were less pronounced. In response to these findings, the company took triple action:

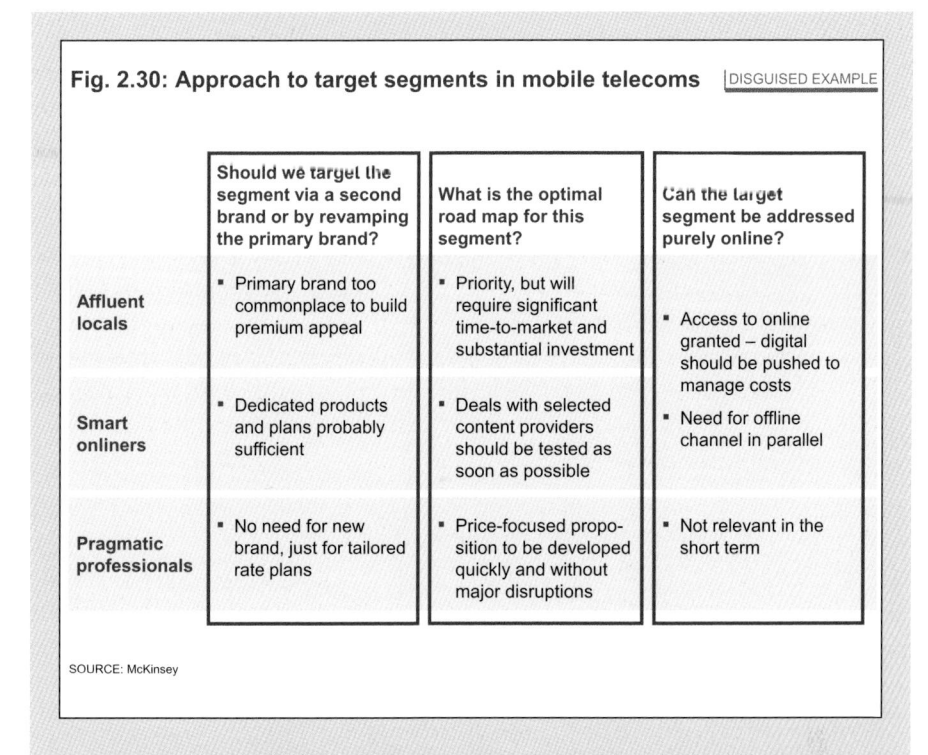

**Fig. 2.30: Approach to target segments in mobile telecoms**  DISGUISED EXAMPLE

|  | Should we target the segment via a second brand or by revamping the primary brand? | What is the optimal road map for this segment? | Can the target segment be addressed purely online? |
|---|---|---|---|
| Affluent locals | • Primary brand too commonplace to build premium appeal | • Priority, but will require significant time-to-market and substantial investment | • Access to online granted – digital should be pushed to manage costs |
| Smart onliners | • Dedicated products and plans probably sufficient | • Deals with selected content providers should be tested as soon as possible | • Need for offline channel in parallel |
| Pragmatic professionals | • No need for new brand, just for tailored rate plans | • Price-focused proposition to be developed quickly and without major disruptions | • Not relevant in the short term |

SOURCE: McKinsey

- *Fine-tune roaming costs* for pragmatic professionals. The option to pay a moderate monthly fee to get a substantial discount on all international calls was introduced.
- *Introduce new services* for smart onliners. Tailor-made products were created, for example, subscriptions to preferred types of content, such as music or games.
- *Launch new brand* for affluent locals. To provide the exclusivity valued by these users, the company is preparing to launch a second fully differentiated brand.

While the launch of the second brand was still in progress at the time of writing, the new rates and services had already been introduced. Ever since these actions took effect, the company has seen a rapid rise in new postpaid contracts, fewer contract cancellation requests, and less migration from postpaid to prepaid rate structures.

The company has recently expanded the focus of its mobile broadband data offerings and introduced product bundles for fixed and mobile services. Segmentation techniques similar to those outlined above have been applied to this growing playing field as a basis for further targeted propositions.

### Big Data: McKinsey Consumer Marketing Analytics Center (CMAC)

Direct customer relationships are a privilege, but they also generate massive amounts of data. This wealth of information holds the potential to drive real frontline differentiation, if companies have the right tools and approaches to make the most of this unique asset.

In response, McKinsey has founded the Consumer Marketing Analytics Center (CMAC) with the objective to leverage advanced analytics on »big data« to make better business decisions (Figure 2.31). CMAC is a network of global experts anchored by a growing number of regional hubs and accessible to teams at McKinsey's 100 global offices. It also includes the full range of required enablers – such as hardware, software, and intellectual property (e.g., algorithms, tools, processes) – to operate along the entire value chain of data analytics. If they wish, clients can outsource their entire analytics work to McKinsey. The offerings of CMAC are organized in service lines focusing on specific content areas – such as customer life cycle management, pricing, marketing mix modeling – or specific industries – for example, telecommunication, banking, retail. CMAC is designed to absorb data from a host of sources, whether client transaction records, third-party research, or proprietary social media screening. This ever-growing data pool is subject to an advanced analytical engine that draws from the latest insights mining techniques, predictive modeling, and industry-specific business rules. CMAC is not a temporary project, but the backbone of an initiative that is built to last and create impact for clients in three respects:

- Generate and integrate big data across touch points
- Derive and synthesize commercially relevant insights
- Empower executives to use insights for more informed daily decisions.

CMAC translates these success factors into an integrated approach to sustainable data-driven value creation; it comprises diagnosis, optimization, and transformation. A growing global team of dedicated affiliates has successfully brought CMAC methodology to retail clients in DIY, apparel, and grocery, covering hands-on marketing topics from category management to pricing and promotions.

One of the most prominent CMAC tools is what we call the Insights Factory, an integrated toolkit that generates new insights from existing client and third-party data, lends decision support to executives, and monitors business performance. The Insights Factory includes a category-level Localization Scorecard that helps companies tailor their propositions to regional needs. The Pricing Module integrates historical data, competitive analyses, and information on the impact of a given item on overall price perception. Based on this data, the tool calculates the optimal retail price. It can also pinpoint specific SKUs for value-maximizing promotions.

Specific tools we use to help companies include the CMAC Heatmap and a five-step improvement program. The Heatmap (Figure 2.32, example for retail) enables companies to gauge their performance at all intersections of relevant data sources, such as loyalty cards, and business levers, such as repeat purchase rate. Based on these diagnostic insights, companies can embark on a systematic improvement program to transform their marketing paradigm from product centricity to consumer centricity.[67]

2.2 From Insight to Impact: Customer Insights and Segmentation for Better Brand Management   129

**Fig. 2.31: The missing link**

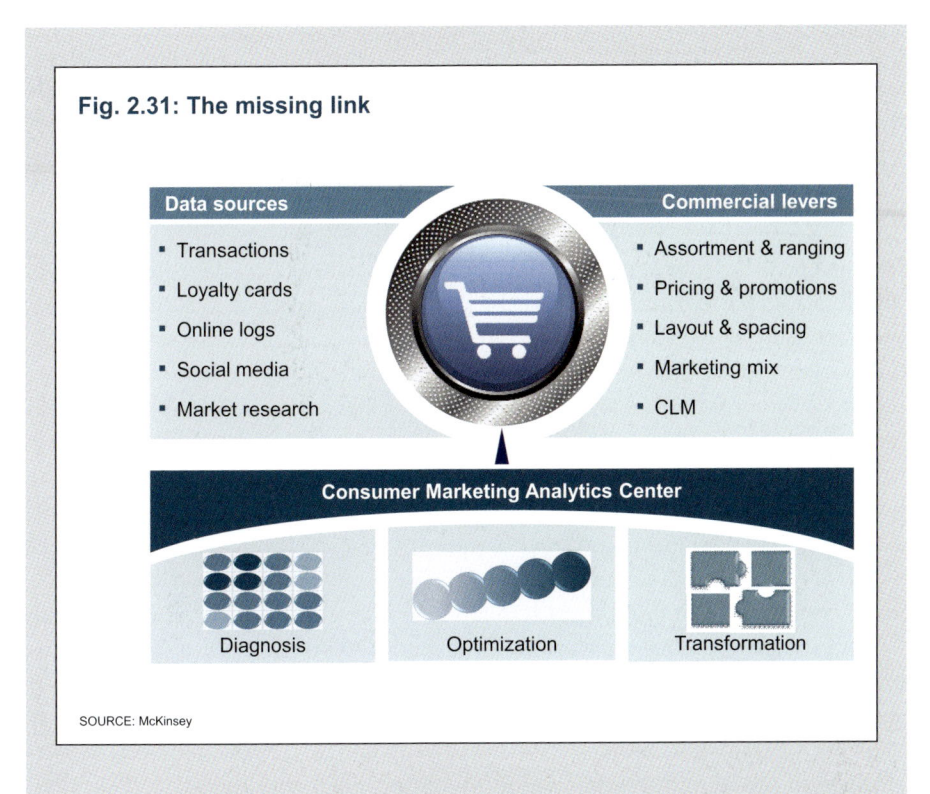

**Data sources**
- Transactions
- Loyalty cards
- Online logs
- Social media
- Market research

**Commercial levers**
- Assortment & ranging
- Pricing & promotions
- Layout & spacing
- Marketing mix
- CLM

**Consumer Marketing Analytics Center**
- Diagnosis
- Optimization
- Transformation

SOURCE: McKinsey

**Fig. 2.32: The heatmap**

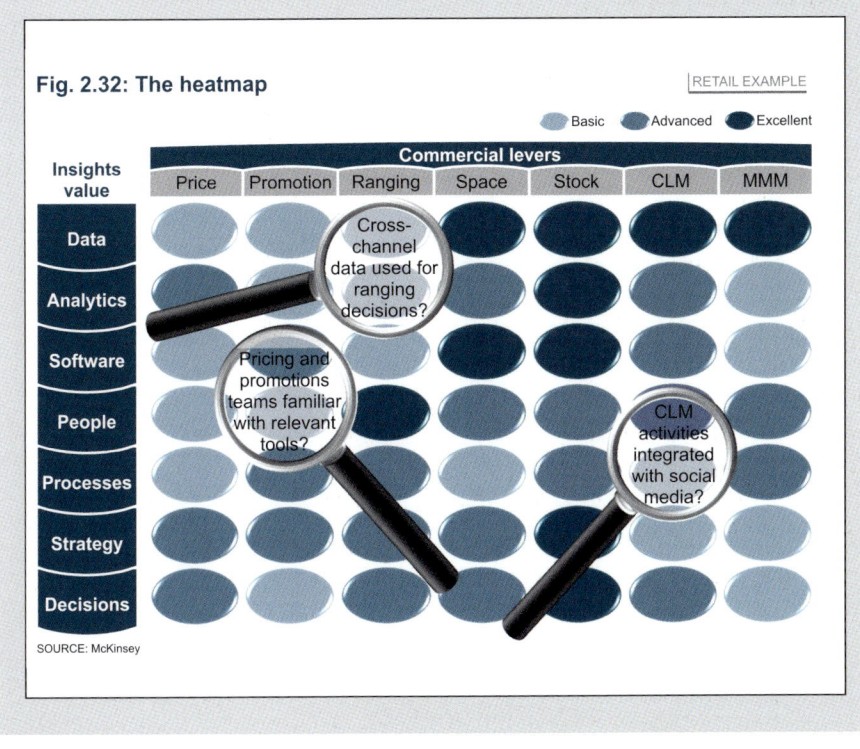

RETAIL EXAMPLE

Basic ● Advanced ● Excellent

Insights value (rows): Data, Analytics, Software, People, Processes, Strategy, Decisions

Commercial levers (columns): Price, Promotion, Ranging, Space, Stock, CLM, MMM

- Cross-channel data used for ranging decisions?
- Pricing and promotions teams familiar with relevant tools?
- CLM activities integrated with social media?

SOURCE: McKinsey

## 2.3 The Brand Purchase Funnel

The crucial question that needs to be answered in quantifying the performance of the brand is how the brand image and consumer attitude influence purchase behavior. These aspects can be quantitatively measured and assessed; this is the core of Brand-Matics®.

Establishing a correlation between the brand image and the attitudes and behavior of consumers is vital in successfully developing and managing brands. But brand managers often underestimate this aspect. In many cases, awareness of brands and global image value remain the exclusive indicators of brand success. These two criteria are even reflected in the business targets of the senior management of many top companies, despite the fact that neither brand awareness nor global image value says anything about the actual economic success of the brand (with the exception of certain brand value analysis approaches that reflect both brand strength and financial performance). As an additional indicator of brand performance, advertising recall has been widely used for some time now. However, this is chiefly due to the fact that it can be easily measured and is being widely offered by tracking agencies. Yet recall is not directly tied to bottom-line impact either. Despite the proven effect of creative advertising (see Chapter 1, Section 1.2), a popular television commercial, an eye-catching billboard poster, or a celebrated social media campaign does not necessarily drive sales.

### Measuring brand performance using the brand purchase funnel

A brand's impact on behavior can be measured using the brand purchase funnel (also referred to here as the brand funnel). The funnel structure is based on the AIDA model (Attention, Interest, Desire, Action) from the realm of behavioral science. It typically represents the purchase process in five idealized stages:

1. What percentage of the target group is aware of the brand?
2. What percentage is familiar with its products and services?
3. What percentage is considering the brand for purchase?
4. What percentage has already purchased the brand at least once?
5. What percentage would purchase it again or recommend it to others?

Strong brands tend to be successful at all stages: they achieve a high degree of awareness, are included in the consideration set, are purchased, and finally convert buyers into loyal customers. The last two stages of the brand funnel are crucial; this is where consumer behavior has a direct impact on the level of sales and earnings.

In order to measure the performance of a brand in the brand funnel, market research data on consumer behavior is collected at each stage. Using this data, it is possible to calculate the respective number of customers the brand retains from stage to stage. Figure 2.33 illustrates the schematic operation of the brand funnel in the automobile industry.

**Fig. 2.33: Applying the brand funnel to cars**

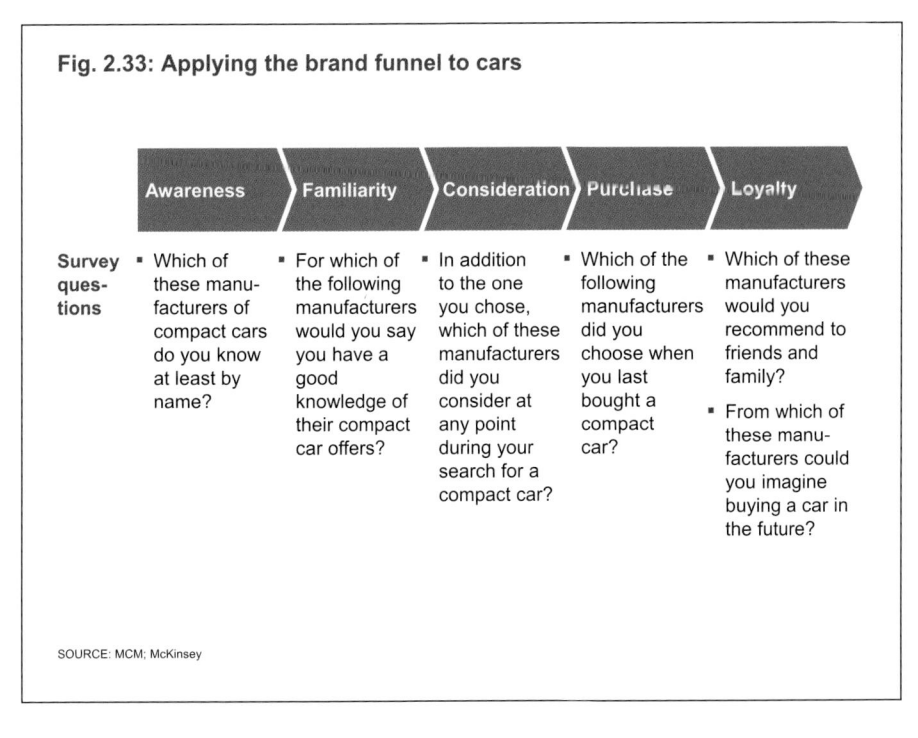

| | Awareness | Familiarity | Consideration | Purchase | Loyalty |
|---|---|---|---|---|---|
| Survey questions | Which of these manufacturers of compact cars do you know at least by name? | For which of the following manufacturers would you say you have a good knowledge of their compact car offers? | In addition to the one you chose, which of these manufacturers did you consider at any point during your search for a compact car? | Which of the following manufacturers did you choose when you last bought a compact car? | Which of these manufacturers would you recommend to friends and family?<br><br>From which of these manufacturers could you imagine buying a car in the future? |

SOURCE: MCM; McKinsey

In principle, the brand funnel can be applied to any B2B or B2C market – and to physical products as well as to services – though it will need to be adapted to the industry segment under investigation. The number and structure of the stages will vary by industry. It is useful to look at a number of examples to see how this can be done. For fast-moving consumer goods – such as candy bars, shampoo, or mineral water – the »will consider« stage can be replaced or supplemented by »trial (purchase).« In this way, occasional purchases of the products can be reflected accurately, since these are important to the brand. For financial investments, the stages of »ownership« or »contract« and »main investment« (declared loyalty) would be integrated into the final stages of the purchase funnel. When applying the purchase funnel to the retail domain, the first stages would include »visiting the shop« or »visiting the store department.« The brand funnel can even be employed in non-business environments, for instance, in analyzing commitment to political parties. In this case, the final »purchase« and »repeat purchase« stages of the funnel would be replaced by »have voted for« and »will vote for again.«

Due to its broad foundation in behavioral science, purchase funnel analysis has been applied in marketing practice for a considerable time and is now a well-accepted tool for nearly all agencies and management consulting firms. In fact, many companies have implemented brand purchase funnel measurement as a permanent diagnostic tool in the form of software solutions – such as the McKinsey Brand Navigator – in which key indicators are updated as new market research becomes available; compare the insert in Chapter 4, Section 4.5. Such applications enable brand managers to track the impact of their decisions over extended periods of time.

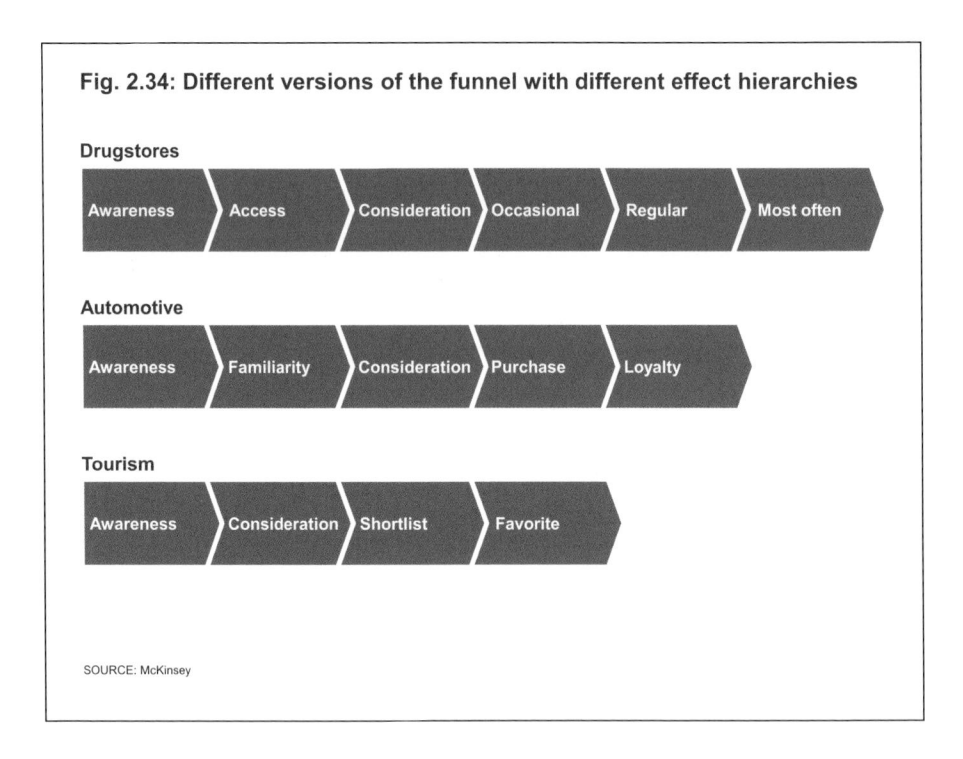

**Fig. 2.34: Different versions of the funnel with different effect hierarchies**

**Drugstores**

Awareness › Access › Consideration › Occasional › Regular › Most often

**Automotive**

Awareness › Familiarity › Consideration › Purchase › Loyalty

**Tourism**

Awareness › Consideration › Shortlist › Favorite

SOURCE: McKinsey

It is important to note that, despite fundamental similarities, the approaches often differ in the number of stages that are included in the funnel. This is an important distinction, because the number of stages determines the »effect hierarchy« that is under investigation in a given case (Figure 2.34):

- Most companies use the classical version of the brand purchase funnel as outlined above. It comprises five stages: awareness, familiarity, consideration, purchase, loyalty. The names of the stages can vary. For example, »loyalty« is often rendered as »repurchase.«
- In some cases, a more granular analysis of brand performance is needed. For example, retailers often use a six-stage funnel: awareness, accessibility (i.e., is there a store in my neighborhood?), consideration, occasional purchase, regular purchase, most often (or preferred) purchase.
- For certain purposes, fewer than five stages are sufficient. When examining the relative performance of competing tourist destinations, for example, four stages are common: awareness, consideration, shortlist, favorite destination.

When they are first confronted with the purchase funnel, many users concentrate only on the absolute values of the stages, although this can be highly misleading. Especially high absolute values in the early stages, such as awareness or familiarity, can be »bought« through advertising. More important from a management point of view are the conversion or transfer rates, which can be derived from the absolute values of the process stages. These indicate at which points in the purchase process a brand loses potential customers, thus revealing bottlenecks in the purchase process. By making

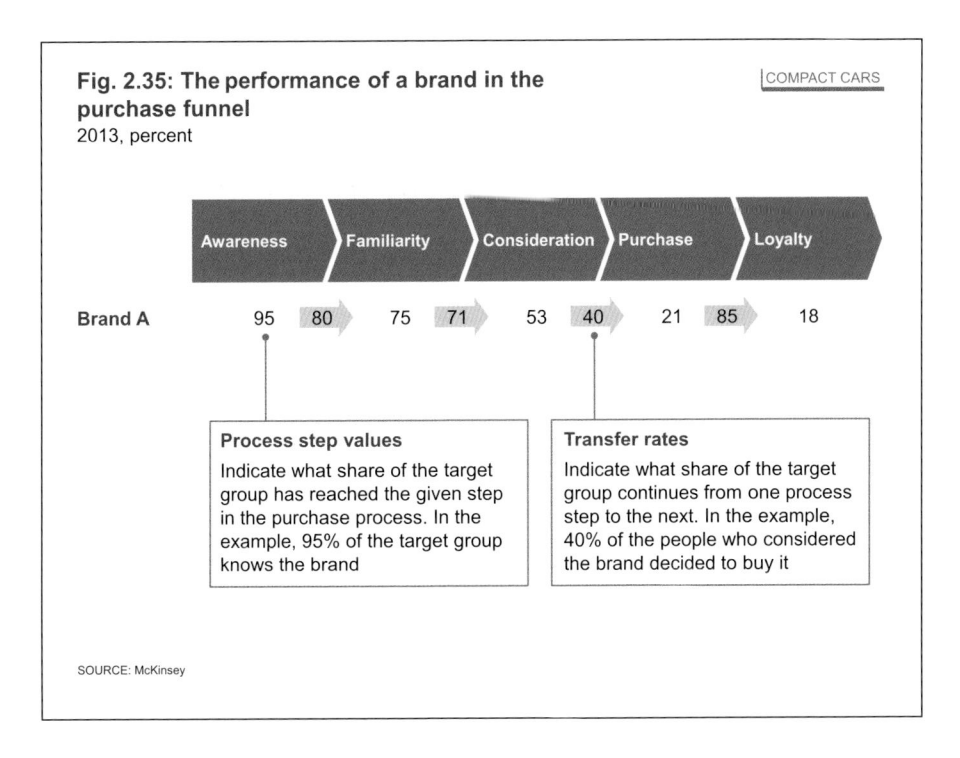

**Fig. 2.35: The performance of a brand in the purchase funnel**
2013, percent

COMPACT CARS

| | Awareness | | Familiarity | | Consideration | | Purchase | | Loyalty |
|---|---|---|---|---|---|---|---|---|---|
| Brand A | 95 | 80 | 75 | 71 | 53 | 40 | 21 | 85 | 18 |

**Process step values**
Indicate what share of the target group has reached the given step in the purchase process. In the example, 95% of the target group knows the brand

**Transfer rates**
Indicate what share of the target group continues from one process step to the next. In the example, 40% of the people who considered the brand decided to buy it

SOURCE: McKinsey

management aware of weak points in the brand's performance, funnel analysis helps to focus investment on the most effective brand drivers (as discussed in the next chapter).

This interrelationship is illustrated using the example of the performance of a brand in the compact car category (Figure 2.35); the survey was conducted independently in a European market in late 2013 and early 2014.[68] Some 95 percent of respondents were aware of the brand in this category. As expected, at each successive stage of the purchase funnel the brand lost (potential) customers. Ultimately, 18 percent of those surveyed remained loyal customers. At first sight, this may appear to be a low level of customer loyalty.

It is hard to interpret these figures meaningfully, however, until they are compared with another car brand. A comparison with a competing brand confirms that the loyalty rate of brand A is in fact very respectable. It is three times that of brand B, chiefly because brand A is so successful at converting familiarity into consideration – with an edge of 25 percentage points over brand B – and consideration into purchase (Figure 2.36). When it comes to purchase generation, however, brand B has an even more serious performance gap. Whereas brand A converts a full 40 percent of considerers to the »purchase« stage, brand B only achieves a conversion rate of 28 percent. From this, it is clear that brand A was significantly more successful than brand B in turning potential compact car customers into actual buyers.

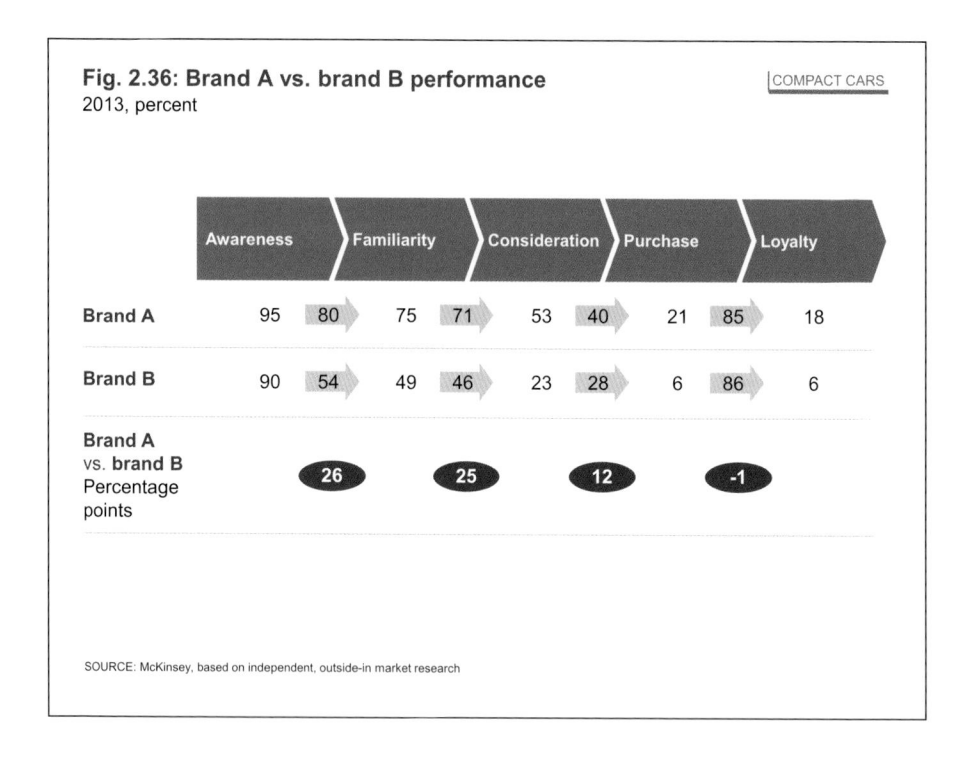

### Fig. 2.36: Brand A vs. brand B performance
2013, percent — COMPACT CARS

| | Awareness | | Familiarity | | Consideration | | Purchase | | Loyalty |
|---|---|---|---|---|---|---|---|---|---|
| Brand A | 95 | 80 | 75 | 71 | 53 | 40 | 21 | 85 | 18 |
| Brand B | 90 | 54 | 49 | 46 | 23 | 28 | 6 | 86 | 6 |
| Brand A vs. brand B Percentage points | | 26 | | 25 | | 12 | | -1 | |

SOURCE: McKinsey, based on independent, outside-in market research

### Example brand purchase funnel applications

The funnel is not limited to specific industries in principle, or even to physical products. If something is branded – be it a product, a service, or an experience – the funnel can be used to measure the performance of the brand in question. While consumer goods have long been a brand-driven industry, brand relevance is currently on the rise in service categories, such as consumer banking and energy; compare Section 2.1 in this chapter. And increasingly, companies in these industries are turning to experts for advice on brand performance measurement and fact-based brand optimization. That said, certain industries call for a more in-depth analysis of different customer groups than the traditional brand funnel allows for. For example, brands operating in categories driven by impulse purchases may want to differentiate between habitual buyers – who always choose from a narrow set of brands – and spontaneous buyers – who will readily try out a brand they know next to nothing about.

Figure 2.37 shows how the funnel can be adapted to the energy market. Although energy – a contractual category as opposed to product categories, such as cars or candy bars – does require some adjustments in the way the questions are phrased, the funnel stages as such are no less applicable. While candy bars are typically purchased at a store in the narrow sense of the word, purchasing insurance or energy is equivalent to signing a contract with a provider. Note that »loyalty« in the energy example is defined to include the intention to recommend the brand to friends or to sign a contract with the provider in the future.

Fig. 2.37: Applying the brand funnel to energy

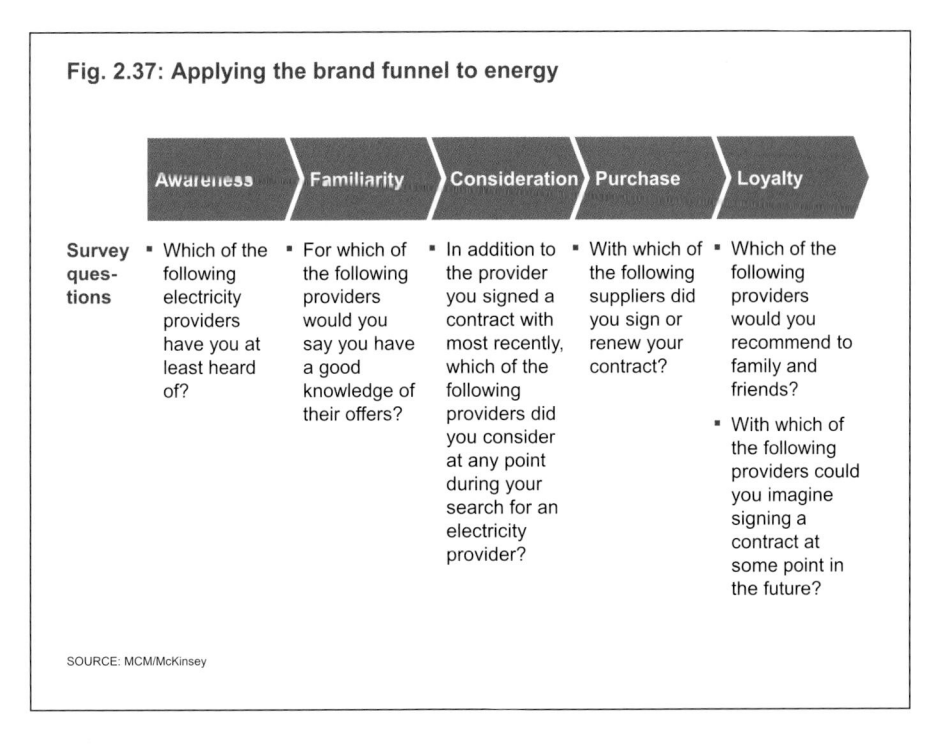

| | Awareness | Familiarity | Consideration | Purchase | Loyalty |
|---|---|---|---|---|---|
| Survey questions | Which of the following electricity providers have you at least heard of? | For which of the following providers would you say you have a good knowledge of their offers? | In addition to the provider you signed a contract with most recently, which of the following providers did you consider at any point during your search for an electricity provider? | With which of the following suppliers did you sign or renew your contract? | Which of the following providers would you recommend to family and friends?<br><br>With which of the following providers could you imagine signing a contract at some point in the future? |

SOURCE: MCM/McKinsey

Figure 2.38 shows the relative performance of Provider 1 versus Provider 2 in a European national energy market; the survey was conducted independently in early 2014.[69] At first sight, these two brands are at very similar levels of brand performance, reflecting their market positions as the country's leading energy providers. More than 90 percent of switchers are aware of both brands. They achieve very similar purchase rates and identical levels of loyalty. When we look at the transfer rates, however, it becomes apparent that Provider 1 is particularly successful at converting consideration into purchase, while Provider 2 outperforms Provider 1 on all other transfers, if only by relatively narrow margins.

Figure 2.39 shows another real-life example of brand funnel research, in this case conducted in the German drugstore market in 2012 as an independent, outside-in survey. It shows that dm and Rossmann achieve the same brand strength throughout the early stages of the funnel from awareness all the way to occasional purchase. Further down the line, however, dm pulls away from its rival Rossmann. For a third of all consumers in the sample, dm is the drugstore at which they shop »most often,« compared with about a fifth for whom Rossmann is the default drugstore. This gap is all the more remarkable in light of Rossmann's slightly larger store network comprising some 1,600 outlets, compared with only about 1,250 for dm (at the time when the research was conducted). In order to close this performance gap, Rossmann would need to focus on building loyalty rather than awareness.

A further example of the flexibility of the brand purchase funnel is demonstrated in its use in assessing competing tourist destinations (Figure 2. 40). A market research study

## 2. Measuring Brands

**Fig. 2.38: Provider 1 vs. provider 2 performance**
2013, percent
[ENERGY]

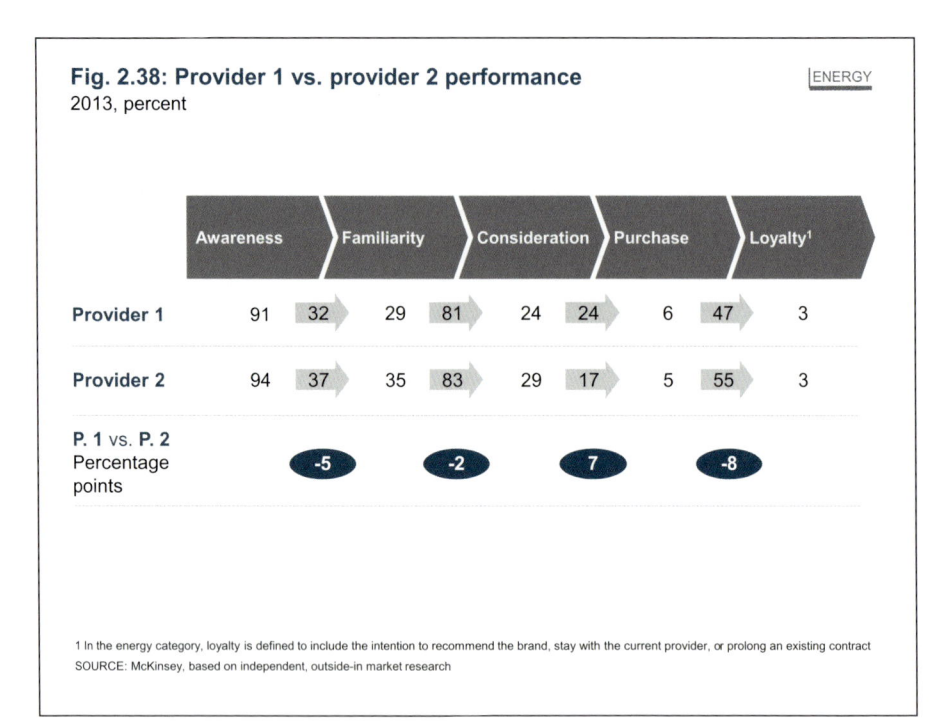

| | Awareness | | Familiarity | | Consideration | | Purchase | | Loyalty[1] |
|---|---|---|---|---|---|---|---|---|---|
| **Provider 1** | 91 | 32 | 29 | 81 | 24 | 24 | 6 | 47 | 3 |
| **Provider 2** | 94 | 37 | 35 | 83 | 29 | 17 | 5 | 55 | 3 |
| **P. 1 vs. P. 2 Percentage points** | | -5 | | -2 | | 7 | | -8 | |

1 In the energy category, loyalty is defined to include the intention to recommend the brand, stay with the current provider, or prolong an existing contract
SOURCE: McKinsey, based on independent, outside-in market research

---

**Fig. 2.39: Performance of competing retail brands**
Percent (n = 982)
[DRUGSTORES, GERMANY]

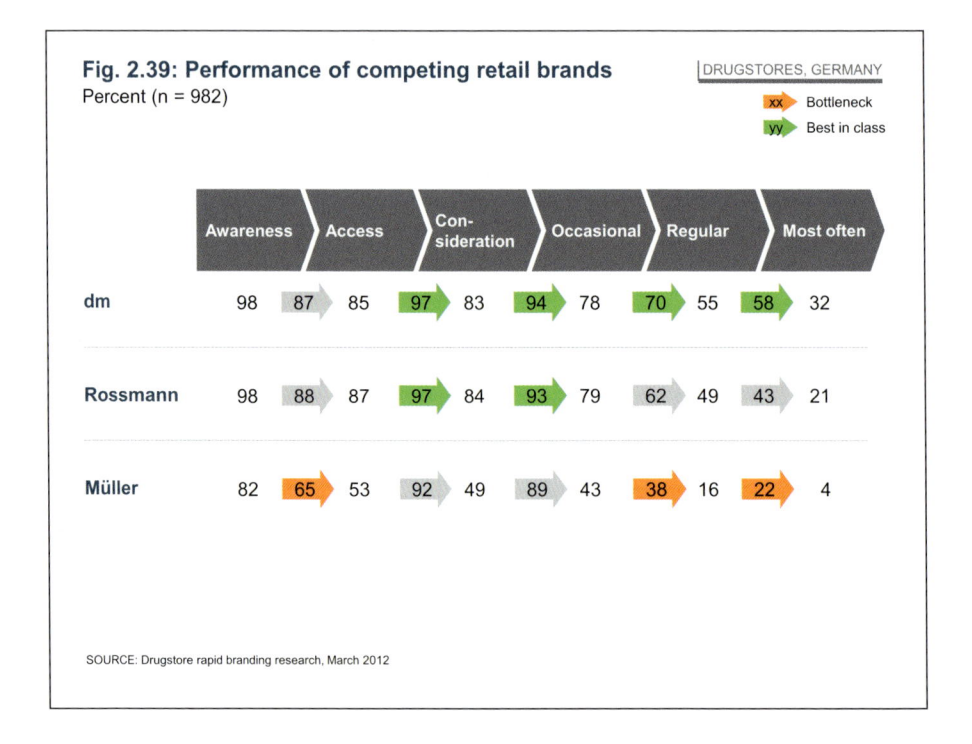

xx▶ Bottleneck
yy▶ Best in class

| | Awareness | | Access | | Con-sideration | | Occasional | | Regular | | Most often |
|---|---|---|---|---|---|---|---|---|---|---|---|
| **dm** | 98 | 87 | 85 | 97 | 83 | 94 | 78 | 70 | 55 | 58 | 32 |
| **Rossmann** | 98 | 88 | 87 | 97 | 84 | 93 | 79 | 62 | 49 | 43 | 21 |
| **Müller** | 82 | 65 | 53 | 92 | 49 | 89 | 43 | 38 | 16 | 22 | 4 |

SOURCE: Drugstore rapid branding research, March 2012

carried out in Germany examined the various stages of the purchase funnel for holiday destinations in Austria and Switzerland. This analysis showed that, for German tourists, Austrian destinations were well ahead of Swiss ones. The major reason why is found in the front end of the purchasing funnel. In response to the question, »Do you know any Austrian tourist destinations?«, percent of those surveyed answered »yes,« while only 58 percent said they knew Swiss ones. Similarly, the conversion rate from »awareness« to »consideration« was 11 percentage points higher for Austria as a destination than for Switzerland. At the time, experts agreed that Switzerland would need to invest in its tourism marketing in order to build familiarity with its destinations and catch up with Austria. One interesting aspect of the analysis is that it shows comparatively high loyalty rates for those who have already visited Swiss holiday destinations. In other words, once tourists get to Switzerland, they enjoy the experience and are likely to come back. So-called taster offers to drive »sampling« of Switzerland as a holiday destination might therefore help the country to secure a bigger slice of the German tourism pie. A few years later, Switzerland launched a tourism campaign that press reports describe as »the most expensive summer campaign of all time.« Observers estimate that Switzerland invested CHF 60 million to boost its popularity abroad. One of the headline topics of the campaign was »Tales of the city,« an attempt to familiarize potential visitors with two dozen destinations. The campaign cuts across media and now includes an interactive electronic brochure that highlights breakfast spots, shopping tips, cultural attractions, and weekend getaways.[70]

**Additions to the brand purchase funnel[71]**

The funnel as presented above has been widely established for some time now as the default method for comprehensive brand performance measurement. It is widely used across industries and companies – both in B2C and B2B environments – to assess and optimize the performance of brands relative to their competitors. In our own practice, we have seen the brand purchase funnel applied to all kinds of brand management decisions in industries that include consumer goods, retail, automotive, telecommunications, personal finance, and professional services.

We are in continuous contact with those who apply BrandMatics® in their daily work, with leading academics, and experienced market research experts.[72] Since the last edition of *Power Brands* was published in 2009, we have observed a number of structural changes in the way brands are perceived and developed:

- **Consumer behavior.** Consumers are more flexible, more educated, and more resourceful than they used to be when it comes to brand assessment, purchase decisions, and recommendations. They often take unexpected short cuts and side steps in their decision journeys. Sometimes they skip a step, revisit an earlier stage of their deliberation, or, on occasion, even circle back on themselves.[73]
- **Digital tools.** Online platforms and mobile applications are facilitating and accelerating consumer decision making, from information gathering to customized comparisons of products, features, and prices. Examples include online peer review por-

**Fig. 2.40: Switzerland vs. Austria**
2005, percent

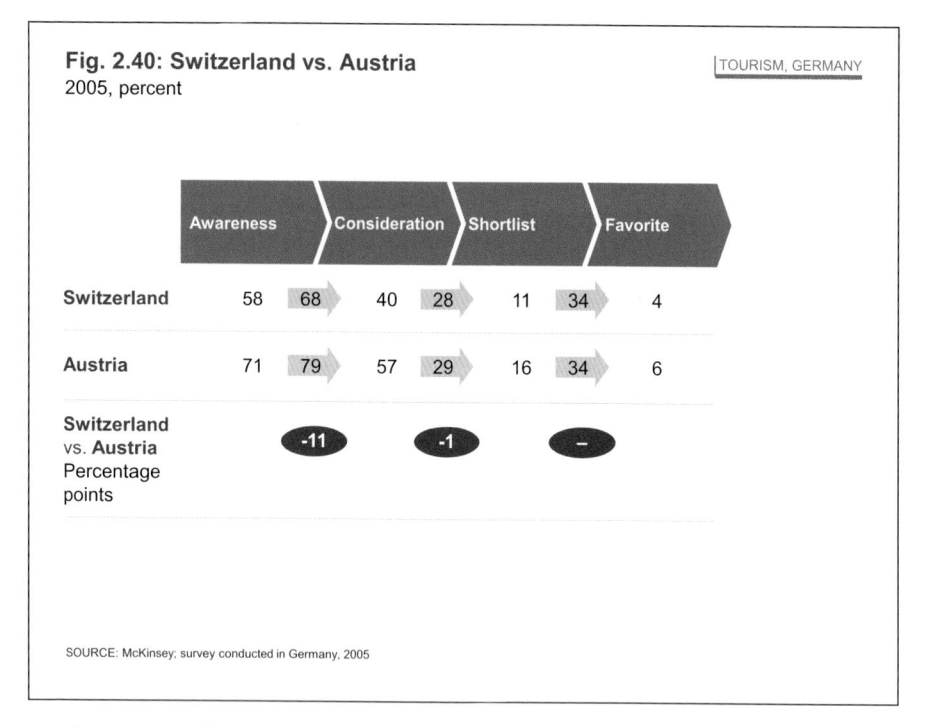

TOURISM, GERMANY

| | Awareness | | Consideration | | Shortlist | | Favorite |
|---|---|---|---|---|---|---|---|
| Switzerland | 58 | 68 | 40 | 28 | 11 | 34 | 4 |
| Austria | 71 | 79 | 57 | 29 | 16 | 34 | 6 |
| Switzerland vs. Austria Percentage points | | -11 | | -1 | | – | |

SOURCE: McKinsey; survey conducted in Germany, 2005

tals, automated prize comparison sites, or mobile applications that allow for last-minute comparison shopping in stores.
- **Industry dynamics.** A new generation of power brands – from Amazon and Google to Facebook and Twitter – is rewriting the rules for consumer decision making, and many of these players are integrating IT-enabled consideration sets with their very business models. Examples include Amazon's recommendation engine (see Chapter 4) and Google Shopping (formerly Google Product Search).[74]

To present the companies most affected by these changes with an alternative to the traditional funnel, we have developed two optional add-ons (Figure 2.41). While the proven purchase funnel – including the calculation of transfer rates and brand drivers – remains unchanged and fully compatible with existing applications, we have made two additions that companies can deploy if and when they are needed.

First, we have introduced a differentiation between »initial purchase« and »repeat purchase.« Initial purchasers, or *new customers*, are defined as those who have never bought a product or service from the brand in question before. In contrast, repeat purchasers, or *prior customers*, are defined as those who have already bought products or services from the brand in question. This differentiation is especially relevant for companies aspiring to develop fact-based strategies for customer lifetime management, that is, to attract new customers effectively, as well as to detect, understand, and prevent customer churn. In general, the differentiation provides two benefits:

- An explicit distinction between intended, or psychographic, loyalty (»I will buy again,« »I will stay with my provider,« or »I will recommend this brand to others«) and actual or behavioral loyalty (»I have bought this brand before«).

- The opportunity to perform brand driver analysis and other such deep dives for new customers and prior customers separately – and to derive tailor-made actions for new customer acquisition on the one hand and customer retention on the other.

In effect, we are applying the proven differentiation between »stated« and »observed« behavior to a new area of brand performance measurement. Previously, this differentiation was only applied to what customers value – for example, quality, innovation, design, or value for money. Now it can also be applied to how customers show their loyalty towards specific brands. While even first-time buyers of a certain car brand might say that they will probably buy that same brand again – and tell you what they like about it – only actual prior purchasers have gone through the motions at least once before, and hence are able to offer insights into their actual reasons why during further analysis. Note that the traditional funnel can also be used to track the performance of different customer groups, although not at a single glance. Separate analyses would be conducted for different subsamples or segments. In contrast, the enhanced approach makes the relative performance in different customer groups apparent at a single glance.

Second, we are accounting for the fact of nonlinear decision journeys and last-minute changes to a consumer's mental shortlist of brands by introducing *direct entry* to consideration. Direct consideration is defined as the addition of a specific brand (that was not initially considered) during the evaluation phase, that is, immediately prior to purchase or contract renewal. Such direct entries might be triggered by last-minute recommendations from friends, advice given at the POS, or the appearance of an unknown brand in an online comparison portal. This second addition to the funnel is particularly relevant to categories dominated by impulse purchases and last-minute decision making. In contrast, brands driven by premeditated purchases and long-term investments – such as car manufacturers and all B2B players – will find this addition less relevant and keep using the traditional purchase funnel for performance tracking. In general, the enhanced purchase funnel is meant to complement the traditional funnel rather than substitute it. The principal purpose of the additions is to accommodate the increasingly dynamic decision journeys observed in some industries, and to allow for deep dives that will enable companies to develop appropriate strategies. Note that both versions can be used in parallel – for example, the traditional funnel for continuous tracking and the enhanced version for occasional deep dives.

To illustrate the additions, we have conducted independent market research in three different countries and three different industries, with a total sample of more than 5,000 cases. Industries include energy, compact cars, and candy bars. Countries include Germany, the United Kingdom, and the US. The respective surveys were conducted in late 2013 and early 2014. The samples were defined as follows:

- *Compact cars:* Respondents who have bought a new compact car in the last 12 months (manufacturer level only, no model brands).
- *Energy:* Respondents who have switched their energy provider or signed a new contract with their prior provider within the last 12 months.

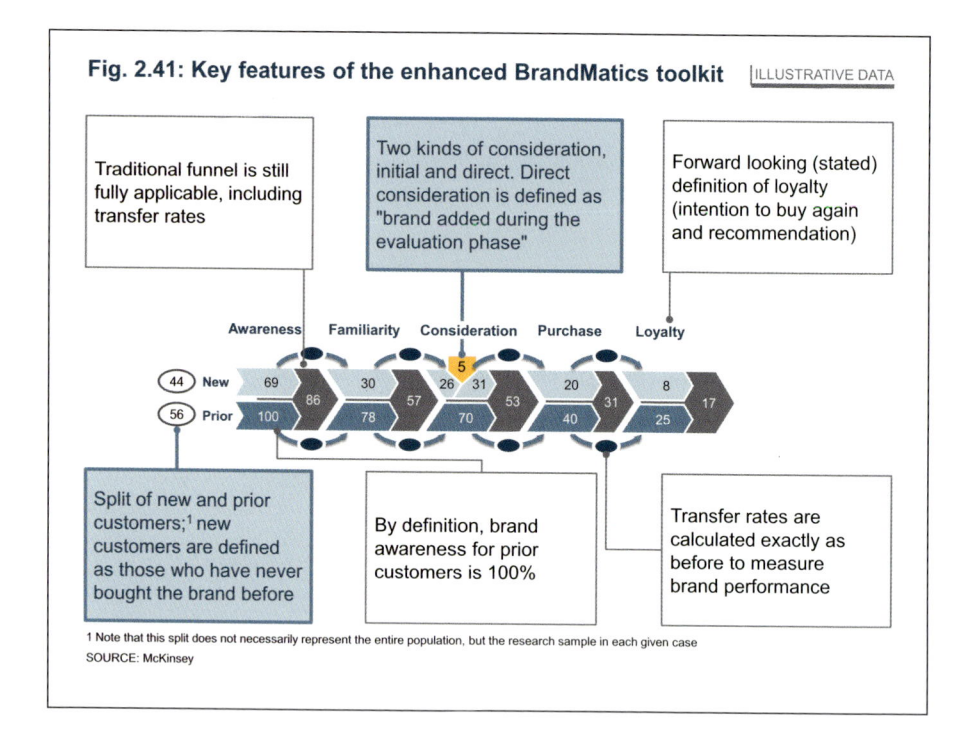

## Fig. 2.41: Key features of the enhanced BrandMatics toolkit — ILLUSTRATIVE DATA

**Traditional funnel is still fully applicable, including transfer rates**

**Two kinds of consideration, initial and direct. Direct consideration is defined as "brand added during the evaluation phase"**

**Forward looking (stated) definition of loyalty (intention to buy again and recommendation)**

| | Awareness | Familiarity | Consideration | Purchase | Loyalty |
|---|---|---|---|---|---|
| New (44) | 69 | 86 / 30 | 57 / 26 — 5 → 31 | 53 / 20 | 31 / 8 |
| Prior (56) | 100 | 78 | 70 | 40 | 25 → 17 |

**Split of new and prior customers;[1] new customers are defined as those who have never bought the brand before**

**By definition, brand awareness for prior customers is 100%**

**Transfer rates are calculated exactly as before to measure brand performance**

[1] Note that this split does not necessarily represent the entire population, but the research sample in each given case
SOURCE: McKinsey

- *Candy bars:* Respondents who have bought a candy bar in the last three months; prior purchase was defined as »have bought a given brand three out of the last ten times.«

The most important observation is that the funnel as such is stable, even over extended periods of time. The new, enhanced version is fully compatible with the existing version 1.0. This means that data sets created using the enhanced methodology can be compared with those created using the original method. This is especially important for companies who have built a database of funnel data in the past. The enhanced funnel allows these companies to apply a refined methodology without sacrificing the benefit of comparing current and future performance with existing data from past waves.

Also, the observed values for the »purchase« stage remain largely in line with the market shares of the respective brands, that is, survey-based data matches actual sales. Finally, the new constructs – the differentiation between new and repeat customers on the one hand and direct entry to consideration on the other – differentiate plausibly between brands and industries. This means that the additions expand the fact base for targeted brand management decisions in a meaningful way.

In general, we encourage companies to use the BrandMatics® toolkit in a modular fashion, depending on the nature and urgency of the decisions they face. One company might just need a snapshot of brand performance – for which the traditional funnel is sufficient. Another company might require a deep-dive analysis of the root causes that govern direct entry among new customers, or the brand attributes that drive actual loyalty among their existing customer base. As we look at some examples in more detail, it will become apparent which kinds of industries might derive the biggest benefit from the additions, and for which industries the straightforward, linear funnel is sufficient.

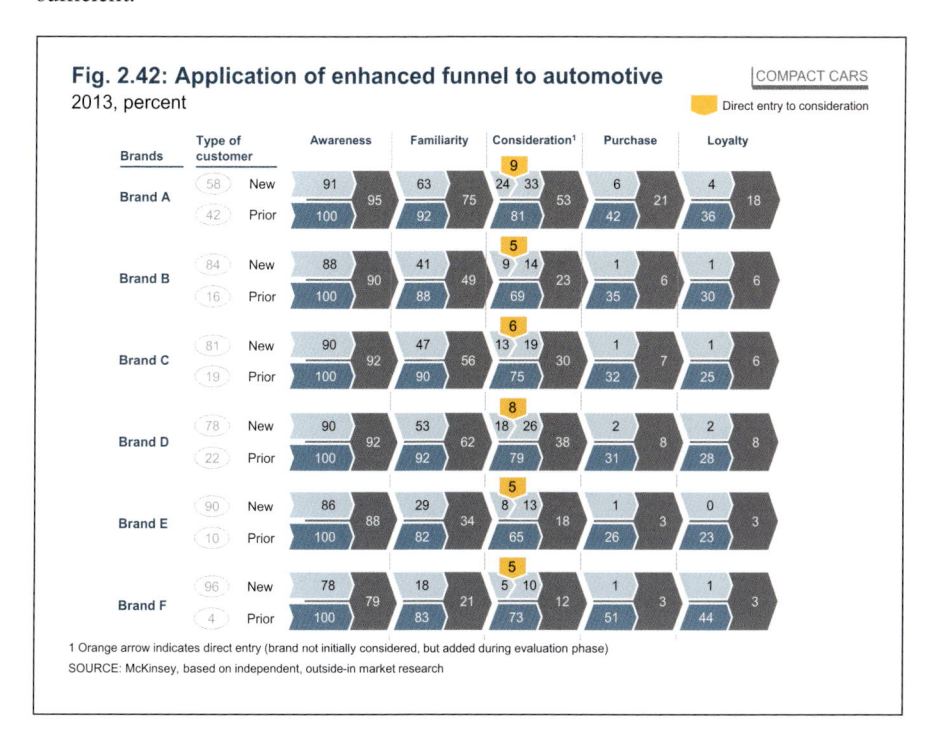

**Fig. 2.42: Application of enhanced funnel to automotive**
2013, percent — COMPACT CARS
Direct entry to consideration

| Brands | Type of customer | Awareness | Familiarity | Consideration¹ | Purchase | Loyalty |
|---|---|---|---|---|---|---|
| Brand A | 58 New | 91 → 95 | 63 → 75 | 24 33 → 53 | 6 → 21 | 4 → 18 |
|  | 42 Prior | 100 | 92 | 81 | 42 | 36 |
| Brand B | 84 New | 88 → 90 | 41 → 49 | 9 14 → 23 | 1 → 6 | 1 → 6 |
|  | 16 Prior | 100 | 88 | 69 | 35 | 30 |
| Brand C | 81 New | 90 → 92 | 47 → 56 | 13 19 → 30 | 1 → 7 | 1 → 6 |
|  | 19 Prior | 100 | 90 | 75 | 32 | 25 |
| Brand D | 78 New | 90 → 92 | 53 → 62 | 18 26 → 38 | 2 → 8 | 2 → 8 |
|  | 22 Prior | 100 | 92 | 79 | 31 | 28 |
| Brand E | 90 New | 86 → 88 | 29 → 34 | 8 13 → 18 | 1 → 3 | 0 → 3 |
|  | 10 Prior | 100 | 82 | 65 | 26 | 23 |
| Brand F | 96 New | 78 → 79 | 18 → 21 | 5 10 → 12 | 1 → 3 | 1 → 3 |
|  | 4 Prior | 100 | 83 | 73 | 51 | 44 |

1 Orange arrow indicates direct entry (brand not initially considered, but added during evaluation phase)
SOURCE: McKinsey, based on independent, outside-in market research

Let's look at how the new features apply to compact cars (Figure 2.42). It is immediately apparent that this is a market governed by loyalty. In general, prior customers have a much better funnel performance than new customers. One in four prior buyers of brand E (26 percent) and almost one in two prior buyers of brand A (42 percent) stick to their brands. At the same time, direct consideration is of relatively low importance for most brands in this category. For example, less than every third considerer of brand A is a direct entrant (9 percent direct consideration versus 33 percent total consideration). Similar ratios apply to the other brands. This is in line with the fact that cars are a high-involvement category. Buying a new car is a big decision; ticket prices are high, and most buyers hold on to a new car for many years. To minimize the risk of a bad choice, customers go through a lengthy process of information gathering and research. As a result, all major brands are relatively well known to most potential buyers.[75] There are, however, two notable exceptions to this rule. For brand F, a foreign manufacturer, one in two considerers is a direct entrant. Brand E, also a foreign brand, has a similar ratio of direct considerers (5 percent) to total considerers (13 percent). Although few new customers who do not have prior experience with these brands actually end up buying a foreign car (12 percent for brand F and 18 percent for brand E), these manufacturers could benefit from targeted programs to trigger direct consideration – be it through online marketing or promotions at multibrand dealerships, where prospective buyers might stumble upon a brand that they did not consider initially. As a first step, however, brand managers will want to invest in further research into the needs of direct considerers to derive tailor-made actions.

In contrast, established local brands will benefit the most from keeping current customers happy – for example through superior aftersales service, attractive trade-in offers, or special events to strengthen their ties to the brand. While all this is true for compact cars in this market today, the picture will look different for other types of cars, in other national markets, or at other points in time.

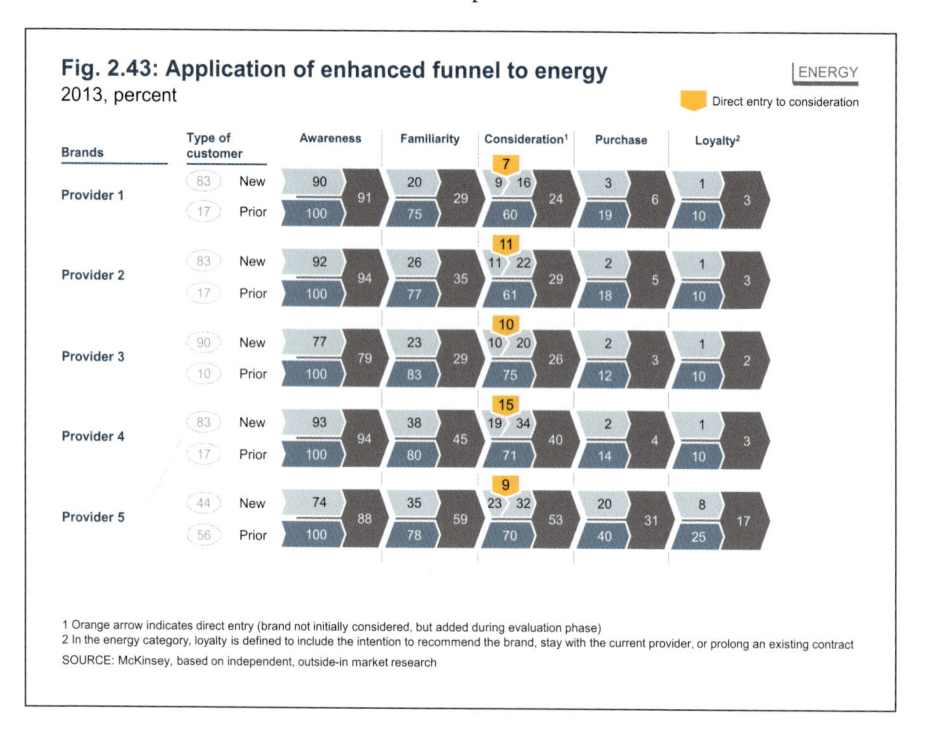

**Fig. 2.43: Application of enhanced funnel to energy**
2013, percent — ENERGY — Direct entry to consideration

| Brands | Type of customer | Awareness | Familiarity | Consideration[1] | Purchase | Loyalty[2] |
|---|---|---|---|---|---|---|
| Provider 1 | 83 New | 90 → 91 | 20 → 29 | 7 / 9 16 → 24 | 3 → 6 | 1 → 3 |
| | 17 Prior | 100 | 75 | 60 | 19 | 10 |
| Provider 2 | 83 New | 92 → 94 | 26 → 35 | 11 / 11 22 → 29 | 2 → 5 | 1 → 3 |
| | 17 Prior | 100 | 77 | 61 | 18 | 10 |
| Provider 3 | 90 New | 77 → 79 | 23 → 29 | 10 / 10 20 → 26 | 2 → 3 | 1 → 2 |
| | 10 Prior | 100 | 83 | 75 | 12 | 10 |
| Provider 4 | 83 New | 93 → 94 | 38 → 45 | 15 / 19 34 → 40 | 2 → 4 | 1 → 3 |
| | 17 Prior | 100 | 80 | 71 | 14 | 10 |
| Provider 5 | 44 New | 74 → 88 | 35 → 59 | 9 / 23 32 → 53 | 20 → 31 | 8 → 17 |
| | 56 Prior | 100 | 78 | 70 | 40 | 25 |

1 Orange arrow indicates direct entry (brand not initially considered, but added during evaluation phase)
2 In the energy category, loyalty is defined to include the intention to recommend the brand, stay with the current provider, or prolong an existing contract
SOURCE: McKinsey, based on independent, outside-in market research

Compared with buying a new car, signing a contract with an energy provider is a low-involvement event. One would expect this to be reflected in the way energy brands perform in the purchase funnel. And in fact, last-minute decision making is a highly relevant topic for energy providers according to our independent pilot research conducted in early 2014 (Figure 2.43). Apparently, direct entry into consideration is nearly as important in this market as the traditional, linear path from awareness via familiarity to premeditated consideration. In the cases of brands like Provider 2 and Provider 3, the two sources of consideration are in fact equally important (11 percent and 10 percent respectively). This means that half the new customers (22 percent and 20 percent respectively) contemplating a contract with these brands had not initially considered them. Because of the relatively low involvement in the category, consumers might simply not be aware of certain brands, especially if they are relatively new to the market. As a result, these brands will become apparent and relevant only immediately prior to a given purchase decision. This may, for example, be triggered by a top rank on price comparison portals, such as verivox, check24, or toptarif. It seems there is a window of opportunity for young challenger brands to capture the attention of switchers with attractive propositions, despite the fact that these brands may be considerably less well known than the incumbents.

The third category we looked at in our pilot research – candy bars in the US – caters to highly capricious customers (Figure 2.44). Although almost everyone knows all the major brands, customers change their minds all the time. For every brand, new customers are overwhelmingly more important than prior customers.[76] What is more, direct entrants to consideration are at least as important as initial considerers. In two cases (Kit Kat and Twix), spontaneous consideration is in fact the most important source of new customers. More than half of all new customers only start considering these brands at the last minute. This is not surprising since candy bars are usually bought on impulse rather than as a planned purchase. In many cases, the purchase decision is triggered by the way candy bars are placed and promoted at the point of sale. According to an industry study conducted in the US, candy accounts for 30 percent of all purchases at the checkout.[77] A qualitative study commissioned by Wrigley concludes that customers at the checkout »are relieved to be done with their shopping and glad to discover products to reward themselves.«[78] The major takeaway for brand managers in this category is to focus their efforts on attracting the attention of spontaneous considerers. It seems that some of the somewhat less prominent brands, such as 3 Musketeers, are slightly more successful at grabbing the attention of new customers and direct considerers than top dogs like Snickers. This effect may be explained by the fact that most buyers seek variety if the cost of switching is low.[79] And if variety is what shoppers seek, a slightly less familiar brand may actually have a psychological advantage over its more established competitors. This is also why candy bar makers keep creating new flavors and limited editions of existing products. Examples for Snickers include Snickers Almond, Snickers Peanut Butter, Snickers 3x Chocolate, Snickers More Nuts, Snickers More Caramel, Snickers Gold, and Snickers Adventure Bar, to name just some of the more prominent instances.[80] As a result, Snickers enjoys the highest loyalty rates in the category by far, both in terms of stated loyalty (21 percent) and in terms of repeat purchases.

To increase the resolution of the analysis even more, new and repeat customers can be displayed separately for a narrower selection of brands. This allows for a direct comparison of transfer rates for competing brands in the respective disciplines – new customer acquisition on the one hand, and loyalty creation on the other.

Figure 2.45 shows the funnel performance for compact cars differentiated by type of customer. Obviously, brand A is ahead of the competition in almost all respects, or at least on par with its peers. Among new customers, the brand is far more successful than brand E, and still superior to brand D when it comes to converting awareness

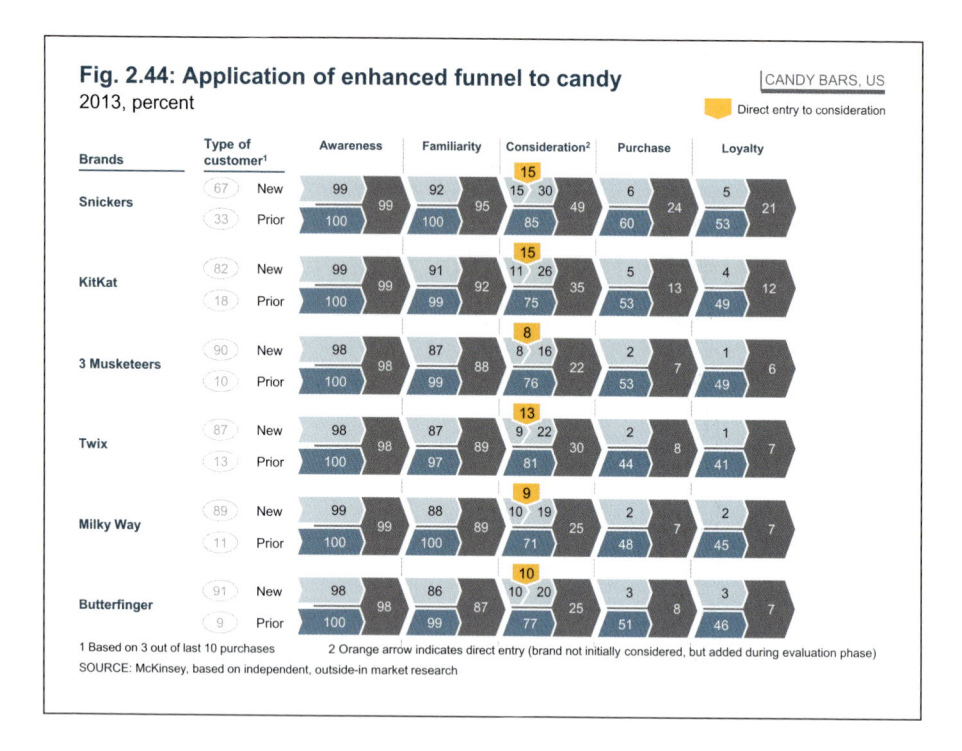

## Fig. 2.44: Application of enhanced funnel to candy
2013, percent — CANDY BARS, US
Direct entry to consideration

| Brands | Type of customer[1] | | Awareness | Familiarity | Consideration[2] | Purchase | Loyalty |
|---|---|---|---|---|---|---|---|
| Snickers | 67 | New | 99 / 99 | 92 / 95 | 15 / 30 / 49 | 6 / 24 | 5 / 21 |
| | 33 | Prior | 100 | 100 | 85 | 60 | 53 |
| KitKat | 82 | New | 99 / 99 | 91 / 92 | 15 / 11 / 26 / 35 | 5 / 13 | 4 / 12 |
| | 18 | Prior | 100 | 99 | 75 | 53 | 49 |
| 3 Musketeers | 90 | New | 98 / 98 | 87 / 88 | 8 / 8 / 16 / 22 | 2 / 7 | 1 / 6 |
| | 10 | Prior | 100 | 99 | 76 | 53 | 49 |
| Twix | 87 | New | 98 / 98 | 87 / 89 | 13 / 9 / 22 / 30 | 2 / 8 | 1 / 7 |
| | 13 | Prior | 100 | 97 | 81 | 44 | 41 |
| Milky Way | 89 | New | 99 / 99 | 88 / 89 | 9 / 10 / 19 / 25 | 2 / 7 | 2 / 7 |
| | 11 | Prior | 100 | 100 | 71 | 48 | 45 |
| Butterfinger | 91 | New | 98 / 98 | 86 / 87 | 10 / 10 / 20 / 25 | 3 / 8 | 3 / 7 |
| | 9 | Prior | 100 | 99 | 77 | 51 | 46 |

1 Based on 3 out of last 10 purchases  2 Orange arrow indicates direct entry (brand not initially considered, but added during evaluation phase)
SOURCE: McKinsey, based on independent, outside-in market research

into loyalty, and loyalty into consideration (at 69 and 38 percent respectively). In this market, brand A apparently owns the compact car category, and the brand capitalizes on its domination in communication. Brand D, in contrast, is particularly successful at generating stated loyalty, regardless of whether it was a first or a repeat purchase (84 percent among first-time buyers and 91 percent among repeat buyers). It seems that once you have bought and driven a new compact made by brand D, other brands pale in comparison.

In energy, the analysis of funnel performance by type of customer reveals some subtle differences between providers (Figure 2.46). Provider 1 – arguably one of the most established brands – leads the pack when it comes to contract renewal. For example, 32 percent of considerers among prior customers renew their contract with Provider 1, compared with 30 percent for Provider 2 and only 16 percent for Provider 3. Provider 3, however, is slightly more successful than its competitors when it comes to creating familiarity among new customers (30 percent transfer rate, compared with only 23 percent for Provider 1). At the same time, Provider 3 is considerably less well known among potential new customers than both Provider 1 and Provider 2 (77 percent awareness for Provider 3 versus 90 percent for Provider 1 and 92 percent for Provider 2).

Finally, let's look at the dual funnel for candy bars. It shows that Snickers owns this category in the US (Figure 2.47). Snickers achieves top transfer rates all the way through purchase, both among new and prior customers. Kit Kat, however, manages to create high stated loyalty even among first time purchasers; 90 percent of trial purchasers say they will buy Kit Kat again or recommend it to others. That value increases

## 2.3 The Brand Purchase Funnel

**Fig. 2.45: Performance among new and prior customers**
2013, percent

COMPACT CARS
- Bottleneck[1]
- Best in class
- Direct entry

| | Awareness | | Familiarity | | Consideration[2] | | | Purchase | | Loyalty |
|---|---|---|---|---|---|---|---|---|---|---|
| Brand A | 91 | 69 | 63 | 38 | 24 | 33 | 18 | 6 | 77 | 4 |
| Brand D | 90 | 59 | 53 | 34 | 18 | 26 | 8 | 2 | 84 | 2 |
| Brand E | 86 | 33 | 29 | 27 | 8 | 13 | 6 | 1 | 58 | 0 |

Direct entry values: 9 (Brand A), 8 (Brand D), 5 (Brand E)

New / Prior

| Brand A | 100 | 92 | 92 | 87 | 81 | 52 | 42 | 86 | 36 |
|---|---|---|---|---|---|---|---|---|---|
| Brand D | 100 | 92 | 92 | 86 | 79 | 39 | 31 | 91 | 28 |
| Brand E | 100 | 82 | 82 | 80 | 65 | 40 | 26 | 88 | 23 |

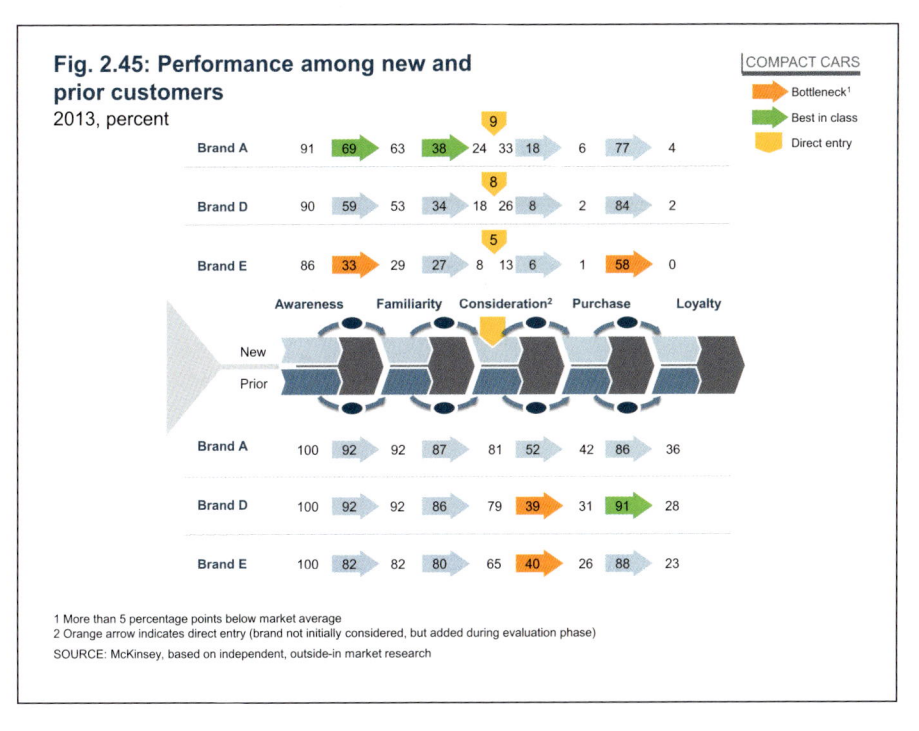

1 More than 5 percentage points below market average
2 Orange arrow indicates direct entry (brand not initially considered, but added during evaluation phase)
SOURCE: McKinsey, based on independent, outside-in market research

---

**Fig. 2.46: Performance among new and prior customers**
2013, percent

ENERGY
- Bottleneck[1]
- Best in class
- Direct entry

| | Awareness | | Familiarity | | Consideration[2] | | | Purchase | | Loyalty[3] |
|---|---|---|---|---|---|---|---|---|---|---|
| Provider 1 | 90 | 23 | 20 | 47 | 9 | 16 | 19 | 3 | 43 | 1 |
| Provider 2 | 92 | 28 | 26 | 44 | 11 | 22 | 9 | 2 | 56 | 1 |
| Provider 3 | 77 | 30 | 23 | 43 | 10 | 20 | 10 | 2 | 57 | 1 |

Direct entry values: 7 (Provider 1), 11 (Provider 2), 10 (Provider 3)

New / Prior

| Provider 1 | 100 | 75 | 75 | 80 | 60 | 32 | 19 | 50 | 10 |
|---|---|---|---|---|---|---|---|---|---|
| Provider 2 | 100 | 77 | 77 | 78 | 61 | 30 | 18 | 55 | 10 |
| Provider 3 | 100 | 83 | 83 | 91 | 75 | 16 | 12 | 83 | 10 |

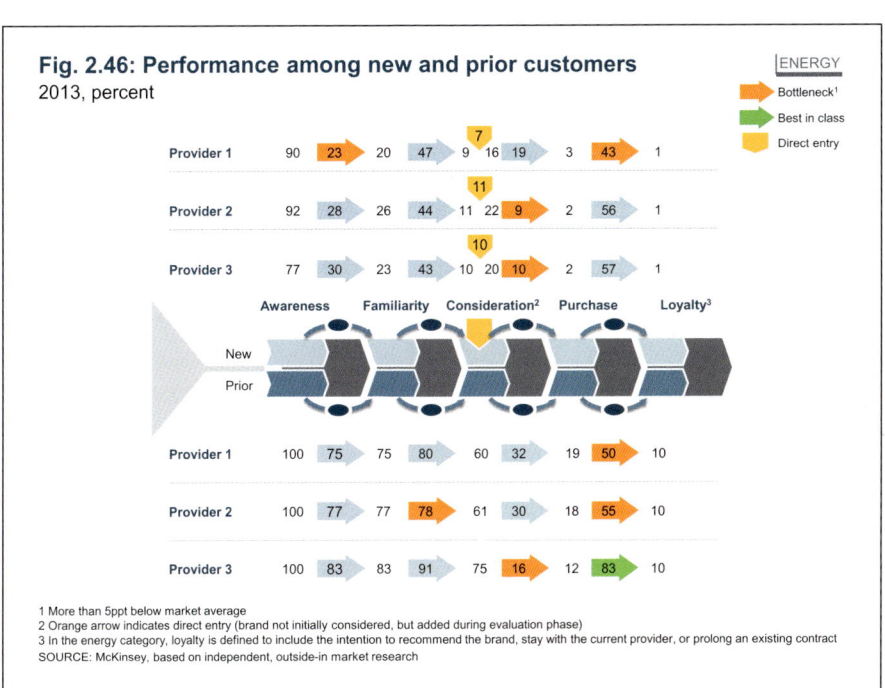

1 More than 5ppt below market average
2 Orange arrow indicates direct entry (brand not initially considered, but added during evaluation phase)
3 In the energy category, loyalty is defined to include the intention to recommend the brand, stay with the current provider, or prolong an existing contract
SOURCE: McKinsey, based on independent, outside-in market research

to 92 percent for repeat Kit Kat buyers. In a market that is driven by variety, this kind of loyalty is clearly an asset. In a deep-dive analysis of loyalty drivers, brand managers at Kit Kat might want to explore what it is that makes customers come back to the brand time and again and do more of this. Twix, in contrast, might want to conduct further research to find out why only 54 percent of its prior customers buy Twix again, compared with 71 percent for Snickers and 70 percent for Kit Kat. That said, the candy bar category calls for further research to shed light on different purchase occasions. For example, stocking up on multipacks of the family's favorite brand from an aisle shelf is psychologically very different from picking a single bar at the checkout for immediate consumption. Also, shopping alone will typically be nothing like shopping with a nagging child. The respective decision journeys, as well as the relevant purchase drivers, are likely to be quite different for these cases.

To substantiate our initial observations, further research in neighboring categories should be conducted. For example, while direct consideration rates for candy bars appear to be substantial compared with cars, it remains to be seen what levels of direct consideration are typical for other impulse categories, such as chewing gum or soft drinks. Similarly, energy figures should eventually be compared with those for other contractual services – such as telecommunication or insurance – for calibration.

**Initial findings and future applications**

The additions to the funnel have proven both robust and relevant in our pilot research. The insights they provide are plausible, and they add value by revealing brand strengths and weaknesses in great detail – and by reflecting structural changes in customer decision making, technology, and industry dynamics. Key findings in our three pilot categories include:

- Established brands are particularly successful in generating actual loyalty in the form of repeat purchases. In contrast, challenger brands, are more successful when it comes to attracting new and impulsive customers.[81]
- Direct entry to consideration is of relatively low importance for purchases characterized by high ticket prices, high involvement, and low frequency, such as compact cars. For established brands in these categories, it is of even lower relevance compared with less established brands.
- High values for direct entry can be observed in the candy bar category. Apparently, customers in this market are quite willing to try an unknown brand, given the low risk. This is supported by the observation that attributes such as »fun advertising« are surprisingly relevant in this category (see next chapter).

While this level of detail is both insightful and instructive, not every given case will require the full analysis arsenal (Figure 2.48). This is especially important because the enhanced methodology may call for larger sample sizes to ensure that inferences at the more granular level of different customer groups remain statistically significant. To allow for full flexibility, the new methodology is modular and can be tailored to a variety of different situations and challenges. The »traditional« funnel is sufficient for

## 2.3 The Brand Purchase Funnel

### Fig. 2.47: Performance among new and prior customers
2013, percent

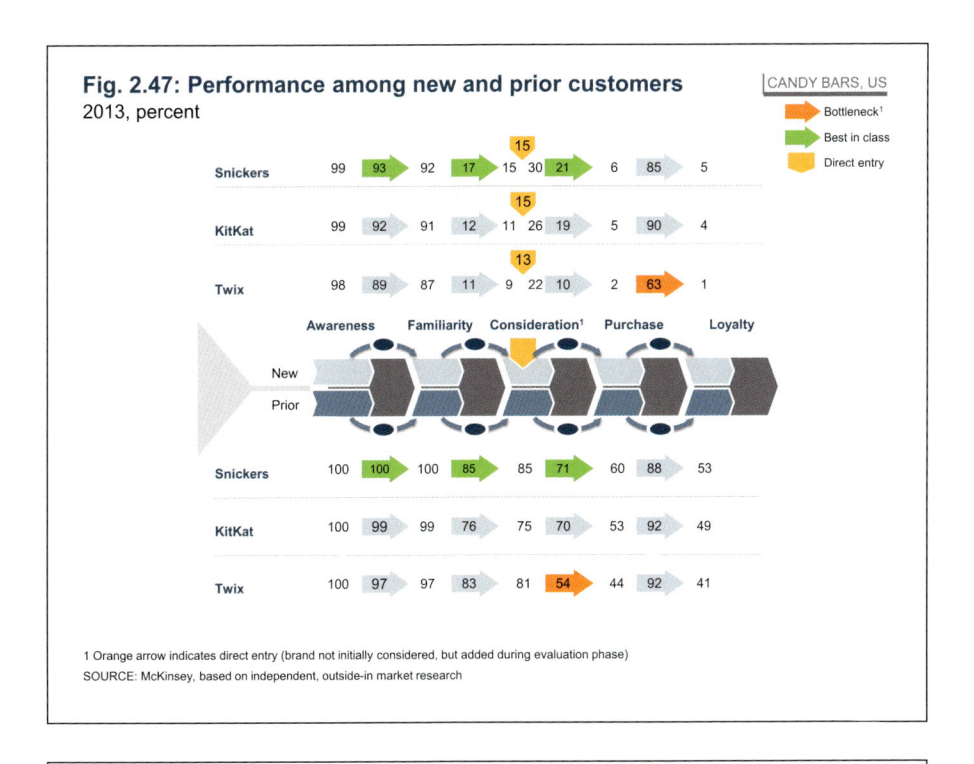

CANDY BARS, US
- Bottleneck[1]
- Best in class
- Direct entry

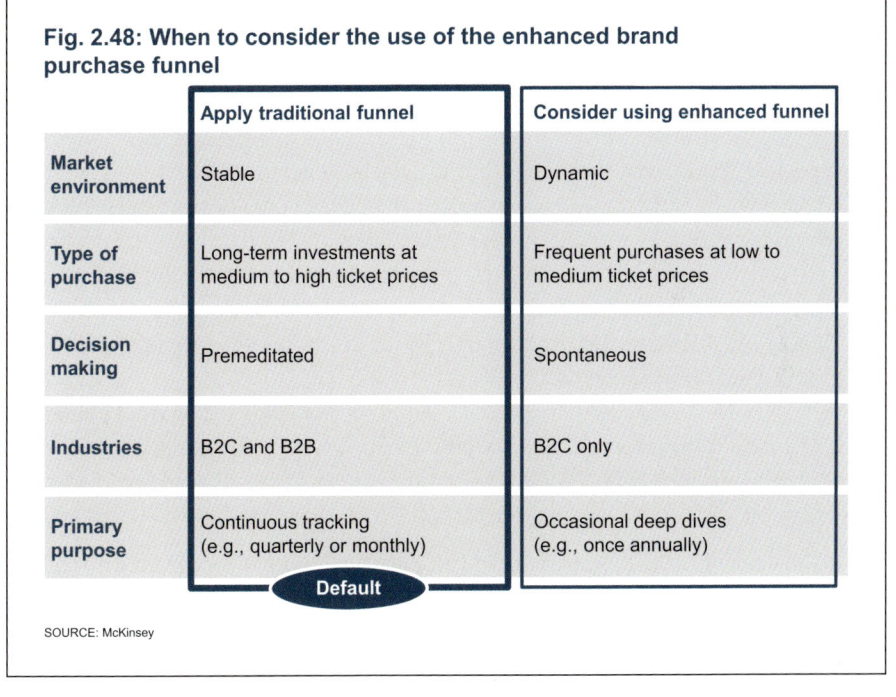

**New**

| | Awareness | | Familiarity | | Consideration[1] | | Purchase | | Loyalty |
|---|---|---|---|---|---|---|---|---|---|
| Snickers | 99 | 93 | 92 | 17 | 15 / 15 / 30 | 21 | 6 | 85 | 5 |
| KitKat | 99 | 92 | 91 | 12 | 15 / 11 / 26 | 19 | 5 | 90 | 4 |
| Twix | 98 | 89 | 87 | 11 | 13 / 9 / 22 | 10 | 2 | 63 | 1 |

**Prior**

| | Awareness | | Familiarity | | Consideration[1] | | Purchase | | Loyalty |
|---|---|---|---|---|---|---|---|---|---|
| Snickers | 100 | 100 | 100 | 85 | 85 | 71 | 60 | 88 | 53 |
| KitKat | 100 | 99 | 99 | 76 | 75 | 70 | 53 | 92 | 49 |
| Twix | 100 | 97 | 97 | 83 | 81 | 54 | 44 | 92 | 41 |

1 Orange arrow indicates direct entry (brand not initially considered, but added during evaluation phase)
SOURCE: McKinsey, based on independent, outside-in market research

---

### Fig. 2.48: When to consider the use of the enhanced brand purchase funnel

| | Apply traditional funnel | Consider using enhanced funnel |
|---|---|---|
| Market environment | Stable | Dynamic |
| Type of purchase | Long-term investments at medium to high ticket prices | Frequent purchases at low to medium ticket prices |
| Decision making | Premeditated | Spontaneous |
| Industries | B2C and B2B | B2C only |
| Primary purpose | Continuous tracking (e.g., quarterly or monthly) | Occasional deep dives (e.g., once annually) |

Default

SOURCE: McKinsey

quick and frequent snapshots of overall brand performance as well as for industries characterized by high involvement, high ticket prices, and low purchase frequency. Deep dives into different types of customers, in contrast, will help to build highly targeted customer acquisition and retention programs, especially in commitment-based industries. While an incumbent brand with a relatively high market share will benefit from detailed insights into the behavior and the needs of its prior customers, challenger brands will want to investigate potential first-time customers in more detail. Finally, brands operating in impulse categories will find that the analysis of direct entry to consideration greatly enhances the fact base for marketing activities geared at getting the attention of ever evolving groups of spontaneous buyers.

# Interview with Erwin van Laethem and Dorkas Koenen of Essent: »Differentiating in the middle«

Essent N. V. is the leading Dutch energy provider. The company has a market share of about 25 percent and provides energy to 2.7 million households. In 1999, Essent was established through the merger of two major energy groups based in the South and the North of the Netherlands respectively. The company provides gas, electricity, and energy services to its customers. Energiedirect.nl, a subsidiary of Essent, is the company's second brand. In 2009, Essent was acquired by RWE AG, one of the leading energy companies in Europe.

Erwin van Laethem is Essent's Chief Executive Officer. He joined the company in 2006, initially as the Director Service & Sales for Essent Netherlands and CEO for Essent Belgium. He was appointed Chief Commercial Officer in 2009, and Chairman of the Executive Board of Essent as Chief Executive Officer in 2012. Mr. van Laethem has previously worked in various executive positions in the global energy industry.

Dorkas Koenen is Essent's Chief Marketing Officer. Appointed to his current position in 2010, Mr. Koenen has previously filled senior marketing roles in the financial services and telecommunications industries. At Essent, his responsibilities include marketing planning, product management and development, pricing, marketing communication, and brand portfolio management.

**McKinsey:** What was the overall strategic situation like when you assumed commercial leadership at Essent, Mr. van Laethem?

**Erwin van Laethem:** When RWE acquired Essent, the customer base had been eroding for some years, and the company was under attack from all sides. So RWE actually set the value of the customer base at zero; the sizeable investment was targeted at the acquisition of the production assets.

**McKinsey:** What was the market like in terms of marketing and branding at that time?

**Erwin van Laethem:** It was totally undifferentiated, a commodity market. At the time, customers did not make a distinction between Nuon, Eneco, or whatever. They got their energy from what they thought of as »the utility.« On the one hand, it was a challenge. No apparent preferences, and no differentiated brands either. On the other hand, it was a big opportunity. A clean slate, at least in theory. There was, however, already a marketing department that was relying at least as much on anecdotes and gut feeling as on facts and analyses. In other words, there was a lot to do. That's when we said, okay, how do you get the organization focused? How do you rally everybody around a few clearly defined target segments?

**McKinsey:** How was the target group of the Essent brand defined at that time?

**Erwin van Laethem:** We identified B2C, B2B, SMEs (small and medium-sized enterprises), horticulture, and local energy services as profit centers. Within those large buckets, however, it was unknown at the time what the high-value segments were, and where to focus our efforts. As a next step, we established two cross-functional units. One around sales portfolio management on the sourcing side, and above all, one around marketing. The intent was to make marketing the engine of the whole commercial transformation. We wanted to establish a strong fundament and become the undisputed commercial leader in the Netherlands in three respects: value of the customer base, customer satisfaction, and external recognition, e.g., in terms of being top of mind for customers who value service.

**McKinsey:** How did you start this transformation?

**Erwin van Laethem:** The challenge was to attract the right people. At the time, there was no internal reference frame for good marketing. I mean, we had 80 people or so in marketing, and many of them had formerly worked for A-brands in the consumer goods industry. But they had no common language or approach among themselves, nor with the rest of the company. And therefore, the department was not being very effective. So I said, okay, let's build a high-performing leadership team to drive the commercial transformation, and attract a really powerful professional as the chief marketing officer to lead the transformation. Let me tell you, it was really hard to find the right person. But I said, we can't compromise on this. We need a combination of the best professional and the best team player. Marketing drives too much value to put it in the wrong hands. Despite enormous pressure, I ended up keeping the position open for a really long time until Mr. Koenen came on board.

**McKinsey:** What did you do while you were waiting for the right person?

**Erwin van Laethem:** I said, even the best leader needs an environment in which that person can be effective. So we started preparing what I call the »landing strip.« It's a combination of the right coalition of people and a specific way of working. Around that time, someone gave me the *Power Brands* book. And I read it in a single weekend, cover to cover. What impressed me were the simple language and the systematic approach to brand management, from positioning to implementation. I was particularly excited about the concept of internal activation, getting people to know and feel what the brand is all about, and then live it. That's what I wanted to do with Essent.

**McKinsey:** How did you go about preparing the landing strip for Mr. Koenen?

**Erwin van Laethem:** The intent was to get ready to reposition the Essent brand in the market. I was certain that if, in this undifferentiated market, we identified the most relevant drivers of customer behavior, we would have the potential for double-digit growth. Because a small difference on the right driver will make a big difference as far as competitive differentiation is concerned. Additionally, we pretty much needed to invent energy marketing in the Netherlands. The concept simply did not exist. It was nothing like consumer goods, where marketing is so advanced that you are just optimizing the figures behind the comma. In energy, we were pioneers.

**McKinsey:** So would you say that the upside of great branding in energy is actually bigger than in, say, consumer goods? Because most people would say it's the other way around. I've heard people say that branding is for chewing gums and cigarettes. But forget energy. There's no relevance.

**Erwin van Laethem:** I disagree. In an undifferentiated market, where there's no tradition of marketing and branding, the same effort will give you a bigger impact than in more marketing-driven industries. However, as there are fewer drivers to play with, it requires more skill from your marketing team. Today, we have the track record to prove we got it right. By finding the relevant drivers and delivering the best performance across all touch points to differentiate ourselves in the market, we were able to turn around the Essent brand – both in terms of customer base development and profitability. In the first year, we broke even. In the second year, we delivered three-figure operating results; and in the third year, we doubled it again. We've seen profitability, as well as the customer base, grow three years in a row now. Customers are highly satisfied, and we also get the external recognition. We are meeting, or in fact surpassing all the objectives that we set ourselves.

**McKinsey:** Mr. Koenen, please tell our readers about the energy market in the Netherlands, especially since it was deregulated in the 1990s.

**Dorkas Koenen:** The energy market in the Netherlands has seen disruptive change over the last decade. It evolved from a completely regulated market into a highly competitive market. I would say it is now the most competitive market in continental Europe. The switch rate is high and still growing, and a lot of new entrants are capturing market share from the three large incumbents. The incumbents are Essent, Nuon, and Eneco. About seven years ago, these three had almost 100 percent market share. Today, they have a combined market share of about 80 percent. So 20 percent of the market has already been eaten away by challenger brands. Most of these new entrants offer no real innovation, no deeper brand promise, only low prices to fight the established energy industry. This has started a vicious cycle of price cuts that we have decided to get out of. Competing on price would eventually have decreased the value of the entire market. That's why, about five years ago, we started repositioning the Essent brand.

**McKinsey:** What was the status of the Essent brand when you started the branding effort? Any particular strengths or weaknesses?

**Dorkas Koenen:** There were a few striking things at that time. Large energy brands had no real brand characteristics. They claimed all kinds of values, like reliability, and told high-profile stories about the future of energy, but they had no real connection to the market and its customers. At that point, the providers were more or less steered with a narrow set of stakeholders in mind: politicians, civil servants, and so on. Instead of making a connection with the customer through a clear profile, all three incumbents were blurred. In a spider chart, the lines of the three brands came out as more or less identical (Figure 2.49).

Nobody was using the brand to build a connection with the customer. In this price-dominated, potentially self-destructive market, I saw our brand as the only source of

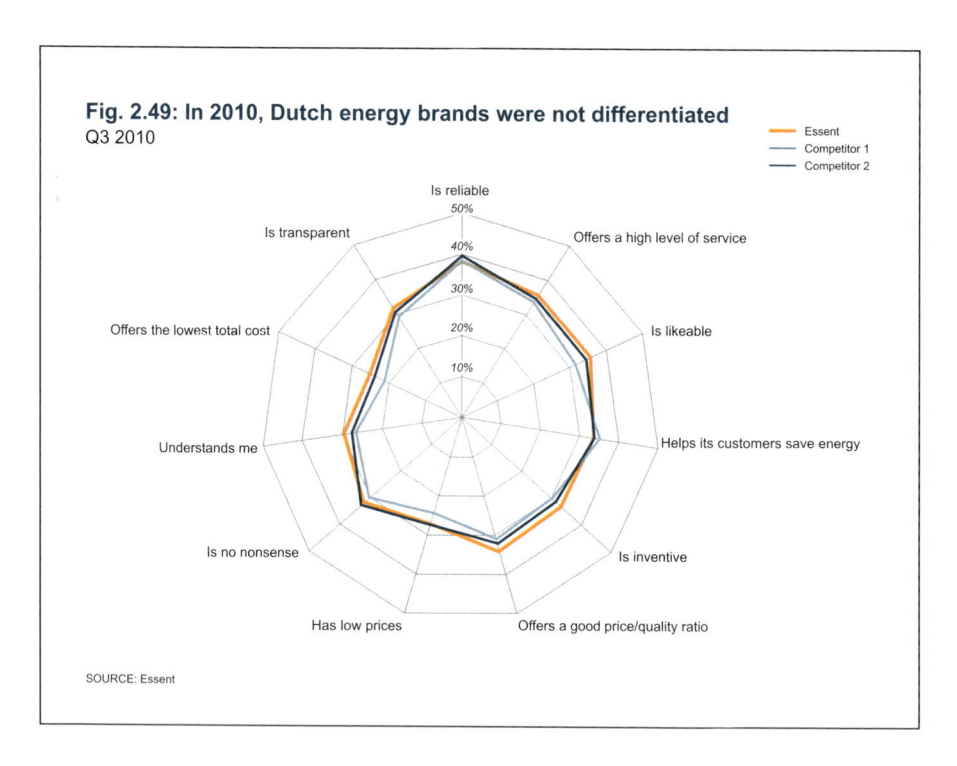

**Fig. 2.49: In 2010, Dutch energy brands were not differentiated**
Q3 2010

— Essent
— Competitor 1
— Competitor 2

Axes: Is reliable, Offers a high level of service, Is likeable, Helps its customers save energy, Is inventive, Offers a good price/quality ratio, Has low prices, Is no nonsense, Understands me, Offers the lowest total cost, Is transparent

SOURCE: Essent

competitive differentiation that we would be able to sustain over a longer period of time. As an incumbent, it was our aspiration to make a difference in the middle of the market. We were convinced that a strong brand could make a difference even in a price-dominated market.

**McKinsey:** How did you go about repositioning the Essent brand? To what extent did you rely on quantified data and analytical tools?

**Dorkas Koenen:** We did something that we had never done before, and that, quite frankly, probably no one has ever done before. We did not start on the creative side. In a situation like this, most companies would conduct an advertising agency pitch, and hope that art directors solve their problems with miracles and fairy tales. We, however, started with science. Our decision to make a difference in the middle of the market through our brand was a big bet. We were about to invest heavily in this, and we wanted to know whether it would pay off. So we really needed a solid foundation of facts that we could build on. We launched a major fact-finding exercise, not only in the market, but internally as well. That was our first step in what we internally called »fact-based marketing.«

**Erwin van Laethem:** Initially, there was no connection between our customers and the brand. So we said, before we do anything, let's first create that connection between Essent customers and the Essent brand. To get there, we ran the »mother of all market researches.« This was the foundation for our market segmentation, for identifying the target segments, and then formulating the value propositions to those segments. And

I think our customer base is still evolving. For example, the »energy unconscious« are starting to wake up, and they will eventually become energy conscious. So as the customer base is evolving, we will also need to adapt our propositions to the different segments. This is also where the multibrand approach comes in. In general, we aspire to make all our brands as distinct as possible to meet the needs of our target segments that deliver value now, and we will continue to do so in the future.

**Dorkas Koenen:** So in a first step, we conducted quantitative market research that we cross-checked with panel research and deep-structure interviews with customers. This helped us to get a sense of the market opportunity. In a second step, we looked at the internal perception of our brand, our values, and our capabilities. We used research, supported by group discussions. This second step was vital, since whatever you promise as a brand will ultimately have to be delivered by people at the front line. Externally, everything is changing very quickly. So you have to have stability at least on the inside to be able to stick to your promises.

We then combined the opportunities that we saw in the market with the strengths that people referred to internally. The fact that we paid so much attention to attitudes and capabilities in the company got us off to a strong start. Top management was immediately on board – because they saw a perfect combination of an external opportunity and an internal capability set. Our employees were also on board because they had been involved from day one. They felt that they were part of the process, and they were confident that the new brand positioning would express what they liked about Essent.

**McKinsey:** Please describe the primary target group you selected for Essent, and please let our readers know why you picked it.

**Dorkas Koenen:** We found a few different segments in the market. We saw right away that Essent was already well-positioned to cover some of these segments. Other segments we would first have to build a connection with, and yet others we would have to activate over a longer period of time. As a major incumbent, our prime directive was not to chase away existing customers. Given our size, we would have to try and be everybody's friend. If you are repositioning a large brand in a commoditized market, your only sustainable option is to differentiate in the middle, and we did just that by matching needs we saw in the market with our unique capabilities. And although the market has changed a lot in the past five years, our positioning still delivers value. New competitors have entered the market, new channels have appeared, and some have already disappeared again. Nevertheless, our positioning framework is still the same and still relevant.

Before we started the repositioning effort, Essent was working with no less than 16 consumer segments, 10 of which we were targeting, but nobody in the company could name more than two of them. We decided to cut this rank growth back to only a few segments that everybody can remember, and to describe them in a way that appeals to intuition and common sense. This simplification alone made a big difference to the way we think about consumer needs today.

The specific segments that we found in the Dutch market were the »energy involved,« the »cost controllers,« the »bargain hunters,« and the »pragmatists.« But in a commodity market, you cannot position the brand for just one or two of these groups. You have to have a story for everybody that you can refer to in the context of an overall umbrella positioning. If you chase away the pragmatists, you chase away 30 percent of the market. If you chase away the bargain hunters, that's another 25 percent. We chose to focus on the energy involved, the cost controllers, and the pragmatists. From a long-term perspective, we were most excited about the energy involved, since these customers might also be interested in products beyond energy, such as solar panels, boilers, and insulation. Above the line, we stayed away from the bargain hunters to shield our brand from any semblance of sellout. But below the line, we devised some activities to capture our fair share of that segment as well, especially because it was growing at the time. In general, we chose to build our stories around how people want to be served, rather than around price, because we consider service a source of sustainable differentiation.

**McKinsey:** In a nutshell, how would you describe the new positioning of the Essent brand? How does it differ from competitors?

**Dorkas Koenen:** Our differentiating attributes include transparency, inventiveness, and delivery (Figure 2.50). Transparency is something that the market demands. hen we asked customers what they expect, they almost unanimously said that they wanted a brand that does what it says, period. Inventiveness comes from our own

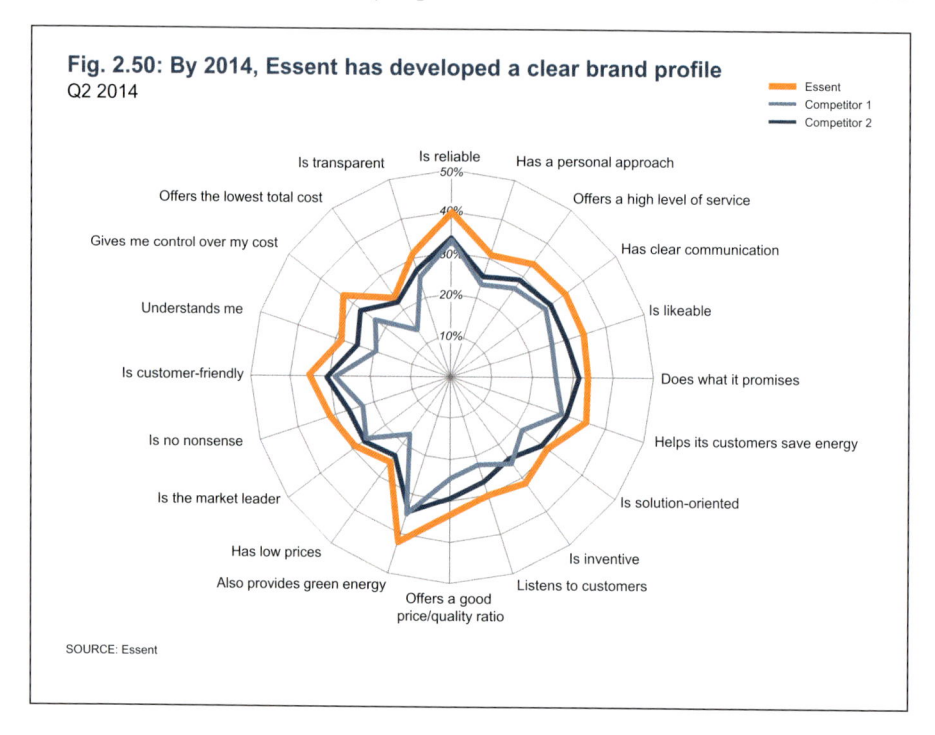

Fig. 2.50: By 2014, Essent has developed a clear brand profile
Q2 2014

SOURCE: Essent

DNA. It's something we really wanted, because it embodies our ambition to be at the forefront of the market, to be the first ones to introduce new propositions and new standards of customer service to the market. Delivery is the connection. Inventiveness without delivery is nothing, and transparency without delivery is only a promise. Our commitment to deliver on our promise is encapsulated in our claim, »Essent levert,« or »Essent delivers« in English.

So transparency, inventiveness, and delivery are our core values. In addition, we also are committed to longevity, reliability, and empathic leadership, although we do not claim these commitments directly. If you claim these things explicitly, people don't believe you. So we chose to let our actions speak for themselves. One example of how brand values shape our behavior is the use of WhatsApp as a customer service channel, an innovation that we were the first to introduce to the Dutch market in mid-2014. The message we are sending with innovations like this is that we are the brand that drives the market by doing whatever it takes to deliver superior customer service. In fact, repositioning the brand was only one of several steps we took to drive customer growth. In parallel, we worked on pricing and channel development to ensure a consistent face to the market.

**McKinsey:** Did you consider introducing additional brands to be able to reach a bigger share of the market? A no-frills brand, perhaps, to serve the bargain hunters?

**Dorkas Koenen:** We had a second brand in our portfolio, energiedirect.nl, and that brand was more or less doing the same as the main brand. If you don't provide clear steering for brands in a commodity market, they will all veer to the middle, because there is a lot to gain in the middle of the market. So we repositioned Essent as a service-driven brand, focusing on »delivery,« »doing what you say,« and »being a leader.« Simultaneously, we reignited the second brand, energiedirect.nl, and we differentiated this second brand through price leadership combined with online service and sales. Energiedirect.nl targets the bargain hunters explicitly, and it even says so in the brand claim, »altijd grip op je knip« in Dutch; that translates into English as »always control over your wallet.«

Serving bargain hunters, however, is not the only purpose of energiedirect.nl. It also helps us protect Essent, the main brand. Trying to cover a commodity market in its entirety will always put a single brand under a lot of strain. Although cheap electricity and gas contracts are only a part of the story, competitors will always challenge you on price. Unlike energiedirect.nl, Essent stands for the belief that bringing your energy bill down is not just about your tariff, but also about the quality of energy that you use and about your behavior, and Essent helps its customers find the type of service that suits their needs. In contrast, energiedirect.nl competes on price more directly and more explicitly. As a group, this makes you much less vulnerable. Two complementary brands make it much harder for competitors to play against you. If you have only one brand, competitors will always pull you into the price corner, simply because one fourth of all customers will switch providers because of price alone.

**McKinsey:** How did you arrive at the decision to have one main brand and one bargain brand? Why not four brands to serve every segment with a tailor-made proposition?

**Dorkas Koenen:** We've had a portfolio of brands for years, and we've now brought it into balance. I've told you about the four customer segments, but that may not be the last word. Needs are changing all the time, and new segments might well arise. If they do, we are willing and prepared to launch additional brands. In fact, we may well need at least one more brand in the future. For the time being, we decided to focus on managing two brands with distinct identities properly, not just in terms of the brand promise, but also in terms of the business model. The large brand, Essent, is the premium brand. It covers more than electricity and gas. It provides an entire set of home energy solutions and added services, delivered through multiple channels. Energiedirect.nl does not provide any of that. It is only accessible online, and its core promise is cost control. We always have to remind ourselves to keep them different, since all brands are drawn to the middle of the market where you can make a lot of money.

So if you want to manage multiple brands, the first checkpoint is to see whether you can manage two without veering back to the middle. Now we have proof of principle, and that gives us the time and the space to add further brands to our portfolio if need be. Depending on how the market develops, it may not even be an energy brand, at least not in the narrow sense of the word. At any rate, if you have two brands, you can think about three. But don't jump from one to three. It's one – two – three.

**McKinsey:** After the repositioning, how is Essent different from Eneco?

**Dorkas Koenen:** Eneco is a brand banking on its sustainability image. And they can, too, because they have a production park that is 100 percent sustainable. So they have a sweet spot in the market based on a promise they can deliver upon. Stakeholders love it. In daily practice, however, sustainability will grow into a hygiene factor for everybody. So Eneco has a good position today, but its longevity is subject to debate. Compare the car industry. Twenty years ago, having a catalytic converter was a source of differentiation. Today, all cars have one. That doesn't mean I don't admire Eneco. I do. They have a great, creative atmosphere. Eneco also has a second brand, Oxxio, their price fighter. For Nuon, it's more difficult, since they don't have a second brand. They have only one brand, covering the entire market. And repeatedly, they have been forced to compete on price. They try to combine price with other attributes, but after a few months, they always find themselves drawn back into a price war. And they cannot afford to miss out because they have no second brand.

In contrast, Essent competes neither on price nor on sustainability. It competes on service. I believe that service is the new marketing. You can always improve your service, so you can sustain this competitive advantage over long periods of time. Ten years ago, customers wanted to be able to call us. Three years ago, they wanted to e-mail us. Now they want to have an online environment. In one year, they will get their service through Twitter, and in two years, they may get it through WhatsApp predominantly. If you can keep up with these developments, and live up to customer expectations, you can sustain your competitive advantage. The trick is to differentiate your brand in an area of the market in which you can continue to differentiate it beyond the next two or three years.

**McKinsey:** Can you tell our readers about the implementation of the new brand promise, both in terms of external communication and internal activation? What did you do to ensure the brand promise is delivered at all relevant touch points?

**Erwin van Laethem:** The first stage was to focus on the customer and, let's say, develop the positioning outside in. And then we complimented that by going from the inside out. So we were really defining the sweet spots both from a market perspective and from the perspective of the organization. Once we had come up with »Essent levert,« that resonated really well in the organization. People were mobilized by that because it clearly hit a sweet spot. So we started with customers, but engaging employees was crucial as well. Everything is now simpler for the customer, it's simpler for the employees, and it's simpler for the IT systems. We are serious about customer centricity, and we have simplified core processes from 25 steps to 12 steps or even as few as 7 or 8 steps.

**Dorkas Koenen:** If you promise that »Essent delivers,« which is our claim, then you have to deliver. To make this happen, we combined the marketing transformation with what we call the »House in Order« program and our Customer Value Center.

Once we had decided that this was the way to go – that we want to be the leaders in the way we provide service to customers, and to be the first ones with new propositions – it became clear that we had to put our house in order. We quickly agreed that if this is what we promise, we would have to have the easiest onboarding process. If this is what we promise, we would have to have the best moving process. If this is what we promise, we have to have an online service platform that extends to social media. We got a lot of pull at all levels of the organization, from top management to service professionals. Our teams were acutely aware that if this was to be our new brand promise, they would have to connect customers as quickly as possible. So we used the new promise to kick off a customer excellence program – largely driven by an operational excellence perspective – in order to elevate our service level to a position well above the market average. That was the first step, the »House in Order« program.

In a second step, we established the Customer Value Center. It teaches our teams to ask themselves a simple question, no matter whether they are in a phone call or providing online service: How can I deliver in a way that serves the customer, the company, and me as an employee? This triangle was the second device that we used to make sure our promise is kept at all times. You must not reposition a brand in a way that is disconnected from everything else that happens in the company. In a service industry, you cannot take the brand in a direction that is out of touch with the front line. You have to piggyback on existing trends and traits – for the benefit of the company as whole, not just for the benefit of the marketing department. In the end, I get paid by the company. The brand has to help the company, and the company has to help the brand.

**McKinsey:** How did the repositioning help Essent become the company that it is today? What was the impact on brand perception and business performance?

**Dorkas Koenen:** There is impact in three areas: brand preference, customer growth, and loyalty. Most importantly, the repositioning helped us to become the brand with highest brand preference in the energy market – not only for private customers, but also for small and medium-sized enterprises. We did not have that position five years ago, but now we do, in B2C as well as in SME. That's a big accomplishment. We have surpassed Nuon, the traditional brand leader. Secondly, it drove customer growth for three years in a row. For an incumbent brand, that's also quite remarkable. How did we do it? In order to live up to the brand promise, we started creating all kinds of new propositions. Obviously, it's not the new brand positioning alone that brings in new customers. It's the right combination of proposition, brand, and channel. What the brand did contribute, however, was the motivation for marketing and sales to come up with a lot of new ideas on how to provide better service to customers. Thirdly, it helped sustain the level of loyalty in an eroding market. On average, churn has almost doubled over the course of the last five years. In general, loyalty rates are declining for everybody.

People think that you use your brand to generate more sales. But in contractual industries, such as energy, that isn't always the case. As the churn rate in such markets increases, you use your brand primarily to keep your customers loyal. The brand is your best loyalty instrument. If you use the brand to give people the feeling they are well-served at a fair price, and that they don't miss out on anything that they need, they will stay with you – even when it would be easy to switch. If people feel emotionally connected to your brand, that's the best switch barrier.

**McKinsey:** What were the big surprises along the way? Any »aha« moments that you would like to share with our readers?

**Dorkas Koenen:** The first »aha« was that this repositioning got the company out of paralysis. It gave so much new energy to the company and its commercial development. The brand gives direction, and if you give the brand itself a good direction, it will lead the way for the entire company. Before, we were more or less paralyzed from a commercial perspective. Now, everybody is cut loose. People are looking for opportunities in order to live up to the brand promise. In the two and a half years before the repositioning, we did not invent a single new proposition. Today, customers are sending me letters complaining that we are introducing too many new things, and that they have a hard time following us. I would call that a luxury problem. The second »aha« moment was a role reversal. Previously, marketing had to ask for brand investments. Now, people elsewhere in the company are building business cases to validate brand investments, instead of challenging them. They now have a clear sense of how the brand helps their business. And the third »aha« moment was that the repositioning introduced a real »fact-based marketing« mentality to Essent. People thought, if we can do fact-based brand positioning, then why not run the entire marketing department based on facts? My team is really motivated to establish a fact-based way of doing marketing now. They aspire to become fully accountable for all our marketing investments. The whole effort brought the marketing department to new levels of professionalism and confidence. If you combine science, art, and craft to develop your brand, it encourages people to apply science, art, and craft to everything that they do.

**McKinsey:** Mr. van Laethem, when you look back on this whole journey, what advice would you give someone who starts on a similar journey?

**Erwin van Laethem:** To deliver results, you need to have the right people on board. Don't compromise on that. Leave the positions open until you to get the right people, regardless of whether you attract them externally or develop them internally. At the same time, make sure you actively create an environment for these people to be successful. Establish a common approach, create a common language, and align the organization across all functions, from product development and pricing to sales and service. As a CEO, it's your job to make sure the marketing team can focus on marketing. When I talk to our staff now, I'm amazed to see how well it worked. When I ask someone in the call center, why do you do it this way, they will say, I do it this way because I know it's good for the customer and I know it's good for the company, because I save costs or I add value. And it's also good for me because I am able to have a meaningful and value-added conversation with the customer, so I feel good as well. So the customer feels good, the employee feels good, and it's good for the company. I'm really impressed that people actually manage to internalize the framework and reproduce it in their own words. The customer determines, and Essent delivers.

# Notes

1. http://interbrand.com/de/best-global-brands/2013/sector-overviews/financial-servces.aspx.
2. Sattler, Henrik (ed.), Praxis von Markenbewertung und Markenmanagement in deutschen Unternehmen, PwC Deutsche Revision, 2nd edition, Frankfurt: Fachverlag Moderne Wirtschaft, 2001, and Dr. Jutta Menninger, Annette Marschlich, Henrik Sattler, Siegfried Högl, Oliver Hupp et al., Praxis von Markenbewertung und Markenmanagement in deutschen Unternehmen 2005, Januar 2006.
3. http://www.ceer.eu/portal/page/portal/EER_-HOME/EER_PUBLICATIONS/NATIONAL_REPORTS/National%20reporting%202008/NR_En/E08_NR_Germany-EN_Summary.pdf.
4. https://www.ofgem.gov.uk/about-us/how-we-work/promoting-value-money.
5. For recent changes regarding brand relevance in the energy sector, see our insert on recent developments in B2C branding below.
6. Extensive primary market studies for both the B2C and the B2B sectors were carried out in conjunction with the market research institute, Marketing Centrum Münster (MCM) at the University of Münster, Germany. The research was directed by Professors Backhaus and Meffert.
7. Representativeness refers to the distribution of age and gender in the population.
8. Premium or luxury cars were not part of the survey.
9. To allow a meaningful comparison, the ratings were transferred into a standardized scale so that differences between countries become more obvious.
10. Hofstede, Geert, Culture's Consequences: Comparing Values, Behaviors, Institutions, and Organizations Across Nations, 2nd edition, Thousand Oaks, CA: Sage Publications, 2003.
11. Seat capacity share for international flights in 2007 according to Official Airline Guide (OAG).
12. All waves were overseen by Professor Marc Fischer, Chair for Marketing and Market Research at the University of Cologne in Germany.
13. For details on the methodology, we refer to Fischer, Völckner, and Sattler (2010): Fischer, Marc, Franziska Völckner, and Henrik Sattler (2010), »How Important Are Brands? A Cross-category, Cross-country Study,« Journal of Marketing Research, 47 (October), 823-839.
14. At the time of writing, Karstadt was about to change hands again: http://www.faz.net/aktuell/wirtschaft/unternehmen/benko-uebernimmtkarstadt-der-naechste-bitte-13098857.html.
15. DIW, German Council of Economic Experts.
16. http://de.statista.com/statistik/daten/studie/1224/umfrage/arbeitslosenquote-in-deutschland-seit-1995/ (Retrieved on October 1st, 2014).
17. http://www.plmainternational.com/industry-news/private-label-today.
18. http://www.crossmedia.de/news/auszeichnungfuer-kampagne-hornbach-hammer/.
19. Frühlingserwachen in der Baumarktbranche, absatzwirtschaft 7–8/2013.
20. http://www.spiegel.de/wirtschaft/unternehmen/baumarktkette-praktiker-stellt-insolvenzantrag-a-910617.html.
21. http://www.boerse-online.de/nachrichten/aktien/OTS-PCG-Project-Consult-GmbH-Ein-Jahrnachder-Praktiker-Pleite-Bilanz–1000201524.
22. In the energy markets of other countries, competitive intensity (and, perhaps, brand relevance as well) is higher than in Germany. In this respect, Germany might be considered to be moving towards a new normal.
23. For details, please compare the brochure »Energize your brand,« published by the authors of this book in 2011.
24. http://interbrand.com/en/best-global-brands/previous-years/best-global-brands-2009.aspx.
25. http://eur-lex.europa.eu/legal-content/EN/TXT/PDF/?uri=CELEX:32003L0033&from=EN; http://eur-lex.europa.eu/LexUriServ/LexUriServ.do?uri=OJ:L:2007:332:0027:0045:EN:PDF.
26. Sophie Borland, A step closer to plain cigarette packaging, Daily Mail, April 2, 2014.
27. http://www.tagblatt.ch/aktuell/schweiz/schweizsda/Bundesrat-will-Zigaretten-Werbungverbieten;art253650,3818490; Jonas Hoskyn, »Neues Tabakgesetz bedroht Art-Sponsoring,« Basler Zeitung, August 12, 2014.
28. https://www.destatis.de/DE/PresseService/Presse/Pressemitteilungen/zdw/2014/PD14_017_p002pdf.pdf?__blob=publicationFile.
29. Lena Schipper, »Letzte Runde im Pub an der Ecke,« Frankfurter Allgemeine Sonntagszeitung, August 17, 2014.
30. http://www.gevestor.de/news/der-bierkonsumnimmt-weltweit-zu-aber-nicht-in-deutschland-716313.html.
31. http://www.euromonitor.com/luxury-goods-inpoland/report.
32. http://www.welt.de/motor/article1966183/Moskau-ist-die-Hauptstadt-des-Maybach.html.
33. http://www.thisismoney.co.uk/money/markets/article-2704647/IMF-gloom-Russia-Ukrainesanctions-fuel-anxiety-Europe.html.
34. Gregory, James R. and Donald E. Sexton, »Hidden Wealth in B2B«, Harvard Business Review, March 2007 (data for 2006).
35. Caspar, Mirko, Achim Hecker, and Tatjana Sabel, »Markenrelevanz in der Unternehmensführung: Messung, Erklärung und empirische Befunde für

B2B-Märkte,« Arbeitspapier Nr. 4, ed. Klaus Backhaus et al., Düsseldorf, 2002. A total of 48 product markets were surveyed, of which 45 fulfilled the necessary requirements for validity.
36 Compare de Chernatony, Leslie and Malcolm McDonald, Creating Powerful Brands in Consumer Services and Industrial Markets, Oxford: Butterworth-Heinemann, 1998.
37 http://www.mckinsey.de/sites/mck_files/files/b2b_branding.pdf.
38 For details on the 2012 B2B brand relevance survey and its implications for B2B brand managers, compare our brochure »Business Branding,« published by McKinsey's Marketing and Sales Practice in March 2013, and the McKinsey Quarterly article »How B2B companies talk past their customers, « published in October 2013. Also compare Lennartz, Eric M., Marc Fischer, Manfred Krafft and Kay Peters (2014), »Drivers of B2B Brand Strength Insights from an International Study Across Industries,« Schmalenbach Business Review, forthcoming.
39 http://www.gimmesomeoven.com/aldi-101-why-ishop-at-aldi/.
40 Ehrnrooth Hanna , Gronroos Christian , (2013) »The hybrid consumer: exploring hybrid consumption behaviour«, Management Decision, Vol. 51 Iss: 9, pp.1793 – 1820.
41 Strauss, Ralph E.: Marketing Planning by Design. Systematic planning for Successful Marketing Strategy, John Wiley & Sons Ltd., Chichester, 2008.
42 White Strip sales according to Felix Oberholzer-Gee and Dennis Yao, »Brighter Smiles for the Masses – Colgate vs. P&G,« Harvard Business School, 21 Mar 2007. Henkel sales according to Bear Sterns Report »The Drag of Invested Capital, « 10 Sep 2007. X-ite launch as announced on http://www.henkel.de/de/content_data/PM_Theramed_X-itel.pdf. Tooth fairy campaign according to http://www.kosmetiknachrichten.de/2013/02/11/theramed-x-ite-die-legende-von-derzahnfee-geht-auf-2-0/.
43 Hölscher, Ansgar, »Customer Insights«, in Hajo Riesenbeck/Jesko Perrey (eds.): Marketing nach Maß, Heidelberg, 2007.
44 Deardorff, Julie, »Americans flocking to fortified water,« Chicago Tribune web edition, Associated Press, and John Sicher/Beverage Digest, 27 Sep 2007. 2013 sales figures according to Soft Drinks: Euromonitor from trade sources/national statistics; date exported 05/08/2014.
45 Wolfe Bieler, Kirsten, »Behind the Yellow Tail«, Beverage Media, Mar 2006; »The Wine Paper 7 Wine Marketing Australasia«; http://www.drinksint.com/files/Most_admired/PDFWorld_s_Most_Admired_Wine_Brands_PDF_March_2014.pdf; http://www.winepages.com/organise/yellow-tail.htm.

46 http://www.forbes.com/sites/steveolenski/2014/02/21/a-fortune-500-brand-and-the-ever-changingrole-of-consumer-insights/ (retrieved Aug 14, 2014); McKinsey literature search.
47 web.sys.virginia.edu/files/capstone_old_projects/.../2001-02.doc.
48 H.W. Schroiff quote according to July 28, 2005 Henkel press release (»Reconnaissance«).
49 http://www.s2customerinsight.com/casestudies/coca-cola-case-study.pdf.
50 http://online.wsj.com/news/articles/SB10001424053111904194604576578691502178606.
51 Web research; database search; company information (http://www.heinzdipandsqueeze.com/), retrieved in August 2014.
52 Ramge, Thomas, »Ratatazong! Die Hilti ist der Rolls-Royce auf dem Bau. Nur innovativer. Wie machen die das? Vier Fragen zum Erfolgsmodell. Und deutlich mehr Antworten,« Brand Eins, Dec 2007.
53 Web research; ConExpo 2011, MC2; http://www.b2bmarketing.net/knowledgebank/branding/features/campaign-month-john-deerelaunches-its-own-chat-show; http://www.betterroads.com/deeres-bright-ideashybrid-diesel-electric-wheel-loader-new-line-ofskid-steers-and-compact-track-loaders/.
54 http://investor.ea.com/financials.cfm.
55 Internet search, Dewmocracyhub.com; Adweek 2010 »What Mountain Dew Learned from ›DEWmocracy.‹«
56 Horizont/TNS Emnid, »Verbraucher werden Markenprodukten untreu,« 26 Mar 2003. http://www.riechstoffverband.de/fakten-rs/fragen_antworten_riechstoffe/.
57 This is neither a debate about the merits and disadvantages of market segmentation nor a scientific discussion of the methods and techniques of determining target groups. The current marketing science literature provides comprehensive answers to nearly all these questions (e. g., Bonoma/Shapiro 1984, Meffert 2000).
58 Marketing Executives Networking Group, 2007.
59 Schellekens, Maarten, »Segmentierung,« in Hajo Riesenbeck/Jesko Perrey (eds.): Marketing nach Maß, Heidelberg, 2007; PepsiMax performance according to PepsiCo Trade Marketing Manager Nicky Seal; http://wheresthesausage.typepad.com/my_weblog/2010/03/leaders-are-hard-to-beat-coke-zero-vspepsi-max.html; http://www.cnbc.com/id/38346760#.
60 Sellers, Patricia, »Starbucks: The Next Generation,« Fortune, 4 Apr 2005.
61 Euromonitor, 2013.
62 http://daxueconsulting.com/shampoo-market-inchina/.
63 Haley, R.I., »Benefit Segmentation: A decision oriented tool,« Journal of Marketing, Jul 1968, pp. 30 – 35.

64 Perrey, Jesko and Ansgar Hölscher, »Nutzenorientierte Kundensegmentierung: Eine Zwischenbilanz nach 35 Jahren,« Thexis 20, No. 4, 2004, pp. 8–11; Bonoma, Thomas V. and Benson P. Shapiro, »Evaluating Market Segmentation Approaches,« Industrial Marketing Management 13, 1984, pp. 257–268; Perrey, Jesko, Nutzenorientierte Marktsegmentierung: Ein integrativer Ansatz zum Zielgruppenmarketing im Verkehrsdienstleistungsbereich, Wiesbaden: Gabler, 1999, p. 129.

65 Voeth, Markus, Nutzenmessung in der Kaufverhaltensforschung: Die Hierarchisch Individualisierte Limit Conjoint-Analyse (HILCA), Wiesbaden: Deutscher Universitätsverlag, 2000.

66 http://www.forbes.com/sites/steveolenski/2014/02/21/a-fortune-500-brand-and-the-ever-changingrole-of-consumer-insights/.

67 For a broader discussion of how technology is affecting retail, see by Stefan Niemeier, Andrea Zocchi, Marco Catena, »Reshaping Retail: Why Technology is Transforming the Industry and How to Win in the New Consumer Driven World«, Wiley 2013.

68 All funnel research referred to in this chapter was conducted at McKinsey's expense. The brands in question were not involved in the way the research was prepared, conducted, or analyzed. The automotive sample consisted of people who had bought a new compact car within the 12 months preceding the date of the survey.

69 The sample for energy is representative only of consumers who had switched their energy provider, or signed a new contract with their prior provider, within the 12 months preceding the date of the survey.

70 http://www.tagesanzeiger.ch/wirtschaft/unternehmen-und-konjunktur/Die-teuerste-Sommerkampagne-aller-Zeiten/story/29787656; http://www.myswitzerland.com/en/tempting-citybreaks-ipad.html.

71 The survey referenced in this section was conducted independently in late 2013 and early 2014 to illustrate the BrandMatics approach.

72 We gratefully acknowledge the contribution of Professor Dr. Marc Fischer, Chair for Marketing and Market Research at the University of Cologne, to the development of the enhanced funnel, and for his help with the pilot research conducted in 2013 and 2014.

73 David Court, Dave Elzinga, SusanMulder, Ole Jørgen Vetvik, The consumer decision journey: »Consumers are moving outside the purchasing funnel_changing the way they research and buy your products.«, McKinsey Quarterly, June 2009; http://www.mckinsey.com/insights/marketing_sales/the_consumer_decision_journey.

74 See our section on digital brand management below for details.

75 In future waves of research, it will be interesting to see whether the dynamic is the same in the US market, where many car buyers are less involved and will take their pick from what is available at the dealer lot, rather than order directly from the manufacturer.

76 Note that a »prior customer« in the candy bar category is defined as someone who has »bought the brand at least 3 times out of last 10 purchases in the category.«

77 http://consumerist.com/2009/12/10/you-must-buycandy-at-checkout/.

78 http://lebensmittelpraxis.de/sortiment/1565-zumguten-schluss%20.html.

79 http://www.britannica.com/EBchecked/topic/623470/variety-seeking-buying-behaviour.

80 http://en.wikipedia.org/wiki/Snickers.

81 While this observation might seem trivial at first sight, it really reveals the need to differentiate between prior customers and new customers, at least in certain industries. Obviously, they react to different purchase triggers, and companies would be well-advised to adjust their acquisition and retention strategies accordingly.

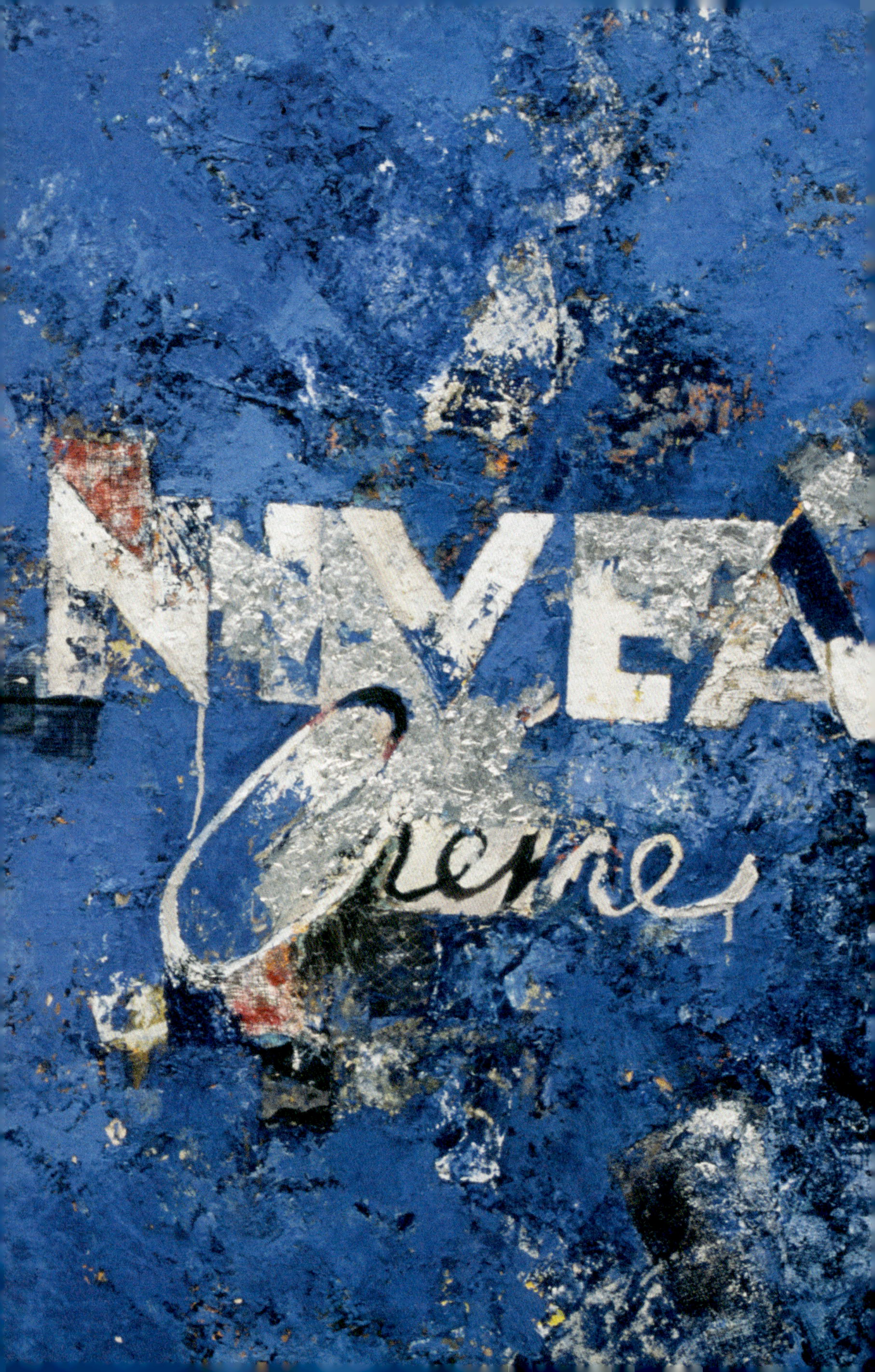
NIVEA
Creme

# 3. Making Brands

Brands are mostly made, not born. They do not arise accidentally. Their growth and development can be measured and predicted. This is the main message of this book.

The success of a brand is measurable at every stage along its path: tools and methods exist that can measure the status of a brand in the competitive environment. We have already introduced three such tools and methods in Chapter 2:

- **Brand relevance measurement**: Determines how relevant brands are in influencing purchasing decisions in a particular market.
- **Customer insights and market segmentation**: Identifies, evaluates, and specifies a brand's target customer groups.
- **The brand purchase funnel**: Measures customer recognition, affinity, and commitment to a brand at the various stages that lead to (and follow) purchase.

Brand managers need to be familiar with these analytical tools and methods and know how to apply them. They reveal the facts of the matter, but they do not tell you what to do to strengthen the brand. Thus, brand managers face many unanswered questions. What can be done to restore a luxury brand to its former glory? How can strong brands be protected from the competition and get even stronger? Can the existing brand and its promise be adjusted, or is it necessary to develop a completely new positioning? What impact will it have to follow the recommendation of an advertising agency and make a given brand more emotional? To help brand managers answer these and similar questions, this chapter introduces a range of tools that are central to the »making« of power brands: brand driver analysis, the resulting matrix of options, brand portfolio management, and brand leverage.

## 3.1 Mapping Brand Image

The brand purchase funnel measures the performance of the brand at the various stages leading to purchase and loyalty. It reveals where there are gaps in comparison with relevant competitors, quantifies these gaps, and ranks them according to their significance. This analysis creates transparency about a brand's strengths and weaknesses, but it leaves brand management with a serious question: How can these gaps be closed if at all? To be more precise: How can the brand be repositioned relative to its competitors so that current and potential customers will better notice it, and how can it capture the untapped sales indicated by the brand potential analysis? Looking back at the examples discussed in earlier chapters, brand managers need to understand what factors are responsible for shortcomings along the purchase funnel.

- What accounts for a brand's dominance in the compact car category?
- Which brand elements drive purchase decisions in the energy market?
- Why do German tourists prefer Austria to Switzerland as a destination?

## Two types of brand benefits

Strong brands generate an unmistakable image in the minds of consumers. Companies must understand the nature of this image and its influence on consumer behavior. This knowledge is the basis for developing the brand image in a way that helps trigger the decision to purchase. Successfully influencing behavior in this manner will increase the value of the brand.[1]

As the basis for reliable measurement of brand performance, the image of a brand has to be captured holistically and reliably across all its relevant dimensions. If the list of attributes is incomplete, there will be gaps in the subsequent analysis of customer behavior, since BrandMatics® uses attributes to explain brand performance and consumer behavior. If companies miss out on certain such attributes, they will possibly miss out on opportunities to understand and activate their target audience.

In marketing science, both the foundations and the creation of brand image have been studied extensively.[2] Numerous approaches have been developed based on behavioral science and with the aid of brand equity research. These approaches seek to understand and structure brand associations.[3] Nearly all these concepts feature a hierarchical structure that differentiates between attributes, benefit perceptions formed from these attributes, and the resulting global attitudes or associations.

Building on the work of others and working closely with Professor Christoph Burmann of the University of Bremen, McKinsey has developed an approach to capture brand image that revolves around the following hierarchical assumptions:

- Benefits drive behavior.
- The brand can provide either functional or symbolic benefits.
- Such benefits are experienced, and need to be substantiated, at all relevant customer touch points.[4]

McKinsey's approach captures the characteristics of a given brand holistically. It distinguishes between two fundamental brand functions, or types of benefits (Figure 3.1):

**Functional characteristics** are the objective features of a given brand and its products that can be counted, weighed, or measured, such as »low consumption« for a car brand, »strong regional presence« for a service provider, »good sound quality« for a mobile phone brand, or »quick energy« for a type of candy bar. These elements vary greatly across industries and need to be identified with the help of industry experts.

**Symbolic characteristics** are the elements that define the subjective image or personality of a brand in the customer's mind. While there is no standard battery of these attributes, they tend to be more similar across industries than functional characteristics, although they vary across countries because of cultural differences. Examples include trustworthiness, likeability, simplicity, exclusivity, or fun.

Figure 3.2 shows some examples of both functional and symbolic brand attributes for the industries we have examined from the perspective of the brand funnel in Chapter 2, Section 2.3, and will examine in more detail in what follows.

3.1 Mapping Brand Image

### Fig. 3.1: Two types of brand characteristics

CONCEPTUAL

|  | Functional | Symbolic |
| --- | --- | --- |
| What it is | Characteristics than can be weighed and measured | Values<br>Attitudes<br>Personality traits |
| How it is perceived | Directly<br>Objectively | Indirectly<br>Subjectively |
| Primary brand functions | Risk reduction<br>Information efficiency | Image benefit |
| Examples | Good value for money<br>Reliable | Likeable<br>Makes me feel good |

SOURCE: McKinsey M&S Practice

### Fig. 3.2: Examples of brand characteristics

ILLUSTRATIVE

|  | Functional | Symbolic |
| --- | --- | --- |
| Automotive | High resale value<br>Good dealer network<br>Low fuel consumption | Fun to drive<br>Trustworthy<br>Makes me proud |
| Energy | Low prices<br>Long-term financial benefit<br>Good customer service | Simple<br>Likeable<br>Reliable |
| Candy | Best value for my money<br>Available everywhere<br>Relatively quick energizer | Satisfies my craving<br>Has fun advertising<br>… |

SOURCE: McKinsey M&S Practice

## The brand diamond

These two fundamental categories of brand image – functional and symbolic – are helpful to get an initial sense of the characteristics that drive a given market. For a more comprehensive mapping, these characteristics can be further subdivided into benefits and attributes. Combining the two dimensions – functional versus symbolic and benefits versus attributes – yields the brand diamond, McKinsey's framework of choice to capture brand image at the high level of detail required by BrandMatics® (Figure 3.3):

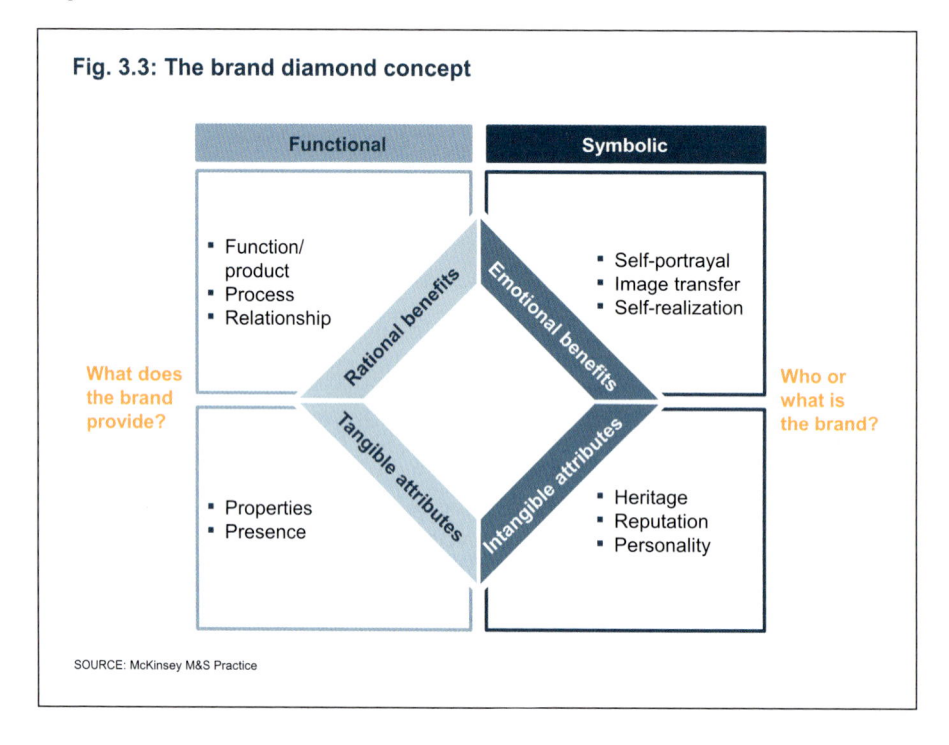

**Fig. 3.3: The brand diamond concept**

**Functional** | **Symbolic**

- Function/product
- Process
- Relationship

- Self-portrayal
- Image transfer
- Self-realization

What does the brand provide? | Who or what is the brand?

Rational benefits / Emotional benefits
Tangible attributes / Intangible attributes

- Properties
- Presence

- Heritage
- Reputation
- Personality

SOURCE: McKinsey M&S Practice

The diamond captures both the attributes that are inherent in the brand (lower half), independent of its consumption, and the benefits it provides to the consumer (upper half). The brand diamond represents all the associations linked to a brand and their relationship with one another.

With this method, the attribute and benefit associations of brand image can be divided into four categories. Moving clockwise from the bottom left, these categories are:

- **Functional characteristics** (left side of the diamond)
  - *Tangible attributes.* The associations in this category are generally those that arise first in the perception of the consumer. This category includes all the characteristics that can be perceived by the senses. They form the basis for the strength of a brand's image in the minds of consumers. They can be physical or functional in nature, such as engine horsepower or product design, as well as related to a brand's presentation – as communicated in advertising, for instance.

- *Rational benefits.* All the measurable benefits the brand brings the consumer fall into this category. Rational benefits can be expressed in the product or its function (e.g., comfortable seats), the transaction process (convenient transaction handling), or in the relationship of the consumer to the brand or provider (good consultation from friendly staff). Rational benefits are directly related to tangible brand elements. A high-speed train, for instance, offers the rational benefit of reduced travel time.
- **Symbolic characteristics** (right side of the diamond)
  - *Emotional benefits.* Consumers associate an emotional benefit with a brand if it reinforces their personal self-image (image transfer) or self-expression. Brands can be used in this manner as status symbols that provide prestige. Examples include a Louis Vuitton handbag, a Porsche sports car, or an Apple iPhone.
  - *Intangible attributes.* This category comprises all the characteristics associated with a brand's origin, reputation, and personality that cannot be sensed directly but are nonetheless important to the consumer's understanding of the brand. These include associations such as »a brand with tradition« or »an innovative brand.« The intangible brand elements typically build on tangible ones.

The brand diamond can be used as the basis for an exhaustive analysis of the brand image in three steps. The first step is to determine all the relevant or potentially relevant brand associations in the pertinent market environment. The four dimensions of the brand diamond act as a structural aid that helps to ascertain accurately all the attributes influencing the brand image. These attributes are identified through a combination of management workshops, interviews, and preliminary quantitative market research. The old adage of »garbage in, garbage out« applies here as well, of course. If attributes that are important in influencing the brand image are not measured adequately or are neglected completely, the risk of drawing incorrect inferences for brand management is high. This is particularly true in analyzing the emotional benefits of the brand (the upper-right corner of the brand diamond). In the B2B sector, for instance, many companies have reservations about addressing the emotional benefits of the brand (»We're talking about the forklift market where the only thing that matters is what it can do and what it costs.«). In reality, the landscape of B2B brands today is no less varied than that of B2C brands, and it is not all about rational attributes either. While a forklift brand like OM claims values such as ergonomics and safety, Linde emphasizes responsibility towards customers and stakeholders – and Jungheinrich prides itself in the company's long tradition and the heritage of its founder.[5]

In fact, a detailed analysis does demonstrate how strongly the brand effect depends on the emotional benefit. These are revealed in such forms as »a brand you can trust,« »you can depend on it,« or »it fits my company.« These types of attributes are of vital importance in fulfilling a brand's fundamental risk-reducing function, even in B2B environments. In the forklift market, for example, there is a substantial segment of relationship-driven buyers. They make their brand choices based primarily on attributes such as »long tradition« and »good name« (see Chapter 2, Section 2.1 for further details on brand relevance in B2B).

In the four dimensions of the brand diamond, a total of 20 to 50 specific aspects of the image are typically taken into consideration in a brand image analysis. Selecting the right number for the brand is a trade-off between cost and reliability (of the market research) on the one hand and actionable insight (gained through additional knowledge) on the other. Companies will be inclined to include as many attributes as possible in the battery of brand characteristics. However, more than about 50 statements can rarely be implemented in market research. Also, the holistic scope of the initial long list is more important than the total number of statements that are ultimately included in the survey questionnaire. To this end, it makes sense to involve stakeholders from several functions outside marketing – such as product development, sales, and service – at an early point in the process. Existing market research can often be used to create an initial list of brand characteristics to start the discussion.

Once the image dimensions have been selected, the second step is to have these dimensions evaluated by (potential) customers in quantitative market research. A given brand's performance on these specific dimensions is typically measured using rating scales.

The third and final step is to compare the image of the company's own brand with that of competing brands. In principle, it would be possible to make a comparison for each of the dimensions of brand image. However, to avoid excessive complexity and costs, it is better to make a comparison of only those dimensions in which the brand possesses critical strengths or weaknesses.

Looking at how the brand diamond works in practice can prove helpful. In an outside-in independent market research study, McKinsey used the brand diamond to analyze brand B compared with brand A (Figure 3.4); note that this research was conducted in 2002. Results revealed that the image of brand B was superior to that of brand A in terms of symbolic value at the time. Apparently, brand A had not yet succeeded in completely shedding its image of being somewhat unexciting when the analysis was conducted. Were we to conduct the same analysis today, we would expect brand A to show an altogether more attractive image. At least that is what the superior performance of the brand in the purchase funnel suggests (see Chapter 2, Section 2.3), and the 2013 analysis of brand strengths below points in the same direction.

As this example illustrates, a brand typically evokes several categories of association. The tangible brand elements, for instance, might include a superior product concept or a creative advertising presence, which might be derived directly from the rational benefits of the brand. Though these are critical elements in a brand's success, an analysis of hundreds of brand diamonds in some dozens market environments – both in mature and emerging markets – confirms that the secret to the success of strong brands lies in the combination of rational and emotional benefits, as the leading brands demonstrate. Successful brand management needs to recognize this principle – regardless of whether the brand is in confectionery, the detergent market, or the steel industry.

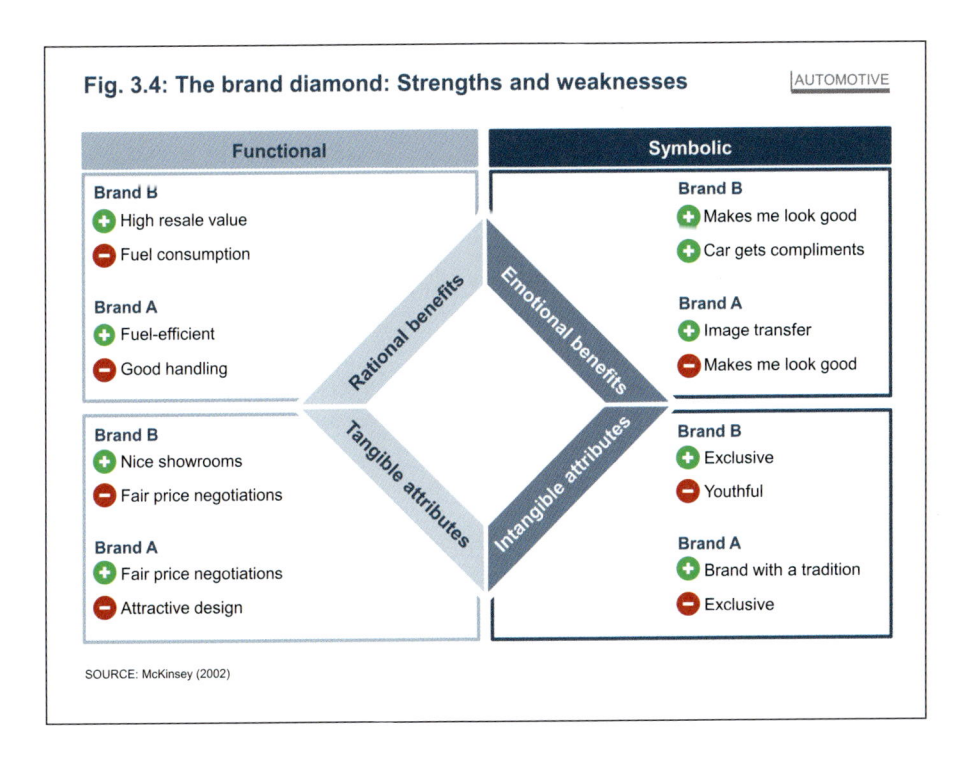

**Fig. 3.4: The brand diamond: Strengths and weaknesses** | AUTOMOTIVE

| Functional | Symbolic |
|---|---|
| **Brand B**<br>➕ High resale value<br>➖ Fuel consumption | **Brand B**<br>➕ Makes me look good<br>➕ Car gets compliments |
| **Brand A**<br>➕ Fuel-efficient<br>➖ Good handling | **Brand A**<br>➕ Image transfer<br>➖ Makes me look good |
| **Brand B**<br>➕ Nice showrooms<br>➖ Fair price negotiations | **Brand B**<br>➕ Exclusive<br>➖ Youthful |
| **Brand A**<br>➕ Fair price negotiations<br>➖ Attractive design | **Brand A**<br>➕ Brand with a tradition<br>➖ Exclusive |

Diamond axes: Rational benefits / Emotional benefits / Tangible attributes / Intangible attributes

SOURCE: McKinsey (2002)

Once the brand diamond has been used to reveal all the associations linked to the brands being studied, the next task is to shape the brand's image in the desired direction. For this purpose, it is important to gain a quantitative understanding of how the image of a brand that consumers form will influence their behavior.

## 3.2 Brand Drivers: What is Really Important for the Consumer?

The brand purchase funnel measures the performance of a brand at the various stages leading to purchase and loyalty. It reveals where there are gaps in comparison with relevant competitors, quantifies these gaps, and ranks them according to their significance. This analysis creates transparency regarding a brand's strengths and weaknesses, but it leaves brand management with a serious question: How can these gaps be closed if at all? To be more precise: How can the brand be repositioned relative to its competitors so that current and potential customers will better notice it? Looking back at the examples discussed above, brand managers need to understand what factors are responsible for consumers' paths through the purchase funnel.

- Which brand attributes drive purchase decisions in the compact car category?
- How can Switzerland improve its competitive position among German tourists?
- What can energy providers do to attract the attention of new customers?

To be able to establish what is really important for the consumer, we first need to identify all the necessary elements of the brand image in order to lead consumers from one stage of the purchase funnel to the next. We refer to these critical brand attributes as brand drivers. Comparing your own brand's performance with that of competitors on key brand drivers yields a profile of strengths and weaknesses. Brand drivers and their respective strengths can then be combined to form a matrix. From this matrix, it is then possible to derive what options management has for growing the brand and setting its strategic direction.

Thus, after compiling all the brand elements, the next step is to ensure that the brand drivers are correctly identified. To accomplish this, all the potential drivers along with the current ones must be taken into consideration. It is best practice to structure all foreseeable drivers using the brand diamond. Figure 3.5 shows a template of the potential drivers of brand image used as the starting point for a broad analysis of brand drivers in the retail trade.

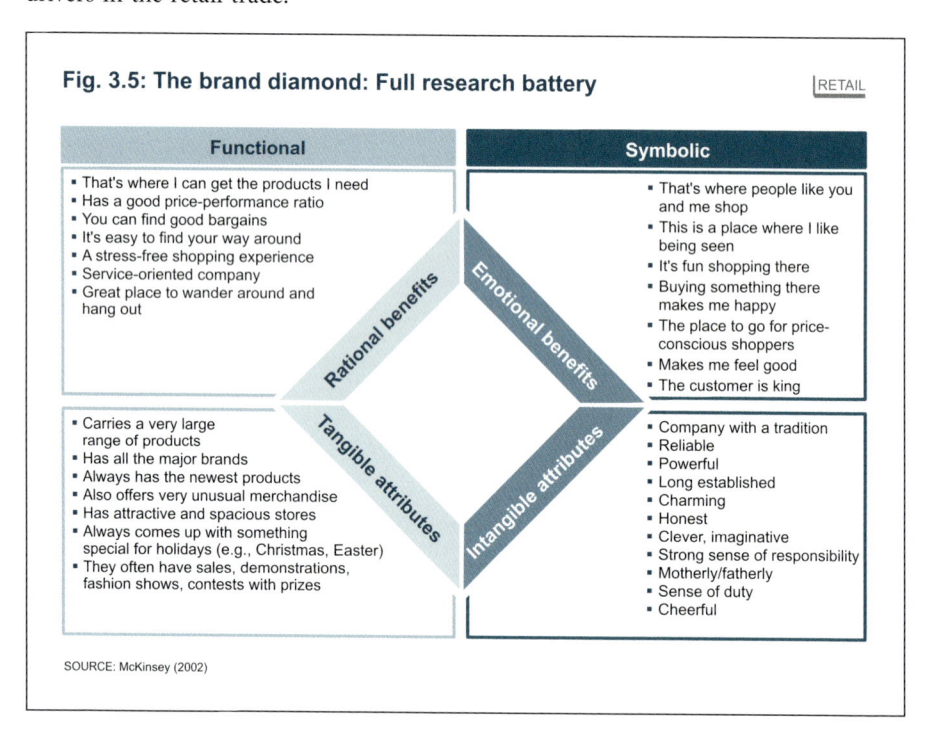

**Fig. 3.5: The brand diamond: Full research battery** — RETAIL

**Functional**
- That's where I can get the products I need
- Has a good price-performance ratio
- You can find good bargains
- It's easy to find your way around
- A stress-free shopping experience
- Service-oriented company
- Great place to wander around and hang out

**Symbolic**
- That's where people like you and me shop
- This is a place where I like being seen
- It's fun shopping there
- Buying something there makes me happy
- The place to go for price-conscious shoppers
- Makes me feel good
- The customer is king

Tangible attributes:
- Carries a very large range of products
- Has all the major brands
- Always has the newest products
- Also offers very unusual merchandise
- Has attractive and spacious stores
- Always comes up with something special for holidays (e.g., Christmas, Easter)
- They often have sales, demonstrations, fashion shows, contests with prizes

Intangible attributes:
- Company with a tradition
- Reliable
- Powerful
- Long established
- Charming
- Honest
- Clever, imaginative
- Strong sense of responsibility
- Motherly/fatherly
- Sense of duty
- Cheerful

(Rational benefits / Emotional benefits)

SOURCE: McKinsey (2002)

The associations shown in Figure 3.5 are based on surveys of consumer focus groups and discussions with market experts. Qualitative research techniques such as these are especially insightful at this early stage of the positioning process. They help to capture the richness of consumers' brand perceptions, including critical items possibly considered irrelevant by the marketing department, for example, »a meeting place for people like me,« »great place to wander around,« or »also offers very unusual merchandise.« Further details are provided in the insert on qualitative research in Chapter 2, Section 2.2. The brand associations elicited from tangible elements essentially describe operational levers, such as the quality of product assortment (»always has the newest products«), the layout of the sales floor (»has attractive and spacious stores«), or distribution (»has a good location«). The other fields of the brand diamond comprise associations that reflect the perceived customer benefit or intangible brand elements.

This kind of mapping produces a complete map of brand elements, analogous to the retail example above. The map of potential drivers is the starting point for actual brand driver analysis. The next step is to establish which associations are responsible for the consumer behavior in the purchase funnel (the brand drivers) and to determine how strongly the individual elements of the brand diamond are linked to a given brand (the brand image). The results indicate which brand elements best account for customer conversion at each stage in the purchase funnel, and how a given brand is performing on these conversion drivers.

Numerous methods of market research are available to analyze the behavioral relevance of the brand elements. A simple method frequently used is the direct customer survey based on the most important attributes. It is important, however, to note that the results of such surveys can be misleading. The fact that all consumers would like the best possible performance for the least possible money actually tells you very little. Market researchers refer to this as expectation inflation. Also, consumers have a tendency to cite rational reasons for decisions that are in fact driven at least as much by emotions, especially if a rational decision is considered socially desirable. Choosing a particular car brand for its superior safety ratings, for example, is deemed more socially acceptable than deciding based on design, performance, or image.

So instead of asking consumers directly for the reasons behind their decisions, it is more reliable to determine their actual priorities indirectly with the help of analytical methods. Although a range of multivariate techniques can be used to achieve this, the most common technique is to compare the average values. The average values of all brand attributes and benefits are compared at two sequential stages of the purchase funnel.[6] Those statements that show the greatest improvement in the average values from one stage to the next are the main brand drivers. In contrast, brand benefits and attributes whose average values do not change in the transition from one stage to the next are not significant for that step in the purchase funnel.

A good example of what this means in practice is the attribute of airline safety. The mean values of this attribute will not differ at the purchase and loyalty stages. This is because the safety of major airlines is likely to be considered equally important by both onetime users and loyal customers. The situation might be very different, however, for an attribute such as punctuality. The punctuality (or lack thereof) of an airline might well be of great significance in encouraging (or discouraging) the transition from being a onetime customer to that of becoming a loyal customer. SAS, for example, claims punctuality as its differentiating attribute in brand communication »we're on time«), while Lufthansa focuses on the emotional aspects of travel (»great escapes,« »above the clouds«). Delta claims service as its competitive advantage.

The analysis presented in Figure 3.6 confirms that the priorities cited by consumers directly can differ considerably from those derived analytically, reinforcing the point

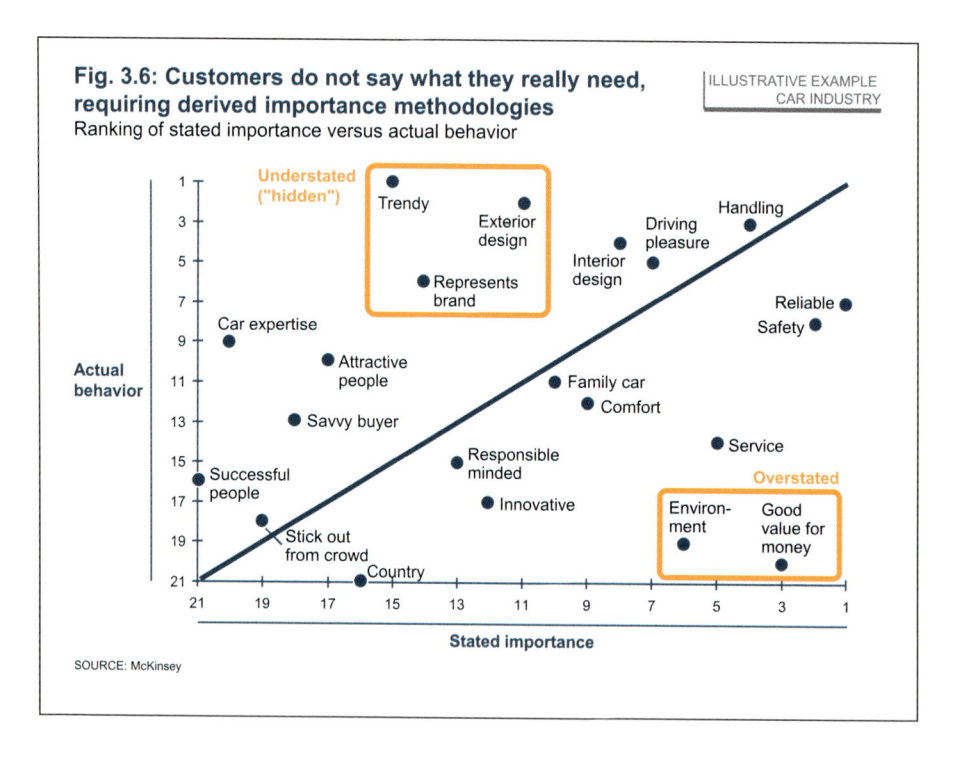

**Fig. 3.6: Customers do not say what they really need, requiring derived importance methodologies**
Ranking of stated importance versus actual behavior

ILLUSTRATIVE EXAMPLE
CAR INDUSTRY

Understated ("hidden"): Trendy, Exterior design, Represents brand

Other points: Handling, Driving pleasure, Interior design, Reliable, Safety, Car expertise, Attractive people, Family car, Comfort, Savvy buyer, Service, Responsible minded, Successful people, Innovative, Stick out from crowd, Country

Overstated: Environment, Good value for money

Axes: Actual behavior (vertical, 1–21); Stated importance (horizontal, 21–1)

SOURCE: McKinsey

that brand managers need to be cautious when using direct measurement methods.[7] The reality is that people do not always do what they say they will, and that they are not always fully aware of why they do what they do. For example, car buyers will say that »value for money« is what made them buy the brand they chose. But when this statement is tested, economic considerations do not turn out to be truly relevant as a brand driver in purchasing a car. Other attributes – such as trendiness and design – are more important drivers of consumers' behavior than they are willing or able to admit.

An analysis of consumer priorities needs to be performed for each stage of the purchase funnel. Once complete, this analysis will paint a clear picture of a consumer's path through each subsequent stage of the purchase funnel. Brand managers should, however, keep in mind that this method works best for mature and relatively stable markets. In general, brand driver analysis is unlikely to pick up on innovation as a potential market or brand driver, let alone potential product features. Often, this is simply due to the fact that researchers have a hard time identifying brand attributes that might turn out to be relevant in the future. For example, imagine Apple, Sony, or Samsung had tried to find out about the importance of »fast mobile Internet access« as a product brand attribute for cellular phones based on market research 15 years ago when the Web itself was brand new. Chances are respondents would not even have understood the question, if anyone had even had the foresight to include it in a survey. Because of this built-in delay, brand driver analysis is more appropriate for brand positioning relative to competitors in a fairly stable environment than for the development of growth opportunities beyond the current solution space.

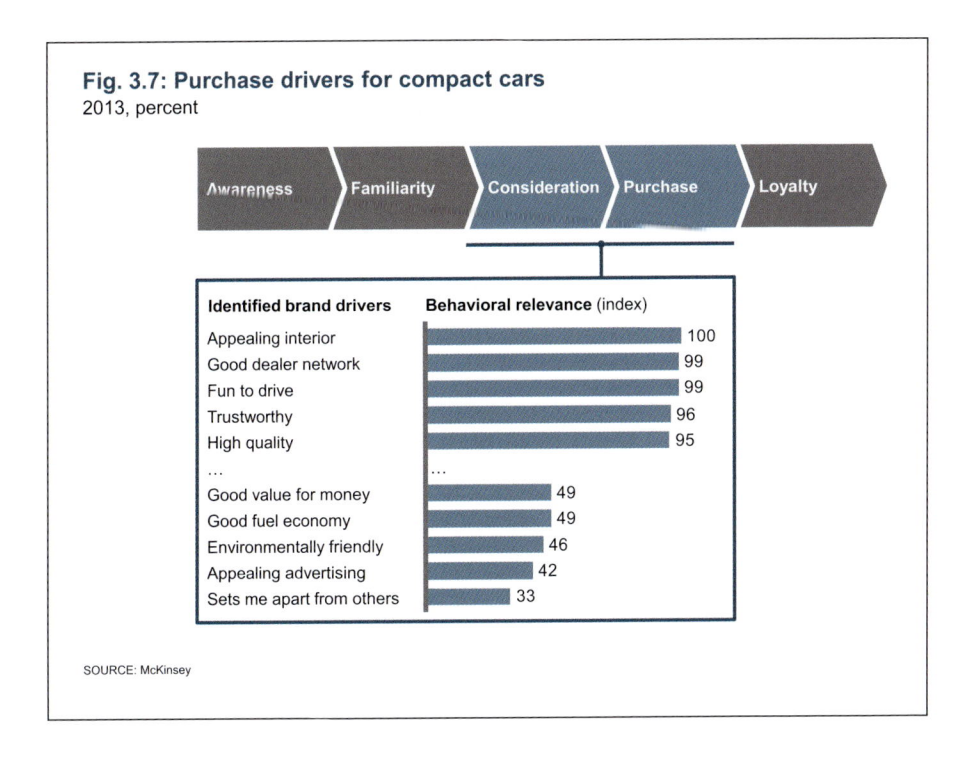

## 3.2 Brand Drivers: What is Really Important for the Consumer? 175

**Fig. 3.7: Purchase drivers for compact cars**
2013, percent

Awareness → Familiarity → Consideration → Purchase → Loyalty

| Identified brand drivers | Behavioral relevance (index) |
|---|---|
| Appealing interior | 100 |
| Good dealer network | 99 |
| Fun to drive | 99 |
| Trustworthy | 96 |
| High quality | 95 |
| ... | ... |
| Good value for money | 49 |
| Good fuel economy | 49 |
| Environmentally friendly | 46 |
| Appealing advertising | 42 |
| Sets me apart from others | 33 |

SOURCE: McKinsey

Figure 3.7 shows the results of brand driver analysis in the compact car category based on the research conducted in 2013 and 2014. The relative importance of the brand drivers is determined using the behavioral relevance index, with the top driver set to 100 percent. Apparently, the principal moment of truth in this category occurs when potential buyers get into a car they consider. If the interior appeals to them, the likelihood they will pick that particular brand will increase and vice versa. More generally, the ranking indicates that compact car buyers make their purchase decisions based on a mix of emotional criteria, such as »fun to drive,« and rational criteria, such as »good dealer network.« More mundane attributes, however, such as »value for money« and »fuel economy,« are apparently less relevant to their behavior. In this respect, nothing has changed since 2002, despite the increases in fuel costs and the advent of the hybrid drive. Today's cars may be partly powered by electricity, but primarily, consumers still want them to look nice and handle well. Perhaps BMW has squared the circle with the i8, an aggressively styled hybrid sports car with four-wheel drive and 300 HP.[8]

In the last chapter, we found that compact car brand A outperforms its key competitor, brand B, in terms of the transfer from consideration to purchase by a margin of 12 percentage points in the compact car category (Figure 2.36). When we look at how brand A is rated on the top purchase drivers, it becomes clear why the brand is so successful. Brand A is perceived as stronger than the market average on eight out of the top ten purchase drivers, and on every single one of the top five (Figure 3.8). Brand A's dealer network coupled with the high quality and resale value of its products are perceived as particularly prominent strengths, as indicated by a variance from the

### Fig. 3.8: Brand A performance on market drivers
Variance from average, percent

COMPACT CARS

| Drivers ranked according to importance | Variance (Negative / Positive) |
|---|---|
| Appealing interior | 11 |
| Good dealer network | 27 |
| Fun to drive | 1 |
| Trustworthy employees | 6 |
| High quality | 35 |
| Unique advantages | -8 |
| Trustworthy brand | 19 |
| High resale value | 79 |
| Good after-sales service | 4 |
| Attractive exterior styling | -7 |
| ... | ... |
| Environmentally friendly | -5 |
| Good fuel economy | 6 |
| One of a kind | -43 |

Average

SOURCE: McKinsey 2013/14

---

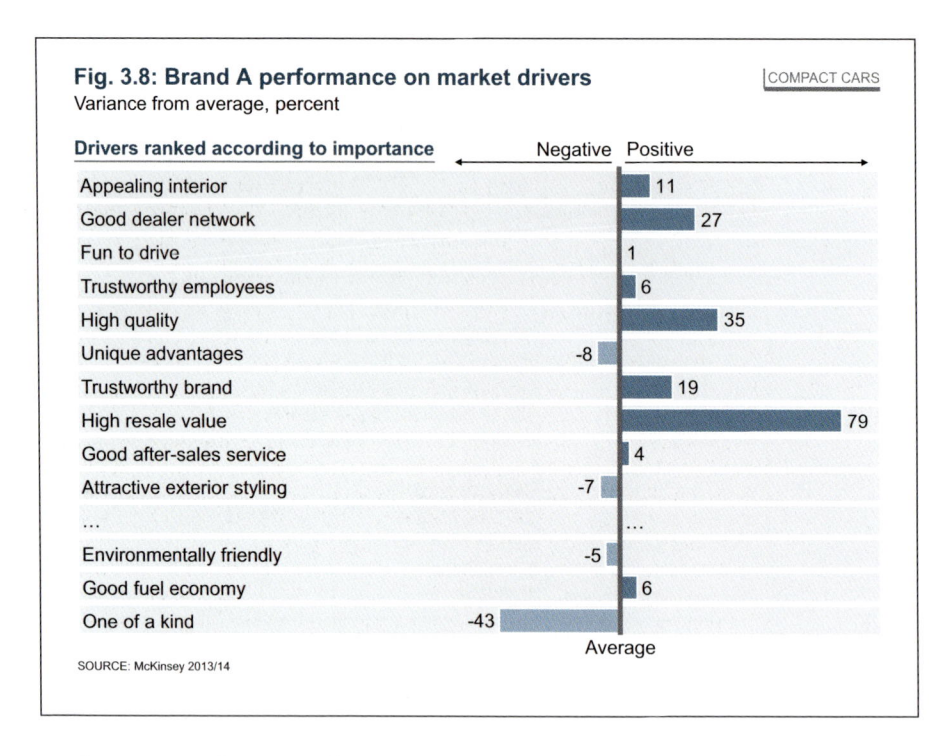

market average of 27, 35, and 79 percent respectively. What little weaknesses brand A shows are mostly restricted to attributes of low purchase relevance, such as »environmentally friendly« and »one of a kind.« The slight weakness on »unique advantages« (the full statement reads »offers advantages I won't find elsewhere«) may be attributed to the democratic appeal of brand A and the ubiquity of its products on the road.

It is all well and good to know which attributes drive a given market. But from a brand manager's perspective, it is at least as important to understand how well their brand is performing on these attributes relative to its competitors. A brand that is perceived by consumers to perform well on the purchase drivers has an advantage over its competitors. For example, a car brand that is perceived to have a »good dealer network« will be more likely to secure purchases in the compact car category than competitors that do not meet this expectation.

So once the brand drivers have been determined, the next step is to carry out an analysis of the brand's strengths and weaknesses. Quite simply: in this analysis, the benefits and elements of a company's brand are compared with those of the market average or the most important competitors, taking all the brand drivers prioritized for each stage of the brand funnel into consideration. This comparison reveals where a company's brand has been able to establish a strong, differentiated position, and in which brand drivers it lags behind the competition.

In the analysis comparing Switzerland and Austria as tourist destinations, Switzerland trailed Austria as a possible destination at the brand funnel stage »consideration.« A segment-specific evaluation shows that Switzerland's brand image – and the concomitant brand drivers – differed considerably across segments at the time the study was conducted, depending on the age group of the potential tourists. For those under 40, the most important criteria when it comes to considering a vacation destination were a »trendy destination« and »charming.« For the segment over 40, the most important drivers were »good value for money« and »high quality« (Figure 3.9). The segment specific analysis also shows that Switzerland's image was far more negative among younger people at the time.

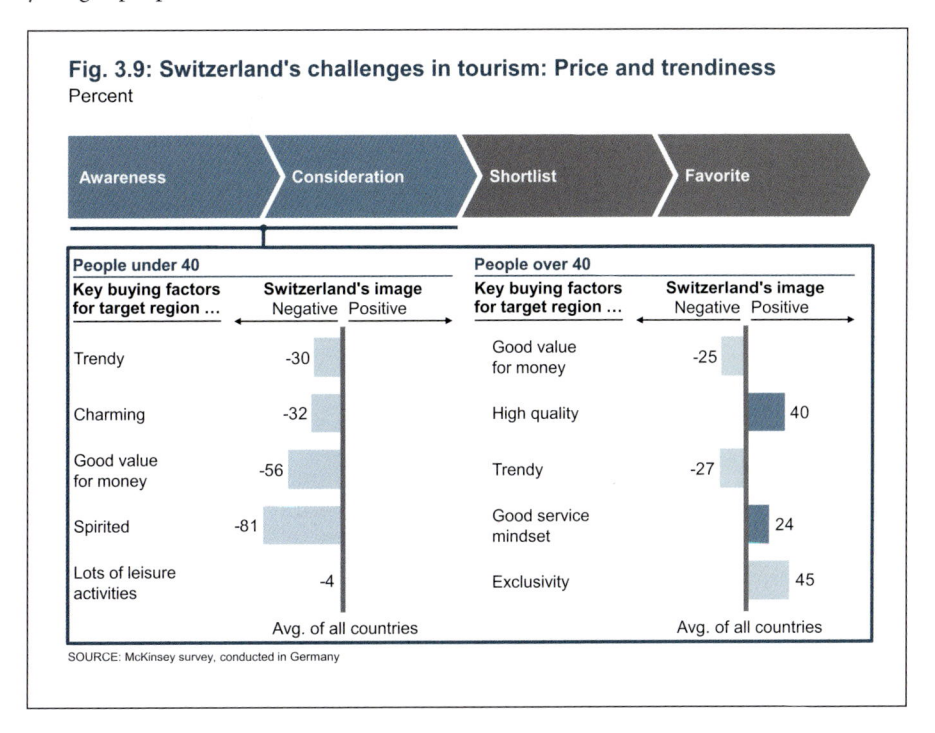

**Fig. 3.9: Switzerland's challenges in tourism: Price and trendiness**
Percent

| People under 40 | | People over 40 | |
| --- | --- | --- | --- |
| Key buying factors for target region ... | Switzerland's image Negative Positive | Key buying factors for target region ... | Switzerland's image Negative Positive |
| Trendy | -30 | Good value for money | -25 |
| Charming | -32 | High quality | 40 |
| Good value for money | -56 | Trendy | -27 |
| Spirited | -81 | Good service mindset | 24 |
| Lots of leisure activities | -4 | Exclusivity | 45 |
| Avg. of all countries | | Avg. of all countries | |

SOURCE: McKinsey survey, conducted in Germany

To appeal to the younger age group, a country in Switzerland's position would need to rejuvenate its image. For example, Swiss tourism marketing has since introduced an »adventure« section on its online portal myswitzerland, along with a range of »High Active« packages for younger visitors.[9] There is also a wide range of smartphone and tablet apps, ranging from snow reports to an interactive »Wonderland« app that takes users on a tour of the marvels of Switzerland in seven episodes – from Geneva's watchmakers to the Aletsch glacier.[10]

For the older target group, Switzerland would have wanted to emphasize the perception that it offers value for money. These days, Swiss tourism marketing is drawing the attention of prospective tourists to budget accommodations that still offer a unique experience – such as monasteries and yurts – thus combining the promise of good value (previously perceived as a weakness) with exclusivity (a perceived strength, even in 2005).[11] This example of using brand driver analysis in tourism clearly demonstrates that the brand purchase funnel is most effective when the various purchasing stages are segmented and considered target group by target group.

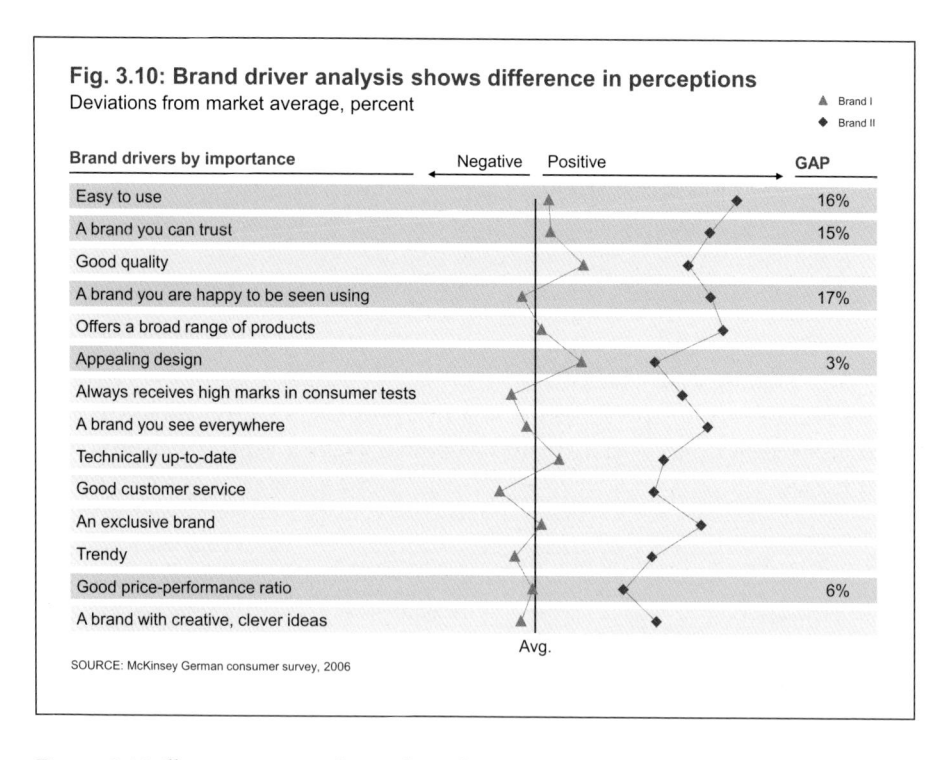

### Fig. 3.10: Brand driver analysis shows difference in perceptions
Deviations from market average, percent

▲ Brand I
♦ Brand II

| Brand drivers by importance | | GAP |
|---|---|---|
| Easy to use | | 16% |
| A brand you can trust | | 15% |
| Good quality | | |
| A brand you are happy to be seen using | | 17% |
| Offers a broad range of products | | |
| Appealing design | | 3% |
| Always receives high marks in consumer tests | | |
| A brand you see everywhere | | |
| Technically up-to-date | | |
| Good customer service | | |
| An exclusive brand | | |
| Trendy | | |
| Good price-performance ratio | | 6% |
| A brand with creative, clever ideas | | |

SOURCE: McKinsey German consumer survey, 2006

Figure 3.10 illustrates strengths and weaknesses analysis using the examples of two competing brands in the consumer electronics market. In this disguised example, brand II is obviously superior to brand I in all respects. Its lead is particularly pronounced regarding drivers such as »easy to use« and »a brand you are happy to be seen using.« What's more, the inferior brand I also lags behind the market average on almost all attributes, with the exceptions of »good quality« and »appealing design,« where it gets at least close to the market average. Given that the shortcomings of brand I are the biggest on the drivers that matter most, this brand will have a very hard time catching up with brand II. The analysis indicates, for example, that brand I will have to make sure its devices are perceived as much more »easy to use« to stay competitive – or even relevant – from the consumer's perspective.

The examples of brand analysis discussed so far are based on the traditional, linear brand purchase funnel. It allows brand managers to determine drivers for different markets, brands, and purchase funnel stages. The enhanced purchase funnel as presented in the last chapter adds the option to differentiate drivers for different types of customer. As before, drivers can be calculated for the funnel as a whole (»market drivers«), or they can be calculated for the transfer of all customers from a given funnel stage to the next – for example, from awareness to familiarity or from consideration to purchase, as in the previous examples. Additionally, the enhanced funnel allows for two types of deep dives:

- Drivers behind direct entry to consideration, that is, the attributes that trigger the last-minute addition of brands into the consideration set.
- Performance of a given brand among potential new customers on the one hand and prior customers on the other.

Based on such deep dives, companies will be able to develop targeted programs to increase the direct entry of their brands into consumers' consideration sets at the last minute, as well as separate programs for customer acquisition and customer retention. For example, consider the fact that a statement such as »Has branches very close to my home or place of work« is a top driver for consideration among new customers in many retail categories. In reaction, several retailers have launched downtown and neighborhood formats of stores with smaller floor plans and reduced assortments. Examples include REWE (Rewe to go) in Germany; Denner (Denner Express) in Switzerland; Morrisons (M Local) and Waitrose (Little Waitrose) in the UK; Asda (Asda supermarket) in Northern Europe; and Ahold (Ahold to go) in the Netherlands.[12]

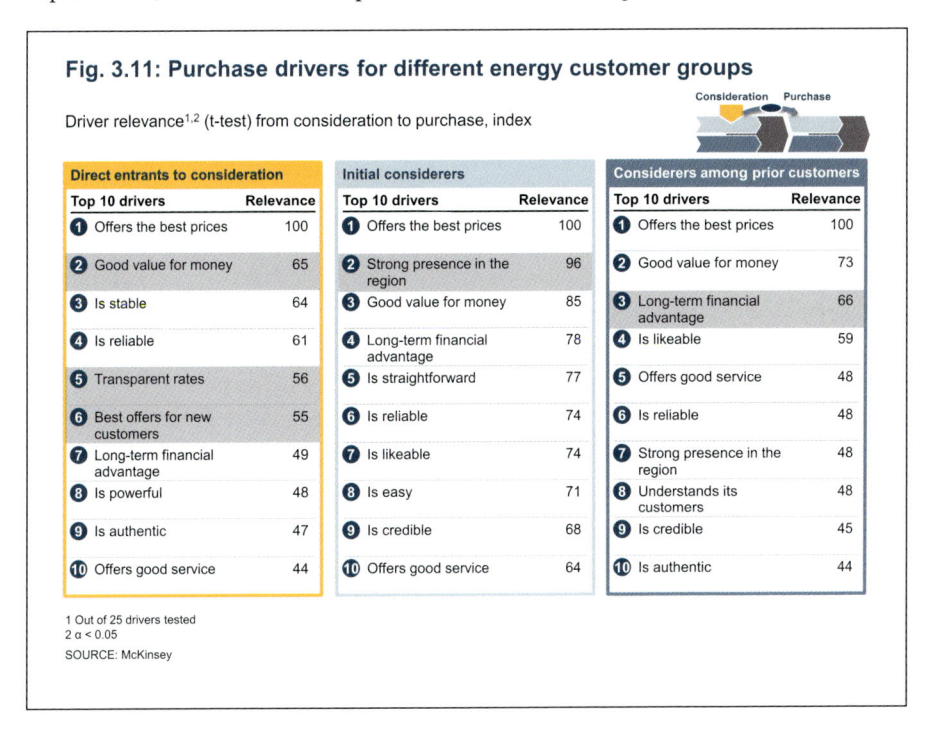

**Fig. 3.11: Purchase drivers for different energy customer groups**

Driver relevance[1,2] (t-test) from consideration to purchase, index

| Direct entrants to consideration | | Initial considerers | | Considerers among prior customers | |
|---|---|---|---|---|---|
| Top 10 drivers | Relevance | Top 10 drivers | Relevance | Top 10 drivers | Relevance |
| 1 Offers the best prices | 100 | 1 Offers the best prices | 100 | 1 Offers the best prices | 100 |
| 2 Good value for money | 65 | 2 Strong presence in the region | 96 | 2 Good value for money | 73 |
| 3 Is stable | 64 | 3 Good value for money | 85 | 3 Long-term financial advantage | 66 |
| 4 Is reliable | 61 | 4 Long-term financial advantage | 78 | 4 Is likeable | 59 |
| 5 Transparent rates | 56 | 5 Is straightforward | 77 | 5 Offers good service | 48 |
| 6 Best offers for new customers | 55 | 6 Is reliable | 74 | 6 Is reliable | 48 |
| 7 Long-term financial advantage | 49 | 7 Is likeable | 74 | 7 Strong presence in the region | 48 |
| 8 Is powerful | 48 | 8 Is easy | 71 | 8 Understands its customers | 48 |
| 9 Is authentic | 47 | 9 Is credible | 68 | 9 Is credible | 45 |
| 10 Offers good service | 44 | 10 Offers good service | 64 | 10 Is authentic | 44 |

1 Out of 25 drivers tested
2 $\alpha < 0.05$
SOURCE: McKinsey

Given sufficiently large samples that enable statistically valid calculations at the highest level of granularity, drivers can be used to explore the differences between alternative points of entry to consideration – and between different customer groups. Figure 3.11 presents an analysis of the attributes that drive three different paths to purchase: from direct consideration among new customers, from initial consideration among new customers, and from consideration among prior customers. Note that the columns are color-coded to conform with the various elements of the enhanced funnel as presented in Chapter 2 (Section 2.3). Initial observations in energy include:

- Getting the »best prices« is an important purchase driver for everybody – across points of entry and customer groups. In this industry, a good price apparently constitutes what is sometimes referred to as a »table stakes« or a »hygiene factor« – a requirement that any brand has to meet to qualify as a relevant option for consumers. This observation is in line with the relatively low involvement on the part of energy customers. No one wants to overspend on something they don't really care about all that much. This trend is also reflected by the growth of price comparison portals and applications. In the US, 70 percent of smartphone owners have used their phones for comparison shopping. In Germany, a price comparison portal called check24 is ranked as one of the country's leading Web sites in terms of revenue generation (EUR 157 million in 2013), ahead of Google's »play« store and YouTube.[13]
- Direct entry to consideration is often related to the perception that a provider offers attractive, transparent tariffs for new customers. These drivers are unique to the top ten for direct entry (left-hand column). So to trigger the last-minute consideration of their brands for purchase, companies will want to take special care that their tariffs are transparent and meet the needs of new customers. In a given case, qualitative research may be needed to find out what those needs are.
- While prior customers (right-hand column) – that is, those looking at contract renewal – are more concerned about long-term financial advantages, initial considerers among potential new customers (middle column) value the strong presence of an energy provider in their region. This means that all providers will want to assure their current customers of the long-term financial benefits of renewing their contract, for example, by offering loyalty rewards. Finally, providers who cannot claim or build a strong regional presence will have to achieve above-average performance on perceived good prices to secure their share of new customers. In light of these observations, it is not surprising that local energy providers are investing in sponsorship activities to strengthen their ties to the local community. Beneficiaries include projects, charities, and other institutions in areas such as education, arts, sports, and environmental protection.[14]

Similar observations can be made in other industries. In the candy bar category, for example, satisfying their »craving for something sweet« is the most important reason for new customers to consider a specific brand (Figure 3.12, left and middle columns). Repeat customers of a brand, however, come back for the »consistency« and the »taste« of their preferred candy bar (right column). In this category, »value for money« is a hygiene factor all customer groups care about to some extent, although it is of much lower behavioral relevance than, for example, good taste. This observation is not surprising, given the low ticket price of most mainstream candy bars. Apparently, most customers will readily spend a few extra cents for a candy bar that »tastes good.«

In the car industry, repeat purchase (Figure 3.13, right column) is correlated with »good long-term service,« while direct and initial considerers place higher importance

## 3.2 Brand Drivers: What is Really Important for the Consumer?

### Fig. 3.12: Brand drivers in the US candy bar market by customer type

Driver relevance[1,2] (correlation with stated loyalty[3]), index

Consideration — Purchase

**Direct entrants to consideration**

| Top 10 drivers | Relevance |
|---|---|
| ❶ Satisfies my craving for something sweet | 100 |
| ❷ Tastes good | 88 |
| ❸ Has a consistency I enjoy | 81 |
| ❹ Is known for superior quality | 51 |
| ❺ Provides the best value for my money | 44 |
| ❻ Has fun ads | 36 |
| ❼ Is a relatively quick energizer | 34 |
| ❽ Is available anywhere | 28 |

**Initial considerers**

| Top 10 drivers | Relevance |
|---|---|
| ❶ Satisfies my craving for something sweet | 100 |
| ❷ Tastes good | 96 |
| ❸ Has a consistency I enjoy | 89 |
| ❹ Is known for superior quality | 84 |
| ❺ Is a relatively quick energizer | 79 |
| ❻ Is available anywhere | 59 |
| ❼ Provides the best value for my money | 51 |
| ❽ Has been around for a long time | 40 |
| ❾ Has fun ads | 39 |

**Considerers among prior customers**

| Top 10 drivers | Relevance |
|---|---|
| ❶ Has a consistency I enjoy | 100 |
| ❷ Tastes good | 76 |
| ❸ Satisfies my craving for something sweet | 67 |
| ❹ Is available anywhere | 55 |
| ❺ Is a relatively quick energizer | 50 |
| ❻ Is known for superior quality | 49 |
| ❼ Provides the best value for my money | 41 |
| ❽ Has been around for a long time | 34 |

1 Out of 10 drivers tested
2 α < 0.05
3 T-test did not find statistically significant drivers for direct consideration
SOURCE: McKinsey

### Fig. 3.13: Purchase drivers for different compact car buyers

Driver relevance[1,2] (correlation with stated loyalty), index

Consideration — Purchase

**Direct entrants to consideration**

| Top 10 drivers | Relevance |
|---|---|
| ❶ Is trustworthy | 100 |
| ❷ Is high quality | 88 |
| ❸ Is a car I can be proud of | 86 |
| ❹ Has trustworthy employees | 86 |
| ❺ Is fun driving | 83 |
| ❻ Is convenient | 79 |
| ❼ Offers good long-term service | 76 |
| ❽ Intuitive handling | 75 |
| ❾ Is powerful | 72 |
| ❿ One of a kind | 72 |

**Initial considerers**

| Top 10 drivers | Relevance |
|---|---|
| ❶ Is fun driving | 100 |
| ❷ Attractive exterior design | 94 |
| ❸ Has trustworthy employees | 86 |
| ❹ Is trustworthy | 86 |
| ❺ Offers advantages I cannot find elsewhere | 84 |
| ❻ Is elegant | 82 |
| ❼ Intuitive handling | 82 |
| ❽ Is a car I can be proud of | 81 |
| ❾ Is convenient | 80 |
| ❿ Is high quality | 80 |

**Considerers among prior customers**

| Top 10 drivers | Relevance |
|---|---|
| ❶ Is trustworthy | 100 |
| ❷ Is fun driving | 92 |
| ❸ Offers advantages I cannot find elsewhere | 76 |
| ❹ Offers good long-term service | 76 |
| ❺ Is high quality | 74 |
| ❻ Attractive exterior design | 72 |
| ❼ Is a car I can be proud of | 71 |
| ❽ Has trustworthy employees | 69 |
| ❾ Is safe | 69 |
| ❿ Has a high resale value | 68 |

1 Out of 27 drivers tested
2 α < 0.05
SOURCE: McKinsey

on the presence of »trustworthy employees« at the point of sale. »Attractive exterior« design is something both initial considerers among new customers (middle column) and prior customers (right column) care about, while customers who had not previously considered a given brand (left column) place higher importance on »high quality.« Apparently, success in this category is not only about the product. The brand driver analysis suggests that car brands depend on superior performance at the front line, especially the quality of sales and service employees. In general, the needs, the demands, and the habits of car buyers are changing fundamentally. »They used to go to a car dealer five times before they bought a new car,« says McKinsey's Detlev Mohr. »Now, they go just once.« It seems the window of opportunity to make a good impression is getting smaller. In response, upscale manufacturers like Audi, Mercedes, and BMW are investing in entirely new store concepts. New-generation showrooms feature large-scale interactive displays, lounge areas, and advisors who help customers navigate the ever-expanding variety of drivetrains, interior packages, and options.[15]

### 3.3 The Matrix of Options

In order to specify the options to influence the brand available to management, the brand drivers and strengths and weaknesses analyses are combined to produce a matrix of options for action. This matrix will highlight key issues for management:

- If a company's brand shows weaknesses in key brand elements, these are potential starting points in improving the brand image. Strongly negative brand elements need to be addressed immediately; they must be eliminated or at least minimized in order to improve the brand's performance in the purchase process.
- Conversely, if the brand demonstrates strengths in important elements, these should be maintained or expanded. Less important brand attributes on which the brand performs particularly well may also help to differentiate the brand; however, it is important to remember that these have only indirect impact on purchasing behavior.

Figure 3.14 shows an example of this type of actionable matrix of options for brand A as perceived by compact car buyers (based on the 2013/2014 research). As we have already seen, brand A is perceived as very strong on highly relevant purchase drivers such as »high resale value,« »high quality,« and »long tradition« (upper right-hand corner of the matrix). The brand may want to put even more emphasis on these strengths in its brand communication to capture their full value. Brand A's weaknesses on highly relevant purchase drivers are few and far between. For example, while »fun to drive« is a highly relevant driver in the purchase process, the brand is perceived only as average in this dimension, and it lags behind on »attractive exterior.« Both of these statements might serve as starting points for brand image optimization. Brand A should not worry too much about relative weaknesses on items such as »good value for money« or »one of a kind,« in contrast, because of their low purchase relevance.

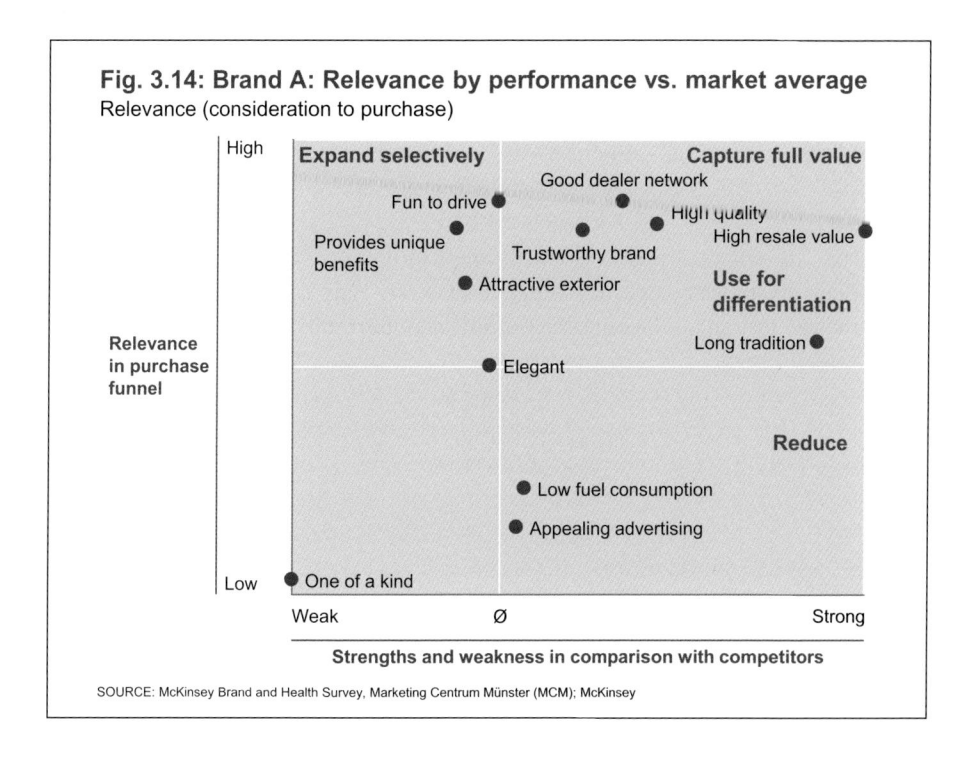

### Fig. 3.14: Brand A: Relevance by performance vs. market average
Relevance (consideration to purchase)

|  | Weak | Ø | Strong |
|---|---|---|---|
| **High** | Expand selectively<br>• Fun to drive<br>• Provides unique benefits | • Good dealer network<br>• Trustworthy brand<br>• Attractive exterior<br>• Elegant | Capture full value<br>• High quality<br>• High resale value<br>Use for differentiation<br>• Long tradition |
|  |  |  | Reduce |
| **Low** | • One of a kind | • Low fuel consumption<br>• Appealing advertising |  |

Relevance in purchase funnel (y-axis) · Strengths and weakness in comparison with competitors (x-axis)

SOURCE: McKinsey Brand and Health Survey, Marketing Centrum Münster (MCM); McKinsey

## Selecting benchmarks

In order to apply brand driver analysis effectively, it is necessary to assess each stage of the purchase funnel separately and to select appropriate benchmarks for each stage.

**Take the purchase funnel stage into account:** The individual brand drivers do not possess the same relevance at all stages of the purchase funnel. Price, for instance, is very important at the transition from consideration to purchase. In establishing customer loyalty, however, price plays only a secondary role in many industries; dimensions of emotional benefit are much more important at this stage, as demonstrated in the examples above. Similarly, a product's perceived price does not always correlate with actual price points. To improve a brand's performance on »value for money,« you don't necessarily have to lower prices (see Chapter 4 on brand delivery for details).

A matrix of options for action can, of course, be generated for each stage of the purchase funnel, but the matrix that addresses the stage with the highest potential for improvement is always of special interest for a brand. If no single stage stands out in purchase funnel analysis, it makes sense to generate an aggregate matrix of options for action. This ensures that all the main drivers of all purchase funnel stages can be examined together.

**Choose the right benchmarks:** In the matrix of options for action, the strengths and weaknesses of a brand are always assessed in relation to those of a benchmark. This benchmark is usually either a single competitor brand or an industry average. Benchmark selection should reflect a given brand's history, current position, and aspiration. For a relatively new brand, for instance, selecting the market leader as the sole benchmark is unlikely to identify anything other than significant weaknesses in the matrix of options for action. This wouldn't be very helpful, since it would make it almost impossible to choose a meaningful strategic option for building the brand. Instead, by considering a more conservative benchmark – in this case, the market average or another new entrant, for instance – more useful results can be developed. In certain cases, it can make sense to create subcategories for a given industry to delineate a more relevant peer group for brand performance« measurement and positioning. An airline might, for example, want to measure the performance of its brand relative to either traditional full-service airlines or low-cost carriers, depending on its own position and strategy, since purchase occasions (e.g., business versus private travel) and decision paths (e.g., corporate travel plans versus online price comparison shopping) will often differ significantly between the two. In contrast, for an airline that aspires to change its position or expand its target group, it may be advisable to choose a broader competitive set. Consider the case of Air Berlin. Founded in 1979 and initially focused on shuttling tourists to Mediterranean holiday destinations at low prices, the airline ventured into business travel in 2008, quickly secured thousands of corporate travel contracts, and received the German Brand Award for brand leverage in 2011.[16] It remains to be seen how Air Berlin will cope with other strategic challenges beyond branding in the future.

**Changing direction**

Brand driver analysis allows management to determine the strategic direction of the brand using the matrix of options for action. Orienting the brand strategy toward selected brand drivers will lead to improved brand performance at the respective stages of the purchase funnel. The unanswered question here is whether or not the competitors' brand strategy should also be taken into account.

It is a fundamental principle of brand management that a brand must be distinctive. One way to look at this is what is sometimes referred to as the »3 a.m. test.« When you wake someone in the middle of the night and ask them what a given brand stands for, what will they say? Will it match what employees perceive as the brand's profile internally? And will they all have similar associations? These questions can be helpful in shaping both a brand's position and its activation in communication. While it is by no means necessary to outperform competitors on all dimensions, power brands are consistently perceived as superior on the most relevant brand drivers, and they display a clear profile that sets them apart from other brands. Often, it can even be sufficient to achieve only average performance on table-stakes type attributes such as safety or affordability if the brand is sufficiently and prominently differentiated on a narrow set of highly relevant attributes. For example, a French fashion house may care very little about being perceived as the leader in »durability« as long as a sufficient number of A-list celebrities are seen (and photographed) with its handbags which, by association, become highly desirable »it« bags. If all brands in a given category relied on the same brand drivers (simply because they are relevant), they would be interchangeable from the consumer's perspective. In other words, market differentiation would disappear, commoditizing the category and the brands that play in it. To avoid this, it is important to examine whether a selected strategic direction potentially leads to:

- The brand assuming a position already held by another competing brand (in single-brand decisions, such as those faced by »branded houses« like Apple in consumer electronics or Ikea in furniture retail); or
- The brand being oriented in such a way that it will conflict with another of the company's own brands (in portfolio management decisions, such as those faced by »houses of brands« like of the Volkswagen group in automotive, Procter & Gamble in consumer goods, or LVMH in luxury).

Of course, in certain cases, it may be in management's interest to attack the position of a competitor by repositioning a brand. Most of the time, however, sustainable brand building will aim towards differentiation from the competition. See our interview with Dorkas Koenen and Erwin Van Laethem of Essent in Chapter 2 for details on how to avoid playing somebody else's game.

Balancing a brand's distinctive identity with the requirements of the competitive arena often proves to be especially challenging in multiple-brand strategies. Brand portfolio management typically attempts to optimize positioning in the overall market based on the selective positioning of single brands.[17] In a group of companies with several brands, however, single brands will often be repositioned without considering the consequences for the overall portfolio. In such circumstances, making the right decisions about prioritization while also balancing all the cost and profit effects presents a major challenge. The next section discusses these challenges and describes how the BrandMatics® approach can help deal with it in a systematic manner.

### Applying the Matrix of Options

Brand managers are often faced with making fundamental decisions based on assessing the matrix of options for action, a framework that plots brand attributes according to their relevance in the market and a given brand's perceived profile. Often this presents them with a dilemma: which of the two matrix dimensions – »strength« or »relevance« – should be given preference? Should a company's own strengths – and thus its differentiation from competitors – be expanded first, even if the importance of these elements in the marketplace is relatively low? Or would it be better to eliminate existing weaknesses in important elements that are crucial to customers' purchase decisions?

There is no universal answer to this question; a case-by-case approach is necessary. What is indisputable, however, is that any weaknesses in important »hygiene factors« or »table stakes« need to be eliminated first. This means, for instance, that airlines must be safe, taxi services on time, and personal care products gentle on the skin. If a brand does not achieve at least average performance on this kind of attribute, it loses the right to play. For example, Coke's British bottled water brand, Dasani,[17] never fully recovered from a 2004 analysis revealing that the water was contaminated with bromate, a cancer-causing chemical. The brand was discontinued in the UK and – against Coke's original plan – never introduced in Germany and France.[18]

As brand managers move beyond the table stakes to select further brand-defining elements, the checklist outlined above will help to prioritize potential attributes. In making such decisions, brand managers need to weigh market requirements (the outside-in perspective, or market-based view) against their own resources (the inside-out perspective, or resource-based view). When taking an inside-out perspective, brand managers need to consider staff and management capabilities and knowledge, as well as financial resources and timing. The best theoretical brand promise is useless if it would take too long to deliver it effectively, or if the company lacks the capabilities and resources to carry it out.

Consequently, a compromise will often need to be made between a purely market-based approach and one that takes a more pragmatic line with the resources required to execute it. In effect, »strengthening your strengths« will usually take priority over »eliminating your weaknesses,« with the exception of weaknesses in table-stakes areas, such as safety (Figure 3.15). By proceeding in this manner, management can ensure that the brand remains unique and can retain its distinct profile in the competitive environment.

Be careful, however. A brand's identity is worthless if the attributes that it conveys are not appreciated by customers. Managing a brand along its identity – an approach outlined in numerous textbooks – does not free the brand manager from the responsibility of analyzing and improving the company's brand image in terms of the outside-in customer perspective. Regardless of how meticulous and cautious one is in developing brand identity, a brand's best assets – whether tangible or intangible – are of no use if they don't generate relevant associations among current and potential customers. A long-established retailer, for instance, might rely on its tradition as much as it wants, but if this image is outdated – or simply irrelevant to consumer decision making – it will fail. In other words, an inside-out approach that focuses purely on a brand's heritage and key strengths does not guarantee success in the marketplace. Examples of players who have succeeded in retail without much heritage to speak of include Zara (founded in 1975) and Hollister (founded in 2000), both of which bank on trendiness and fast fashion rather than tradition or durability.

Focusing exclusively on overcoming a brand's weaknesses is also a poor approach in most cases because it is likely to lead to »me too« decisions. In the worst case, the company never gets off the treadmill of trying to catch up with more affordable, more luxurious, or more flexible competitors. Focusing too much on weak points can lead a company to invest in brand elements or positions that are already better covered by competitors' strong brands. Since these competitors will likely be striving to improve their strengths, this is very shaky ground on which to build. For example, a premium car brand might never catch up with the market average on »value for money,« but may well lose its luxury appeal – or even its profitability – in the process. In contrast, a middle-of-the-road carmaker should think twice about aspiring to build premium appeal, lest it put the loyalty of its current customers at risk. This dilemma is what leads many companies to build brand portfolios by acquiring, launching, or spinning off new brands. Consider the car brands Lexus and Acura, both of which were established to

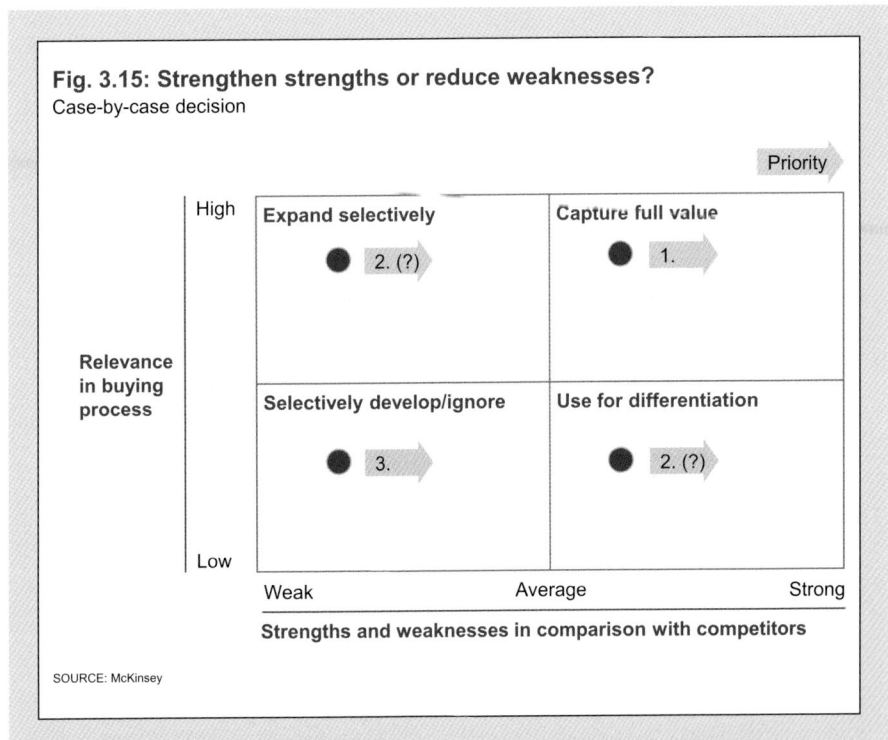

**Fig. 3.15: Strengthen strengths or reduce weaknesses?**
Case-by-case decision

|  | Weak | Average | Strong |
|---|---|---|---|
| **High** Relevance in buying process | Expand selectively — 2. (?) | | Capture full value — 1. (Priority) |
| **Low** | Selectively develop/ignore — 3. | | Use for differentiation — 2. (?) |

Strengths and weaknesses in comparison with competitors

SOURCE: McKinsey

serve a segment of the US car market that was considered inaccessible to the main brands of their respective parent companies Toyota and Honda.[19]

To sum up: in order to define the »right« brand promise, brand managers need to analyze and evaluate the market perspective, including the brand's current strengths and weaknesses as well as the company's internal perspective with respect to its resources and capabilities. Bear in mind that the time horizon is of critical importance in this context. While a brand may aspire to develop a promise that differs from its current position and perception, it would be commercial suicide to communicate such an aspirational promise before the organization it set up to keep it. In other words, be careful not to talk about what you wish you could do before you can actually do it.

Brand driver analysis and the matrix of options for action help companies determine which brand elements drive the purchase process, which are the best options in terms of positioning, and what effect these options will have on the competitive environment. But brand building is more than merely specifying strategic direction. For details on how to deliver a given strategy at all relevant customer touch points and across decision journeys, see Chapter 4.

## 3.4 Brand Portfolio Management

As we have seen in the last section, virtually no brand is an island these days. Many manufacturers of branded goods have reacted to the increasing fragmentation of their markets with larger and larger brand portfolios. This fragmentation is a consequence of the consumer trend towards individualization and self-expression. Theorists refer to »hybrid,« »multioptional,« and even »paradox« consumers who exhibit less and less brand loyalty. Building or acquiring new brands was intended to appeal to the various individual market segments. Those consumers switching brands were to be given the opportunity to select a different brand within the portfolio and thus remain as a customer of the company. At the same time, management hoped to capture synergies along the entire chain of value creation. And while some portfolios are still growing, others are being consolidated. This is due to the fact that, in some cases, brand proliferation has left companies with countless brands, only a few of which are adding substantial value. Compare our interview with Kasper Rorsted on portfolio consolidation at Henkel.

Nevertheless, the portfolios of global players, such as Unilever, Henkel, Nestlé, and Procter & Gamble, still comprise hundreds of brands and sub-brands. But brand portfolios are no longer a phenomenon limited to the consumer goods industry. In many industries, proliferation of consumer segments and consolidation of manufacturers has led to the coexistence of multiple brands under the same roof; such as Skoda, Seat, Audi, and Volkswagen, to name but the biggest brands in the Volkswagen portfolio. While some automobile manufacturers have successfully expanded their brand portfolios, others are revising their multiple brand strategies. Ford, for example, sold Jaguar and Land Rover to Tata Motors in 2008[20] (Figure 3.16). Global automobile manufacturers compete around the world with various umbrella brands and numerous product brands, derivatives, and models.

### Fig. 3.16 : Multiple-brand strategies in the automotive industry

| Volkswagen AG | | Fiat[1] | | |
|---|---|---|---|---|
| Audi | SEAT | Fiat | Chrysler | Ferrari |
| Bentley | Škoda | Alfa Romeo | Jeep | Maserati |
| Bugatti | VW | Lancia | Dodge | |
| Lamborghini | Porsche | Abarth | | |

| BMW | Daimler | Ford[2] | Honda | PSA |
|---|---|---|---|---|
| BMW | Mercedes-Benz | Ford | Acura | Peugeot |
| Mini | Smart | Lincoln | Honda | Citroën |
| Rolls-Royce | | Mazda | | |

| GM[3] | | Toyota | Renault Nissan | Hyundai |
|---|---|---|---|---|
| Buick | GMC | Daihatsu | Renault | Hyundai |
| Cadillac | Holden | Lexus | Nissan | Kia |
| Chevrolet | Opel | Scion | Dacia | |
| GM | Vauxhall | Toyota | Infiniti | |
| Daewoo[4] | | Hino | Datsun | |

1 Full control of Chrysler acquired by Fiat in Jan. 2014
2 Jaguar and Land Rover were sold to Tata in 2008; Aston Martin was sold to private investors in 2007
3 Production of Hummer, Pontiac, Saturn discontinued in 2010; Saab sold to Spyker in 2010
4 South Korea only

SOURCE: Company annual reports, Company Web site, Global Insight, McKinsey

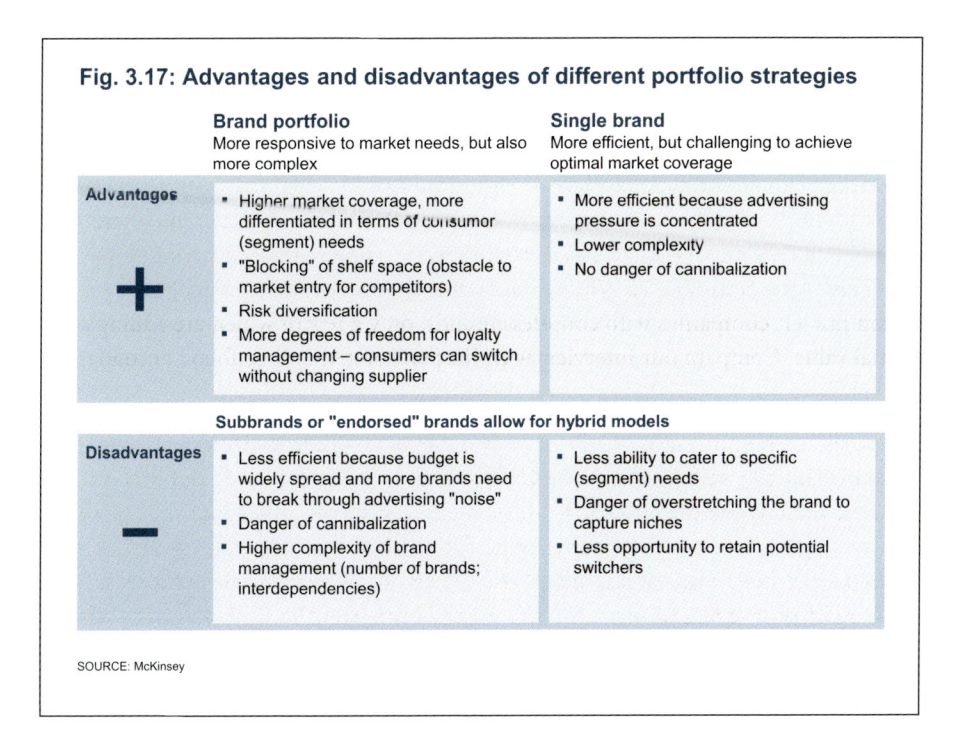

### Fig. 3.17: Advantages and disadvantages of different portfolio strategies

|  | **Brand portfolio**<br>More responsive to market needs, but also more complex | **Single brand**<br>More efficient, but challenging to achieve optimal market coverage |
|---|---|---|
| **Advantages +** | • Higher market coverage, more differentiated in terms of consumer (segment) needs<br>• "Blocking" of shelf space (obstacle to market entry for competitors)<br>• Risk diversification<br>• More degrees of freedom for loyalty management – consumers can switch without changing supplier | • More efficient because advertising pressure is concentrated<br>• Lower complexity<br>• No danger of cannibalization |
|  | Subbrands or "endorsed" brands allow for hybrid models |  |
| **Disadvantages −** | • Less efficient because budget is widely spread and more brands need to break through advertising "noise"<br>• Danger of cannibalization<br>• Higher complexity of brand management (number of brands; interdependencies) | • Less ability to cater to specific (segment) needs<br>• Danger of overstretching the brand to capture niches<br>• Less opportunity to retain potential switchers |

SOURCE: McKinsey

The primary objective of brand portfolio management can be summarized as: profitably, capturing as much market potential as possible in the relevant market segments by positioning your own brands in such a way as to ensure that they do not cause cannibalization. In practice, this is a highly complex task. Both multiple-brand and single-brand strategies carry specific advantages and disadvantages that call for careful trade-off decisions. Figure 3.17 provides a direct comparison of extreme cases in a widely diversified portfolio and a single-brand strategy to bring out the upside and the downside of either approach.

A fine example of how a brand portfolio can be leveraged to improve customer retention is provided by Condé Nast. The publisher's fashion magazine portfolio comprises among other titles, *Teen Vogue* and *Vogue* itself. *Teen Vogue* readers grow up to become *Vogue* readers. This type of brand hierarchy allows Condé Nast to capture the value of brand loyalty even in the face of changing needs. The success factor at work in this case is structuring the brand portfolio in a way that enables customers who wish to switch brands simply to select a different brand within the same portfolio, instead of migrating to the competition. Hugo Boss – founded in 1924 and now owned by Permira – pursues a similar approach with its family of brands. While all subbrands leverage the power and the heritage of the umbrella brand, they appeal to different types of customer, thus allowing for greater market coverage. In 2013, Hugo Boss reported growing sales in what the company calls a stagnating market environment.[21] In mid-2014, Permira was reportedly planning to divest up to 7.9 million of its Hugo Boss shares, hoping to generate more than EUR 800 million from the sale.[22]

This kind of portfolio is often referred to as a »branded house,« as opposed to a »house of brands« as managed by the likes of Procter & Gamble or Unilever. Like most automotive companies, Toyota is leaning towards the latter with several independent brands. To expand its coverage of the US car market, for example, it introduced the Scion brand as a stand-alone entry-level brand for younger car buyers in the US »with its combination of affordability, customization possibilities, and reputation for reliability.«[23] At 39, the median age of Scion buyers was almost 20 years below that of Toyota drivers in 2007.[24] While Toyota and Scion have distinct consumer-facing identities, the fact that both brands are distributed by the same dealers makes switching easier as drivers mature and their requirements for roominess and performance grow – along with their buying power. Recent Scion models include the iQ, an ultra-compact car launched in 2011, and the sporty FR-S launched in 2012.[25]

In these cases, the success of brand portfolios was based on needs differentiation. But multiple brands also help achieve competitive advantages associated with scale. A larger portfolio, for example, can strengthen your position when negotiating with suppliers. Larger portfolios can, in effect, also create obstacles to market entry for competitors, while distributing market risk across many brands. In the retail trade, for example, expanding shelf area can improve a company's competitive position. Unilever, for instance, largely dominates shelves of most German food retailers in the margarine segment with its brands Rama, Sanella, Becel, Lätta, Du darfst, and Bertolli. According to Euromonitor, three out of the top five brands in this category are owned by Unilever.[26] The dilemma for management, however, is that an ever-increasing number of brands will tend to reduce each individual brand's market share. At the same time, brand management costs will increase, because additional resources will be required in research and development, marketing, procurement, distribution and sales, and channel management – while ensuring that resources are well coordinated and effectively and efficiently deployed.

Unilever also found that brand proliferation comes at a price. Any advantages in market coverage and economies of scale need to be carefully balanced with the complexities that arise from portfolio management. Consolidation and brand expansion, repositioning and elimination, acquisition, launch, and restructuring are the key words in the strategy jungle. It comes as no surprise that the former enthusiasm for portfolios among the major market participants has long since given way to something resembling disillusionment. In 2000, Unilever initiated a restructuring program it called »Path to Growth,« the objectives of which were to decrease complexity, reduce costs, and increase efficiency by concentrating on the 400 core brands that accounted for 75 percent of its revenues in 1999 (Figure 3.18). The resources freed up by this program were to be used for researching and communicating successful brands. By the end of 2003, Unilever had reduced its portfolio from 1,600 brands to some 600; by 2004, it had whittled down the portfolio to 400. The target for the remaining 400 core brands was to achieve an annual growth rate of 5 to 6 percent and an operating margin of 16 percent.[27] In 2014, the portfolio included »over 400 brands« according to the Unilever Web site.[28] Unilever reported revenue »growth ahead of its markets« at 4.3 percent for

**Fig. 3.18: Unilever: 75% fewer brands in 5 years**

| Year | Brands |
|---|---|
| 2000 | 1,600 |
| 01 | 900 |
| 02 | 800 |
| 03 | 600 |
| 2004ff[1] | 400 |

Start of "Path to Growth" initiative (2000) — -75%

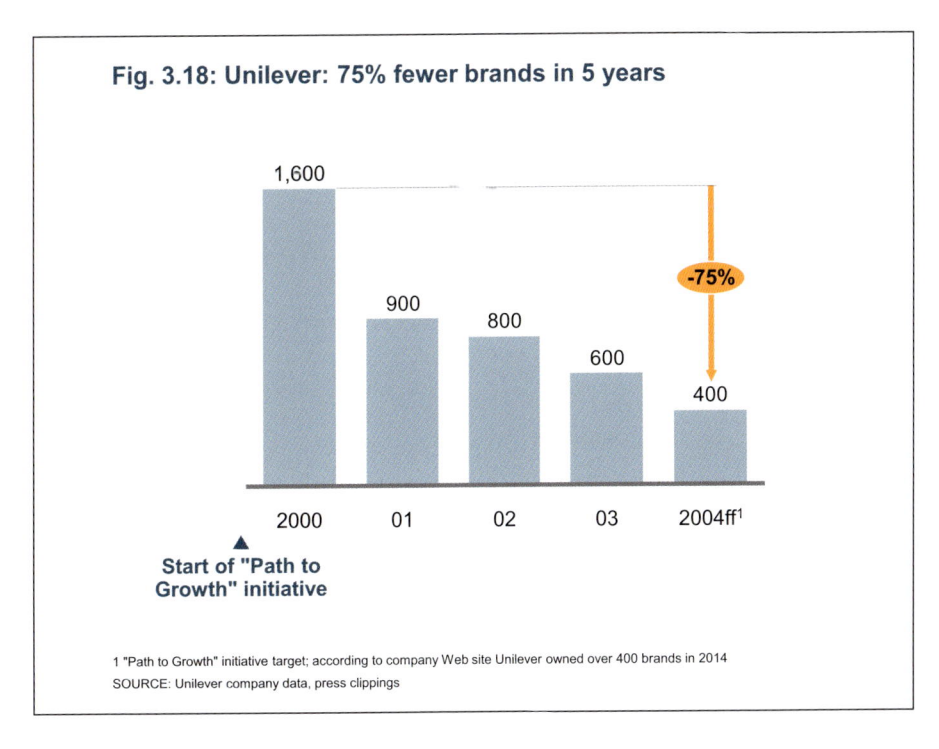

1 "Path to Growth" initiative target; according to company Web site Unilever owned over 400 brands in 2014
SOURCE: Unilever company data, press clippings

2013.[29] Unilever's competitors are making similar efforts. While both Procter & Gamble and Nestlé are reportedly engaged in portfolio restructuring,[30] Henkel says it has »consolidated the number of brands from more than 1,000 to under 400, while sales from our top ten brands represented 44 percent at the end of 2012 compared with 38 percent at the end of 2008.«[31] Also compare our interview with Kasper Rorsted in Chapter 4.

But which is the right strategy for your company? What brands should you abandon and which should you strengthen? In answering this, we come back to the three questions that need to be answered in the context of single-brand optimization: What are the true needs of potential customers? How attractive – both economically and strategically – are the respective segments? How successful are your brands in reaching these segments?

### 3.4.1. Defining and segmenting the relevant market: Start with the customer

As with the process of single-brand optimization (see previous sections), the optimization of a brand portfolio begins with defining and segmenting the relevant market and the relevant categories in a manner that the customer can understand (for an example, see Figure 3.19). PepsiCo, for instance, had discovered that its customers in the US market select their soft drinks from among all alcohol-free beverages, not just from carbonated ones. This insight shaped PepsiCo's decision to acquire additional brands (Tropicana in 1998, Gatorade in 2001, Naked Juice in 2006), to develop new

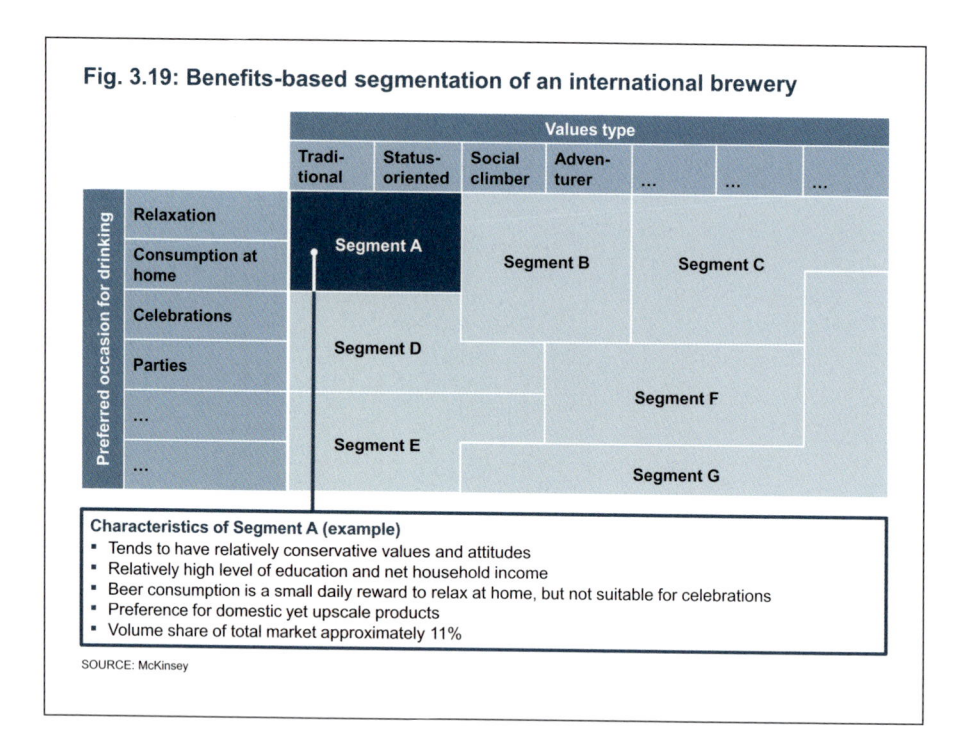

**Fig. 3.19: Benefits-based segmentation of an international brewery**

|  | Values type |  |  |  |  |  |  |
|---|---|---|---|---|---|---|---|
| Preferred occasion for drinking |  | Traditional | Status-oriented | Social climber | Adventurer | ... | ... | ... |
| | Relaxation | Segment A | | Segment B | | Segment C | | |
| | Consumption at home | | | | | | |
| | Celebrations | Segment D | | | | | |
| | Parties | | | | Segment F | | |
| | ... | Segment E | | | | | |
| | ... | | | | Segment G | | |

**Characteristics of Segment A (example)**
- Tends to have relatively conservative values and attitudes
- Relatively high level of education and net household income
- Beer consumption is a small daily reward to relax at home, but not suitable for celebrations
- Preference for domestic yet upscale products
- Volume share of total market approximately 11%

SOURCE: McKinsey

products (Aquafina, for example), and to enter into joint ventures (ready-to-drink coffee in cooperation with Starbucks). By 2006, Pepsi had secured US market leadership in sports drinks (Gatorade), PET water (Aquafina), chilled juices and juice drinks (Dole and Tropicana), enhanced water (Propel), ready-to-drink coffee (in cooperation with Starbucks), and ready-to-drink tea (Lipton in cooperation with Unilever). According to Euromonitor, non-carbonated drinks, including water, juices, and ready-to-drink teas, accounted for about one third of PepsiCo's volume in 2014.[32]

### 3.4.2. Analyzing the brand portfolio: Assess the attractiveness of segments and brands

Once the relevant market has been segmented distinctly, the next task is to assess the economic potential of the corresponding segments, similar to the procedure described in Chapter 2, Section 2.2. This kind of economic assessment is anything but trivial, since the segments are very seldom identical with classic product or market definitions.

Evaluating the size and profitability of these segments often requires using a sophisticated combination of existing data on segment shares, growth rates, and the channel mix. Trends in consumer behavior, categories, and products can give insight into the potential development of the market and its future profitability. This is one end of the analysis. The other end involves assessing the company's brands. How well does their value contribution and future potential match the segments under consideration? It makes sense to assign the existing brands to the segments that have been identified.

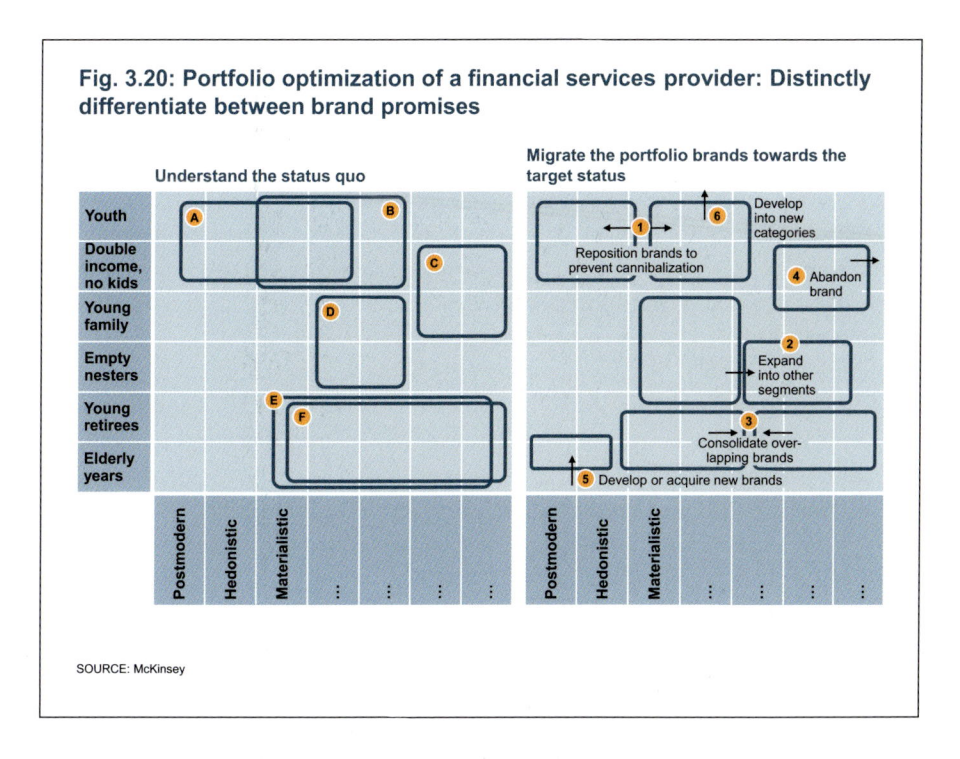

**Fig. 3.20: Portfolio optimization of a financial services provider: Distinctly differentiate between brand promises**

[Figure showing two segmentation maps. Left map "Understand the status quo" shows current brand positions A, B, C, D, E, F across segments (Youth; Double income, no kids; Young family; Empty nesters; Young retirees; Elderly years) and lifestyles (Postmodern, Hedonistic, Materialistic). Right map "Migrate the portfolio brands towards the target status" shows target positioning with actions: (1) Reposition brands to prevent cannibalization, (2) Expand into other segments, (3) Consolidate overlapping brands, (4) Abandon brand, (5) Develop or acquire new brands, (6) Develop into new categories.]

SOURCE: McKinsey

Analytical methods such as factor analysis or multidimensional scaling can be used to place the brands of a portfolio together with relevant competitors in a »segmentation map« (Figure 3.20); compare our in-depth discussion of segmentation in Chapter 2, Section 2.2.

Comparing the identified target segments on the basis of their economic and strategic potential with the reality of the company's own brand portfolio provides the initial indications of the potential options for optimization. This makes clear where the company has »white spaces« (where relevant segments are not targeted by a brand currently) and brand overlaps. It is important not to jump to premature conclusions, however: an approach using »one brand per segment« may be incorrect. Sometimes, in fact, it makes sense to offer several brands to target customers in a single segment. For example, some breweries offer different brands for different consumption occasions. While the consumer prefers one brand »on tap« with friends at a bar, the same person may turn to a different brand when buying bottled beer for in-home consumption. Similarly, brand preference within a single segment has been found to differ in a category such as baked goods. While brand A is preferred for on-the-go snacks, the same consumer will turn to brand B when shopping for groceries.

A detailed understanding of the optimization options requires an economic analysis of portfolio performance (please refer to the insert on BrandMatics® Advanced at the end of this chapter for details). The basic data required for this includes market shares, profitability, and growth rates of the individual brands in their target segments. Additionally, the analysis tools discussed in Chapter 2 – in particular the purchase funnel

(Section 2.3) – should be applied to each individual brand. Including special portfolio figures in the analysis makes it easier to understand exactly what the relationships are between the individual brands of a portfolio.

One method involves migration analysis: when formerly loyal customers migrate away from (or towards) another brand in the portfolio, this is referred to as positive or negative participation. These figures provide detailed information about brand competitiveness. The rates of purchase consideration in the brand funnel (second-choice data) can also be used to assess competition within the portfolio. These rates indicate what brand a consumer would have preferred if the brand actually purchased had not been available. In this manner, it is possible to differentiate between actual cannibalization and portfolio loyalty. In order to achieve an integrated overview of these economic interactions between individual brands, the key figures can be summarized in a »portfolio balance,« or net economic impact assessment. The insert at the end of this chapter on the brand portfolio map provides an example of how the simulation of net effects can inform the assessment of different positioning options for multiple brands in a single category.

These analyses often reveal that certain individual brands are relatively weak and thus candidates for elimination. Apparent brand overlap can be corrected by consolidation or repositioning, but only after the reasons for this overlap have been explored in detail. A segment-specific analysis of brand performance in the brand purchase funnel, combined with an analysis of the brand drivers as discussed in Section 3.1, can be very helpful here.

In industries that depend on intermediaries for products to reach the consumer (sometimes described as B2B2C, for business-to-business-to-consumer), portfolio considerations need to reflect additional criteria. For example, manufacturers of consumer goods often find themselves fighting for sufficient, and sufficiently prominent, retail shelf space to display their products in stores. In these cases, companies sometimes end up picking battles not only with competitors, but with themselves as well, that is, with neighboring brands in their own portfolios. To optimize their trade spend in today's multi-channel reality, many manufacturers are limiting their investments to secure shelf space in physical stores to a few high-profile brands, while niche brands are increasingly promoted online. In any case, criteria that reflect a company's distribution strategy should be part of portfolio analysis for players in B2B2C industries – to avoid channel conflicts and consumer confusion.[33]

### 3.4.3 Managing the brand portfolio: Decide on the right strategy, implement it, and refine it continually

The comprehensive analysis of the market segments – in combination with the current standing of your own brands – forms the basis for deciding on the right strategy. In addition, in prioritizing the strategic options, the potential reactions of competitors must also be taken into account along with the capabilities of your own organization. For instance: if the repositioning of several brands makes sense fundamentally, the next question is whether the company has access to the necessary resources (financial means, employee capabilities, etc.) to carry this out effectively and efficiently. Independent of this strategy selection, articulations of the distinct brand promise for each brand need to be formulated for all the brands remaining in the portfolio (analogous to the procedure described in Section 3.2). These brand promises need to be made tangible at all relevant customer touch points.

Developing a mathematically sophisticated, multicausal optimization approach for deriving the perfect portfolio constellation usually only makes sense if the company can apply the approach in the long run. In most cases, it is more practical to develop and evaluate an easily manageable number of plausible scenarios.

Developing the strategy is the relatively easy bit. Now great courage and perseverance are required: courage to make difficult decisions and to see them through, and perseverance, since implementing a portfolio strategy is anything but a short-term project.

However difficult dropping a cherished brand might be, retaining it can prove worse. When weak brands are maintained, these resources cannot be deployed elsewhere, thus weakening the performance of the entire portfolio. But dropping a brand is just the start. For many companies, full implementation is a long-term project. (At Unilever, the »Path to Growth« project mentioned above started in 2000 and took about five years.)[34]

In short, deriving and implementing a viable portfolio strategy is a complex, dynamic task. Implementing a brand portfolio strategy requires even more endurance than single-brand optimization, since the target positions can often only be achieved through a carefully staged migration plan. Note that a given portfolio strategy should also be reflected in the way the marketing function is organized. Depending on the number, value tier, and international reach of brands, very different organizational models apply. Compare our discussion of brand organization in Chapter 4.

## 3.5 Brand Leverage[35]

Fragrant perfume and smoldering cigars: it's hard to imagine two products more diametrically opposed. It may initially seem inconceivable to sell the two under the same name. But with the worldwide success of its Cool Water fragrance, the Davidoff cigar brand has proved otherwise. Sir Richard Branson's successful extension of the Virgin brand from entertainment (Virgin Records; Virgin Media) to travel (Virgin Atlantic; Virgin America; Virgin Australia, formerly known as Virgin Blue) and communication (Virgin Mobile) is another classic example.[36]

More and more companies are taking advantage of this type of brand transfer, referred to as *brand leverage*. This applies not only to consumer goods but to services, automobiles, and industrial goods as well. The big question is why some of these projects are hugely successful while others fail miserably. Obviously, the brand considered for leverage has to be strong enough in its original category. But even a true power brand does not guarantee success in a new category.

McKinsey research has looked at the conditions that make successful brand transfer possible. In cooperation with the German Brands Association (Markenverband e. V.), a survey of some 40 companies in Germany was conducted in December 2004 and January 2005 to understand the specific objectives companies pursue in brand transfer. Of those surveyed, the vast majority (82 percent) considered these activities to be successful. One in five companies surveyed now develops more than 40 percent of its total revenues through new products derived from the parent brand.

The following five statements summarize the most important survey findings.

### 3.5.1 The true potential of brand leverage can only be achieved by looking beyond the immediate financial impact

Some 95 percent of the companies surveyed were interested primarily in additional profits or sales, while 84 percent hoped to gain easier market access as a result of using an established brand name. In contrast, only 65 percent wanted to expand brand image in a targeted manner and even fewer – just 57 percent – hoped to increase brand awareness. In general, the trend to leverage strong brands in new or neighboring categories persists, and it is used as a source of competitive advantage by innovative players in categories as diverse as food and personal care. Recent winners of the German Brand Award (»Marken-Award«[37]) for brand leverage include:

- Rügenwalder Mühle (2014). Previously focused on old-school cold cuts, the company has successfully added snack sausages to its portfolio.
- Nivea (2013). Responding to a dormant consumer need, Nivea has combined shower gel and body lotion to create »Nivea In-Dusch«.
- Rotbäckchen (2012). Originally known for dietary supplements, the cult brand has successfully introduced a range of functional juices.

Yet it appears from the survey that many companies underestimate the impact of brand transfer on the parent brand, be it positive or negative. This is surprising, for other companies have found that brand leverage can – in addition to brand capitalization – serve as an outstanding opportunity to:

- Develop, change, or rejuvenate the image of the parent brand.
- Increase awareness of the brand outside the group of regular users.
- In some cases, help increase sales of the brand in the parent category.

Perhaps the best examples of how this can be done are found in the luxury goods market. Jil Sander, for instance, did not develop into the successful fashion brand it is today until the company had first entered the fragrance market.[38] Many other fashion brands that started out as couture houses also generate a significant proportion of their current sales in adjacent categories such as leather goods, footwear, accessories, cosmetics, and fragrances. Conversely, nearly all best-selling fragrances bear fashion-house labels; Chanel and Calvin Klein are among the most prominent examples. Compare our more comprehensive discussion of brand extension in luxury below.

## 3.5.2 A close connection between the transfer product and the parent brand is a prerequisite for success

Brand leverage works especially well when consumers can recognize a logical, relevant, and credible brand fit between the parent brand and the transfer product. The companies surveyed use a range of approaches to establish such a connection: some 82 percent emphasize a common basis of expertise in manufacturing the parent product and the transfer product; a similar number also focuses on the products' common lifestyle and brand environments (Figure 3.21). As long as consumers perceive logical commonalities – in that the transfer product and the brand concept relate well with one another in terms of the brand – there are few other limits to the nature of the transfer. Caterpillar, for instance, using its well-defined brand attributes of »enduring,« »highest quality,« and »down-to-earth,« has seen impressive results from the transfer of its parent brand in construction machinery to its licensed merchandise lines of rugged work shoes and hiking boots.[39] Similarly, Apple has successfully enhanced and rejuvenated its traditional computer business by launching the iPod, the iPhone, and the iPad, venturing into categories that are sufficiently close to personal computers to make Apple a credible player, yet novel enough to attract new business. In 2012, actual computers contributed only about 15 percent to Apple's sales. In contrast, the iPhone and the iPad collectively accounted for 75 percent of sales.[40]

## 3.5.3 Transfer products require their own marketing

Of those surveyed, 95 percent use a similar price positioning for the transfer product as for the parent product. A number of significant differences were observed, however, in distribution and communication.

Some 38 percent of the companies use alternative distribution channels for the transfer product. The advantage of a different channel is that it opens up new groups of customers for the brand, while increasing the loyalty of existing customers by exposing them to products from the parent business in new environments. McDonald's, for instance, sells its ketchup at grocery stores in Germany, Bosch offers toy versions of its equipment at toy stores across Europe, and Harley Davidson markets its leather clothing at fashion retailers worldwide. Other examples include Starbucks' bottled Frappuccino (with PepsiCo) and ground coffee products sold at supermarkets,[41] or Mars Inc., Nestlé, or Cadbury candy products sold as ingredients in or toppings for desserts served at McDonald's restaurants.

Just over half of the companies (54 percent) surveyed design independent communication strategies for the transfer product. Successful companies have learned that the key to brand leverage is competitive marketing of the transfer product in its target category. Masterfoods, now Mars Inc., demonstrated its understanding of this success factor when first entering the ice cream category in 1989 in the United Kingdom.[42] With Mars Ice Cream, the company effectively created ice cream bars as a new subcategory next to sticks, cones, and scoops. Mars further differentiated the product by

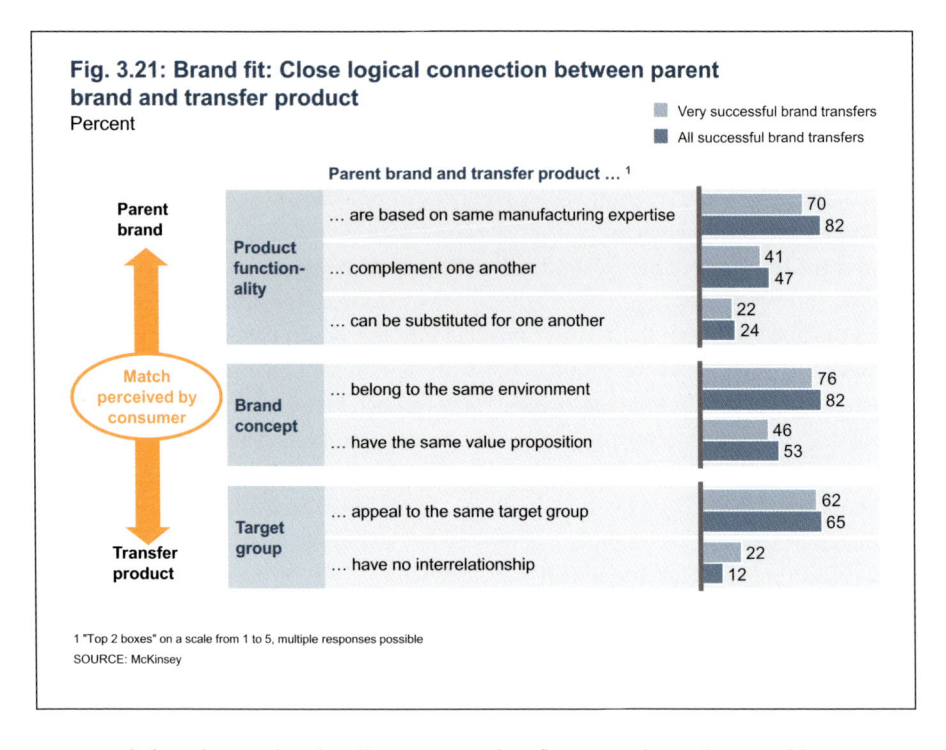

### Fig. 3.21: Brand fit: Close logical connection between parent brand and transfer product
Percent

■ Very successful brand transfers
■ All successful brand transfers

Parent brand ↕ Transfer product — Match perceived by consumer

Parent brand and transfer product ...[1]

**Product functionality**
- ... are based on same manufacturing expertise: 70 / 82
- ... complement one another: 41 / 47
- ... can be substituted for one another: 22 / 24

**Brand concept**
- ... belong to the same environment: 76 / 82
- ... have the same value proposition: 46 / 53

**Target group**
- ... appeal to the same target group: 62 / 65
- ... have no interrelationship: 22 / 12

[1] "Top 2 boxes" on a scale from 1 to 5, multiple responses possible
SOURCE: McKinsey

using real chocolate and real milk, as opposed to flavors and powders used by competitors. To work around the fact that most in-store ice cream freezers holding portion packs for immediate consumption were owned and exclusively stocked by incumbent ice cream manufacturers, Mars launched its ice cream bar through the grocery sector. That is, it offered Mars Ice Cream in bulk packs for in-home rather than impulse consumption, worked its way into the fiercely competitive impulse sector with the aid of consumer pull, and eventually installed its own freezers. Within months, Mars accounted for a large part of the impulse market's ice cream segment. Following the successful launch of Mars itself, a number of other popular confectionery lines including Bounty, Snickers, Galaxy Dove, and Opal Fruits have appeared as wrapped impulse ice cream products. Ten years later, Mars continued to outsell Nestlé in the wrapped singles sector. The market share captured by Mars Ice Cream was based on a combination of three factors: First, leveraging existing strengths acquired in the impulse candy category – that is, branded bar-shaped premium snack products with high-quality ingredients. Second, carefully selecting, or more accurately, creating a neighboring category in which these strengths mattered – that is, wrapped, bar-shaped ice cream (Mars never bothered with cones, sticks, or scoops). Third, deeply understanding the broader target category (wrapped impulse ice cream), especially its unique distribution dynamics resulting from the forward integration of incumbent manufacturers.[43] This differentiated approach was specific to Masterfoods' marketing approach in the United Kingdom; in the United States, the company chose to take on the incumbents more directly. Also compare our discussion of novelty and variety as consideration triggers in the US candy bar category in 2014 (Chapter 2, Section 2.3).

### 3.5.4 Good preparation increases the chances of success

One remarkable finding is that few companies hire managers familiar with the target market or consult professional external advisors or licensing agencies prior to launching the transferred brands (Figure 3.22). Although two-thirds (68 percent of those surveyed) do use quantitative market research, the vast majority (89 percent) rely primarily on their own internal experts. This is astounding, considering the high failure rates of new product launches and brand transfers.

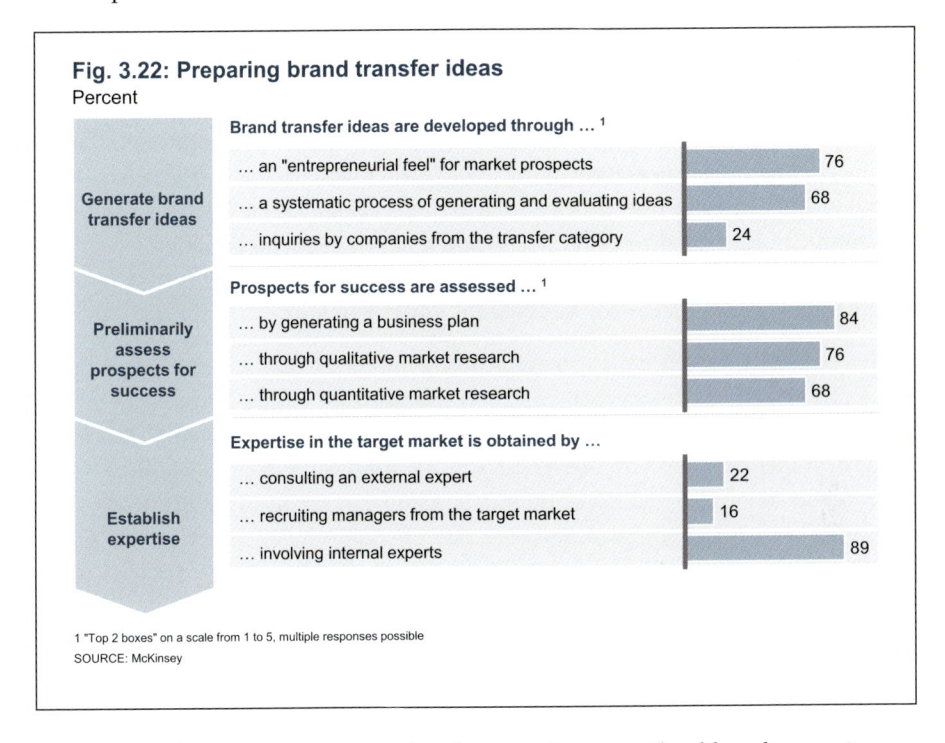

**Fig. 3.22: Preparing brand transfer ideas**
Percent

Generate brand transfer ideas
- Brand transfer ideas are developed through ... [1]
  - ... an "entrepreneurial feel" for market prospects — 76
  - ... a systematic process of generating and evaluating ideas — 68
  - ... inquiries by companies from the transfer category — 24

Preliminarily assess prospects for success
- Prospects for success are assessed ... [1]
  - ... by generating a business plan — 84
  - ... through qualitative market research — 76
  - ... through quantitative market research — 68

Establish expertise
- Expertise in the target market is obtained by ...
  - ... consulting an external expert — 22
  - ... recruiting managers from the target market — 16
  - ... involving internal experts — 89

[1] "Top 2 boxes" on a scale from 1 to 5, multiple responses possible
SOURCE: McKinsey

A company that wants to increase its chances of success should under no circumstances do without expertise in the target market and professional market research. Companies with little or no experience in classic consumer marketing should seek external advice well in advance, or better yet, develop this expertise internally. The need for expertise in the new market is all the more critical because failure in brand transfer can dilute or even permanently damage the parent brand. A company that overextends its brand or chooses the wrong licensing and distribution partners can likewise dilute the brand. The once-exclusive designer brand Pierre Cardin, for instance, was overextended in the 1980s and has since lost much of its cachet.[44] Fine foods manufacturer Mövenpick of Switzerland recently withdrew its license for premium chocolate from Katjes Fassin, saying its brand was »not a top priority« for Katjes. Mövenpick selected Halloren Schokoladenfabrik – a maker of premium chocolates dating back to the early 1800s – as the new license holder.[45] Halloren has since made further acquisitions (e.g., Die Steenland Chocolate BV in 2011) and entered into new strategic partnerships (e.g., with Bouchard in 2013). In August 2014, Halloren reported year-on-year revenue growth of 22 percent for the first two quarters.[46]

### 3.5.5 There are many models for successful brand leverage

The survey shows that a variety of business models are very successful in leveraging the parent brand. Regardless of the business model selected, the crucial issue is to strike the right balance between adapting the new product to the target market and ensuring identity with the parent brand. This requires close monitoring and adequate control mechanisms, especially in the areas of product development, communication, and quality control.

The company that owns the parent brand has a good deal of freedom in deciding how to manage the actual production and distribution of the transfer product. Some 76 percent of the companies surveyed carry out brand transfer within their own company or in its subsidiaries, while 19 percent choose to use licensing. The success of licensing depends on the close cooperation of the brand owner with its business partner. There is obviously a degree of risk involved here, so a good foundation for this partnership is a common understanding of the brand and a match of business cultures.

**Summary of prerequisites for successful brand transfer**

Many companies have been successful in using brand leverage to launch new products, open up new customer groups, and even develop new business models. Entrepreneurial instinct and intuition in operational implementation have often played a key role. The numerous brand transfer failures prove, however, that an established brand and a certain amount of instinct by no means guarantee successful brand transfer. The chances of success can be significantly increased by following these few simple rules:

- Ensure independent, competitive transfer product marketing in the target market.
- Establish a relevant and credible connection to the parent brand.
- Ensure professional preparation of the transfer.

Those who follow these rules are capable of selling smoldering cigars, fragrant perfume, and even premium cognac under a single brand.

To illustrate how these success factors play out in different categories, we will look at two cases in more detail, Lego and Meissen. While Lego's efforts to capitalize on its brand in categories beyond toys date back many decades, Meissen has started venturing beyond porcelain only recently. After going through a rough patch in 2003 and 2004, Lego is now on a solid growth trajectory anchored by core values like creativity and fun, while Meissen is still in the process of transforming itself from an admittedly prestigious porcelain maker into a multi-category luxury brand (Figure 3.23).

**Lego: From plastic toys to interactive entertainment**

Based in Billund, Denmark, Lego is a maker of plastic toys that are sold in more than 130 countries worldwide. Started in 1932 by Ole Kirk Kristiansen, the company is still owned by the founder's family. The name Lego is derived from the Danish »leg godt« that translates as »play well.« In 1958, the company started making the signature plas-

**Fig. 3.23: Brand leverage examples: Lego and Meissen**

| Brand | Origin | Extension | Links | Impact[1] |
|---|---|---|---|---|
| LEGO | Plastic toys | • Theme parks<br>• Video games<br>• Movies | • Creativity<br>• Fun<br>• Social experience | • Revenues up 101%<br>• Operating margin up 9.2 pp |
| MEISSEN COUTURE 1710 | Fine porcelain tableware | • Jewelry<br>• Home furnishings<br>• Apparel | • Art<br>• Craftsmanship<br>• Discreet luxury | • Revenues up 14%<br>• Operating margin up 6.4 pp |

1 2009 - 2012
SOURCE: Press search; Web research; company reports

tic bricks that can be assembled to create almost any structure. In 2013, Lego was the world's second largest manufacturer of toys, trumped only by Mattel, the maker of Barbie dolls, Fisher-Price technical toys, and Matchbox miniature cars.[47]

Lego's first venture beyond its traditional toys was Legoland, an amusement park established near the company's headquarters in Denmark in 1968. It features models of architectural landmarks and other structures built to scale using Lego bricks as well as a number of themed rides. Subsequently, similar parks were opened in Germany, the UK, the US, and Malaysia. In 2005, the four Legoland parks that existed at the time were acquired by the Blackstone Group.[48] At the time of writing, Legoland parks were owned by the Merlin Entertainments Group. Globally, Merlin is second only to Disney in terms of number of visitors.[49] Both Blackstone and the Kristiansen family are among Merlin's current owners.

More recently, Lego began leveraging its brand in interactive entertainment. Starting in the late 1990s, Lego developed a growing range of video games, often working in association with Warner Bros and its major motion picture franchises targeting children and teenagers. Examples include Lego Star Wars, Lego Harry Potter, Lego Indiana Jones, Lego Batman, and Lego Pirates of the Caribbean. Many of these games let players build or modify themed virtual worlds from virtual Lego bricks to create a link with the offline Lego experience. By 2010, Lego video games had generated more than 50 million unit sales. »One of the things that sets the Lego brand apart is that it allows kids to express their creativity, and the games we develop [...] are not just great fun but also inspire kids to play with their Lego bricks, exploring our different play themes

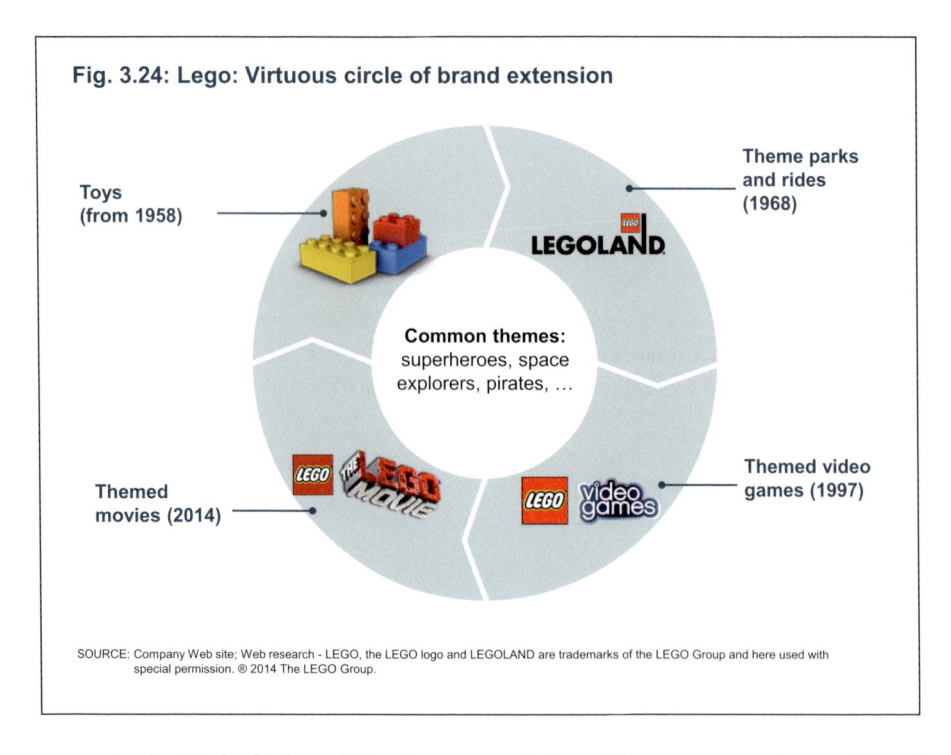

**Fig. 3.24: Lego: Virtuous circle of brand extension**

- Toys (from 1958)
- Theme parks and rides (1968)
- Themed video games (1997)
- Themed movies (2014)
- Common themes: superheroes, space explorers, pirates, …

SOURCE: Company Web site; Web research - LEGO, the LEGO logo and LEGOLAND are trademarks of the LEGO Group and here used with special permission. ® 2014 The LEGO Group.

more deeply. We […] take a distinctive approach to making games creative, social and non-violent, which makes them a valuable part of the broader Lego experience,« said Henrik Taudorf Lorensen, Vice President of Lego Digital at the time.[50]

In early 2014, *The Lego Movie* distributed by Warner opened in theaters worldwide (see Figure 3.24 for Lego's brand extensions). At the time of writing, gross revenues exceeded USD 250 million.[51] Jill Wilfert, Lego's Vice President for Global Licensing and Entertainment, says: »A lot of people might think, ›OK, this is all about them trying to sell the most toys.‹ For us, this was always about building the Lego brand.« Characters featured in the movie are available for sale from Lego shops; examples include Superman, Wonder Woman, and Abraham Lincoln. According to *The Financial Times*, Warner is already working on another Lego movie scheduled for release in 2017.[52]

After a rough patch marked by losses of EUR 174 million in 2004, Lego sales are now thriving. Between 2009 and 2012 alone, revenues more than doubled. At the same time, business has become substantially more profitable. Over the four-year period ending in 2012, the company's operating margin went from 24.8 percent to an impressive 34.0 percent.[53] According to Lego's annual reports, income from licenses only accounts for about 1 percent of total revenues. While the direct contribution of interactive and filmed entertainment to Lego's total sales of more than EUR 3.4 billion may be limited, its impact on the brand and its overall appeal is tremendous. Between 2009 and 2012, Lego's brand strength increased by 29 percent, according to Landor Associates: »In the past three years, Lego's product extensions, licensing deals, and new media activations have embraced the company's commitment to being a medium for creativity.«[54]

The fact that Lego is successful today despite a period of declining sales in 2003 and 2004 shows that brand leverage is not only about the courage to enter new categories that add value, but also about the consequence to get out of the ones that don't. During the subsequent clean-up, the company went through a process of what observers describe as »a mix of cost-cutting, philosophical renewal, [...] and simplicity.« The effort was as painful as it was cathartic. »What we realised is that the more we're true to ourselves, the better we are,« CEO Jorgen Vig Knudstorp[55] sums up the brand's growth philosophy. To date, Lego has made more than some 400 billion plastic bricks and reached some 400 million children who play with them.[56] In September 2014, *The Wall Street Journal* reported that revenues from *The Lego Movie* had helped Lego take the top spot as the world's leading toy company from Mattel, if only by a slim margin.[57]

**Meissen: From fine porcelain to home furnishings**

Meissen – originally established in 1710 by King Augustus the Strong as a maker of fine porcelain – is one of Germany's top luxury brands and is considered by many to be a major cultural asset. It was the first Western company to master the art of porcelain making. To protect its exclusivity, Meissen introduced the hand-painted crossed swords as its logo in 1720. This makes the crossed swords – originally derived from a Saxon coat of arms – one of the oldest trademarks in the world.[58] To this day, fine china tableware is the company's core category. As the brand's 300$^{th}$ anniversary was approaching, Meissen found itself struggling with a waning demand for its traditional baroque figurines and intricately embellished tableware. By that time, many of Meissen's traditional competitors had already gone out of business. In 2008, Christian Kurtzke came on board as the company's new CEO. To expand the company's relevant market and save as many jobs as possible, Kurtzke decided to enlarge the product portfolio considerably and start turning Meissen into a global luxury lifestyle brand: »We want to build a Saxon Hermès, or Chanel.«[59] The driving force of this expansion was the transfer of the brand's core – the artful craftsmanship of discreet European luxury, to new categories. Meissen has since entered the markets for jewelry (Joaillerie), home furnishings (Home) (Figure 3.25), fine art (Fine Art), and high-end apparel (Couture). CEO Christian Kurtzke says: »The essence of the brand Meissen is not fashion, but art. For this reason, the focus will be the use of the best materials, combined with the highest standards of craftsmanship and creativity.«[60]

The brand's creative director, Markus Hilzinger, is going to great lengths to make sure that every new design is connected in some way to the company's roots. For example, one of the signature fabrics in the Home collection features a Chinese dragon, just like the one displayed on the company's most famous traditional hand-painted porcelain. Similarly, the legendary crossed swords have made a reappearance as a semiabstract pattern on carpets and fabrics. Beyond this, the brand's trademark colors are present in all categories of the Meissen collection: a rich yellow gold, pale blue, greyish brown, rusty red, black, ivory, and grey – all of which have been in use at Meissen for centuries. To celebrate its broader footing, the company opened Villa Meissen in Milan on the occasion of the 2012 furniture fair.[61] The villa is an Italianate palazzo that displays the brand's new interior furnishings, along with a vast array of assorted china. The Villa is a testimony to the brand's aspiration to provide everything a grand contemporary house might need, from lamps to carpets and from furniture to porcelain.

While the jury is still out on the longevity of the new product categories, the expansion has certainly helped reinvigorate the brand, and the recent numbers reflect this trend. Between 2009 and 2012, revenues went up by 14 percent. In 2012, Meissen's operating margin was 1.6 percent, up from a negative 4.8 percent in 2009.[62] That said, the company is still a small fish in a big pond. Today, the likes of Hermès and Chanel are roughly 100 times the size of Meissen in terms of revenues. However, the new direction is drawing compliments even from the competition. Says Peter Ting, a renowned designer for Royal Crown Derby, the oldest maker of porcelain in the UK, and for Garrard & Co., the long-time Crown Jeweler to Her Majesty the Queen: »The surprise of Meissen Home is that the same language of elegance in porcelain has been translated into fabrics and furniture. It's as if the hundreds of years of making beauty is used as an incubator for this great leap forward.«[63]

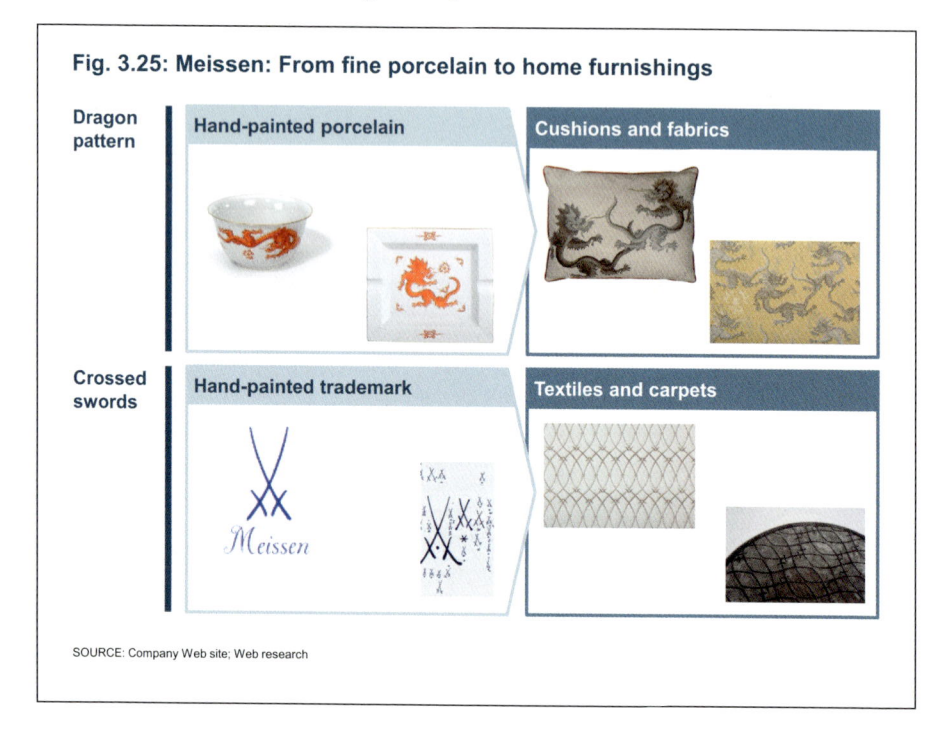

**Fig. 3.25: Meissen: From fine porcelain to home furnishings**

| | Hand-painted porcelain | Cushions and fabrics |
|---|---|---|
| Dragon pattern | | |
| Crossed swords | Hand-painted trademark | Textiles and carpets |

SOURCE: Company Web site; Web research

**Outlook on other strategies**

While Meissen is primarily using the extension of its strong brand to generate additional revenues in new categories, Lego has ventured into entertainment to strengthen its brand and generate additional sales in its core category. Between these objectives, there is room for many different paths and strategies.

Some brands run on the charisma and the identity of a single person. Consider the example of Martha Stewart. Starting with a small-scale catering business and a single cookbook first published in 1982, Martha Stewart Living is now a USD 160 million business that includes print publishing, broadcasting, various services, and a wide variety of home goods and decoration materials available by direct mail order and through retailers such as Macy's, The Home Depot, and J.C. Penney. According to company information, merchandizing accounted for 37 percent of total turnover in 2013. The importance of the founder to the company's continued success, however, may eventually threaten its sustainability: »Our success depends in part on […] the reputation and popularity of Martha Stewart […]. Ms. Stewart's efforts, personality and leadership – including her services as an officer and director – have been and continue to be critical to our success.«[64]

Some of the world's most highly leveraged brands can be found in the luxury industry. Many of these brands date back decades if not centuries, and a few of them started out as suppliers to the kings and queens of an age gone by. In our examination of the trajectories of such brands – based chiefly on the sequence of their category extension efforts – we have found two typical patterns of brand leverage (Figure 3.26):[65]

- Luxury brands with a *technical* core – such as makers of jewelry or watches – tend to be quite circumspect in their extension efforts. Frédéric de Narp, President and CEO of Harry Winston, says: »There are soft luxury goods, which stand for fashion, and hard luxury goods, which stand for timelessness. Timelessness in hard luxury goods does not easily allow for lifestyle expansion, while fashion brands would lend them-

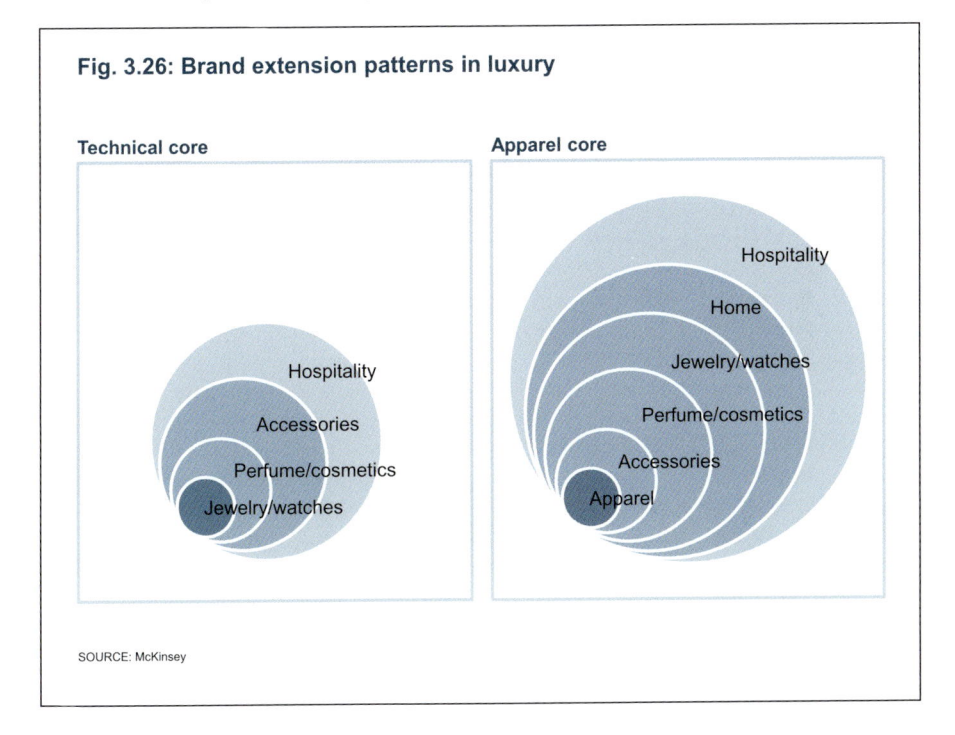

Fig. 3.26: Brand extension patterns in luxury

Technical core
- Hospitality
- Accessories
- Perfume/cosmetics
- Jewelry/watches

Apparel core
- Hospitality
- Home
- Jewelry/watches
- Perfume/cosmetics
- Accessories
- Apparel

SOURCE: McKinsey

selves more easily to extension.« Some jewelry brands have, however, successfully added perfume, cosmetics, and accessories over time. Examples include Cartier (leather goods, glasses, fragrances) and Bulgari (fragrances, leather goods). Also compare our interview with Bulgari's CEO, Jean-Christophe Babin at the end of this chapter.

- Luxury brands with an *apparel* core are perhaps the most prolific pacemakers of brand extension. Many of them have moved into perfume in the 1980s and 1990s, added jewelry, watches, and home products in the 2000s, and entered the hospitality business over the course of the last few years. Successful examples include Givenchy and Roberto Cavalli. Some players – typically those that already feature rather broad assortments – have transgressed the realm of products altogether by adding various types of experiences to their offering, such as hospitality services. Although hotels and restaurants may only generate a fraction of an apparel maker's total revenues, these services often are key contributors to the brand's identity.

Arguably, Armani has taken brand leverage further than almost any other brand. The brand portfolio now includes Armani Privé, Giorgio Armani, Armani Collezioni, Armani Junior, Emporio Armani, EA7, Armani Jeans, AX, and Armani Casa. As one of Italy's most valuable brands,[66] Armani reportedly derives some 40 percent of its EUR 7 billion in revenues from non-apparel categories. These include accessories, fragrances, watches, and home furnishings.[67] Armani is also among the most active players in the hospitality arena, operating more than a dozen cafés, two restaurants, and several hotels. Giorgio Armani explains: »You are only in danger of diluting the brand principles if you do not have a strong guiding aesthetic vision. It is absolutely imperative to ensure that each piece truly possesses the Armani signature. This is how I work with all my collections – clothing, accessories, and interiors.«[68]

### BrandMatics® Advanced

#### Background: Managing interdependencies of brands in the same category

Brand Portfolio Management is all about managing interdependencies. To decide whether offering multiple brands in the same category makes sense, the advantages of differentiation and market coverage have to be weighed carefully against the risks of management complexity and cannibalization. This trade-off is the staff of life at consumer goods giants like Unilever or Procter & Gamble, both of which manage several hundred brands in a wide range of categories. But the fundamental questions remain the same no matter whether you manage 20 or just two brands. In fact, clear and fact-based relative positioning of neighboring brands is even more critical with a small number of brands, simply because the individual brands tend to have higher relative value for the company, and the potential downside of cannibalization is disproportionately large. The more brands you have, the more leeway there is for experiments like test launches and repeated repositioning. With only a few brands, you have to get it right the first time. This insert looks at recent advances in positioning and portfolio management methodology that help to take a holistic, multiple-brand perspective when assessing the risks and benefits of brand launches and brand positioning efforts within the same category combined with the proven tools described in previous sections, the approach outlined below forms the kernel of »BrandMatics® Advanced.«

### The positioning dilemma of Alphabet Inc.

Think of a company, Alphabet Inc., that offers brands A and B in the same category. A and B are complementary in several respects: while A is traditional, reliable, and medium-priced, B is a high-profile premium brand offering unique tangible and intangible benefits. Where A is »charming« and »trusted,« B is both »indestructible« and »glamorous.« Because of high entrance barriers, there are only a few competitors, including Numerical Inc.'s brands 1 and 2. To expand its market coverage in the category, Alphabet Inc. is thinking about relaunching its third brand, C. To date, C has a very limited share in most markets, a comparatively low profile, and no clear-cut position (Figure 3.27).

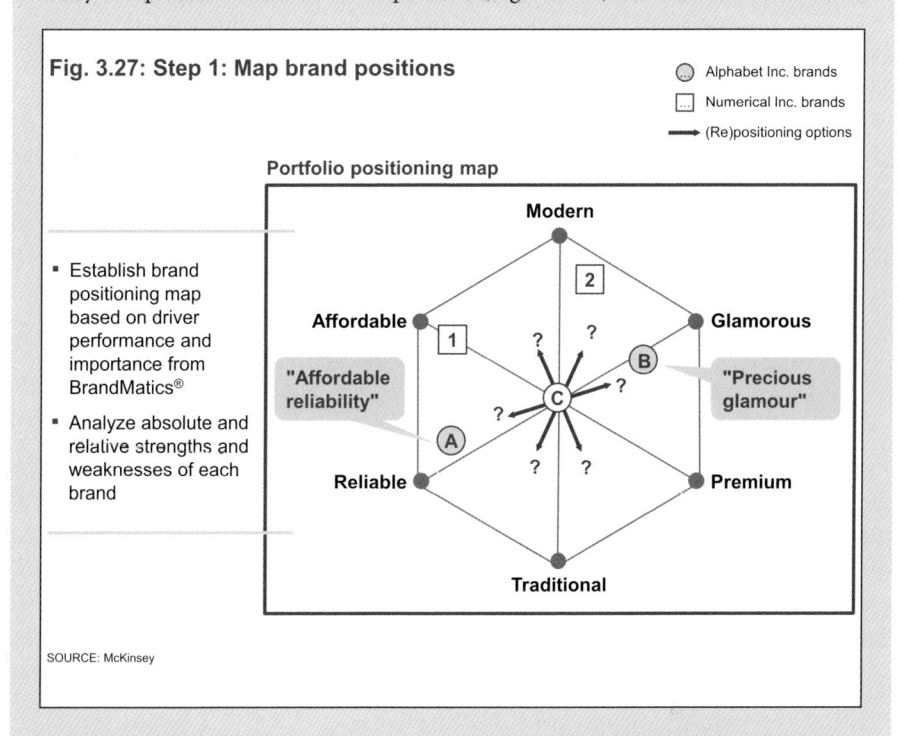

**Fig. 3.27: Step 1: Map brand positions**

- Alphabet Inc. brands
- Numerical Inc. brands
- (Re)positioning options

Portfolio positioning map

- Establish brand positioning map based on driver performance and importance from BrandMatics®
- Analyze absolute and relative strengths and weaknesses of each brand

"Affordable reliability"

"Precious glamour"

Modern — Glamorous — Premium — Traditional — Reliable — Affordable

SOURCE: McKinsey

Because of advances in technology and manufacturing, Alphabet Inc. has been able to improve and refine the intrinsics of brand C. C now shares many of B's premium characteristics, but can be offered at a price that is much closer to A, the company's mid-price bread-and-butter brand. The question is whether the potential upside of pushing C as a major third brand outweighs its potential cannibalization of A and B. Specifically, Alphabet Inc. wants to know how to position C in order to minimize that cannibalization and, hence, maximize C's net benefit. Ideally, C would gain market share mostly at the expense of Numerical Inc.'s brands 1 and 2, with minimal damage to the sales and market share of Alphabet's A and B. Any changes to C's positioning affect its performance in the purchase funnel (for a description of how brand attribute perception drives the purchase funnel, see Chapter 2, Section 2.4 and Chapter 3, Section 3.1). In the category in question, brand attributes such as »affordable« and »glamorous« act as drivers between the funnel stages »familiarity« and »consideration,« and

»consideration« and »purchase.« Let's assume »glamorous« is a key driver that has a high impact on the transfer of consumers from »consideration« to »purchase.« This implies that, if Alphabet Inc. succeeds in repositioning and establishing C as a more »glamorous« brand, this move would help to increase C's performance on purchase, hence its market share. But it doesn't stop there. Repositioning C also would have an effect on its neighboring brands A and B. Since B is also positioned as »glamorous,« part of C's gains would eat into B's market share. At the same time, promoting C as »value priced« could cannibalize the sales of A, which is also positioned as an affordable brand.

## How BrandMatics® Advanced helps to assess positioning alternatives

McKinsey has developed the BrandMatics® Advanced portfolio positioning map to assess and optimize the net effect of such (re)positioning efforts. To identify potential positions for C, the first step is to create a brand positioning map based on quantitative brand driver research not just for C, but for the entire category. This first step creates transparency about the current positions of existing brands in the category as shown in Figure 3.27. If two given positions, for example, »affordable reliability« and »precious glamour« are already occupied, C could either attack one of these head on (which would make sense only if the incumbent is a competitor brand) or assume an intermediate position, for example, »affordable glamour.« The map helps to identify such positioning alternatives; the arrows in the chart indicate potential repositioning directions for C. In the next step, the analytics behind the BrandMatics® Advanced positioning map simulate the net portfolio impact of the various possible positioning alternatives for C.

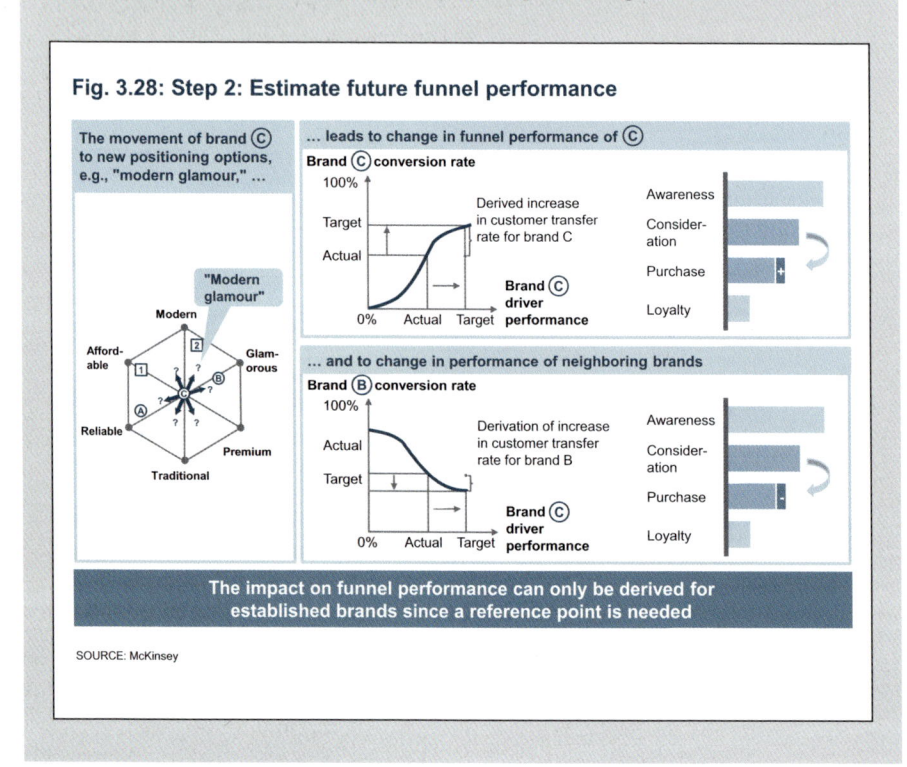

**Fig. 3.28: Step 2: Estimate future funnel performance**

SOURCE: McKinsey

Effectively, the tool estimates the repositioning impact on the funnel by way of quantified changes in brand attributes that act as funnel drivers; the illustrative results are shown in Figure 3.28. The simulation then subtracts the value of any market share captured from A and B; it is even set up to recognize indirect effects such as usage of C as an ingredient brand in either A or B. The result is a clear and fact-based ranking of positioning alternatives according to their net portfolio effect as shown in Figure 3.29. As the length of the »net gain« bars in the figure indicates, »modern glamour« is the most attractive position from a portfolio perspective. Accordingly, Alphabet Inc. decided to relaunch C as a more modern, more natural, and slightly more affordable alternative to B, the premium brand. This position combines the advantage of appealing to a younger, more open-minded audience than A with the benefits of attracting a more price-conscious target group than B, effectively damaging neither in-house brand in any substantial way, but growing mostly at the expense of Numerical Inc.'s competing brands.

## Potential applications

The new portfolio positioning method is applicable both to companies that find themselves with multiple similar brands in the same category in a postmerger situation and to incumbents contemplating the discontinuation, repositioning, or (re)launch of individual brands in the same category. Its main limitation is that the simulation module works with alternative positions and compares their net benefit with any given existing position. This means the methodology may be applied to launches from scratch only if the company in question already operates at least one similar brand in the target category. In other words, it works for most in-category portfolio management challenges, but not for new category entry.

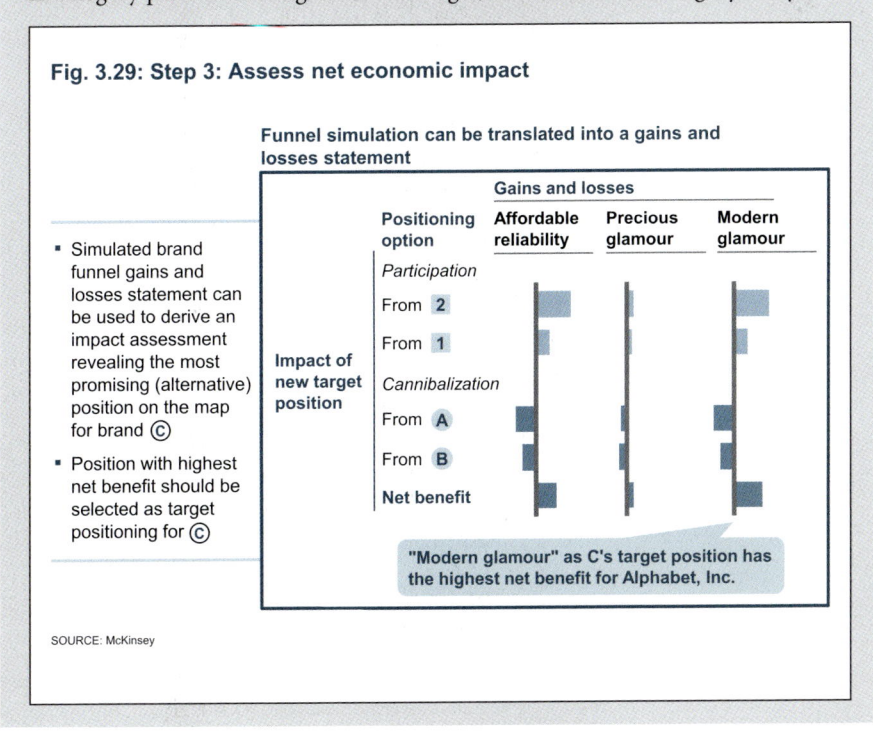

**Fig. 3.29: Step 3: Assess net economic impact**

Funnel simulation can be translated into a gains and losses statement

- Simulated brand funnel gains and losses statement can be used to derive an impact assessment revealing the most promising (alternative) position on the map for brand Ⓒ
- Position with highest net benefit should be selected as target positioning for Ⓒ

| Impact of new target position | Positioning option | Affordable reliability | Precious glamour | Modern glamour |
|---|---|---|---|---|
| | Participation | | | |
| | From 2 | | | |
| | From 1 | | | |
| | Cannibalization | | | |
| | From A | | | |
| | From B | | | |
| | Net benefit | | | |

"Modern glamour" as C's target position has the highest net benefit for Alphabet, Inc.

SOURCE: McKinsey

Because it estimates the impact of positioning changes based on past purchase funnel performance, the BrandMatics® Advanced portfolio positioning map is ideally suited to the requirements of repositioning efforts. The good news is that the starting point of the impact estimate can be a brand already owned by the company in question as well as a competitor brand operating in the target category or market.

Potential applications include, among others:

- Automotive companies managing multiple brands in the same category, for example, premium passenger vehicles.
- Makers of branded components that act as alternative ingredients in third-party products in the same category, such as functional fabrics used in apparel or computer hardware components.
- Pharmaceuticals and healthcare companies that manage multiple branded drugs or products for the same indication or application, such as sleeping medication or antiaging skincare products.
- Fast-moving consumer goods manufacturers that want to optimize their brand portfolio within a given category, for example, breakfast snacks or kitchen tissues.

No matter what the exact application, BrandMatics® Advanced will help make portfolio management decisions more fact-based and more reliable by linking the estimation of their net impact to quantified market research and the proven methodology of potential brand value calculation based on the purchase funnel.

# Interview with Jean-Christophe Babin of Bulgari: »Everything we do is brand management«

Established in Rome as a jewelry shop at the end of the 19th century, Bulgari is one of the world's leading brands in the luxury sector with a product portfolio that includes – beyond jewelry – watches, perfumes, accessories, and hotels. Bulgari is currently part of the LVMH Group (Louis Vuitton Moët Hennessy).

Jean-Christophe Babin is the CEO of Bulgari. Appointed to this position in 2013, he has most recently served as the chief executive for TAG Heuer, another LVMH subsidiary. A graduate of the École des Hautes Etudes Commerciales in Paris, Mr. Babin has previously worked for Procter & Gamble, the Boston Consulting Group, and Henkel.

**McKinsey**: For over 130 years, Bulgari has been the key player in luxury jewelry in Italy. What are the fundamental values of the brand on which you have built this success?

**Jean-Christophe Babin**: With 130 years of history, Bulgari has progressively established itself as an emblem of Italian excellence and sophisticated luxury. Today, it is a global and diversified player in the luxury market. Bulgari is unique because of its Roman birthplace. Rome, the eternal city, is unrivalled in the world. For 2,700 years, the city has been one of the leading centers for art, architecture, and design. This has created a peculiar cultural context, with a strong impact on the Bulgari family and on all the craftsmen who have worked for the company. This also explains the architectural character of Bulgari's jewelry. Bulgari's style is, in fact, a balanced mix of classicism and modernity in a continuous search for innovative design and materials, with a special attention to color combinations. The sense of volume, the love for linearity and symmetry, and certain details recalling art and architecture are renowned hallmarks of the Bulgari creations.

**McKinsey**: What are the most important choices that, in your view, have enabled Bulgari to build up its own brand without ever betraying its very essence?

**Jean-Christophe Babin**: Jewelry – which is what we do in Italy – is our work, our specialty, where our heart is. It's quite simple, actually. We have been a jewelry brand for the past 130 years, and that is what we have just been celebrating. The company was launched with jewelry – right from the start with silver, in fact – and then we moved rapidly to more precious materials and extraordinary color combinations. Once Bulgari became part of the LVMH Group in 2011, it was fundamental to reassert its very essence as the Italian jeweler *par excellence*. This is what distinguishes our brand from the other luxury players in the group: we are the Italian jeweler, with 130 years of history, 2,700 years of Roman heritage, and a long track record of expertise in craftsmanship. Our products are made in Italy, relying on the unique *savoir faire* of our master artisans.

**McKinsey**: Let's talk about brand extension. Bulgari has proven capable of stretching from jewels to watches, from accessories to resorts. What have been the main elements on which you have built the move from one category to another, and how have you managed to maintain the coherence of the Bulgari brand?

**Jean-Christophe Babin:** Over the years, the brand has been diversified into many sectors. Today, we have six production sites in Switzerland and seven in Italy. We are not the only ones who expanded the scope of our activities. Other jewelers have adopted the same strategy by offering leather goods, perfumes, etc. But unlike our competitors, we have established a framework: use our jeweler's formula in each new territory that we enter. The bags we sell today are *Serpenti*, inspired by one of Bulgari's iconic jewelry emblems. In watchmaking, our business as jewelers is never too far away, if you consider the design, the material processing, and the workmanship. Also for perfume, the fragrances take inspiration from the jewelry world. Omnia Indian Garnet, for example, is reminiscent of the mandarin garnet, the precious stone. Also, the Bulgari hotels are the ultimate expression of the brand, and they help to reinforce its image. These diversifications, in consistency with Bulgari's jeweler soul, have allowed the brand to grow much faster than other luxury brands.

**McKinsey:** Bulgari has always been linked to the celebrity world, but has also undertaken very interesting initiatives for the community, such as the campaign alongside Save the Children. What is the role of celebrities on the one hand and social initiatives on the other?

**Jean-Christophe Babin:** The partnership with Save the Children is part of Bulgari's DNA as it reflects the characteristics of our company, which is certainly very demanding, but always dedicated to people.

To date, the specially designed Save the Children ring has helped raise more than EUR 20 million in donations. The sum by far exceeds the ambitious objective set in 2009, when the partnership began. On its 130th anniversary and to boost its support for Save the Children, Bulgari has launched a new silver and ceramic Save the Children pendant, with another ambitious objective of generating an additional EUR 1 million to save the lives of children. The renowned photographer Fabrizio Ferri has actively supported this initiative with his time and talent. Over the years, he has photographed over 170 celebrities wearing the ring – and recently, the pendant – in support of Bulgari's commitment to quality education for the world's neediest children. Several of the celebrities involved in the partnership have participated in field visits to Save the Children programs funded by Bulgari to observe the impact of this partnership with their own eyes.

This partnership shows how you can align common interests, by enhancing Bulgari's corporate reputation and Save the Children's philanthropic reach with the world of the celebrities that become ambassadors of the brand's values.

**McKinsey:** What do you particularly like about the Bulgari brand?

**Jean-Christophe Babin:** A Bulgari creation is not just a piece of jewelry. It is something that tells a story and carries a heritage of values, realized with excellent workmanship. All this is contained in each piece of jewelry we make. While this spirit is rooted in jewelry, we also apply it to watches, accessories, fragrances, hotels, to our stores, and to our advertising campaigns. In all we do, you will always recognize the Bulgari style.

**McKinsey:** How important is the influence of customers' tastes and of your style choices?

**Jean-Christophe Babin:** Particularly for high jewelry, there is a relationship based on great trust and loyalty between Bulgari and the clients. Bulgari has a very strong identity and attracts customers who identify with the same values. Our creative director, Lucia Silvestri, says that she knows the tastes of our customers so well that sometimes when she is buying a precious gem, she can already imagine how the jewelry creation could evolve to match the taste of a certain client. As a result, you have a product that reflects the Bulgari style and, at the same time, the taste of clients that identify with the brand's values.

**McKinsey:** How much time do you spend on brand management?

**Jean-Christophe Babin:** Basically, everything we do is also brand management. Product creation, the stores, the advertising campaigns, the events, the packaging, the exhibitions: everything is aimed at cultivating the brand's identity and communicating it to people.

**McKinsey:** The way people get in touch with luxury products is changing. For more than 50 percent of consumers, the purchase process starts with online research today. How does digital development influence the Bulgari brand?

**Jean-Christophe Babin:** The digital world is certainly a dimension on which the luxury brands must count for both customer loyalty and for the entire brand communication. Bulgari not only renewed its Web site and will launch a new bulgari.com by the end of the year, it is also active on several social platforms – such as Facebook and Instagram – enriching them with almost daily news and also covering brand events in real time.

**McKinsey:** Please tell us how the new workshop you are building in Italy will help strengthen Bulgari's brand identity, especially the brand's continuing commitment to excellent craftsmanship.

**Jean-Christophe Babin:** Bulgari's commitment to the highest quality in craftsmanship has always been a strength that defines the brand. The high jewelry collections, for example, are realized in a workshop in Rome where master goldsmiths create perfectly crafted jewelry. Sometimes, they will work on a single piece over the course of five to six months, to give every Bulgari creation an exceptional suppleness and extraordinary quality.

Building a new jewelry factory in Piedmont to replace the two existing sites in Solonghello and Valenza has the objective of streamlining the organizational structure and optimizing production chain efficiency by keeping the highest standards in craftsmanship and our unique *made in Italy* savoir faire.

**McKinsey:** Also thinking about other sectors, which brand do you most admire?

**Jean-Christophe Babin:** Porsche. With the 911 – derived from the 356 – they have managed to create an icon, and they have had the patience and courage to build it and evolve it. Based on its success, Porsche was able to diversify the brand in order to attract a broader user base with the creation of a younger, more feminine, more affordable entry point – the Boxter, and then the Cayman. At the same time, they have created an evolutionary step for families with the Cayenne and the Panamera, built on the 911 concept yet identifying and leveraging industrial synergies between VW Group models and platforms. With this evolution, Porsche has become not only the most desired sports car brand in the world, but also the most profitable. Hats off.

# Notes

1 Fanderl, Harald, Ansgar Hölscher and Oliver Hupp, »Der Charakter der Marke – Die Messung der Markenpersönlichkeit: Das Brand Personality Gameboard,« Part 1, Markenartikel, Mar 2003, pp. 28–33; and Hölscher, Ansgar, Achim Hecker and Oliver Hupp, »Der Charakter der Marke – Die Messung der Markenpersönlichkeit: Das Brand Personality Gameboard,« Part 2, Markenartikel, Apr 2003, pp. 36–43.
2 Aaker, Jennifer L., »Dimensions of Brand Personality,« Journal of Marketing Research 34, Aug 1997, pp. 347–356.
3 One such approach is called the BPI (brand potential index). The 10 attitudinal components of the BPI are allegiance, acceptance of premium pricing, quality, awareness, uniqueness, empathy, trust, identification, willingness to recommend, and buying intention. See Hupp, Oliver, Sven Mussler, Ken Powaga, »Evaluation of the Financial Value of Brands,« GfK/PWC (German society for consumer research/PricewaterhouseCoopers), March 2004.
4 For details on how the benefits promised by a brand promises are delivered, experienced, and substantiated at customer touch points, see Chapter 4 below.
5 http://www.the-linde-group.com/en/about_the_-linde_ group/index.html; http://www.jungheinrich.com/en/about-us/ our-brand/; http://www.om-bg.com/index.php?l=1&p=2 (retrieved in August 2014).
6 Depending on the specific research, other methods may be superior, such as logarithmic regression analysis.
7 Note that this analysis is based on research conducted in 2002 in the market for mid-size cars. Were we to repeat this study today, chances are we would find some shifts. For example, fuel economy and environmental concerns would probably turn out to be more relevant as drivers of actual behavior than they were a decade ago.
8 http://live.wsj.com/video/bmw-launches-i8-hybridall-wheel-drive-supercar/89A7C998-6E40-4C00 880C-CC2ABEB9D489.html#!89A7C998-6E40-4C00-880C-CC2ABEB9D489.
9 http://www.myswitzerland.com/en/interests/adventure-sports-winter.html.
10 https://www.youtube.com/watch?v=9jesRMas8eY.
11 http://www.myswitzerland.com/en/accommodation/other_types.html.
12 Dennis Spillecke and Jesko Perrey, »Store brand portfolio management« (p. 77), in Retail Marketing and Branding, Wiley 2013.
13 http://www.ukprwire.com/Detailed/Computers_Internet/Shopping_Comparison_Engines_market_worth_120m-_140m_in_2005_says_Econsultancy_1648.shtml; http://www.horizont.net/aktuell/medien/pages/protected/Statista-Dieumsatzstaerksten-Content-und-Service-Portale-in-Deutschland_119907.html.
14 http://www.stadtwerke-bochum.de/privatkunden/unternehmen/engagement/sponsoring/bericht.html; https://www.stadtwerke-muenster.de/unternehmen/verantwortung/unser-angebotfuersie/sponsoring/unsere-werte.html; https://www.swp-potsdam.de/swp/de/stadtwerke-potsdam/ueber-uns-swp/verantwortung/st_sponsoringbericht.php (retrieved in August 2014).
15 Mit dem Avatar zum Autokauf, Frankfurter Allgemeine Zeitung, June 6, 2014.
16 http://www.marken-award.de/marken-award/preistraeger/2011.php.
17 Meffert, Heribert and Jesko Perrey, »Mehrmarkenstrategien,« Markenmanagement, ed. Heribert Meffert, Christoph Burmann, and Martin Koers, Wiesbaden: Gabler, 2002, p. 201 ff.
18 http://edition.cnn.com/2004/WORLD/europe/03/25/uk.dasani/.
19 Aaker, David A.: Brand Portfolio Strategy: Creating Relevance, Differentiation, Energy, Leverage, and Clarity, Free Press, 2004, p. 253.
20 http://www.nytimes.com/2008/03/26/business/worldbusiness/26cnd-auto.html?_r=0.
21 http://geschaeftsbericht-2013.hugoboss.com/das-geschaeftsjahr/konzernumsatz-undertragslage.html.
22 http://www.handelsblatt.com/finanzen/boerse-maerkte/boerse-inside/modekonzern-investorverkauft-erneut-hugo-boss-aktien/10645522.html.
23 http://www.boston.com/cars/news-and-reviews/2014/08/22/scion-sports-coupe-that-turn-heads/prHNsenkOwGJO3YkNtctaK/story.html.
24 Ohnsman, Alan and Jeff Bennett, »Toyota Puts Hipness Ahead of Sales for New Scion Cars,« Update 4, 8 Feb 2007, www.bloomberg.com.
25 http://www.scion.com/cars/ (retrieved on September 17, 2014).
26 Euromonitor database.
27 Unilever company information, »Path to Growth Summary and Implementation, Third Quarter 2003,« www.unilever.com.
28 http://unilever.com/aboutus/introductiontounilever/.
29 http://www.unilever.com/mediacentre/pressreleases/2014/Unileverreportsgrowthaheadofmarketsin2013.Aspx.
30 http://www.horizont.net/marketing/nachrichten/Procter–Gamble-90-Marken-sollen-verkauft-oder-zusammengelegt-werden-121637.
31 http://annualreport2012.henkel.com/the-company/k6.html.

32 Beverage Digest Factbook 2014; https://www.pepsicobeveragefacts.com/home/timeline; PepsiCo Annual report 2006; Euromonitor database.
33 http://www.mckinsey.com/insights/consumer_and_retail/how_retailers_can_keep_up_with_consumers.
34 Nandram, Sharda S., Samsom, Karel J.: The spirit of entrepreneurship, Springer, 2006, p. 133.
35 Based on an article by Baumüller, Nicole and Christoph Erbenich, »Wege zum Erfolg: Fünf Thesen zum Markentransfer,« Markenartikel, Jun 2005.
36 Most recently, the company has started conquering not only new categories, but entirely new territories with the Virgin Brand as well: Africa, namely Nigeria, and India.
37 http://www.marken-award.de/.
38 http://www.fashionmodeldirectory.com/brands/jilsander/.
39 http://www.piercom.com/knowledge-center/blog/posts/2011/august/avoiding-brand-extension-failures/.
40 http://www.theatlantic.com/business/archive/2012/04/apples-monster-quarter-in-4-charts/256311/; http://www.theatlantic.com/business/archive/2013/01/these-charts-tell-you-exactly-how-and-whereapple-makes-money-right-now/272463/.
41 http://www.businessweek.com/stories/1996-08-04/starbucks-does-not-live-by-coffee-alone.
42 http://businesscasestudies.co.uk/masterfoods/how-mars-transformed-the-ice-cream-market/#axzz3Eo1VzVOg.
43 »The Market for Impulse Ice Cream,« A report on the supply in the UK of ice cream for immediate consumption, London: British Competition Commission, 1994 and 2000.
44 http://hbr.org/2005/12/how-not-to-extend-your-luxury-brand/ar/1.
45 Janotta, Anja, »Mövenpick gibt Katjes den Laufpass, « Werben & Verkaufen, 28 Jan 2008, www.wuv.de.
46 http://www.halloren.de/ (retrieved in August 2014).
47 Till Krause, Steinreich, Süddeutsche Zeitung Magazin, April 4, 2014; http://www.businessweek.com/news/2014-02-27/lego-beats-u-dot-s-dot-toymaker-rivals-as-fullyear-revenue-jumps-10-percent.
48 http://www.bloomberg.com/apps/news?pid=newsarchive&sid=a_AY6q7HA3cA.
49 http://www.teaconnect.org/pdf/TEAAECOM2013.pdf.
50 http://nintendoeverything.com/lego-systems-andtt-games-publishing-extend-global-exclusivepartnership-for-development-of-lego-videogamesthrough-2016/.
51 http://www.imdb.com/title/tt1490017/?ref_=nv_sr_1.
52 http://www.businessweek.com/articles/2014-02-05/lego-movie-toy-brands-minifigs-entrusted-towarner-bros-filmmakers; http://www.ft.lk/2014/02/28/after-topping-box-office-lego-movie-sequel-setfor-may-2017/.
53 Lego Annual report 2012.
54 http://www.rankingthebrands.com/;http://www.forbes.com/pictures/ejdd45gefg/lego-branding-a-platform-for-creativity-through-extensions-licensing-and-new-media/.
55 http://www.dailymail.co.uk/home/moslive/article-1234465/When-Lego-lost-head--toy-story-got-happy-ending.html#ixzz3CGFEY4lb (retrieved in August 2014).
56 http://lego.gizmodo.com/5019797/everything-you-always-wanted-to-know-about-lego;http://www.omgfacts.com/Animals/More-than-400-billion-Lego-bricks-have-b/23072 (retrieved in August 2014).
57 http://www.wsj.de/nachrichten/SB10001424052970203966604580133281555808548?mg=reno64-wsjde.
58 http://www.sachsenmagazin.de/en/sightgeistextract/items/luxury-at-home.html.
59 http://howtospendit.ft.com/home-accessories/39083-the-empires-strike-back; http://www.wiwo.de/unternehmen/mittelstand/edel-porzellan-meissen-setzt-jetzt-auf-klamotten/.8313220.html.
60 http://fashiondailymag.com/meissen-couturelaunch/.
61 http://www.centurion-magazine.com/home/style/shopping/meissen-goes-milan.html.
62 Bundesanzeiger DE, company accounts 2013.
63 http://howtospendit.ft.com/home-accessories/39083-the-empires-strike-back.
64 Martha Stewart Living Omnimedia, Inc., SEC 10-K filing for 2013; http://www.sec.gov/Archives/edgar/data/1091801/000109180114000002/mso-12312013x10k.htm.
65 Linda Dauriz and Thomas Tochtermann, Luxury Lifestyle – Business beyond buzzwords, McKinsey June 2012.
66 http://interbrand.com/en/news-room/pressreleases/2008-12-05.aspx.
67 http://www.statista.com/statistics/270437/globalrevenue-share-of-the-armani-group-by-productcategory/.
68 http://www.wallpaper.com/design/giorgio-armaniqa-exclusive/1754.

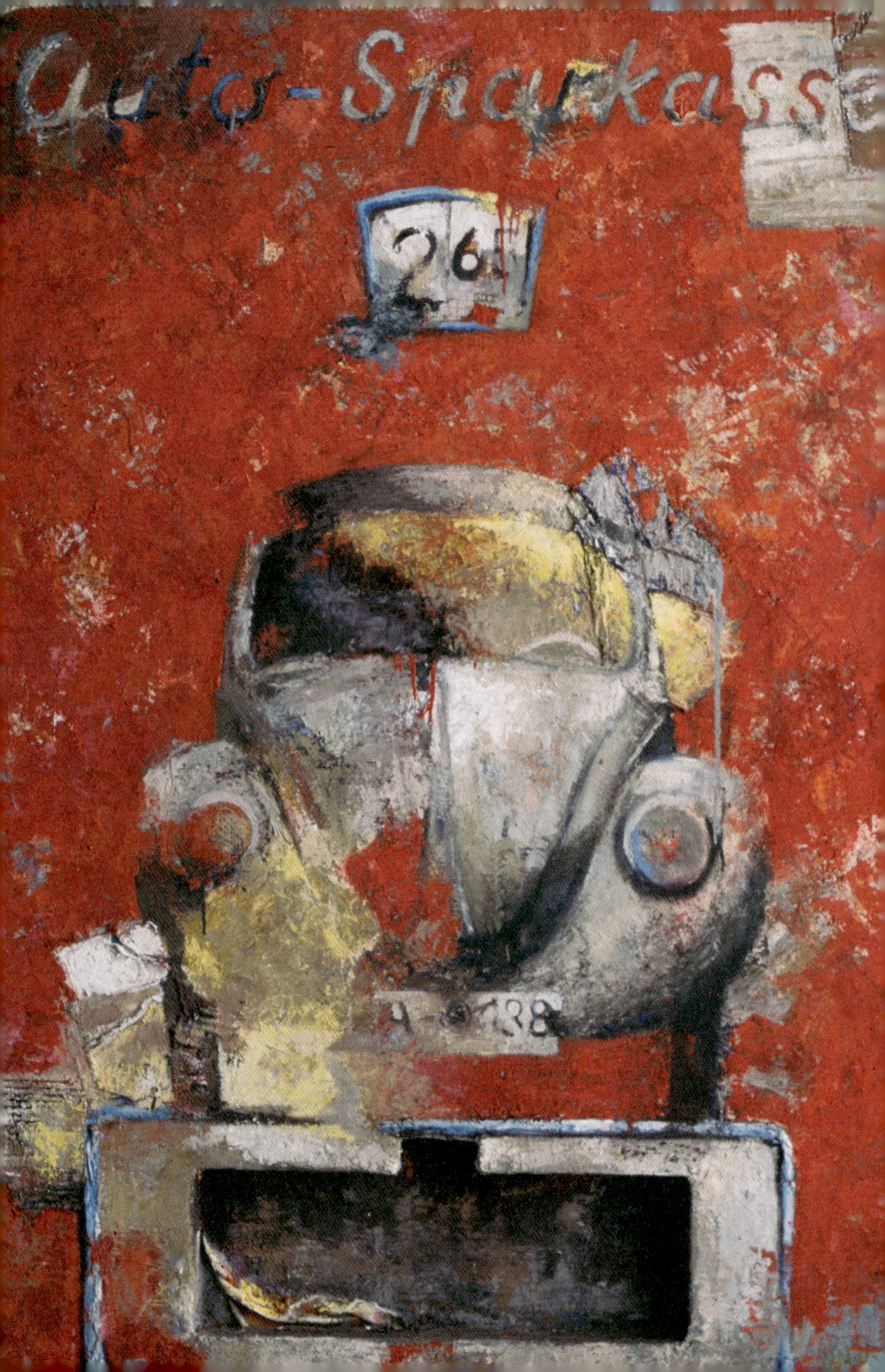
Auto-Sparkasse
26

# 4. Brand Delivery

## 4.1 A Promise is a Promise: Bringing Brands to Life

Imagine a symphony without an orchestra to play the notes of the score. Sounds lifeless? Exactly. That's what a brand without appropriate delivery is like. It takes a conductor who is congenial to the composer's intentions, the right instruments, proper tuning, and well-trained musicians to bring music to life for an audience. Much the same applies to a brand. Unless a brand is properly activated at the right touch points, nobody will get to experience the brand promise the way it is meant to be seen, heard, and touched.

As described in some detail in the preceding chapters, the BrandMatics® toolkit can be used to measure a brand's performance and optimize its positioning. Positioning, however, is just the starting point of effective brand management – just as even the most inspired composition is but the starting point of a great concert. Think of brand delivery as being the ultimate test a brand needs to pass to qualify as a true power brand.

As brand managers proceed from positioning to activation, or from measuring and making to managing, they usually find it helpful to synthesize the essence of what the brand stands for in the form of a brand promise. The brand promise can appear as a short statement or claim; it serves as the guiding light of all brand delivery. Superior delivery of such a promise comprises three complementary – and partly overlapping – disciplines of brand activation (Figure 4.1):

- *Customer experience management*, that is, the continuous optimization of the brand's performance at all relevant intersections of the brand and a customer's life, be they individual points in time and space (»touch points«) or processes (»journeys«).
- *Media management*, that is, the fact-based selection of relevant communication channels and the allocation of funds to these channels, governed by marketing return on investment (MROI) as the principal metric.
- *Internal activation*, that is, the totality of activities, tools, and processes that help a company's employees live the brand and become its ambassadors in all interactions with customers, business partners, and the general public.

To make sure the brand promise is kept and brought to life comprehensively and consistently, a true power brand needs to excel in each of these disciplines. We will start by examining brand promise development and customer experience management in this section, and then proceed to MROI-based media selection and internal activation in subsequent sections in this chapter. In addition, we will take a closer look at digital brand management.

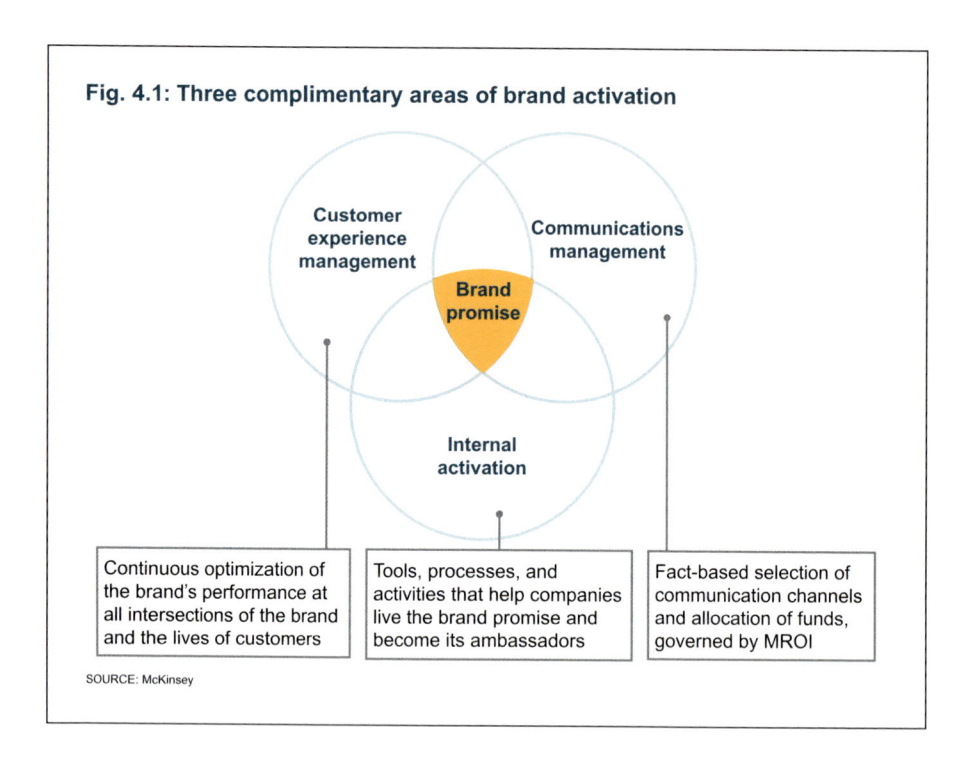

**Fig. 4.1: Three complimentary areas of brand activation**

- Customer experience management — Continuous optimization of the brand's performance at all intersections of the brand and the lives of customers
- Brand promise / Internal activation — Tools, processes, and activities that help companies live the brand promise and become its ambassadors
- Communications management — Fact-based selection of communication channels and allocation of funds, governed by MROI

SOURCE: McKinsey

### Defining the brand promise

BrandMatics® provides answers to the questions about which brand elements drive consumer decisions, which are the best options in terms of positioning, and what effect these options will have on a brand's position in its competitive environment:

- *The brand purchase funnel* (see Chapter 2, Section 2.3) measures brand performance and highlights gaps to relevant competitors (e.g., the brand may have an issue converting consideration to purchase).
- *Brand driver analysis* (see Chapter 3, Section 3.2) helps brand managers pinpoint the attributes driving critical transfers in the funnel (e.g., the top attribute driving the transfer to purchase may be the »contemporary design« of the brand's products).
- The *matrix of options* (see Chapter 3, Section 3.3) balances a brand's perceived strengths (e.g., »good resale value«) with attributes that matter to keep its promise and succeed in the market (e.g., »contemporary design« and other such attributes).

But brand building is more than analyzing performance and specifying strategic direction. This direction must also be synthesized into an overall concept and then translated into operational terms, so that all employees are aware of exactly what individual contributions they can make in implementing the strategy. The brand promise serves as the link between brand measurement and brand management. It takes into account the analysis of the brand and any strategic considerations. The promise should describe the essence of a brand and its differentiation in two respects:

- Relative to other brands in the company's own portfolio or hierarchy (if applicable).
- Relative to competing brands from the perspective of current and potential customers.

Ideally, the brand promise culminates in a concise phrase, even if brevity comes at the cost of detail. At the same time, the promise must be applicable to concrete actions, such as product design, customer communication, and aftersales service.

Summarizing the brand positioning in a brand promise is one of the most challenging tasks for executives. Even if all the analyses are available, it is not easy to distill their essence. This is all the more challenging as the brand promise needs to include – in a concise yet complete manner – its differentiating attributes, that is, the aspects that make it stand out from its competitors. Although the process may be tedious, we are convinced that it is a rewarding way for brand managers to spend their time and energy. Our work with clients has shown the value and the power of the concept of a short brand promise statement. It forces brand managers to clarify the brand's identity and prevents executives from cultivating »private« perceptions that may eventually result in a diluted brand identity and lead to inconsistencies regarding its activation. The brand promise serves as an internal touchstone for all major brand management decisions, although not all companies use the brand promise as a client-facing claim. Some brands are explicitly meant to speak for themselves externally, especially in the luxury goods sector.[1] Even if there is a claim or brand essence statement for internal purposes, it will not normally appear in advertising or other forms of external communication.

The starting point for brand promise definition is to ask what the brand represents from the consumer's point of view. In answering this question, agencies and specialists often come up with seemingly endless lists of visions, missions, values, attributes, beliefs, personalities, identities, and so on. Frequently, the same clusters of buzzwords are applied to very different brands, and often without empirical evidence of any sort.

A certain retailer, for instance, defined its brand promise using fifteen brand value statements, including »inspiration,« »ingenuity,« »fun,« »self-confidence,« »trust,« and »good value for money.« Nothing was left out. With this degree of fuzziness, the retailer might arguably represent all conceivable formats, from Giorgio Armani to H&M or The Gap. Additionally, the company addressed nearly all conceivable dimensions of value. Who wouldn't want to shop there? When one of the authors of this book read aloud another colorful medley of positioning attributes, such as »friendly,« »honest,« and »helpful« to his spouse, her guess as to the identity of the brand was: »It must be a church!«

Another example is a service provider that not only compiled a long list of general statements about its brand promise, but also went so far as to arrange them into a number of categories: from »value proposition« and »core values« to »inner-directed values,« »outer-directed values,« and »personality traits.« The brand promise seemed to be trying to answer questions that no one was asking. To top it off, the service provider took more than 100 words to define who its target customers were. By contrast, promises like BMW's »Ultimate Driving Machine,« Apple's »Think Different,« Toyota's »Moving Forward,« Nationwide's »Nationwide is on your side,« or Tim Horton's »Comfortably Canadian« are so simple and self-explanatory that they make immediate sense. They stick almost as soon as you hear them.

**Fig. 4.2: Nivea and Sixt: Precise brand promises pay off**

| Nivea | | Sixt | |
|---|---|---|---|
| When I use | Nivea | When I rent from | Sixt |
| instead of | products made by another personal care manufacturer | instead of | another car rental company |
| then I get | gentle skin and beauty care | then I get | a lot of car for a little money |
| because | Nivea attaches great value to gentle ingredients and has decades of experience in preparing them | because | only Sixt offers the most attractive cars at the best prices |

SOURCE: McKinsey

Establishing a successful brand promise is by no means child's play. It takes expert craftsmanship to reduce a brand to its essence without sacrificing its individual appeal. While such efforts should always be based on solid fact, that is, the *science* of brand measurement as introduced in Chapter 1 and laid out in Chapters 2 and 3, the presentation of the resulting synthesis can take many forms. One particularly popular form is the »Brand Key« used by Unilever.[2] When the company acquired the Ben & Jerry's ice cream brand, one of the first things the new owners did was to develop a Brand Key for the new member of the Unilever family of brands.[3] As a framework, the Brand Key combines four aspects of brand identity:

- *Benefits:* Which functional and emotional benefits does the brand provide compared with its competitors?
- *Values and personality:* Which values does the brand stand for? What is its personality?
- *Reason to believe:* Why would consumers believe that this brand is right for them, and that it will keep its promise?
- *Unique selling proposition:* Which unique advantage does this brand provide as opposed to all its competitors?

In a final step, these elements are condensed to the brand core: What is the essence that remains the same for a substantial period of time, and applies to all products and categories? For Dove, Unilever's leading personal care brand, the essence was once described as the aspiration to »help more women feel beautiful every day.«[4] The food brand Bertolli – also part of Unilever's portfolio – strives to embody »the Italian passion for food and life.«[5] When marketing executives at Ben & Jerry's proceeded to define the brand's first-ever Brand Key more than a decade ago, they captured the brand essence as »Joy for the belly and the soul.« It still holds today.[6] Figure 4.2 shows a similar approach, using Nivea, the personal care company, and Sixt, the car rental company, as examples.

Depending on the degree of aspiration involved, the brand promise may reflect current as well future strengths of a given brand, but should not deviate too far from the brand's heritage. BrandMatics®, as outlined in the preceding chapters, will help brand managers narrow down the list of attributes for consideration. Common criteria to derive and assess the brand promise include:

- *Distinctiveness:* Concentrate on unique and distinctive brand elements that set you apart from competitors.
- *Relevance:* Take into consideration the important brand elements that drive customers' purchase decisions.
- *Credibility:* Ensure that the brand promise is credible and reflects current strengths in brand perception as much as possible.
- *Consistency:* Maintain consistency with past brand image and brand heritage, especially if your brand is the market leader and depends on the loyalty of current customers.
- *Feasibility:* Secure internal performance capabilities. The company needs to possess the internal resources and capabilities necessary to ensure that the brand promise can be fulfilled consistently in all its contacts with customers. It is especially important to take into consideration the costs of implementing the brand promise.

The criteria included in the checklist (Figure 4.3) will form the basis for assessing and prioritizing the brand elements. If needed, the criteria can be transformed into a simple scoring model. As with all scoring models, the key question is how to weight the criteria. Their weighting in the checklist should be oriented first and foremost towards the initial situation of the brand and the associated strategy. In a stable environment (e.g., in the case of market leaders such as BMW, Henkel's leading German detergent brand Persil, or Beiersdorf's Nivea), the most important criteria are certainly consistency and internal feasibility. In such cases, this exercise would typically not produce an entirely new brand promise, but would update and enhance the existing one. Nevertheless, there is no doubt that the brand promise represents an important, if not the decisive, component of a successful brand. But the brand promise is only a true guarantee of success if it is embedded in all business units and implemented in a consistent manner at every touch point.

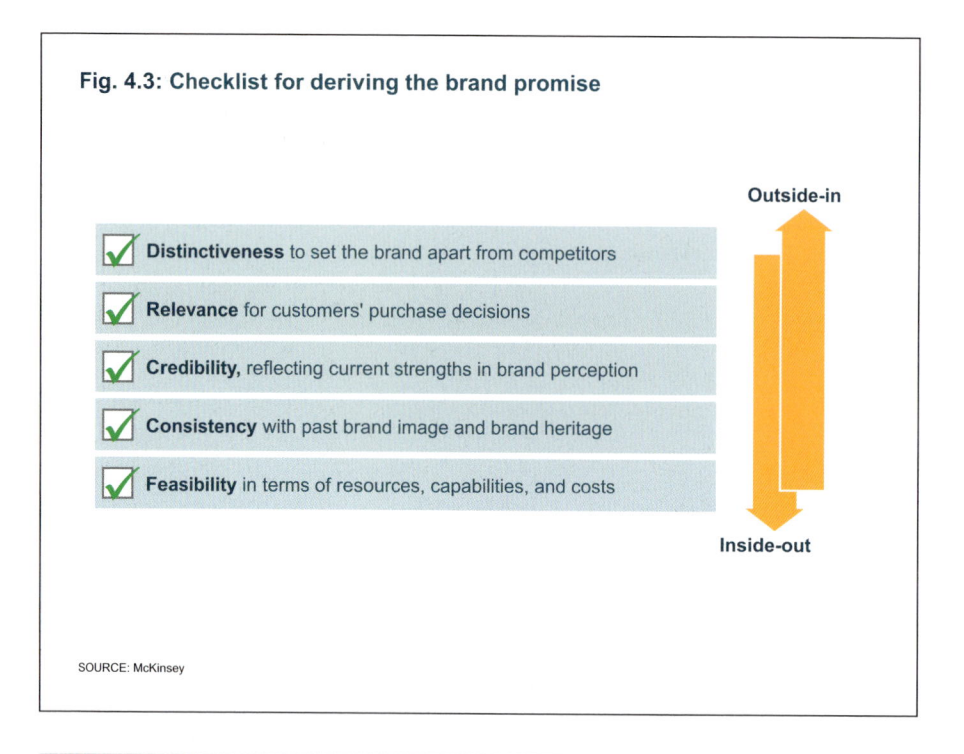

**Fig. 4.3: Checklist for deriving the brand promise**

Outside-in

- ✓ **Distinctiveness** to set the brand apart from competitors
- ✓ **Relevance** for customers' purchase decisions
- ✓ **Credibility,** reflecting current strengths in brand perception
- ✓ **Consistency** with past brand image and brand heritage
- ✓ **Feasibility** in terms of resources, capabilities, and costs

Inside-out

SOURCE: McKinsey

---

**Brand promise definition in B2B: Science meets craft**

Faced with fierce competition in a global oligopoly, a leading capital goods conglomerate set out to define a new brand promise. Because the group had been formed through a series of international mergers and acquisitions, the challenge was to find a proposition for the umbrella brand that would fit not only the company as a whole, but a vast array of business units and national subsidiaries as well. To create a robust fact base for this effort, the BrandMatics® toolkit was used to take stock of brand perception across several stakeholder groups, including customers, employees, external experts, and the general public. The survey covered both tangible attributes, such as »superior product quality« and »competitive prices,« and intangible attributes, such as the perception of the brand as »modern,« »traditional,« or »innovative.«

Based on the brand's perceived strengths and weaknesses on key market drivers, the CMO's team developed four options for the future brand promise. While these options were based on solid analysis, they were deliberately phrased in a pointed, even provocative way to trigger productive discussions among senior leaders:

- »Providing the best customer service.«
- »Being the most caring company.«
- »Delivering the highest quality.«
- »Leading through cutting-edge innovation.«

For example, the option »being the most caring company« would incorporate differentiating attributes such as »sustainable supply chain« or »a fun work environment«; »delivering the highest quality« would be anchored by statements such as »performs above the market average in tests« and »the first choice for critical applications.«

In a second step, these options were evaluated using a predefined set of criteria that included distinctiveness, relevance, credibility, consistency with the company strategy, and feasibility. This evaluation was conducted on three levels: at the corporate center, for each major business unit, and in all countries. The shortlist of options and the initial results of the evaluation were discussed in a series of workshops and breakout discussions with the C-suite, division managers, and selected external opinion leaders. Over the course of several weeks, the four options were narrowed down to the two most realistic routes, »best customer service« and »cutting-edge innovation.«

In a third and final step, the remaining two routes were tested with an even wider group of stakeholders. Specifically, mixed groups of line managers discussed what either route would mean for the way they do business in their divisions – from new product development to aftersales service. This was a crucial reality check, since it forced managers not only to think about the implications for their own business areas, but to listen to the needs and concerns of their peers in other areas as well. As part of this exercise, the groups spelled out in detail how either option would be implemented in each division, and what they would have to deliver in the future to keep the brand promise.

The executive board weighed both the BrandMatics® results and the expertise of their direct reports. Ultimately, the company settled on the promise to provide the best customer service, a proposition that fits both the company as a whole and its divisions.

## Activating the brand promise

Any musician will tell you that composing and performing are altogether different things. Similarly, it is one thing to measure a brand's performance and to get its target positioning, including the brand promise, right analytically and strategically. However, it is another thing to make sure the brand is brought to life and sustained where it matters most – in the eyes and the ears, the hearts and the minds of everyone it touches.

Customer touch points can take many shapes and forms. Communication in the form of advertising or public relations is, of course, very important. But in every industry there are many other touch points that are of equal, or even greater, importance. Think about the airline industry, where the customer's experience during reservation, check-in, boarding, or baggage claim, can have a much more significant impact on the brand image than any advertising campaign. In a world of viral media, the behavior of a single employee can literally make or break the image of a brand; compare the case of the airline in Section 4.4 on digital brand management. In the automotive industry, the car itself is and its presentation in advertising is but the center of gravity for touch points that range from online configurator tools to dealerships and from call centers to racing teams. All these touch points need to be managed carefully to ensure the customer's experience at these interfaces reflects the value proposition and desired image of the brand (Figure 4.4).

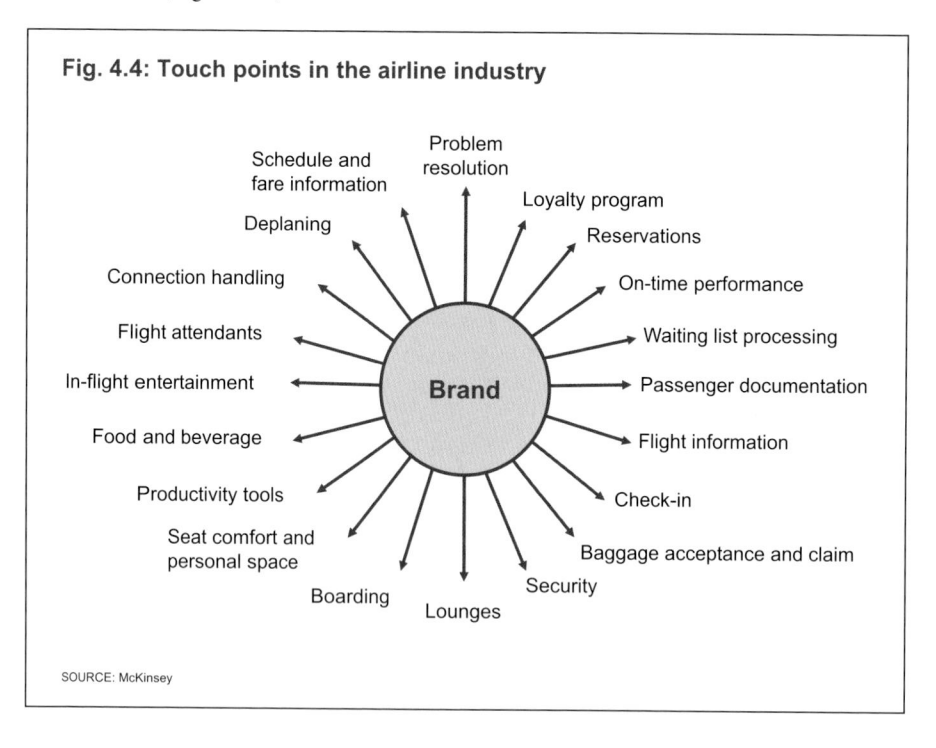

**Fig. 4.4: Touch points in the airline industry**

- Schedule and fare information
- Problem resolution
- Loyalty program
- Deplaning
- Reservations
- Connection handling
- On-time performance
- Flight attendants
- Waiting list processing
- In-flight entertainment
- Passenger documentation
- Food and beverage
- Flight information
- Productivity tools
- Check-in
- Seat comfort and personal space
- Baggage acceptance and claim
- Boarding
- Security
- Lounges

SOURCE: McKinsey

How often have you heard something like the following dialog? The director of the marketing department is presenting the findings of the most recent market research as well as a new creative brand claim that was developed on the basis of the research. He tells his audience: »We must design our products so that the brand perception corresponds to customers' need for security.« A murmur goes around the room, and the speaker is immediately bombarded with questions. »And what does that mean, in concrete terms, for our product design?« asks the director of research and development. »How can we implement this at the point of sale?« the sales manager enquires. »It seems that it really has nothing to do with employee training then,« the head of personnel comments.

Some of the differentiating elements of a given brand can be translated intuitively into operational actions, such as an »attractive purchase price« for a car brand. The devil is in the details, however. A good price or inexpensive optional equipment undoubtedly contributes to customers perceiving the brand products in question as attractively priced. But what makes more sense in the end? A lower starting price, low prices for popular optional equipment, or both? Or would it be even better to optimize the prices of the higher-performance models instead of the starting price? Then how is »high performance« defined? At 90, 100, or 150 horsepower?

This problem is aggravated when the differentiating attribute is more emotional than functional in nature. It is often the intangible brand elements – that is, emotional benefits along with associations of origin and reputation – that emerge as especially relevant brand drivers in the purchase funnel.

## Disaggregating brand drivers to drive brand operations

To ensure sustainable success for a brand, it is crucial to tie its operations to the brand promise and to brand attributes that drive its performance in the purchase funnel. Perception may be reality in many ways, but broken promises are bound to come back and haunt the brand manager sooner or later. To stay successful beyond the short term, brand operations need to match the brand's benefits proclaimed by the brand promise and communicated in advertising. Let's quickly recapitulate the tools and methods outlined so far to bring out the role a brand's operations play to drive its performance in the purchase funnel:

- Brand relevance measurement, customer insights, and segmentation are used to select and profile attractive target groups for a brand in a given category.
- For these segments, quantified purchase funnel research is conducted to assess how the target group's attitudes towards the brand compare with its competitors, thereby identifying gaps in funnel transfer rates for targeted improvement.
- The brand diamond and brand driver analysis help identify the image attributes that are critical to move consumers from stage to stage in the purchase funnel, especially those drivers that will help to close any transfer gaps.
- These critical brand drivers can be broken down into operational actions at relevant touch points to improve the brand's performance on these attributes and to close the transfer gaps in the purchase funnel for which they act as drivers.

So there is a direct link from day-to-day operations to a brand's image and funnel performance that – by way of the »purchase« stage – ultimately translates into market share. Selecting both the appropriate touch points and the most relevant messages or actions is essential to make sure the brand promise is kept at the front line in interaction with customers (Figure 4.5). Let's assume a given brand lags behind the competition in transferring its target customers from »purchase« to »loyalty.« Let's also assume that the image attribute »good service« is a key driver behind this transfer. In order to close its gap in creating loyalty, the brand in question needs to improve its perceived performance as a provider of »good service.« One obvious step the company can take is to convey a service promise in its above-the-line communication. But provident brand managers will also want to know how »good service« can effectively and efficiently be activated at other touch points. How can they put »good service« into practice at the point of sale, in customer call centers, and in aftersales relationship management?

The challenge is to disaggregate the components of the brand promise, such as »good service,« into concrete recommendations that management can act upon. Is the con-

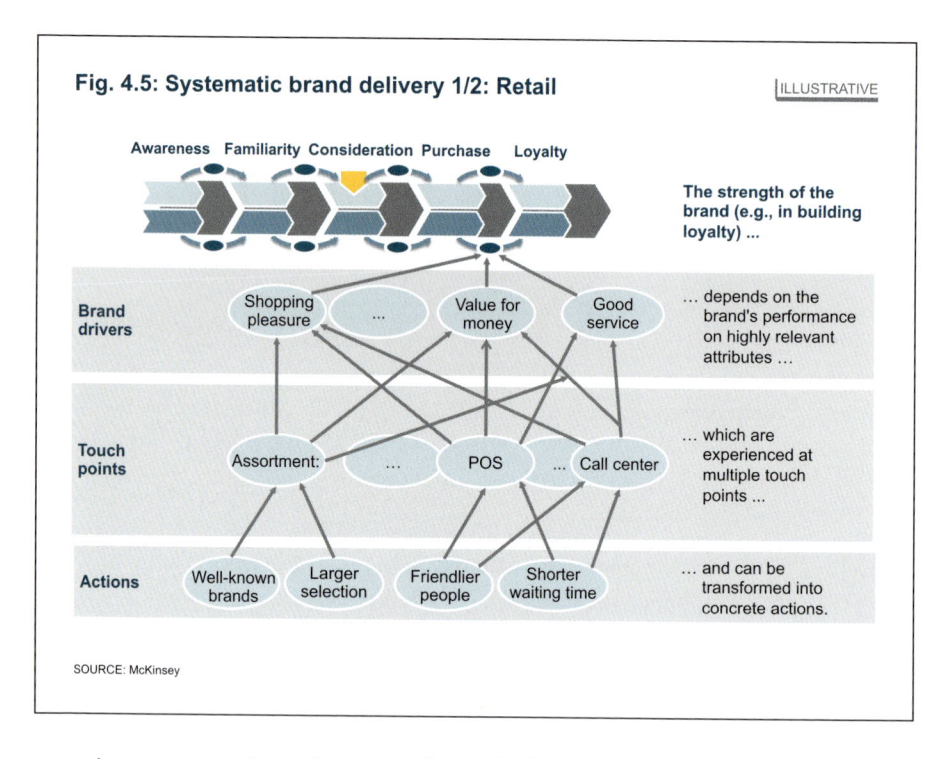

## Fig. 4.5: Systematic brand delivery 1/2: Retail  ILLUSTRATIVE

Awareness → Familiarity → Consideration → Purchase → Loyalty

The strength of the brand (e.g., in building loyalty) …

**Brand drivers**: Shopping pleasure, …, Value for money, Good service

… depends on the brand's performance on highly relevant attributes …

**Touch points**: Assortment, …, POS, …, Call center

… which are experienced at multiple touch points …

**Actions**: Well-known brands, Larger selection, Friendlier people, Shorter waiting time

… and can be transformed into concrete actions.

SOURCE: McKinsey

sumer's perception of »good service« driven by friendly staff, shorter waiting times at the POS, faster responses to e-mails, or something else entirely (Figure 4.6)? Which actions promise the biggest impact on the perception of the brand as a provider of »good service«? To help brand managers and their teams answer these questions, a range of multivariate analysis techniques is available, including pathways analysis, causal analysis, and partial least square algorithms. The common denominator of these techniques is their objective to translate abstract brand elements into concrete actions at touch points such as product design, sales, and service. The causal relationships and interdependencies of brand elements are examined mathematically, and brand attributes are disaggregated into their operational components to facilitate and monitor action planning.[7]

A simplified example of a mail-order company (Figure 4.7) will help us demonstrate how brand driver disaggregation works. The individual brand elements are depicted in the boxes. The arrows represent the causal relationships between these elements. The brand promise consists of the brand essence »I like shopping here« and the differentiators »I feel good shopping here,« »consistently good service,« and »shopping here shows that you value good clothing.« The strength of the causal relationship between the attributes is represented by the path coefficient. These coefficients are similar to correlations. Thus, the attribute »I feel good shopping here« has the strongest impact on the brand essence, as indicated by a coefficient of 0.49.

4.1 A Promise is a Promise: Bringing Brands to Life  **229**

**Fig. 4.6: Systematic brand delivery 2/2: Automotive** — ILLUSTRATIVE

Awareness   Familiarity   Consideration   Purchase   Loyalty

**Brand drivers:** Contemporary design · Good resale value · Good service

**Touch points:** Showroom · Printed materials · Online configuration · Dealership · Call center

**Actions:** Tailor design to model · Review corporate colors · ?

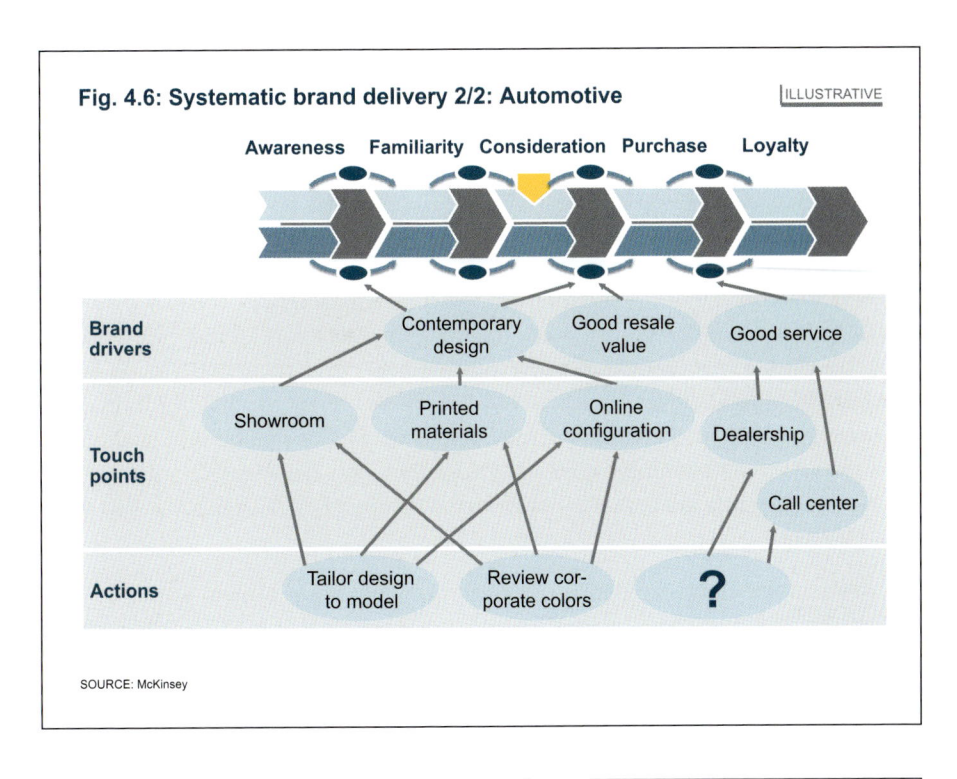

SOURCE: McKinsey

---

**Fig. 4.7: Pathways analyses help identify the right operational definitions and targets to fulfill the brand promise** — MAIL-ORDER SALES

**Operational steps**

Stronger focus on specialized mailings and targeted CRM:
- Mailings are exactly tailored to my needs — 0.36
- Always sends me up-to-date offers — 0.25
- …

Alongside efficiency, train, measure, and communicate "friendliness":
- Fast delivery service — 0.23
- Simple return procedures — 0.23
- Helpful customer service — 0.32
- …

Focus assortment on quality merchandise and communicate this fact explicitly:
- Offers quality merchandise — 0.38
- Fashionable clothing — 0.32
- Unusual clothing — 0.19
- …

**Elements of the brand promise**

- I feel good shopping here — 0.49 → I like shopping here
- Consistently good service — 0.47 → I like shopping here
- Shopping here shows that you value good clothing — 0.27 → I like shopping here

● = Strength of causal connection (0 = non-existent; 1 = very high)

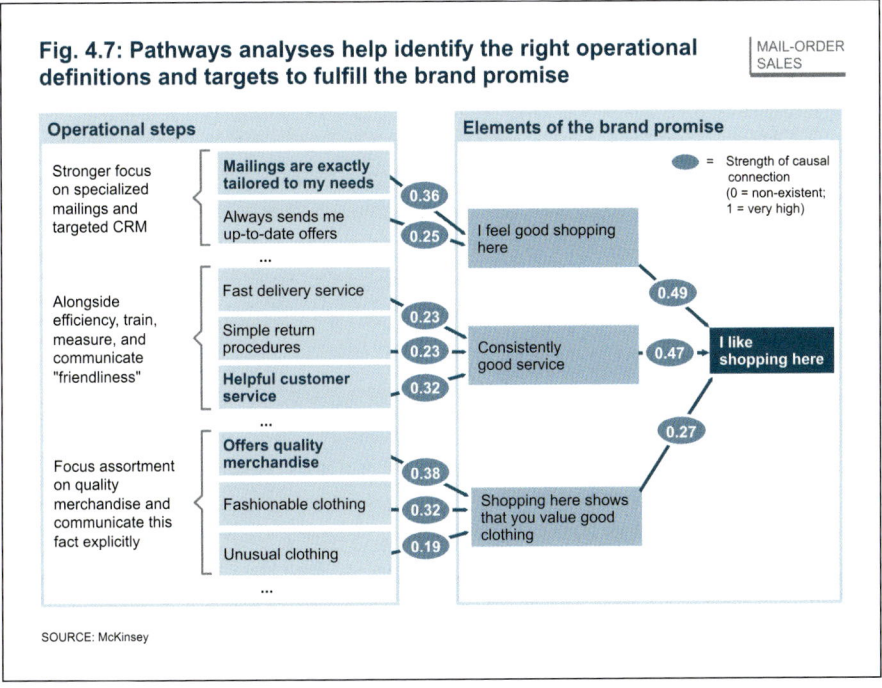

SOURCE: McKinsey

The causal interrelationships can now be subdivided until the operational level is reached. This analysis shows that the perception of the brand driver »I feel good shopping here« can be promoted through customized mailings in particular. This realization leads to concrete measures for the mail-order company, such as greater concentration on segment-specific mailings, or a targeted customer relationship management program. The analysis also yields concrete guidelines for personnel management. The service image of the mail-order company is apparently determined less by efficient processes and much more by the company's perceived willingness to help during contact with the customer. In other words, to strengthen its image as a service-oriented company, management should focus on improvements in customer interaction rather than back-office operations. Finally, in its product assortment, the mail-order company should pay particular attention to maintaining consistent standards of quality: unusual or high-fashion clothing apparently contribute less than reliable, quality products to increasing its score on the brand driver »shopping here shows that you value good clothing.«

The causal model shown for a mail-order company is based on simple outside-in market research. To this extent, it represents only a subsection of the complete problem context. In daily business, both the brand promise and how it is put into operation along all dimensions of the brand diamond need to be spelled out in more detail.

The dimensions of brand benefit discussed above serve as an aid in structuring the causal relationships in the pathways analysis. The functional elements – e.g., »has all the major brands,« »has a large product selection,« »has friendly and helpful staff« – represent the operational brand levers that can be influenced by refining the marketing mix, including components such as product, price, distribution, and communication. The perception of these functional elements does not bring about any direct benefit, but it does impact the perception of the remaining symbolic dimensions of a brand – for example, »company with a tradition,« »a major brand,« »a dynamic brand« – that collectively constitute a brand's personality. Recognizing both the functional and the symbolic aspects of a brand enables brand managers to translate the differentiators defined in the brand promise into targeted programs for action, employing all tools of the marketing mix.

Let's take a look at the example of an apparel retailer to see how causal analysis of brand image attributes can be combined with the purchase funnel framework to derive operational actions (Figure 4.8). The apparel retailer in question is struggling with insufficient brand loyalty compared with its competitors. Its market share remains high, but this is primarily driven by the broad presence of its outlets at premium downtown locations, that is, by distribution power rather than true brand assets.

First, the brand drivers are identified through a factor analysis of 30 individual statements. Figure 4.8 shows the causal relationships between the brand drivers and loyalty, again quantified as pathway coefficients. The brand driver »shopping pleasure,« for instance, has the highest significance in establishing loyalty. The next step involves

**Fig. 4.8: In brick-and-mortar clothing retail, assortment is still more important than price and service**

DISGUISED EXAMPLE

Standardized pathway coefficients[1]

| Brand drivers[2] | Effect on loyalty | Marketing levers ||||||
|---|---|---|---|---|---|---|---|---|
| | | Assortment | Service | Decor | Price | Advertising | Events | Distribution |
| Shopping pleasure | 0.55 | 0.55 | 0.27 | 0.25 | | | | |
| Value-priced shopping | 0.35 | | | | 0.64 | 0.32 | | |
| Individual shopping world | 0.10 | 0.10 | 0.17 | 0.09 | | 0.17 | 0.31 | |
| Customer orientation | 0.12 | | 0.37 | 0.11 | | 0.25 | | 0.17 |
| Familiarity | 0.11 | | | | | | | 0.29 |
| Total effect on loyalty[3] | | **0.31** | 0.21 | 0.16 | 0.22 | 0.16 | 0.03 | 0.05 |

| Individual assortment indicators | Importance |
|---|---|
| • Has all the major brands | High |
| • Carries many products of good quality | High |
| • Carries a very large range of products | High |
| • Always has the latest products in stock | Medium |
| • Also offers very unusual merchandise | Medium |
| • ... | ... |

1 Other relationships not significant
2 Result of the factor analysis of 30 individual statements
3 Factor weightings (loadings) multiplied by total contribution to the effect of the factor

SOURCE: McKinsey consumer survey, GfK market research

examining what marketing activities especially influence »shopping pleasure.« It turns out that the product assortment is of highest significance, followed by service and decor (i.e., ambience and merchandise presentation). The remaining marketing levers have no significant influence on this brand driver. As expected, the brand driver »value-priced shopping« is related first and foremost to price. In addition, however, advertising also promotes the image of value-priced shopping. Overall, the model shows that the product assortment is of overwhelming significance for customer loyalty. Price, service, decor, and advertising trail at some distance. In contrast, »events« and »distribution« are of little importance in strengthening loyalty. This does not mean that they are completely irrelevant. Distribution, in particular, is of relatively high importance in the early steps of the purchase funnel; »events« and special sales are of medium importance in the conversion from the stage of familiarity to visiting the store. While pathway analysis does not provide yes-or-no answers, it helps brand managers set priorities to help them focus on the most effective marketing levers.

Driver disaggregation not only provides the insight that assortment is the most effective means of increasing customer loyalty for this leading clothing retailer, it can also identify the subcomponents of individual marketing levers such as assortment (see bottom of Figure 4.8). In this example, the main indicators are availability of major brands, products of good quality, and a large range of products. This level of granularity enables the retailer to derive a specific program for brand building. Potential initiatives can be assessed and prioritized in terms of their contribution to brand attributes that drive loyalty. These examples illustrate that the pathways approach is a sophisticated, yet highly practical analysis tool that can be used to translate the abstract brand promise into operational guidelines for all business units.

Multivariate analysis methods allow brand managers to get even one step closer to concrete marketing action planning – provided the market research used is sufficiently detailed and marketing levers can be broken down to different performance levels. Imagine an insurance company that has identified »processes my requests quickly« as one of the top differentiators in its brand promise. One of the most important service levers, determining whether the brand is perceived to be performing well on this driver, is »speed of mail correspondence.« But just how speedy does the claims department have to be in order to satisfy consumer expectations? From the policyholder's perspective, it may not make much difference whether it takes a day or a week for a request to be processed, as long as it is less than a month. But from a resource and cost perspective, the difference between these service levels is, of course, tremendous. The concept of customer-driven redesign helps to address this issue by reflecting consumers' elasticity of perception. In other words, any optimization should be based on an assessment of the expected gain in consumer satisfaction, addressing questions such as: How big a difference does an improvement from a five- to three-day lead time really make? This knowledge enables brand and marketing management to decide whether it's worth going the extra mile for all key drivers identified, and where to focus their investments.

Figure 4.9, a disguised insurance example, shows an illustrative output for »better performance than others« and »processes my requests quickly,« which are the key drivers behind purchase for a specific segment in this case. Similar insights can be derived for most rational benefits and tangible brand elements. Prominent examples include call center performance, service component selection, or performance levels achieved in tests. For example, achieving a top JD Power quality ranking in the car industry may be very costly, yet not really necessary. Being ranked above average by a consumer or expert panel may be fully sufficient to be perceived as a brand that »performs better than others.« The impact of achieving specific performance levels is captured by the »gain in satisfaction« score. Depending on the research design, this kind of score can even be operationalized as »willingness to pay (more).«[8]

It is exactly this type of fact-based operational definition of business actions that will help branding shed its reputation as a »soft« discipline. Linking specific actions to key components of the brand promise enables executives both in the marketing function and elsewhere in the organization to improve a brand's performance in a targeted and cost-efficient way. Armed with pathway coefficients as quantified indicators of how marketing investments drive brand equity, the CMO may even get the CFO's attention when it comes to resource allocation discussions.

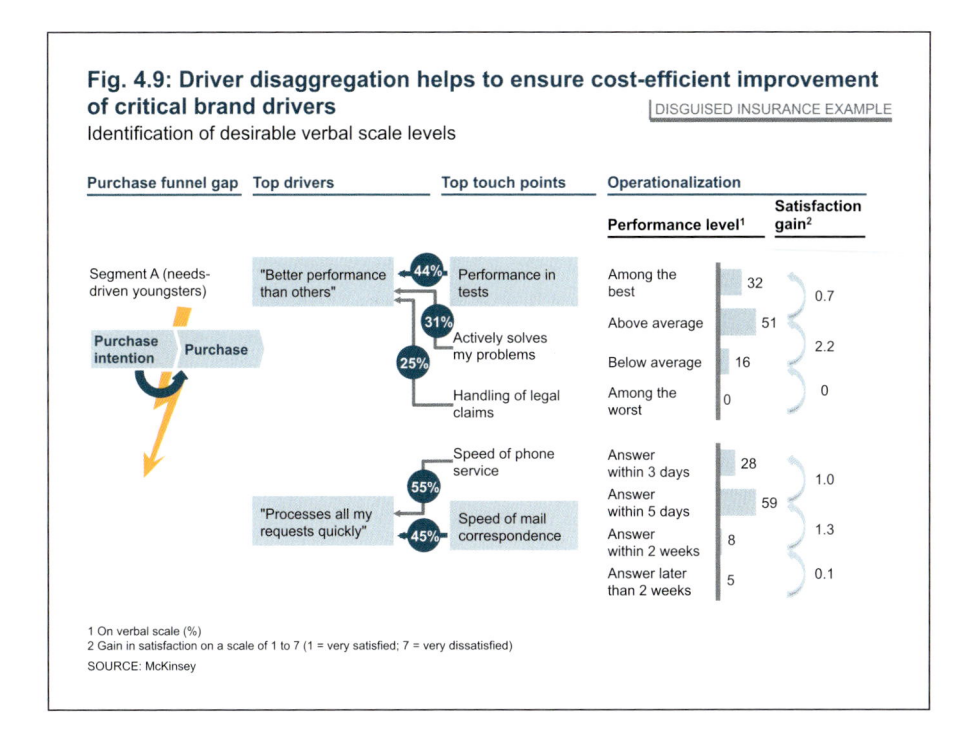

**Fig. 4.9: Driver disaggregation helps to ensure cost-efficient improvement of critical brand drivers**

DISGUISED INSURANCE EXAMPLE

Identification of desirable verbal scale levels

| Purchase funnel gap | Top drivers | Top touch points | Operationalization | | |
|---|---|---|---|---|---|
| | | | Performance level[1] | | Satisfaction gain[2] |

Segment A (needs-driven youngsters) — "Better performance than others" — 44% — Performance in tests
- Among the best: 32 — 0.7
- Above average: 51 — 2.2
- Below average: 16
- Among the worst: 0 — 0

Purchase intention → Purchase
- 31% Actively solves my problems
- 25% Handling of legal claims

"Processes all my requests quickly" — 55% — Speed of phone service
- 45% Speed of mail correspondence
- Answer within 3 days: 28 — 1.0
- Answer within 5 days: 59 — 1.3
- Answer within 2 weeks: 8
- Answer later than 2 weeks: 5 — 0.1

1 On verbal scale (%)
2 Gain in satisfaction on a scale of 1 to 7 (1 = very satisfied; 7 = very dissatisfied)
SOURCE: McKinsey

**Optimizing entire journeys**

Making sure that the brand promise is kept at critical touch points is a powerful way of bringing brands to life. It is usually the first order of business for many companies, especially if resources are restricted and a single touch point stands out in terms of purchase relevance as measured by the brand funnel. Our experience shows that high-frequency touch points have above-average impact on brand perception and customer satisfaction (Figure 4.10). For example, always having to stand in line at the supermarket checkout will quickly frustrate shoppers and create an impression of poor service that may be hard to rectify once it has taken hold in the consumer's mind. Companies will want to resolve this kind of issue as quickly as possible – and monitor the touch point in question continuously to make sure the improvements are sustained. Yet some retailers may consciously choose to allow for long lines to project an image of scarcity and value for money, implying that they are offering something of superior value that customers will readily wait for. In categories such as fashion and accessories, a deliberate shortage of supply and lack of convenience can, in fact, become part of the brand promise, assuming that if people are willing to wait or even fight for something, it must be worth it. Some luxury companies go as far as making limited editions available only to a hand-picked group of brand ambassadors who can be relied on to spread the word among their peers, thus increasing the brand's allure.

Fig. 4.10: Brand delivery optimization:
Individual touch points vs. entire journeys

|  | Start with optimizing individual touch points | Consider optimizing high-priority customer journeys |
| --- | --- | --- |
| Market maturity | Low to medium (relatively fragmented, dynamic market) | Medium to high (consolidated and/or saturated market) |
| Customer involvement | Low to medium (impulse purchases, commodities) | Medium to high (contractual services, major milestones) |
| Purchase frequency | Medium to high (daily, weekly, or monthly) | Low to medium (quarterly, annually, or less frequent) |
| Ticket price | Low to medium | Medium to high |
| Touch point relevance | Brand perception is dominated by a narrow set of touch points | Brand perception evolves during multiple interactions at several touch points |

SOURCE: McKinsey

Sometimes, however, optimizing brand performance at individual touch points is not enough. In some industries, customers chiefly experience brands as they go through specific processes, or journeys, that typically span several interactions and call for a consistent approach. In musical terms, think of a journey as of a symphony, that is, the interplay of several sections and instruments, in contrast to the solo performance given at individual touch points. On such a journey, a customer engages with a brand across multiple touch points, rather than just at a single one. A prospective car buyer going on a test drive, for example, may interact with the chosen brand through its Web site to arrange an appointment, at the dealership when picking up the car, during the actual drive, and possibly by phone when requesting additional information later on. In the insurance industry, common journeys include purchase, claims processing, contract change, billing, and complaints. In the case of a claim, the journey typically starts in the policyholder's home, where he or she will review documents and gather information on claim settlement. It continues with telephone conversations to clarify terms and conditions, followed by correspondence to request and dispatch an assessor, and may culminate in court proceedings to settle the claim (Figure 4.11).

Each customer embarking on such a journey has specific expectations, and the degree to which they are met has a direct effect on customer satisfaction. This makes it important that the experience is consistent across all touch points, both in terms of the information that is conveyed and in terms of the actual interaction. To make this happen, all employees must have access to the latest customer touch point history. The key to a seamless and satisfactory brand experience for the customer is the interplay

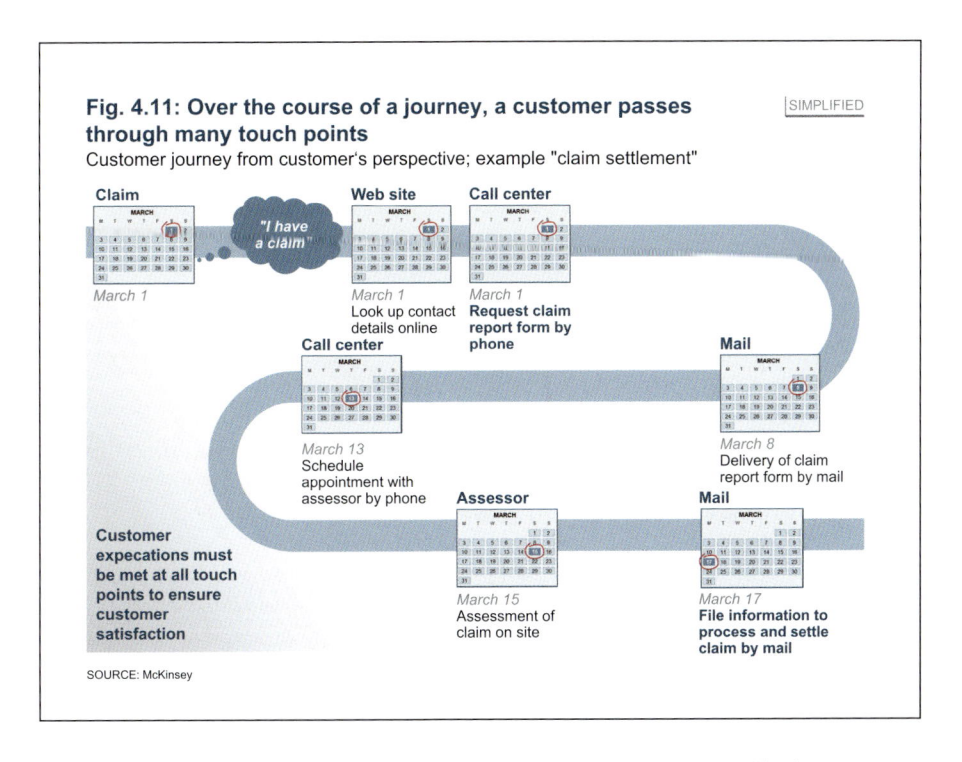

**Fig. 4.11: Over the course of a journey, a customer passes through many touch points**
Customer journey from customer's perspective; example "claim settlement"

SIMPLIFIED

Claim
March 1

Web site
March 1
Look up contact details online

Call center
March 1
Request claim report form by phone

Call center
March 13
Schedule appointment with assessor by phone

Assessor
March 15
Assessment of claim on site

Mail
March 8
Delivery of claim report form by mail

Mail
March 17
File information to process and settle claim by mail

"I have a claim"

Customer expectations must be met at all touch points to ensure customer satisfaction

SOURCE: McKinsey

between the Web site, the call center, and the departments that handle the transmission and processing of documents. This is a challenge for many companies, both in the insurance industry and in other sectors. Most organizations are still structured as »silos« without clearly defined responsibility for the overall customer journey. Our experience shows that it pays to bring down these organizational barriers. One international auto insurance company analyzed its customer processes for all relevant journeys, determined the required level of service from the customer's perspective, and set out to optimize the customer experience not just at individual touch points, but across entire journeys. Before, customers went through complicated processes that involved a wide variety of departments. And although every individual touch point had already been optimized, the overall experience was still fragmented and characterized by an abundance of interactions with many different service professionals. After this effort, all relevant journeys were much smoother, and customer satisfaction went up. Ultimately, the company recorded an increase in revenues by USD 200 million.

Consistency, however, is only one aspect of a satisfying customer experience. Brand managers should keep in mind that the entire journey is only as good as its weakest episode, and that some parts of the experience are more important to the customer than others. A leading theme park operator, for example, found that the time it takes visitors to find their car in the parking lot can make or break the entire day. Customers said in interviews that once their kids are crying because of an overly long walk, the day is ruined, no matter how much fun they had before with rides and other attractions.

More generally, we find the benefits of holistic customer journey optimization to be threefold:[9]

- *Delighting customers.* Whether the unexpectedly rapid processing of a claim, or the smooth completion of a contract via a combination of online and offline channels, a positive experience goes a long way toward delighting customers and increasing their satisfaction. This can result in revenue gains of up to 10 percent.
- *Motivating employees.* Concentrating on a shared, overarching objective motivates employees and creates a sense of common purpose, provided the objective is easily understood and widely supported. Leading practitioners have seen employee motivation levels increase by up to 35 percent. Additionally, absentee rates and employee churn can often be reduced as well.
- *Increasing efficiency.* Processes structured around customer journeys rather than individual touch points can help decrease the number of contacts required to resolve a request and reduce costs by up to 25 percent. The integration of Web sites, call centers, and frontline staff has proven particularly powerful.

Compare Figure 4.12 for disguised impact examples. While optimizing customer journeys is often tied to comprehensive brand performance measurement, it may also be conducted independently, that is, without prior BrandMatics® diagnostics to identify purchase funnel gaps and brand drivers. In such a case, most companies use customer satisfaction as the dependent variable and optimize the most important journeys accordingly, balancing incremental implementation cost with the expected impact on satisfaction. In fact, many companies find that customer satisfaction increases while

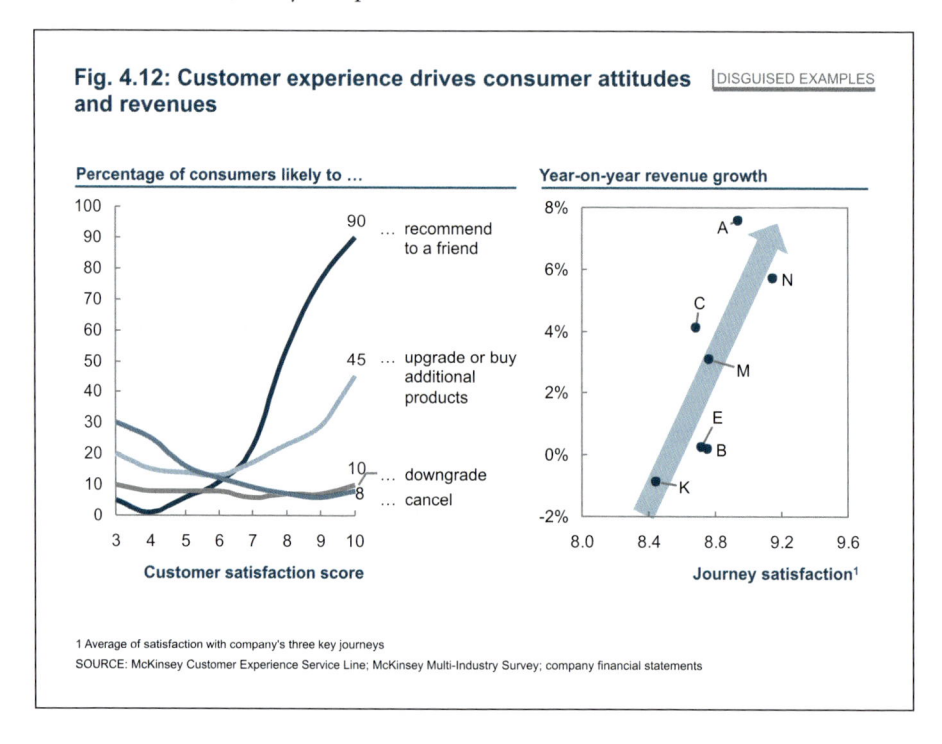

**Fig. 4.12: Customer experience drives consumer attitudes and revenues** [DISGUISED EXAMPLES]

1 Average of satisfaction with company's three key journeys
SOURCE: McKinsey Customer Experience Service Line; McKinsey Multi-Industry Survey; company financial statements

costs can be decreased. This is due to the fact that understanding the drivers behind satisfaction enables them to focus their funds on what customers really care about, and reduce investments in less important areas. An existing brand promise, or brand positioning statement, can be used to cross-check operational actions for their compliance with the brand's identity. Moving all customer interactions online, for example, may work well for a no-frills brand promising low prices, while a premium brand taking pride in its personal touch would be ill advised to cut back on direct interaction with service staff at the POS or over the phone.

Journey-based customer experience optimization has successfully been applied to a wide range of different industries (see Figures 4.13 and 4.14). For example, a North American chain of car dealers found that their leadership teams were overly focused on their own department at the expense of a smooth customer experience. There was no protocol in place for the transition of car buyers from sales to aftersales service, nor was there an established process for how to refer service customers to the sales department. This turned out to be a major opportunity for additional revenues. As part of a customer experience diagnostic, the dealership discovered that many service customers were, in fact, contemplating the purchase of a new car. If their current car was relatively old, had high mileage, or required major work, customers felt they might be better off with a new car. Additionally, some customers were facing changes in needs, for example, because their family was outgrowing their current vehicle. In up to a third of all cases, however, these customers never even got close to a purchase because sales agents were unavailable or failed to present a set of relevant options. By establishing a smooth handover process from service to sales, and a flexible new protocol for sales pitches to service customers, the company was able to increase their gross profits by 15 percent, generated by improved service to sales conversion alone. In general, the company was able to increase both sales and customer satisfaction by establishing new handover procedures, more flexible scheduling, and dynamic capacity management.

Similarly, a retail bank based in South America used journey-based optimization to give their brand a boost after the financial crisis that had left the entire industry in disarray. The bank combined experience optimization with the creation of client clusters that deepened the company's understanding of their customers' needs. In the case of a telecommunications company, the situation was slightly different. The cable provider had historically focused on minimizing cost-to-serve rather than the customer experience. Separate targets were set for different departments. As a result, customers would see one face of the brand when they signed a contract, but an entirely different face when equipment was installed or repaired. By redesigning key journeys and conducting a range of cross-functional customer experience pilots, the company was able to increase both sales and satisfaction dramatically. Additionally, the pilot program helped to generate higher employee pride and empowerment.

But the concept of the customer journey can even be brought to bear on industries beyond its most common application to contractual businesses. An international airport in the southeastern US, for example, was faced with an increase in passengers while

### Fig. 4.13: Customer experience optimization – Industry examples

DISGUISED EXAMPLES

|  | Automotive | Financial services | Telecommunications |
|---|---|---|---|
| Company | - Car dealership | - Retail bank | - Cable provider |
| Challenge | - Silo thinking inhibiting service-to-sales conversion | - Lack of customer needs understanding | - Focus on cost rather than customer experience |
| (Mini-) journeys in focus | - Sales<br>- Service | - Claims<br>- Mortgages | - Onboarding<br>- Installation |
| Biggest changes | - Dynamic scheduling and capacity management | - Introduction of needs-based client clusters | - Cross-functional experience pilots |
| Impact | - + 8% in sales<br>- + 2% in satisfaction | - + 10% in value creation<br>- + 15pp in net promoter score (NPS[1]) | - + USD 100 million in sales<br>- + 20% in satisfaction |

1 NPS is based on questions such as: "How likely is it that you would recommend our brand to a friend or colleague?"
SOURCE: McKinsey

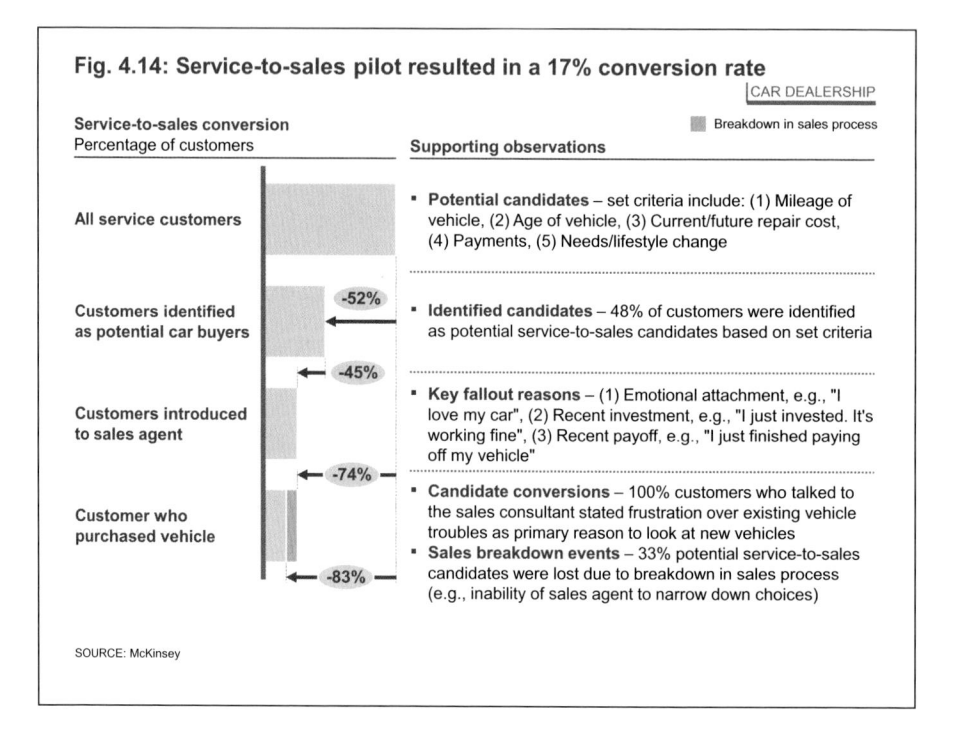

### Fig. 4.14: Service-to-sales pilot resulted in a 17% conversion rate

CAR DEALERSHIP

**Service-to-sales conversion**
Percentage of customers

■ Breakdown in sales process

- All service customers
- Customers identified as potential car buyers ← -52%
- Customers introduced to sales agent ← -45%
- Customer who purchased vehicle ← -74%
← -83%

**Supporting observations**

- **Potential candidates** – set criteria include: (1) Mileage of vehicle, (2) Age of vehicle, (3) Current/future repair cost, (4) Payments, (5) Needs/lifestyle change
- **Identified candidates** – 48% of customers were identified as potential service-to-sales candidates based on set criteria
- **Key fallout reasons** – (1) Emotional attachment, e.g., "I love my car", (2) Recent investment, e.g., "I just invested. It's working fine", (3) Recent payoff, e.g., "I just finished paying off my vehicle"
- **Candidate conversions** – 100% customers who talked to the sales consultant stated frustration over existing vehicle troubles as primary reason to look at new vehicles
- **Sales breakdown events** – 33% potential service-to-sales candidates were lost due to breakdown in sales process (e.g., inability of sales agent to narrow down choices)

SOURCE: McKinsey

passenger satisfaction was declining. In one of the industry's more common rankings, the airport had dropped from the mid-60s to the 150s over a period of just five years. Perceived performance was low on many important drivers of passenger satisfaction, such as seating, entertainment, and information. But it turned out that the bigger issue was a general lack of customer orientation. In an effort to drive satisfaction, a cross-functional team examined the »departure« journey more closely, from curbside arrival and check-in to security and boarding. The team found that the staff at each touch point were doing their best in their immediate sphere of influence, but failed to recognize the implications for passengers upstream and downstream on their journey. For example, check-in counters would open an hour prior to boarding, disregarding the fact that the vast majority of passengers arrived at least two hours prior to their scheduled departure. As a result, passengers waiting to check their luggage found themselves stranded in the crammed landside part of the terminal, rather than the more spacious airside area beyond security. The airport is currently redesigning larger parts of its operations and signage from the perspective of the passenger's journey, a particularly complex effort because of the many different stakeholders involved, from airline personnel and security staff to airport employees and third-party service providers.

## Using method, not magic, to create a memorable customer experience[10]

Implementing improvements across touch points can be challenging even for the most customer-centric brands and leaves many companies wondering whether it is worth the considerable effort. McKinsey has discussed this challenge with about 100 companies from a variety of sectors worldwide.[11] It turns out that devotion to customer service pays handsome dividends. Companies offering an exceptional customer experience can exceed their peers' gross margin by more than 26 percent.[12] Emotionally engaged customers are typically three times more likely to recommend a product and to repurchase it themselves. Delivering an exceptional end-to-end experience is especially important in a world where customers interact with a brand at many different points – in person, through social networks, online. Analyses reveal that performing well across these customer journeys is often linked with greater impact on market success rather than individual touch point performance. Companies that had a one percentage point lead over their peers in key customer journeys typically enjoyed a two percentage point advantage in revenue growth. In addition, companies that deliver excellent customer journeys increase employee satisfaction by 30 percent.

Yet corporate initiatives to improve customer experience struggle to make a tangible difference where it matters most: at the front line. Call center agents read from rigid scripts and get paid for keeping calls short rather than for resolving complaints. Web sites try to drive upsell rather than help customers find what they're looking for. According to the results of McKinsey's work with the Disney Institute, the best way for companies to create emotional connections with their customers is by ensuring that every interaction delights them. To do this, brands need more than great products. What they need most is a motivated, empowered team at the front line. Several companies have emerged as champions of customer experience management.

Among them are the following:

- JetBlue, an airline that frequently comes out on top in customer satisfaction rankings, believes that if you want friendly service, you should hire friendly people. The company has embedded this conviction in its front-line hiring process. To recruit individuals with a natural service bent, JetBlue uses group interviews. Watching how applicants interact with each other enables the interviewer to assess candidates' communications and people skills to an extent that wouldn't be possible in a one-to-one setting.
- Best Chevrolet, a large auto dealership in Massachusetts, is another believer in »hiring for nice.« Since adopting and sustaining this approach over several years, it has seen a rise in employee retention and a flow of testimonials from satisfied customers – not to mention a customer satisfaction rating more than ten percentage points above the industry average. It also has achieved a 69 percent retention rate of customers who still return for services five years after purchase, compared with an industry average of 40 percent.
- Wawa is an innovative convenience-store chain based on the East Coast of the US. Knowing that its store managers understand local customers' needs better than any desk-bound analyst ever could, it grants them considerable latitude over what they sell. One enterprising manager decided his customers would welcome a coffee bar and more fresh food options. When customer traffic and profits soared, Wawa's head office noticed and quickly dispatched a team to investigate. On their return, the team explained how the manager had boosted sales and presented a plan for rapidly replicating the innovation across other stores in the network.

Let's take an even closer look at the Nespresso brand, one of the pioneers of consistent customer experience management in Europe. Nespresso goes to great lengths and expense to make sure its brand promise of exclusivity is kept across the entire customer journey, regardless of whether coffee is purchased through the company's Web site or at a Nespresso boutique. Nespresso coffeemakers, for example, come with a high-end welcome package. After an initial purchase, customers are provided with the latest customer magazine and invited to join the Nespresso Club. Perks include a telephone hotline staffed by highly motivated, passionate coffee specialists. Capsules ordered online can be delivered to club members' homes or picked up at the customer's Nespresso boutique of choice. The company monitors satisfaction levels by asking club members about their experience through customized online satisfaction surveys. By polling all customers who have been in touch with remote support, Nespresso leverages customer perception for continuous improvements.[13] In 2013, Interbrand named Nespresso one of the top Swiss brands, valued at CHF 2.2 billion: »Its club concept […] and its service orientation are the reasons that the brand is unequaled despite numerous copycats.«[14]

Companies aspiring to improve customer experience along key journeys and drive satisfaction typically take a four-step approach:

- *Identify relevant journeys.* Journeys should be prioritized by applying metrics – such as customer volume and churn rates – and by applying appropriate research tools such as focus groups and online customer journey tracking (e.g., ClickFox). In addition, the availability and quality of data needs to be assessed: Does the company already have detailed data?
- *Develop the target state.* Companies often choose to optimize prioritized journeys in a way that focuses on the degree to which they conform with the brand promise or value proposition. The scope and aspiration level of the optimization effort should be determined depending on a given company's overall situation, current performance, resources, and level of analytical sophistication:
  - *Fix the basics* quickly at key stations of relevant journeys, for example, to harness contract renewal churn in a turnaround situation, to prepare for an IPO, or to allow for smooth onboarding of new subscribers in a fast-growing environment.
  - *Fine-tune performance* over a longer period. Contractual businesses, for example, may find themselves faced with conflicting objectives, such as the short-term need to increase profitability and the long-term need to add new customers. Since newly acquired customers typically yield a negative profit contribution in the first year, companies is this situation might want to focus on contract renewal journeys initially and move on to acquisition journeys later.
- *Determine improvement potential.* A feasibility study will help companies determine to which extent, and how quickly, the target state can be achieved. The result of the feasibility study is a transition plan detailing which journeys and touch points should be tackled in light of expected improvements.
- *Implement and monitor improvements.* Once they are defined, touch point and journey improvements need to be integrated with a company's organizational structures and operational processes. For example, call center capacity may need to be ramped up, or functional silos may need to be restructured to conform to the need for a seamless experience. Additionally, customer satisfaction measurement should be translated into KPIs as part of periodic performance metrics. Success monitoring ensures that management's attention remains focused on the topic. It is not sufficient, however, to look only at the overall journey to improve satisfaction. It is much more effective to evaluate the individual touch points within the respective journey along with the most important elements within the touch points – based on internal KPIs and customer perceptions.

Superior brand delivery management also needs to reflect the interplay of physical and virtual brand experience. This is particularly pressing for brands operating in a dynamic multichannel environment, such as retail. These brands need to take special care to ensure that their physical presence (e.g., branded apparel retail stores or supermarkets) are well-aligned with other touch points, such as online content, newsletters, or mobile services (see Figure 4.15), to create a seamless brand experience.[15] In contrast, brands operating in industries with limited physical customer contact, such as utilities, should initially focus on call center quality and robust online resources.

**Fig. 4.15: Digital media are relevant all over the shopper's decision journey**

SOURCE: McKinsey

## 4.2 MROI-based Communications Management

Brand communication is a central element of brand delivery. It is about telling consumers what a brand stands for, what its specific proposition is, which products it offers, and where to find it. Today's media landscape comprises all kinds of channels and formats for brands to get the word out. If their budgets were unlimited, brand managers would probably use them all. According to a survey conducted by *Forbes* magazine, »72 percent of CEOs say marketers are always asking for more money, but can rarely explain how much incremental business this money will generate.«[16]

In the real world of finite funds and fierce competition for corporate resources, the challenge is to select those channels that promise the biggest return on marketing investment. Yet, according to a recent McKinsey survey among marketing practitioners, less than one-fifth of all advertisers say they have a clear understanding of the contribution made by each individual communication channel, confirming the legendary observation: »Half of my advertising money is wasted. I just wish I knew which half!« Not unlike its subject matter, the origin of the quote is much disputed. Some attribute it to mass production pioneer Henry Ford, others to Lord Leverhulme – the founding father of Unilever – and yet others to department store mogul John Wanamaker of Philadelphia.

Although advertising is often one of the biggest line items in a company's budget – especially in the consumer goods sector – it seems to escape the rigorous review most other positions have long been subject to. At first sight, this is surprising, considering the scale of expenditure involved. Consumer goods companies typically invest more than 10 percent of their revenues in advertising, the equivalent of billions of dollars for some of the bigger players in the industry. Procter & Gamble, for example, spent USD 9.4 billion, or 11.2 percent of sales, on advertising last year, up from USD 3.7 billion, or 9.5 percent of sales, in 2002 according to *Advertising Age*.[17] Unilever is spending at similar levels, both in absolute and in relative terms. In light of this magnitude, a growing group of stakeholders – other business functions, corporate controlling, and investors – is putting pressure on brand managers to account for their actions. Why invest in advertising rather than product development or sales force effectiveness? Brand managers need to demonstrate that they are generating sufficient returns, and that they are spending their budgets wisely. According to a global McKinsey survey among chief marketing officers (CMOs), *marketing* MROI is their top priority today.

To face the accountability challenge, brand managers need to answer three questions:

- How do we allocate our budget to investment units, such as brands and countries?
- Within investment units, how do we allocate the budget to specific media?
- How can we optimize the effectiveness and the efficiency of individual media?

In this section, we address the first two questions: allocation to investment units and allocation to specific media. We will examine the third element – individual instrument optimization – in a separate section, using digital media as an example. More generally speaking, optimizing marketing spend is but the first step on the path to true and sustainable MROI excellence (Figure 4.16).

**Fig. 4.16: Levers of marketing spending excellence**

Marketing ROI

5. **Smart purchasing** — Ensure fact-based selection and efficient management of vendors
4. **Excellent execution** — Maximize impact of spend through best-in-class creation and execution
3. **Instrument allocation** — Select touch points based on "apples-to-apples" comparison, e.g., of reach, cost, and quality
2. **Message definition** — Determine relevant messages and stories for key target segments
1. **Spending priorities** — Align marketing spending with business objectives (categories, products, brands, regions, etc.)

SOURCE: McKinsey

### Creating transparency

Fact-based budgeting starts with transparency generation. At first sight, this appears to be a simple task. In our experience, however, it takes much more time and effort than companies expect. Time and again, we find that acquiring detailed information on targets, spending, and communication activities for an entire brand is a real challenge (Figure 4.17).

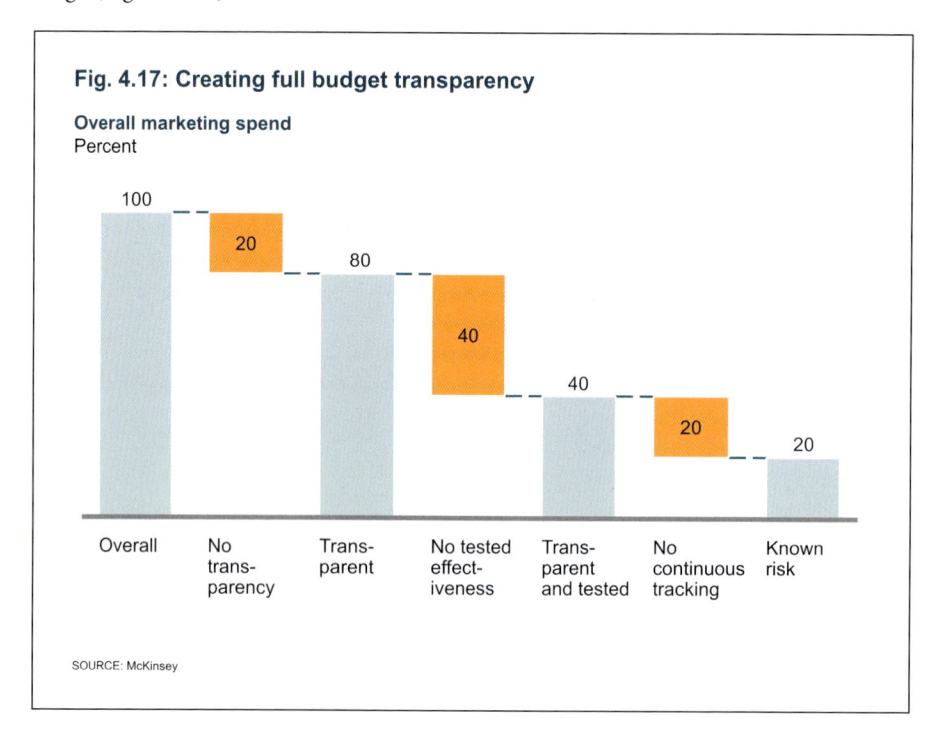

**Fig. 4.17: Creating full budget transparency**

Overall marketing spend
Percent

| Overall | No transparency | Transparent | No tested effectiveness | Transparent and tested | No continuous tracking | Known risk |
|---|---|---|---|---|---|---|
| 100 | 20 | 80 | 40 | 40 | 20 | 20 |

SOURCE: McKinsey

Initially, spending on marketing activities should be broken down by brand, product, and country. In a second step, the budget should be differentiated by media and customer touch points. Difficulties often arise because budgets are split between different parts of the organization, each of which has its own controlling department and accounting system. Traditional marketing budgets, for example, are run by the marketing division or a special advertising unit together with product management. The public relations budget is handled by the PR department or the board itself. Events and promotions come under the promotions division. Further touch points might generate costs in several departments. The corporate home page, for instance, might be shared between IT, PR, marketing, and several other business units. Beyond this, there may be marketing spending on outdoor advertising, sports sponsorship, or co-branding that has been planned and committed many years in advance. In some cases, this type of marketing is not arranged by the marketing department at all, partly for contractual and partly for historical reasons. As a result, these areas are out-of-bounds for regular reviews, so the company ends up excluding them from the current marketing spending. These »overlooked investments« might include the sponsorship of a local event initiated by a former CEO, or a long-term sponsorship contract which can't be cancelled, but does not play an active role in the communication strategy anymore. Yet all these activities either strengthen or weaken a brand and should thus be included in the drive towards achieving transparency.

The larger and more complex the company, the more difficult it is to get hold of full, transparent data, especially historical data. Many marketing managers and controllers appear unable to pin down how much was spent on advertising in the past, or to say exactly how the budget was spent. Sometimes one level of the organization will carry out advertising for another level, or one part will pay another part to do its marketing. Thus a subsidiary might reap the benefits of a marketing campaign carried out by the parent company or another country, while at the same time being involved in sponsorship carried out together with a partially owned subsidiary. The same goes for spillover effects between multiple brands under the same roof. Land Rover, for example, may benefit from Range Rover investments and vice versa. From an efficiency perspective, killing two birds with one stone seems tempting. But in reality, such multipurpose marketing activities often represent a considerable challenge for companies trying to produce a rational framework for fact-based budgeting.

For traditional advertising, a useful tool for investigating overall spending and media mix is to compare the visible spending in the market (as tracked by NielsenMedia Research, for example, or other such providers of ad tracking data) and the costs recorded internally by the company. In general, outside observers perceive companies as spending about one-and-a-half times what they actually do because of discounts. Any significant deviation from this ratio should sound alarms for the company and be investigated thoroughly in order to determine what is causing the discrepancy.

The quest for transparency needs to apply to all items in the budget. Cooperative marketing arrangements represent a further complication when studying budgets. This is especially true in cases where a company both receives payments from suppliers to run joint marketing campaigns (incoming payments) and supports sales partners to fund further joint campaigns (outgoing payments) – as in the retail sector, or between mobile operators and mobile phone producers. Financial controllers need to include these payments in the quest for transparency since these also impact the brand, in the presentation of goods, packaging, advertising by commercial partners, and so on. Some controllers face a rude awakening when they look into the effect of such cooperative payments. In retailing, for example, free advertising (i.e., that paid for by the campaign partner) is often tied to bundled goods. In the worst case, miscalculations can lead to the company suddenly finding itself in possession of large stocks of surplus merchandise. It cannot be assumed that the objectives of both partners in a cooperative campaign are exactly the same. Often, the supplier subsidizing the marketing is thinking purely in terms of sales or revenue targets with little regard to the impact on the brand. Thus, caution is prudent. Just because such cooperative advertising is free does not mean that it makes strategic or economic sense. Companies must also take into account the consequential costs for write-offs.

Full budget transparency will only be achieved if investments in all the customer touch points are taken into account. Call centers, customer service, the corporate home page, and sales can be considered touch points, and improving services, offering rewards and discounts, or subsidizing funding will all impact sales and marketing. Since all customer touch points influence customer behavior, they need to be considered part of marketing expenditure.

### Prioritizing investment units

Obviously, transparency regarding past and current investments is only the beginning of fact-based budgeting. A company's marketing activities never take place in a void. They compete with competitor activities for customer attention. In a noisy environment, it is important for a brand's own tune to be heard above the general hum. Perhaps the most common indicator of the relative marketing intensity is marketing expenditure as a percentage of sales. This metric varies greatly by segment and country, but it is a quick and easy way of determining whether a company is spending within a healthy range. According to the Schonfeld database, ad-to-sales ratios can range from 2 percent in retail to more than 20 percent in logistics.

In general, determining the appropriate overall budget level for future planning periods requires the combination of three approaches:

- Bottom-up budgeting based on past and present budgets, marketing objectives, and marketing activity planning.
- Top-down budgeting based on competitive benchmarking, such as the share of voice required to cut through the clutter in a given industry.
- Efficiency modeling and saturation analysis to avoid overspending in areas of deteriorating returns.

In most cases, brand managers will want to combine these approaches to arrive at a robust figure for their total budget.[18] But how much of this should be spent on a specific country, region, brand, or product? The key to success is to overcome the »tyranny of the average« and find the pockets of growth to prioritize investments accordingly (Figure 4.18). An average national market sales growth rate of 6 percent, for example, may not appear particularly exciting at first sight. But if you slice the growth rates to represent increasingly granular investment units, a much more differentiated picture often emerges – one with a spread that may range from -10 percent to more than 20 percent in a given case. To stimulate overall growth, advertisers will want to cut spending on low-growth investment units and focus their funds on high-growth units. To determine the appropriate level of granularity for use in the budget prioritization, the advertiser will need to establish which of its spending units or groups of them are sufficiently homogeneous to justify a unified approach – as opposed to those units that are sufficiently different from each other to warrant customized solutions.

When determining the appropriate geographical cut, you will first need to answer a series of questions:

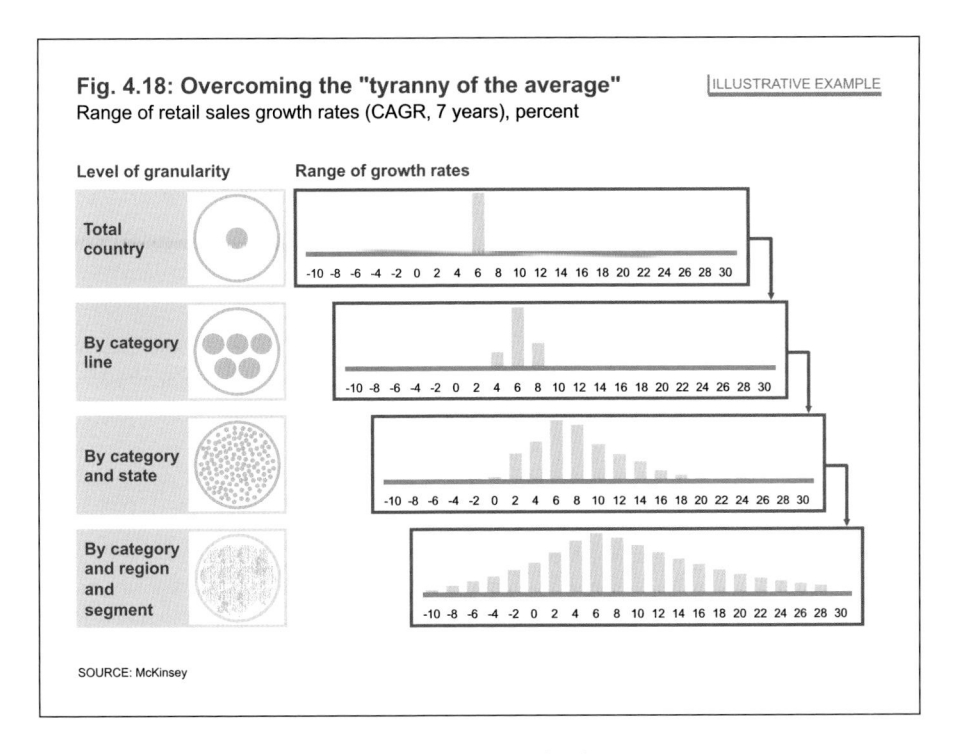

**Fig. 4.18: Overcoming the "tyranny of the average"**
Range of retail sales growth rates (CAGR, 7 years), percent

ILLUSTRATIVE EXAMPLE

| Level of granularity | Range of growth rates |
|---|---|
| Total country | -10 -8 -6 -4 -2 0 2 4 6 8 10 12 14 16 18 20 22 24 26 28 30 |
| By category line | -10 -8 -6 -4 -2 0 2 4 6 8 10 12 14 16 18 20 22 24 26 28 30 |
| By category and state | -10 -8 -6 -4 -2 0 2 4 6 8 10 12 14 16 18 20 22 24 26 28 30 |
| By category and region and segment | -10 -8 -6 -4 -2 0 2 4 6 8 10 12 14 16 18 20 22 24 26 28 30 |

SOURCE: McKinsey

- Are there local differences in the competitive landscape?
- Do consumer preferences differ from region to region?
- Is there a higher growth ambition in certain regions?

In cases where there are major local or regional differences, it makes sense to break down the budget accordingly to be able to adjust its allocation to local requirements. In general, higher budgeting granularity promises a more targeted marketing investment. But sometimes a very detailed budget breakdown will create more work than added value. For example, if an advertiser does not have detailed information on its regional markets, such as the share of voice or growth rates – then there is no point in differentiating the budget for these regions. Similarly, highly granular budget allocation is not likely to be worthwhile if a company does not have the operational means and processes to derive true value from it. It makes no sense, for example, to determine the budget for 300 Italian fashion retail outlets at the individual store level if there is no activity plan in place to make sure these funds are used to the benefit of the individual stores.

Once the total budget and the granularity of the investment units has been determined, the next step is to decide on the criteria by which the budget will be allocated to the investment units. For want of a more systematic approach, many companies take a percentage of sales or use similar allocation keys. The main challenge in making the allocation is to ensure that the criteria used support the overall business objectives of the company. If the company's ambition is to grow sales in a few selected regions while maintaining current sales levels in all others, for example, it would make sense to use regional growth targets or budgeted revenues as the allocation criterion. If, in addition, a number of local markets are planning new store openings or product launches, another meaningful factor might be the number of new stores or products per market. As a rule of thumb: the greater the business complexity, the greater the number of criteria required. In all cases, however, a weighted average should be used as the ultimate allocation key.

The most common allocation key is revenues per investment unit. In general, this makes a lot of sense. Its weakness, though, is that it does not take relative competitive intensity or specific local opportunities into account. Because of such factors, it may make sense to fine-tune investment manually. A region with high market share typically needs less marketing support to be visible in the market place than a region in which the company has a low market share. In order to pick the right budget allocation criteria, it is critical for the brand manager to have a deep understanding of the company's business objectives:

- What are the company's long-term objectives?
- Does the company aspire to expand in a certain area?
- Have new competitors entered the marketplace?

Among the well-established metrics for marketing investment decisions are: sales, sales growth, sales growth versus market rate (share gain), market share, profitability, competitive intensity (e.g., measured as competitor ad spend or share of voice in a given segment or area), and media cost (Figure 4.19). But even when a set of relevant

**Fig. 4.19: List of potential criteria for budget prioritization**

| | Criteria | Operationalization (example) |
|---|---|---|
| **Financial** | Revenues | • Net revenues of business unit by region |
| | Revenue growth | • Net revenue growth of business unit by region |
| | Gross profit on sales | • Net revenues minus cost of goods sold by business unit and region |
| | Gross profit growth | • Change in net revenues minus cost of goods sold for business unit by region |
| **Strategic** | Growth opportunity | • Market size not captured in EUR, e.g., (1 – market share) x addressable share factor (considering local competition) |
| | Industry competition | • Brand building and promotional spend of competitors |
| | Relative individual growth | • Company or segment growth (e.g., discount) of business unit in region |
| **Marketing-oriented** | Marketing cost factor | • For example: local cost for typical marketing basket |
| | Brand status | • Brand awareness according to market research |
| | Event communication | • Store openings, etc. |

SOURCE: McKinsey

criteria has been agreed upon, there is still room for error. Often, there is no common understanding of how a specific metric is or should be defined. Take growth ambition: most marketing managers will agree that units with more ambitious targets will need and deserve more funds. But what is growth ambition? Is it revenue growth as a percentage? Using this metric would lead to a bias toward units with low current sales levels. Alternatively, is it the absolute growth in EUR or USD? No matter how high this amount is, the level of growth could still be at or even below market growth – which should not justify extra funds. So in this case, absolute growth above market level or above market share gain would be the best choice. This is just one example that shows how different interpretations of the same metric can lead to fundamentally different budgeting decisions.

Once there is a shared understanding of which criteria should inform the prioritization, the relative importance of these criteria can be specified by weighting them. The basic choice is whether to focus on stability or growth. If the primary objective is to defend current sales, the greatest weight should be given to past or current sales as allocation criteria. If the primary objective is growth, greater weight should be attributed to growth targets or metrics capturing opportunity – for example, the size of the market not yet captured.

**Allocation to instruments**

Within the investment units, the budget needs to be allocated to specific media, or more generally, to customer touch points; compare Section 4.1 on brand delivery for details. In this section, we will focus on allocating investment unit budgets to specific media. One of the advertisers we spoke with as part of our survey on media management said: »We're still far from having anything resembling a ›common currency‹ that covers all the media we use« (compare the OWM insert for details).[19] MROI – or marketing return on investment – is that common currency. In principle, there are four approaches to manage the media mix and optimize MROI:

- Testing and learning.
- Comparative heuristics: the Reach-Cost-Quality (RCQ) approach.
- Econometric modeling: marketing mix modeling (MMM).
- Consumer decision journey (CDJ).[20]

While testing and learning works well for individual instruments, such as direct marketing campaigns, comparative heuristics and econometric modeling are more appropriate to optimize the entire marketing mix across a wide range of media. Comparative heuristics ranks the efficiency of media relative to one another, while econometric modeling ties marketing investment to its real impact on business performance and generates a »dollar-for-dollar« ROI for various vehicles. CDJ-based approaches take advantage of consumer surveys that help determine and optimize the impact of marketing investments at specific stages of a consumer's decision journey.

## Testing and learning

Testing and learning is about tracking the effects of specific campaigns or other marketing activities. Perhaps the most established example of this technique is the analysis of direct marketing activities that include a response element, a coupon for example. The ROI assessment of such activities is calculated as »sales (or profit) triggered by response element« over »campaign cost.« To refine the campaign, brand managers test multiple executions of the same concept on a small scale. The winning execution will be selected for broader rollout. Sometimes this approach is also used to track activities that are not directly geared to sales stimulation, such as brand image campaigns. In this case, the advertiser would assess the pre-campaign image perception and compare it with the image observed after the campaign. The delta will express the campaign's »return.«

Because it typically uses customer responses to assess the impact of a campaign directly the advantage of testing and learning is that campaign refinement can be very hands-on and detailed – and this does not require complex arithmetical methods. You simply go with what works best and then build on that. But the approach has its limitations. To give one example: it is often difficult to isolate the test campaign's effect because of impact from other marketing activities that are being carried out in parallel.

Testing and learning is appropriate for optimizing individual activities – as opposed to the entire media mix – since it is usually impossible to test all campaigns in all channels simultaneously. The approach works best for direct marketing activities: if these feature prominently in the marketing mix, or the advertiser operates in a market characterized by push marketing, then testing and learning should be the tool of choice. Also, testing and learning makes fewer demands on analytical capabilities than the other approaches featured in this chapter.

## Comparative heuristics: Reach-Cost-Quality (RCQ)

The Reach-Cost-Quality (RCQ) approach is a quantitative method for evaluating, comparing, and selecting different media on a like-for-like basis. It relies on the concept of a common metric across all marketing touch points: real cost per actual reach (Figure 4.20). RCQ enables brand managers to increase actual reach at no extra cost (effectiveness), or to reduce cost without compromising advertising impact (efficiency).

- The first step in RCQ is to define *cost* in a comprehensive way – as the »total cost of ownership«. Media buying is the first item that comes to mind, but it is by no means the only one. Other relevant positions include agency fees, production, research, creative rights, distribution, and maintenance. This step often is quite an eye-opener. Some vehicles will immediately look less expensive than previously thought, while others may well turn out to be a lot more costly.
- The second step is to determine actual *reach* – the actual number of people a given vehicle reaches among an advertiser's relevant target groups. All consumers who do not match the target group characteristics in terms of demographics, sociographics,

**Fig. 4.20: Reach-Cost-Quality approach**

**① Efficiency**

**Cost**
Total costs
- Creation
- Production
- Activation
- Total

**② Effectiveness**

**Reach**
Unique individuals reached in target group

**Quality**
Contact → Consumer

**③ Performance**

**RCQ ranking**
Instruments
- Leaflets
- Local print
- Radio
- …
- …
- …

Cost per reach | Quality rating | Cost per actual reach

SOURCE: McKinsey

---

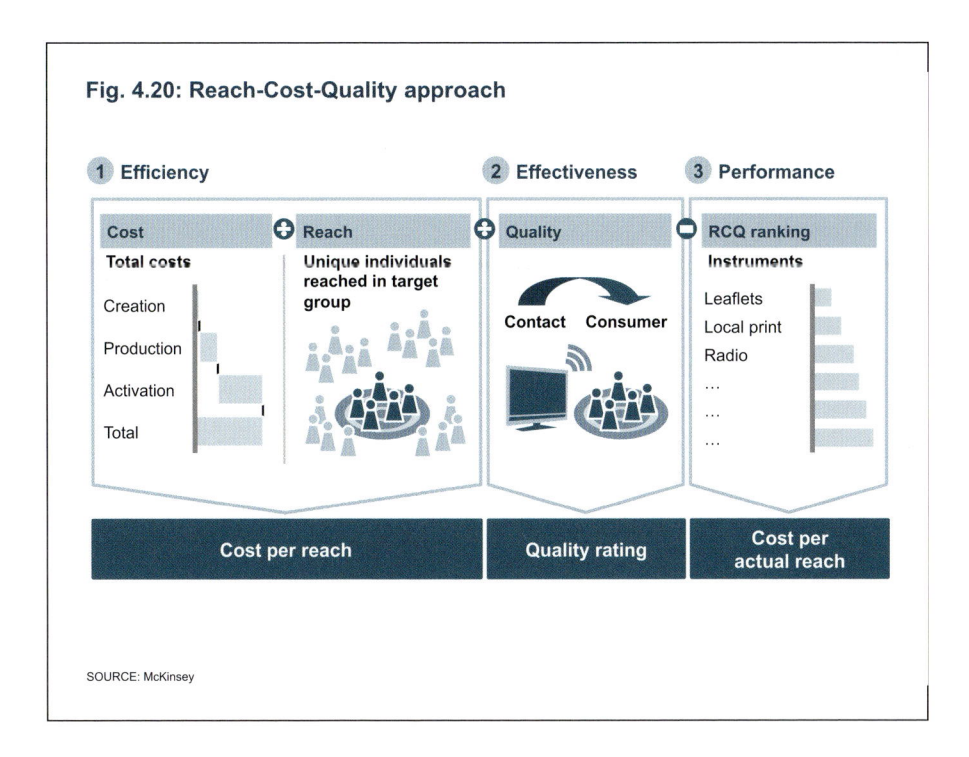

or psychographics need to be removed. This step yields gross reach. To derive net reach, divide the gross reach by the average contact frequency. Finally, subtract all individuals who may have been exposed to your communication, but have not actually received the message (»tune-out« factor).

- The third step is to assess contact *quality*, defined as the impact of a given advertising activity on each consumer reached. This is the most challenging aspect of RCQ – and it relies on the judgment of experienced marketing practitioners. Typically, they will look at three aspects: the ability of a touch point to convey information (cognitive quality), its suitability to evoke emotion (affective quality), and its ability to trigger action (behavioral quality). Advertising pretesting can help in checking the quality of a given execution. As an example of high affective quality, consider the presence of automotive brands at car shows. While the reach of such events is certainly limited, the opportunity to experience the goods in real life makes shows and fairs much more powerful as touch points than print ads, television commercials, or glossy brochures.

The resulting RCQ score is the basis of an apples-for-apples comparison of different media (Figure 4.21) that enables advertisers to optimize their media selection within and across specific instruments, and it provides advertisers with a fact-based frame of reference for the purposes of briefing and measuring media agencies. Of course, RCQ also has its limitations. Its output goes beyond experience and judgment, but also falls short of the rigidity of fully-fledged econometric marketing mix modeling (MMM) as described below. Unlike MMM, RCQ neither yields vehicle saturation curves, nor

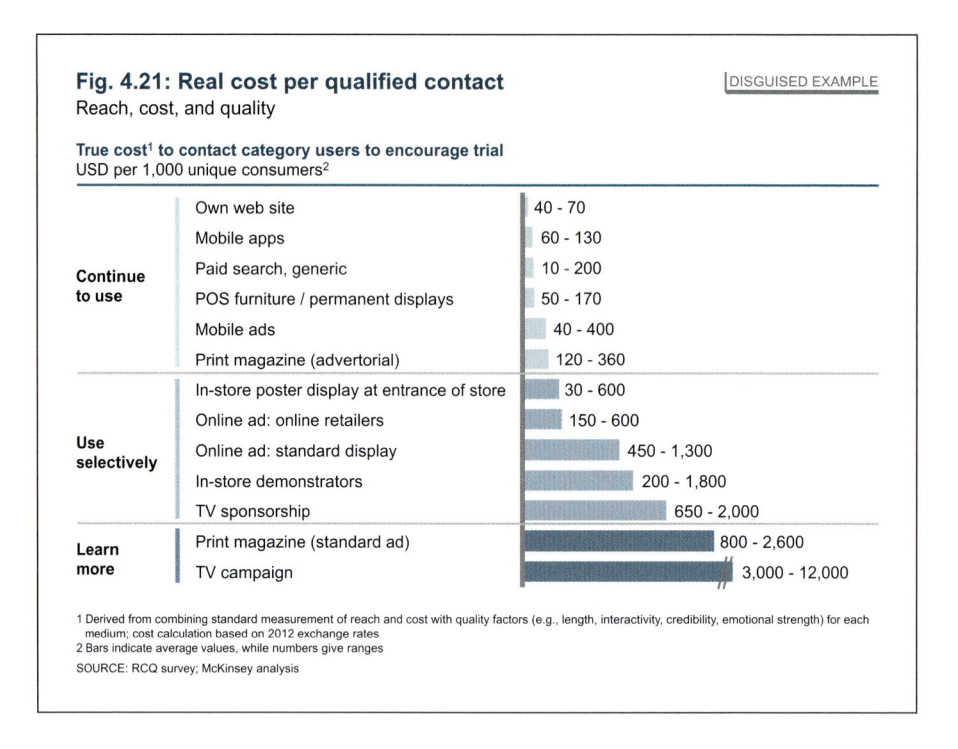

### Fig. 4.21: Real cost per qualified contact
Reach, cost, and quality

DISGUISED EXAMPLE

True cost[1] to contact category users to encourage trial
USD per 1,000 unique consumers[2]

| | | |
|---|---|---|
| **Continue to use** | Own web site | 40 - 70 |
| | Mobile apps | 60 - 130 |
| | Paid search, generic | 10 - 200 |
| | POS furniture / permanent displays | 50 - 170 |
| | Mobile ads | 40 - 400 |
| | Print magazine (advertorial) | 120 - 360 |
| **Use selectively** | In-store poster display at entrance of store | 30 - 600 |
| | Online ad: online retailers | 150 - 600 |
| | Online ad: standard display | 450 - 1,300 |
| | In-store demonstrators | 200 - 1,800 |
| | TV sponsorship | 650 - 2,000 |
| **Learn more** | Print magazine (standard ad) | 800 - 2,600 |
| | TV campaign | 3,000 - 12,000 |

1 Derived from combining standard measurement of reach and cost with quality factors (e.g., length, interactivity, credibility, emotional strength) for each medium; cost calculation based on 2012 exchange rates
2 Bars indicate average values, while numbers give ranges
SOURCE: RCQ survey; McKinsey analysis

does it allow for holistic budget optimization. It is, nevertheless, a solid choice for advertisers who are waking up from years of going by gut feeling and rules of thumb. For example, a manufacturer of consumer goods found that the cost per actual reach of their online banners ranged from EUR 0.04 to 1.45 (USD 0.03 to 1.15). By canceling the more expensive banner placements, the company cut their cost for this vehicle by 60 percent without reducing its actual reach. Similarly, a grocery retailer compared its cost per actual reach for different TV campaigns and observed a cost range from EUR 0.15 to 0.55 (USD 0.12 to 0.44). In light of this, the company reviewed and adjusted its campaign plan, effectively increasing its proportion of high-impact campaigns on television.

### Econometric modeling: marketing mix modeling (MMM)

MMM is a data-intensive method that utilizes econometric modeling techniques to link marketing investments to business objectives. While RCQ relies on the expertise of executives to assess the quality of specific media, MMM uses actual historical performance data. It enables advertisers to measure the performance of their current marketing mix and optimize it not only across advertising media, but also across all marketing instruments, including pricing and sales support. It helps brand managers identify the true drivers of top-line performance among dozens of instruments, to quantify the business impact of marketing investments, and to optimize the allocation of funds to media and other touch points accordingly. The heart of MMM – its analytical engine – models the relative impact of a wide range of levers on revenues and other performance metrics, such as traffic or price perception (Figure 4.22).

**Fig. 4.22: MMM: High-level technical architecture** — SIMPLIFIED

Data sources:
- Internal data
- Market research data
- Competitor market data

MMM proprietary tool:
- Fully integrated database
- Econometric model
  - Multiple linear regression
  - Penalized linear regression
  - Bootstrap model validation
- User interface
  - Actual vs. plan gap analyses and explanation
  - "What if" scenario simulation
  - Guidelines based on commercial expertise

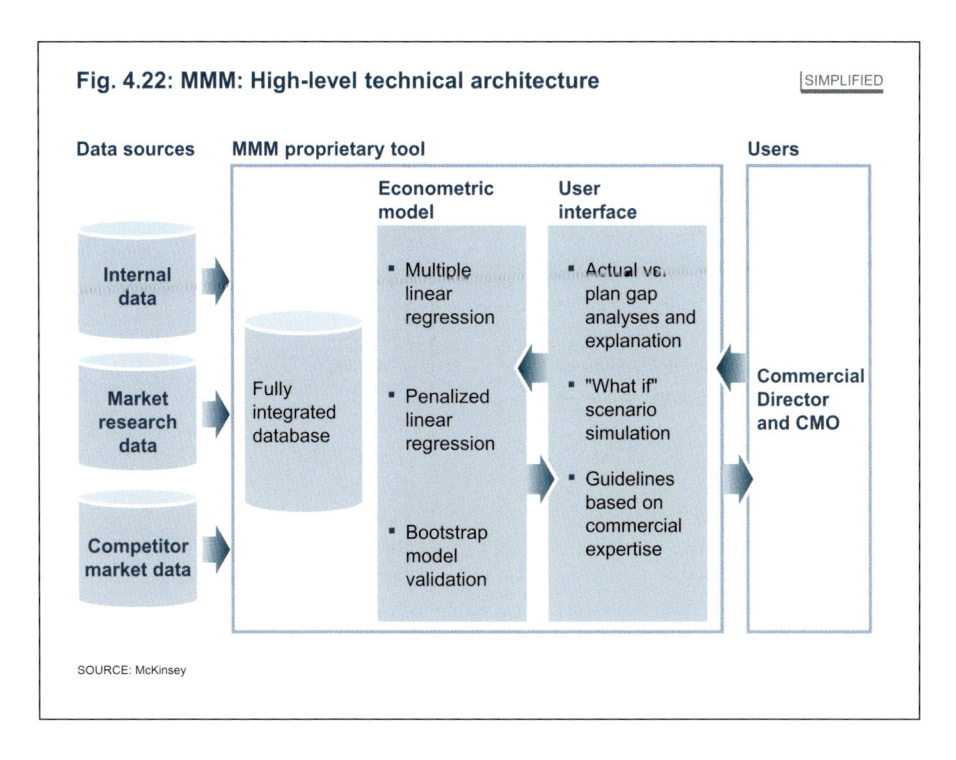

Users:
- Commercial Director and CMO

SOURCE: McKinsey

The output of a state-of-the-art MMM tool helps advertisers separate external factors – such as the overall market growth or demographic trends – from the levers they can address themselves – such as promotional strategy or advertising investment. MMM also provides revenue impact measurements across all marketing levers in order to assess their relative business contribution. Ultimately, MMM provides brand managers with the means to investigate the likely consequences of their actions before they act, enabling them to make fact-based decisions, instead of relying on intuition (Figures 4.23 and 4.24). MMM does, however, make heavy demands on the scope and the quality of input data:

- *Sufficient scope and granularity.* Two or three years of past weekly or daily data are needed to stabilize the model. The data set must be sufficiently detailed to encompass all relevant influencing factors, and sufficiently granular to capture relevant differences between regions and categories. The more detailed the input data is, the more accurate and the more meaningful the MMM results will be. But granularity also depends on a company's business model. While retailers will want daily data, weekly data is typically sufficient for most service providers or manufacturers of products with low purchase frequency.
- *High reliability and accuracy.* »Garbage in, garbage out« applies to MMM as much as it applies to any other advanced modeling effort. Extra care is required to detect and fix any gaps or inconsistencies in the data basis, since both market data and in-house reporting are susceptible to error and corruption. Meticulous merging, cleaning, and validating of data sources are indispensable prerequisites.

## 254    4. Brand Delivery

### Fig. 4.23: MMM tool brings transparency to ROI across all marketing levers

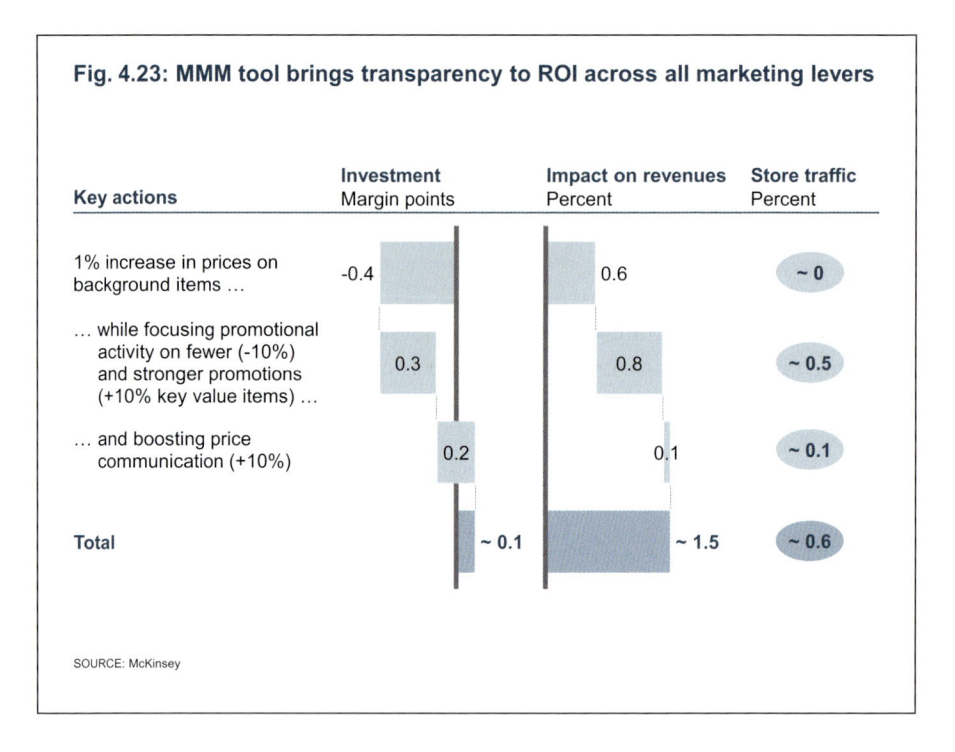

| Key actions | Investment<br>Margin points | Impact on revenues<br>Percent | Store traffic<br>Percent |
|---|---|---|---|
| 1% increase in prices on background items … | -0.4 | 0.6 | ~ 0 |
| … while focusing promotional activity on fewer (-10%) and stronger promotions (+10% key value items) … | 0.3 | 0.8 | ~ 0.5 |
| … and boosting price communication (+10%) | 0.2 | 0.1 | ~ 0.1 |
| **Total** | ~ 0.1 | ~ 1.5 | ~ 0.6 |

SOURCE: McKinsey

### Fig. 4.24: MMM is mainly used to optimize the allocation of funds to "paid media"

Response curves for incremental customer acquisitions

DISGUISED EXAMPLE

○ Current budget level
● Optimized budget level
➤ Optimization

**Incremental customer acquisitions**

- TV
- Paid search
- Specialist print
- Display
- Affiliates
- General print
- TV halo

Spend

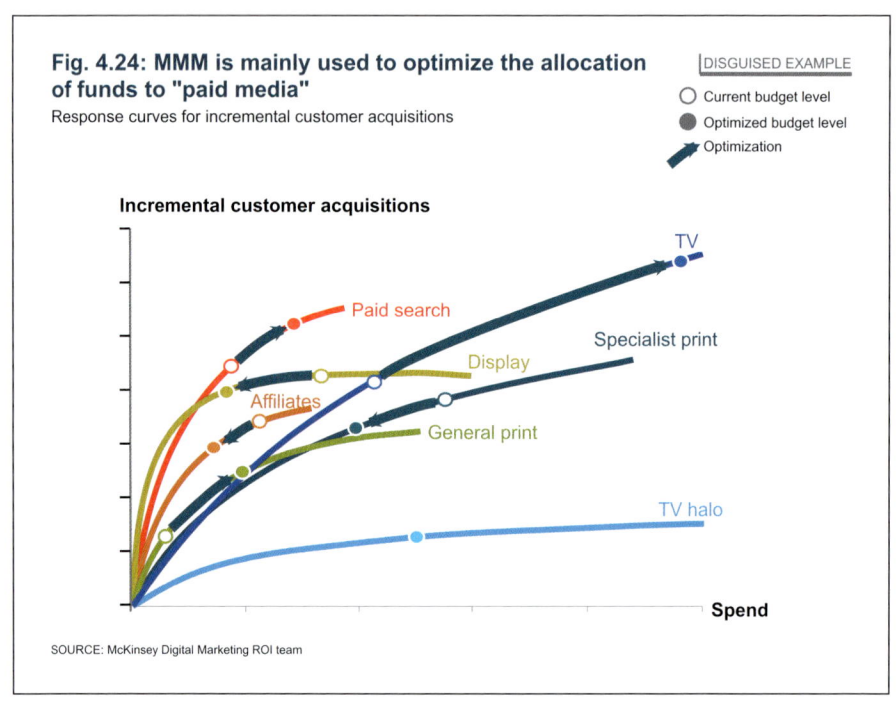

SOURCE: McKinsey Digital Marketing ROI team

- *Constant care.* To ensure MMM remains meaningful and relevant over the longer term, the database needs to be fed with new input data on a regular basis, whether using automated or manual updates. Frequent input updates enable the model to capture market evolution and changes in competitive dynamics. If the data is uploaded automatically, extra care is required to ensure its compatibility with the analytical engine in terms of formats and units.

Given the data requirements and analytical sophistication, MMM is not typically a quick fix, but neither should it be a once-in-a-lifetime effort for brand managers. Its true power lies in its continuous and consistent application. As an integral part of a marketing management information system, it is a comprehensive decision support tool that yields transparency at a holistic level as well as at the level of individual marketing activities. Despite its analytical allure, MMM should not take the place of experience and common sense. It is a decision support tool, not a marketing management robot. Like any tool, it depends on the wisdom of its users.

In a given case, a telecoms player used MMM to determine which time slots, channels, and sellers provide the best contact-to-ad spend ratio in their target group for television advertising. Based on econometric modeling that linked the number of gross new subscribers to advertising spending, the company decided to move its television advertising from prime time (after 7:30 p.m.) to pre-prime time slots (6:30 p.m. to 7:30 p.m.). Additionally, they switched to an advertising sales house with higher effective discounts. As a result of these efforts, the company increased the return on its television advertising investment by more than 60 percent (Figure 4.25) without compromising brand awareness or advertising recall.

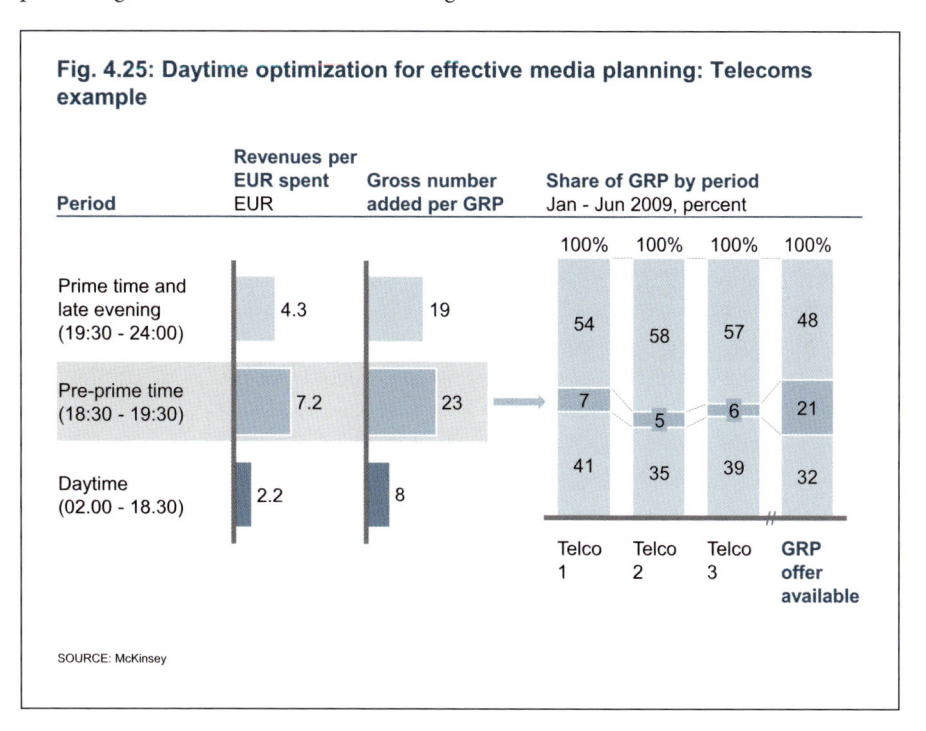

Fig. 4.25: Daytime optimization for effective media planning: Telecoms example

| Period | Revenues per EUR spent EUR | Gross number added per GRP | Share of GRP by period Jan - Jun 2009, percent |  |  |  |
|---|---|---|---|---|---|---|
| | | | Telco 1 | Telco 2 | Telco 3 | GRP offer available |
| Prime time and late evening (19:30 - 24:00) | 4.3 | 19 | 54 | 58 | 57 | 48 |
| Pre-prime time (18:30 - 19:30) | 7.2 | 23 | 7 | 5 | 6 | 21 |
| Daytime (02.00 - 18.30) | 2.2 | 8 | 41 | 35 | 39 | 32 |

SOURCE: McKinsey

### The pitfalls of attribution modeling in digital marketing

The availability of »big data« is tempting many marketing executives to try and quantify the dollar-for-dollar impact of their digital marketing investments. There are now tools that allow companies to monitor and record almost every consumer action online and on mobile devices: What searches have they performed? Which types of online advertising have they been exposed to, and how often? Have they clicked through to e-commerce stores, and if yes, which products have they looked at, added to their virtual shopping baskets, and ultimately purchased? Surely having this kind of information would lead to more accurate impact assessments and investment decisions. If the majority of consumers who have seen a particular pop-up ad ended up purchasing the product that was promoted in the ad, then running more of those pop-up ads would certainly be a good use of the marketing budget. Or would it?

The trouble is that the consumer decision process is subject to important influencing factors that lie beyond the scope of online logs and cookie-based consumer tracking. This is why marketing decisions that rely only on digital data can be significantly biased. There is a general tendency, especially among some service providers, to measure only those factors that are easy to measure – such as Web site visits, click-through rates, and online shopping behavior – even if the explanatory value for consumer decision making is questionable or insufficient. What about classic advertising consumers may have seen on television or in magazines en route to their ultimate online purchase? What about word of mouth? What about the buzz that may have been generated in social media by other consumers? What about competitor activities?

Ignoring these and other factors outside the narrow scope of online tracking can lead brand managers to overestimate the sales impact of digital marketing activities substantially, thus inflating the MROI of digital marketing investments. The distortion will be even greater for brands that pursue multichannel approaches – those brands that sell their products both through online channels and in brick-and-mortar stores.

### Consumer decision journey

The consumer decision journey approach to MROI involves the optimization of marketing investments at each stage of the consumer decision journey from initial consideration and active evaluation to the moment of purchase and the post-purchase experience (Figure 4.26). The impact of marketing investments on consumers' attitudes towards a given brand is assessed with the help of consumer surveys. Examples for dependent variables in CDJ-based MROI optimization include the likelihood of a given brand to be included in the consideration set, or to be selected at the moment of purchase. This assessment is used to optimize both the media mix and the respective investment levels, enabling advertisers to spend more on media that have a high impact on consumer attitudes toward their brand.

Specifically, CDJ can help advertisers determine which stages of a consumer's decision journey have the highest impact on ultimate purchase decisions. In a recent survey among consumers in the US, McKinsey found that car insurance is purchased as a

**Fig. 4.26: What is CDJ?**

Consumer decision journey (CDJ) is focused on key battlegrounds and provides critical insights to inform marketing and MROI objectives

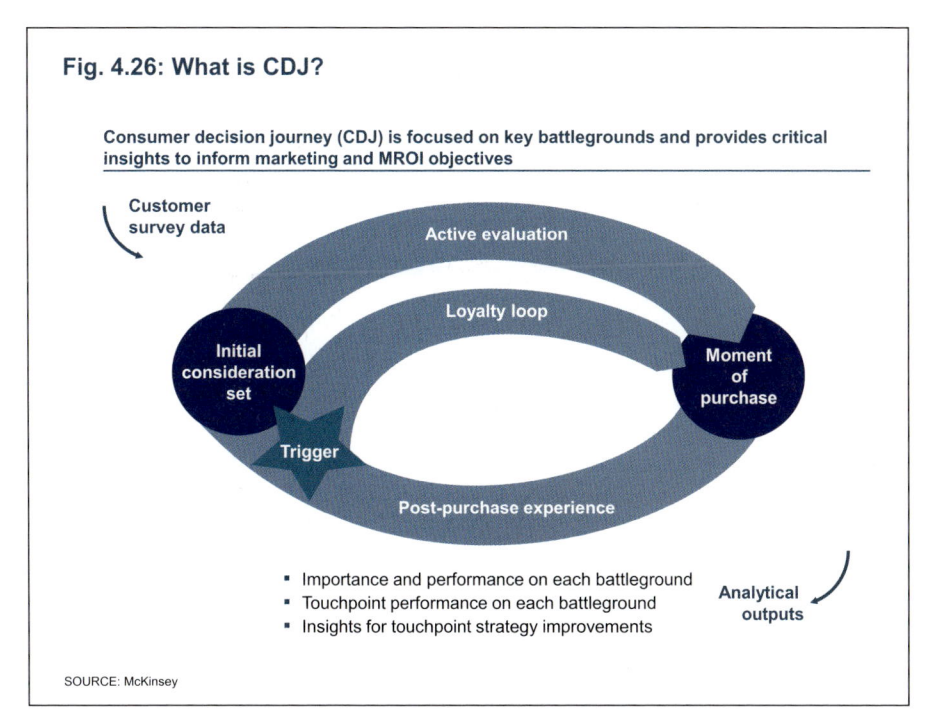

- Importance and performance on each battleground
- Touchpoint performance on each battleground
- Insights for touchpoint strategy improvements

Analytical outputs

SOURCE: McKinsey

result of the »loyalty loop« in more than three quarters of all cases.[21] This means that the overwhelming majority of purchase decisions are based on previous purchases. From this perspective, investments by insurance companies in an improved product experience – such as faster claims management – would be money well spent. In other industries, such as skin care, »initial consideration« and »active evaluation« are far more influential stages of the decision journey, warranting reallocation of marketing funds to touch points and activities that impact those earlier stages. Examples may include sampling, POS materials, or product advice provided online.

**Combining multiple approaches**

Every media allocation approach has its specific merits, but none of them is perfect. The good news is that these approaches are not mutually exclusive in application, but can be combined in recognition of their relative strengths and weaknesses. Each of these approaches has certain blind spots where some of the other approaches can help shed light. The principal dimension of difference is the source of input data:

- Testing and learning: controlled experiments based on actual performance data.
- MMM: modeling based on actual performance data.
- RCQ: standardized comparison based on management expertise.
- CDJ: optimization based on consumer surveys.

This overview shows that we have not compiled the choice of approaches at random. They are collectively exhaustive and can be combined for a balanced allocation of funds to media, other touch points, and entire journeys to improve the end-to-end brand experience. For example, approaches that rely on historical data – such as testing and learning along with MMM – are blind to the impact of new marketing instruments that were not part of the media mix in the past. This gap can be filled by relying on management expertise as RCQ does, or on consumer feedback as CDJ would. On the other hand, relying exclusively on a consumer's current decision journey as the basis for optimization would blot out the long-term impact of marketing investments in brand equity and might result in the eventual starvation of the brand. Compare the insert below for a discussion of the specific challenges of attribution modeling, a subcategory of MMM as applied to digital media.

Ideally, brand managers will want to combine all sources of information on all available touch points and journeys to generate a complete and unbiased understanding of how their media mix performs and how it can be improved: actual performance data, management expertise, and consumer surveys. In real life, however, certain limiting factors will prevent most companies from pursuing this holistic course: lack of data availability or compatibility, excessive analytical complexity, and – last but certainly not least – prohibitively high costs. The important thing to note is that no single media allocation approach is flawless. Multiple approaches can and should be combined to minimize blind spots and bias for the overall benefit of the brand.

**MROI impact examples**

Time and again, systematic marketing ROI management has proved its merit. Companies have often been able to reduce their marketing spending by 5 to 15 percent in the short term, without adversely influencing marketing effectiveness or revenues. In the medium term, they have frequently realized revenue growth of 5 to 10 percent depending on the sector, by redirecting expenditure to bottlenecks in their performance relative to other brands. Specific examples include the following:

- With the help of a marketing ROI program, a European beverage company determined that between 14 and 22 percent of its marketing expenditure had very little impact. The wasted expenditure included the expensive sponsorship of sporting events that had no relevance for the target group. At the same time, the beverage company carried out media effectiveness analysis that resulted in the decision to redirect a fifth of its budget to media that were more effective in fulfilling the company's marketing objectives.
- An apparel retailer was able to realize short-term efficiency gains of 10 to 15 percent while redirecting almost a third of its budget to areas that were more effective in achieving its new marketing strategy. Sometimes, a simple comparison of how much is spent to raise brand awareness or familiarity by a single percentage point is enough to reveal the potential savings in switching from one medium to another. Though the targets remain the same, the money is used more effectively.
- A leading consumer goods company that had sponsorship deals spanning multiple years and costing over USD 400 million was able to use a customized version of the RCQ approach to compare the effectiveness of these to tradi-

> tional media benchmarks. By developing additional criteria for measuring the ancillary benefits of sponsorship deals and creating a clear marketing assets strategy focused on priority channels, the company was able to divest ineffective sponsorships and to renegotiate contracts for which effectiveness was less than that of traditional television. Savings amounted to more than EUR 40 million annually.

At DHL, the express delivery giant, fact-based marketing allocation and MROI optimization was implemented in more than 20 of the largest countries since 2004. This lead to an estimated increase in brand value of more than USD 1.3 billion over five years, corresponding to an ROI of 38 percent and an internal rate of return of 24 percent. Beyond the financial success, the implementation of the approach also had a major impact on DHL's strategy and organization:

- **Improved communication.** MROI modeling had considerable impact on the understanding and application of brand management in the company – but even more importantly, on DHL's overall culture. The application of a fact-based approach and the connection of brand attributes with hard sales data made brand management tangible not only for marketing managers, but for executives in other functions as well.
- **Improved controlling.** The brand assessment tool is also used as a controlling tool. It enables management to clearly specify and monitor responsibilities. It is the vehicle to transport and communicate the global brand concept's three core values. The tool helps align objectives and metrics for brand management among the company's managers around the world.
- **Improved employee identification.** Finally, establishing DHL as the second major brand alongside Deutsche Post strengthened the identity and culture of the DHL organization overall. Today, DHL employees feel proud of being members of one single global DHL organization. They also recognize the contribution their actions as DHL employees can have on the overall success of the Deutsche Post DHL Group.[22]

The marketing ROI approach represents a major revolution in brand management. As Lord Kelvin once observed: »If you cannot measure it, you cannot improve it.« Now, companies have precise tools at their disposal to manage and monitor budget allocation. This will inevitably lead to important changes in the size and structure of marketing spending. Eventually, it will change the face of the function fundamentally. MROI will transform brand management into a more sober, a more scientific, and a more accountable affair. Having said that, creative campaigns and common sense will always remain important elements of brand management. Allocating money to high-impact touch points is, after all, a means to end, not an end in itself.

**Interactive decision support tools**

To embed MROI optimization in their marketing organizations and ensure it is used for front-line decision making, brand managers should consider the implementation of interactive decision support tools. Simulation tools that rely on MROI modeling enable marketing practitioners to evaluate different scenarios for their future marketing plans.

One example of such tools is McKinsey's Marketing Navigator. It helps managers use advanced analytical methods to answer questions such as:

- Which countries and brands should I focus my spending on?
- Which messages should I send to my target groups?
- Which channels should I invest in to get the highest return?

The Marketing Navigator integrates and combines the strengths of the different approaches discussed in this section: Econometric models (»marketing mix modeling«), pragmatic models based on rules (»reach, cost, and quality«), methods based on customer insights (»consumer decision journey«), and attribution modeling.

Figure 4.27 shows an illustrative screenshot from the Marketing Navigator. Also compare our discussion of the Brand Navigator in Section 4.5 on the brand cockpit. While the Marketing Navigator is focused on marketing spending, the Brand Navigator covers all aspects of brand performance.

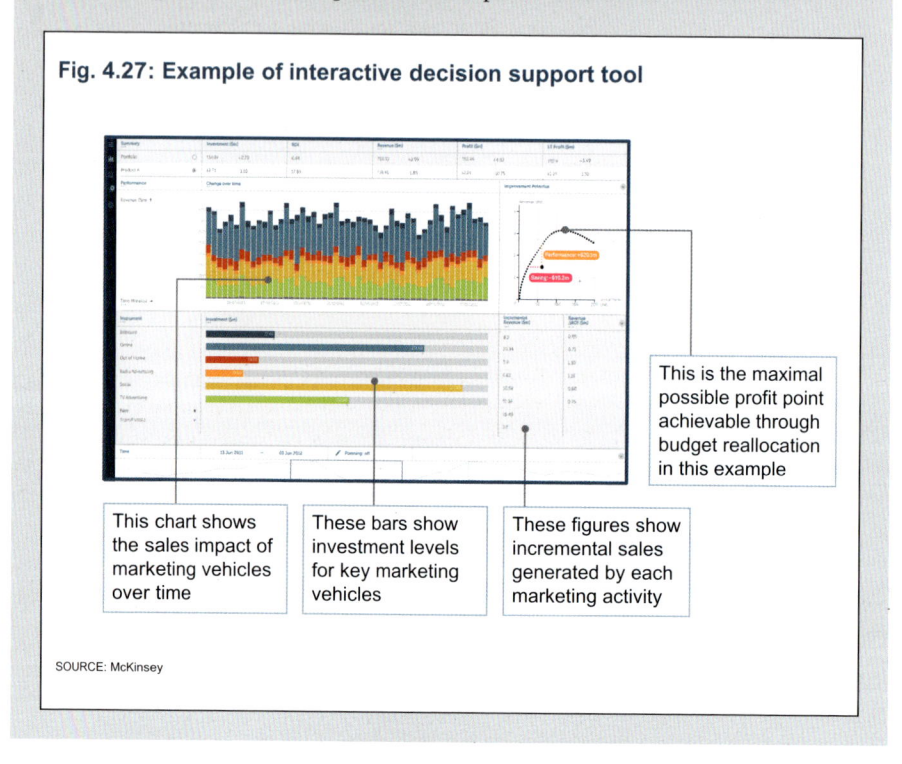

**Fig. 4.27: Example of interactive decision support tool**

This chart shows the sales impact of marketing vehicles over time

These bars show investment levels for key marketing vehicles

These figures show incremental sales generated by each marketing activity

This is the maximal possible profit point achievable through budget reallocation in this example

SOURCE: McKinsey

## 4.3 Internal Activation: Creating a Brand Mindset

For many industries, branding in its holistic sense of *science*, *art*, and *craft* is still a fairly new concept. Often, many people within an organization understand the concept of branding only in an advertising or logo context.

This is why successful brand delivery entails a long transformational process to create the right mindset and make sure that every employee understands his or her role and responsibility in creating a consistent brand experience for customers. This is especially critical in service industries, where many employees directly manage customer touch points and journeys.

Two aspects need to be managed in this process:

1. **Employees need to understand the concept of »brand delivery along all customer touch points and journeys.«** This makes every one of them a brand ambassador. They must understand that every action directed toward a customer – implicitly or explicitly – influences that customer's perceptions. In order to motivate members of the organization to act as responsible brand ambassadors, strong top management backing and involvement is a prerequisite. Recognizing this, Helmut Maucher, long-time CEO of Nestlé, said: »If you consider [your brand] to be the most important asset, brand management responsibility has to be a C-level issue.«[23] While organizations may theoretically understand that frontline employees are accountable for the full customer experience, they often fail to empower them or show them the kind of respect they deserve. As one frustrated call center manager at a leading telecommunications company reported: »As long as we are treated as second-class citizens in charge of protecting management from ›pesky customers,‹ our company will fail to keep its promises.«[24] Workshops, training sessions, manuals, and other reinforcing mechanisms will help the organization stress the importance of each customer interaction and help the staff gradually adopt a brand mindset. Of course, such activities can only complement, but not substitute visible top management commitment to the brand and its promise.

2. **Identification with the brand promise.** The brand will be »lived« only if employees truly believe in what they are asked to deliver or – even better – are proud of what they do every day to satisfy their customers. An effective tool in this context can be a brand book – a document that is shared widely across the organization, that defines the core brand identity, and that provides a common language for consistent brand execution. Organizations with strong brands like IBM, Nivea, or DHL have created such brand books and use these together with additional internal communication vehicles – like »brand days,« awards for behavior in line with the brand promise, or sweepstakes – to deepen employee identification with the brand promise.

In the day and age of 360-degree brand communication, brand managers need to think ever more holistically about delivering the promise of their brands. To come full circle, brand delivery planning needs to recognize that brand positioning is not only an outbound game. Brands must be built consistently at all touch points and along all crucial journeys. Numerous touch points involve direct interaction or communication with the customer – for example, the sales force, store design, or customer service. But there are also touch points at which customers are indirectly influenced by employees. Think, for example, of the image projected by the human resources department's employer branding efforts and recruiting events. Similarly, every marketing manager's idea of the brand influences the image conveyed in advertising materials. So when we say brands must be built at all touch points, that is meant to include a company's staff as well as their customers. Says Colin Mitchell of Ogilvy & Mather: »When you think of marketing, you more than likely think of marketing to your customers. But another ›market‹ is just as important: your employees; the very people who can make the brand come alive for your customers.«[25]

Often, executives assume that by defining a (new) brand positioning, their work is essentially done. They send out memos or even brand books to key players in their organizations and hope for the best. But a brand doesn't come to life in employees' hearts and minds on cue, nor does it happen automatically. According to a McKinsey survey, 60 percent of transformation efforts are considered failures – often because of a perceived lack of senior commitment, confusion among employees, and insufficient project management.[26] In fact, there is an entire subprocess behind the first stage described in Figure 4.28, »Creating a brand mindset«. From numerous transformational programs at clients, a set of guiding principles has been identified for internal branding. To show how these success factors play out in practice, an example has been included for each factor:[27]

- **Ensure CEO sponsorship.** The best sponsor for internal brand building is the CEO. Although a purely top-down communication can lead to »not invented here« reactions, there is nothing like inspirational leadership when it comes to creating enthusiasm for the brand among your staff. At Virgin, CEO Richard Branson leads by example. He enters new categories and businesses simply because he feels passionately about them, manages his company in a hands-off fashion from his private yacht to give his executives greater autonomy, and puts people first: »Our first priority should be the people who work for the companies, then the customers, then the shareholders.«[28] At DHL, the early endorsement by CEO Klaus Zumwinkel was vitally important to the establishment of fact-based brand management.[29]
- **Choose the right moment.** Employees have to understand »why now.« Suitable triggers for major internal brand-building efforts can be the arrival of a new CEO, fundamental changes in company structure, or business dynamics. British Petroleum (BP) used the occasion of its merger with Amoco and Arco to create a new, distinctive identity for employees of all premerger companies. Positioning itself as an energy company »beyond petroleum,« BP ventured to transform itself from an old-school corporation into an open, collaborative company. An internal survey conducted subsequent to the integration confirmed two-thirds of the staff were aware of and supported the new brand values.[30]

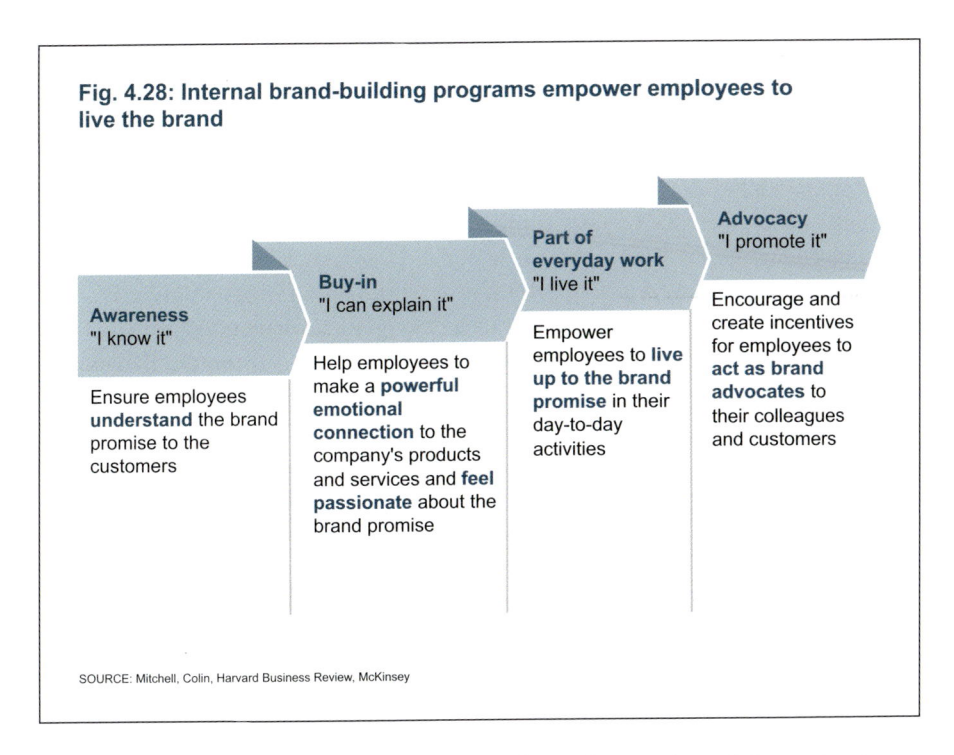

## 4.3 Internal Activation: Creating a Brand Mindset

**Fig. 4.28: Internal brand-building programs empower employees to live the brand**

**Awareness** — "I know it"
Ensure employees **understand** the brand promise to the customers

**Buy-in** — "I can explain it"
Help employees to make a **powerful emotional connection** to the company's products and services and **feel passionate** about the brand promise

**Part of everyday work** — "I live it"
Empower employees to **live up to the brand promise** in their day-to-day activities

**Advocacy** — "I promote it"
Encourage and create incentives for employees to **act as brand advocates** to their colleagues and customers

SOURCE: Mitchell, Colin, Harvard Business Review, McKinsey

- **Apply holistic change management.** To shift mindsets and capabilities, simply announcing the (new) brand identity is not sufficient. Successful transformation takes clear instructions, role modeling, talent development, and formal reinforcement. When low-cost carrier JetBlue set out to »bring humanity back into the airline industry,« it made sure there were clear guidelines for key touch points (»BluePrint« and »BlueBook«), management got involved in passenger-facing operations at peak times, new employees were invited to a brand value training camp, and an annual brand value »speak up« survey was conducted to monitor the implementation of the new brand values.[31]

- **Stick to it.** Internal brand building requires consistency; a one-shot effort is not enough. Leading players such as Ritz Carlton, Marriott's standalone luxury brand, have built continuous internal branding into their corporate DNA. Top management delivers inspirational speeches to the staff of every hotel several times a year, always building on the corporate credo »We are ladies and gentlemen serving ladies and gentlemen.« New hires go through two days of corporate philosophy training and are accompanied by a coach during their first four weeks. The first 15 minutes of every shift are set aside to discuss one of the 20 »brand basics.«[32]

- **Link internal to external brand building.** Linking inbound to outbound brand communication gives employees a strong sense of direction and purpose. Sending one consistent message to internal and external audiences was IBM's top priority when it launched its e-business initiative. What was perceived as a normal marketing campaign externally, doubled as an internal effort to push the company to achieve objectives previously thought out of reach. It helped change the way employees thought about processes, product development, product naming, and sales force organization, keeping in mind customer perceptions and expectations of the brand as a provider of superior e-business solutions. Examples such as these illustrate that internal brand building – let alone internal brand transformation – doesn't happen overnight. It requires thorough preparation, a detailed road map, and rigorous implementation monitoring. In many ways, it isn't all that different from external brand building. This is all the more true in large and complex corporations. As a consequence, understanding, segmenting, and addressing different internal target groups is one of the key prerequisites of successful internal branding. Internal target groups – whether they have direct customer contact or not – have different profiles, should play different roles in brand transformation efforts, and must receive tailored communication (Figure 4.29). Nader Tavassoli of the London Business School claims: »One-size-fits-all programs simply will not work when trying to win over people. Segmenting people based on their various mindsets is critical to taking the organization to the next level.« A group brand manager at an international multicategory conglomerate agrees: »You need to segment your internal population just as you would your external audience and communicate appropriately.«[33]

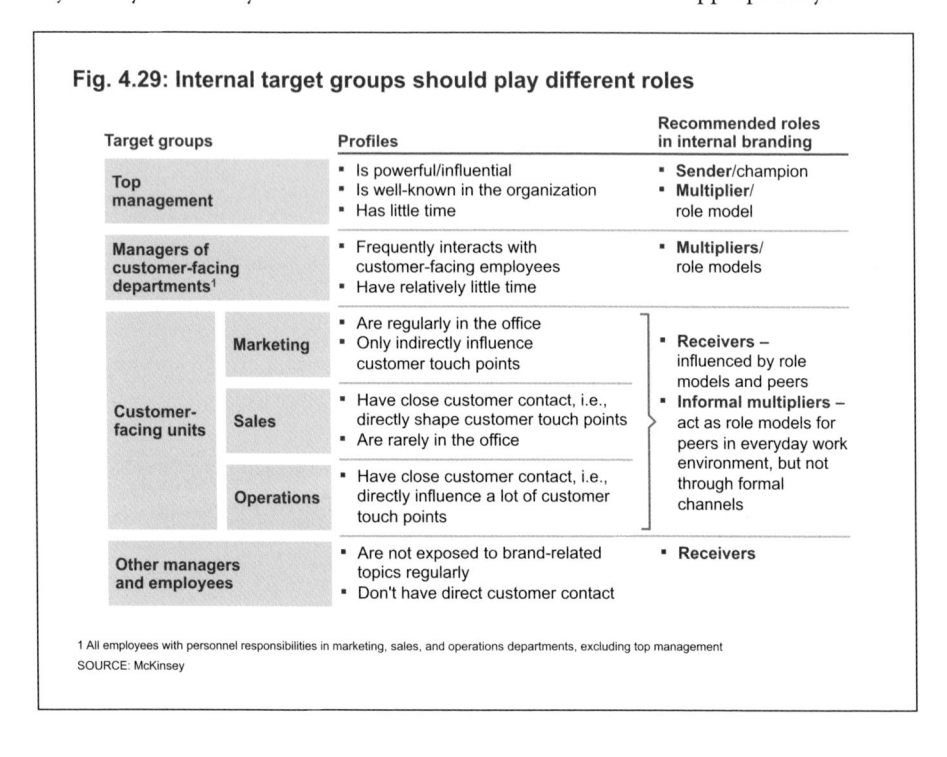

**Fig. 4.29: Internal target groups should play different roles**

| Target groups | | Profiles | Recommended roles in internal branding |
|---|---|---|---|
| Top management | | • Is powerful/influential<br>• Is well-known in the organization<br>• Has little time | • Sender/champion<br>• Multiplier/<br>role model |
| Managers of customer-facing departments[1] | | • Frequently interacts with customer-facing employees<br>• Have relatively little time | • Multipliers/<br>role models |
| Customer-facing units | Marketing | • Are regularly in the office<br>• Only indirectly influence customer touch points | • Receivers – influenced by role models and peers<br>• Informal multipliers – act as role models for peers in everyday work environment, but not through formal channels |
| | Sales | • Have close customer contact, i.e., directly shape customer touch points<br>• Are rarely in the office | |
| | Operations | • Have close customer contact, i.e., directly influence a lot of customer touch points | |
| Other managers and employees | | • Are not exposed to brand-related topics regularly<br>• Don't have direct customer contact | • Receivers |

1 All employees with personnel responsibilities in marketing, sales, and operations departments, excluding top management
SOURCE: McKinsey

### Brand delivery across customer touch points

A motivated staff is the basis for delivering the brand promise to the customer. However, customers will experience the brand promise only if they constantly encounter a consistent brand message at every customer touch point.

Accordingly, the brand promise should generally be translated along the entire business system, including territories well outside the traditional purview of the marketing department, such as research and development or production. For example, BMW's clearly defined value proposition of »The Ultimate Driving Machine« is being translated into tangible research and development objectives for the chassis frame so that it will support driving pleasure, using clearly defined guidelines for the product design. As former CEO Dr. Helmut Panke put it: »The BMW brand stands for a promise of fascinating, distinctive automobiles, and we shall continue to keep our promise in this respect. A part of this promise is never to build a boring BMW [...]. We will only break into new segments if we remain true to the BMW image.«[34] Apparently, this also applies to the new i3. On the occasion of its launch in 2013, the company said: »The BMW i3 – the BMW Group's first pure electric, series-produced model – has the same sporting genes as every BMW and is characterized by sheer driving pleasure.«[35] To make sure the entire organization knows and lives the brand values, BMW established the BMW Group Brand Academy in 2002. This is a training center that brings to life the three main brands – BMW, Mini, and Rolls-Royce – for managers from all departments. Upon graduating from the academy, they return to their teams and divisions as persuasive brand ambassadors.[36]

To develop and reinforce integrated end-to-end delivery of the brand promise, cross-functional workshops are a useful format. Bringing together the expertise and experience from multiple functions, such workshops help to develop brand delivery programs that go well beyond classic communication. Typically, the workshops follow a three-step approach:

- *Generate ideas.* Once the desired brand positioning and implicit value proposition have been specified and understood, new ideas for a targeted implementation are generated in workshops held within the various corporate functions.
- *Transform ideas into programs.* These ideas are then refined and aggregated into specific activities that influence customer interactions. Programs are developed to facilitate the implementation of these activities.
- *Prioritize and develop action plans.* The various programs need to be prioritized according to their improvement potential (cost/benefit) and the resources required to bring them to life.

**Long-term institutionalization**

Once the plans for the brand's delivery are in place throughout the organization, the next step is to ensure the brand's long-term institutionalization. Achieving this usually depends on three key dimensions: people, processes, and tools. In the people dimension, it is critical to design a marketing organization that not only works effectively within itself but also connects well with the rest of the business system, such as product development. Good marketers have well-established processes in place that link marketing and customer insights to each relevant business process using objective milestones and specifying clear responsibilities. This often means bringing qualified personnel into the organization and anchoring responsibility with the brand manager.

## 4.4 Digital Brand Management

It all started with Super Mario's gold coins, earned the hard way by jumping and running all around the Mushroom Kingdom. Then the Linden Dollar, the common currency in that half-forgotten parallel universe known as Second Life. Then the Bitcoin, the online gambler's chip of choice. Who knows what's next? Any way you look at it, the digital realm seems to be all about money, even if it is mostly virtual. But does it also have the power to help brand managers make real-world money?

When marketing executives look at the development of the digital world, what they usually see is a threat to the equity of their brands and to the return on their marketing investments. Audiences tune out of broadcast media and may never come to see that costly TV commercial. Consumers compare prices and put everybody's margins under pressure. Shoppers cheat traditional retailers out of their revenues by browsing in physical stores next door, but buying online. Bloggers unleash vicious cycles of publicity and put decades of reputation building at risk. So is the Internet bad news for brands?

It can be, but is doesn't have to be. In fact, we believe that the digital (r)evolution can make strong brands even stronger. But to make it happen, brand managers need to deepen their knowledge and their skills in three areas:

- How do key digital trends affect consumer behavior, business dynamics, and brand management?
- Which digital value creation opportunities are emerging at various stages of a consumer's journey?
- Which success factors are critical for competitive differentiation in the world of digital brand management?

In this section, we set out to explore these questions and provide inspiration for executives who aspire to turn potential threats posed by digital developments into real-life opportunities for their brands.

### How do key digital trends affect consumer behavior, business dynamics, and brand management?

Digitalization is transforming not only marketing communication and consumer behavior, but entire business models and even industries. These changes are not brought about by the invention of a single device, the introduction of any given killer application, or the IPO of a specific company. It is the result of persistent trends that work in conjunction and reinforce one another. In this section, we look at six such trends that are here to stay and will have lasting effects on brand management (Figure 4.30).

### Power to the people

Digital technology opens up a wealth of value creation opportunities for brands. But first of all, it empowers consumers to make more informed choices. They now have

**Fig. 4.30: Six major digital trends**

| | What is the trend? | What is going on? | What does it mean? |
|---|---|---|---|
| 1 | Power to the people | The digital world offers consumers nearly total brand and price transparency | Brands face growing price/margin pressure and need for clear differentiation |
| 2 | The data explosion | Companies can access unprecedented volumes of consumer data | Brands need to turn "big data" into "smart data" to create real benefit |
| 3 | New brands and business models | Digital pioneers like Amazon are reshaping the economy | Incumbent brands need to review and sharpen their value propositions |
| 4 | Touch point evolution | Digital touch points form an entire ecosystem in itself | Brands need to strategize and prioritize their digital marketing and channel mix |
| 5 | Viral marketing | Digital snowball effects can multiply creative marketing efforts | Brands have the chance to let consumers do marketing for them |
| 6 | Negative buzz | Negative consumer sentiment can get out of control in social media | Brands need to engage in online listening and active crisis management |

SOURCE: McKinsey

real-time access to a richer fact base than ever before – from price comparisons to product reviews. If they want, consumers can attain almost total transparency through online research and comparison shopping. The impact of this development is multiplied by what is now commonly referred to as »constant connectivity« – the fact that a growing share of consumers is online anytime and anywhere. Smartphone penetration more than doubled between 2009 and 2013 in the US. In China, an estimated 800 million smartphones are now in circulation.[37] Tablet penetration doubled within a single year, from 2011 to 2012, and increased by a factor of five between 2010 and 2013 in the US (Figure 4.31). Mobile devices bring price transparency and the ensuing margin pressure to the brick-and-mortar sales floor. As a result, branded downtown retailers find themselves competing with online price breakers for shopper attention, sales conversion, repeat visits, and repeat purchases.

**The data explosion**

Customers may benefit from greater transparency than ever before, but the same is true for brands. They have access to consumer data at an unprecedented level of detail. »Big data« allows for more differentiated profiling and interaction, down to personalized offers for target groups of one. Players like Amazon and Netflix are using these tools to generate individual recommendations to repeat customers or subscribers, and a lot of users seem to value these services. In addition, there is a window of opportunity for an ever more precise measurement of marketing effectiveness and MROI. This puts brand managers in a position to move beyond the guesswork and

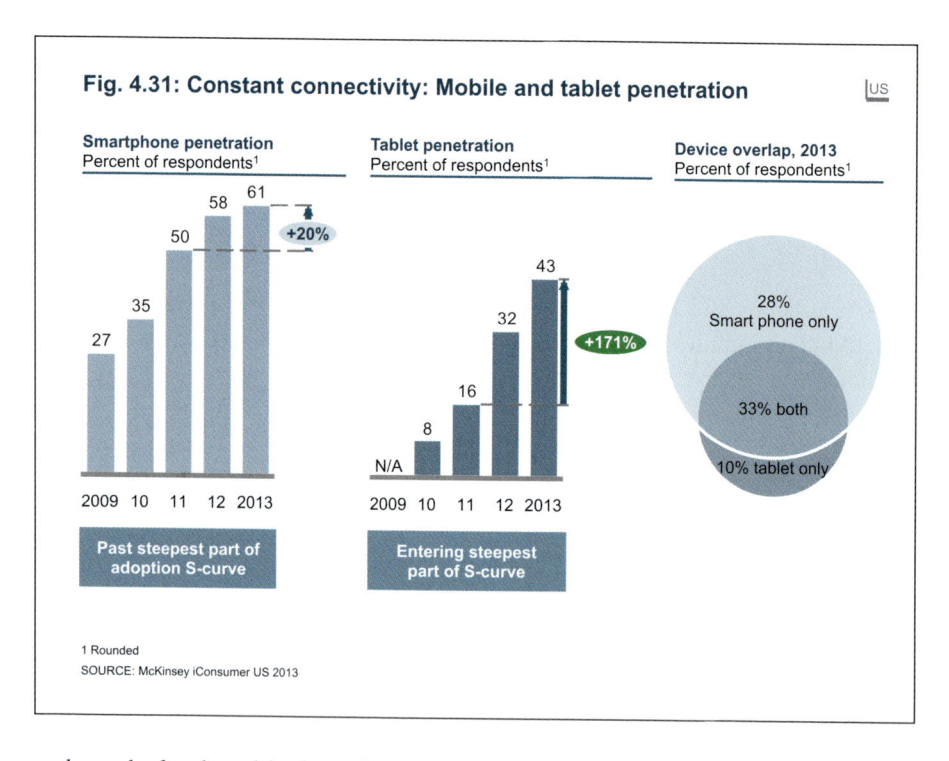

**Fig. 4.31: Constant connectivity: Mobile and tablet penetration** |US

**Smartphone penetration**
Percent of respondents[1]

- 2009: 27
- 10: 35
- 11: 50
- 12: 58
- 2013: 61

+20%

Past steepest part of adoption S-curve

**Tablet penetration**
Percent of respondents[1]

- 2009: N/A
- 10: 8
- 11: 16
- 12: 32
- 2013: 43

+171%

Entering steepest part of S-curve

**Device overlap, 2013**
Percent of respondents[1]

- 28% Smart phone only
- 33% both
- 10% tablet only

1 Rounded
SOURCE: McKinsey iConsumer US 2013

make truly fact-based budget allocation decisions, provided they have the tools and skills to do so; compare Section 4.2 on MROI for details. At the same time, executives are under pressure to turn the vast ocean of »big data« into »smart data« by identifying the bits that matter. Where do you start? How do you know what to look for? And once you find it, how do you make sure it has an impact on the marketing mix?

**New brands and business models**

The digital revolution has given rise to some of the biggest success stories in the history of capitalism. Digital business models and the brands that embody them have skyrocketed. Apple, Google, Amazon, eBay, and Facebook come to mind. These five brands alone are collectively valued at some EUR 235 billion by Interbrand (2013), roughly the equivalent of the GDP of the nation of Israel. What is more, all of these brands have seen double-digit year-on-year growth. In 2013, Apple and Google are topping the Interbrand list, displacing Coca-Cola, the brand that had held the top spot ever since the brand value ranking was first compiled in 2000. And already, the next generation of digital business models is emerging, either as part of the growing portfolios of established digital players, or through new start-up ventures. Examples include free delivery of online purchases on the same day or even within 90 minutes of ordering, paid access to personal profiles in social media, and a growing number of peer-to-peer platforms for trading, swapping, or short-term rentals. To stay relevant and defend their fair shares, incumbent brands need to adapt flexibly to this evolving environment, for example, based on partnerships with pure players or refinements of an existing business model.

## Touch point evolution

A decade ago, »online« was a single line item in a brand manager's list of touch points. Today, the multitude of digital touch points constitutes an entire ecosystem in itself – from search engine marketing to online aftersales service. Moreover, a growing number of these touch points are interactive. Examples include live chats with consumers on the company homepage, such as Ikea's »Ask Anna« interface,[38] or consumer co-creation and customization as promoted by the likes of Adidas and Nike. The evolution of touch points is further fueled by the fact that social network users spend more than 10 billion minutes on Facebook, watch 4 billion videos on YouTube, and send 400 million tweets every day. In response, some brands have moved large parts of their customer interaction to social media. In general, companies face a trade-off between the number of digital touch points they cover and the resources they can commit to manage each touch point.[39]

## Viral marketing

Media usage is changing fundamentally. Parallel usage of traditional and new media is increasing, but it doesn't stop there. Today's consumers create almost as much content as they consume. For example, 100 hours of video are uploaded every minute to YouTube alone, according to company information. If brand managers take advantage of user-generated content, they can let consumers do the marketing for them. There are two ways to set in motion such virtuous cycles of user-generated content and online advocacy: proactive triggers, such as the appearance of a company-controlled flash mob in a public place, or reactive measures, such as original responses to major news events. Audi, for example, took advantage of the 2013 Super Bowl power outage at the Mercedes Benz Super Bowl by tweeting »Sending some LEDs to the @MBUSA Superdome right now,« eventually generating almost 10,000 retweets (at the time of writing). Both proactive and reactive triggers need to be sufficiently creative and unusual to get the ball rolling among online opinion leaders. At the same time, brands should stay true to their identity and heritage even in fast-moving media.

## Negative buzz

Viral effects can not only strengthen but also damage a brand. In a networked world, consumers have unprecedented power to make themselves heard through blogs, reviews, or social media posts – sometimes as ardent advocates, and sometimes as fierce critics of a given brand or product. In the past, this kind of feedback would reach only a handful of friends. But now, it is potentially available to a worldwide audience of followers. Take the example of a passenger's guitar that was broken during a flight. The airline refused to compensate the passenger for the loss, quoting company policy. The passenger reacted by recording and uploading a musical complaint to YouTube. The music video got millions of views. To protect their brands, managers will want to engage in active listening and ready themselves for constructive interventions as soon as a storm is brewing.

In light of the game-changing impact of digital technology on brand management, brands cannot opt out anymore: if they don't compete in the digital arena, consumers will drag them into the ring by way of online word of mouth and social media posts. In short, the question is not *whether* to play. The question is *where* and *how* to play.

### Which digital value creation opportunities are emerging at various stages of a consumer's journey?

Where and how on a consumer's decision journey should brands employ digital technology to engage their audience, to sharpen their profile, and to improve their operations? Leading players such as Amazon demonstrate that a digital presence can add substantial value along the whole value chain – from insights generation and effective marketing to sales stimulation and highly efficient services. Below, we will outline specific value creation opportunities in each of these areas (Figure 4.32).

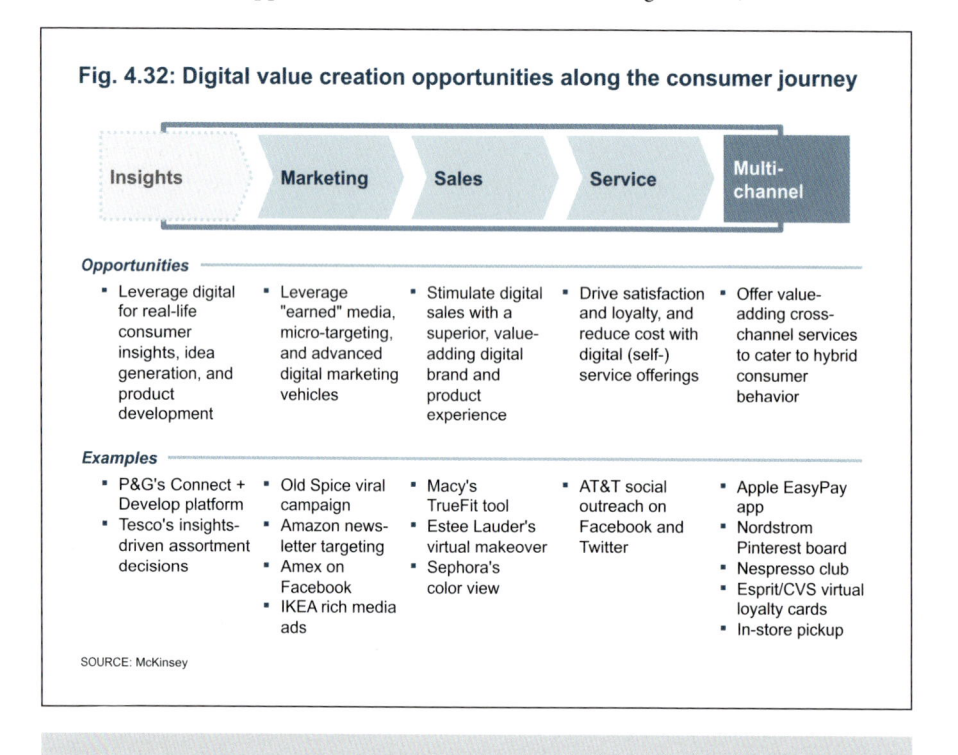

**Fig. 4.32: Digital value creation opportunities along the consumer journey**

Insights → Marketing → Sales → Service → Multi-channel

**Opportunities**
- Leverage digital for real-life consumer insights, idea generation, and product development
- Leverage "earned" media, micro-targeting, and advanced digital marketing vehicles
- Stimulate digital sales with a superior, value-adding digital brand and product experience
- Drive satisfaction and loyalty, and reduce cost with digital (self-) service offerings
- Offer value-adding cross-channel services to cater to hybrid consumer behavior

**Examples**
- P&G's Connect + Develop platform
- Tesco's insights-driven assortment decisions
- Old Spice viral campaign
- Amazon news-letter targeting
- Amex on Facebook
- IKEA rich media ads
- Macy's TrueFit tool
- Estee Lauder's virtual makeover
- Sephora's color view
- AT&T social outreach on Facebook and Twitter
- Apple EasyPay app
- Nordstrom Pinterest board
- Nespresso club
- Esprit/CVS virtual loyalty cards
- In-store pickup

SOURCE: McKinsey

### Social media GRP

To put social media on equal terms with other media and enable companies to assess their social media performance relative to competitors, McKinsey has transferred the well-known concept of gross rating points (GRPs) from traditional media to social media. GRPs measure the advertising intensity of a campaign or activity in its target group. They are calculated by multiplying reach (reached share in target group) with frequency (number of campaign contacts in target group). To accommodate the specific nature of social media, our approach counts

> all posts mentioning a company on a given platform, taking into account the reach of every post. Drawing on a wide range of sources – such as social media monitoring, panel data, and Facebook insights – a GRP value represents an integrated KPI. Additionally, GPR analysis captures sentiment – the attitude towards the brand or company in question expressed in a given post. This provides companies with additional insights into how their messages resonate with their target group.
>
> In a recent case, this analysis was used to calculate the magnitude of negative buzz in social media and its effect on customer acquisition (-8 percent) along with its root cause: poor customer service. Based on these insights, the company was able to derive a set of targeted countermeasures. (See McKinsey's publication »Turning buzz into gold« – available through the authors of this book – for details).

### Customer insights

Digital natives are very generous when it comes to information about their likes and dislikes, their needs and preferences, even their purchasing behavior. While they browse and shop, consumers generate millions of data points. These include transactions, click-stream pathways, and preferences posted online, such as »likes« on Facebook, or retweets on Twitter. This wealth of information has given rise to new approaches to market research that are based on real-life consumer behavior. Within the boundaries of data protection acts and privacy regulation, digital platforms offer rich opportunities for companies to gather insights about current and potential customers. Social listening services help companies mine the depth of blogs, message boards, and social networks for messages mentioning a brand, a product, or a company. Other types of service providers build communities or panels of users who receive coupons or free product samples in exchange for feedback on their brand and product experience.

Additionally, there is a window of opportunity for digital idea generation and product development. Procter & Gamble is among the pioneers in this field. A decade ago, the company initiated its »Connect+Develop« program, declaring that 50 percent of all future product innovations should leverage external idea generation.[40] As a key component of the program, Procter & Gamble set up their own social platform to invite contributions and discussions from dedicated consumers and professionals. Ideas are logged in the company's »Eureka Catalog« on the corporate intranet, accessible to executives and R&D teams worldwide who gauge the business potential of submissions. One of the innovations that originated from the program was the Swiffer range of cleaning products, collectively contributing about a billion dollars in annual sales.

### Digital marketing

It took most brands some time to adapt to the world of digital marketing. Today, however, many companies allocate substantial shares of their marketing budget to digital media. The global net advertising market for digital channels is now worth more than USD 100 billion,[41] and its share of all advertising is still growing. Online display advertising more than doubled in the US and more than quadrupled in the UK between 2003 and 2013,[42] while investments in TV and print advertising stagnated or decreased over the same period. All over Europe, online advertising keeps growing at the expense of traditional media (Figure 4.33). Mobile advertising is the fastest-growing vehicle by far. Print advertising, in particular, is suffering from the growing budgets allocated to online vehicles such as search engine and mobile marketing (Figure 4.34). In 2013, global mobile advertising revenue jumped to USD 19 billion, according to a new report from the Interactive Advertising Bureau, IAB Europe, and research firm IHS. North America captured the largest share at 42 percent, followed by Asia-Pacific at 39 percent. The growing importance of mobile advertising is also apparent in the revenue mix of leading online players. eMarketer predicts that mobile advertising will contribute 68 percent to Facebook's advertising revenues in the US in 2014, up from 47 percent in 2013. According to *The Wall Street Journal*, eMarketer also predicts that by 2016, Google's mobile advertising business will account for over half its ad revenues.[43]

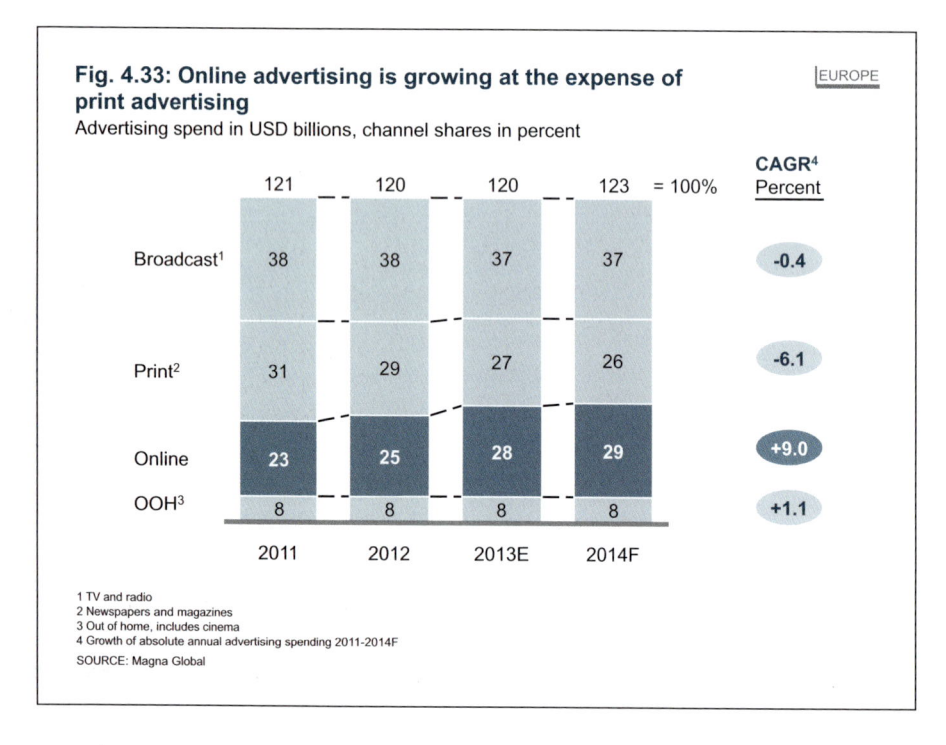

**Fig. 4.33: Online advertising is growing at the expense of print advertising**
Advertising spend in USD billions, channel shares in percent

EUROPE

| | 2011 | 2012 | 2013E | 2014F | CAGR[4] Percent |
|---|---|---|---|---|---|
| Total | 121 | 120 | 120 | 123 = 100% | |
| Broadcast[1] | 38 | 38 | 37 | 37 | -0.4 |
| Print[2] | 31 | 29 | 27 | 26 | -6.1 |
| Online | 23 | 25 | 28 | 29 | +9.0 |
| OOH[3] | 8 | 8 | 8 | 8 | +1.1 |

1 TV and radio
2 Newspapers and magazines
3 Out of home, includes cinema
4 Growth of absolute annual advertising spending 2011-2014F
SOURCE: Magna Global

Digital marketing, however, is much more than a question of budget level and allocation. It has triggered nothing short of a paradigm shift. Traditional terms like »above-the-line« and »below-the-line« are insufficient to capture and manage the multitude that is digital marketing. Today's landscape comprises »bought« media, such as paid online advertising or search engine marketing, »earned« social media, such as blogs and Facebook, and »owned« media, such as a company's own Web site or service portal. All of these can be platforms for effective brand building.

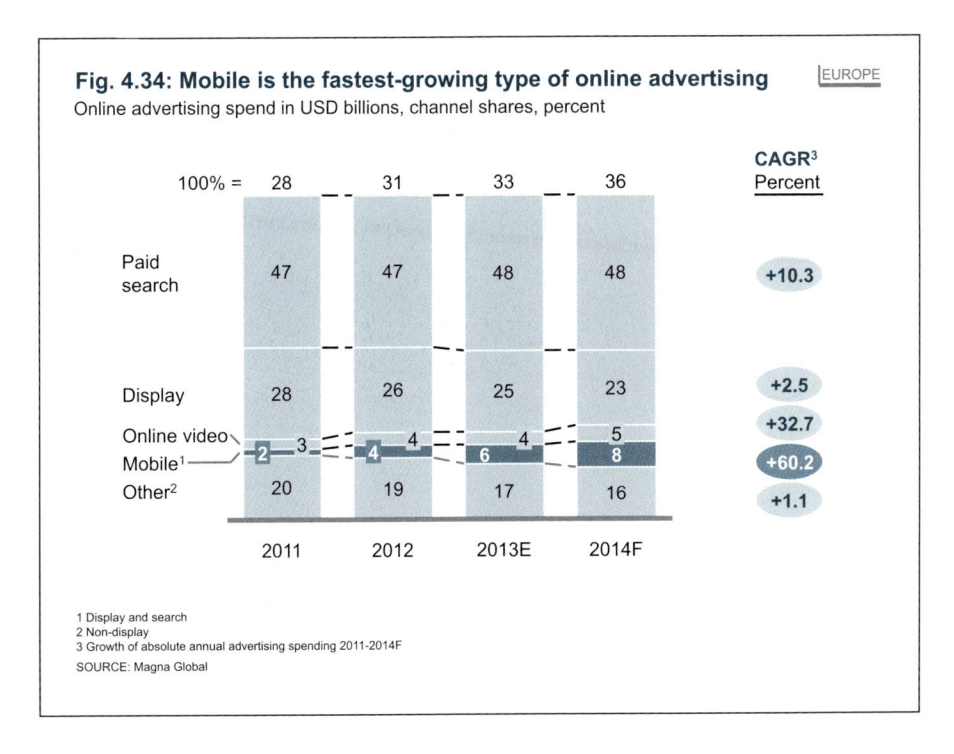

**Fig. 4.34: Mobile is the fastest-growing type of online advertising** [EUROPE]
Online advertising spend in USD billions, channel shares, percent

| | 2011 | 2012 | 2013E | 2014F | CAGR[3] Percent |
|---|---|---|---|---|---|
| 100% = | 28 | 31 | 33 | 36 | |
| Paid search | 47 | 47 | 48 | 48 | +10.3 |
| Display | 28 | 26 | 25 | 23 | +2.5 |
| Online video | 3 | 4 | 4 | 5 | +32.7 |
| Mobile[1] | 2 | 4 | 6 | 8 | +60.2 |
| Other[2] | 20 | 19 | 17 | 16 | +1.1 |

1 Display and search
2 Non-display
3 Growth of absolute annual advertising spending 2011-2014F
SOURCE: Magna Global

Examples of good practices in digital marketing include:

- American Express driving interest in new card applications by inviting social media users to share their passion for charitable causes on a dedicated Web platform, »The Members' Project.« The initiative has attracted millions of new unique visitors to the Amex Facebook page and also resulted in free TV coverage.[44]
- Ikea employing rich media advertising as an online embodiment of its do-it-yourself philosophy. Players of the award-winning »Unbox the banner« game receive discounts for assembling the ad themselves, following a typical Ikea-style manual. One in four participants clicks through to the Ikea Web store.[45]

The paradigm shift we are witnessing brings powerful new digital marketing vehicles, such as retargeting, real-time bidding (RTB), and shopping links embedded in online versions of consumer magazines. What is more, it also brings new metrics and new operational requirements. On the one hand, digital marketing benefits from more precise and more direct MROI measurement than ever before; compare the discussion of attribution modeling in Section 4.2 on MROI. On the other hand, marketing managers also need to adapt their operating mode. Online marketing is not just about finding digital equivalents to offline channels. Online media planning, targeting, and payment models differ substantially from those employed in the offline world. Search engine advertising, for example, is procured through live auctions based on preselected keywords, an advertiser's willingness to pay, and the expected yield on a given space.[46]

Digital marketing vehicles differ from more traditional media not only in terms of procurement and operations, but also in terms of service provider management. In the past, most brand managers used to work with a single media agency that took care of all media buying for them. Today, there are specialists for almost every digital marketing vehicle, and marketing departments depend on their expert knowledge, as well as on their command of specific advertising planning and budget management tools. Compare our insert on media and communication management below.

**Digital sales**

Should a given brand sell online? In some categories, consumer behavior does not leave brand managers much of a choice. In a retail survey conducted by McKinsey in 2012, »can be easily reached« emerged as the second most important market driver, trumped only by »the store I trust most.«[47] And these days, easy accessibility equals online shopping for an increasing number of customers. A few categories have already »gone to digital« for all practical purposes; examples include computers, consumer electronics, and video games. In these categories, both pre-purchase research and the purchase itself happen online in more than 50 percent of all cases, as examined in McKinsey's proprietary iConsumer survey. And other categories are catching up quickly. When considering the purchase of a large appliance or a mobile phone, about half of all shoppers conduct online research before they make their choice. The actual purchase, however, still happens in stores in the majority of cases. These and similar categories collectively constitute the »digital battleground.« They will see fierce competition for the growing share of online purchases in the immediate future. A third group of product categories is currently »still in store,« usually because consumers associate too high a risk with online purchases in these categories. This may be due to substantial variations in product quality or high product complexity. In most countries, this is true for groceries (Figure 4.35).

These inherent differences between categories indicate that not every type of product is equally suited for digital sales. Yet even some complex and heterogeneous products can be made to appear tangible and tempting online with the help of detailed information and multimedia presentation. In their efforts to differentiate their offering and create added value for consumers, digital sales pioneers often go beyond an ordinary online product presentation:

- Macy's helps shoppers find the apparel brands, products, and sizes that fit them well through its proprietary TrueFit tool. Based on a shopper's personal profile, the software provides a rating of how suitable a given item is for the person's body and recommends the appropriate size.[48]
- Estee Lauder provides users with a virtual makeover tool, Taaz, on the brand's Web site. It enables prospective buyers to upload their photo and try the effects of various combinations of makeup and hair color prior to making a purchase. The results can be saved, printed, and shared on networking sites.[49]
- Sephora tracks past purchases and samples a user has tried to generate targeted offers, filtered by up to 25 criteria that include target age, ingredients, and price. Recommended products are displayed by »color views« that provide an impression of how the color in question will look on the user's skin.[50]

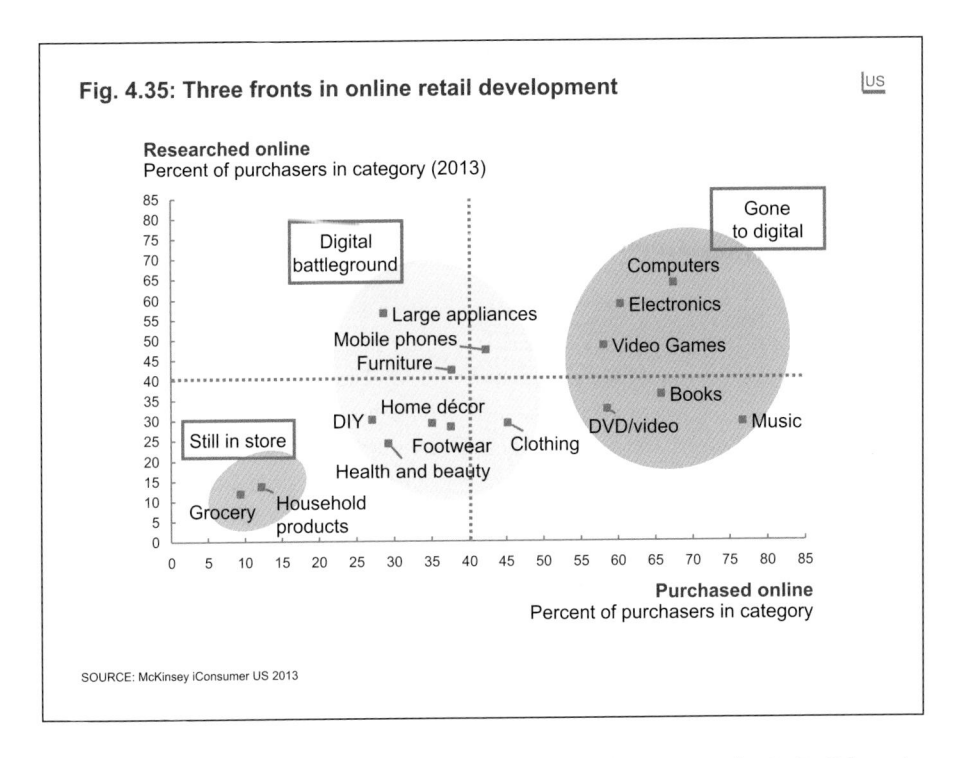

**Fig. 4.35: Three fronts in online retail development** — US

Researched online
Percent of purchasers in category (2013)

- Digital battleground: Large appliances, Mobile phones, Furniture
- Gone to digital: Computers, Electronics, Video Games, Books, DVD/video, Music
- Still in store: Grocery, Household products, DIY, Home décor, Footwear, Clothing, Health and beauty

Purchased online
Percent of purchasers in category

SOURCE: McKinsey iConsumer US 2013

The question whether to sell online at all is particularly pressing for B2B2C brands, that is, manufacturers of consumer products who do not have their own offline store network and work with retailers to reach consumers. To make the call, executives of B2B2C players will want to employ the following criteria:

- What is the value at stake for our brand if we start selling online?
- Is our brand strong enough to support and sustain its own online sales?
- To what extent will online sales threaten or substitute existing offline sales?

So far, most manufacturers of consumer goods have not yet dared to launch their own digital sales channel – but there are some exceptions. Fiji offers online shoppers an annual subscription for bottled water at a discount of up to 30 percent on regular prices.[51] Subscribers receive convenient monthly deliveries of 12, 24, or 36 bottles. Evian offers a similar service, »Chez Vous,« that comes with its own »Smart Drop« wireless ordering device.[52] In contrast, Levis uses a Facebook plug-in to re-create the experience of shopping with friends in a physical store.[53] Users can share their decision journey with their network of friends, seek recommendations, and comment on each other's choices.

Finally, before any brand starts selling online, a clear definition of the role of the prospective e-commerce channel is required: Is it primarily meant to stimulate overall sales, possibly even as a cost center that acts as a marketing vehicle? Or should the Web shop pay for itself and drive profitability, for example, by cutting out retail partners? Depending on the answers to these questions, brand managers may have to adjust their offline cost structure as well. Once the overall purpose of an online channel is defined, digital sales managers need to select and profile their online target segments, choose the products to be made available for online sales, specify their digital go-to-market approach, and spell out the digital operating model. Specifically, they will want to develop an organizational structure that provides sufficient freedom and supports the fast decision-making processes any online channel needs to succeed. When a major competitor launches a ground-breaking mobile shopping app, or a new entrant changes the rules of the game by cutting out intermediaries altogether, there may simply not be enough time to call a committee meeting. Within reasonable limits, online brand managers must be free to act swiftly, test new ways of working, and counter competitive action.

### Digital services

Using digital media as a service channel can drive customer satisfaction, strengthen brand loyalty, and even help reduce service costs – provided digital channels are generally accepted, well established, and frequently used by customers in a given market.

### Multichannel excellence

Despite the game-changing potential of digital development, many traditional brands struggle with integrated multichannel strategies, especially if brick-and-mortar stores remain an important element in their channel mix. Online and offline channels may move at different speeds and follow different rules, but today's customers are not either offline customers or online customers anymore. They switch channels at will, even during the same decision journey, for example, by researching products and prices online prior to a purchase in a physical store. This phenomenon has become known and hyped as ROPO (research online, purchase offline). But in reality, its opposite is no less common: customers may visit a physical store to sample fragrances or try on clothes, but they end up ordering their product of choice from an online player.

In recognition of hybrid customer behavior, digital brand management needs to play its role as one aspect of multichannel management. Pioneering players differentiate their propositions by linking their digital offering to their physical stores, and vice versa. In fact, the creative interplay of channels may give multichannel operators an edge over pure players. Examples of creative multichannel management include:

- **Rewards.** McDonald's delivers coupons for discounts or free products directly to a registered user's phone. Guests can redeem coupons simply by passing their phone over near-field communication (NFC) reader next to the register. The same touch-free technology is used to sign up for the program.[56]
- **Social shopping.** Nordstrom, the apparel company, has set up dozens of themed boards on Pinterest, the photo sharing site. Boards are updated as seasons and collections change. At the time of writing, Nordstrom had attracted almost 4.5 million followers on Pinterest. In stores, Nordstrom labels »top pinned items« to help shoppers identify online favorites.[57]

- **Cross-channel club.** Nespresso, the coffee company, operates a small network of premium stores in urban locations that are as much lighthouses of the brand as they are retail outlets. To achieve coverage, the physical network is complemented by the company's online store and a mobile app that allows Nespresso club members to order coffee capsules and schedule delivery.[58]
- **In-store pickup.** Bed, Bath & Beyond, the household goods retailer, has fully integrated its e-commerce channel with its network of physical stores. An easy-to-use interface enables customers to order online, locate the nearest store, and pick up their purchase there or select home delivery. Thanks to the seamless shopping experience, almost half the company's sales now originate online.[59]

Some of the more advanced multichannel loyalty programs have already abandoned the concept of a physical loyalty card and rely on smartphone apps instead. Such apps act as virtual loyalty cards and can be used to collect and redeem rewards both offline and online. Examples include Esprit's »Friends« program and the virtual »ExtraCare« loyalty app offered by CVS. Most recently, CVS even introduced tailored versions of its weekly specials for ExtraCare members. *The New York Times* reports that the »initiative, under the rubric of myWeekly Ad, will use data gathered by CVS from Extra-Care members' purchases to do things like suggest sale items based on previous purchases and make available in one place all ExtraCare savings and rewards offers.«[60]

Multichannel marketing can even be the source of tongue-in-cheek humor. Imitating Apple's highly ritualized product presentations, Ikea introduced its 2015 printed catalogue as a ground-breaking gadget, the so-called »bookbook«, highlighting its unique features: A light-weight, wireless device with eternal battery life, instantaneous page loading, and easy bookmarking functionality. Within 24 hours, the viral video got more than 1.5 million views. After a week, it had hit the eight million mark.[61]

**Which success factors are critical for competitive differentiation in the world of digital brand management?**

The challenges of brand management in the digital world are numerous and substantial, but the vast opportunities for value creation make it well worth the while. As detailed in the examples above, there are many specific opportunities along the consumer's journey. More generally, there is also a set of overarching success factors for digital transformation efforts. These apply irrespective of the specific value creation opportunity at hand – be it big or small – and will help sustain the impact of digital brand management in an environment characterized by fierce competition from energetic new players and their quickly evolving business models.

- **Innovation.** Winning players succeed by standing out from the crowd – be it through mutually beneficial partnerships, value-added propositions and services, or by beating pure players at their own game in a specific segment or niche.
- **Boldness.** Many companies see digitalization as a threat and underestimate its potential for brand building. E-commerce is by no means the only opportunity. A digital presence can also drive brand equity, aid offline sales, and build loyalty.

- **Flexibility.** Digital transformation is not a one-off effort, but a continuing challenge. As new brands and business models appear on the scene, only those who think on their feet will attract visitors and convert them into loyal shoppers.
- **Integration.** Consumers cut across channels, and so should brand managers. It takes a true multichannel approach to ensure the brand is activated consistently offline and online, regardless of the respective roles of these channels.
- **Insight.** The potential of big data is vast, but data does not equal insight. Brand managers must employ best-in-class data gathering and analysis techniques to generate the kinds of insights that will add value to each customer interaction.
- **Delivery.** Operational excellence is the top loyalty driver in the digital world. If you disappoint your customers once, you may never see them again. So keep your promises every step of the way, from transparent pricing to hassle-free returns.
- **Readiness.** Most organizations are averse to change. To pull off a digital transformation, companies need to rethink their entire structure, talent pool, capabilities, and HR processes. Top management should lead the way.
- **Speed.** Being the first mover is an asset in many contexts, but in digital brand management, it is essential. Network effects and the dynamics of peer-to-peer recommendations lead to disproportionate rewards for early movers.

If they play by these rules, companies will be able to cash in on the clicks their brands attract – generating real brand equity and hard cash from digital activities, not just the funny money that abounds in the virtual realms of games and simulations. The online world may be special in many ways, but it has long become far more than a playground. Thirty years have passed since the introduction of the PC. The Internet as we know it took shape 20 years ago. Even smartphones have been around for more than a decade now. It is high time to get serious and subject the digital domain to the same standards of effectiveness and efficiency as any other channel.

When you read this, chances are that new fads will have come and gone. By paradoxical necessity, any discussion of online phenomena – such as social networks – in offline media – like this book – will be old even when it's new. Still, we are confident that the principles laid out above will stand the test of time, even as some of the instruments and applications change.

## 4.5 The Brand Cockpit: Collecting and Using Data Systematically and Effectively

Marketing and financial control: are they even compatible with each other? In modern, professionally managed companies, the financial controller supervises even the most remote links in the chain of value creation – including materials purchasing and processing/manufacturing all the way to sales and distribution. With the aid of division-specific indicators, the effectiveness and efficiency of decisions, activities, processes, and contracts are analyzed and audited to maximize company success. On a regular basis – at the end of the month or quarter at the latest – the management board requests controlling data on the profit contribution of its profit centers and the efficiency of its cost centers. It concludes its work at the end of the day, confident that the financial department will continue to closely monitor all business areas the following day. But does it really monitor all of them? Not quite. The marketing department was one of the last corporate functions to be subject to controlling mechanisms. For example, the standard reference, *Measuring Brand Communication RoI* by Don E. Schultz of Northwestern University, first came out in 1997.[62]

If the marketing department has not managed to avoid the grasp of financial control completely, it often happens that the only thing that gets checked is budget compliance. Until very recently, few chief financial officers demanded fact-based arguments regarding the order of magnitude of expenditure or its distribution between the various media and campaigns. The problem has been that it is unclear what financial indicators should be used. As a result, even »old hands« such as David Ogilvy complain about the lack of advertising effectiveness.

Even when the marketing department documents the effectiveness of its own activities and expenditures – by tracking advertising or surveys of brand awareness, for instance – there is almost never any kind of coordination with the controlling department. This can lead to discrepancies between the two departments' views of the actual expenditure. Despite widespread efforts of brand managers to improve MROI, there is still major variation in the ratio of advertising spending to sales. For example, ad-to-sales ratios varied between 2.2 and 8.1 for pay-TV players, or 3.6 to 7.9 for pharmaceutical companies in the US in 2013 (Figure 4.36). This raises the question whether some players are using their funds more efficiently than others, and whether there is room for improvement for the big spenders. Or take the example of the car industry. In Germany, why did Toyota spend more than three times as much as Volkswagen on above-the-line advertising per newly registered vehicle at some point?[63] Admittedly, this type of question is hard to answer in any meaningful detail. Besides, the ad-to-sales ratio – or even share of voice versus share of market – is only a rough indicator of whether spending is in the right neighborhood. But how do you even get to a state of affairs where you know exactly how much you're spending, what you're spending it on, and what the money is or isn't doing for you?

Obviously, transparency is key. In many companies, there is hardly any clarity in terms of objectives, in the desired content of the marketing campaign and expenditures, or in success in marketing or brand communication. Despite heated discussions of content and implementation, how many companies have launched expensive advertising campaigns that weren't based on any kind of clear measurement parameters?

Although this situation – in which advertising expenditure appears wildly variable in nature – is unsustainable in the longer term as CEOs come to demand the same control over marketing as over other areas of their business, it is nonetheless understandable to some extent. Measuring marketing effectiveness and efficiency is more difficult than in other areas for at least two reasons.

**Fig. 4.36: There is a wide variation of ad-to-sales ratios even within individual industries** | US, 2013

**Pay TV**

| Company | Ad spending to sales Percent |
|---|---|
| Viacom | 8.1 |
| 21st Century Fox | 7.8 |
| Time Warner | 7.7 |
| Dish Network | 3.4 |
| DirecTV | 2.2 |

**Pharmaceuticals**

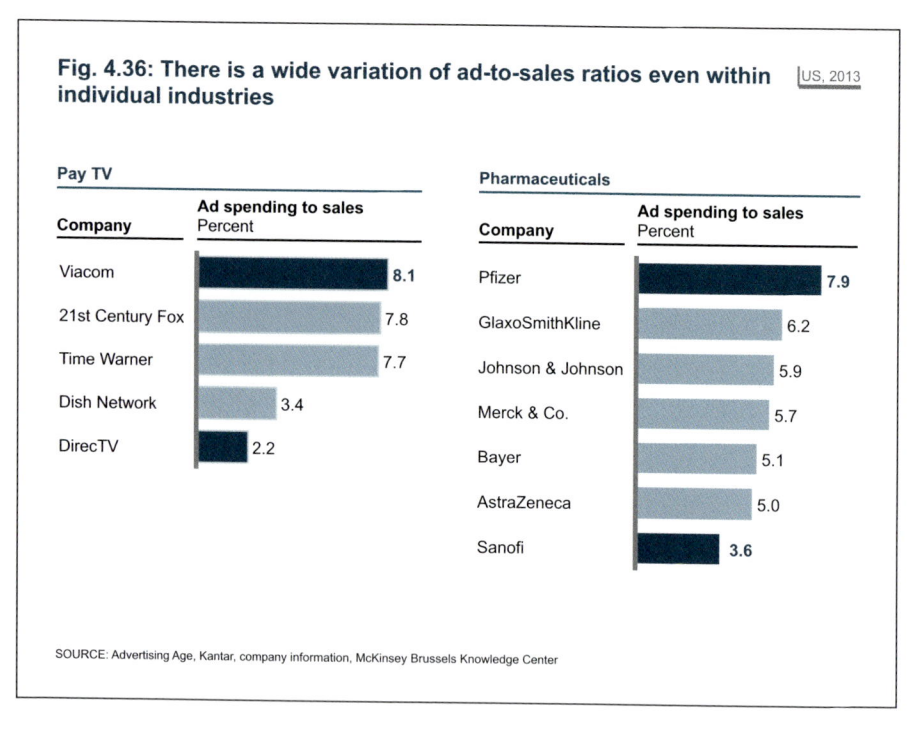

| Company | Ad spending to sales Percent |
|---|---|
| Pfizer | 7.9 |
| GlaxoSmithKline | 6.2 |
| Johnson & Johnson | 5.9 |
| Merck & Co. | 5.7 |
| Bayer | 5.1 |
| AstraZeneca | 5.0 |
| Sanofi | 3.6 |

SOURCE: Advertising Age, Kantar, company information, McKinsey Brussels Knowledge Center

First, marketing has an effect that is primarily indirect for many companies. Pricing, product design, and sales structures can be linked directly to established parameters such as number of units, revenues, or contract fulfillment. Marketing, however, typically has an indirect impact on success by building the brand. This »indirectness« often results in an almost fatalistic attitude about assessing the impact of marketing: »But it's something you can't even measure!«

Second, the fast pace of marketing also makes measuring difficult. Run times for advertising campaigns and promotions are typically much shorter than most product cycles, contract periods, or customer relationships. The automotive industry provides a good example of this.

The good news for management is that these challenges can be overcome through the use of financial indicators, key performance indicators, monitoring cycles, and control processes. Many large companies have already had positive experiences using such tools. The key to their success is a combination of three components:

- Systematically logging input (investment) and output (effectiveness) data at regular intervals.
- Providing actionable reporting that shows causal relationships between investment and effect.
- Ensuring targeted use of selected indicators for effectiveness and efficiency to inform decision making.

McKinsey calls the combination of these components the *brand cockpit* (Figure 4.37).

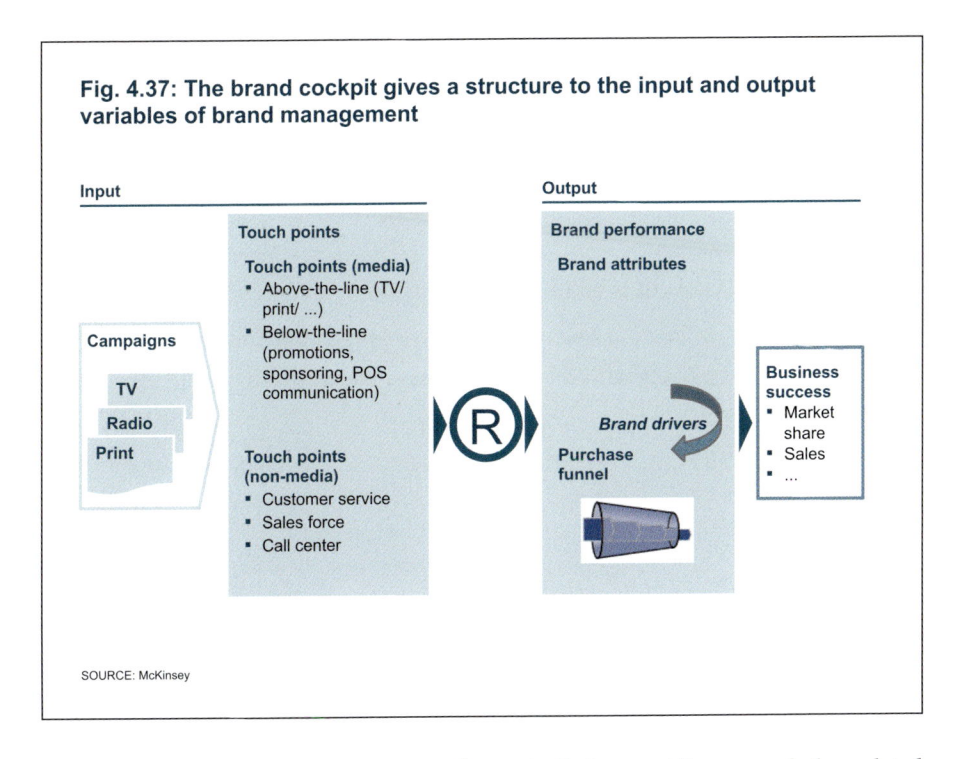

**Fig. 4.37: The brand cockpit gives a structure to the input and output variables of brand management**

Input:
- Campaigns
  - TV
  - Radio
  - Print
- Touch points
  - Touch points (media)
    - Above-the-line (TV/print/ ...)
    - Below-the-line (promotions, sponsoring, POS communication)
  - Touch points (non-media)
    - Customer service
    - Sales force
    - Call center

Output:
- Brand performance
- Brand attributes
- Brand drivers
- Purchase funnel
- Business success
  - Market share
  - Sales
  - ...

SOURCE: McKinsey

A brand cockpit increases transparency dramatically by providing a regularly updated representation of brand communication or marketing activities according to expenditures and results. This information enables financial controlling and management to direct the effectiveness and efficiency of marketing. The concept of MROI – as discussed in Section 4.2 – provides the contextual framework for fact-based brand management. The brand cockpit should be understood as the next stage of brand development and as a universal brand management tool. Think of the brand cockpit as the hard-wired version of an MROI effort: not as a single project, but as an ongoing process embedded in the company. The highest level of development is an integrated marketing cockpit detailing comprehensive data and interrelationships, including content and monetary input – campaigns, expenditures for communication, and other elements of a marketing mix – and their effects on brand image, drivers, purchase funnel performance, and company earnings.

This may be the point when the marketing manager – who works largely independently of financial control – slams the book shut and hopes that it never occurs to the management board or the controlling unit to seriously consider implementing such »technocratic whims.« This is why it is important to emphasize once again that successful brand management is dependent on the combination of *art, science,* and *craft.* Although the brand cockpit is referred to here as the pinnacle of quantitative brand management, this is not to say that creative work should be given up in favor of automated marketing management. Controlling of performance figures is a necessary but not sufficient means. No one would conduct a brand campaign as if it were a form of production planning or product life cycle management. Automating brand management not only carries the danger of producing countless »me-too« campaigns, which will quickly become ineffective. It would also make brand management unattractive to young marketing executives. No marketing department can survive without a constant influx of new creative managers – reason enough to stay away from a »science only« approach.

## The brand cockpit provides transparency and control

Once correctly installed and maintained, the brand cockpit offers users fact-based insights into three problem areas: input transparency, output transparency, and performance assessment.

*Input transparency.* A brand cockpit needs to ensure that the objectives, content (messages and campaigns), spending, and customer touch points of brand communication or marketing are compiled and depicted systematically over time. This supports financial control by providing clarity about the when, what, and where of marketing spending. It shows what amount of expenditure is directed to which target group. Depending on the sector, this might include current and potential customers, dealers, and distribution partners. The core of the cockpit's function is to categorize expenditures according to clearly defined customer touch points (Figure 4.38). Which of the individual customer touch points are involved depends largely on the type of business (e.g., B2C versus B2B, contract-based versus case-by-case purchase decisions) as well as on market size, products, target groups, legal regulations, geographic features, and on the nature of the company itself.

To lend some structure to the wide range of marketing and communication vehicles, the brand cockpit differentiates between above-the-line and below-the-line communication on the one hand and non-media touch points on the other. High precision is necessary initially in compiling campaign and spending data so as to maximize input transparency. It pays to think ahead about how to represent the defined touch points in effectiveness-oriented market research projects. What marketing manager wouldn't like to know what the company's head of distribution support wants to do with EUR 3 million for »point-of-sales materials«? At the same time, it is impossible to examine the impact of every single flyer without spending a disproportionate amount of time and money on the analysis.

*Output transparency.* As with the objectives, content, spending, and customer touch points on the input side, companies need to systematically compile and interpret data and information regarding developments directly or indirectly influenced by brand communication and marketing activities in order to make interrelationships between input and output transparent. This data includes overall brand image performance, the most important brand drivers in the purchase funnel, and the performance of the brand in the purchase funnel itself. The second output category – not always directly linked to brand performance – is the development of economic indicators such as revenues or market share by brand. Any interrelationships that have been ascertained

### Fig. 4.38: Checklist of possible customer touch points

| Category | | Touch points |
|---|---|---|
| **Communication** | Above-the-line | • TV (commercials, presentations)<br>• Print (newspapers, magazines, inserts)<br>• Radio<br>• Cinema<br>• Outdoor<br>• Banner (online)<br>• … |
| | Below-the-line | • Public relations<br>• Sponsoring (sports, entertainment)<br>• Trade fairs/exhibitions<br>• Points of sale (e.g., posters, displays)<br>• Promotions<br>• Direct marketing<br>• Customer communication (e.g., customer magazine)<br>• … |
| **Other parameters** | Experience (rather than communication) | • Sales support<br>• Promotion allowances (partly media-related)<br>• Discounts and bonuses<br>• Call center<br>• … |

SOURCE: McKinsey

through onetime or repeat market research can be integrated into the structure and the priorities of the cockpit. Such data might include, for instance, the touch points that influence specific brand attributes, the media that influence the various individual stages of the purchase funnel, the elements that drive customer transfer through the purchase funnel, and the financial indicators that are influenced (where possible, directly) by specific marketing activities.

Like the input factors, the output factors need to be differentiated according to company, brand, business model, product, and so on. The relevant brand drivers, structure of the purchase funnel, and economic indicators depend largely on the nature of the business involved; for instance, whether the company and its marketing are targeting private or business customers, or whether the business model revolves around relatively long-term contracts (e.g., pay-TV, subscriptions, mobile communication services), occasional large acquisitions (e.g., cars, household appliances), or repeat single purchases (e.g., fast-moving consumer goods and retail).

*Performance assessment.* The function of a brand cockpit from the perspective of management and financial controlling is to check the effectiveness and efficiency of marketing spending. Depending on the stage of cockpit development and the availability of data, there are three principal options for integrating the cockpit into the company's overall performance management system:

- The first is to assess performance relative to targets: Are activities as effective and efficient as expected?

- The second is to assess performance relative to earlier time periods: Are they more effective/efficient than last year?
- The third is to assess performance relative to competitors: Are they as effective as those of the strongest competitor?

The systematic monitoring of performance using what is perhaps the simplest reference parameter, the company's own targets, is often very enlightening – not lastly because such an approach forces the company to specify concrete targets for itself, its brands, and its products in advance.

**The heart of the cockpit: Deriving key performance indicators**

Let's now focus on the main task and the *raison d'être* of the brand cockpit: the sustainable assessment, control, and optimization of the effectiveness and efficiency of marketing spending. To support fact-based decisions about marketing expenditure, the cockpit must help create meaningful key performance indicators (KPIs). With the help of action-oriented scorecards, these will be used to answer questions about the performance of the marketing function.

Figures 4.39 and 4.40 provide typical examples of questions about marketing expenditures and corresponding KPIs categorized in terms of whether they relate to effectiveness or to efficiency.[64]

*Effectiveness.* Did our most recent campaign achieve the intended target awareness of 70 percent among 14 to 49 year olds? Did we achieve an improvement in brand perception in the main loyalty driver »forward-looking«? The corresponding KPIs can be calculated, for instance, as the awareness growth ratio over the course of the campaign, or as the ratio of actual-to-desired score for the driver »forward-looking.« Leading companies include not only funnel performance, but also actual economic impact – such as sales, market share, or net customer gains – in their set of effectiveness KPIs, even if these are not under the marketing department's exclusive control. Holding marketing executives accountable for the performance of the company as a whole is, after all, as much a question of mindset as it is one of controlling.

*Efficiency.* What is the connection between brand or marketing spending and revenues? How much did the increase in awareness cost? How much was spent on below-the-line efforts in the past quarter per percentage point of additional buying propensity? Corresponding KPIs might include the ratio of brand or marketing spending to revenues or company earnings, the percentage increase in awareness relative to total advertising expenditure, or the ratio of below-the-line expenditure to the increase in »propensity to buy« in the brand funnel in terms of percentage points per quarter. Much more complex interrelationships can also be translated into performance indicators, such as the relationship between brand spending and the company's business results as indicated, for instance, by shareholder value. Note, however, that even sophisticated KPIs cannot capture the exact correlation between input and output. For that purpose, marketing mix modeling is required. Compare our discussion in Section 4.2.

## 4.5 The Brand Cockpit: Collecting and Using Data Systematically and Effectively

**Fig. 4.39: Performance indicators for campaign tracking** — ILLUSTRATIVE

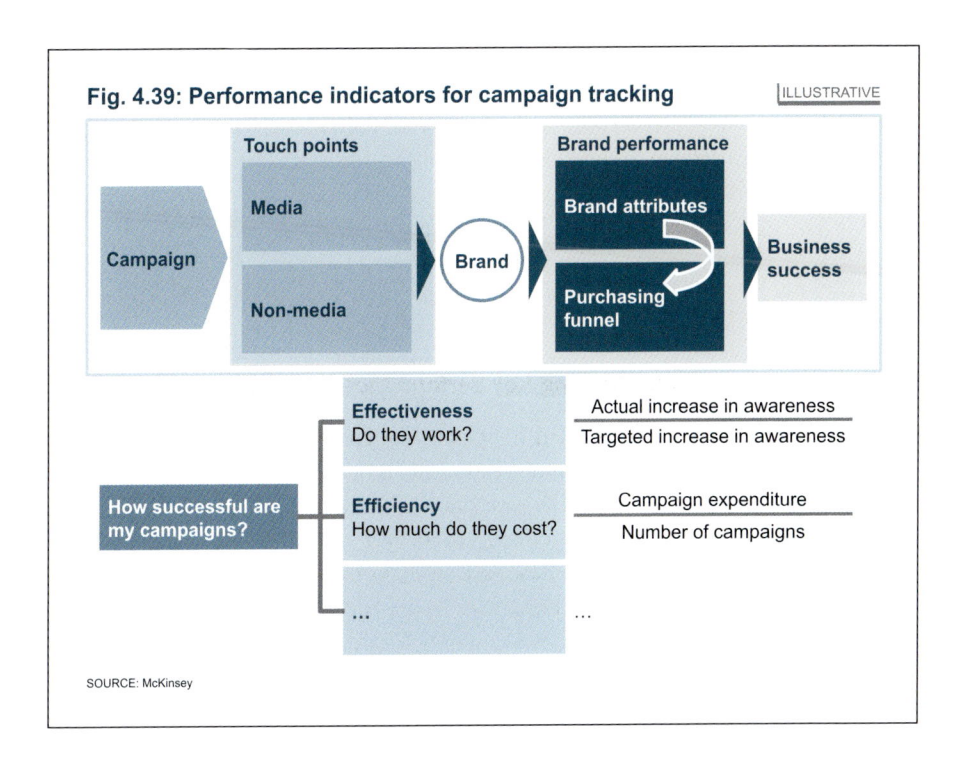

Campaign → Touch points (Media, Non-media) → Brand → Brand performance (Brand attributes, Purchasing funnel) → Business success

How successful are my campaigns?
- **Effectiveness** — Do they work?
  - Actual increase in awareness
  - Targeted increase in awareness
- **Efficiency** — How much do they cost?
  - Campaign expenditure
  - Number of campaigns
- …

SOURCE: McKinsey

**Fig. 4.40: Performance indicators for brand management** — ILLUSTRATIVE

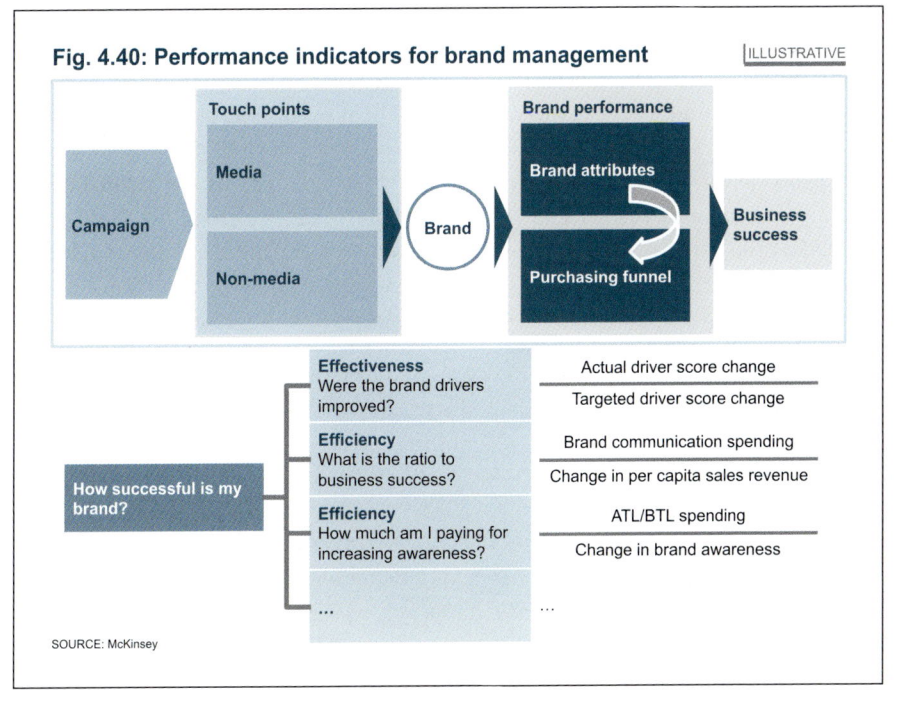

Campaign → Touch points (Media, Non-media) → Brand → Brand performance (Brand attributes, Purchasing funnel) → Business success

How successful is my brand?
- **Effectiveness** — Were the brand drivers improved?
  - Actual driver score change
  - Targeted driver score change
- **Efficiency** — What is the ratio to business success?
  - Brand communication spending
  - Change in per capita sales revenue
- **Efficiency** — How much am I paying for increasing awareness?
  - ATL/BTL spending
  - Change in brand awareness
- …

SOURCE: McKinsey

A scorecard based on these KPIs – generated semiannually or annually for the director of marketing, the marketing controller, or, depending on the organizational design, even the CEO – might include, for instance, two sets of data on input and effect over a specified period of time. The input side would include marketing spending categorized by touch points and campaign; the output side would show change in brand awareness or achievement of brand awareness targets and the three most important brand drivers in the purchase funnel. Such an overview makes it easy to see whether marketing expenditures were successful in reaching their targets over the specified period of time, as indicated by objective performance criteria. If corrections are necessary, marketing managers can use the detailed KPIs to derive options for optimizing the amount and mix of expenditures. The higher up in the organization a given user of the brand cockpit resides, the more important aggregated indicators – such as total marketing spending over sales, or actual brand awareness over targeted brand awareness – will become. While full clarity regarding input and output is important for day-to-day marketing management, top management will be looking for composite performance indicators, relative to predefined targets, to other brands in the company's portfolio, or to competitors. Some executives find it easier to make sense of the KPIs when they are visualized as a color-coded scale – for example, in the form of a traffic light.

The objectives include product-, brand-, customer-, and capabilities-oriented categories and therefore encompass more than a mere brand tracking tool. The corresponding KPIs need to be selected based on the following criteria:

- *Actionability*: Does the KPI enable decision making, such as budget allocation or activity prioritization?
- *Controllability*: Does it improve the influence of the respective stakeholder?
- *Educational effect*: Does tracking or monitoring the KPI improve the brand orientation of the organization?
- *Data availability*: Can the KPI data be easily acquired or generated, either internally or externally?
- *Comparability*: Does the KPI metric allow for consistent application and comparison across businesses, brands, and markets?

**No turnkey cockpit solutions**

A cockpit's degree of detail, structural complexity, data collection frequency, and graphic interface depend largely on the underlying economic and organizational conditions. A standardized brand cockpit does not and will never exist, as any turnkey solution will fall short of the specific marketing requirements of a company's brand or brands. The content, structure, update frequency, and organizational integration of a well-designed cockpit should reflect the company's specific strengths and challenges. The brand cockpit for the management board of a large international conglomerate with numerous single brands will obviously differ from the cockpit for a single-country consumer goods producer with one brand or the cockpit used by the marketing department for tracking the performance of a particular campaign. Yet, solutions catering to these different types of demand can, of course, be integrated into a modular »master« cockpit. It is important, however, to balance the costs of data collection with the required level of detail or timeliness of the data carefully. The finest, most detailed cockpit is useless if its upkeep requires an entire department, thus making it prohibitively expensive.

Overall responsibility for the cockpit should rest at senior level, above functional interests, and may be supported by internal or external auditing as necessary. Leading companies have established functional controlling as the default owner of the brand cockpit to ensure that both financial and functional expertise go into its design and maintenance. Functional controlling can either be part of the CFO's team or reside in the marketing function itself.

Regardless of the stage of cockpit development, it is always worthwhile to involve external partners, such as media and advertising agencies, early on in its design and execution. Especially with respect to the interaction of individual media, agencies are often good sources of conceptual and practical expertise whose potential should not go untapped. Agencies are also frequently helpful in reconciling different sources of data, such as gross versus net, spending versus placements, and so on. Cutting-edge companies even get their key providers to send them periodic hard-coded updates of market research or advertising tracking. By minimizing manual data entry, the brand cockpit becomes more cost efficient to maintain and less susceptible to reporting errors.

**The three stages of cockpit development**

Three stages of complexity and sophistication can be observed in the development of the brand cockpit, each of which makes different demands in terms of structure, content, and organizational foundation (Figure 4.41). The path of development from the early days of campaign tracking to a comprehensive brand cockpit, in other words, from the descriptive to the explanatory to the prescriptive, should always be understood as an iterative process. Refinement takes time; as the adage has it: »Learn to walk before you run.« In addition to the two basic cockpit modules, a more advanced and comprehensive marketing cockpit would reflect additional customer touch points, brand performance, and company success.

The first stage of development is that of tracking campaign success. This will indicate whether targets have been fulfilled over time, and whether the expenditure is warranted by the results. As part of this, it is also useful to use prelaunch tests to estimate the likely outcome of the campaign. Such prelaunch tests are often more effective in deriving causal relationships than extrapolating from the outcomes of previous campaigns. It is vital to track the campaign's success in terms of the effectiveness of the concept, its execution, and its compliance with the advertising schedule.

The second stage in the development of the brand cockpit is to move to tracking all spending at media-based customer touch points. Tracking should cover performance

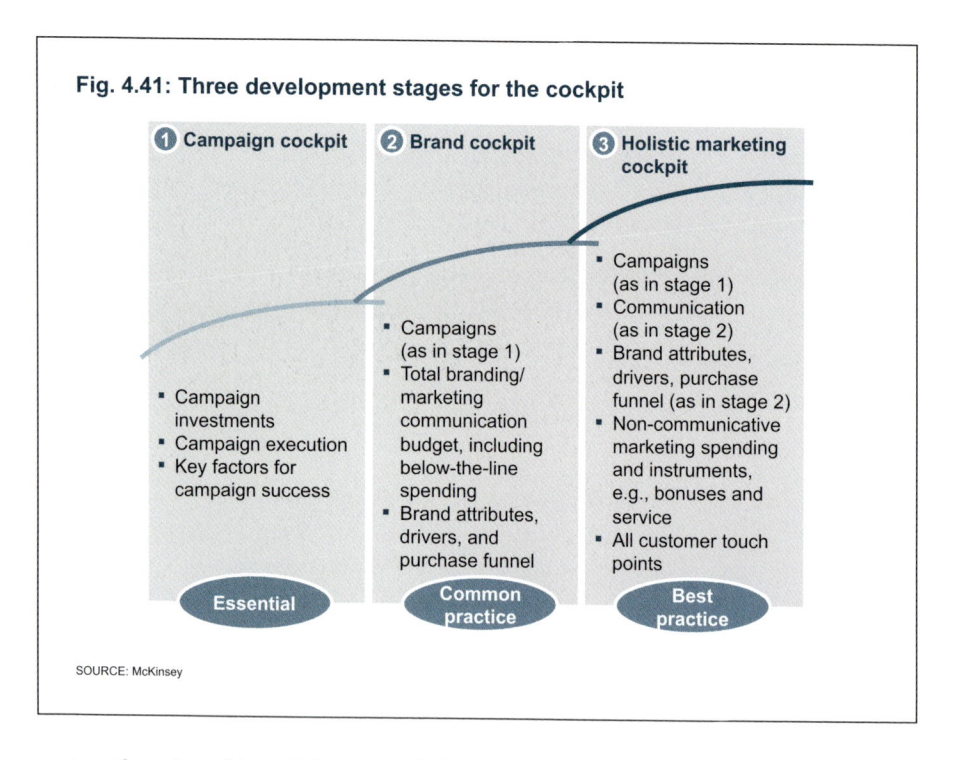

### Fig. 4.41: Three development stages for the cockpit

**① Campaign cockpit** — Essential
- Campaign investments
- Campaign execution
- Key factors for campaign success

**② Brand cockpit** — Common practice
- Campaigns (as in stage 1)
- Total branding/marketing communication budget, including below-the-line spending
- Brand attributes, drivers, and purchase funnel

**③ Holistic marketing cockpit** — Best practice
- Campaigns (as in stage 1)
- Communication (as in stage 2)
- Brand attributes, drivers, purchase funnel (as in stage 2)
- Non-communicative marketing spending and instruments, e.g., bonuses and service
- All customer touch points

SOURCE: McKinsey

metrics for selected brand drivers and the various stages of the purchase funnel. From the results, it is possible to derive content-related, touch-point-based interrelationships and correlations. This is essential for companies in marketing-intensive sectors or competitive environments, since it ensures that the marketing budget is invested at the most effective points and in a sufficient but not uneconomic manner. This data will provide the basis for the ongoing optimization of brand investments in the context of a company-wide optimization of MROI.

The third and final stage of refinement is a comprehensive brand cockpit that also includes non-media touch points and factors of influence. On the input side, this will cover investments for distribution channels, call centers, customer service, products, and prices – and all essential market performance indicators for all products, brands, and countries. This type of integrated marketing cockpit makes it possible to derive trade-offs between the individual cost and profit centers throughout the company. It

is also suitable as a component in a brand portfolio management system. Although this model is certainly ideal from a corporate point of view, it can only be the outcome of strategic customer management and might be beyond the skills and scope of most brand communication and marketing departments.

Generally speaking, it is as tempting as it is dangerous to go overboard with the level of detail and technical sophistication. Various departments are making demands on the scope of the cockpit. Marketing planners request features that enable them to slice and dice the data any way they want, enabling them to pull reports on a by brand, by product, by country, by type of advertising spending, by campaign – essentially, a by anything – basis. If the IT department is involved, chances are they will get excited about the user interface and, more importantly, the technical back end of the cockpit. Before you know it, they will be implementing hotlinks to the company's data warehouse and automated uploads from the market research agency. But experience shows that it is usually the simple solutions that survive and help to change management thinking. Ten years ago, some of the most successful solutions took the tangible form of a laminated, pocket-sized chart displaying the top indicators for the CMO and the team to carry around. Today, cutting-edge brand scorecard solutions are implemented as applications for tablet computers or even mobile phones (Figure 4.42).

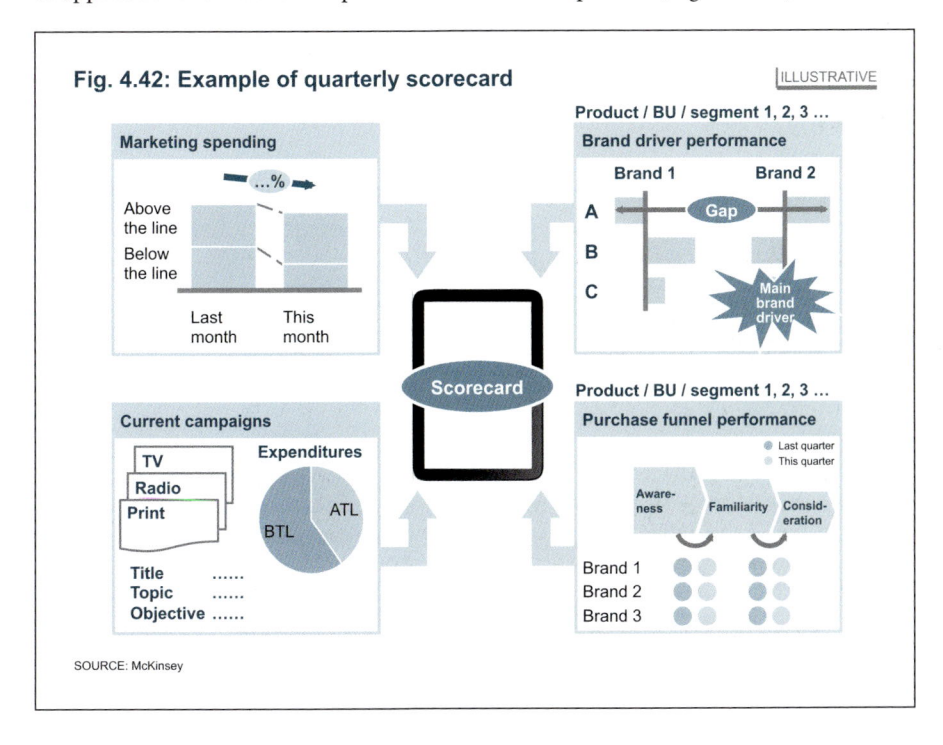

Fig. 4.42: Example of quarterly scorecard

SOURCE: McKinsey

## Ongoing compilation of input and output data

For the brand cockpit to be successful, it is necessary to collect selected input and output data in a careful and meticulous manner and on a regular basis. The scope and frequency of this compilation depends, as already described, on the nature of the organization. The essential input factors for a typical brand cockpit include data on individual campaigns and their content, target groups, and objectives over defined time periods on the one hand, and spending on brand communication or overall marketing by touch points on the other. The most important output dimensions fall into two categories:

- *Brand perception,* that is, perceived strengths and weaknesses on brand drivers, such as »high quality« or »value for money« relative to competitors or earlier periods.
- *Brand performance,* that is, conversion rates in the purchase funnel – for example,

from »consideration« to »purchase,« and, depending on development stage, key indicators of a company's success such as revenues or market share.

It is not a simple task to ensure the quality and consistency of this data. It involves both vertical (cross-sector) and horizontal (temporal) comparability: if, for instance, spending information is recorded in one place as budgeted amounts, in another as actual expenditure, and in a third as actual expenditure to date plus an updated forecast. In any case, it is important that potential limitations to the accuracy and granularity of the data are themselves made transparent; otherwise, the cockpit will generate a false impression of reality.

Following a limited test phase within the organization, the process of data collection and evaluation should be automated – at least partially. Whether a well-developed brand cockpit can be updated and maintained regularly and conscientiously in the end depends on good coordination with the respective marketing or controlling unit's data warehouse. Of equal importance for its success is the dovetailing of the brand cockpit into the organization's processes for decision making and action. There is little point in investing in a brand cockpit if the insights are not considered in designing future marketing plans and campaigns.

Experience and training in applying this powerful tool are essential for its success. Even a theoretically outstanding tool is useless if it is not implemented with a good portion of common sense.

### Brand Navigator

McKinsey's Brand Navigator was made with the brand manager in mind. Based on the BrandMatics® toolkit, the Navigator translates complex research and analysis into straightforward, intuitive visualizations for brand managers and their teams. Brand Navigator makes consumer insights easily accessible and helps marketers across widespread organizations do what they are supposed to do with data: make better brand management decisions (Figure 4.43).

Its modular analytical platform and expert services build on McKinsey's proven BrandMatics® frameworks – such as the brand purchase funnel and brand driver analysis – to help brand managers build strong brands, monitor changes in performance, and manage MROI. The tool goes beyond analytics by incorporating more than ten years of McKinsey client experience and practical insights based on real-world situations.

Brand Navigator addresses critical branding questions such as:
- How do your brands perform compared with the competition?
- How does this vary across countries and consumer segments?
- How can you improve your brand positioning and communication to fuel growth?

Brand Navigator helps to improve brand performance and growth, while enabling companies to make the most of their brand equity. It pinpoints bottlenecks in the brand purchase funnel at the customer segment level, identifies the brand attributes and benefits that will help brands overcome the bottlenecks, and shows how

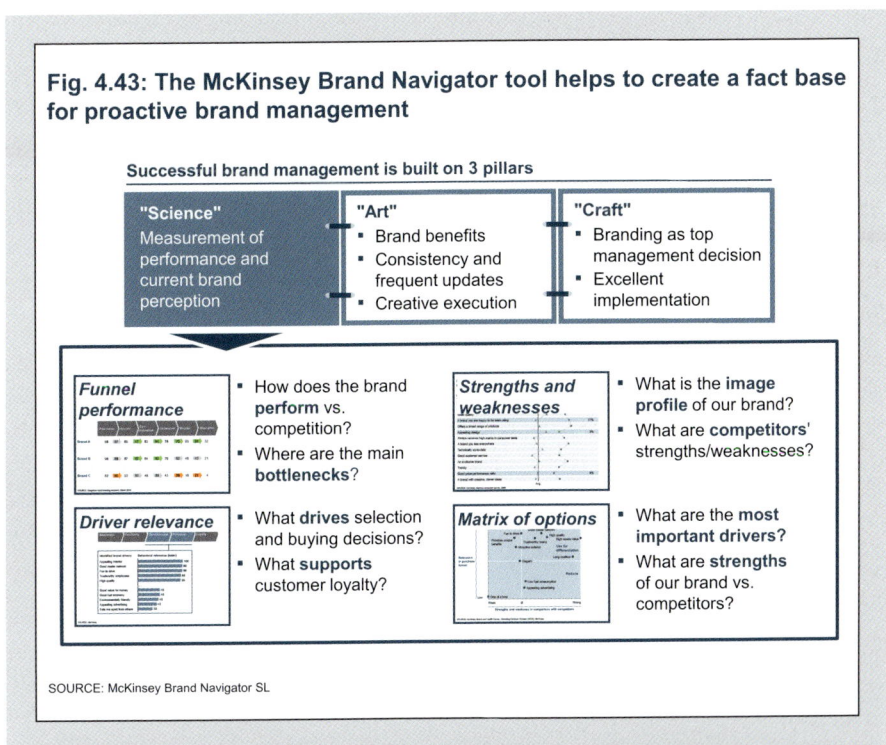

**Fig. 4.43: The McKinsey Brand Navigator tool helps to create a fact base for proactive brand management**

Successful brand management is built on 3 pillars

| "Science" | "Art" | "Craft" |
|---|---|---|
| Measurement of performance and current brand perception | • Brand benefits<br>• Consistency and frequent updates<br>• Creative execution | • Branding as top management decision<br>• Excellent implementation |

**Funnel performance**
- How does the brand **perform** vs. competition?
- Where are the main **bottlenecks**?

**Driver relevance**
- What **drives** selection and buying decisions?
- What **supports** customer loyalty?

**Strengths and weaknesses**
- What is the **image profile** of our brand?
- What are **competitors'** strengths/weaknesses?

**Matrix of options**
- What are the **most important drivers**?
- What are **strengths** of our brand vs. competitors?

SOURCE: McKinsey Brand Navigator SL

the brand is perceived on those relevant decision factors by customer segment and versus the competition. As an optional feature, it can also highlight the most effective touch points for delivering specific propositions and messages to the target group. Key benefits include:

- *Superior insights.* Track how your brands perform by running real-time analyses across geographies, products, and customer segments.
- *Greater productivity.* Streamline repetitive tasks by using the automated Web interface to upload market research, run customized analyses, and produce graphical output that can be easily incorporated into reports to facilitate decision making.
- *Sustainable improvements.* Build in-house capabilities and embed best-practice approaches to measure, manage, and upgrade brand performance.

Generally, it takes three to six weeks of application to generate insights that typically help companies achieve 3 to 5 percent in annual revenue growth, or a reduction of up to 20 percent in marketing spending. Brand Navigator is part of McKinsey's broader Marketing Navigator solution. Brand Navigator can be used as a standalone application or in conjunction with the other modules of the Marketing Navigator, such as portfolio allocation and campaign deployment.

## 4.6 The Brand Organization: Structural Success Factors

Successful brand management demands a powerful brand organization, including an appropriate structure, suitable management qualifications, and the right decision-making processes. Many companies appear to believe that installing the right structure alone will be decisive. It is as if they expect a new organization chart will suffice to ensure marketing success.

That such a misconception should persist more than a quarter century after the publication of Tom Peters' and Robert Waterman's best seller *In Search of Excellence* is hard to believe.[65] Their research showed, among other things, that the »ideal« organizational structures do not guarantee success. The structure of a company not only has to fit its strategic objectives, but also orient the processes and systems of the organization and the talents and skills of its people toward the same ends. In other words, the structure of the organization is only part of the solution. There is no point in employing talented and highly qualified brand managers if they do not have sufficient authority within the organization – be it formal or informal – to make a difference to the outcome. Often, this is not primarily a question of boxes, lines, decision-making authorities, and job descriptions, but of the role and recognition of the executive in charge of a given brand. Since the power wielded by a brand manager ultimately depends on the qualifications of the individual in question, hiring and developing top brand management talent is a critical component of successful brand organization.

Only an executive of sufficient caliber and credibility will be able to ensure the brand is recognized as a valuable asset well beyond next year's EBIT, whether the brand is managed as a profit center in its own right or not. A CEO at a major European service company recently told the authors of this book that he would rather keep the brand manager's position open than hire the wrong person, implying that the brand was too valuable an asset to be placed in the wrong hands. No matter what the short-term business targets may be, it is the brand manager's paramount goal to safeguard and develop the brand for the future. It's obvious that this role sometimes requires tough decisions; consider Skoda's much disputed but ultimately successful strategy of staying away from high-margin, lifestyle vehicles to protect its no-nonsense brand image. It takes an executive of considerable standing with strong support from the board for the brand manager to deliver on this the promise as the brand's caretaker and watchdog. In recognition of this challenge, many companies have created the role of CMO. IBM, Pepsi, and Procter & Gamble were among the pioneers to hire CMOs, thus effectively moving brand management to executive or even supervisory board level. And with good reason. As the Skoda example shows, sustainable brand management is of the utmost importance from a shareholder perspective.

In this section, we will examine five aspects of brand organization:

- Origins and best practices, from 1919 to the present day.
- The CMO as the brand integrator.
- The trade-off between centralization and decentralization.
- Performance-based service provider management.
- The future of media and communications management.

## Best practices in the brand manager organization

The origins of the brand manager organization can be traced back to 1919 at Libby, McNeill & Libby, which was the first company to place emphasis on managing individual brands (Figure 4.44).[66] It was Procter & Gamble, however, that introduced the classic brand manager organization in 1931, with one brand manager responsible for one product.[67] This was in accordance with the Procter & Gamble belief that a product must have distinct tangible and rational benefits, which were then communicated through the product's brand.

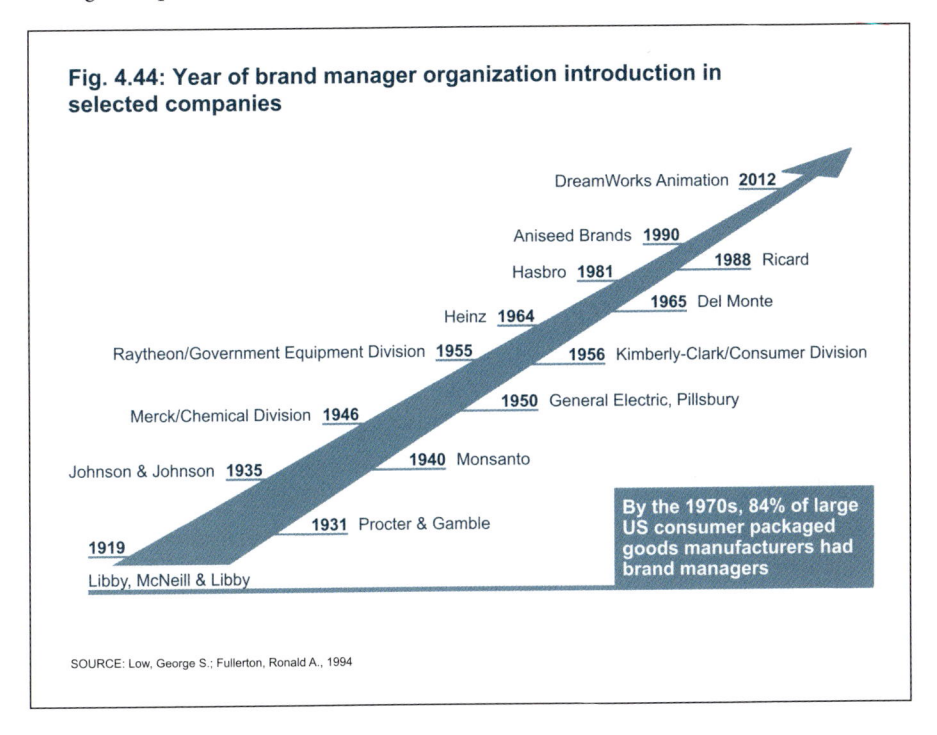

**Fig. 4.44: Year of brand manager organization introduction in selected companies**

- DreamWorks Animation **2012**
- Aniseed Brands **1990**
- **1988** Ricard
- Hasbro **1981**
- **1965** Del Monte
- Heinz **1964**
- **1956** Kimberly-Clark/Consumer Division
- Raytheon/Government Equipment Division **1955**
- **1950** General Electric, Pillsbury
- Merck/Chemical Division **1946**
- **1940** Monsanto
- Johnson & Johnson **1935**
- **1931** Procter & Gamble
- **1919** Libby, McNeill & Libby

By the 1970s, 84% of large US consumer packaged goods manufacturers had brand managers

SOURCE: Low, George S.; Fullerton, Ronald A., 1994

As manager of Procter & Gamble's marketing department, Neil McElroy, recognized that his company's own brands were struggling unsuccessfully for market share against competing products. He developed a plan in which every Procter & Gamble brand would be managed by independent brand managers and brand assistants. The brand manager would be responsible for advertising and all other marketing activities of that single brand. By approving the plan, Procter & Gamble's president Richard Deupree established the world's first formal brand manager organization.

The previous forms of brand organization typical at that time had a coordination problem. Responsibility for a brand was distributed across several functional managers, resulting in poor coordination of activities. But Procter & Gamble found a solution. The brand manager alone was responsible for sales figures, market share, and brand profit (Figure 4.45). A secondary objective of this new form of organization was to foster stronger competition between multiple brands under the same corporate

**Fig. 4.45: Example of brand management organization**
P&G organizational structure

|  | Worldwide business units |  |  |  |  |  |  | Corporate functions |
|---|---|---|---|---|---|---|---|---|
| **P&L responsibility** → | Baby care | Beauty/ personal care | Textile and household care | Feminine hygiene | Food and beverages | Health care and corporate new ventures | Hygienic papers | • Finance |
| **Marketing and sales responsibility** ↓ |  |  |  |  |  |  |  | • HR |
| North America |  |  |  |  |  |  |  | • Legal |
| Central and Eastern Europe |  |  |  |  |  |  |  | • Supply chain |
| Middle East/Africa general export |  |  |  |  |  |  |  | • PR |
| Western EU markets |  |  |  |  |  |  |  | • IT |
| ASEAN/India/ Australia |  |  |  |  |  |  |  | • Marketing |
| Japan/Korea |  |  |  |  |  |  |  | • R&D |
| Greater China |  |  |  |  |  |  |  |  |
| Latin America |  |  |  |  |  |  |  |  |

(Market development organization)

**Worldwide services**
- Accounting
- Benefits
- Payroll
- IT
- Order management

**Development of corporate strategy and important initiatives**

SOURCE: Press clippings

---

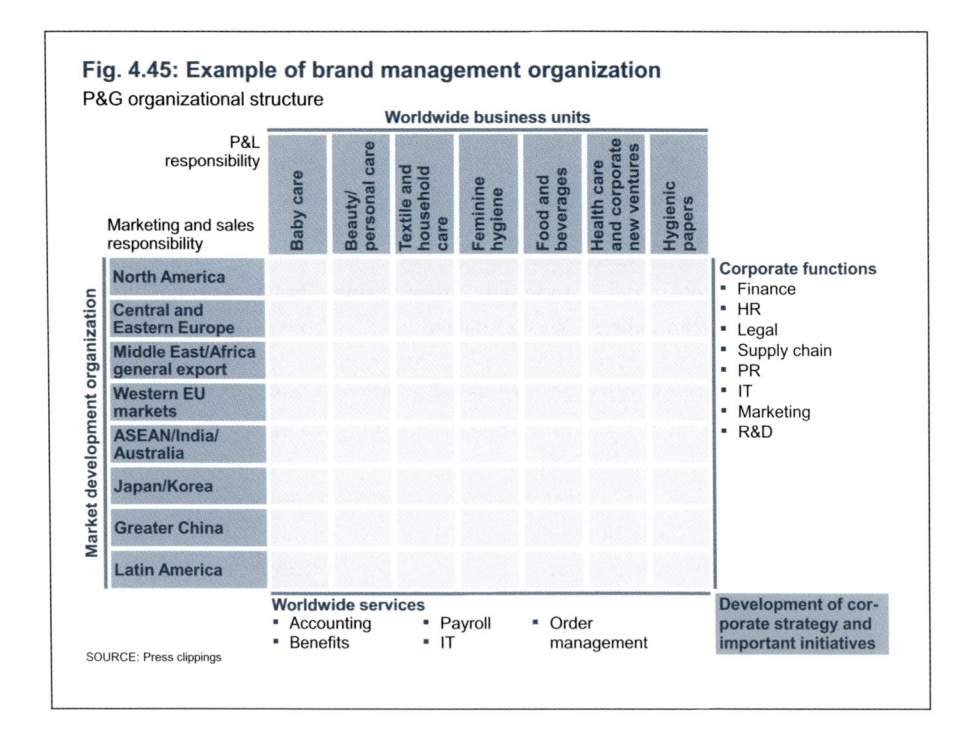

roof. McElroy believed that it was better to lose market share to his own Procter & Gamble products than to competitors.[68]

Soon Procter & Gamble's system was widely imitated by consumer goods companies. Even today, the Procter & Gamble model characterizes the structures of marketing-oriented companies in many industries. In the years of strong growth following the Second World War, it was this brand management system that helped many companies to establish and maintain innovative products and new brands.

More recently, companies have gone to great lengths to ensure that the brand organization keeps up with the evolution of media consumption habits and consumer decision making. Given the growing number of touch points where customers now interact with companies, marketing often cannot do what is needed all on its own. CMOs and their C-suite colleagues must collaborate intensively to adapt their organizations to the way customers now behave, and in the process, redefine the traditional marketing organization. PepsiCo, for example, has sought to provide a single point of contact for its digital marketing efforts by creating the role of chief digital officer (CDO): An executive without line responsibility who drives the application of best practices across the beverage group's global digital efforts.[69] Examples of other companies that have recently hired CDOs include McDonald's, the NFL, and Aviva. Gartner predicts that 25 percent of businesses will have a CDO by 2015.[70]

Companies also need a clear approach for monitoring touch points and renewing them as needed. At one major hotel chain, for example, a single group circumnavigates the globe acting as a rapid-response »monitor and fix« team. It meets with hotel licensees, educates them about the company's customer engagement approach and management of key touch points, demonstrates new behavior, and trains the staff in new operational processes. Given the speed of information sharing today, constant monitoring and adaptation – indeed, continuous improvement of the sort that came to the operations world long ago – is bound to infiltrate marketing and grow in importance.

Today's successful brand organizations are not only able to adapt to external changes, but are also more in touch and in tune with other business functions internally. John Hayes, CMO at American Express, says: »I haven't met anybody – and I talk to a lot of my colleagues in the marketing world – who feels they have the organization completely aligned with where this revolution's going, because it's happening so fast and so dramatically. Marketing is touching so many more parts of the company now. It touches on service; it touches on product development. We need to organize in a way that starts to break down the traditional silos in the business.«[71] Honoring the maxim that strong brands should deliver a consistent experience across touch points and journeys, one global financial institution, for example, has created a governance council with representatives from all customer-facing business units. The company's objectives were to ensure that data and analytics are shared, that customers receive the same experience regardless of channel, and that IT systems meet the customer's digital engagement needs.

For brand managers operating in B2B2C environments, robust formal and informal partnerships with distribution partners are becoming more critical too. Nestlé, for example, manages its relationship with Wal-Mart via what it calls the Nestlé/Wal-Mart team. This unified cross-business, cross-functional group is responsible for everything from in-store activity to promotions, logistics, innovation, and product design. As a result, Wal-Mart has a single point of contact with one of its largest suppliers, Nestlé enjoys a stronger relationship with the retailer, and critically, both companies gain a better understanding of and engagement with packaged goods consumers.[72]

## The CMO as brand integrator

Brand management has to emanate right from the top. It requires great clarity of vision to develop a company from a single product brand into an umbrella brand with a complex group of companies or subsidiaries that have a diverse range of products, target customer segments, sales channels, and countries of distribution. Whether the responsibility rests with the chair of the management board or an executive relatively high in the corporate hierarchy, those involved must have a deep understanding of the company's brand positioning as well as the potential and limits for expanding the brand into other products, sales channels, and countries. In addition to painstaking market research – which is, of course, necessary for systematic planning – interpretation is always required, along with the occasional executive decision on expansion alternatives.

Brand management requires a broad range of expertise: in product and supply, pricing, promotions management, sales channel management, customer service management, market research, and insights, all of which cannot be provided by one person alone. Instead, these capabilities must be brought together in a marketing team under the head of marketing's supervision. This person thus plays a vital role as the coordinator – or perhaps we should say the integrator – of the brand process.

The brand integrator has a major task in ensuring that all aspects of brand management are given adequate attention and held in balance, always keeping the long-term health and value creation potential of the brand in mind. Activities aimed at individual target groups and individual brands need to be orchestrated as part of the development of the umbrella brand. Similarly, product development and marketing need to share a common language about what they are trying to achieve as well as a set of complementary objectives. All too often, pricing, sales, and marketing can be at loggerheads or can unwittingly undo whatever the other sets out to achieve. Promotions need to work towards the same ends as advertising. Similarly, the brand integrator needs to manage the external specialists brought in to develop the brand (such as marketing research and advertising experts) and ensure that they are also focused on this same set of common objectives.

A crucial part of this task is to determine what special marketing expertise is required for the organization, and whether this is available in-house or needs to be acquired externally. This requires the marketing leadership to keep up to date with the state of the art in marketing knowledge. It is important for this group to scrutinize the know-how of internal and external specialists and ensure that it is robust and applied well. If they fail to do so, marketing organizations face the risk of never moving beyond the conventional answers to important questions. It is all too easy for a successful company to become comfortable with the conventional and complacent about change. Coca-Cola, a well-managed brand, also fell into this trap by being slow to adapt to the general fitness and wellness trend – and in particular, to the growing popularity of mineral water as a branded lifestyle product, rather than a no-name commodity. »The emerging consumer trends in health and wellness were missed,« admitted CEO Isdell in 2004.[73]

SAP, the worldwide market leader in business administration software, is another example of a strong company initially missing out. SAP did not recognize the importance of the Internet revolution early enough. Assuming this invention was just a fad, it underestimated the importance of the innovation. Once it recognized this, SAP adjusted its brand and charted a new course into the network era by developing the mySAP.com software. Within three years, it once again started to close the gap to its competitors and is currently the indisputable market leader.[74]

One of the most critical roles in marketing is that of the integrator. It is also one of the most difficult to fill, since only rarely can the necessary skills be acquired through training in special marketing departments or through job rotation between marketing, sales, and other departments. As a manager, the integrator needs to have the fundamental capability of being able to find the right balance between science, art, and craft and then to make decisions that are consistent in the longer term – while meeting shorter-term targets, or at least managing expectations surrounding them. Ideal brand integrators do much more than just love the brand; they must be able to demonstrate this love on a daily basis – both internally to the company's employees, and externally. This is the capability that Jeff Bezos displays at Amazon, Jeff Immelt at GE, Michael O'Leary at Ryanair, and Sir Richard Branson at Virgin. The organization's leadership needs to be able to make effective use of marketing expertise in their decision-making processes. Conversely, this expertise shouldn't be allowed to hold the organization hostage. As brand leaders, integrators need to be receptive to special knowledge on the one hand, but on the other, they must be prepared to make independent decisions. Only when this balance is maintained can speed of action be ensured. In the fast-moving world of brands, letting things degenerate into consensus-seeking can spell disaster.

### Centralize or decentralize?[75]

By Paul Magill, CMO at Abbott, a healthcare company based in Chicago, Illinois

Many CMOs ask themselves: to centralize or not to centralize? To have a marketing organization that does a better job of coordinating across units and gaining efficiencies in shared services, or one that decentralizes marketing activities to the units where they can be closer to the customers and business unit priorities they are meant to support?

CMOs have created a pendulum effect, in which they accede to the demands of business units to have greater control over »their« marketing, and then a few years later face the backlash of dramatically inconsistent brand expressions and customer experiences. Businesses need to move away from this pendular debate. It's unhelpful because it muddles the conversation and forces people to think in »either/or« terms. What they need to understand is that for organizations to grow into customer engagement engines, they have to take a »both/and« approach.

We're seeing the emergence of »both/and« in the integrated marketing organization. Marketing activities are decentralized to business units where interaction with customers happens, but the organization has the capability to act on a coordinated basis when needed. One global bank we've worked with swung from a highly centralized marketing approach to one that was highly decentralized. While decentralization initially delighted most business units, the downside soon emerged. It became difficult to attract talent in key areas – such as data analytics – because the decentralized system didn't allow for any clear bank-wide career progression. Projects that should have been bank-wide, such as Web site development or social media programs, were hard to coordinate. Money was wasted on duplicated activities. As one executive put it, »We're a bunch of marketing islands, with our own language and ways of doing things.«

Rather than simply swinging the pendulum back again, the bank leaders decided to »grow a new organizational muscle« that allowed the bank to act in a coordinated way. They layered on strips of standardization:

- A unified language describing marketing job functions.
- A model of bank-wide career paths.
- Communities of practice with designated »global conveners« that allowed marketing personnel from different units to take coordinated action – such as agreeing on a shared database or consolidating around particular market research partners.

- New governance bodies such as a brand council.
- Key processes – such as customer engagement and experience, and new market development.

All of which, marketing should be running for the bank in all units.

As a result, the marketing organization was able to stop debating centralized versus decentralized, and instead position itself as a unifying force in the organization. Teams moved away from debating whether, say, data analytics must be centralized or decentralized, and started asking questions such as »which specific activities in data analytics could benefit from being shared across units?« The units have been able to increase the ROI of their marketing programs – mainly by increasing returns, in some cases by lowering investment – by calling on top-quality pooled skills in shared centers of excellence. The corporate brand is more consistent and better coordinated with unit programs, resulting in a better customer experience across brand touch points, improved customer satisfaction, and higher retention. Consolidation in marketing activities – such as vendor management and metrics reporting – has yielded cost savings of about 25 percent, along with increased professionalism.

To reshape the brand organization and reap the dual rewards of the »both/and« approach, CMOs should follow three simple rules:

- Articulate the vision of marketing's dual role, both at business unit and cross-unit levels. The C-suite needs to have a clear vision for the roles marketing plays within units and across them, and then be able to articulate this throughout the organization.
- Prioritize the work of marketing. It's a lot easier to coordinate a more focused set of marketing activities. Many marketing organizations perform a range of legacy activities that, in fact, the business no longer values.
- Be specific and creative in designing the integrated marketing model. It's no use talking about »market intelligence« or »data analytics« as a whole. You need to break them down to see the real opportunities. Maybe database analytics queries need to be designed at the business unit level, but the coders who develop the software algorithms to execute them could be shared. Maybe social media response should be done close to the customer in the business units, but elements of digital content creation can be shared.

Customers are increasingly looking beyond specific products and units to their experience interacting with the company as a whole that stands behind them. Marketing organizations need to function at both the business unit and company level so they can deliver on those high expectations. When faced with the choice between centralized and decentralized marketing functions, companies should simply say: yes.

## Performance-based service provider management

Every brand will need to engage external assistance at many points along its journey to success. Any successful brand that hasn't done so is the exception that proves the rule. Selecting the right providers for assignments as diverse as creation, production, media planning, and brand research is an art in its own right. However, the science of fact-based performance management is no less important to the long-term success of the brand.

Advertising campaigns, market research methods, and other external services need to be reviewed periodically. As much as is practicable, the performance of external service providers should be included in the brand cockpit metrics. Leading companies are in the process of forming mixed teams that comprise experts from their brand management, procurement, functional controlling, and market research departments to ensure consistent and sustainable agency performance monitoring.

Each external provider will require a different method of assessment. Ideally, this should involve a handful of tailored key performance indicators. A market research institute, for example, can be assessed in terms of its precision and the quality of its forecasts based on its own market research. An advertising agency can be evaluated against the targets it achieves in the rates of awareness, recall, and recognition, as well as in the comprehension of its advertising messages. Including such metrics in a brand cockpit, and using the cockpit for agency performance monitoring, is a way of tying management to measurement. It also helps to align the steering of service providers with the wider BrandMatics® approach. Core BrandMatics® frameworks, such as the brand purchase funnel, are well established these days, even in the agency world. As a consequence, changes in funnel-related attitudinal metrics – such as brand awareness, familiarity, or purchase intention – are well suited to monitoring the performance of agencies that provide client-facing services such as advertising campaigns, media planning, point-of-sales materials, or loyalty programs.

The process of evaluation need not become overly burdensome. It is sufficient to calculate a few performance indicators for each external service provider. This is not to underestimate the importance of the evaluation, however. Indeed, the corporate center's role in evaluating the performance of the marketing organization needs to be directed largely towards the performance of external service providers. As is the case in all other business functions, performance indicators are often only taken seriously if they are compiled by a neutral third party.

The classic agency compensation model – a commission fee on total advertising spending (typically 5 to 10 percent for creative agencies and 2 to 6 percent for media agencies) – has many obvious disadvantages. Not only does it incite agencies to favor »expensive« classic media over potentially more efficient or innovative below-the-line touch points. It also gives companies an incentive to cut back on upfront planning and keep requesting reworks from their agencies, simply because they come at no additional cost. Thus, it's no surprise that a 2007 survey among German advertisers (GWA) shows that the traditional commission is going out of style. The use of this model has decreased by 60 percent over the past few years. At the same time, performance-based compensation is spreading. According to industry estimates, as early as 2003 a total of 80 to 90 percent of new contracts signed with agencies included performance-based components. In a survey conducted by the Association of National Advertisers (ANA) in the United States in 2013, 61 percent of all respondents said

**Fig. 4.46: Agency payment practices**
Percent

Use of performance incentives in agency compensation

| 1991 | 1994 | 1997 | 2000 | 2003 | 2007 | 2010 | 2013 |
|------|------|------|------|------|------|------|------|
| 13   | 19   | 30   | 35   | 38   | 47   | 46   | 61   |

+7% p.a.

> It is possible that marketers are gravitating to **performance incentives as a simpler and more precise way to tie** at least some of their **agency compensation to performance accountability**. Incentives can be **easily tailored to different types of agencies**, especially as the capabilities and tools for measuring marketing communications performance have grown and become more sophisticated.
> 
> – Association of National Advertisers (ANA), "Trends in Agency Compensation 2013"

SOURCE: Association of National Advertisers (ANA), 2013

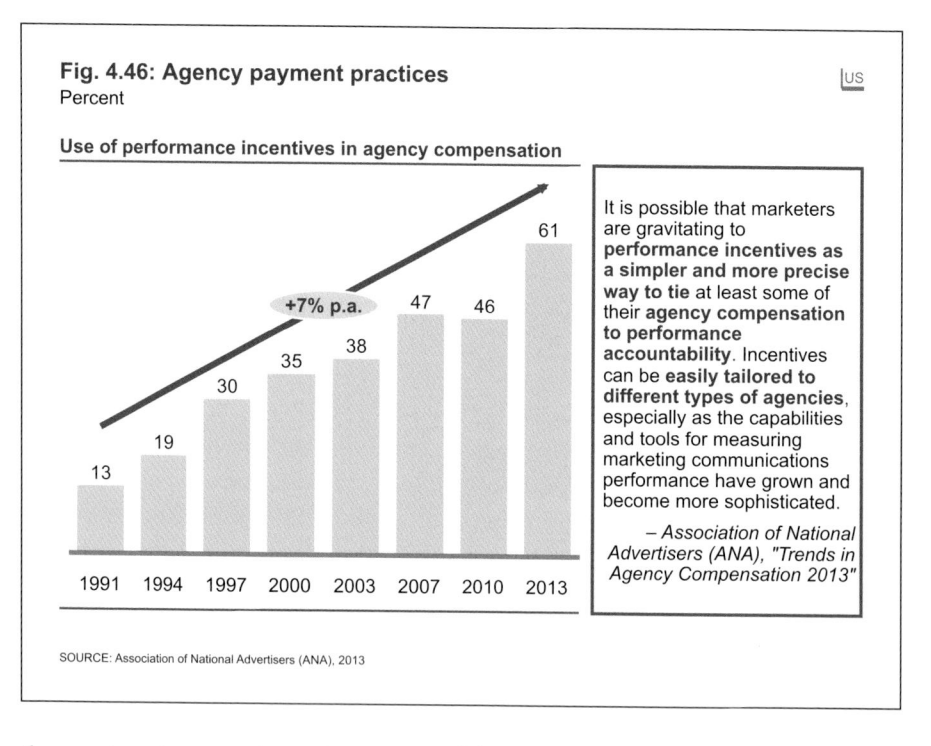

they used performance incentives as part of their agency compensation systems. More than 70 percent say this helps to maintain (13 percent) or improve (62 percent) agency performance, and an overwhelming majority of advertisers surveyed say they will continue to use performance incentives (80 percent). As the basis for such incentives, most players (69 percent) use a combination of client and agency performance. Popular indicators include agency performance review scores (75 percent) and client sales (48 percent), or client brand/advertising awareness (54 percent). Only a minority uses market share (23 percent) or media performance targets (25 percent).[76]

In typical performance-based models, a share (often 20 percent) of the payment depends on achieving objectives as contractually stipulated. As indicated by the ANA survey results, these objectives are most commonly quantitative targets, but qualitative criteria are also widely used. Common quantitative targets include achieving planned sales figures, acquiring new customers or leads, or changes in market share. Communication-related quantitative targets include indicators of awareness building, recall values, customer attitudes towards the product, and brand loyalty. The qualitative criteria include assessments of how well the partnership is functioning, the quality of the services provided, and the overall impression of the agency's creative work.[77] Many of these performance models already seem to be standard, or at least this is what most companies would argue. At any rate, advertisers say they increasingly use performance incentives as part of their agency compensation (Figure 4.46), although it is not equally common in all industries. While almost all consumer goods companies use performance incentives, only two in three service providers and one in two B2B players do the same (Figure 4.47).

**Fig. 4.47: Almost all consumer goods companies use performance incentives**
Percent

Use of performance incentives by industry

| Industry | Percent |
| --- | --- |
| Consumer durables | 100 |
| Fast-moving consumer goods | 89 |
| Services | 64 |
| B2B | 50 |
| Other | 33 |

66 (Average)

SOURCE: Association of National Advertisers (ANA), 2013

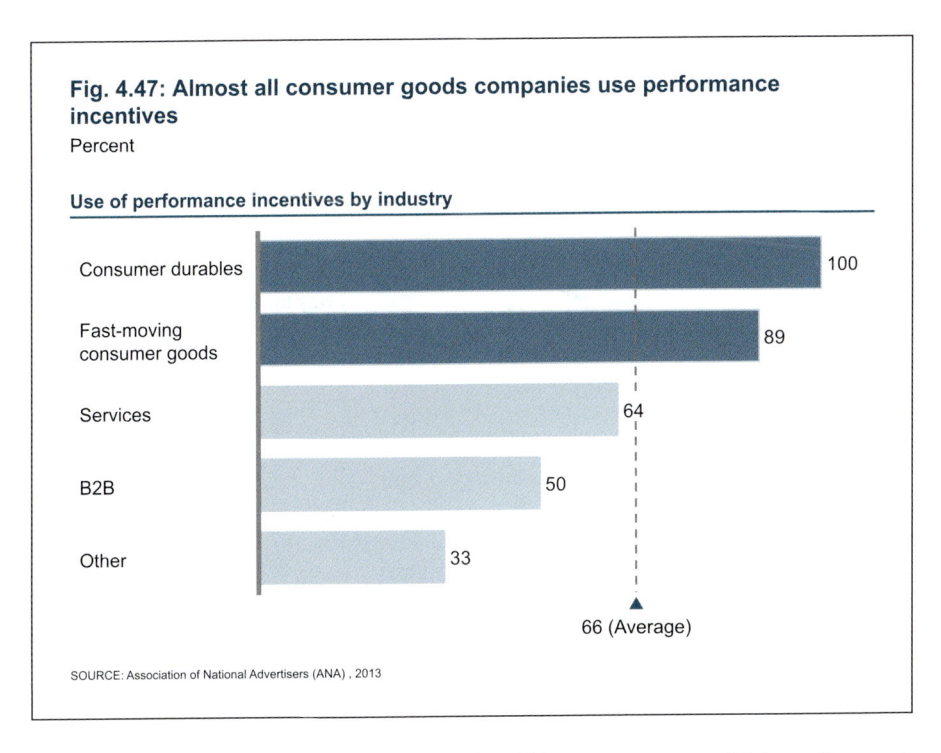

The objective of all remuneration systems should be to compensate high-quality work fairly, to maintain the objectivity of the external service provider, and to secure its interest in the success of the brand. It is also clear that concentrating on price components may lead to unsatisfactory or unprofessional work by the service provider. This problem is independent of whether the remuneration model is input-oriented or output-oriented. The outcome ultimately depends on the level and quality of effort invested in the service performed. The recent increase in criticism of and dissatisfaction with the creative work of agencies is not surprising in light of the increasingly price-driven selection processes, including unpaid pitches. Good services require good money. This rule applies as much to the war for talent as it does to the selection and compensation of external service providers. The *art*, *craft*, and *science* that go into building successful brands are very different from raw materials or energy. While it may make sense to bargain for supplies that can be easily replaced, it can be just as rational to pay above-average fees for superior creative and professional services. Brilliant ideas are anything but a commodity. Creative agencies in particular tend to do their best work as their clients' performance partners. Trying to pinch a few pennies in agency fees has, on occasion, proved a risky strategy. Few companies would want to suffer the drain in expertise and experience that comes from their creative agency dropping the account in favor of a larger, more exciting, or more generous competitor. In other areas – such as media buying and advertising production – cost cutting and hard bargaining are less risky. Bundled buying, requests for quotes, and resolute auditing can yield substantial savings without any perceptible changes to the services provided. As has already been stressed, strong brands require strong partnerships with external providers. One implication of this is that switching service providers over the short term needs to be avoided. Too much change – with the hectic coming-and-going of external partners – can weaken the brand. The basics of any relationship between the brand management and external service providers are those of strong motivation, long-term dedication, and trust-based cooperation.

Agencies themselves can play an active role in improving relationships. New incentives, such as licensing, could be deployed as part of the agency's remuneration package to reduce the risk of agency hopping. With this approach, agencies would receive a corresponding license fee in exchange for their highly creative work during the time their work is used by the company. Hence, if the company plans to switch agencies, then its use of the agency's work would either cease, or alternatively, the rights to the work would be purchased by the subsequent agency. Of course, a single agency alone, regardless of its quality, cannot achieve such a revolution in payment practices. The umbrella organizations of the advertising industry – such as the World Federation of Advertisers (WFA) or its local counterparts like the OWM in Germany – need to pave the way for such changes. Compare the insert on the future of media and communications management below.

### The future of media and communications management

McKinsey has partnered with the German Advertisers Association – the Organisation Werbungtreibende im Markenverband (OWM) – to investigate challenges and opportunities for media and communications management in Germany today. Key topics include organizational structures, cooperation with agencies, job profiles, and required capabilities. This insert captures the essence of qualitative interviews among some 30 senior executives and a quantitative survey among 122 advertisers, agencies, and media owners. Founded in 1995, the OWM now has more than 100 corporate members from a wide range of industries such as consumer goods, telecommunications, car manufacturers, financial services, pharmaceutical industries, and energy. Collectively, the members represent an annual advertising volume of more than EUR 8.5 billion.[78]

#### Three current challenges

Almost all interviewees agreed that the accelerating rate of change makes any long-term planning almost impossible. One executive claimed: »We have no idea what the marketing function will look like in a few years.« Specifically, our respondents identified three current challenges for media and communications management:

- Complexity is growing at an increasing rate.
- Advertisers are out of touch with their investments.
- Managers are struggling to account for the value they add.

#### Complexity is growing at an increasing rate

The pace of change in media and communications management has grown dramatically. More than three quarters of respondents said that the complexity of media management has increased substantially in the past five years. In particular, advertisers feel insufficiently equipped to cope with the requirements of new media that did not even exist a few years ago, such as mobile marketing and social media. Beyond this, most players feel they lack the facts they need to make informed decisions. Only some 15 percent of advertisers said they know how much a specific communication activity is contributing to corporate success.

**Advertisers are out of touch with their investments**

Companies should manage their agencies, not the other way around. However, years and years of outsourcing have robbed many advertisers of the required capabilities. Especially large advertisers handling budgets in excess of EUR 10 million have largely outsourced most aspects of media management, particularly media planning and media buying (Figure 4.48). As a result, marketing managers often feel unable to grasp their agencies' recommendations fully, let alone challenge them. They concede that they lack transparency regarding volume discounts, and that they have no way of knowing whether their agencies give them a good deal. »Advertisers focus on soft factors and neglect the real cash flows,« one interviewee said.

**Managers are struggling to account for the value they add**

»Our finance department keeps suggesting these obscure KPIs to measure the impact of marketing,« one executive complained in an interview, indicating that these numbers rarely reflect actual marketing performance. But in an increasingly ROI-minded environment, managers are under pressure to quantify the added value of each and every cost position. For want of meaningful metrics, 60 percent of respondents believe that top managers do not even know the key facts about the company's communication and media strategy. As a result, executives uniformly feel the need to invest in developing a system of appropriate performance indicators.

**Five potential remedies**

In response to these challenges, our survey participants have identified five levers to increase the effectiveness of media and communications management (Figure 4.49):

- Manage media performance more closely.
- Build skills to close critical competence gaps.
- Establish creative performance partnerships.
- Expand the fact base for informed decision making.
- Optimize performance measurement and tracking.

**Manage media performance more closely**

Outsourcing media management is commonplace, and pretty much everybody does it. But whoever does also says that this calls for meticulous efficiency management and performance tracking. Currently, many companies admit they do not live up to this aspiration. Many of them feel they depend on their service providers, even in core areas such as media strategy development. And although media is usually the biggest marketing cost block, it tends to receive less attention than creative input. In response to these challenges, advertisers pledge to manage their media agencies more actively and monitor their performance more closely.

## 304  4. Brand Delivery

**Fig. 4.48: Media strategy, planning, and buying are largely outsourced**

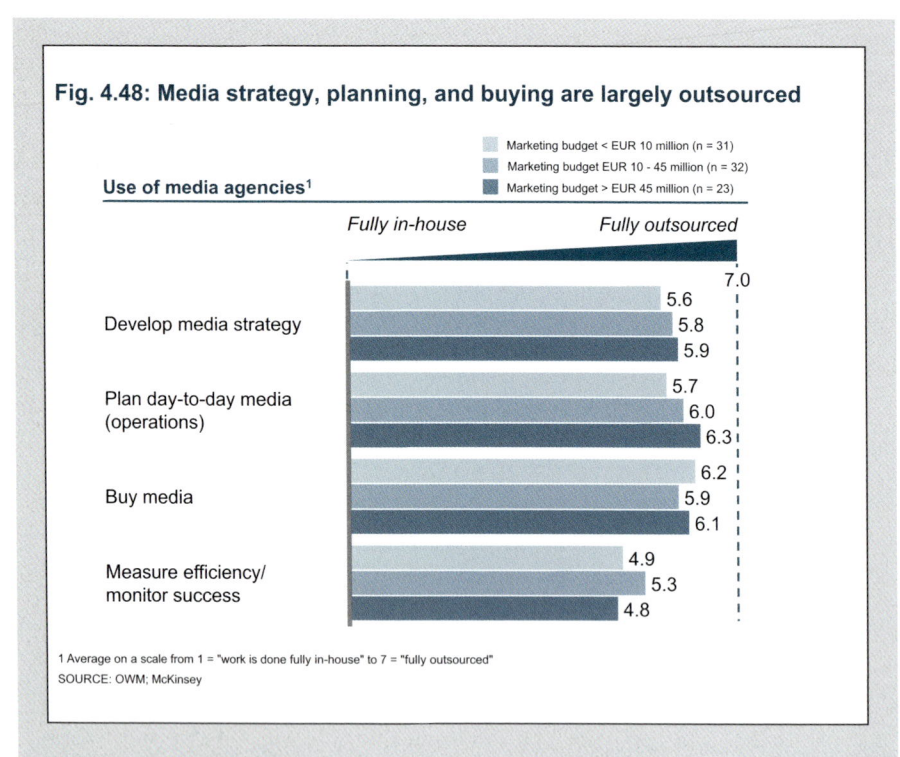

Use of media agencies[1]

Legend:
- Marketing budget < EUR 10 million (n = 31)
- Marketing budget EUR 10 - 45 million (n = 32)
- Marketing budget > EUR 45 million (n = 23)

Scale: Fully in-house ← → Fully outsourced

| Activity | <10M | 10–45M | >45M |
|---|---|---|---|
| Develop media strategy | 5.6 | 5.8 | 5.9 (7.0) |
| Plan day-to-day media (operations) | 5.7 | 6.0 | 6.3 |
| Buy media | 6.2 | 5.9 | 6.1 |
| Measure efficiency/monitor success | 4.9 | 5.3 | 4.8 |

1 Average on a scale from 1 = "work is done fully in-house" to 7 = "fully outsourced"
SOURCE: OWM; McKinsey

---

**Fig. 4.49: Depending on the marketing budget, companies mainly rely on more media performance or more competence building**

Prioritized target system (average[1])

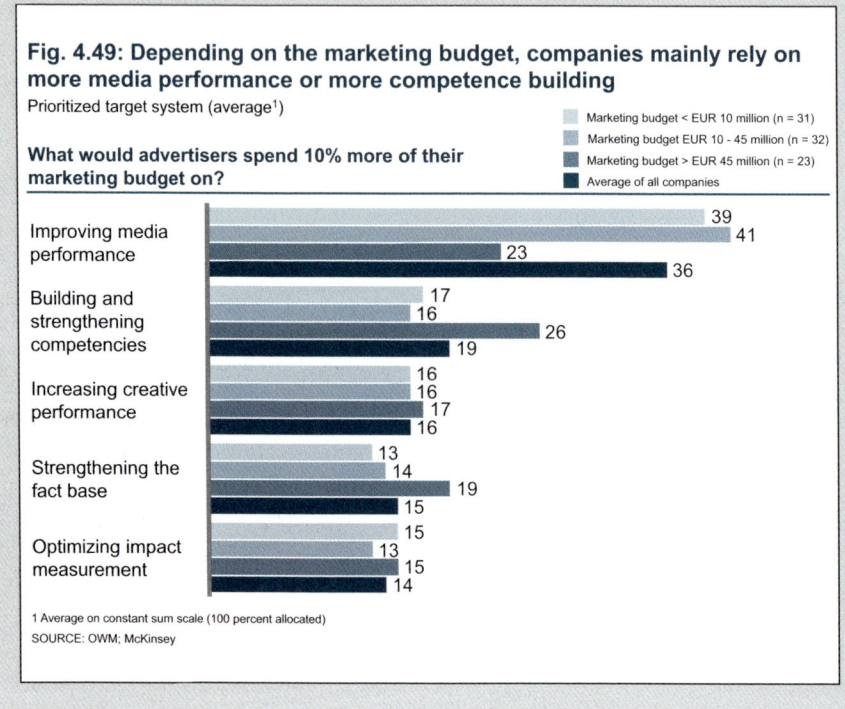

What would advertisers spend 10% more of their marketing budget on?

Legend:
- Marketing budget < EUR 10 million (n = 31)
- Marketing budget EUR 10 - 45 million (n = 32)
- Marketing budget > EUR 45 million (n = 23)
- Average of all companies

| Category | <10M | 10–45M | >45M | Avg |
|---|---|---|---|---|
| Improving media performance | 39 | 41 | 23 | 36 |
| Building and strengthening competencies | 17 | 16 | 26 | 19 |
| Increasing creative performance | 16 | 16 | 17 | 16 |
| Strengthening the fact base | 13 | 14 | 19 | 15 |
| Optimizing impact measurement | 15 | 13 | 15 | 14 |

1 Average on constant sum scale (100 percent allocated)
SOURCE: OWM; McKinsey

### Build skills to close critical competence gaps

Our respondents strongly feel that media and communications management have become more demanding in the past five years. Executives observe that knowledge and managerial skills depreciate more quickly than they used to. While media and communications managers feel comfortable handling traditional communication channels, such as print and TV advertising, they are a lot less confident when it comes to more recent media like mobile marketing, social media, and search engine marketing. To make things worse, these modern media are also perceived as particularly important for the future of brand communication (Figure 4.50). In short, media managers have a self-diagnosed gap where it matters most.

And there is no easy way out either. Very few survey participants believe that expert knowledge can be acquired »on the job,« implying that the opportunities for effective internal skill building are limited. Especially large advertisers will have to hire external experts and lure fresh talent to ensure an influx of new knowledge.

### Establish creative performance partnerships

When it comes to working with agencies, media managers are of two minds. On the one hand, they expect their agencies to »cover all aspects of integrated communication.« On the other hand, they want providers of creative services to be specialists in their respective fields, such as print advertising, direct mail, or social media marketing. Advertisers handling smaller budgets (below EUR 10 million) are particularly keen on »one-stop shopping.« They look for full-service agencies that will be able to handle all communication channels for them. But in reality, very few such players exist. Most agencies tend to employ either generalists or specialists.

The way out is for advertisers to focus on what they really need. As Figure 4.48 shows, most advertisers admit to specific gaps in areas such as online videos or search engine optimization. Specialized agencies can help advertisers fill these gaps in a spirit of partnership – provided corporate media managers stay on top of communication strategy and assign clear roles to their service providers in accordance with the company's overall marketing objectives.

### Expand the fact base for informed decision making

Media and communication management do not always get the attention and the funds they deserve in light of their contribution to the bottom line. This is especially true in companies with advertising budgets below EUR 10 million. One of the root causes of this imbalance is a lack of reliable information. Media managers often have a hard time demonstrating the value their functions add. Many of them complain that »controlling works with obscure indicators,« and that their companies have no clear sense of how specific communication activities drive corporate success. This lack of reliable indicators puts them at a disadvantage in their struggle for corporate resources. As a result, funds are often allocated to functions that can quantify their return on investment more easily, such as operations or sales. To improve their fact base and substantiate their claims to relevance, media and communications managers suggest conducting more market research, improving access to customer information, and making better use of the data available.

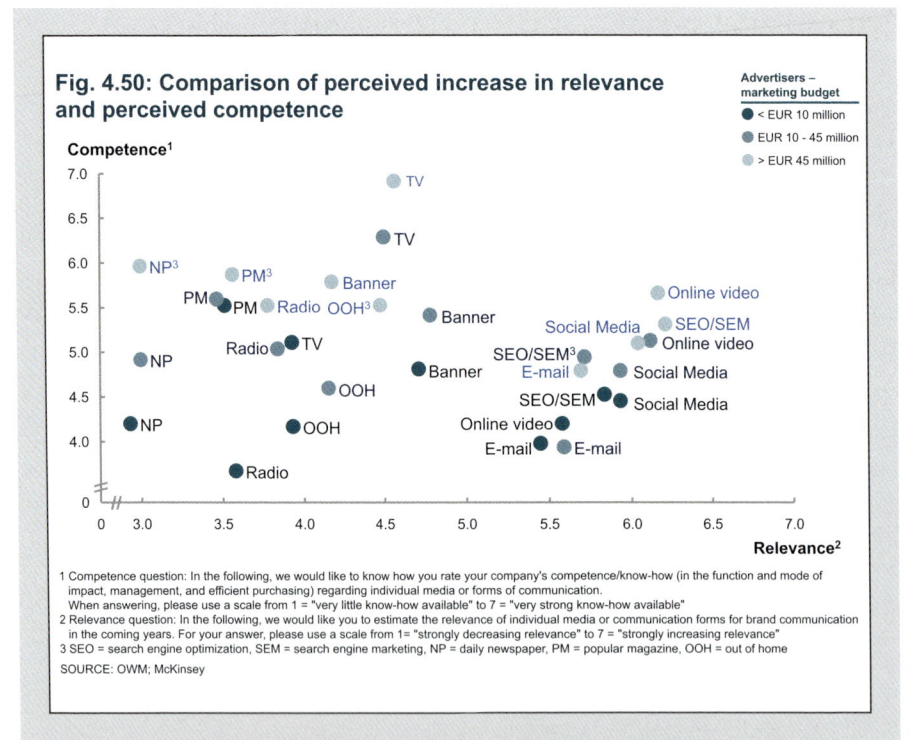

## Fig. 4.50: Comparison of perceived increase in relevance and perceived competence

Advertisers – marketing budget
- < EUR 10 million
- EUR 10 - 45 million
- > EUR 45 million

1 Competence question: In the following, we would like to know how you rate your company's competence/know-how (in the function and mode of impact, management, and efficient purchasing) regarding individual media or forms of communication. When answering, please use a scale from 1 = "very little know-how available" to 7 = "very strong know-how available"
2 Relevance question: In the following, we would like you to estimate the relevance of individual media or communication forms for brand communication in the coming years. For your answer, please use a scale from 1 = "strongly decreasing relevance" to 7 = "strongly increasing relevance"
3 SEO = search engine optimization, SEM = search engine marketing, NP = daily newspaper, PM = popular magazine, OOH = out of home

SOURCE: OWM; McKinsey

### Optimize performance measurement and tracking

Advertisers, agencies, and media owners agree that more reliable performance data is needed to transform media and communications management. Less than 4 percent of all respondents »fully agree« that they already have the information it takes today. Agencies and media owners are even more aware of the power of data than advertisers themselves. Yet even the most optimistic respondents understand that data-driven transformation will not take place overnight. Instead, they think of it as of a step-by-step process.

Regardless of the size of their budgets, advertisers believe that developing an appropriate system of performance indicators is an important stepping stone towards more professional media and communications management. Additionally, they want their agencies to engage in more systematic performance management and tracking.

### Outlook

Media and communication managers in our sample are surprisingly self-critical. They are acutely aware of their growing knowledge gaps. They feel their companies tend to underinvest in media and communications. They even admit they don't always know what exactly they need from their agencies. Yet, collectively, they already have the answers that will help them make their functions more professional, more accountable, and more impactful: resume control of the essentials, build new skills, partner with specialists, expand the fact base, and track performance.[79]

# Interview with Kasper Rorsted of Henkel: »Get the strategy and the team right«

Based in Düsseldorf, Henkel is a manufacturer of home and personal care products and adhesive technologies. Henkel's roster of brands includes Persil detergent, Dial soap, Fa deodorant, and Loctite glue. In recent years, the 137-year-old company has fared well – to a large extent, by boosting its presence in emerging markets, which today account for 45 percent of its global revenues of around EUR 16.5 billion. Henkel employs about 47,000 people from more than 120 nations, working in over 75 countries.

Kasper Rorsted has been CEO of Henkel since 2008. Born in Aarhus, Denmark, Mr. Rorsted has previously worked for Hewlett Packard and Compaq. He serves on the boards of international media conglomerate Bertelsmann and Denmark-based industrial company Danfoss. Mr. Rorsted is married with four children. He recently shared his views on his tenure at Henkel and the company's plans for the future with McKinsey's Klaus Behrenbeck. The full interview was first published in »Perspectives on retail and consumer goods«. It is reprinted here with Mr. Rorsted's kind permission.

**McKinsey:** If all goes according to plan, emerging markets will account for half of Henkel's sales by 2016.

**Kasper Rorsted:** That's right. We have set the ambitious target of generating EUR 20 billion in sales by 2016, EUR 10 billion of which we expect to come from emerging markets. We're aiming for growth in both emerging and mature markets. To be very clear: we are concentrating on markets where we hold leading positions or are able to generate sustainable growth. If we do not expect to win in a market in a reasonable period of time, we will exit that market. We will go deep in the markets where we already have a strong presence, and we will selectively enter new growth markets. Last year we opened our »Dragon Plant« in Shanghai—it's the world's largest adhesives factory. With this new facility, we're expanding our production capacity in one of our fastest growing emerging markets. We will continue to strengthen our position in growth markets like China, Russia, and Brazil. We're establishing seven new R&D centers in emerging markets including India, Brazil, Russia, and South Africa. We expect that in 2016, 12 of Henkel's 20 highest-revenue countries will be in emerging markets.

**McKinsey:** At the 2013 World Economic Forum in Davos, you told reporters that »the price for high growth is volatility.« What are some of the steps Henkel has taken to manage volatility in emerging markets?

**Kasper Rorsted:** Large, international corporations tend to become complex organizations, which makes them inflexible. But in fast-growing emerging markets, you cannot expect the same stable conditions that we are used to in mature markets – just think of the political unrest in the Middle East, for example. To succeed in an increasingly volatile market environment, we need simple structures and processes. We are constantly adapting our structures to become faster and more flexible. In the future, we want fewer but larger manufacturing sites and a reduced number of global suppliers. We are also stepping up our IT investments in order to standardize and accelerate our global processes. And we will continue centralizing functions in shared service centers.

**McKinsey:** What are your plans for mature markets?

**Kasper Rorsted:** Mature markets will remain important for us. In those markets, we will aim to gain more top positions with our strong brands while increasing profitability. One example is our home market, Germany, where we're making very high capital investments; with around 13 percent of sales, it's our second-most important market after the United States, and it will remain a cornerstone of our success. But I expect Europe will continue to face an extremely challenging period over the next few years.

**McKinsey:** You mentioned the role of your strong brands. Since becoming CEO, you've significantly reduced the number of Henkel's brands. Will you continue to do this?

**Kasper Rorsted:** When I joined the company, Henkel had about 1,000 brands. Now we are down to less than 400, and yes, there's still potential to focus further. While our ten top brands currently account for 46 percent of sales, we're aiming for 60 percent by 2016. At the same time, however, we will continue to invest in innovation. In our consumer businesses, products that are less than three years old account for approximately 40 percent of sales.

**McKinsey:** One of your newest product lines is Gliss Restore & Refresh, developed specifically for Middle Eastern women who wear veils. Tell me more about how Henkel came up with that product line.

**Kasper Rorsted:** To succeed in the highly competitive consumer-goods environment, we need both a management team that reflects the diversity of markets in which we operate and the innovation capabilities to address a broad range of varying consumer needs. The innovation you mentioned is a remarkable example of targeted customer relationship management. In the Middle East, which is one of our growth regions, many women wear veils. Their hair is covered for hours every day and, as a result, needs special care. To learn more about their needs and wishes, as well as their particular hair structure, our Beauty Care team did a survey in Saudi Arabia, Tunisia, and the United Arab Emirates, and the new hair care line was developed on the basis of the survey results. One of our values at Henkel is, »We put our customers at the center of what we do.« We have to understand their needs and wishes and enter into a dialog with them.

**McKinsey:** To that end, Henkel set up a ShopperLab and a Beauty Care Lighthouse. How do these two concepts help generate consumer insights?

**Kasper Rorsted:** The ShopperLab is a room that re-creates the shelves of a real store. We designed it to help us further understand customer behavior in shopping environments. We can study the impact that product designs have on shelf appearance and occupancy, point-of-sale materials, and the various aspects of buying behavior. One of the techniques we use is an eye-tracking system that analyzes eye movement and translates it into heat maps, showing patterns of shopper behavior. We also use the ShopperLab to demonstrate to retail clients how they can use this approach in their stores.

The Beauty Care Lighthouse is a unique venue where we host customers, business partners, or investors. Specific areas of the Lighthouse are devoted to topics that are important to us, such as sustainability or digital innovation. It's a space where customers can try out, for instance, new digital tools that let them test hair colorants at the point of sale. This creative atmosphere helps us engage and interact with our customers more deeply.

Only when we are close to consumers can we offer them products that cater to their specific needs. To give another example, in our Laundry & Home Care Business, we have a global consumer insights program that includes visits to local households by our team. Sometimes it's that easy: simply talk to people. Henkel managers from marketing or R&D regularly visit households. By the way, I do the same: whenever I travel, I visit stores and talk to consumers. What do you like about the product? What do you miss? Where do you see room for improvement?

**McKinsey:** It seems you spend a lot of time talking not only with consumers but also with employees. Do you feel that's important to do as a CEO?

**Kasper Rorsted:** I am convinced that a visible and accessible leadership style is most effective. My door is open; I encourage colleagues to call me directly. Our employees know who I am and what I'm doing. I eat with employees in our canteens whenever I am traveling or here at headquarters. You cannot run a global company from your desk. That's why I spend around 170 days per year abroad, meeting employees – from top executives to young high-potential individuals – as well as customers and business partners. As CEO, I believe that a primary task for me and the management board is to shape Henkel's growth strategy and clearly communicate it to all employees. Last year, to present our growth strategy for 2016, the management board and I visited 28 sites in 22 countries. Overall, more than 70 town hall meetings have taken place around the world. And of course, a critical part of my role is to make sure Henkel has the right team in place. So in summary, those are my key tasks as CEO: get the strategy and the team right.

**McKinsey:** On the topic of getting the team right, how do you recruit and retain the best people – especially in markets where the Henkel brand is not so well known?

**Kasper Rorsted:** It's certainly a challenge to find and keep good local employees, especially in emerging markets. The turnover rate in China is around 25 percent. In these markets, a large number of companies is competing for a relatively small, although steadily growing, pool of candidates. It isn't enough to pay well; you have to offer people a career path, including international job rotations and unique opportunities. Developing an employer brand takes time. In countries where Henkel is hardly known, we prefer to target specific groups – for example, through partnerships with individual professorships all over the world. We also increasingly recruit cross-border: at international recruitment fairs, we meet highly qualified candidates studying abroad and encourage them to work for Henkel in their home countries.

And once we recruit them, we have to retain them. We do that in part by investing in their development. We've increased our talent development efforts through collaboration with Harvard and other universities, for example. This enhances our position as an attractive employer. We have a results-driven performance culture. We put great emphasis on internal promotion and talent development. Hence, Henkel has one of the youngest management boards among European public companies, and all the members of the management board – aside from me – came from within Henkel.

**McKinsey:** Can you tell us how Henkel is taking advantage of multichannel opportunities brought about by the digital revolution?

**Kasper Rorsted:** We have just established a Digital Council to coordinate Henkel's digital activities, develop a digital vision through 2020, and explore digital opportunities for our businesses. Currently, e-commerce plays a minor role for us. Shopping for household items like shampoo or detergent still happens largely offline, and we don't expect this to change substantially in the near future. Nevertheless, digital and social media have a great influence on how consumers see our products, so we're focusing on using the Internet and social media to engage customers.

As an example, we aim to promote responsible use of our products. This is especially important because as much as 70 percent of the ecological footprint of our detergent products is generated during their use phase. On the Persil Web site, for instance, consumers can learn about reducing the water temperature in their washing machines and saving money at the same time, without compromising the superior performance of Persil.

**McKinsey:** Is there anything else you'd like to share with our readers?

**Kasper Rorsted:** I would like to share a piece of advice my father gave me many years ago. He told me, »If you do something, do it with your full heart and do it properly. Then you'll be successful.« This advice has become my life motto. Whether it's your studies, sports, or your job, if you're not willing to do it with all your energy, you should leave it. Another piece of advice that I've taken to heart: stick to your goals, but be flexible in how you achieve them.

# Notes

1. Linda Dauriz, Thomas Tochtermann, »Luxury Lifestyle – Business Beyond Buzzwords,« McKinsey, June 2012.
2. Cf. Kapferer, Jean-Noel, »The new strategic brand management,« London 2008, p. 179–180.
3. Martinson, Jane, »Interview – Yves Couette, Chief Executive, Ben & Jerry's – The keeper of corporate cool,« in: The Guardian, 18 Aug 2001, p. 34.
4. http://www.prnewswire.com/news-releases/dove-campaign-for-real-beauty-to-help-foster-self-esteem-in-girls-55138272.html.
5. http://www.holmesreport.com/casestudy-info/10304/Bertolli-Into-The-Heart-Of-Italy.aspx.
6. Please see the latest German edition of this book, »Mega-Macht Marke,« published by Redline, for details.
7. This section complements the discussion of customer decision making in preceding sections; both decision process analysis and driver disaggregation are tools to identify critical touch points and relevant messages or actions to improve the performance on key brand drivers and corresponding transfers in the purchase funnel.
8. Fanderl, Harald and Fabian Hieronimus, »Consumer Driven Redesign – Capturing New Potential Through Customer Insight,« Recall No. 1, Düsseldorf: McKinsey & Company, 2008.
9. Fanderl, Harald, Stefan Roggenhofer, and Kai Vollhardt:»The customer experience – delighting customers, motivating employees, and increasing profits,« McKinsey handbook.
10. This section is partly adapted from Beltran, Fernando, Dilip Bhattacharjee, Harald Fanderl, Bruce Jones, Scott Lippert, and Francisco Ortega, »The Secret to Delighting Customers? Put Employees First,« January 2014. http://disneyinstitute.com/blog/2014/01/the-secret-to-delighting-customersput-employees-first-/233/ (retrieved in June 2014).
11. Fanderl, Harald, Stefan Roggenhofer, Kai Vollhardt, »The customer experience – delighting customers, motivating employees, and increasing profits«, McKinsey handbook, 2013.
12. http://www.communicoltd.com/pages/1076_four_-key_strategies_for_building_emotional_connections_with_your_customers.cfm.
13. »Nespresso makes feedback part of the brand experience«, retrieved 10 May 2014, from http://www.enterprisefeedbacksuite.com/solutions/marketing/customer-satisfaction-survey/case-study.html.
14. http://interbrandonline.com/bestswissbrands/; retrieved 15 May 2014.
15. Perrey, Jesko and Dennis Spillecke, »Retail Marketing and Branding, A Definitive Guide to Maximizing ROI,« Second Edition, John Wiley & Sons, 2013.
16. «Five ways marketers lose credibility with the C-suite.» Forbes, July 2011.
17. http://adage.com/article/news/unilever-adspending-hits-heights/239348/.
18. For a detailed discussion of each approach, compare the chapter on budget sizing in Perrey/Spillecke, »Retail Marketing and Branding: A Definitive Guide to Maximizing ROI,« Wiley 2013.
19. Perrey, Jesko, and Dennis Spillecke, »Retail Marketing and Branding: A Definitive Guide to Maximizing ROI,« John Wiley & Sons, 2013.
20. In the context of CDJ, journey is a technical term that refers to active evaluation, the post-purchase experience, and the loyalty loop.
21. McKinsey CDJ survey, 2009.
22. Fischer, Marc, Wolfgang Giehl, and Tjark Freundt, »Managing Global Brand Investments at DHL. Submission to the 2010 Competition for the Franz Edelman Award,« February 2010.
23. »Werbung ist out,« manager magazin, March 1999, p. 98.
24. James, Allen, Frederick F. Reichheld, Barney Hamilton, and Rob Markey, »Closing the delivery gap,« Bain & Company, 2005, www.bain.com.
25. Mitchell, Colin, »Selling the Brand Inside,« Harvard Business Review, 1 Jan 2002.
26. LaClair, Jennifer A., »Helping Employees embrace change,« The McKinsey Quarterly 4, 2002, www.mckinseyquarterly.com.
27. Corporate Web sites, McKinsey research (Nov 2007), Harvard Business Review.
28. Parsley, Andy, »Employee Engagement: the What, Why and How,« Management Issues, 6 Dec 2005, www.management-issues.com.
29. Fischer, Marc, Wolfgang Giehl, and Tjark Freundt, »Managing Global Brand Investments at DHL. Submission to the 2010 Competition for the Franz Edelman Award,« February 2010.
30. Mitchell, Colin, »Selling the Brand Inside,« Harvard Business Review, 7 pages. Publication: 01 Jan 2002, http://hbr.org/2002/01/selling-the-brand-inside/ar/1.
31. Leberecht, Tim, »True Blue – Internal branding as a strategic corporate communications tool, A case study of JetBlue Airways,« http://www.brandchannel.com/images/papers/210_true_blue.orig.pdf.
32. Elswick, Jill, »Puttin' on the Ritz: Hotel chain touts training to benefit its recruiting and retention,« Employee Benefit News, Vol. 14 Issue 2, February 2000.
33. Chandrasekar, Mythili, »Internal branding,« Business Line, 7 Sep 2006.
34. Panke, Helmut, Speech at the Paris Motor Show, 2002.

35 https://www.press.bmwgroup.com/global/pressDetail.html?title=bmw-i3-world-premiere-innew-york-london-and-beijing (retrieved in August 2014).
36 www.bmw.com (November 2007).
37 Ankenbrand, Hendrik, »Die One-Man-Show,« Frankfurter Allgemeine Sonntagszeitung, 31 Aug 2014.
38 http://curbed.com/archives/2010/09/23/anna-ikeas-chatbot-graciously-answers-proust-questionnaire.php; http://www.engadget.com/2014/05/16/mi-adidas/.
39 See McKinsey's publication »Turning buzz to gold,« (available through the authors of this book) for details on how to identify and manage the most important touch points.
40 http://hbr.org/2006/03/connect-and-develop-inside-procter-gambles-new-model-for-innovation/ar/1.
41 IDC 2012 estimate.
42 Magna Global/IPG Mediabrands 2013.
43 http://blogs.wsj.com/cmo/2014/08/13/mobile-ad-revenue-soars/.
44 »American Express Members Project: A Marketing 50 Case Study,« Advertising Age, published on 17 Nov 2008, http://adage.com/article/print-edition/american-express-members-project-a-marketing-50-case-study/132427/.
45 Perrey, Jesko and Dennis Spillecke, »Retail Marketing and Branding, A Definitive Guide to Maximizing ROI,« Second Edition, John Wiley & Sons, 2013.
46 For an in-depth discussion, see »Search engine marketing« in Perrey/Spillecke, »Retail Marketing and Branding: A Definitive Guide to Maximizing ROI.«
47 McKinsey rapid branding research (March 2012).
48 »The Goal: a Perfect First-Time Fit,« The Wall Street Journal, updated March 23, 2012, http://online.wsj.com/news/articles/SB10001424052702304724404577293593210807790.
49 Van Willemskwartier, K., »Taaz: The Makeover Tool That Also Recommends Cosmetic Brands,« published on 28 May 2013, http://bwrite.biz/en/taaz-the-makeover-tool-that-also-recommends-cosmetic-brands/.
50 »Sephora Gives Its Shopping Experience a Makeover,« April 2012. Mashable.com, http://mashable.com/2012/04/08/sephora-makeover/.
51 Company Web site: http://store.fijiwater.com/.
52 »12 mini trends to run with now,« by trendwatching.com, September 2012, http://trendwatching.com/trends/pdf/2012-08%20MINITRENDS.pdf.
53 Anderson, Hilding and Rob Gonda, »Facebook Open Graph and the Future of Personalization,« Sapient Nitro, 2010, http://www.sapient.com/assets/imagedownloader/652/49281332_facebook_open_graph_and_the_future_of_personalization.pdf.
54 Communitelligence, Forrester, AntsEyeView.
55 »A Radical Transformation: B2B Commerce is Learning from B2C, Developing More Touchpoints, Becoming More Consistent – and More Complex,« by INTERSHOP, Fall 2013, http://www.intershop.de/files/Intershop/media/downloads/en/studies/2013-Intershop-E-Commerce-Report.pdf.
56 http://www.clickz.com/clickz/news/2319429/mcdonald-s-tries-out-mcd-coupon-app-in-select-markets.
57 PISACANE: »Retailers get creative with Pinterest to boost sales,« by The Associated Press, 25 Apr 2014, http://www.denverpost.com/business/ci_25639478/retailers-get-creative-pinterest-boost-sales.
58 http://www.nespresso.com/de/en/pages/services-mobile ; International Journal of Competitive Intelligence, Strategic, Scientific and Technology Watch, SciWatch Vol. 5, Issue 3, December (2012), »Nespresso's strategy: an idea of exclusiveness and personal touch« (page 3), Elizabeth PRIMO, http://hexalog.files.wordpress.com/2012/06/article2.pdf.
59 »Where Is Bed Bath & Beyond's E-Commerce Business Headed?,« Forbes, published 11 Sep 2014, http://www.forbes.com/sites/greatspeculations/2014/09/11/where-is-bed-bath-beyonds-e-commerce-business-headed/).
60 NYT 11 Oct 2013.
61 http://www.escapistmagazine.com/news/view/137266-IKEA-Catalog-BookBook-Video-Parodies-Apple-Ipad; https://www.youtube.com/watch?v=MOXQo7nURs0 (retrieved September 2014).
62 Schultz, Don E., »Measuring Brand Communication ROI,« Association of National Advertisers, 1997.
63 Nielsen Media Research, Kraftfahrtbundesamt, 2005 – 2007.
64 The RCQ model, described in Section 4.2, provides an excellent basis for structuring these types of questions.
65 Peters, Thomas J. and Robert H. Waterman, »In Search of Excellence: Lessons from America's Best-Run Companies,« New York: Warner Books, 1982.
66 Low, George S. and Ronald A. Fullerton, »Brands, Brand Management, and the Brand Manager System: A Critical-Historical Evaluation,« Journal of Marketing Research 31, No. 2, 1994, pp. 173 – 175.
67 Decker, Charles, Winning with the P&G 99: 99 Principles and Practices of Procter and Gamble's Success, London: Harper-Collins, 1998.

68 Low, George S. and Ronald A. Fullerton, »Brands, Brand Management, and the Brand Manager System: A Critical-Historical Evaluation,« Journal of Marketing Research 31, No. 2, 1994, p. 173.
69 French, Tom, Laura LaBerge, and Paul Magill, »We're all marketers now,« McKinsey Quarterly, July 2011.
70 http://adage.com/article/news/mcdonald-s-chiefcreative-marlena-peleo-lazar-departs/294814/; http://www.usatoday.com/story/tech/2014/09/04/nfl-now-digital-network-apple-microsoft-verizonroger-goodell/15068521/; http://www.computerworlduk.com/news/careers/3539053/aviva-appoints-chief-digital-officer/; https://www.umbel.com/blog/influence/chiefdigital-officer/ (retrieved in September 2014).
71 http://www.mckinsey.com/insights/marketing_sales/how_we_see_it_three_senior_executives_on_the_future_of_marketing.
72 French, Tom, Laura LaBerge, and Paul Magill, »We're all marketers now,« McKinsey Quarterly, July 2011.
73 »Coca-Cola hofft auf Wachstum durch Mineralwasser,« Financial Times Deutschland, 18 Mar 2002, p. 5; »Stille Wässer pushen Branche,« Lebensmittel Zeitung, 17 Jan 2003, p. 14; Teather, David, »Coca-Cola Reduces Profit Targets,« The Guardian, 12 Nov 2004, p. 24.
74 Zepelin, Joachim, »Turm im Sturm. Die Softwarebranche ist in einer Krise wie nie zuvor,« Financial Times Deutschland, 9 Jul 2002, p. 25.
75 Based on »The central question for CMOs,« by McKinsey alumnus Paul Magill, originally published as part of the compendium »The marketing organization of the future,« McKinsey, November 2012.
76 According to Frank-Michael Schmidt, head of J. Walter Thomson, and Tom Felber, financial manager of BBDO, »In die Enge getrieben,« Werben & Verkaufen, 16 May 2003, pp. 42–45. Also see GWA, »Frühjahrsmonitor 2007« and Association of National Advertisers (ANA), »Trends in Agency Compensation 2007.« For a more in-depth discussion of agency compensation, see Uzelac, Gordana, »Vergütungsmodelle von Werbeagenturen« (academic paper), Karlsruhe, 2007.
77 See, e. g., Krenn, Ulrich, »Großer Friede, keine Freude,« Werben & Verkaufen, 30 Jan 2004.
78 http://www.owm.de/index.php?id=76.
79 51 »Today's changing marketing landscape and the future of agency partnerships«, McKinsey white paper, Spring 2013.

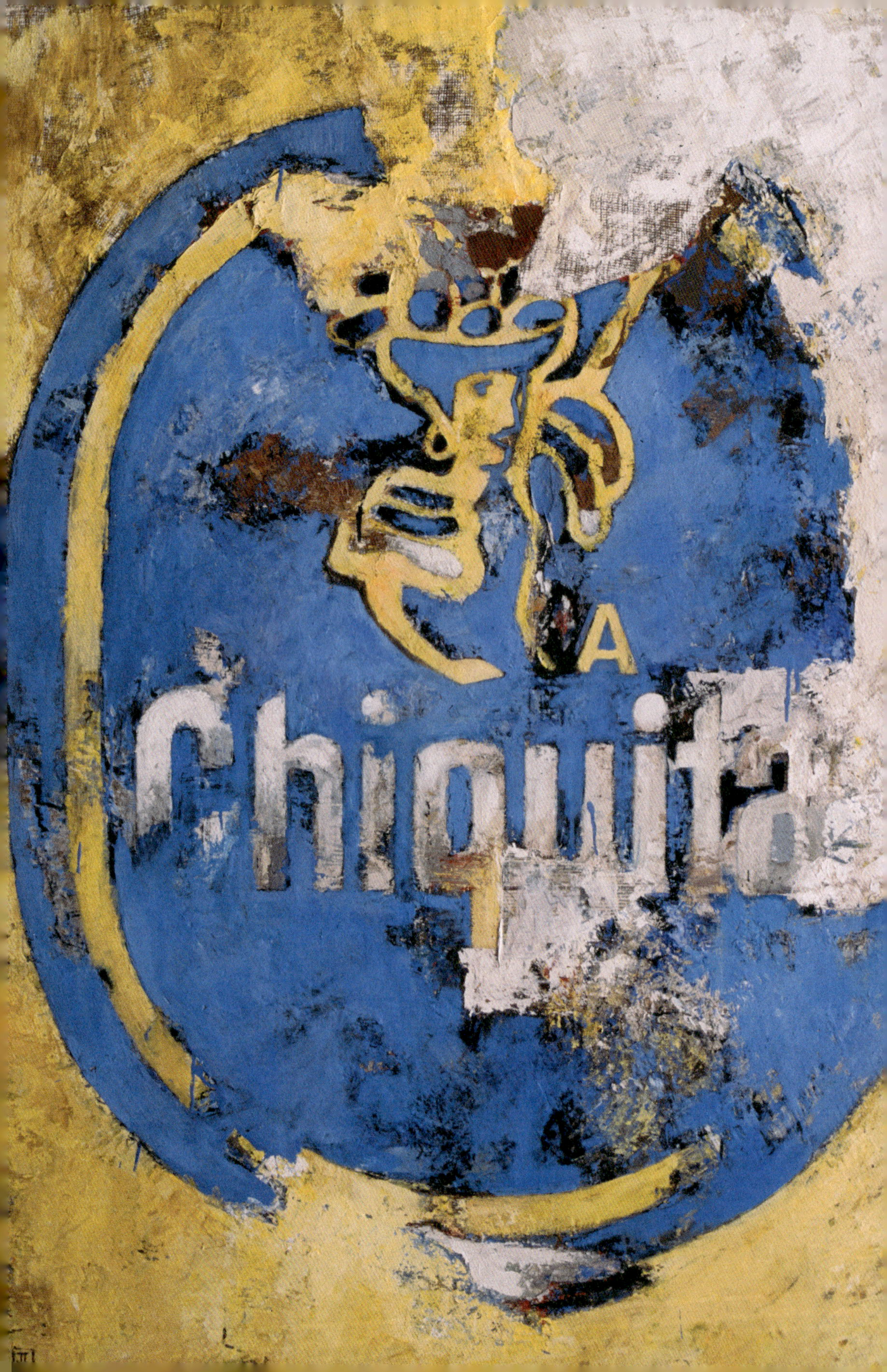
Chiquita

# 5. Power Brands: Ten Perspectives

With this book, the authors have attempted to present a model for effective brand management. Our aim was to describe the model as clearly and comprehensively as possible for readers in a wide range of disciplines. We believe that executives can succeed in measuring, making, and managing their brands better than ever before, provided they apply the right set of instruments. Is that all there is to it? No, the bar is a little higher. Indeed, it is so high that many managers may be reluctant to try to clear it. Do companies that have achieved a perfect mastery of all of the techniques and processes even exist? Can any company ever apply all of the instruments in an optimal way? Perhaps not. But that's no reason to hang back. The quest for relevance and consistency is no excuse to sit and wait. This is why we have chosen to sidestep the classic closing summary. Instead, we present ten points to get brand managers started.

### 1. Apply a more systematic approach; don't rely on gut feeling

As in all business functions, a systematic approach to branding should become a given. Those who apply the tools available for measuring, making, and managing brands will quickly see tangible results and become less dependent on gut feeling or guesswork.

### 2. Focus on one target group; don't try to be everybody's darling

Many companies find it hard to focus their brands on one target group only and to optimize their value proposition for this group. But those who try to be everybody's darling run the risk of creating run-of-the-mill offerings that no one really cares about.

### 3. Use your brand to tell a story; don't just send messages

It's hard to get noticed in a noisy world. Those who create a story that elevates their brand above its individual attributes stand the best chance of building an emotional connection with consumers, creating loyalty, and triggering word of mouth – both offline and online.

### 4. Keep it simple; complex stories don't travel well

Strong brands stand out by virtue of clearly differentiated promises. Aspire to tell the kinds of stories that people will easily remember and readily share with others. Focus on the first thing that should come to their minds when you ask them about your brand.

### 5. Strive for consistency; avoid incessant change

Strong brands are characterized by consistency and continuity in image and in management. Changes should be made very cautiously, and only to meet the needs of customers, never for the sake of a newly minted manager's self-marketing campaign.

### 6. Make the brand a C-level topic; avoid fragmentation

Most companies assign clear responsibilities for core assets such as patents and factories. The brand, however, is often a playing field for everyone in the company. Put an end to this. Put the brand where it belongs: In the hands of the C-suite.

### 7. Move the organization; moving marketing managers is not enough

The brand is the promise that the entire company must keep. Identify the challenges and the stories that are compelling enough to rally today's global organizations. To keep brands strong, all functions must do their part – from production to public affairs.

### 8. Treat external specialists as partners; not as subordinates

As long as brand managers treat agencies and institutes as mere service providers, they will miss out on new ideas and honest feedback. Strong brands depend on the hearts and the minds of the best specialists, regardless of whether they are on the payroll.

### 9. Connect and interact with your team; nobody can know it all

Command and control may work in warfare, but not in brand management. The best brand managers surround themselves with great people from all walks of life, listen to what they have to say, and synthesize their various viewpoints into clear resolve.

### 10. Speed, speed, speed

Consumer preferences, market dynamics, product specifications, and channels change with increasing velocity. Brand organizations need to speed up and become more agile to keep pace. Think of digitalization as an opportunity, not a threat.

# Interview with Oliver Bierhoff of the German national soccer team:
# »I never stop thinking about the national team brand«

The German national soccer team has won four World Cups and three European Championships. Although just a medium sized business in terms of revenues, it enjoys 100 percent awareness. As the manager of the German national soccer team, Oliver Bierhoff is used to constant media scrutiny. When he accepted his new post ten years ago, approval ratings for the national team were low. »The public perception was of a team of young millionaires, and many people didn't want to support a team they saw as aloof and spoiled,« says Mr. Bierhoff. Building on the »summer's tale« that unfolded during the 2006 World Cup in Germany, both the team and its manager worked to change public opinion. There were financial benefits as well: the national team now generates 70 percent of the budget for the German Football Association (DFB).

Oliver Bierhoff became manager of the German national soccer team in 2004. The son of a board member at RWE, he studied business management during his time as a player. In 1996, he scored two goals in the European Championship final, helping Germany to a much-celebrated championship victory. We first spoke with Mr. Bierhoff in 2012. The interview was originally conducted for *Akzente*, a periodical published by McKinsey's German Retail and Consumer Practice.

**McKinsey:** Mr. Bierhoff, the national team is riding a wave of approval, it is a much sought-after advertising partner, and it makes a significant financial contribution to the DFB. What are the key factors in this success?

**Oliver Bierhoff:** Everything is built on success in the sport. Back when I arrived with Jürgen Klinsmann in 2004, we'd already decided that the team needed to do more than just win games. We wanted the team to endorse values, passion, and an attractive way of playing. Since then, we have focused on building up approval. We've gradually eliminated the »closed shop« mentality by initiating targeted public appearances, such as during training sessions. Those often attract up to 40,000 people. We've created a tangible brand, a brand that people can and want to identify with. Of course, breathtaking skills also help.

**McKinsey:** It used to be said that soccer players were difficult to market. Today's national team players are in great demand as brand ambassadors. How did this turnaround come about?

**Oliver Bierhoff:** In this country, it was left to me to break through that barrier when I began marketing myself professionally in the 1990s. Soccer has changed a great deal since then. We have interesting players, successes, an elaborate professional infrastructure with ultramodern stadiums, and we are much more creative and professional in terms of marketing. Obviously, these marketing strategies have also given rise to a clientele that is receptive to these messages and related products.

**McKinsey:** Are there ever any conflicts between the national team's advertising obligations and advertising contracts held by individual players?

**Oliver Bierhoff:** Given that we don't have contracts with the players, we do have to be incredibly sensitive in that respect. Of course there are clashes when, for example, Miroslav Klose is linked with Audi through his club, but appears for our main sponsor Mercedes Benz as a player in the national team. We are very careful to make sure that national team players only ever appear for our partners as a group, never as individuals. That way, it does not appear as though the sponsor has a special contract with any particular player. A sponsor is always a partner to the national team.

**McKinsey:** As a standalone business, the national team brings in around 70 percent of the DFB's income, but only costs around 25 percent of the DFB budget. Do you measure the team's success primarily in euros?

**Oliver Bierhoff:** We don't see ourselves as a profit center, but as an engine that drives the association. That said, TV rights, sponsorships, and ticket sales for the national team do make up the lion's share of the DFB's income. As a charitable organization, the DFB has to distribute this income to the grassroots clubs. So we cannot just say that we're going to spend half of that on the national team. And those 26,000 grassroots clubs are also the source of our future national team players.

**McKinsey:** The national team is ever-present in advertising, particularly during major tournaments. Aren't you worried about inflating the brand? Isn't there a risk of oversaturation?

**Oliver Bierhoff:** I never stop thinking about the national team brand. Clearly, there is a risk of oversaturation, especially since the team and its reputation are often used in relation to social issues. And the media is always there. Not only that, but more and more games are being broadcast on television – and not just national team games. Still, TV ratings and our own market research show that we are nowhere near the point of oversaturation. We have to ensure that the product – meaning the game – is of high quality. To do that, we need to make sure that the number of obligations relating to games and advertising appearances stays manageable for the players.

**McKinsey:** The national team brand is not your typical brand: It is made up of individual people. Presumably, that doesn't make brand management any easier?

**Oliver Bierhoff:** The human factor makes the whole thing unpredictable. Regardless of how likeable the players may seem, if we lose key parties, then a flood of criticism follows and the team's approval ratings can sink rapidly. Fans, friends, and partners to the national team have high expectations of and close emotional ties to the team. That can quickly turn into massive disappointment. Representations in the media are also becoming more extreme, and of course we have no control over them. That is what makes brand leadership for the national team more challenging than for a normal product where most things can be meticulously controlled. But at the same time, this makes everything more exhilarating.

**McKinsey:** You have a national team of immensely self-aware young people, all of whom also have their own advisors. How do you get a group like that to tread a common line?

**Oliver Bierhoff:** We don't always want a »common line.« What we want is a shared understanding. And the best way to achieve that is through continued conversations and convincing arguments. I cannot and do not want to force anyone to do anything – although our monopoly position is an asset. If you want to play at the European or world championship level and make that leap to becoming a top international player, then you have to play in the national team. You must go through the eye of that needle. So far, we have been able to communicate really well what it means to be a national player. The group dynamics also help; there's no need for pressure.

**McKinsey:** Clearly, things have not always been as harmonious – there have been regular shake-ups. Are today's players different?

**Oliver Bierhoff:** Personalities have changed. Each generation – and this is something we see reflected in the economy as well – has its own style and chooses its own path. Our players are very professional and have outstanding team spirit. Then again, they also have clear ideas of what they want and ask to be more involved in decision making than they used to be.

**McKinsey:** Have you ever attempted to define the value of the national team brand?

**Oliver Bierhoff:** We haven't ever asked ourselves that question, but it would be extremely interesting to find out. Until now, we've carried out market research at the end of every tournament to discover how our fans see the national team, and how much approval and attention we draw.

**McKinsey:** Although the attention usually focuses on individual stars, you consistently position the entire team as the star. Does that sometimes conflict with your sponsors' wishes?

**Oliver Bierhoff:** A brand needs a profile. The national team raises its profile through strong player types. We want personalities, players with rough edges who stand for an opinion, an ideal, or a value, and don't just parrot platitudes. Nevertheless, we always demand that the players make a real effort. Sponsors prefer those players who really shine at the sport. If they also have massive charisma, all the better.

**McKinsey:** Why does the national team need its own online presence – is that a conscious attempt to distance the team from the DFB?

**Oliver Bierhoff:** It's not about distancing; it's about raising the profile. I think there is an analogy to the car industry. There are manufacturers who offer various product lines, from luxury to sports to economy. They approach different customers in different ways. The more segments I have to cover, the less of a profile my brand has. That is why we opted for our own Web site and our own logo. We are a premium brand in the DFB. Uniformity never helped anyone. Differentiation, creating nuances, that's what we want to achieve. It is an individual approach that reinforces cohesion. A strong brand comes from a strong core.

**McKinsey:** At times, the national team has been advertising up to 300 products. At what point do you think a brand becomes overstretched?

**Oliver Bierhoff:** The number of strong, major partners is strictly limited. We have one main general sponsor, Mercedes Benz, and one main general outfitter, Adidas. We also have a maximum of six premium sponsors. Most of those have been working with us for a long time already, and all of them are among the premium brands in their respective fields. That suits us perfectly. We shoot a maximum of four ads per tournament for our partners. The other products we advertise are mainly merchandizing articles. We have an agency that handles that for us. But for each and every product, we decide whether it makes sense to create that connection with our brand. We get closer to our fans while working for the brand.

**McKinsey:** Consumer goods firms are your most frequent advertising partners. What can you offer them?

**Oliver Bierhoff:** Millions of fans, all of whom are also consumers and like products that are linked to the national team. Consumer goods and the companies behind them find it easiest to create links with the emotionality of soccer as a product, and thus to their customers' emotions.

**McKinsey:** Soccer has definitely broadened its appeal in recent years. Have you managed to tap into new target groups for the national team?

**Oliver Bierhoff:** The proportion of female fans has grown steadily and has now reached around 50 percent. Our national team exemplifies the family experience, even more so than club soccer, both in front of the TV and in stadiums. We are trying to be »the team for Germany.«

**McKinsey:** Soccer used to be seen as a pursuit for the lower classes. How has that changed?

**Oliver Bierhoff:** That sounds disrespectful. People from all walks of life enjoy our team and find the games exciting. And that is also reflected in education levels within the team itself. The 2006 World Cup in Germany helped overcome many prejudices. In the modern stadiums, the audience gets to experience just how great the atmosphere is during a soccer game. This has helped us attract a lot of people from tennis and golf. Soccer has thus acquired new target groups, and that is why companies today are finding more courage to invest in it. This sport offers something for everyone.

**McKinsey:** The national team is subjected to greater media scrutiny than industry brands. How do you deal with that?

**Oliver Bierhoff:** I try and stay relaxed when dealing with the media. For me, my work always takes priority, not the drama, speculations, or ratings. The occasional hysterical report is just part of the job today. During the 1990 World Cup, the team was accompanied by 60 media representatives. At the last European Championship, there were five times as many. There is more pressure on the journalists and an almost infinite number of distribution channels. Internet, print, radio, TV, digital channels, social networks, bloggers: everything is published instantly, often after no or far too little research. People are looking for the emotion, not necessarily the story. The half-life of news can now only be measured in seconds. Proactive media relations are our attempt to help reporters understand contexts easier and faster, although that hasn't stopped the unending tide of scandals derived from trivialities. At times like those, I tell myself that even this type of publicity is merely a reflection of the high interest in the team. But I in no way endorse the saying »there's no such thing as bad publicity.«

**McKinsey:** What is your opinion of social media – do Facebook, Twitter, etc. represent an opportunity or a problem?

**Oliver Bierhoff:** We use social media intensively. The national team has more than four million Facebook friends. However, social media does come with its own challenges. Every player tweets or is on Facebook. If someone has an injury and we are still thinking about how to share that information with the press, it's possible that the player will tweet all about it before we get the chance. It is becoming more and more difficult to control the flow of information, but so far we have a good handle on things in the national team.

**McKinsey:** Congratulations on winning the World Cup in Brazil. How will the fourth star affect the national team as a brand?

**Oliver Bierhoff:** First of all, let me be clear about one thing: all of Germany won that fourth star. It is the result of the combined efforts of German soccer over the course of the last ten years. Now we want to keep up the momentum created by the World Cup, maintain our excellent image, and create the kinds of structures in the association that we need in order to stay competitive in the coming years. One key element is the performance center (»Leistungszentrum«), a high-end soccer school. At this time of triumph, we cannot rest on our laurels. The positive image and the fact that people identify with the team to such a high degree will help us increase our sponsoring and licensing revenues – and we will make sure that the proceeds will be invested in meaningful activities.

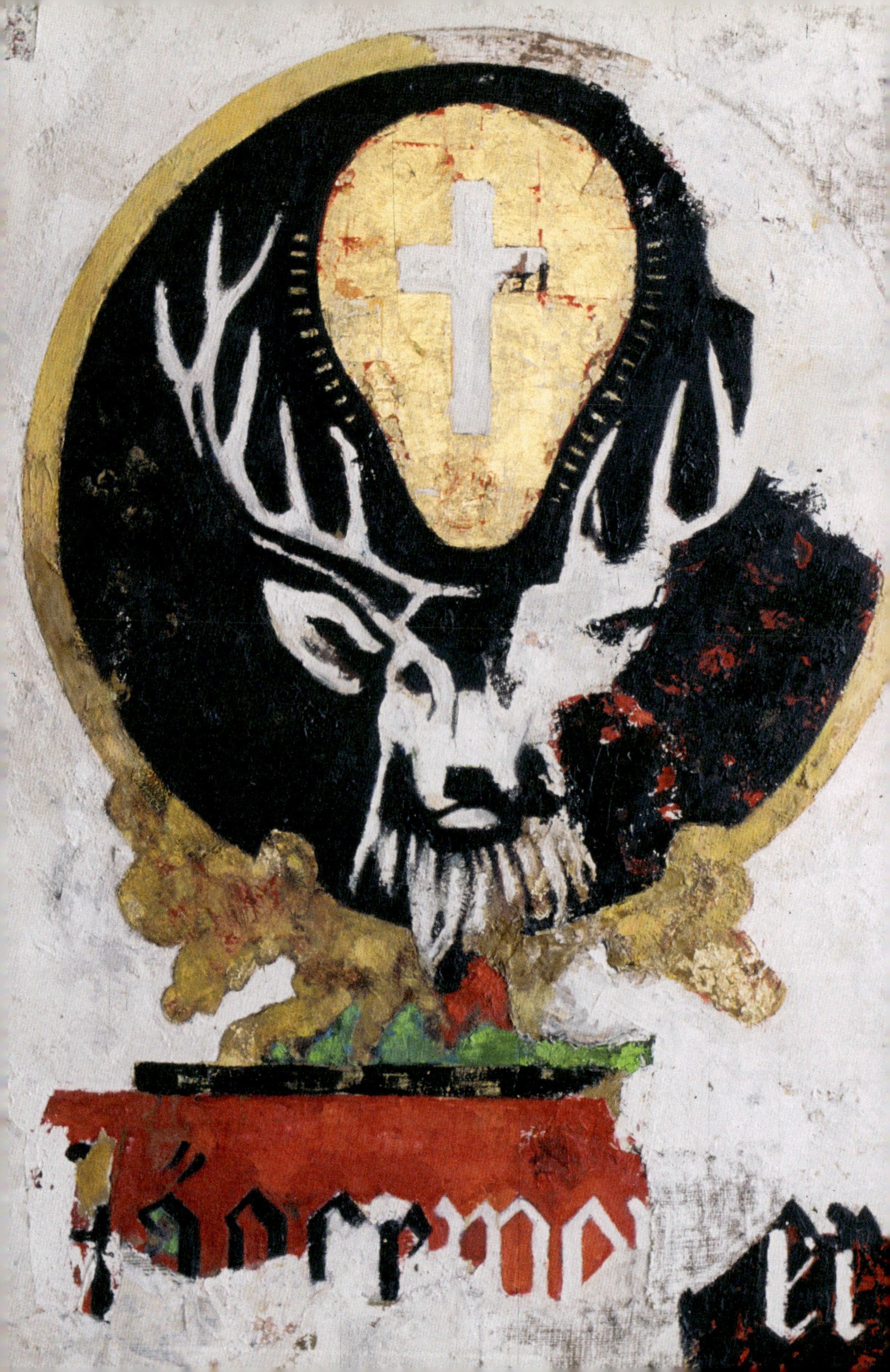

# Table of illustrations

Figure 1.1: Louis Vuitton: Travel heritage in notable marketing campaigns
Figure 1.2: Private label advertising at Aldi
Figure 1.3: Private label share by category
Figure 1.4: Strong brands outperform the index in financial markets
Figure 1.5: Brands fullfill three basic functions
Figure 1.6: Three elements underpin excellent brand management
Figure 1.7: The cowboy is constant: The camel wanders
Figure 1.8: How Samsung uses customer insights to drive product innovation
Figure 1.9: Febreze 2012 Olympics campaign visuals
Figure 1.10: Criteria for advertising assessment: Creativity and content fit
Figure 1.11: Both creativity and content fit contribute to economic success
Figure 1.12: Overview of Google's portfolio of products and services
Figure 1.13: Ikea: Expertly developed into a global brand
Figure 1.14: Samples of »branded« artworks: Chanel by Andy Warhol
Figure 1.15: Red Bull: Painstaking planning gave the brand wings


Figure 2.1: Overall relevance ranking in B2C: How important are brands to consumers in different product categories around the world?
Figure 2.2: Ranking of selected B2C product markets by brand function
Figure 2.3: Brand relevance ranking across countries: In which countries do consumers focus most on brands?
Figure 2.4: Ranking of brand relevance by function across countries: Which brand function is most important?
Figure 2.5: Variance of brand relevance across countries in selected product categories
Figure 2.6: Brand relevance by country: How important are brands to consumers across product categories in Western European countries?
Figure 2.7: Brand relevance by country: How important are brands to consumers across product categories in the world's largest economies?
Figure 2.8: Brand relevance by country: How important are brands to consumers across product categories in Eastern European countries?
Figure 2.9: Development of brand relevance by industry group
Figure 2.10: Development of brand relevance in retail over time
Figure 2.11: Four categories made the top 10 in all waves
Figure 2.12: Needs-based customer segmentation reveals key buying factors beyond price
Figure 2.13: Advertising spending by providers of electrical energy
Figure 2.14: German tobacco industry: Share of total marketing spending
Figure 2.15: Relevance ranking in B2B: How important are brands to business people?
Figure 2.16: Ranking of selected B2B product markets by brand function

Figure 2.17: Brands drive decisions in B2B
Figure 2.18: Brands help companies reduce risk in B2B
Figure 2.19: Press report about hybrid consumption
Figure 2.20: Building blocks of a consumer-centric company
Figure 2.21: Example of insights-based product innovation at John Deere
Figure 2.22: Overview of qualitative research techniques
Figure 2.23: Three-step segmentation process
Figure 2.24: Clarifying the frame of reference is one of the most important steps in the segmentation process
Figure 2.25: Relevant market definition determines revenue potential
Figure 2.26: Needs provide the deepest insights into consumer motivation
Figure 2.27: Need states combine attitudes and needs in occasions worn
Figure 2.28: Example of segmentation-based action planning for mobile phone operators
Figure 2.29: Overview of creative techniques to bring segments to life
Figure 2.30: Approach to target segments in mobile telecoms
Figure 2.31: The missing link
Figure 2.32: The heatmap
Figure 2.33: Applying the brand funnel to cars
Figure 2.34: Different versions of the funnel with different effect hierarchies
Figure 2.35: The performance of a brand in the purchase funnel
Figure 2.36: Brand A vs. brand B performance
Figure 2.37: Applying the brand funnel to energy
Figure 2.38: Provider 1 vs. provider 2 performance
Figure 2.39: Performance of competing retail brands
Figure 2.40: Switzerland vs. Austria
Figure 2.41: Key features of the enhanced BrandMatics® toolkit
Figure 2.42: Application of enhanced funnel to automotive
Figure 2.43: Application of enhanced funnel to energy
Figure 2.44: Application of enhanced funnel to candy
Figure 2.45: Performance among new and prior customers
Figure 2.46: Performance among new and prior customers
Figure 2.47: Performance among new and prior customers
Figure 2.48: When to consider the use of the enhanced brand purchase funnel
Figure 2.49: In 2010, Dutch energy brands were not differentiated
Figure 2.50: By 2014, Essent has developed a clear brand profile

Figure 3.1: Two types of brand characteristics
Figure 3.2: Examples of brand characteristics
Figure 3.3: The brand diamond concept
Figure 3.4: The brand diamond: Strengths and weaknesses
Figure 3.5: The brand diamond: Full research battery
Figure 3.6: Customers do not say what they really need, requiring derived importance methodologies

Figure 3.7:    Purchase drivers for compact cars
Figure 3.8:    Brand A performance on market drivers
Figure 3.9:    Switzerland's challenges in tourism: Price and trendiness
Figure 3.10:   Brand driver analysis shows differences in perceptions
Figure 3.11:   Purchase drivers for different energy customer groups
Figure 3.12:   Brand drivers in the US candy bar market by customer type
Figure 3.13:   Purchase drivers for different compact car buyers
Figure 3.14:   Brand A: Relevance by performance vs. market average
Figure 3.15:   Strengthen strengths or reduce weaknesses?
Figure 3.16:   Multiple-brand strategies in the automotive industry
Figure 3.17:   Advantages and disadvantages of different portfolio strategies
Figure 3.18:   Unilever: 75% fewer brands in 5 years
Figure 3.19:   Benefits-based segmentation of an international brewery
Figure 3.20:   Portfolio optimization of a financial services provider: Distinctly differentiate between brand promises
Figure 3.21:   Brand fit: Close logical connection between parent brand and transfer product
Figure 3.22:   Preparing brand transfer ideas
Figure 3.23:   Brand leverage examples: Lego and Meissen
Figure 3.24:   Lego: Virtuous circle of brand extension
Figure 3.25:   Meissen: Frome fine porcelain to home furnishings
Figure 3.26:   Brand extension patterns in luxury
Figure 3.27:   Step 1: Map brand positions
Figure 3.28:   Step 2: Estimate future funnel performance
Figure 3.29:   Step 3: Assess net economic impact

Figure 4.1:    Three complimentary areas of brand activation
Figure 4.2:    Nivea and Sixt: Precise brand promises pay off
Figure 4.3:    Checklist for deriving the brand promise
Figure 4.4:    Touch points in the airline industry
Figure 4.5:    Systematic brand delivery (1/2): Retail
Figure 4.6:    Systematic brand delivery (2/2): Automotive
Figure 4.7:    Pathways analyses help identify the right operational definitions and targets to fulfill the brand promise
Figure 4.8:    In brick-and-mortar clothing retail, assortment is still more important than price and service
Figure 4.9:    Driver disaggregation helps to ensure cost-efficient improvement of critical brand drivers
Figure 4.10:   Brand delivery optimization: Individual touch points vs. entire journeys
Figure 4.11:   Over the course of a journey, a customer passes through many touch points
Figure 4.12:   Customer experience drives consumer attitudes and revenues

Figure 4.13: Customer experience optimization – Industry examples
Figure 4.14: Service-to-sales pilot resulted in a 17% conversion rate
Figure 4.15: Digital media are relevant all over the shopper's decision journey
Figure 4.16: Levers of marketing spending excellence
Figure 4.17: Creating full budget transparency
Figure 4.18: Overcoming the »tyranny of the average«
Figure 4.19: List of potential criteria for budget prioritization
Figure 4.20: Reach-Cost-Quality approach
Figure 4.21: Real cost per qualified contact
Figure 4.22: MMM: High-level technical architecture
Figure 4.23: MMM tool brings transparency to ROI across all marketing levers
Figure 4.24: MMM is mainly used to optimize the allocation of funds to »paid media«
Figure 4.25: Daytime optimization for effective media planning: Telecoms example
Figure 4.26: What is CDJ?
Figure 4.27: Example of interactive decision support tool
Figure 4.28: Internal brand-building programs empower employees to live the brand
Figure 4.29: Internal target groups should play different roles
Figure 4.30: Six major digital trends
Figure 4.31: Constant connectivity: Mobile and tablet penetration
Figure 4.32: Digital value creation opportunities along the consumer journey
Figure 4.33: Online advertising is growing at the expense of print advertising
Figure 4.34: Mobile is the fastest-growing type of online advertising
Figure 4.35: Three fronts in online retail development
Figure 4.36: There is a wide variation of ad-to-sales ratios even within individual industries
Figure 4.37: The brand cockpit gives a structure to the input and output variables of brand management
Figure 4.38: Checklist of possible customer touch points
Figure 4.39: Performance indicators for campaign tracking
Figure 4.40: Performance indicators for brand management
Figure 4.41: Three development stages for the cockpit
Figure 4.42: Example of quarterly scorecard
Figure 4.43: The McKinsey Brand Navigator tool helps to create a fact base for proactive brand management
Figure 4.44: Year of brand manager organization introduction in selected companies
Figure 4.45: Example of brand management organization
Figure 4.46: Agency payment practices
Figure 4.47: Almost all consumer goods companies use performance incentives
Figure 4.48: Media strategy, planning, and buying are largely outsourced
Figure 4.49: Depending on the marketing budget, companies mainly rely on more media performance or more competence building
Figure 4.50: Comparison of perceived increase in relevance and perceived competence

# About the authors

Dr. Jesko Perrey is a director of McKinsey & Company, Inc., and based in the Düsseldorf office, which he joined in 1999. He is the global knowledge leader of McKinsey's Marketing & Sales Practice. Jesko serves clients in the consumer goods, retail, financial services, and logistics industries. The functional focus of his work is on brand management and MROI.

Dr. Tjark Freundt is a principal of McKinsey & Company, Inc., and based in the Hamburg office, which he joined in 2001. He is a core member of McKinsey's European Marketing & Sales Practice and a leader in the global Branding Practice. Tjark serves mainly energy providers along with companies in the logistics and manufacturing industries. He specializes in brand strategy, MROI, and customer-centric transformations.

Dr. Dennis Spillecke is a principal of McKinsey & Company, Inc., and based in the Cologne office, which he joined in 2001. As the leader of McKinsey's Marketing & Sales Practice in Germany, Dennis specializes in MROI, brand management, and multichannel/digital marketing. He primarily serves logistics companies, energy providers, retailers, and consumer goods companies.

# About the illustrations

Jens Lorenzen provided an artist's interpretation of the brand names, corporate logos, and company products gracing the pages of our book. With his fresco-like paintings and collage work, Lorenzen – born in Schleswig in 1961 and now living in Berlin – has made a name for himself both in the art world and in the world of business. After his studies at the Academy of Art in Braunschweig, Lorenzen exhibited his works in galleries, museums, and major corporations. His pictures are included in collections belonging to Commerzbank Berlin, Volkswagen Bank Braunschweig, Norddeutsche Landesbank Hannover, and the Axel Springer Verlag Hamburg.

(www.jens-lorenzen.com)